D1103876

MULTIMEDIA SECURITY TECHNOLOGIES FOR DIGITAL RIGHTS MANAGEMENT

MULTIMEDIA SECURITY TECHNOLOGIES FOR DIGITAL RIGHTS MANAGEMENT

Edited by

Wenjun Zeng

University of Missouri - Columbia

Heather Yu

Panasonic Princeton Laboratory

Ching-Yung Lin

IBM Research, Qibin Sun
Institute for Infocomm Research

AMSTERDAM • BOSTON • HEIDELBERG • LONDON
NEW YORK • OXFORD • PARIS • SAN DIEGO
SAN FRANCISCO • SINGAPORE • SYDNEY • TOKYO

Academic Press is an imprint of Elsevier

Academic Press is an imprint of Elsevier
30 Corporate Drive, Suite 400, Burlington, MA 01803, USA
525 B Street, Suite 1900, San Diego, California 92101-4495, USA
84 Theobald's Road, London WC1X 8RR, UK

This book is printed on acid-free paper. ∞

Library of Congress Cataloging-in-Publication Data
Multimedia security technologies for digital rights management/edited by Wenjun Zeng,
Heather Yu, and Ching-Yung Lin.
    p. cm.
Includes bibliographical references and index.
ISBN-13: 978-0-12-369476-8 (casebound : alk. paper)
ISBN-10: 0-12-369476-0 (casebound : alk. paper) 1. Computer security. 2. Multimedia
systems–Security measures. 3. Intellectual property. I. Zeng, Wenjun, 1967- II. Yu, Hong
Heather, 1967- III. Lin, Ching-Yung.

QA76.9.A25M875 2006
005.8–dc22

                    2006003179

British Library Cataloguing-in-Publication Data
A catalogue record for this book is available from the British Library.

ISBN 13: 978-0-12-369476-8
ISBN 10: 0-12-369476-0 05-07-07

For information on all Academic Press publications
visit our Web site at www.books.elsevier.com

Printed in the United States of America
06 07 08 09 10   9 8 7 6 5 4 3 2 1

Table of Contents

ABOUT THE EDITORS

Wenjun Zeng is an Associate Professor in the Computer Science Department of University of Missouri, Columbia, MO. He received his B.E., M.S., and Ph.D. degrees from Tsinghua University, China, the University of Notre Dame, and Princeton University, respectively. His current research interests include content and network security, and multimedia communications and networking.

Prior to joining Univ. of Missouri-Columbia in 2003, he had worked for PacketVideo Corporation, San Diego, CA, Sharp Labs of America, Camas, WA, Bell Laboratories, Murray Hill, NJ, and Matsushita Information Technology Lab, Panasonic Technologies Inc., Princeton, NJ. From 1998 to 2002, He was an active contributor to the MPEG4 Intellectual Property Management & Protection (IPMP) standard and the JPEG 2000 image coding standard, where four of his proposals were adopted. He has been awarded 11 patents. Dr. Zeng has served as an Organizing Committee Member and Technical Program Committee Chair for a number of IEEE international conferences. He is an Associate Editor of the *IEEE Transactions on Multimedia,* and is on the Editorial Board of *IEEE Multimedia Magazine*. He was the Lead Guest Editor of *IEEE Transactions on Multimedia's Special Issue on Streaming Media* published in April 2004.

Heather Yu is a Senior Scientist at Panasonic Princeton Laboratory. She received her B.S. degree from Peking University, her M.A. and Ph.D. degrees from Princeton University all in Electrical Engineering. In 1998, she joined Panasonic where her major focus is multimedia communications and multimedia information access R&D. Her current research interests include digital rights management and multimedia content access and distribution in consumer networks. In the multimedia security area, she holds two US patents, has many patents pending, published a variety of technical papers in prestigious conferences and journals, and has given three tutorials at IEEE multimedia, communications, and consumer electronics conferences.

Currently, Dr. Yu serves as Chair of IEEE Communications Society Multimedia Communications Technical Committee, Editor for ACM Computers in Entertainment, IEEE Multimedia Magazine, and Informing Science Journal, Conference Steering Committee Member of IEEE ICME (IEEE International Conferences on Multimedia and Expo) and IEEE CCNC (IEEE Consumer Communications and Networking Conference), and Technical Program Co-chair of IEEE ICC2007 Multimedia Symposium. From 1998-2002, she served as Associate Editor for IEEE Trans. on Multimedia and conference technical program chair, associate chair, session chair, technical committee member, best paper award committee member, keynote speaker, panelist, panel chair, and steering committee member for many conferences.

Ching-Yung Lin received his Ph.D. degree from Columbia University in Electrical Engineering. Since Oct 2000, he has been a Research Staff Member in IBM T. J. Watson Research Center, where he is currently leading projects on the IBM Large-Scale Video Semantic Filtering System. He is also an Adjunct Associate Professor at the University of Washington and Columbia University. His research interest is mainly focused on multimodality signal understanding, social computing, and multimedia security. Dr. Lin is the Editor of the Interactive Magazines (EIM) of the IEEE Communications Society, an Associate Editor of the IEEE Trans. on Multimedia and the Journal of Visual Communication and Image Representation. He served as a Guest Editor of the Proceedings of IEEE – Special Issue on Digital Rights Management, and EURASIP Journal on Applied Digital Signal Processing – Special Issue on Visual Sensor Network. Dr. Lin is a recipient of 2003 IEEE Circuits and Systems Society Outstanding Young Author Award. He is the (co-)author of more than 100 journal articles, conference papers, book, book chapters and public release software. Dr. Lin is a Senior Member of IEEE, and a member of ACM, INSNA and AAAS.

ABOUT THE CONTRIBUTORS

Scott Moskowitz. Founder of Blue Spike, Inc., rights management expert, inventor and technology architect, author of *So this is Convergence?*. In 1992, Mr. Moskowitz entered the entertainment industry doing agency work for a large U.S. wholesaler of music-related products increasing high gross margins while realizing whole revenues of $ 120 million. Mr. Moskowitz had previously founded a Tokyo-based trading company involved in the consulting, representation and export sales of American consumer products to Japan. He designed initial plans for the High Definition Television's market entry in the U.S. and worked on other related strategy for Sony's Monitor Group in Tokyo as Sony Japan's first undergraduate intern. Mr. Moskowitz earned two cum laude degrees at The Wharton School and College of Arts and Sciences at the University of Pennsylvania. He is a member of the Institute of Electrical and Electronics Engineers ("IEEE"), Association for Computing Machinery ("ACM") and The International Society for Optical Engineering ("SPIE") organizations. Mr. Moskowitz holds 15 U.S. Patents with dozens of pending patent applications. scott@bluespike.com

Marina Bosi is Chief Technology Officer at MPEG LA, LLC – a firm specializing in the licensing of multimedia technology. Prior to that, Dr. Bosi was VP-Technology, Standards and Strategies with Digital Theater Systems (DTS) and was at Dolby Laboratories where she worked on AC-2 and AC-3 technology and coordinated the MPEG-2 AAC development.

Dr. Bosi has participated in numerous activities aimed at standardizing digital secure content coding, including the DVD Forum, the SDMI, and is currently involved in the ANSI/ISO MPEG, ATSC, DVB, and SMPTE standard setting process. Dr. Bosi is also a founding member and director of the Digital Media Project, a non-profit organization that promotes successful development, deployment and use of Digital Media. Fellow and Past President of the Audio Engineering Society (AES), Dr. Bosi is a Senior Member of IEEE and a Member of ASA.

Consulting Professor at Stanford University's Computer Center for Research in Music and Acoustics (CCRMA) and also in Stanford's Electrical Engineering department, Dr. Bosi holds several patents and publications in the areas of coding and digital rights management including the textbook "Introduction to Digital Audio Coding and Standards", published by Kluwer Academic Publishers. MBosi@mpegla.com

Leonardo Chiariglione graduated from the Polytechnic of Turin and obtained his Ph. D. degree from the University of Tokyo.

He has been at the forefront of a number of initiatives that have helped shape media technology and business as we know them today. Among these the Moving Pictures Experts Group (MPEG) standards committee which he founded and chairs and the Digital Media Project of which he was the proponent and is the current president. Dr. Chiariglione is the recipient of several awards: among these the IBC John Tucker award, the IEEE Masaru Ibuka Consumer Electronics award and the Kilby Foundation award. Since January 2004 he is the CEO of CEDEO.net, a consulting company advising major multinational companies on matters related to digital media. leonardo@chiariglione.org

Bin B. Zhu has been with Microsoft Research (MSR) Asia as a researcher since Dec. 2001, where he has been working on content protection and digital rights management, watermarking, multimedia processing and communications, P2P networks, encryption algorithms, etc. Before he joined MSR Asia, he worked as a cofounder and Lead Scientist at Cognicity for more than 4 years. Cognicity was a pioneer in the field of audio watermarking and music promotion and advertising enabling technologies. Dr. Zhu is a senior member of IEEE. He has published four book chapters and more than 40 peer-reviewed journal and conference papers. He has been awarded 8 US patents with more than 10 pending US patent applications. Dr. Zhu received his B.S. degree in physics from the University of Science and Technology of China in 1986, and M.S. and Ph. D. degrees in electrical engineering from the University of Minnesota, Twin Cities in Sept. 1993 and Dec. 1998. binzhu@microsoft.com

Dajun He received BS degree from Tsinghua University, China in 1991 and MS degree from Shanghai Jiaotong University, China in 1994, and PhD degree from National University of Singapore, Singapore in 2005.

From 1994 to 1995, he was a lecturer in Shanghai Jiaotong University, where he developed the first HDTV simulation system in China. From 1996 to 2001, he was a senior engineer in AIWA Singapore, in charge of developing audio and visual consumer products. From 2001 to 2005, he was a scientist in Institute for Infocomm Research (I2R) in Singapore. Now, he is a deputy director of engineering in

Shanghai Zhangjiang (Group) Co., Ltd., China. His main research interests include media security, image/video processing and compression.

Qibin Sun is currently leading the Media Semantics Department at the Institute for Infocomm Research (I2R) in Singapore, conducting research and development in media (text, audio, image, video) analysis, retrieval and security. He is also the Head of Delegates of Singapore in ISO/IEC SC29 WG1(JPEG). Dr. Sun actively participates in professional activities in IEEE ICME, IEEE ISCAS, IEEE ICASSP and ACM MM, etc. He is the member of Editorial Board in IEEE Multimedia Magazine, the associate editor in IEEE Transactions on Circuits and Systems for Video Technology and the member of Editorial Board in LNCS Transactions on Data Hiding and Multimedia Security. djhe@i2r.a-star.edu.sg & qibin@2r.a-star.edu.sg

Ahmet M. Eskicioglu received the B.S. degree from the Middle East Technical University (METU), Ankara, Turkey, and the M.S. and Ph.D. degrees from the University of Manchester Institute of Science and Technology (UMIST), England. He was with the Computer Engineering Department, METU from 1983 to 1992, the Department of Computer Sciences, University of North Texas from 1992 to 1995, and Thomson Multimedia Corporate Research, Indianapolis from 1996 to 2001.

Dr. Eskicioglu is with the Department of Computer and Information Science, Brooklyn College of the City University of New York. He has actively participated in the development of several national and international standards for copy protection and conditional access in the US and Europe. Dr. Eskicioglu's teaching and research interests include data security, conditional access, digital rights management, copy protection, digital watermarking, and multimedia applications. He has been a National Science Foundation panelist, and a guest lecturer at several universities and research organizations. Dr. Eskicioglu is a Senior Member of the IEEE. eskicioglu@sci.brooklyn.cuny.edu

Ning Liu received the B.E in Electrical Engineering from the Sichuan University, China in 1995, and the M.E in Signal Processing Engineering from the Tongji University, China in 2001. Since Fall 2002, he has been a Ph.D. student in the Department of Electrical and Computer Engineering, Stevens Institute of Technology, Hoboken, NJ, where he works in the MSyNC. His research interests include quantizer based steganography and stego-games, digital image/video watermarking, joint source channel coding.

Palak Amin received the B.E. and the M.E. degree both in Computer Engineering from the Department of Electrical and Computer Engineering, Stevens Institute of Technology, Hoboken, NJ in 2003. He is currently working towards the Ph.D. degree in Computer Engineering at Stevens Institute of Technology, Hoboken, NJ. He was with the MedSW-West Lab, Siemens Medical Solutions at Iselin, NJ for 2001–2002. His research interests include multimedia security-digital image/video watermarking, statistical security, distributed source channel coding (DSCC), and multiple description coding (MDC)

Aruna Ambalavanan is currently working towards her Ph.D degree in Electrical Engineering at Stevens Institute of Technology, Hoboken, NJ. She received her Masters degree in Electrical Engineering from the University of South Florida, Tampa, FL in 2002 and Bachelors degree in Electrical Engineering from the University of Madras, India in 2000. Her research interests include Steganalysis, information forensics and security.

Dr. K.P. Subbalakshmi is an Assistant Professor at the Electrical and Computer Engineering department at Stevens Institute of Technology, where she co-founded and co-directs the Multimedia Systems, Networking and Communications (MSyNC) Laboratory. Her research interests lie in the areas of: Information and Network Security, Wireless and Multimedia Networking and Coding. She chairs the Special Interest Group on Multimedia Security, IEEE Technical Committee on Multimedia Communications. She received the Stevens President's Research Recognition Award in 2003. She is the Guest Editor of the IEEE Journal on Selected Areas of Communication, Special Issue on Cross Layer Optimized Wireless Multimedia Communications. ksubbala@stevens.edu

Anil Jain is a University Distinguished Professor in the Department of Computer Science & Engineering at Michigan State University. He received his B.Tech. degree from Indian Institute of Technology, Kanpur and M.S. and Ph.D. degrees from Ohio State University in 1970 and 1973. His research interests include statistical pattern recognition and biometric authentication.

He received awards for best papers in 1987 and 1991 from the Pattern Recognition Society. He also received 1996 IEEE Transactions on Neural Networks Outstanding Paper Award. He is a fellow of AAAS, ACM, IEEE, IAPR and SPIE. He has received Fulbright, Guggenheim and Humboldt Research Awards. He received the 2003 IEEE Computer Society Technical Achievement Award.

Holder of six patents in fingerprints, he is the author of a number of books on biometrics: Handbook of Multibiometric Systems, Springer 2006, Biometric Systems, Technology, Design and Performance Evaluation, Springer 2005, Handbook of Face Recognition, Springer 2005, Handbook of Fingerprint Recognition, Springer 2003, BIOMETRICS: Personal Identification in Networked Society, Kluwer 1999. He is an Associate editor of the IEEE Transactions on Information Forensics and Security and is currently serving as a member of

The National Academies committees on Whither Biometrics and Improvised Explosive Devices.

Umut Uludag received the B.Sc. and M.Sc. degrees in Electrical and Electronics Engineering from Bogazici University, Istanbul, Turkey in 1999 and 2001, respectively. He is currently working toward the Ph.D. degree in the Department of Computer Science and Engineering, Michigan State University, East Lansing. He was a researcher in Information Technologies Institute, Marmara Research Center, from 1999 to 2001. He also spent four summers (2002–2005) with Intel Corporation, Santa Clara, CA, National Institute of Standards and Technology, Gaithersburg, MD, Siemens Corporate Research, Princeton, NJ, and Symbol Technologies, Holtsville, NY.

His research interests include biometrics, pattern recognition, multimedia, digital security, watermarking, image processing and computer vision. He is a member of the IEEE and Computer Society. jain@cse.msu.edu

John Apostolopoulos is a principal research scientist and project manager for the HP Labs Streaming Media Systems Group. Since 2000, he has also been a Consulting Assistant Professor of electrical engineering at Stanford University. He joined HP Labs in 1997 after receiving his B.S., M.S., and Ph.D. degrees from MIT. In graduate school he worked on the U.S. Digital TV standard, and received an Emmy Award Certificate for his contributions. He received a best student paper award for part of his Ph.D. thesis, the Young Investigator Award (best paper award) at VCIP 2001 for his work on multiple description video coding and path diversity for reliable video communication over lossy packet networks, and in 2003 was named "one of the world's top 100 young (under 35) innovators in science and technology" (TR100) by Technology Review. His work on media transcoding in the middle of a network while preserving end-to-end security (secure transcoding) has been adopted by the JPEG-2000 Security (JPSEC) standard. He is currently vice-chair of the IEEE Image and Multidimensional Digital Signal Processing (IMDSP) technical committee, and he has served as associate editor of IEEE Transactions on Image Processing and IEEE Signal Processing Letters. His research interests include improving the reliability, fidelity, scalability, and security of media communication over wired and wireless packet networks.

Susie Wee is the Director of the Mobile and Media Systems Lab (MMSL) in HP Labs. She is responsible for research programs in multimedia communications and networking, wireless sensor networks, and next-generation mobile multimedia systems. MMSL has activities in the US, Japan, and England, and includes collaborations with partners around the world. Wee's research interests broadly embrace design of mobile streaming media systems, secure scalable streaming over packet networks, and efficient video delivery to diverse clients over dynamic networks. In addition to her work at HP Labs, Wee is a consulting assistant professor at Stanford University, co-teaching a graduate-level course on digital video processing. She received Technology Review's Top 100 Young Investigators award in 2002, served as an associate editor for the IEEE Transactions on Image Processing, and is currently serving as an associate editor for the IEEE Transactions on Circuits, Systems, and Video Technologies. She is currently a co-editor of the JPEG-2000 Security standard (JPSEC). Wee received her B.S., M.S., and Ph.D. degrees in electrical engineering from the Massachusetts Institute of Technology (MIT). john_apostolopoulos@hp.com & susie.wee@hp.com

Jeffrey Lotspiech (BS and MS Electrical Engineering, Massachusetts Institute of Technology, 1972) has been working in the content protection industry for over 12 years for IBM, and more recently as a private consultant. He has over 50 patents in this area, including the basic key management schemes used for both the Content Protection for Recordable Media (CPRM) and Advanced Access Content System (AACS). He has worked on the detailed specifications for both systems. He has been a leading proponent of broadcast encryption in general, and especially as it is applied to content protection of entertainment applications. lotspiech@almaden.ibm.com

Hongxia Jin is a Research Staff Member in IBM Almaden Research Center in San Jose, California. She obtained her Master and Ph.D degree in Computer Science from the Johns Hopkins University. Her main research interests are information security and privacy, content protection, Digital Rights Management, and software engineering.

Jessica Fridrich holds the position of Associate Professor at the Dept. of Electrical and Computer Engineering at Binghamton University (SUNY). She has received her PhD in Systems Science from Binghamton University in 1995 and MS in Applied Mathematics from Czech Technical University in Prague in 1997. Her main interests are in Steganography, Steganalysis, Digital Watermarking, and Digital Image Forensic. Dr. Fridrich's research work has been generously supported by the US Air Force. Since 1995, she received 17 research grants totaling over $ 5mil for projects on data embedding and steganalysis that lead to more than 70 papers and 7 US patents. Dr. Fridrich is a member of IEEE and ACM. fridrich@binghamton.edu

Tian-Tsong Ng received his M.Phil degree in Information Engineering from Cambridge University in 2001. He is currently pursuing his PhD degree in Electrical Engineering at the Columbia Univeristy Digital Video and Multimedia

Laboratory. His research focuses on passive-blind image forensics. His paper received the Best Student Paper Award at the 2005 ACM Multimedia Conference.

Shih-Fu Chang is a Professor in the Department of Electrical Engineering of Columbia University. He leads Columbia University's Digital Video and Multimedia Lab (http://www.ee.columbia.edu/dvmm), conducting research in multimedia content analysis, video retrieval, multimedia authentication, and video adaptation. Systems developed by his group have been widely used, including VisualSEEk, VideoQ, WebSEEk for image/video searching, WebClip for networked video editing, and Sari for online image authentication. He has initiated major projects in several domains, including a digital video library in echocardiogram, a content-adaptive streaming system for sports, and a topic tracking system for multi-source broadcast news video. Chang's group has received several best paper or student paper awards from the IEEE, ACM, and SPIE. He is Editor in Chief of IEEE Signal Processing Magazine (2006–8); a Distinguished Lecturer of the IEEE Circuits and Systems Society, 2001–2002; a recipient of a Navy ONR Young Investigator Award, IBM Faculty Development Award, and NSF CAREER Award; and a Fellow of IEEE since 2004. He helped as a general co-chair for ACM Multimedia Conference 2000 and IEEE ICME 2004. His group has also made significant contributions to the development of MPEG-7 multimedia description schemes. sfchang@ee.columbia.edu

Jeffrey A. Bloom has been working in the field of multimedia content security research since 1998 at Signafy, Inc. and later at NEC Research Institute. He was jointly responsible for advanced image and video watermarking technologies at Signafy and participated in the development of the NEC and Galaxy DVD copy control proposals for the Copy Protection Technical Working Group. Dr. Bloom then lead watermarking research and development at Sarnoff Corporation where his team developed digital watermarks specifically targeted at the digital cinema forensic application before joining Thomson in 2005. He currently manages the content security research group in Princeton New Jersey.

In addition to his contributions to numerous technical conferences, journals, and patents, Dr. Bloom is a co-author of *Digital Watermarking,* the leading text book in the field. This book is considered the primary source of fundamental watermarking principles.

Dr. Bloom holds B.S. and M.S. degrees in electrical engineering from Worcester Polytechnic Institute, and a Ph.D. from the University of California, Davis. He has expertise in the areas of multimedia content security, signal and image processing, image and video compression, and human perceptual models. His current research interests include digital watermarking, digital rights management, and machine learning. Jeffrey.Bloom@thomson.net

Xin Wang is the Chief Scientist and Director of DRM Architecture and Language at ContentGuard Inc., which is a spin-off company from the Xerox Palo Alto Research Center based on the Digital Rights Management project he initially worked on since 1996. He has in-depth expertise and extensive experience in developing DRM technologies, designing DRM systems, and creating novel business and usage models for multimedia content in the entertainment and enterprise environments. He holds more than 30 US and international patents in the areas of DRM and security. He has been one of the key editors of the ContentGuard XrML (eXtensible rights Markup Language), the MPEG-21 REL (Rights Expression Language), and the ContentGuard CEL (Contract Expression Language). Over the last six years, he has been participating and contributing to a number of DRM related standards groups including MPEG, OeBF, and ISMA.

He is an Adjunct Faculty member of Computer Science at the University Southern California, Los Angeles, where he teaches and researches in the areas of algorithms, security, and parallel and distributed computing. He is also an associate editor for the Journal of Computer and System Sciences. He received his B.S. and M.S degrees from Tsinghua University, Beijing, China, and Ph.D. degree from the University of Southern California. Xin.Wang@CONTENTGUARD.COM

Zhongyang Huang received his Master degree in Information Engineering from Nanyang Technological University (Singapore) in 2001 and Bachelor degree in Biomedical Engineering from Shanghai Jiaotong University (China) in 1993 respectively. From 1994 to 1999, he worked as a senior engineer for medical apparatus development in medical image processing area with China-America Joint Venture KangMing Biomedical Engineering Ltd. in China. Since 2001 he has been working as a Senior R&D Engineer at Panasonic Singapore Laboratories in Singapore. During this period, he has been actively involved in the standardization activities such as MPEG (MPEG-2/4/7/21), OMA, AVS, ISMA in the field of Digital Media distribution and management, particularly in the Digital Rights Management area. He has made some important contributions to these standardization groups. ZhongYang.Huang@sg.panasonic.com

Shengmei Shen is currently an R&D Manager of Panasonic Singapore Laboratories after she worked as a Senior Staff Engineer for 5 years from 1992 to 1997 in the same company. She has been involved in MPEG1/2/4 standardization and related product development for 12 years, particularly in Video Coding.

Since 2000 she has participated in MPEG IPMP Standardization and made important contributions together with her team. She also led a team to work on DTV, content distribution & management, as well as audio product development.

She received her Bachelor Degree in Electrical Engineering and Master Degree in adaptive signal processing in North-west Telecommunications Engineering Institute, in Xi'an (now Xidian University) in 1984 and 1986, respectively.

She worked in the Electrical Engineering Laboratories in the same University for two years before she went to Japan where she worked for 3 years in the area of medical signal processing. ShengMei.Shen@sg.panasonic.com

Gregory A. Stobbs is a partner in the patent law firm of Harness, Dickey & Pierce with over 25 years of experience in patent law, specializing in information and computer software technologies. He is author of two patent law treatises: Software Patents and Business Method Patents. stobbs@hdp.com

PREFACE

The explosive combination of digital signal processing, computing devices and digital networks have enabled pervasive digital media distribution that allows flexible and cost-effective multimedia commerce transactions. The digital nature of information also allows individuals to access, duplicate or manipulate information beyond the terms and conditions agreed upon. For instance, widespread piracy of copyrighted audio or video content using peer-to-peer networking has caused significant tension between members of the entertainment industry and free-speech advocates regarding the *fair use* of digital content. The large-scale acceptance of digital distribution rests on its ability to provide legitimate services to all competing stakeholders. This requires secure e-commerce systems that allow convenient use of digital content while equitably compensating members of the information distribution/consumption chain. Digital Rights Management (DRM), a critical component of such secure e-commerce systems, defines a set of tools that manage the trusted use of digital media content on electronic devices, ranging from personal computer, digital video recorder, DVD player, Music player, PDA, to mobile phones and other embedded devices. Various multimedia security technologies, such as encryption, watermarking, key managements, etc., have been designed to achieve this goal. To make DRM systems trustworthy to all players is more than just a technical issue. A truly effective approach requires solid engineering as well as a social, business and legal infrastructure. The market for DRM products and services is burgeoning and the search for the balance has been on-going.

Target Audience

While DRM has been in the spotlight in recent years, there had not been a single book that addresses all aspects of DRM. In particular, no book had provided a comprehensive coverage of the technical aspect of DRM. *Multimedia Security Technologies for Digital Rights Management* is the first book that was designed to provide an in-depth and comprehensive coverage on the state-of-the-art multimedia security technologies for the DRM applications.

If you have ever been intrigued by the buzz-word DRM and are interested in finding out more, if you are a manager or engineer developing a DRM system, if you plan to offer topic courses or tutorials on multimedia security, if you are curious about the hacking by a Norwegian teenager of the Content Scrambling System defined to protect the content of DVDs, if you have been alerted to the on-line music sharing debates, or if you are concerned about the potential implications of the recently enacted Digital Millennium Copyright Act in light of the arrest of the Russian programmer who circumvented Adobe Systems' eBook Reader DRM, this book is for you. In particular, this book can be used by graduate or senior undergraduate students who are starting to research in the field of multimedia security and digital rights management. It also serves perfectly as a comprehensive technical reference book on DRM for researchers, system engineers and algorithm developers.

Content and Organization

Multimedia Security Technologies for Digital Rights Management is one continuous book that has been harmonized to provide the audience with a comprehensive coverage of the fundamentals and the latest development of multimedia security technologies targeted for the DRM applications. It also reflects other non-technical (i.e., social and legal) aspects of DRM. The contributors include technology visionary and leading researchers in the field, many of whom are also active DRM standards contributors, industrial practitioners, and copyright lawyers.

The book comprises 18 chapters, and divides into four parts: Overview (Part A), Fundamentals of Multimedia Security (Part B), Advanced topics (Part C), and Standards and Legal issues (Part D). The first three chapters in Part A contain background materials and an overview of the DRM system architecture and deployment issues. Chapters 4 through 8 in Part B describe the fundamental security techniques for multimedia protection. Chapters 9 through 16 in Part C introduce the latest development in multimedia security and DRM. Chapters 17 and 18 in Part D discuss the standards and legal aspect of DRM. We elaborate on the contents of individual chapters in the following.

> **Chapter 1** introduces the subject of DRM, discusses a number of topics that identify the importance of rights management technologies, and shares some insight about the future.

Chapter 2 offers an overview of the general technology structure and capabilities of a DRM system, and presents a flexible, extensible reference model that may be used to characterize current and emerging DRM systems.

Chapter 3 discusses the importance of interoperability and standardization, and how media value-chains can change thanks to interoperable DRM specifications which support traditional rights and usages, and illustrates a toolkit approach to interoperable DRM.

Chapter 4 presents the fundamentals of multimedia encryption, including cryptographic primitives, application scenarios and design requirements, and an overview of some typical multimedia encryption schemes.

Chapter 5 presents the fundamentals of multimedia authentication, including cryptographic primitives, design requirements of multimedia applications, and an overview of some popular approaches.

Chapter 6 presents the fundamentals of conditional access systems in cable, satellite, and terrestrial distribution; digital rights management systems on the Internet, and the protection in digital home networks.

Chapter 7 provides an overview of the digital watermarking technologies, including applications, design considerations, tools and mathematical background, and latest development.

Chapter 8 introduces biometric authentication, and highlights its characteristics as pertained to its application to the digital rights management problem.

Chapter 9 analyzes the security requirements and architectures for multimedia distribution and introduces the general concept of format-compliant content protection to address both content adaptation and end-to-end security.

Chapter 10 addresses secure scalable streaming and secure transcoding, and shows that by co-designing the compression, encryption, and packetization operations, one can enable streaming and mid-network transcoding to be performed without requiring decryption, i.e., one can simultaneously provide end-to-end security and mid-network transcoding.

Chapter 11 presents an overview of scalable encryption and multi-access encryption and key schemes for DRM and other multimedia applications.

Chapter 12 introduces broadcast encryption, a relatively recent development in cryptography, and discusses its interesting advantages as a key management scheme for content protection.

Chapter 13 addresses the practical problem of tracing the users (traitors) who instrument their devices and illegally resell the pirated copies by redistributing the content or the decryption keys on the Internet.

Chapter 14 features steganalysis, the counterpart of steganography, that aims to detect the presence of hidden data.

Chapter 15 reviews an emerging research area - the passive-blind image forensics, which addresses image forgery detection and image source identification.

Chapter 16 addresses prevention of unauthorized use of the motion picture content in digital cinema. Standardization efforts, goals and an example security system are presented.

Chapter 17 presents an overview of activities of a number of standards organizations involved in developing DRM standards, such as MPEG, OMA, Coral, DMP, ISMA, and AACS, and provides a quick-reference list to many others.

Chapter 18 provides an in-depth discussion and analysis of the Digital Millennium Copyright Act and its social and technological implications.

With the above introduction, we hope you enjoy reading *Multimedia Security Technologies for Digital Rights Management*. We learned a great deal putting this book together. We thank all the contributors for their enthusiasm and hard work that make the timely publication of this book possible. We would like to thank Ian Scott and Thomas J. Riehle for their assistance in proofreading some chapters and providing editorial suggestions. We are grateful to the assistance from B. Randall, R. Roumeliotis, R. Adams, L. Koch, B. Lilly and others at Elsevier, Inc. whose expertise has helped make the editing experience much more enjoyable.

Wenjun Zeng
Heather Yu
Ching-Yung Lin

PART **A**

OVERVIEW

1

Introduction—Digital Rights Management

Scott Moskowitz

1.1 PROPERTY AND VALUE

Real property is familiar to most people. We live in houses, work in offices, shop at retailers, and enjoy ball games at stadiums. In contrast with "personality," which includes personal effects and intellectual property, real estate derives from *realty*—historically, land and all things permanently attached. Rights, whether for real property or intellectual property, have communal roots. Security, however, is a term with very subjective meaning. Simply "feeling secure" is not necessarily equivalent with the expectations or actual protections provided. Securing real property can mean locking a door or, for the significantly more paranoid, deploying tanks on one's lawn. Although it can be argued that intellectual property is related to real property, there are inherent and significant differences—the obvious one being that intellectual property is not physical property. The most controversial aspect of intellectual property is the ease at which it can be and is shared. Divergent viewpoints on this issue exist. At the extremes, "information is free," while others assert theft. We will leave the ability to define "piracy" to economists, lobbyists, policymakers, and even jurists with such interests. Clearly, we need to consider the law and the cost of copy protection when making technical decisions about designing the appropriate system. A particular set of problems will need definitions in order for agreement on any "secure" solutions. For this reason, any resource on "Digital Rights Management" (DRM) should include appropriate context. While other chapters of this book focus on technology topics and the development of the burgeoning market for DRM products and services, this chapter covers a number of topics identifying the importance of rights management technologies.

1.2 "ORIGINAL WORK"

It is prudent to provide a cursory outline of copyrights, not in the interests of providing any form of legal advice, but to delineate the impact of how copyright protection has evolved with respect to U.S. copyright law.[1] Copyright is established in the U.S. Constitution. The single occurrence of the word "right" in the Constitution appears in Article 1, Section 8, Clause 8: "[t]o promote the Progress of Science and useful Arts, by securing for limited times to authors and inventors the exclusive *right* to their respective writings and discoveries." As with all U.S. laws, the U.S. Congress first enacts legislation, while the courts provide judicial oversight and interpretation of law. Over time, legislation has been adopted making copyright more consistent with advances in the technology landscape. Lobbying efforts by a variety of stakeholders have provided additional impetus for change for economic reasons. Litigating "copyright infringements" represent additional efforts at defining copyright and its associated protections. However, when one has a copyright, what exactly does that mean? Essentially, a copyright is a form of contract between the creator of the original work and the public. While based on the recognition of property rights, in general, the creator agrees to make his work publicly available in consideration of legal recognition under the law. The Constitution promulgated copyright in the interests of promoting science and the arts for the benefit of society. Subsequent changes, challenges, and context have become arguably more public with the huge success of the Internet and networking technologies in general.

To be a bit more specific, a "work," the copyrighted value to be protected, is "created" when it is fixed in a copy or phonorecord for the first time: where a work has been prepared over a period of time, the portion of it that has been fixed at any particular time constitutes the work as of that time, and where the work has been prepared in different versions, each version constitutes a separate work. A "derivative work" is a work based upon one or more pre-existing works, such as a translation, musical arrangement, dramatization, fictionalization, motion picture version, sound recording, art reproduction, abridgment, condensation, or any other form in which a work may be recast, transformed, or adapted. A work consisting of editorial revisions, annotations, elaborations, or other modifications which, as a whole, represent an original work of authorship is a derivative work. As electronics and digital editing software become the inexpensive tools of the

---

[1]For international copyright issues, one helpful resource is http://caselaw.lp.findlaw.com/data/constitution/article01/39.html.

Information Age, copyright is thought to need additional protections. We do not argue the merits of such a belief, but provide the following milestones as to how we got here from there.

1.3   LOOKING BACK AT THE COPYRIGHT ACT OF 1976

Including a list of burgeoning "copyright protection" software companies, the National Information Infrastructure Copyright Act of 1995 made recommendations to the Copyright Act of 1976 and addressed the potential problems with open networks such as the "Internet." It is a fairly interesting point to start a historical timeline from which rights management technologies have evolved as several of the companies listed in that report made subsequent impacts in the field. For our purposes, it is not necessary to interpret the large body of legal arguments, but it is helpful to provide what limits have been argued and how far the perception of technology impacts DRM. After all, the copyright holder is not the only party with legal rights. While copyright previously concerned "sweat of the brow," what is referred to as "Feist," a modicum of creativity has become the more stringent standard for establishing copyright. An early case, *Lotus Corporation v. Borland* is somewhat emblematic of the early fights over copyright protection of intellectual property.

> In Feist [Feist Publications, Inc. v. Rural Telephone Serv. Co., 499 U.S. 340 (1991)], the court explained:
>
> The primary objective of copyright is not to reward the labor of authors, but to promote the Progress of Science and useful Arts. To this end, copyright assures authors the right to their original expression, but encourages others to build freely upon the ideas and information conveyed by a work.
>
> Feist, 499 U.S. at 349-50. We do not think that the court's statement that "copyright assures authors the right to their original expression" indicates that all expression is necessarily copyrightable. While original expression is necessary for copyright protection, we do not think that it is alone sufficient. Courts must still inquire whether original expression falls within one of the categories foreclosed from copyright protection by 102(b) [1].

Section 107 of the Copyright Act of 1976 provides additional guidance for the wide range of stakeholders who may need to access or manipulate copyrighted works. Perhaps inevitably, reverse engineering and related attempts at circumventing "security" increase the perception that copies of the original work may require layered security and additional legal protections. The least understood aspect of copyright and its place "to promote the Progress of Science and useful Arts" regards "fair use." Bounded by several factors, the relative weights are not provided by the Copyright Act of 1976, and fair use may indeed be the one legal issue that presents the most difficult challenges in engineering solutions to piracy.

Four factors must be considered: (1) the purpose and character of the use, including whether such use is of a commercial nature or is for non-profit educational purposes; (2) the nature of the work; (3) the amount and the substantiality of the portion used in relation to the copyrighted work as a whole; and (4) the effect of the use on the market value of the copied work [2].

The one case at the heart of the most extreme debates in copyright circles may be *Sony Corporation v. Universal City Studios* (1984), concerning the sale of videocassette recorders (VCRs). The U.S. Supreme Court ruled that "[b]ecause recorders were 'widely used for legitimate, unobjectionable purposes,' the recording did not constitute direct infringement of the studio's copyrights .... Absent such direct infringement, there could be no contributory infringement by *Sony* [3]." The key factor being that there was value in personal recording. While citing the concept of fair use, which protects consumers from *some forms* of copyright infringement, the debate did not end with this ruling. Indeed, the concept of fair use has been extended to areas not previously anticipated, including reverse engineering of copyrighted software.

Additionally, the Copyright Act of 1976 laid several other "foundations," though they are still unsettled in the minds of the stakeholders involved. Besides extending the length of copyright protection, library photocopying was changed to make possible preservation and inter-library loans without permission. Section 107 is at the heart of the types of issues for evaluation of DRM system design, even if less than all stakeholders' rights are considered. Fair use is a doctrine that permits courts to avoid rigid application of the copyright statute when to do otherwise would stifle the very creativity that copyright law is designed to foster. One author addresses this notion of relativity in the early days of the Internet Age.

> The doctrine of fair use recognizes that the exclusive rights inherent in a copyright are not absolute, and that non-holders of the copyright are entitled to make use of a copyrighted work that technically would otherwise infringe upon one or more of the exclusive rights. Although fair use originated 'for purposes such as criticism, comment, news reporting, teaching, ... scholarship, or research,' it also applies in other areas, as some of the examples below illustrate. However, courts seem more willing to accept an assertion of fair use when the use falls into one of the above categories. Perhaps more than any other area of copyright, fair use is a highly fact-specific determination. Copyright Office document FL102 puts it this way: 'The distinction between "fair use" and infringement may be unclear and not easily defined. There is no specific number of words, lines, or notes that may safely be taken without permission. Acknowledging the source of the copyrighted material does not substitute for obtaining permission.' The document then quotes from the 1961 Report of the Register of Copyrights on the General Revision of the U.S. Copyright Law, providing the following examples of activities that courts have held to be fair use:—Quotation of excerpts in a review or criticism for purposes of illustration or

comment;—Quotation of short passages in a scholarly or technical work for illustration or clarification of the author's observations;—Use in a parody of some of the content of the work parodied;—Summary of an address or article with brief quotations, in a news report;—Reproduction by a library of a portion of a work to replace part of a damaged copy;—Reproduction by a teacher or student of a small part of a work to illustrate a lesson;—Reproduction of a work in legislative or judicial proceedings or reports;—Incidental and fortuitous reproduction in a newsreel or broadcast, of a work located in the scene of an event being reported [4].

Several other more recent legal and legislative actions should be mentioned to provide a broader consideration of what the fuss is really all about.

Digital Millennium Copyright Act, the "DMCA" (1998). Key among its impact is the provision, known as Section 1201, of a prohibition on circumvention of access restriction controls or technological protections put in place by the copyright owner. If a copyright owner puts an access restriction scheme in place to protect a copyright, unauthorized access is essentially illegal. However, it is still unclear how to define "access restriction" if such measures can be circumvented by holding the shift key at start-up of a personal computer, as in the case of one access restriction workaround or any consumer action that is inherent to the use of general computing devices. The Librarian of Congress conducted a proceeding in late 2000 to provide guidance to Congress.

Digital Theft Deterrence and Copyright Damages Improvement Act (1999). Congress increased damages that can be assessed on copyright infringements from that of $500 to $750 to $20,000 to $30,000. Willful infringement increased from $100,000 to $150,000.

Librarian of Congress Issues Exemptions to the DMCA (2000). Librarian of Congress issues exemptions to the DMCA, Section 1201(a)(1), the Anti-Circumvention Provision, for "classes of works" that adhere to fair use. These two exemptions include: "Compilations consisting of lists of websites blocked by filtering software applications; and Literary works, including computer programs and databases, protected by access control mechanisms that fail to permit access because of malfunction, damage, or obsoleteness." The full recommendation can be found at http://www.loc.gov/copyright/1201/anticirc.html.

Dmitri Skylyarov Arrested under DMCA Provisions (2001). The Russian programmer for ElcomSoft was accused of circumventing Adobe Systems' eBook Reader DRM. Although Adobe later reversed course, government attorneys continued with the prosecution of the case, presumably to test the interpretation of the DMCA. As one of the first criminal cases brought under the DMCA, many observers viewed this as a test case for how far allegations under the DMCA could be pushed into actual indictments. A federal jury returned a verdict of "not guilty" in late 2002.

U.S. Supreme Court Hears Challenge to Sonny Bono Copyright Term Extension Act, the "CTEA" (2002). In copyright debates Lawrence Lessig, a well-known constitutional scholar, has been active in promulgating such mechanisms as the "Creative Commons." His representation of the plaintiffs in *Eric Eldred v. John Ashcroft* extended his experience in the copyright debate. Ultimately, the Supreme Court ruled against the plaintiffs, affirming the constitutionality of the CTEA and affirming Congress's role in intellectual property. Retrospectively, the CTEA extended existing copyrights by 20 years—to 70 years from the life of an author, from 50 years. As well, adding 20 years of protection to future works. Protection was extended from 75 to 95 years for "works made for hire," a common contractual framework used by many corporations.

MGM v. Grokster **(2005).** It is unclear how many rounds of dispute resolution between technology innovators and content owners will go before the courts or Congress. For this reason, it may take some time to understand fully the impact of the *MGM v. Grokster* decision. The most widely quoted aspect of the ruling, thus far, concerns who should determine when a device is "promoted" to infringe copyright. The Supreme Court essentially decided:

> For the same reasons that *Sony* took the staple-article doctrine of patent law as a model for its copyright safe-harbor rule, the inducement rule, too, is a sensible one for copyright. We adopt it here, holding that one who distributes a device with the object of promoting its use to infringe copyright, as shown by clear expression or other affirmative steps taken to foster infringement, is liable for the resulting acts of infringement by third parties. We are, of course, mindful of the need to keep from trenching on regular commerce or discouraging the development of technologies with lawful and unlawful potential. Accordingly, just as *Sony* did not find intentional inducement despite the knowledge of the VCR manufacturer that its device could be used to infringe, 464 U.S., at 439, n. 19, mere knowledge of infringing potential or of actual infringing uses would not be enough here to subject a distributor to liability. Nor would ordinary acts incident to product distribution, such as offering customers technical support or product updates, support liability in themselves. The inducement rule, instead, premises liability on purposeful, culpable expression and conduct, and thus does nothing to compromise legitimate commerce or discourage innovation having a lawful promise [5].

In the world of physical media distribution, there are many channels available, both for broadcast and for physical carriers. Specialized retailers compete for consumer sales by differentiating their efforts from other more generalized retailers. Written content and imagery attracts consumers to publications such as magazines; and spoken content and music selection attracts consumers to radio. The number of possible combinations of content and editorial material provides for rich broadcast opportunities, which have the effect of attracting advertising dollars to the broadcasters. The parallels with online streaming or pay-per-click-type schemes are not a coincidence. Total spending on advertising has continued to grow over time, although the ability to reach a profitable, aggregated group of consumers has grown more difficult. The ability to reach paying audiences is the obvious aim of advertising.

The argument that there is too much entertainment vying for consumers' dollars is beginning to meet the more complicated issue of how to measure actual time for said consumption, while deploying efforts at protecting copyrighted material. Supply meets demand whether measured in units of time (e.g., minutes on a cellular phone), bandwidth (e.g., amount of data per unit of time), or copyrighted CDs, books, and DVDs. Some agreement on the unit of measurement obviously needs consideration. When supply is controlled, as with generalized DRM, the ability to measure demand may become distorted. Though the conclusions are contentious, the arguments can be made from a variety of viewpoints. Simply, can technical controls for accessing copyrighted material cost less than the cost of implementation and maintenance of these same controls? How are new devices and services handled given legacy control systems or even open systems? Is there value in securing copyrights with DRM? What rights of revocation exist, and who should determine the scope and form of revocation? How much open access should be provided to consumers? Is there value in providing copyrighted works for free? What constitutes a consumer's property in contrast with a content provider's property?

1.4   COMMUNICATION THEORY—WHO SCREAMS LOUDEST?

When considering the security of multimedia data, several issues pose challenges. First, multimedia data is compressible and easily transferable. Second, advances in digital signal processing have made the ability to digitize analog waveforms both economic and more commercially viable. Third, ownership and responsibility for any copies made of digitized content are typically a double-edged sword. Manufacturing has been made inexpensive to the owners and licensors, increasing profit margins, but content has increasingly been copied without regard to the interests of those rights holders. More on these issues will be discussed below.

1.4.1   Shannon's Gift

Before delving into technical aspects of DRM, attention must be paid to communications and cryptography. Cryptography has impacted history at several points. World War II was emblematic of the tight relationship between codes, militaries, governments, and politics—before the first microprocessors, but at a time of great technical innovation. The work in cracking the codes of that war was supplemented later by a growing interest in the underlying nature of communications. Largely unknown to the public, the seminal work of Claude E. Shannon in *The Mathematical Theory of Communication* and *Communication Theory of Secrecy Systems* provides helpful analysis in what can be expected theoretically. Developments based on communication theory, including cryptographic systems, are pervasive in modern society. The impact on our daily lives is incalculable. Telephones, financial markets, and even privacy itself have changed in dramatic, often unpredictable, ways. The demand for codes to assist with the secure transport of sensitive data was matched by the increasing importance of computerized networks for dispersal and distribution of such data.

At some point, confidentiality, one of several primitives designed into data security systems, was met by increasing calls for restrictions on the deployment of cryptographic protocols. Separately, but just as important, authentication, data integrity, and non-repudiation—additional primitives of cryptography—assisted in the growth of business over electronic networks. Public key cryptography provides all four of these primitives, in a manner making distribution of codes and ciphers economically feasible for all persons wishing to secure their communications. The landmark failure of the U.S. government's Clipper chip [6] in 1993 was only the beginning of an increased public interest in cryptography. With the proliferation of more bandwidth and anonymity, in many cases based on so-called strong encryption, commercial concerns were also heightened. Here, we deal specifically with copyrighted works such as images, audio, video, and multimedia in general. A basic notion that should be considered in understanding DRM may well be how to balance privacy with notions of piracy. Ironically, the emphasis on protecting privacy has been trumped in many ways by the goal of securing against piracy. Should personal secrets be shared to satisfy the demands of copyright holders? Put another way, is a social security number used to secure a purchase for a song download a fair exchange of value asserted by the copyright holder?

Shannon's conceptualization of communication theory provides a fitting background to copy protection techniques to be explored in this book. Actual performance of real-world systems should be matched against theory to encourage appropriate expectations. Communication theory at its most basic level is about the transmission of information between a sender and a receiver. The information typically has meaning or context. Obviously, there are limitations to communication systems as explored by Shannon and others. The channel and destination of the information being transmitted provide additional parameters to a communication system. Here, we eliminate the simplified arrangements for a noiseless communication channel where the inputs and outputs are equivalent. By noiseless we mean no "chance variables" occur, and thus no redundancy or other error correction is needed to communicate messages.

The ratio of the actual rate of information transmission to capacity in a given channel is called the efficiency of the coding scheme. Efficiency to both the sender and the receiver can have subjective measurements as well. When a more real-istic scheme is analyzed, namely efficient transmission in the presence of noise, it is proven that there are still a finite number of errors (perceptibly "noise") or sets of errors (which can be mathematically generalized to create noise filters). Because binary data is either a "1" or a "0" in a given channel, we can say that each bit of data in the abstract may be completely random by flipping a coin, with 1 or 0 being the limited choices. That is not to say that entropy of any of the elements of the coin flip can be ignored. However, in order to ensure effective com-munication, the entropy of any chance variables, the entropy of the information source, the entropy of the channel, etc. must be taken into account. Error detec-tion, correction, and concealment form a large body of work in dealing specifically with the context of the information, the channel and nature of the transmission, and the entropy of the source impacts the channel capacity. That information may be successfully reproduced and can be expressed mathematically is, in large part, Shannon's legacy. This applies to cell phones and DVDs. Here, we con-cern ourselves with how a perceptible signal can be digitized, or "sampled," to approximate the original analog waveform. However, as is well known in signal processing and in a philosophical sense, the digitized signal can never be a perfect replica, but is an exact facsimile of an otherwise analog and infinitely approxi-mated waveform. The natural limit is quantization itself; however, the limit of the value of the coding scheme in terms of practical use is human perception and the economics of deployment.

In a discrete channel, entropy measures in an exact way the randomness of a "chance variable," which itself may be random. The development of very precise digitization systems representing an "ensemble of functions" used to communicate information has been reduced into a multitude of software or hardware systems. As we delve into cryptography, here, we quickly note that senders and receivers can exchange secrets, or "keys," associated with an ensemble of functions that facilitate agreement over the integrity of the data to be transmit-ted. Similarly, the ensemble of functions assures transmission of the message in the presence of noise in the channel. Keys may be mistaken as noise by other observers. So long as the sender and receiver can agree to the key, the "secret," the associated message can be authenticated. The key is ciphered (i.e., processed by a cryptographic algorithm) in a manner to mimic randomness not compu-tationally easy to discover even if the other observers are in possession of the cipher.

The key is thus a state or index of an ensemble of functions from which the receiver can be assured that the sender of the message did indeed transmit the mes-sage. The data transmission's discrete rate may not exceed the capacity of the communication channel. Finally, relating back to sampled signals, the quantiza-tion error (e.g., what is related to data conversion between analog to digital) must be small relative to the information transmitted in order to establish sufficiently small probabilities that the received signal is the communication intended by the sender. Statistically isolating "perturbing noise" from other errors and bounding upper and lower limits of capacity in a communication channel are presently computationally easy.

The introduction of digital CDs resulted from agreements over trade-offs of the general technologies so far described. As a medium for music, it is fitting to observe this medium for rich discussions on DRM. The CD is itself a discrete communication channel. The reflective material sandwiched between transparent plastic, which can be read by a CD player, is converted into a series of binary data (1s and 0s) as physical pits on the reflective material substrate. This data stream has pre-determined sampling rates and quantization values (16 bits, 44.1 kHz per second, for a Red Book Specification Audio Compact Disc). Again, data bits which have pre-determined locations or modality on the physical CD, are fed through an ensemble of functions which filter the digitized sample information stream into analog audio signal data. This data, of course, may be compressed for more economic use of bandwidth. We hear a song, the binary information sent out to an amplifier to be transduced, but, there is no "perceptually obvious" relationship with the music rendered. The data are presented according to the Red Book standard. We hear the music with our psychoacoustic abilities, our ears, and ultimately, our brains process the music and may associate the music information with some other independent or unrelated information.

Any such "associated information" may be different for every listening experience, every time for every individual listener. We would call this associated information "value added" or "rich" because it can be associated, with other independent information that may have no relationship with the primary communicated information which is the same for all listeners. The "hits" are hits for each individual in different ways that are aggregated in such a manner that they can be called hits—the memorable song for a high school prom, the one played when waking up, or any number of events associated with the copyrighted work in unintended ways, impacting the value attributed to such a work. Money is one obvious measure of success. Acting out a song may reflect the meaning intended by its creator or it may not. What matters with regards to DRM are the decisions made by creators and consumers of copyrighted works to create, seek, and consume with a fixed and limited amount of time and money determined by the harsh realities of the marketplace. Recognizable and potentially valuable multimedia can be rendered by general computing devices. Multimedia having many different interpretations depending on what stake the party has in the work. After all, creators, too, may give their work away for free.

We have generalized that it is computationally feasible to reproduce information, allowing senders and receivers to share the gestalt of information that may be transmitted. We ignore the specifics of digital filters and error correction to stress the point that, conceptually, data can be communicated and communicated securely. If the communication channel is too expensive, based on bandwidth or overall available transmission capacity or, as is central to this book, the cost of protection, it ceases to play a role in enabling security of data. Additionally, if the bandwidth requirements for reproduction are sufficiently high, certain other types of data are not computationally feasible to economically transmit over communication channels. As more information is digitized and, by extension, digitally copied, even if there are imperceptible differences with the original analog waveform, the limit to data transmission becomes closely linked to bandwidth [7].

Interestingly enough, Shannon does address "intelligibility criterion" of information transmissions in providing "fidelity evaluation functions." Because systems must be economically practical, and information is ultimately deemed authentic or genuine by the creator or source of the information (assuming the source is trusted or the information can be verified), human perception does play a role in establishing a close enough proximity of replicated data information, when "exact recovery" is infeasible, given the presence of noise in communications channels. The five examples Shannon provides for measuring acceptable fidelity of a proposed information channel include root mean square (i.e., "RMS," to assist in determining coordinate information of the data), frequency weighted root mean square (essentially weighting different frequency components prior to RMS, which is similar to passing the distance between data through a shaping filter and calculating the average power of data output), absolute error criterion (over the period of zero to a discrete time), human perception (which cannot be defined explicitly, though we can observe how noise is received by our senses and our brain, sufficiently subjective parameters), and the discrete case (differencing input from output and dividing by the total amount of input data).

1.4.2   Kerckhoffs' Limits

In cryptography, the content or bits comprising the message must not be changed in order to provide acceptable levels of confidence in a secure system. However, systems themselves cannot guarantee security. A human can compromise a system by providing passwords or systems may generate weak pseudo-random numbers, making the most seemingly strong "cryptographic algorithm" ("cipher") unsecure. A "keyed" algorithm defines an ensemble of functions with the specific member of the ensemble identified by a unique key. With respect to encryption, the set of all keys defines a plurality of encryption functions. Each element is instantiated by a specific key. Though there may be randomness ("entropy") within the input, the use of the randomness only relates to the manner in which the function operates as a Turing machine (e.g., a general computing device). The random choice of a key to specify the element in the plurality of encryption functions is essential.

As Shannon stressed, communications is concerned with "operations on ensembles of functions," not with "operations on particular functions." Cryptography, too, is about ensembles of functions. The basic difference with coding (i.e., communications) is the exchange of the key. The ensemble of functions occupies a finite set, so that the input and output can be secured by associating the data to be transmitted with a randomly generated key that is pre-determined by both parties by some mutually agreed to means—the cryptographic algorithm or cipher. Kerckhoffs' law is the foundation by which such determinations are made; it is assumed that the adversary possesses the cipher, and thus the security must rest in the key. Auguste Kerckhoffs provided five additional principles, including (1) system indecipherability, (2) the key must be changeable, (3) the system should be compatible with the means of communication, (4) portability and compactness of the system is essential, and (5) ease of use. Of these principles, ease of use and whether security rests with the key have historically made for difficult engineering challenges within DRM. In cases where DRM systems must come in contact with other DRM systems, these challenges are heightened. Some have argued that it is not possible to tamperproof cryptographic systems to sufficiently prevent hacks [8]. This has obvious impacts on DRM.

1.5   CRYPTOGRAPHY—MUCH TO DO

With a basic understanding of communications theory and its relationship with cryptography, we can describe two conventional techniques for providing key-based confidentiality and authentication currently in use: symmetric and asymmetric encryption. Both systems use non-secret algorithms to provide encryption and decryption and keys that are used by the algorithm. This is the basis for Kerckhoffs' law: all security should reside in the key, as it is assumed the adversary will have access to the cryptographic algorithm. In symmetric systems, such as AES, the decryption key is derivable from the encryption key without compromising the security of the message. To assure confidentiality and authenticity, the key should be known only to the sending and receiving entities and is traditionally provided to the systems by secure physical communication, such as human courier. Other systems where a common key may be developed by the sender and receiver using non-secure communications are widely deployed. In such systems, each party to a communication generates a numerical sequence, operates on the sequence, and transfers the result to the other party. By further operation using the transferred result and the locally generated sequence, each party can develop the identical encryption key, which cannot be obtained from the transferred results alone. As implemented for use over the Internet, common encryption systems are those denoted by the Secure Socket Layer (SSL) and IP Security Protocol (IPSEC) protocols.

In asymmetric encryption systems, a first party to a communication generates a numerical sequence and uses that sequence to generate non-reciprocal and different encrypting and decrypting keys. The encrypting key is then transferred to a second party in a non-secure communication. The second party uses the encrypting key (called a public key because it is no longer secure) to encrypt a message that can only be decrypted by the decrypting key retained by the first party. The key generation algorithm is arranged such that the decrypting key cannot be derived from the public encrypting key. Similar methods are known for using non-reciprocal keys for authentication of a transmission. There are also digital signature algorithms. In some cases, as with RSA, encryption and digital signature functionality are properties incorporated by the same algorithm. In a manner parallel with the real-world handwritten signatures, the non-secure public key can be used to tamperproof a message (i.e., providing nonrepudiation) that has been digitally signed using a secure "private" or secret key known only to the originating party—the signer. Thus, the receiving party has assurance that the origination of the message is the party who has supplied the "public" decrypting key. So, how does this relate to DRM? We have devised several areas of interest to establish commonality of the elements typically considered in designing a DRM system, namely authentication, data integrity, non-repudiation, and confidentiality. However, DRM is inherently constrained from legal, economic, and political constraints, as well as consumer expectations—not strictly cryptography or more generally communication theory. Mentioned previously, some argue it is not possible to tamperproof software programs given the inherent foundations of communications. Within the DRM product and service space, terminology and practicality can vary widely. Here, we generalize DRM by discussing "wrapping" and "embedding," so-called "digital watermark," technology.

1.6   DIGITAL RIGHTS MANAGEMENT—WRAPPING AND EMBEDDING

It is not prudent to limit our discussion solely on word choice. Essentially, the terms may not always reflect the utility or functionality of the protections being described. Rights are typically matched by responsibilities. DRM offers up examples of how stakeholders may not share common interests [9]. Copy protection and content extensions generally apply to digitized content, while "scrambling," a scheme related to encryption, may be applied to an analog signal. Such analog scrambling is evident in analog cable and analog cell phone systems. Encryption, as discussed previously, scrambles content, but the number of 1s and 0s may be different after the encryption process. In some scenarios, prior to enabling access to content it must be decrypted, with the point being that once the content has been encrypted, it cannot be used until it is decrypted. Encrypted audio content itself might sound like incomprehensible screeching, while an encrypted image or video might appear as random noise when viewed. The encryption acts as a transmission security measure—access control. One approach has commonly been called "conditional access" when someone or something has the right to access the media. In many scenarios, identifying information or authentication of that party must first be completed prior to decryption of the content or description of the intended scope of use. There may be layered access restrictions within the same scheme. In either case, the transmission protection ends when the content is to be observed.

Encryption is poorly applied in at least two specific areas with respect to copy protection of content. First, so-called "pirates" have historically found ways to crack the protection as it is applied to content. The effect is essentially equivalent to obtaining the decryption key without paying for it. One such technique is "differencing," where an unencrypted version of the content is compared with an encrypted version of the same to discover the encryption key or other protections. Differencing is also a weakness in many digital watermark systems. In some watermark systems, the requirement to maintain original unwatermarked material for comparing and recovering embedded code from a suspect copy of content introduces other problematic issues such as additional data storage requirements at the detection side. Why store watermarked content for protection purposes when unwatermarked content may exist at the same site for decoding said watermarks? Second, and perhaps more complicated to address, is that once a single legitimate copy of content has been decrypted, a pirate is now free to make unlimited copies of the decrypted copy. In effect, in order to make, sell, or distribute an unlimited quantity of content, the pirates could simply buy one copy, which they are authorized to decrypt, and make as many copies as desired. These issues were historically referred to as the "digital copy problem"; others prefer "digital piracy."

Copy protection also includes various methods by which an engineer can write software in a clever manner to determine if it has been copied and, if so, to deactivate the software. The same engineer may be a "rogue engineer" who essentially has the backdoor key to deactivate the copy protection. This is typically the result of a poorly chosen encryption algorithm or means for obtaining a key. Also included are undocumented changes to the storage format of the content. Copy protection was generally abandoned by the software industry, since pirates were generally just as clever as the software engineers and figured out ways to modify their software and deactivate the protection. The cost of developing such protection was also not justified considering the level of piracy that occurred despite the copy protection. That being said, the expansion of software product activation keys, online registration schemes, and registered version upgrades indicates increased interest and benefit in securing even software programs. Software watermarking schemes, including those using "steganographic ciphers," have correspondingly increased over the past few years [10].

Content extension refers to any system attaching some extra information indicating whether a copy of the original content can be made or some other logic with regards to the use and accessibility of the content. A software or hardware system must be specifically built around this scheme to recognize the additional information and interpret it in an appropriate manner. An early example of such a system is the Serial Copyright Management System (SCMS) included in Digital Audio Tape (DAT) hardware. Under this system, additional information is stored on the track immediately preceding each sound recording indicating whether or not it can be copied. The hardware reads this information and uses it accordingly. By wrapping content, we are generally referring to "content extensions." We further formalize concepts below.

When we discuss watermarks, we are addressing steganography, or hiding information in plain view, in combination with cryptographic techniques. They need not be mutually exclusive and in many cases complement each other. Watermarks [11] are a unique technology that embed and protect a "code" by placing "transactional information" intrinsically within the electronic work. The transaction information can specify time, date, recipient, and supplementary information known by the transmitter at the time of the transfer to the recipient. Review of the electronic copy of the media at a later instance reveals the historical record of the electronic copy. Safeguarding from manipulation or deletion, unauthorized modification of the transactional information results in degradation of the perceptual quality of the work. Tampering with watermarked media is, thus, quickly identifiable. More advanced schemes include watermark code which itself interacts with the system. This code, with or without interaction with a key, can upgrade content security systems and can be characterized by a variety of interactions between the protection scheme, associated keys, watermark information, and content to be protected. Before delving into finer detail, we note that it is unclear that any wrapped, embedded, or generally "DRM'd" content has remained wrapped or inaccessible. In parallel, we have not observed clear examples where copyright holders have yet to eschew traditional distribution channels to achieve economic success solely through DRM distribution schemes.

1.6.1   Who Is in Control—Active and Reactive Controls

Protection of copyrighted works may be a proactive control that reduces the potential of loss at the time of an event, while a reactive control provides an audit trail after the fact to conclude what happened and by whom. The two types of controls are complementary and, in many cases, can and should be used concurrently. Such consideration as the time value of the content, that period in which the content is worth most for protection, is subjective and varies among media types, distribution channels, and market forces. Yesterday's newspaper arguably suffers far greater reduction of economic value than long-running hits on Broadway during the time it takes a new edition of the newspaper to appear (changes in critiques of the Broadway work, notwithstanding). Uniqueness over data or data copies assists in establishing responsibility for the data. Similar to the physical world use of receipts for transactions over the "same" material, watermarks act as a control for receipts of digitized data. However, time also plays a significant role in value.

Active controls provide a first line of defense in times of a breach in security. With regard to data security risks, there are several types of commonly established information security controls, generally categorized as physical, procedural, and logical controls. Physical controls are generally building access and alarm systems. Procedural controls include policies, operating procedures, training, and audits. Logical controls are placed at the computer system level and include application and operating system-level access controls, lists, and perimeter protection with firewalls, router security, and intrusion detection systems. With respect to the copying of copyrighted media, the most common type of active controls is "security wrappers," often called ("active") DRM [12]. A wrapper wraps the digital media around a digital structure to prevent extraction of the media from the stored data object. Generally, the wrapper includes encryption of the media, "meta-data" about the media, and may include other logic, encrypted or not. A simplistic explanation follows here.

First, content is encoded with associated meta-data, followed by encryption of the meta-data and media, and any additional non-encrypted data may be placed. Finally, additional information, oftentimes a software wrapper, that must be run to extract the media is added. The data object is stored directly within the software wrapper. That is, the media is blanketed with multiple layers of controls. To obtain the media in a perceptually similar form, the wrappers must be removed. Hence, this is an active control. However, to be useful, the wrapper must be removed, making the media extremely vulnerable at the time of use (viewing, playback, etc., when the media is "in the clear" and susceptible to unauthorized use). The software wrapper may also require active coordination by a third party during the unwrapping process. For instance, the software wrapper may require interaction with the content provider to obtain keys to decrypt the content. This communication requirement adds additional complexity to the process and, if required, places additional constraints when the active DRM-protected media is part of a larger workflow. Watermarks need not be incorporated in the previous example. Instead, meta-data are placed external to the content for operational requirements, and both the meta-data and the media are encrypted. The meta-data, for instance, may provide cryptographic authentication of the media or may provide keys for an external cryptographic operation that must be performed again including upgrades to the system in parts or in its entirety. The placement of watermarks as an additional reactive control provides complementary benefits.

Reactive controls do not actively prevent misappropriation or data transfer from happening. However, the benefits of reactive controls are multifold. To support recovery of losses, so-called "tracing traitors" or "identifying pirates," reactive controls provide an audit trail for actuarial or forensic analysis. As an ancillary benefit to their forensic capability, reactive controls act as a deterrent. Knowing that a copy can be traced back to a pirate is common in traditional commerce. Reactive controls may also assist with authentication or indicate tampering. Furthermore, valuable actuarial information may be obtained through reactive controls, providing marketing information intrinsic to the data objects or distribution channels being utilized. Reactive controls are complementary to active controls and may be used concurrently.

Watermarks are a "reactive" DRM control technique. Unlike wrappers, watermarks are maintained throughout the data workflow. As watermarks are intrinsically embedded into the content, they cannot be removed during processing of the copy of the digital media. Ideally, attempts at removal result in degradation of the content and a corresponding devaluation of the content's economic worth. As the copy of the media is moved through its expected and unexpected workflow, there are no stages requiring removal of the watermark as the media retains its same perceptual qualities. As watermarks do not modify the copy to a new format via wrapping or encryption, processing and workflow used prior to the incorporation of watermarks in the media do not require modification. Previous processes continue to stay the same without the incorporation of new steps or technology. Moreover, the watermark is retained in each step of the workflow rather than being stripped off as is required in many security controls employing encryption or wrappers. Once the wrappers are stripped off, they are ineffective, and the only protection mechanism remaining is the reactive controls. Watermarks can be designed to survive format and data transformations between digital and analog domains for varying degrees of persistence. This persistence assists with analysis of data that exists in different formats or channels.

1.6.2   Traceability and Active Controls

Watermarks, being a part of the media rather than external to it, are not susceptible to problems with wrappers. Moreover, when used in conjunction with an active control, watermarks are not removed during the unwrapping process. By indelibly mapping transaction information to the characteristics of the media, watermarks are presently deployed in several active control environments to manage authentication of the media and enable such features as copy management and even system upgradeability. In a manner parallel to physical money, active controls are comparable to copy protection features, including ink type, paper stock, fiber, angles of artwork that distort in photocopier machines, inserted magnetic strips, and composite art. When all of these security features are reduced to digital data, active and reactive controls can be similarly compared. These controls are intended to make money difficult to reproduce, while the serial number is intended to enable audits of specific transactions. Responsibility over individual media copies via watermarks can be used to enable policies regarding use limitations, first and third party transfers, and any number of active controls.

Though active controls provide a first line of defense, they have many inherent deficiencies. By the very nature of a wrapper, it must be unwrapped to use. Similar to a crab moving out of its shell, at the point of unwrapping the media has no effective protection mechanism. In practice, several technologies have been used to actively protect the media, including physical protection. However, these additional controls have limited effectiveness given the sophistication of hackers, complexity of the wrapper, and inconveniences presented to users. Once hacks have been successfully made, it is relatively easy for less sophisticated users to deploy the same hack with little effort. Wrappers increase overall processing requirements depending on operating systems or file formats limiting persistent protection. Inconvenience is the most significant problem for the users of the media. Unless each step of the workflow is able to unwrap "securely," the process leaves exposed media vulnerable. Active controls limit the movement of information, as each process requires the unwrapping technology associated with it.

1.6.3   Binding Transactions, Not Just a Handshake

The placement of transactional information directly into media works has many benefits. First and foremost, it creates an audit trail embedded directly into the work. This information can include time, place, and the identities of the transferring party and the transferee of the electronic media. Whereas system logs on computers can state prior actions that have taken place on a server, these logs cannot be used to analyze two copies of the same media and state the past history of the works. Yet today, it is not uncommon that multiple copies of the same media are transferred to multiple parties, including internal and external parties. System logs are insufficient to determine cause during a forensic analysis of media discovered at an unauthorized location unless each copy is serialized. System logs also make analysis of first and third party responsibility an unsupported process, if applied alone. In practice, a unique serial or transaction number, rather than the actual, copyable information, is placed as a search index to map back to additional transaction information (e.g., name, date, time, distribution channel, transaction id, etc.) stored in a database. Such hierarchy, or layering of "unique digitized data," is beneficial for workflow separation [13] and assigning responsibility over data as it moves within and beyond an organization's electronic systems.

As a single work (or other electronic media) may be digitally copied into multiple digital works at little or no marginal cost, digital watermarks ensure that each digital work is uniquely serialized. Similar to physical money with serial numbers, each unit is unequivocally different and perceptually equivalent from other copies of the same source. Properly deployed, digital watermarks enable inherent audit trails of digital data in any number of electronic transactions or workflows. For instance, Person A has a copyrighted work with their identity embedded as the watermark "A". In transferring a copy of the digital work to Person B, Person A imprints a watermark with identity "B" into a new copy of the work. This process can be repeated from Person B to Person C and so forth. Similarly, additional transactional information or a unique serial or transaction number may be placed into the work via a watermark. In the process, each electronic copy is digitally unique yet perceptually the same. Hence, each copy incorporates an internally embedded audit trail of its transactional history. The same work may also have been transferred by the same person to two different entities. In this scenario, a work sent to "B" is uniquely different, but perceptually equivalent to a work sent to "C." As the data is digital rather than physical, a recipient may create exact copies. Because of the watermark, each new copy must contain the previous embedded audit trail relating to its past history. Each work, independent of what the watermark contains and the number of watermarks incorporated into the copy, is perceptually the same. From an auditing and forensic point of view, these are unique. A copy with watermark "A, B" relates to a work that was last authorized for transfer from Person A to Person B and was not obtained directly from "C" or from "A."

1.7 NOW, THE FUTURE

Looking backward at the progress of technology, as with any hindsight, is much simpler than projecting forward. The concepts discussed here do not represent the definitive "last word," but an introduction to an important aspect of the technology landscape. DRM is a subject with so many competing stakeholders that new paradigms or business models do not necessarily appear obvious [14], and the viewpoints are not mutually exclusive. However, business is primarily an exercise in seeking profits. Measuring profitability or even accountability are invaluable starting points, but by no means is money the only perspective nor should it be, especially with regards to copyright. It is not just copyrighted multimedia that is impacted by advances and debates over DRM. Arguably, all intellectual property will be subjected to similar pressures. A valuable and fungible asset in the economy, besides time, is trust. Trust itself shapes many of the compromises that are needed in further commercializing networks [15]. An important aside: if we knew what the "blockbusters" would be, we would forgo the agents, promotion, distribution channels, specialty retailers, and all other middlemen and offer the valuable works from the back of our cars. *Caveat emptor.*

ACKNOWLEDGMENTS

Thanks for all of the rich insight and valuable comments received over the past decade. Special thanks goes to Yair Frankel and my family.

REFERENCES

[1] Lotus Development Corporation v. Borland International, Inc., 49 F. 3d 807, 818 (1st Cir. 1995).

[2] P. Durdik. Reverse Engineering As A Fair Use Defense To Software Copyright Infringement, Jurimetrics J., 34:451–470, Summer 1994.

[3] C. Miller. New Technology and Old Protection: The Case for Resale Royalties on the Retail Sale of Used CDs. Hastings Law Journal, 46:217–241, November 1994.

[4] Originally, T. Carroll. A Frequently Asked Questions Document Discussing Copyright Law ftp://ftp.aimnet.com/pub/users/carroll/law/copyright/faq/part2. Updated on September 11, 2002, http://www.tjc.com/copyright/FAQ/.

[5] Metro-Goldwyn-Mayer Studios, Inc. v. Grokster, Ltd. (04-480) 380 F. 3d 1154 (Sup Ct. 2005).

[6] Basically, a chip for encryption with a backdoor for the government.

[7] S. Moskowitz. *Bandwidth as Currency*, IEEE MultiMedia, pp. 14–21, January–March 2003.

[8] Barak, Goldreich, et al. *On the (Im)possibility of Obfuscating Programs*. An extended abstract appeared in *CRYPTO 2001*, pp. 1–43, August 16, 2001.

[9] R.J. Anderson. Cryptography and Competition Policy—Issues with 'Trusted Computing,' 2003 Wenk Lecture related to R.J. Anderson. TCPA/Palladium FAQ, at http://www.cl.cam.ac.uk/users/rja14/tcpa-faq.html/.

[10] Method for Stega-Cipher Protection of Computer Code, U.S. Patent No. 5,745,569, Patent and Trademark Office, 1998.

[11] There are many forms of digital watermarks. We generically use watermark to mean forensic or traceable watermark.

[12] "Active DRM" is our preferred terminology to distinguish between DRM technologies providing active controls and DRM technologies providing reactive controls.

[13] Workflow separation refers to the steps, or identifiable points, data moves as it is being prepared or processed.

[14] W. Fisher. Promises to Keep: Technology, Law, and the Future of Entertainment, PTKIntroduction.doc Draft, pp. 1–21, March 22, 2003. Also see http://www.harvard.edu/Academic_Affairs/coursepages/tfisher/Music.html/

[15] A. Odlyzko. Privacy, Economics, and Price Discrimination on the Internet [Extended Abstract], http://www.dtc.umn.edu/~odlyzko, pp. 1–16, July 27, 2003.

2
Digital Rights Management Systems

Marina Bosi

2.1 INTRODUCTION—WHAT IS DIGITAL RIGHTS MANAGEMENT?

In recent years there has been an inexorable migration of entertainment and other content from analog formats toward digital formats. Examples include the transition from vinyl records and analog tape to CDs, MP3 files, and other digital audio formats; from books to PDF and other e-book formats; from analog TV signals to MPEG-2, HD-TV, and other digital video formats; from celluloid film to the DVD-Video format and digital film distribution; etc. In general, digital media enables enhanced end-user experience and new opportunities for content creation and distributions, as well an increased level of interaction between creators/end-users.

Content owners often look at sales/rentals of digital assets as an important source of revenue and look askance at the increasing prevalence in sharing of files containing copyrighted content. While the nature of analog assets allows for an "implicit" form of content protection, the transition to digital systems raises the specter of unlimited perfect copies of proprietary content being distributed without compensation to the owner.

Digital Rights Management (DRM) refers to technologies that support legal distribution of digital media while protecting appropriate property rights. DRM technology doesn't take a stance on whether or not such content should be shared, but instead provides the tools to manage the access to digital media. In other words, DRM systems define a set of tools that allows digital media to be protected, but the existence of such tools does not imply that all digital media should be protected.

Early implementation of DRM systems emphasized defensive protection from copying digital content, but more modern implementations aim to support specific business use models for the content. Modern implementations flexibly manage access to digital assets via a variety of different distribution channels and devices. For example, the Open Mobile Alliance (OMA) has promoted a set of DRM technologies for cellular phone applications that include such capabilities as "Forward-Lock," which allows content to be downloaded to a specific handset and played unlimited times, but does not allow the content to be forwarded to any other device, and as "Flexible Preview," which allows a pre-specified preview of digital content to be viewed on any device and allows the content to be forwarded to any other device, but does not allow the full content to be accessed without full access rights. Clearly, capabilities such as Forward-Lock and Flexible Preview can support content owners in very different business models for content access.

Enabling proper distribution/deployment of digital media across a variety of contexts and devices not only raises issues of DRM systems interoperability, but also reaches above and beyond DRM systems to moral, business, and legal concerns. Purchasers of full access to a piece of digital content reasonably should expect that the content will work on all of their digital playback devices, putting high hurdles on system interoperability. However, the ability to transfer copies across devices raises the issues of how to limit such transfer. These issues include how many copies should be allowed, what users should be able to view those copies, how long should these users have access to those copies, etc. Not only are technological issues raised, but also legal and ethical issues. Furthermore, users have certain usage rights expectations based on traditional analog usage patterns, and such expectations also raise hurdles on the technological requirements of DRM systems [1].

In this chapter we do not intend to address all of these heady issues. Instead, we hope solely to offer an overview of the general technology structure and capabilities to provide the readers with context as they weigh for themselves the broader legal, ethical, and business issues associated with deploying DRM technology.

2.2   THE BASIC STRUCTURE OF A DRM SYSTEM

In this section we describe the high-level structure of any DRM system. A DRM system needs to address three major areas:

1. Ensuring that the digital asset is packaged in a form that will prevent unauthorized copying/usage
2. Appropriately distributing the digital asset to the end-user
3. Making sure the end-user is able to render the digital asset consistently with his/her rights

In addition, DRM systems increasingly treat packaged content and the rights to access that content as separate entities. This adds a fourth area that a DRM system needs to address:

4. Distribution of usage permissions allowing the user to access the protected content

Furthermore, the creation of a "trusted" environment, where both the rights issuer and the receiving devices are recognized as such, implies the establishment of authentications protocols that ensure safe exchange of information.

Figure 2.1 shows the basic DRM process flow. In the DRM process, rights holders/content providers release digital content that needs to be packaged into a media file format to allow for protection and watermarking/tracking of the enclosed content. The rights holders/content providers also will define the end-user's rights that will allow access to the protected media asset.

Once packaged, the packaged/protected asset is made available for distribution either through physical distribution of media (e.g., DVD or CD sales through a store, purchase of a DVD or CD through Amazon.com) or through online distribution (e.g., download MP3 files from iTunes® [10] onto a PC or MP3 player).

Having the content physically present does not necessarily guarantee that it is playable. Playing content in a DRM system requires that usage rights to that content are also delivered to the end-user. Those rights may come packaged with the asset (e.g., once purchased, a DVD is playable in any DVD player), but they

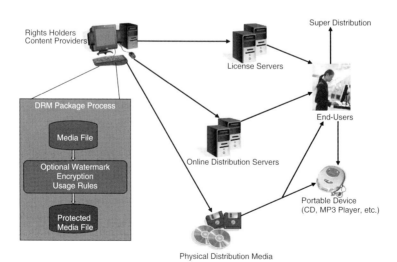

FIGURE 2.1:   Basic structure of a DRM system [2].

also may be distributed separately (e.g., with OMA Flexible Preview the content may reside locally on the user's player, but nothing beyond a preview is allowed prior to receiving a full access license). An integral part of usage rights is not only what types of usage are allowed, but also where such usage is permitted. In some cases the user may have rights to port digital assets to different authorized devices (domain), but in other cases the usage rights may be limited to a single specified device. Also, an end-user may have rights to forward digital assets to a different user who, in turn, would be required to acquire usage rights before full access to the content is allowed.

2.3   EXAMPLE: THE DVD CONTENT SCRAMBLING SYSTEM

To make the high-level structure described in the prior section more tangible, we will present a particular DRM system and show how its components fit into the described structure. The example we will use is that of the Content Scrambling System (CSS) which was designed to protect the digital content of DVDs [3]. The CSS was defined by the DVD Copy Control Association (CCA) and released in 1996. This was one of the first examples of a widely deployed DRM system.

Movies are put on a DVD-Video disc in an encrypted format that requires a key to decode and view the content. A DVD player is only able to play the content if it has such a playback key. The manufacturers of DVD players need to register with the DVD CCA to gain access to the decryption key to embed into their players. Hence, distribution of playback keys to DVD player manufacturers represents the distribution of usage licenses in the general DRM structure. The discs themselves are sold via stores or through phone/Internet purchases, leading to the delivery of a DVD disc to the purchaser; hence, the distribution channel is the physical distribution of the packaged media. Once acquired, the end-user has the ability to watch the content of purchased DVDs an unlimited number of times on any registered player. Hence, the usage rights are for unlimited content access on any licensed player. Moreover, the physical disc can be given to anyone else so that usage is not limited to any particular individual or corporate entity or playback device.

For the interested reader, we add a bit more detail as to how the encryption technology is utilized (see Figure 2.2). The DVD disc itself contains a hidden area in addition to the encrypted digital asset. The hidden area holds a table of encrypted disc keys and the disc key hash needed to decode the encrypted content on the disc. The hidden area itself can be accessed only by a device that is "authenticated." A DVD decoder licensed by the DVD CCA maintains a player key that is required to decrypt the disc key, a region code to verify that the disc has been released for usage in this region (e.g., United States, Europe, Asia), and a nonce (secret key) used in the authentication process with the playback device. The DVD decoder needs to

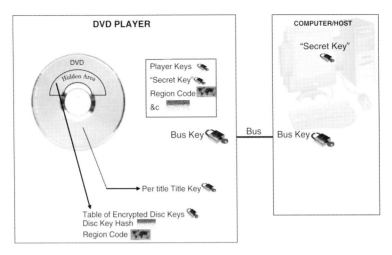

FIGURE 2.2:   DVD CSS system overview [4].

send the decoded audio/video content over a bus to a playback device. The play-back device also contains a secret key used for authenticating itself as a legitimate player of the decoded content. Both the decoder and the player know each other's nonces at the end of the authentication process. During the authentication process, the session (or bus) key is negotiated and created based on the two nonces. The bus key is used to encrypt the disc keys and title key before sending them through the bus so as to prevent "eavesdropping," and the nonces change at every authentication session. The authentication process is here based on a private key.

The process goes through the following steps:

a. Establish trust. The result of this phase is the session key.
b. Decode the disc content. The player keys are used to decrypt the disc key.
c. Title and bus keys are sent to the host.
d. The device sends a data sector to the host.
e. The host decrypts the title key using the disc key.
f. The host reads the data sector using the title and sector keys.

A major issue with the CSS structure is that it includes a fixed encryption scheme that can potentially be hacked. This is not just of theoretical interest as a Norwegian teenager managed to hack the CSS system, and, following dissemination of how he did it, "DeCSS" code has become so prevalent that T-shirts can be purchased with the algorithm on them. (As it turns out, his initial hack was based on getting access to a particular player key. Over time, however, additional hacks have been promulgated which do not require access to any company's particular license information.)

Also, possession of the decryption key allows full access to the content so limited access cannot be easily sold through the DVD-Video format. This limits the business models that can be carried out using DVD-Video content. Recently, discs that self-destruct after limited contact with air have been tried as an attempt to deal with this limitation. Moreover, access to the decryption key allows access to *all* DVDs, so it cannot be used as a basis for online distribution of movies (i.e., the license distribution is not linked to the particular content in any meaningful manner).

2.4   EXAMPLE: THE OMA DRM

Before one can download a ring tone, stream a video clip, or read an article on a mobile phone, a secure system of protection for that material (most of which is copyrighted) needs to be put in place. The OMA is a group of mobile phone operators, IT companies, vendors of wireless equipment, and content providers whose espoused mission "is to facilitate global user adoption of mobile data services by specifying market driven mobile service enablers[1] that ensure service interoperability across devices, geographies, service providers, operators, and networks, while allowing businesses to compete through innovation and differentiation." One of the areas in which the OMA has put together an "enabler" package is the area of DRM. The OMA has been able to unite in its DRM specifications the wireless industry under one standard by consolidating the Wireless Application Project (WAP) Forum, Third Generation Partnership Project (3GPP), SyncML, and Wireless Village. It counts more than 300 members.[2]

Two versions of the OMA's DRM enabler package have been released: OMA DRM version 1.0, which provides basic access control to content via mobile devices, and OMA DRM version 2.0, which extends version 1.0 to provide a wider set of usage rules to access content, increased security, domain, and export. According to the OMA, version 1.0 is meant to provide access to "light media content" (mostly ring tones), while version 2.0 is meant to handle access to "premium" content.

2.4.1   OMA DRM version 1.0

OMA DRM version 1.0 consists of three parts and was finalized in November 2002 [5]. The three parts are:

1. **Forward-Lock** (prevents content from leaving device)
2. **Combined Delivery** (adds specific rights definitions to the content)

---

[1] "Enabler" is the OMA's term of art for an open standard that they have developed.
[2] A complete list of OMA members can be found at http://member.openmobilealliance.org/Common_ display/currentmembers.asp.

3. **Separate Delivery** (provides content encryption and supports legitimate viral distribution by separating the rights definitions from the content)

Forward-Lock is DRM at its simplest. It allows for basic content such as news, sports scores, ring tones, or images to be downloaded to a handset, but it prevents the content from being forwarded on to another user. Once a piece of media is downloaded, that is the end of it. It stays on that phone only or until it is deleted. Forward-Lock can be used on simple phones and is available today on several handsets. Typically, the end-user initiates the download of a media object from a server to a device (phone). The content is packaged in an unencrypted form in a mime-compliant format. Defaults usage rights/limitations include

- Enable the end-user to consume the content (e.g., play, print, or execute)
- Prevent the content from being copied/transferred to another device

Applications include phone ring tones, logos, and wallpaper.

Combined Delivery allows for more complicated rules for usage to be set for a given piece of media and is an extension of Forward-Lock. The usage rules or rights are expressed using OMA Rights Expression Language (REL), which is a subset of the XML-based Open Digital Rights Language (ODRL), a mobile profile of ODRL 1.1 [6]. For example, an image could be downloaded to a phone using Combined Delivery, and the user could view the image a pre-determined number of times before the usage rights expire. Or the usage rights could be set by a time limit instead. The content is wrapped inside of the DRM technology, and the two are inseparable. In other words, the rules of usage are actually embedded in the content. Typically, the end-user initiates the download of a media object from a server to a device (phone). The protected media object and the rights are carried together in a single DRM message. The rights are expressed in terms of specific permissions/restrictions in rendering (e.g., play, print, or execute) the content. In general, the content is prevented from being copied/transferred to another device. The rights are also prevented from being forwarded.

Separate Delivery means that the content itself and the rules for usage (same as in Combined Delivery) are sent as separate and distinct information. In this case the user can download media content and forward it on to a friend, but the rights are not sent. In order for the friend to use the content, she/he needs to agree to a new rights agreement, whether that means making a small payment or something else. It is called "Rights Refresh," and it allows for the kind of viral distribution of content that the wireless medium enables, referred to as "Superdistribution." This technology would give a user the ability to preview a piece of content before deciding whether to purchase it. In this mode the content must be encrypted and converted into DRM Content Format (DCF). DCF provides plaintext headers describing content type, encryption methods, etc. A unique content identifier is also included (ContentURI). A DCF content object cannot be used without a Content Encryption Key (CEK) contained in the separately delivered rights. The rights include a uid which equals the ContentURI. The media object is allowed to pass from mobile device to mobile device where the rights objects are obtainable from the rights issuer (superdistribution). Applications include music distribution services. The separate delivery mode is a precursor to the more sophisticated OMA DRM version 2.0.

2.4.2   OMA DRM version 2.0

OMA DRM version 2.0 was released in July 2004, and it extends version 1.0 in numerous directions [7]. As compared to version 1.0, version 2.0 is intended to provide a more complete DRM system for protecting premium content while giving end-users more flexibility in their access to that content. Basic to the version 2.0 system is the idea that content and rights are separate entities that can be separately controlled. The content is encrypted using a symmetric key (known to the device enabled to consume the content). The DCF and PDCF (Packetized DRM Content Format) file formats are used for discrete media and streaming media, respectively. Licenses are created as Rights Objects (RO) and include header information (URLs, version, time stamp, etc.), security elements (decryption key, signature), and rights information (play, copy, execute, etc.). DCF and RO identify each other by using the information in headers. RO are communicated to the device by using the Rights Object Acquisition Protocol (ROAP). Public key encryption infrastructure (PKI) is utilized to protect rights information. PKI-based key delivery and management are used to authenticate devices and rights issuers and to bind RO to devices.

An RO governs how DRM content may be used. It is an XML document specifying permissions and constraints associated with a piece of DRM content. DRM content cannot be used without an associated RO and may only be used according to the permissions and constraints specified in an RO. The digital REL selected for version 2.0 represents an extension of the ODRL subset defined in OMA DRM version 1.0.[3] PKI technology is used by OMA DRM version 2.0, and the content decryption key is included in the RO so that content cannot be viewed in the absence of its RO.[4]

Version 2.0 provides new functionality so that content providers can offer the following additional capability to end-users:

- Storage and backup: users can move content and/or rights to remote or removable storage and later restore the rights and/or content to device

---

[3]By contrast, MPEG-21 [8] selected XML-based eXtensive rights mark-up Language (XrML) originally developed by ContentGuard.

[4]It should be noted that the public-key encryption algorithm is not part of the OMA DRM specification. Presumably, this is to allow the standard to migrate to new encryption algorithms if the algorithms behind current implementations become hacked (as were the CSS system in DVDs and the system behind Adobe's e-Book system).

- Multiple devices: users can move content and/or rights between several devices owned by the user (second phone, PC, music player, etc.), thus adding a "domain" concept for sharing between devices
- Copy to secure removable media for a mobile music player
- Complementary preview
- Ability to preview superdistributed content before purchase
- Export to other copy protection schemes
- Transfer music to DRM-enabled set-top box or computing device
  It also provides the following additional protections/capability to content providers:

- Individually encrypted rights using a device's public key to provide cryptographic binding
- Integrity protection for content and rights
- Mutual authentication between device and rights issuer
- Device revocation: rights issuer can identify device revocation status
- Rights issuer revocation: device can identify rights issuer revocation status
- Secure multicast and unicast streaming
- Metered time and usage constraints
- Subscription rights for content bundles
- Gifting
- Support for peer-to-peer and messaging
- Superdistribution: viral marketing and reward mechanism

(Please note that the functional requirements alone for version 2.0 are in a standalone document 22 pages long, so I am only summarizing some of the high points. Please also note that some functionalities, although allowed, are not described in detail in version 2.0.)

As stated above, the public key encryption technology (and other parts of the so-called "trust model") used by OMA DRM version 2.0 is not defined in the standard. Four companies (Intel, Nokia, MEI/Panasonic, and Samsung) banded together (February 2004) and created an LLC called the Content Management Licensing Administrator (CMLA) to implement a trust model for OMA DRM version 2.0. Its tasks include

- Issuing, distributing, and management of keys
- Issuing, distributing, and management of certificates
- Revocation mechanisms
- Defining import/export digital outputs

The CMLA trust model defines a compliant implementation of this specification for use with a wide variety of digital client devices and applications (e.g., cell phones, PDAs, and PCs). Although the CMLA trust model is not a required part of the version 2.0 standard nor is the ability to provide a trust model for OMA DRM version 2.0 in any way limited to the CMLA alliance, it is not possible to implement the standard without the type of technology provided by the

CMLA trust model. The CMLA technical specifications deal with issues related to distribution and management of keys and certificates issued by the CMLA. Key generation and provisioning must comply with the CMLA-specified security requirements and involve a compliant central facility for the root Certificate Authority, technical and administrative arrangements for the generation, and distribution of keys and certificates for use by the service providers and client manufacturers. CMLA will generate and distribute millions of keys and certificates. CMLA also maintains a revocation mechanism which makes it possible to prevent further consumption of new content by devices whose keys have become compromised.

2.5 THE MPEG LA® DRM REFERENCE MODEL

My company, MPEG LA, LLC (MPEG LA), is involved with the licensing of technology. When we began looking into DRM applications, we saw that the market was developing a wide variety of technology systems for a wide variety of applications. Moreover, DRM technologies are covered by many patents owned by many patent owners which implies that a company like MPEG LA could provide a useful market service by providing one-stop licensing for DRM systems. Since we were interested in being the license administrator for as wide a technology/application base as possible, we wanted to develop a common framework that could be used to cover as wide a set of potential DRM systems and applications as possible. Our hope was that a common framework would allow technology owners and patent licensors to develop license models for DRM technology that would be reusable across systems. Working with a variety of participants in the DRM market, MPEG LA facilitated the development of a "Reference Model" (RM) describing the various principles and functions of a DRM system to support the evaluation of patents for their essentiality and the creation of joint patent licenses for a wide variety of applications [9].

In general, while DRM has the potential to enable new markets, new products and services, new revenue, and other growth opportunities, the use of the technology requires separate licenses. The development and deployment might be inhibited without convenient access to essential intellectual property(IP). There is a demand from everyone in the distribution chain who will benefit from these services—content providers, service providers, device manufacturers, and consumers—to address this issue. The DRM RM helps remove the uncertainty surrounding the "patent overhang" by providing the basis for convenient access to DRM technologies through alternative licenses. The terms of any license may be determined only by patent holders with essential IP as identified through a patent submission and evaluation process. Everyone in the distribution chain—content owners, service providers, device manufacturers, and consumers—may benefit.

A toolkit of generic DRM processes is specified in the RM through a set of primitive functions. The basic tools include

1. **Packaging assets** with application certification, credentialing, authentication, and verification
2. **Distributing assets** with application certification, credentialing, authentication, and verification
3. **Generating and issuing usage licenses** through REL
4. **Enforcing only licensed usage** by controlling the execution of actions on assets received in packages based on licenses and rights expressions
5. **Protecting asset and license confidentiality** by encryption and integrity protection by signing
6. **Managing keys** used for the asset and license confidentiality and integrity protection

In the RM, Data Flow Diagrams (DFDs) depict the functional processes of the RM. The DFDs organize processes in a hierarchical fashion, with the lowest level representing a primitive of a generic DRM system. Process Specifications (PSPECs) illustrate the primitive processes shown in the DFDs. Control Specifications (CSPECs) illustrate the control processes shown in the DFDs. A requirements dictionary contains the list of the DFDs' data and control flows along with their definitions. In addition, Architectural Flow Diagrams (AFDs) show the physical composition of a system and the data flow between external devices. The highest level of rights management, DFD 0, is shown in Figure 2.3. In DFD 0 four main processes are shown:

a. Package assets (DFD 1)
b. Distribute assets (DFD 2)
c. Generate and issue licenses (DFD 3)
d. Enforce license and consume assets (DFD 4)

Figure 2.3 also shows the input/output data flows for these processes. Processes that do not represent primitives are further described with more detailed DFDs. Only primitive processes have PSPECs. PSPECs provide a description of the primitive process as well as protection specifications (e.g., integrity or confidentiality protection for data or control flows, where integrity protection refers to protection against alteration or corruption of the data in the flow and confidentiality protection refers to protection against revealing the data in the flow; "tamper-resistant" which refers to the same type of confidentiality or integrity protection for the process itself) and identification of protected inputs/outputs.

In this fashion the RM can describe DRM systems with diverse functionalities. The RM does not detail how flows between processes are carried out, but simply shows which flows are required in order to complete a process. For example, credentials are used as input to various processes, but their generation and delivery

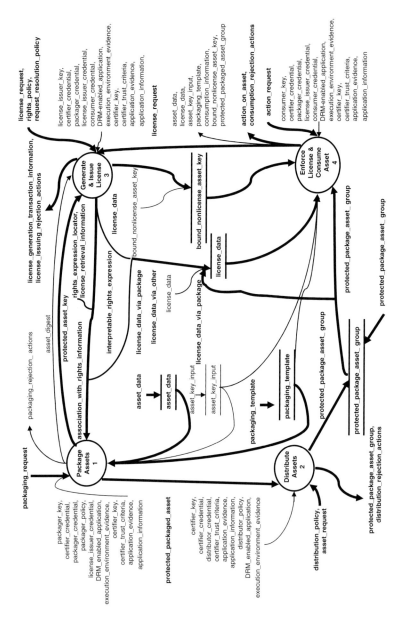

FIGURE 2.3: High-level data flow diagram (DFD 0) for the RM.

are not specified. In addition, the DFDs do not mandate any specific DRM system architecture.

2.5.1 Profiling

Subsets or profiles of the generic DRM technology are also defined to enable support of specific standards and marketplace implementations. The DRM RM can and is expected to continue to be expanded, reflecting emerging market needs.

The current version of the RM is version 3.0. It includes three profiles: the **Black Profile**, the **Blue Profile**, and the **Green Profile**. It should be noted that the Black Profile stands by itself in the absence of the Blue and Green profiles, whereas the Blue Profile is a superset of the Black Profile. Furthermore, these three profiles can be integrated together to form a single unitary model. All profiles are taken into account when patents are evaluated against the DRM RM.

In addition to the three profiles, explicit support for industry applications and standards such as **Internet Music Transfer Services (IMTS)**, the **OMA DRM version 1.0**, and **OMA DRM version 2.0** is included in RM version 3.0.

The **Black Profile** includes the following process groups (see also Figure 2.3):

a. **Package Assets.** The processes of this group are for selecting data for assembly into a package and for assembly of such packages.
b. **Distribute Assets.** The processes of this group are for distributing groups of one or more asset-bearing packages to consumption processes.
c. **Generate and Issue License.** The processes of this group are for generating interpretable rights expressions, generating licenses containing such interpretable rights expressions, and issuing such licenses to consumption processes.
d. **Enforce License and Consume Asset.** The processes of this group are for controlling the execution of actions on assets received in packages based on licenses and interpretable rights expressions.

The Black Profile includes indications of integrity protection, confidentiality protection, or tamper resistance of certain flows and processes. The Black Profile supports both confidential and non-confidential assets, as well as protects the integrity of licenses. It also supports protecting the integrity and confidentiality of an asset key. In Figures 2.3 and 2.6–2.10, the Black Profile processes are shown in bold.

The Blue Profile includes the Black Profile as well as additional processes related to trust and security, including

e. DRM-enabled application certification, credentialing, authentication, and verification
f. Packager, distributor, license issuer, and consumer entity authorization
g. Asset and license confidentiality protection by encryption and integrity protection by signing

   h. Management of keys used for the asset and license confidentiality and integrity protection

The Blue Profile also includes techniques for implementing tamper resistance.

The Green Profile includes tethered devices. An example of architecture diagrams for a tethered device system is shown in Figures 2.4 and 2.5. The system shown in Figures 2.4 and 2.5 includes two devices: a host device (producer) and a tethered device (consumer), where the host is receiving the asset from a source device which precedes the host in the distribution chain. An action_request for asset transfer provided to the host device causes the host device to transfer a content asset to the tethered device. An action_request provided to the tethered device then produces an action_on_asset response such as playing the content. In Figures 2.4 and 2.5, a mechanical link includes any means to generate the appropriate input signals. For example, a mechanical link includes a physical pressing of the "play" button on the tethered device or the soldering of components that emit the required signals into the tethered device. A protected electrical link is an electrical link whose contents are protected.

The IMTS profile (added in RM version 2.0) is an example of an auxiliary profile supporting industry applications. The IMTS profile includes the following tools:

- Confidentiality protect asset using encryption
- Consumer originating asset/license request specifying requested rights

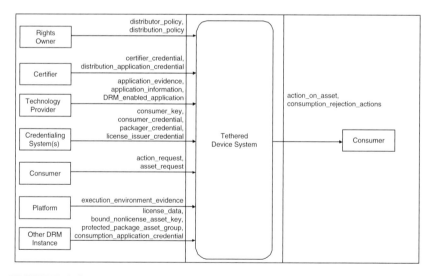

FIGURE 2.4: Example of an architecture context diagram for a tethered system device.

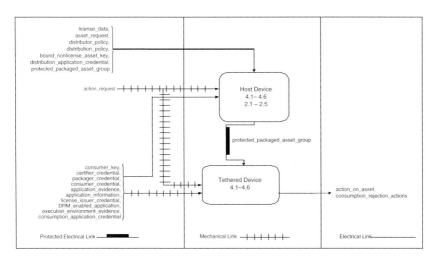

FIGURE 2.5:   Example of an architecture flow diagram for a tethered system device.

- Separately deliver license
- Integrity protect license with public key encryption
- Transfer asset action
- Associate rights with asset
- Distribute package by download/streaming
- Deliver asset key with license
- Integrity protect package and rights
- Transfer rights
- Automated subscription license renewal
- Authentication and verification application
- Verify license for integrity and destination
- Check consumer authorization

Music download services are applications related to the IMTS profile. For example, in the Apple computer's iTunes®, the content is a music file encoded with MPEG Advanced Audio Coding (AAC) and distributed in a file format based on the MP4 file format. The AAC-encoded content is confidentiality protected. The encryption is implemented using a 128-bit AES (Advanced Encryption Standard) method, which is based on a symmetric key algorithm, i.e., encryption and decryption are performed with the same key. An encrypted master key, which is used to decrypt the AAC content, is also stored in the content file. In order to decrypt the master key, a user key is necessary. The user key, which ultimately enables the end-user to enjoy the selected music files, is obtained from a server after purchase of a specific iTunes® item.

Version 2.0 of the RM also includes by reference OMA DRM version 1.0. Version 3.0 of the RM, the current version, expands the reference to OMA DRM version 2.0.

2.5.2   Overview of the RM

In Figure 2.3, DFD 0 is shown to have four main processes, specifically, Package Assets (DFD 1), Distribute Assets (DFD 2), Generate and Issue License (DFD 3), and Enforce License and Consume Asset (DFD 4). In Figures 2.6–2.9, further details of these processes are shown.

Upon a request for packaging, the Package Assets process forms a package. It receives as input at least asset_data (i.e., content), and it outputs the protected_packaged_asset containing the input asset. Other inputs may include a template for packaging the asset and rights information such as license_data, an interpretable_rights_expression, or a locator for these data. Specifically, the association_with_rights_information input specifies the rights data included (see the requirements dictionary for RM 3.0 [9]). The contents of the package may be confidentiality and/or integrity protected.

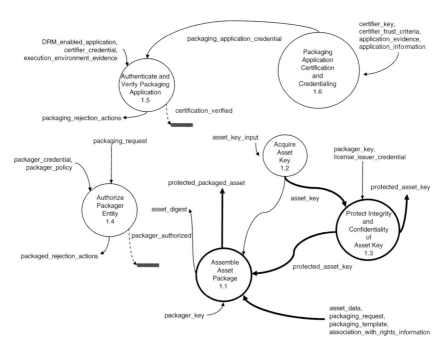

FIGURE 2.6:   Data flow diagram for the Package Assets process (DFD 1).

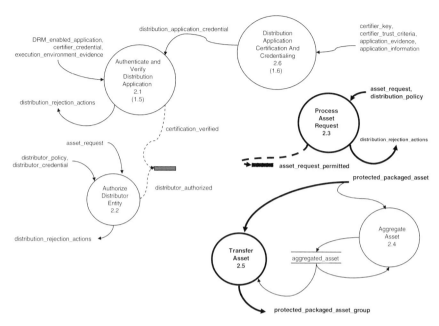

FIGURE 2.7: Distribute Assets process (DFD 2).

The Distribute Assets process reacts to an asset_request providing in output a protected_package_asset_group that reflects a distribution_policy. Multiple separate protected_package_assets_groups can be aggregated. In addition, according to the distribution_policy there may be circumstances under which the assets may not be distributed.

In response to a request for a license, the Generate and Issue License process outputs interpretable_rights_expressions. These can be retrieved or created to form a license_rights_expresssion. In addition, a key utilized by the Package Assets process to protect an asset can be recovered and bound to a specific destination that will receive certain rights to consume the asset. The key can be combined with the license or conveyed separately. The license may be confidentiality and/or integrity protected.

During the Enforce License and Consume Asset process, the license is retrieved, and its integrity and binding to a corresponding asset is verified. The asset key is also retrieved from the license, if available. After receiving a request to render an asset (action_request), the interpretable_rights_expressions for the asset are examined. If the action requested is allowed, then the action is executed. If the asset is encrypted, a decryption of the asset is performed using the asset key.

In general, the processes depicted in Figures 2.6–2.9 do not all represent a primitive process. For example, in Figure 2.10 one of the lower hierarchical

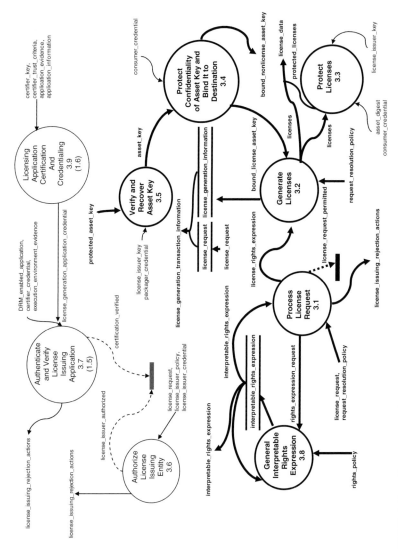

FIGURE 2.8: Generate and Issue License process (DFD 3).

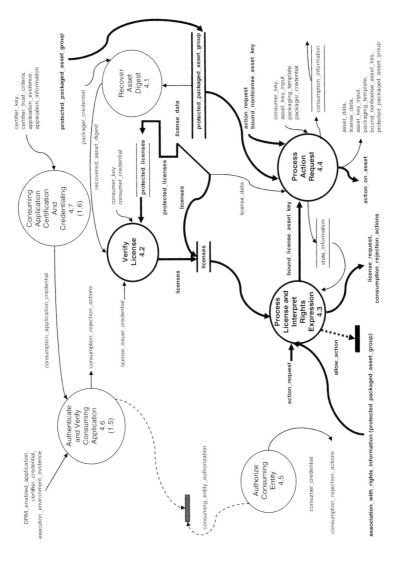

FIGURE 2.9: Enforce License and Consume Asset process (DFD 4).

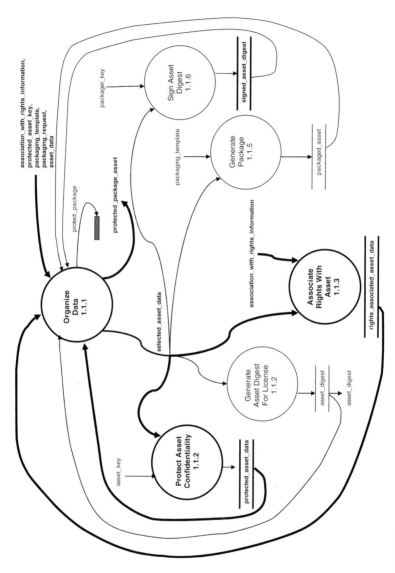

FIGURE 2.10:   Package Asset's Assemble Asset Package (DFD 1.1).

PSPEC 1.1.1: Organize Data
INPUTS: protected_asset_key, signed_asset_digest, packaging_request
OUTPUTS: protected_packaged_asset
PROTECTION SPECIFICATION: Tamper-resistant. Maintain integrity of
packaging_template_identifier, when present in packaging_template. Maintain integrity of
packaging_policy. Maintain integrity of association_with_rights_information,
protected_asset_data,
asset_digest, rights_associated_asset_data, packaged_asset (when signed_asset_digest is absent),
and selected_asset_data. Maintain confidentiality of asset_data when it requires confidentiality
protection. Maintain the above-noted integrity and confidentiality of the above-noted flows,
respectively, (under the conditions mentioned above) when components of selected_asset_data.
PROTECTED INPUTS: packaging_template, asset_digest, protected_asset_data,
rights associated asset data, association with rights information, packaged asset, asset data

---

Select selected_asset_data and protected_packaged_asset from all inputs. Use packaging request
to iterate. When present, iteratively select based on information/instructions found in the
packaging_template. Initially, protect_package is NO and is switched to YES when asset_digest is
available and packaged_asset is to be integrity protected.

FIGURE 2.11: PSPECs corresponding to the Organize Data process (DFD 1.1.1).

levels of the Package Asset process, the Assemble Asset Package DFD 1.1, is shown. The processes shown in Figure 2.10 (DFD 1.1.1 Organize Data, DFD 1.1.2 Protect Asset Confidentiality, etc.) are all considered primitives. Associated with each primitive on the RM, there is the PSPEC that explains the functionalities of the primitive. For example, Figure 2.11 shows the PSPEC that corresponds to the Organize Data process (DFD 1.1.1) in DFD 1.1. For more information about the different primitives and other details of the RM diagrams, please see the RM version 3.0, Part II, Context Diagrams, Data Flow Diagrams, Process Specifications, and Control Specifications, September 2004 [9].

2.6 MAPPING AN APPLICATION ONTO THE MPEG LA® DRM RM

MPEG LA's DRM RM can be used to model the DRM process associated with a specific technology approach. The DRM RM provides primitive structures that give alternative means for carrying out each of the pieces that can be put together into or mapped onto a complete DRM system.

As discussed in Section 2.4, Forward-Lock is DRM at its simplest. It allows for basic content, such as news, sports scores, ring tones, or images to be downloaded to a handset, but it prevents the content from being forwarded on to another user. In Figure 2.12 MPEG LA's RM DFD 0 is shown where the RM is specifically used to model OMA 1.0 Forward-Lock. First, the asset_data is packaged and then, upon a request for the asset, distributed. Based on the Forward-Lock default rights

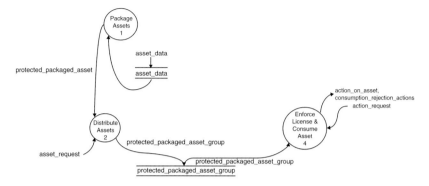

FIGURE 2.12:   DFD 0 for OMA DRM 1.0 Forward-Lock.

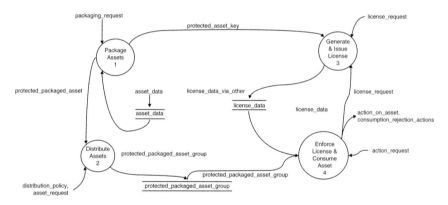

FIGURE 2.13:   DFD 0 for OMA DRM 1.0 Separate Delivery.

(license) and responding to an action request, the asset is rendered (or the action is rejected, depending on the circumstances).

As a somewhat more complicated example, in Figure 2.13 the RM characterizes OMA 1.0 Separate Delivery. Recall that in Separate Delivery the content and the rules for usage are sent as separate and distinct items. First, the asset_data is encrypted and packaged and then, upon a request for the asset, distributed. The asset encryption key is packaged with the license. Upon license request, the license is generated and issued separately from the protected content. When an action is requested, the license data is used to enforce specific consumption/rejection rules.

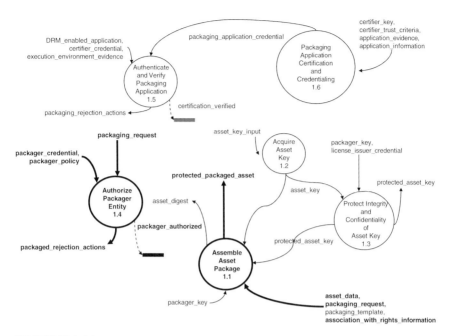

FIGURE 2.14:   DFD 1 for OMA DRM 1.0 Combined Delivery (bold lines).

To get a better idea of what is below the high-level DFD 0 mappings, let's examine in detail the mapping of OMA DRM 1.0 Combined Delivery on the RM. In Figure 2.14 DFD 1 (Package Assets) for OMA DRM 1.0 Combined Delivery is shown. A packaging request is accompanied by content data and associated rights information (license data consisting of an interpretable rights expression). If the request is compatible with the policy, packaging permission is given. The packaging protocol packages content data and associated rights together into a protected package.

In Figure 2.15 DFD 2 (Distribute Assets) for OMA DRM 1.0 Combined Delivery is shown. A distribution request is received and compared with the distribution policy. If the request is compatible with the policy, distribution permission is given. Upon receiving distribution permission, the protected package (i.e., the media file with included rights information) is transferred according to the distribution request.

In Figure 2.16 DFD 3 (Generate and Issue License) for OMA DRM 1.0 Combined Delivery is shown. A license request is received and compared with the request policy. If the request is compatible with the license request policy, license creation permission is given. The requested rights policy is converted into an

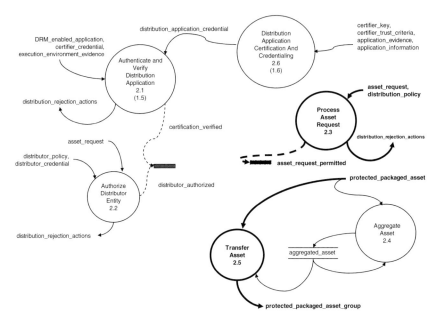

FIGURE 2.15:   DFD 2 for OMA DRM 1.0 Combined Delivery (bold lines).

interpretable rights expression (to be packaged as license data in the protected package).

Finally, DFD 4 (Enforce License and Consume Assets), the last of the four DRM processes for OMA DRM 1.0 Combined Delivery, is shown in Figure 2.17. An action request is received by the player along with a pointer to the protected package (content and license data). The action is compared with the rights in the license data (an interpretable rights expression). If the action request is compatible with the license data, the action is processed and carried out.

2.7   CONCLUSION

We hope this overview of DRM technology provides the reader with a greater sense of what the technology is trying to achieve and the standard steps in carrying out those goals. In addition, we hope the reader also begins to see how MPEG LA's RM can provide a common language and framework for discussing, designing, and offering joint patent licenses for a broad set of DRM technologies and applications. We have worked very hard to try and build a flexible, extensible RM that can be used to characterize current and emerging DRM systems.

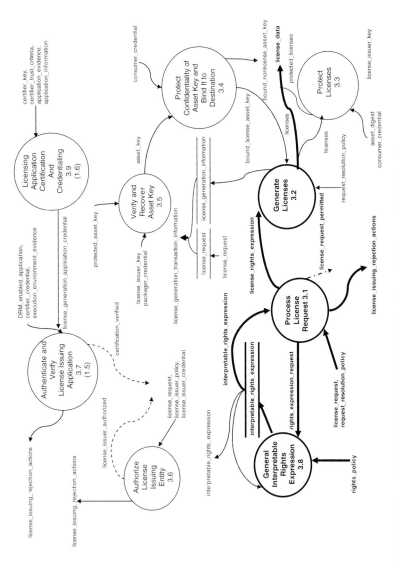

FIGURE 2.16: DFD 3 for OMA DRM 1.0 Combined Delivery (bold lines).

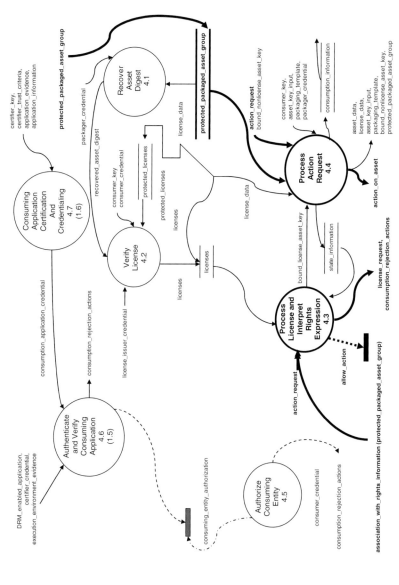

FIGURE 2.17:   DFD 4 for OMA DRM 1.0 Combined Delivery (bold lines).

REFERENCES

[1] DMM, The Digital Media Manifesto, http://www.chiariglione.org/manifesto/.

[2] Digital Rights Management White Paper, http://www.medialab.sonera.fi/workspace/ DRMWhitePaper.pdf.

[3] DVD Content Scrambling System, http://www.dvdcca.org/css/.

[4] Content Scrambling System (CSS), http://www.cs.cmu.edu/~dst/DeCSS/Kesden/.

[5] OMADRM1.0, http://www.openmobilealliance.org/release_program/docs/ CopyrightClick.asp?pck=DRM&file=OMA-DRM-v1_0-20031113-C.zip.

[6] Open Digital Rights Language (ODRL) Version 1.1, August 2002, http://odrl.net/1.1/ ODRL-11.pdf.

[7] OMADRM2.0, http://www.openmobilealliance.org/release_program/docs/ CopyrightClick.asp?pck=DRM&file=V2_C/OMA-DRM-V2_0-20040715-C.zip.

[8] ISO/IEC "Information technology — Multimedia framework (MPEG-21)," ISO/IEC 21000, http://www.iso.ch/iso/on/CatalogueDetailPage.catalogueDetail? CSNUMBER=35366&ICS=35.

[9] MPEG LA's Reference Model 3.0, http://www.mpegla.com/pid/drm/.

[10] iTunes®, http://www.apple.com/itunes/.

3
Putting Digital Rights Management In Context

Leonardo Chiariglione

3.1 INTRODUCTION

Ever since technology was introduced to help creation, distribution, and consumption of media, there has been tension between those who manage "rights to content" (usually called "rights holders"), intermediaries in the media value-chain, and end-users. Still, the technologies in use until some ten years ago, that we will call "analog," were usually so unwieldy that for each new technology a new equilibrium point could be reached, sometimes with the help of legislation and the courts.

The explosive combination of digital signal processing, personal computers, and digital networks, usually called "digital technologies," has empowered intermediaries and end-users to do more with media than they could ever have imagined before. The new situation has exacerbated the contrast that has always existed between these three classes of "users" of the media value-chain. On the one hand, rights holders enforce the rights that have been granted to them by successive legislations, including those granted by recent legislation stemming from the WIPO Copyright Treaty that was planned to cover the use of digital technologies [1]. On the other hand, intermediaries and end-users try to cling to rights and exceptions that were traditionally assigned to them, whose applicability to the new digital space is often disputed by other parties affected.

The result is that in the last ten years the great promises of digital media have not been delivered. What we are witnessing is, on the one hand, the continuous looting of rights holders' assets that seriously affects their economic viability, and, on the other hand, the ongoing deployment of media distribution that is based on Digital

Rights Management (DRM) technologies that limit, in some cases substantially and always unilaterally, the Traditional Rights and Usages (TRU) of media users.

In this situation, we see public authorities either shying away from an issue that is admittedly thorny, but critical for the future of society, or boldly getting into it only to retreat after declaring victory but actually without even scratching the surface of a solution. In this vacuum, other public authorities—the courts—are busy creating the legal framework of digital media by applying laws or court cases that are the legacy of just another age.

The field of civil liberties advocates is obviously very involved in this issue, but, in most cases, these organizations are fighting a rearguard battle. As soon as there is a major clash between the use of digital technologies or regulation with TRU, these organizations promptly side with those affected by the technology or regulation. While it is clear that this role is important in a democratic society, it is a far cry from what is really needed, i.e., actively proposing a way out of this stalemate.

Proposals do come from some quarters, but most of them are, in the opinion of the author, hopelessly idealistic. Indeed, it would be great if a gifted musician could sustain himself by giving away his music because he can make money from his real-time performances. The problem is that bringing a couple of cases where this has happened does not prove that this is a universal solution to a complex problem.

In mid-2003 the author launched the Digital Media Manifesto, a grassroots initiative to discuss the digital media situation outlined above. In less than three months, the movement published the manifesto [2], where a solution to the stalemate was proposed in the form of the Digital Media Project (DMP) [3], a not-for-profit organization with the twin goals of developing technical specifications of interoperable DRM and the practical means to support TRUs in an interoperable DRM framework.

This chapter is about how media value-chains can change, thanks to interoperable DRM specifications which support TRU, and the role of DMP in making them available.

3.2   VALUE-CHAINS

Creating value-chains is a primary function of *homo oeconomicus*. This is true for most activities, but achieves a distinct form in the case of value-chains created to "connect" those who produce with those who consume intellectual creations. In this chapter we will call media value-chains those designed to achieve this goal.

No matter how far back in the past one goes, traces of media value-chains can be found. To produce the Chinese tortoise shells with engraved ancient Chinese characters, a series of economic actors were required. The Egyptian Book of the Dead, required at funerals, demanded a dedicated set of economic actors. Similarly, the Babylonian clay tablets and the Roman wax tablets required at least a semi-industrial arrangement. Very modern, in spite of its 2000 years, is the case of Titus Pomponius Atticus, who used learned slaves to copy manuscripts and then distributed them throughout the Roman Empire. In spite of being "only" 1000 years old, the value-chain that created the medieval manuscripts looks ancient, while the reported cases of Chinese publishers at about the same time performing the same functions with similar concerns as today's publishers, but with manuscripts, looks very modern.

The media value-chains have seen many examples of stately interventions, not always as seen with today's eyes for the better. The royal Assyrian library may have been established to serve sovereign needs, but the Great Library of Alexandria was meant to serve the needs of the people—if by this word we mean the thin layer of Herrenvolk who could afford just minding their own intellectual challenges by virtue of having slaves working for them. But the very burning of the Great Library of Alexandria, setting aside the controversy of how it actually happened, is an example of stately intervention in media value-chains. Medieval amanuenses were another form of stately intervention (religious, which at that time was almost the same), this time for the better. Similar to the case of the Great Library of Alexandria is the burning of Aztec books at the hand of Spaniards in Mexico, while the "imprimatur" system was a powerful means to control the value-chain of books. Finally, the authors' societies, created in Europe mostly at the initiative of the state, are another example of stately intervention to support national cultures by propping up authors and, in some cases, publishers as well.

One should not think of value-chains as something static. As soon as a value-chain is created, there is a need to add more features to it. One important means to achieve this goal is by using technology. So we have seen Arabian paper replacing parchment in Europe, printing replacing the copy of a manuscript, photography replacing portrait painting, telegraphy replacing messengers, CD replacing compact cassette, DVD replacing VHS, MP3 replacing CD, etc. All this requires a word of caution, though. Replacement does not happen "instantaneously," but is the result of a possibly long process.

If the *raison d'être* of a media value-chain is to connect creators and consumers, this does not mean that the two are in the driver's seat. Actually, the more technology there is, the more value-chains are shaped by intermediaries. They are primarily interested in making sure that the entry threshold remains high and the distribution channel is under strict control. These two main goals are achieved by an array of actions, such as making expensive content and rich offers of services, flooding the market with a broad range of content, introducing expensive technologies, concentrating on big hits, etc. There is nothing new here. Merchants on the Silk Road did not behave much differently.

3.3 DIGITAL TECHNOLOGIES

Digital technologies are the combination of Digital Signal Processing (DSP), i.e., the ability to represent efficiently media in digital form, personal computers and digital devices with their ability to process the high bitrate of digital media, and digital networks with their ability to move content instantaneously and inexpensively to anybody in the network.

Digital technologies have proved capable of uprooting the role of many inter-mediaries, as it is so much easier to create, distribute, find, and consume content in the digital space. In other words, most of the reasons that made analog content an object of desire and, therefore, "valuable" disappeared. The question is then: What determines the (monetary) value of digital media?

It is too early to despair, because here are some of the options that people have considered and sometimes implemented to withstand the loss of content value.

- **Create your own value-chain by using security technologies (DRM).** In a way, this is the easiest thing to do because the "analog way" of doing business, namely high entry barrier and distribution control, is essentially preserved. However, DRM is a new cost that is added across a range of value-chain players, and the question of who will pay for the technology does not have a straightforward answer.
- **Rely on the good will of users.** This means to borrow some techniques experimented with computer software (but actually discontinued in that domain a long time ago), such as "Pay, if you want to continue reading my novel" or "Make a donation if you want me to continue creating."
- **Offer service, not content.** This is a view that, since there is so much content around, money should be made from offering services related to content, but not content that everybody can easily get. There is obviously a high degree of speculation in this idea that basically keeps possibly new intermediaries in the driver's seat.
- **Give up hope of being paid for your creation.** It would be great if people could freely create and freely donate their creations and if users could freely access them. This could indeed work if everybody had a fat bank account or was a tenured professor. Unfortunately, this is not the world we know. Many artists struggle to make ends meet and work hard to be successful, if ever they are.

  In designing the world of digital media, it would be advisable to remember the words of the Florentine Secretary [4]:

  > ...for many have pictured republics and principalities which in fact have never been known or seen, because how one lives is so far distant from how one ought to live, that he who neglects what is done for what ought to be done, sooner effects his ruin than his preservation...

3.4 WORKING WITH DIGITAL MEDIA

There is no reason to make a philosophical debate about what should or should not be done based on the experience of analog media, because digital media can let people make their own dreams real. In this chapter we will offer a number of illustrative scenarios where digital media are used in ways that were cumbersome or not possible at all in the analog era.

3.4.1 Open Release

Imagine that I create what I consider an outstanding piece of work, but no one is willing to publish it. With digital technologies I can resort to Open Release, i.e., I create a package with my content, meta-data about the content and usage rules, and then I post the package on my web site.[1] Note that at this stage there is no need to encrypt my content because, if my work becomes famous, I will still be able to exploit it economically as a new release later on, possibly using more robust content control technologies.

3.4.2 Open Search

Imagine now that I run a commercial web site in a world where there is plenty of valuable Open Release content around and I start indexing it using their meta-data and usage rules. I could put in place a business whereby I give away basic authoring and browsing tools, offer free hosting of content on my web site, and then engage in intermediation between sellers and buyers of Open Release content.

3.4.3 Flat-Taxed Content Use

Imagine now that a country decides that its citizens should have free access to all works created in that country and creators should be remunerated in proportion to the use of their works. In other words, creators should register their works and release them, while users would use content freely, every time generating use data. A state-appointed agency would then collect a flat "content use tax," collect use data, and redistribute revenues to creators accordingly.[2]

3.4.4 Personal Photography

If today I take pictures and pass them on to a friend or business partner, I do not know how they will end up being used. But digital technologies allow me to encrypt my pictures, add usage rules to them, and create a file that I can send to

---

[1]Note the similarity of this case with Creative Commons [5]. The difference is that there can be a wider variety of licenses.

[2]This case has been inspired by Fisher [6].

my friend or business partner. He will be the only one to be able to see the pictures because he will get the decryption key from me or from a service provider.

3.4.5   Internet Distribution

Imagine a garage band that after having achieved notoriety by Open Releasing their music tries to actually sell it. Today, the only way is by printing and distributing CDs, a hopeless task without a contract with a publisher. Today's DRM is an even more impossible task as it requires DRM-specific players that the garage band is in no position to get manufacturers to provide. But an interoperable DRM standard would allow the garage band to purchase the necessary authoring and e-commerce tools at a low price from competing suppliers and to rely on a population of deployed devices capable of playing governed content.

This short sequence of examples shows that the digital media world does not necessarily obey the same rules of the analog media world. There is demand to be able to release content by retaining "control" of it, not just from incumbent media companies, but also from small companies and even individuals. "Control" technologies can be used to preserve and enhance the status quo because they enable the establishment of a high entry barrier to content distribution and seal the distribution against competition better than it was ever possible before. On the other hand, "control" technologies can also help break the status quo because they can lower the entry barrier to content distribution and create a competitive market, can support business models based on "long tails" [7], and can help the unknown artist make himself known because of the quality of his work and not because some unknown entity controlling the distribution has decided to back him.

What discriminates the two versions of "control" is a simple word: "interoperability."

3.5   DIGITAL RIGHTS MANAGEMENT

The control we are talking about is what is commonly called DRM.

As for everything that is new and, on top of it, technically hard to understand, there is a lot of confusion with this term. A first step to clear the confusion is to introduce a definition. The one quoted here has been derived by the National Institute of Science and Technology (NIST) in the United States:

> DRM is a system of Information Technology components and services, which strives to distribute and control content and its rights. This, in an environment driven by law, policies, and business models.

The definition is not perfect because it bundles together the two separate functions of "management" and "protection" that too many people confuse. This separation is spelled out in the term "Intellectual Property Management and

Protection" (IPMP), which is used within the Moving Picture Experts Groups (MPEG) [8].

In spite of its possible cause of confusion, in the following we will use the more common term DRM, but it is important to stress that DRM does not necessarily mean protection. All cases considered in the preceding sections can only be realized using some sort of DRM technology. However, while the first and second cases only need management, the third, fourth, and fifth cases would normally require protection. In the digital world, rights enshrined in the 120-year-old Berne Convention [9], such as to have one's authorship recognized, to object to distortion or mutilation of works, to make quotes from works, and to use works for teaching, can more effectively be supported using DRM technologies, but not necessarily of the protection type.

A value-chain is a special type of communication system linking different users of the value-chain, and DRM is a technology that is added to the system for better management and control of the flow of information through it. As for all communication systems, if the specification of the technology is known and open, anybody can communicate with anybody else, possibly with the payment of a fee to a third party. If the specification is not known or, if it is, is not open, and the communication system is owned by a third party, this party becomes a gatekeeper. For this reason, DRM is a "neutral" technology that can be used to either preserve or break the status quo.

If a value-chain or a portion of it employs a DRM system that is closed or cannot be independently implemented (that from now on will be called "non-interoperable"), it is very easy to preserve the status quo, actually the access barrier gets even higher and the distribution control tighter. But if a value-chain or a portion of it employs a DRM system that is based on open specifications that can be independently implemented (that from now on will be called "interoperable"), the advantages of low access threshold to creators and users demonstrated by such social phenomena as MPEG-1 Audio Layer III (MP3) and DivX can be combined with the possibility to control the use of digital media, a condition that is known to work to preserve the creators' incentive to continue creating.

3.6   MAKING DRM INTEROPERABLE

There is growing awareness that an interoperable DRM is needed. But how near are we to having one? The answer is very simple: It's being done by the DMP.

The basic DMP position is that digital technologies are an asset of mankind that should be used so that creators, intermediaries, and end-users all benefit from them. As stated in the DMP statutes [10]:

> ...DMP promotes the development, deployment, and use of digital media that safe-guard the rights of creators to exploit their works, the wish of end-users to fully enjoy

the benefits of digital media and the commercial interests of value-chain players to provide products and services.

The means to achieve this goal is to provide an open DRM specification, i.e., to achieve standardization of appropriate protocols between value-chain users supporting the functions they perform. To remove any doubt about the goals, DMP has provided a **definition of DRM interoperability**:

> The technical ability of value-chain users to perform functions through interfaces and using protocols of open specification that can be independently implemented and provide predictable results.

Converting the general DMP objectives into a work plan that can be practically implemented is not simple. The first problem is that there is no such thing as a "universal DRM system" to develop a standard for simply because there is no such thing as a "universal way of doing business with media." We can only think of a range of *implementations* of DRM systems that satisfy the needs of specific value-chain users.

The second problem is that digital technologies have forced changes on media value-chains and are likely to keep on doing so. Therefore, it is impossible to standardize functions performed in existing value-chains, as we do not know how today's value-chains will evolve in the future. It is even more difficult to standardize functions that will be performed in future value-chains, as the shape they will take is anybody's guess.

However, it is possible to standardize protocols for functions at a more atomic level, called primitive functions, which are executed between value-chain users. Examples are offered by *identification* of content and devices, *expression of rights* to content, *authentication* of devices, *access* to content, etc. Functions performed by value-chain users are obtained through combinations of primitive functions.

Standards are useful because they provide interoperability to users, but in developing a standard one must make sure that it will be possible to continuously inject innovation into the system. The ability to combine primitive functions to create new functions ensures that the system remains open to the introduction of both new primitive functions and new roles in the value-chain. The DMP approach ensures that new technologies can be developed and standardized to enable new functions to be performed in an interoperable fashion.

Currently, DMP is developing a harmonized series of toolkit standards. These specify component technologies, called tools, which support the implementation of interoperable primitive functions. Users of the standard can build solutions suiting their requirements by picking the tools to support the functions of their interest.

The benefits of a toolkit standard are manifold. The first is that value-chains are interoperable, and users can still tailor the technologies to their needs instead of being forced to implement a "one size fits all" type of standard. The second is reduced implementation cost because technologies can be obtained from multiple competing suppliers and reused in multiple instances.

Toolkit standards also have disadvantages. The most relevant is probably that building value-chains may require considerable expertise. We will see later how DMP mitigates this problem.

3.7   THE DMP RESULTS SO FAR

In its two years of existence, DMP has proceeded along the well-established standards organizations process of the following:

1. Identification of the target of its standard (primitive functions, in the case of DMP)
2. Development of the corresponding requirements
3. Publication of calls for proposals
4. Review of submissions received
5. Selection of the most promising technologies
6. Integration of technologies
7. Publication of the standard

DMP has identified the users of a generic media value-chain, made a thorough analysis of the functions performed between them, and derived a comprehensive list of primitive functions [11]. Table 3.1 lists some of the most relevant

Table 3.1:   DMP primitive functions.

Category	Primitive function
Access	Content, License, Tool
Assign	Description, Identifier
Authenticate	Control Device, Tool, User
Certify	Control Device, Tool, User, Work
Identify	Content Format, Content, Device, Device Capability, Domain, License, Tool, User
Manage	Device Capability, Domain, Tool, Use Data
Package	Content, Tool
Process	Backup, Binarize XML, Bind, Copy, Encrypt, Export, Import, Move, Play, Restore, Render, Store,
Represent	Content, Key, Meta-data, Rights Expression, Tool, Use Data
Revoke	Device, Domain
Verify	Data Integrity, Device Integrity

Table 3.2:   Requirements for Assign Descriptors.

Definition	The function performed by an Authority to assign a Descriptor to a Work, a Resource, or a piece of Content
Objective	To facilitate search and find Works, Resources, or pieces of Content

Requirements	• To include the following mandatory fields
	  – Author
	  – Title
	  – Genre of Authorship
	  – Date of Creation of Work
	• Assign Descriptors that facilitate cataloguing Content for B2B distribution

Benefits	Easy and accurate retrieval of Works, Resources, or pieces of Content

primitive functions organized by categories. Requirements for primitive functions have been developed through a process that has seen the involvement of a range of industry representatives: collective management societies, consumer electronics manufacturers, end-users (particularly people with disabilities), public service broadcasters, sheet music publishers, telecommunication companies, etc.

Table 3.2 is an example of how each primitive function is handled in Reference 11. In this case the primitive function is "Assign Descriptors." The third column indicates the source of the requirement.

So far, DMP has produced two calls for proposals. The first Call has been for "Portable Audio and Video (PAV) Devices" [12]. The call was the result of focusing the general DMP requirements to the specific case of devices capable of playing governed content, but without a network or broadcast access [13]. Governed content can reach the device only through another device (e.g., a PC) that has a network connection.

3.8   THE DMP SPECIFICATIONS PHASE I

In just six months, DMP has been able to convert a large number of submissions covering all areas called for by the PAV call into a set of six specifications (called Approved Documents [ADs]). Table 3.3 gives the title of the six ADs. In Table 3.3 "Type" refers to the fact that a given AD must be implemented as specified in order to be able to interoperate with other implementations (normative) or be used as a guide (informative).

In the following, a short overview of the content of the six ADs will be given.

Table 3.3:   DMP Approved Documents, Phase I.

AD	Title	Type	Ref.
#1	Use Cases	Informative	14
#2	Architecture	Informative	15
#3	Interoperable DRM Platform	Normative	16
#4	Value-Chains	Normative	17
#5	Registration Authorities	Normative	18
#6	Terminology	Informative	19

3.8.1   Use Cases

This informative AD provides seven Use Cases:

Use Case No. 1—Open Release
Use Case No. 2—Open Search
Use Case No. 3—Home Distribution #1
Use Case No. 4—Home Distribution #2
Use Case No. 5—Internet Distribution
Use Case No. 6—Smart Retailer
Use Case No. 7—Personal Photography

These are examples of use of governed content that can be implemented with the DMP ADs. Each Use Case has a rationale and a walkthrough illustrating the steps implied by the Use Case. Open Release, Open Search, Internet Distribution, and Personal Photography have already been summarily illustrated in Section 3.4.

3.8.2   Architecture

This informative AD provides a high-level description of the technologies required to support digital media value-chains. It shows how governed content is generated, packaged, passed on, and eventually consumed. The architecture is capable of supporting value-chains that are essentially digital extensions of today's analog value-chains, even though the standard technologies can be used smartly to make media value-chains that are vastly different from today's.

A brief description of the architecture is given below. Note that terms beginning with a capital letter have the meaning of the DMP Terminology [19].

The process starts at the moment a Work is generated by a Creator in the form of a Manifestation that needs to be Instantiated before it can become an Instance carried in a Resource.

- For the purpose of *Identifying* intellectual property objects (i.e., Works, Manifestations, and Instances) uniquely, Creators, Producers, and

Instantiators will typically resort (as already the practice in the analog world) to Registration Agencies generating Meta-data.

- For the purpose of *expressing* the Rights and conditions to Use a Governed Content Item in a License, there is a need for a language to Represent Rights Expressions so that a Device can interpret Rights without human intervention.[3]

- For the purpose of *Representing* the combination of different types of Resources, Meta-data, and Licenses as a single entity, DMP defines the DMP Content Information (DCI). Typically, DCIs will also be uniquely Identified by Registration Agencies.

- For the purpose of *delivering* Content from one User to another, DCI, including its referenced Resources, needs to be Packaged. Phase I provides specifications for Tools to create a file using a file format that DMP calls DMP Content Format (DCF).

- For the purpose of *Accessing* a Content Item with a License that is Bundled within the Content or just the License, DMP standardizes appropriate Protocols.[4] When these are invoked, the establishment of a Trust relationship between Devices is required, which in turn requires the ability to Identify and Authenticate Devices or Domains, i.e., special groups of Devices.

- For the purpose of *Using* a Governed Content Item for consumption, there is a need for the Device to Parse the DCF to obtain the License and, if the Resources are Encrypted, to Parse the License to obtain the Resource Decryption Keys.

3.8.3   Interoperable DRM Platform

This normative AD is called Interoperable DRM Platform (IDP). It provides specifications of basic standard technologies (Tools) that are required to build Value-Chains. The word "Platform" has been selected to indicate that interoperable applications sit on top of the collection of DRM Tools and use them as required. As this is the first version (Phase I) of the IDP, it is currently called IDP-1.

In Table 3.4 (the same as Table 3.1), Tools for the primitive functions specified in IDP-1 are marked in bold.

Table 3.5 provides a summary description of each IDP-1 Tool.

---

[3]A User can deliver Content to another User for free Use, such as when the Content has been put in the public domain, but DMP specification applies only to the case in which a User delivers Content to another User in the form of Governed Content.

[4]Note that the License of the Governed Content Item can be Bundled within the Governed Content or not Bundled within the Governed Content. In the latter case it must be obtained separately from the Content.

Table 3.4: IDP-1 primitive functions (in bold).

Category	Primitive function
Access	**Content, License**, Tool
Assign	Description, Identifier
Authenticate	**Device,** Tool, User
Certify	Device, User
Identify	Content Format, **Content, Device**, Device Capability, **Domain, License**, Tool, Use Context, User
Manage	Device Capability, **Domain**, Tool, Use Data
Package	**Content (file)**, Tool
Process	Backup, **Binarize XML**, Bind, Copy, **Encrypt**, Export, Import, Move, **Play**, Restore, Render, **Store**
Represent	**Content, Key**, Meta-data, **Rights Expression**, Tool, Use Data
Revoke	Device, Domain
Verify	Data Integrity, Device Integrity

Table 3.5: Description of DMP Phase I tools.

Access Content	Protocol that is employed when the Content Item to be Accessed has the License Bundled within it
Access License	Protocol that is employed in order to Access a License for a Content Item that does not have the License Bundled within it
Authenticate Device	Protocols to Authenticate three classes of Devices 1. Devices having unique certificates 2. Devices that are uniquely identified by data 3. Devices without a unique data with certificate proxy
Identify Content	Identification according to the Uniform Resource Names (URN) scheme
Identify Device	Two kinds of Device Identification (comprising the Device Identifier's format, generation scheme, generation protocol, and exchange protocol): 1. "Device info-based identification" generated by a "Device Identification Server" based on Device information 2. "Certificate-based identification" based on an X.509 certificate
Identify Domain	(Done by a Domain Manager in *Manage Domain*)
Identify License	Same as Identify Content

continued

Table 3.5:   Description of DMP Phase I tools.—Cont'd

Manage Domain	Comprises Protocols to:
	1. Set up a Device Domain Context 2. Control the Use of Content within the Domain 3. Manage Device Domain membership (join/leave)
Package Content	File format containing the DCI with some or all of its ancillary Resources, potentially in a single package; it uses a DMP-defined subset of the MPEG-21 File Format
Process: Binarize XML	Tool to Represent a DCI in binary form; it is based on the MPEG BiM technology
Process: Encrypt	Tools to Encrypt/Decrypt (128-bit Key Advanced Exemption Standard (AES) in Cipher Block Chaining (CBC) and Electronic Code Board (ECB) modes) and RSA with a variable Key length
Process: Play	(No specification required)
Process: Store	(No specification required)
Represent Content	Tool to:
	1. Convey Identifiers of Content and Resources/Meta-data 2. Associate DMP-specific information and Meta-data with Content and Resources/Meta-data 3. Associate information with Governed Content.
	It uses a DMP-defined combination of subsets of MPEG-21
	1. Digital Item Declaration (DID) 2. Digital Item Identification (DII) 3. IPMP Components
Represent Key	Tool to Represent Keys; it uses the W3C's name spaces dsig and xenc
Represent Rights Expression	Tool to Represent Rights and Conditions associated with the Use of Content; it uses a subset of MPEG-21 Rights Expression Language

It should be noted that, in most cases, the technologies described above have been developed by other bodies, e.g., MPEG.

3.8.4   Value-Chains

This normative AD specifies how the informative Use Cases described in AD No. 1 can normatively be implemented using the Tools specified in AD No. 3.

By giving a normative value to this AD, DMP does not imply that Use Cases of AD No. 1 can only be implemented as specified in this AD. With this AD, DMP provides an example normative implementation so that Users assembling Tools as specified in this AD will be able to interoperate with other Users who will assemble the Tools in a similar way.

The steps in **Value-Chain No. 1 Open Release** can be implemented as follows:

Creation

Create	Resources
Obtain	Resource Identifiers from Resource Registration Agency (R-Agency)
Create	Meta-data for all Resources
Obtain	Meta-data Identifiers from Meta-data R-Agency
Create	Human-readable license (H-license)
Create	Machine-readable License (M-License) corresponding to H-license
Obtain	License Identifiers from H-license and M-License R-Agency
Create	DCI with Resources, Meta-data, H-license, and M-License
Obtain	Content Identifier from Content R-Agency
Create	DCF from DCI
Release	DCF

Access and Use

Access	DCF
Play	DCF

The steps in **Value-Chain No. 5 Internet Distribution** can be implemented as follows:

Creation

Create	MP3 and other Resources
Create	Meta-data for all Resources in each recording
Obtain	Resource and Meta-data Identifiers from R-Agency
Create	H-license
Create	Corresponding M-License
Store	M-License in a License server
Obtain	H-license and M-License Identifiers from R-Agency
Encrypt	Resources
Create	DCI with Encrypted Resources, Meta-data, H-license, and M-License
Create	DCF
Post	DCF on web site

Access and Use

Access	DCF
Play	DCF

The steps in **Value Chain No. 7 Personal Photography** can be implemented as follows:

Creation

Create	Photos and Meta-data
Obtain	Resource and Meta-data Identifiers from R-Agency
Create	H-license
Create	Corresponding M-License
Store	M-License in the License server
Obtain	H-license and M-License Identifiers from R-Agency
Encrypt	Resources
Create	DCI with Encrypted Resources, Meta-data, and H-license
Create	DCF
Send	DCF to friend

Access and Use

Access	License
Create	New DCF with License Bundled within it
Transfer	DCF to PAV Device
Play	DCF

3.8.5 Registration Authorities

This normative AD collects roles, qualification requirements, appointment procedures, and operation rules of DMP-appointed Registration Authorities who oversee the task guaranteeing the Identity of Entities such as Content, Device, and Domain.

For any type of Entity for which identification is required, DMP appoints the "root" element (Registration Authority). Registration Authorities allocate namespaces and appoint Registration Agencies. Registration Agencies Assign Identifiers.

3.8.6 Terminology

This informative AD collects definitions of terms used in DMP ADs.

3.9   BEYOND TECHNICAL SPECIFICATIONS

3.9.1 Reference Software

DMP is in the process of developing reference software for its Phase I specification. There are three main reasons for this development.

1. Put the text of the specification under test by verifying that the software implementation performs the functions that are expected.

Table 3.6: Licenses for DMP reference software.

Source technology or specification	License of reference software
Technology is unencumbered by IP	Open Source Software
Technology is encumbered by IP with a RAND license	Modify and use source software
Specification from another body provided with reference software	Existing license, if Open Source Software- or Modify and Use Source Software-compatible
Specification from another body provided without reference software	Open Source Software, if possible, otherwise Modify and Use Source Software

2. Boost the use of DMP specifications because users find it easier to adopt the technology.
3. Provide tools for conformance testing (see below).

To the extent possible, DMP will develop reference software with an open source license. When this is not possible because there is Intellectual Property (IP) that is required for the implementation, the reference software has a license that allows modifications of the software and use in products with the condition that the software or its derivative conforms with DMP specifications.

Table 3.6 describes the type of license adopted for DMP reference software.

The DMP reference software for Phase I will be published in February 2006 as a normative Approved Document No. 7. It will contain reference software for all Tools and for some selected Value-Chains.

3.9.2 Conformance

Value-chains are the result of business agreements and are supported by a set of technologies that Value-Chain Users decide to adopt. As DMP specifications can be implemented by anybody, Value-Chain Users can get solutions from multiple sources. However, not every implementer can be equally trusted. Therefore, Users must have the means to make sure that the other Users "play by the rules," i.e., employ conforming products.

DMP will develop Recommended Practices for End-to-End Conformance to be published in February 2006 as Approved Document No. 8. When this is achieved, Value-Chain Users will be able to reference the document in their business agreements.

3.10 ADAPTING TO THE NEW ENVIRONMENT

For DMP, DRM interoperability is a must, but *any* DRM solution, even an interoperable one, has the potential to substantially alter the balance between users that existed in the analog world, particularly when the user is the end-user. If the imbalance is not remedied, the scope of TRU of media users, be they rights and exceptions sanctioned by law or "liberties" that users have taken with media, will be reduced. This reduction may lead to the outright rejection of DRM by some users, particularly end-users.

DMP does not claim that an established TRU necessarily implies a *right* of a user to a particular use of digital media or an exception or something else. DMP only observes that, if users have found a particular TRU advantageous in the analog domain, they are likely interested to continue exercising that use in the digital domain as well. This does not necessarily mean that such usage will be for "free," as the exercise of a TRU in the digital space may have substantially different implications. Leveraging on this interest may offer opportunities for new "Digital Media Business Models" that are attractive to users, but also respectful of rights holders' rights. Such Digital Media Business Models can then be extended to cover usages that were not possible or not even considered in the analog age. During 2004 a large number of TRUs were collected and analyzed [20], and an exercise was carried out to study the effect of a range of scenarios of TRU support [21]. Finally, in April 2005 a Call for Contributions on "Mapping of TRUs to the digital space" [22] with an attached document "Issues in mapping TRUs to the digital space" [23] was published. The latter document contains an analysis of 14 (out of 88) TRUs, as shown in Table 3.7.

Table 3.7:   TRUs analyzed in the TRU Call for Proposals.

#	TRU name
1	Quote
2	Make personal copy
3	Space shift content
4	Time shift content
5	Take playback device
6	Choose playback device
7	Use content whose copyright has expired
14	Edit for personal use
18	Apply a rating to a piece of content
19	Continued access
30	Freedom from monitoring
55	Access content in libraries
67	Make content creation device
69	Access content of one's choice

Table 3.8: Analysis of TRU #55 Access content in libraries.

Nature	A user can draw a book from a public library at nominal or no cost and read it at will for a short, possibly renewable, period of time
Digital support	Scenario 1: Digital support of copyright exceptions for libraries
	Repositories can "lend" Governed Content by using copy-controlled check-in/check-out mechanisms for the borrowed Contents Items
	Scenario 2: Focused online access to Content
	A Repository offers the following services:
	1. Content search services not driven by commercial criteria
	2. Pointers to Content offered by other (possibly commercial) sources
	3. Governed Content when no other sources are available
	4. Content when copyright has expired (see TRU #7)
	5. Content when the repositories hold the copyright
User roles and benefits	Public Authorities
	Enact appropriate legislation to enhance the social role of public libraries in the digital media era

For each analyzed TRU, the following is provided:

1. Nature of TRU
2. Digital support
3. User roles and benefits

Let's see the case of TRU #55 Access content in libraries (Table 3.8):

The latter document requests contributions addressing the following topics:

1. Comments on the methodology utilized for studying TRU support in the digital space
2. Identification and description of new TRUs
3. Comments on the choice of scenarios, the type of measures to support the scenarios, and the effects on the main Value-Chain Users
4. Identification and analysis of new scenarios of TRU support

The DMP has received contributions and started the development of a "Recommended Action on Mapping of Traditional Rights and Usages to the Digital Space." This will be published in October 2006 as Approved Document No. 9.

The Recommended Action is expected to be of use to national legislative or regulatory bodies when defining the scope of TRUs in their jurisdictions.

Table 3.9:   Analysis of TRU #55 Access content in libraries.

Category	Primitive function
Access	**Content, License,** *Tool*
Assign	Description, Identifier
Authenticate	**Device,** *Tool,* **User**
Certify	Device, User
Identify	Content Format, **Content, Device**, Device Capability, **Domain, License,** *Tool*, Use Context, **User**
Manage	Device Capability, **Domain,** *Tool*, Use Data
Package	**Content (file),** *Content (stream)*, **Tool**
Process	Backup, **Binarize XML**, Bind, **Copy, Encrypt**, Export, Import, **Move, Play**, Restore, Render, **Store**
Represent	**Content, Key, Meta-data, Rights Expression,** *Tool*, Use Data
Revoke	Device, Domain
Verify	Data Integrity, Device Integrity

3.11   INTEROPERABLE DRM PLATFORM, PHASE II

In January 2005, DMP issued a new Call for Proposals targeted to "Stationary Audio and Video (SAV) Devices," i.e., Devices capable of Playing Governed Content obtained from a network or a broadcast channel.

In April 2005, submissions were received and working drafts of Approved Documents Nos. 1, 2, and 3 were produced. These drafts add new Tools to existing specifications according to the following philosophy:

1. Reuse Phase I Tools when these do a good job in the SAV case.
2. Extend Phase I Tools when this is needed and can actually be done.
3. Add new (Phase II) Tools when 1 and 2 are not possible.

Table 3.9 lists Tools that are being considered for IDP-2 (Tools underlined are those extended from IDP-1. Tools in bold italic are the new ones.):

The new specifications will enable Pay-TV services that employ receiving devices that are service-provider agnostic, and they can be used to implement Internet Protocol TV (IP TV) terminals capable of playing Governed Content.

The Phase II specifications were approved in February 2006.

3.12   CONCLUSION

The epochal transition between analog and digital media is happening with great pain and is far from completed. One approach that is being implemented is based on proprietary solutions of DRM technologies. This approach, favored by incumbents, can be used to retain a high entry threshold and a tight control of distribution. However, in most cases proprietary DRM solutions neglect the TRU of media users. Another approach advocates the adoption of radical solutions where content is basically free and creativity is repaid by other means, called Alternative Compensation Schemes (ACS).

The DMP, a not-for-profit organization registered in Geneva in December 2003, has been working with the goal of providing specifications of interoperable DRM that accommodate TRUs. The first two sets of specifications were approved in April 2005 and February 2006.

The chapter illustrates the DMP approach to digital media and the advantages for all users of the media value-chains, including creators and end-users.

REFERENCES

[1] WIPO Copyright Treaty, 20 December 1996, http://www.wipo.int/treaties/en/ip/wct/trtdocs_wo033.html.
[2] The Digital Media Manifesto, http://manifesto.chiariglione.org/.
[3] The Digital Media Project, http://www.digital-media-project.org/.
[4] N. Machiavelli, The Prince, http://www.constitution.org/mac/prince00.htm.
[5] Creative Commons, http://creativecommons.org/.
[6] W. Fisher, An Alternative Compensation System, Chapter 6 of Promises to Keep: Technology, Law, and the Future of Entertainment, http://cyber.law.harvard.edu/people/tfisher/PTKChapter6.pdf.
[7] C. Anderson, The Long Tail, *Wired,* October 2004, http://www.wired.com/wired/archive/12.10/tail.html.
[8] The Moving Picture Experts Group, http://mpeg.chiariglione.org/.
[9] Berne Convention, http://www.wipo.int/treaties/en/ip/berne/trtdocs_wo001.html.
[10] The Statutes of the Digital Media Project, http://www.dmpf.org/project/statutes.htm.
[11] Digital Media Projects; Primitive Functions and Requirements, http://www.dmpf.org/open/dmp0277.zip.
[12] Digital Media Projects; Call for Proposals on Portable Audio and Video Devices, http://www.dmpf.org/open/dmp0145.doc.
[13] Digital Media Projects; Requirements for Portable Audio and Video Devices, http://www.dmpf.org/open/dmp0146.doc.
[14] Digital Media Project; Approved Document No. 1 — Technical Reference: Use Cases; 2005/04, http://www.dmpf.org/open/dmp0401.doc.
[15] Digital Media Project; Approved Document No. 2 — Technical Reference: Architecture; 2005/04, http://www.dmpf.org/open/dmp0402.doc.
[16] Digital Media Project; Approved Document No. 3 — Technical Specification: Interoperable DRM Platform; 2005/04, http://www.dmpf.org/open/dmp0403.zip.
[17] Digital Media Project; Approved Document No. 4 — Technical Specification: Value-Chains; 2005/04, http://www.dmpf.org/open/dmp0404.doc.
[18] Digital Media Project; Approved Document No. 5 — Technical Reference: Registration Authorities; 2005/04, http://www.dmpf.org/open/dmp0405.doc.

[19] Digital Media Project; Approved Document No. 6 — Technical Reference: Terminology; 2005/04, http://www.dmpf.org/open/dmp0406.doc.

[20] Collection of TRU Templates, http://www.dmpf.org/open/dmp0270.zip.

[21] TRU Scenario Analysis, http://www.dmpf.org/open/dmp0280.zip.

[22] Call for Contributions on "Mapping of Traditional Rights and Usages to the Digital Space," http://www.dmpf.org/open/dmp0409.doc.

[23] Issues in Mapping of Traditional Rights and Usages to the Digital Space, http://www.dmpf.org/open/dmp0410.doc.

PART **B**

FUNDAMENTALS OF MULTIMEDIA SECURITY

4

Multimedia Encryption

Bin B. Zhu

4.1 INTRODUCTION

Recent advances in multimedia compression and communication technologies and increasing computing capabilities have led to a phenomenal growth of digital multimedia services and applications. Multimedia content can be compressed efficiently and distributed to end-users through physical media such as CD and DVD, wired and wireless networks, etc. Those distribution channels are not secure in general. Technologies should be developed to protect valuable multimedia assets from unauthorized access and consumption. Multimedia encryption is a technology that applies to digital multimedia to protect confidentiality of the media content, prevent unauthorized access, and provide persistent access control and rights management of the content. It is a special application of general encryption that the representation of multimedia is encrypted such that the content cannot be rendered intelligibly or to an acceptable perceptual quality. Multimedia encryption has a number of unique issues that are not seen in text encryption and plays a critical role in modern digital multimedia services and applications. Like general encryption, providing privacy and confidentiality for multimedia services is the goal of multimedia encryption. Many encryption schemes have been developed in the past 15 years or so. Multimedia encryption has found many practical applications. These applications can be roughly classified into the following three categories:

1. **Confidentiality of multimedia content**. Multimedia encryption prevents other people from knowing the multimedia content to be stored, played, or transmitted. Typical applications include teleconferencing, real-time monitoring, storage of sensitive multimedia contents in hard discs, etc.

2. **Access control**. Multimedia encryption allows only authorized users to access and consume protected contents. Typical applications include

pay-per-view channels, premium satellite and cable TV, and other subscription-based multimedia services.

3. **Digital Rights Management (DRM)**. A DRM system provides persistent rights management for multimedia content throughout its life from creation to consumption. This is a much more refined control than access control. DRM systems are presented in Chapter 2. Multimedia encryption is a critical component in a DRM system.

This chapter will focus on the fundamentals of digital multimedia encryption. More advanced topics and specific applications of multimedia encryption can be found in other chapters of this book. We have assumed in this chapter that readers are familiar with multimedia formats and compression technologies.

In Section 4.2 we present a brief overview of relevant results of modern cryptography which will be the foundation of multimedia encryption. Unique issues and general requirements of multimedia encryption are discussed in Section 4.3. Typical multimedia encryption schemes are then described in detail in Section 4.4. The chapter concludes in Section 4.5.

4.2 FUNDAMENTALS OF MODERN ENCRYPTION

Multimedia encryption is based on the conventional encryption which is one of the major topics studied in modern cryptography. To facilitate the description of multimedia encryption in this chapter, we present briefly the fundamentals of modern encryption in this section. Since the core task of multimedia encryption is to ensure confidentiality of the content, this section focuses on the cryptographic technologies that provide confidentiality. Interested readers are referred to the literature [1–3] for further reading.

4.2.1 Cryptosystems

Messages in modern cryptography are treated as numbers or algebraic elements in a space. **Encryption** is a mathematical transformation or algorithm that takes a message as input and transforms it into a different message that hides the original meaning of the input message. The message input to an encryption algorithm is called the **plaintext** or the **cleartext**, and the encrypted message is called the **ciphertext**. In practical applications, an encrypted message must be restored to recover the corresponding plaintext. This means that an encryption transformation has to be reversible. The reversing transformation is called the **decryption**. An encryption algorithm and its corresponding decryption algorithm are also referred to together as a **cipher**. Encryption and decryption algorithms in modern cryptography are parameterized by cryptographic keys. A key might be any one of a large number of values. The set of possible values of the key is called the **keyspace**. A cipher plus the description on the format of messages and keys form a cryptographic system, or a **cryptosystem**.

Definition 4.1 A cryptosystem is a five-tuple (M, C, K, E, D), where the following conditions are satisfied:

- M is a finite set of possible plaintexts over some alphabet.
- C is a finite set of possible ciphertexts.
- K, the keyspace, is a finite set of possible keys. K usually consists of two parts: an encryption keyspace K_E, which is a finite set of possible encryption keys, and a decryption keyspace K_D, which is a set of possible decryption keys.
- For each encryption key $k_E \in K_E$, there is an encryption rule $E_{k_E} \in E$ and a corresponding decryption key $k_D \in K_D$ and rule $D_{k_D} \in D$. Each pair of $E_{k_E} : M \to C$ and $D_{k_D} : C \to M$ are functions such that $D_{k_D}(E_{k_E}(m)) = m$ for every plaintext $m \in M$.

A cryptosystem is shown in Figure 4.1. There are two general types of cryptosystems: symmetric and public key. A **symmetric cryptosystem** is also called a **secret key cryptosystem**. In such a cryptosystem, the encryption key can be calculated from the decryption key or vice versa, and a principal who encrypts a message has to share the encryption key with the principal who will receive and decrypt the encrypted message. In most symmetric cryptosystems, the encryption key and the decryption key are the same. A **public key cryptosystem**, also called an **asymmetric cryptosystem**, on the other hand, is a cryptosystem where the encryption key and the decryption key are different and match each other. Furthermore, the decryption key cannot be calculated from the encryption key, at least in any reasonable amount of time. The encryption key k_E does not need to be kept secret. It can be made public. Anybody, even an absolute stranger, can use the encryption key k_E to encrypt a message, but only the principal who owns the corresponding decryption key k_D can decrypt the encrypted message. In a public key cryptosystem, the encryption key is often called the **public key**, while the decryption key is often called the **private key**. A public key cryptosystem is usually much slower than a symmetric cryptosystem at a similar strength of security. Due to this reason, symmetric cryptosystems are typically applied in the encryption of multimedia content, while the content encryption key might be encrypted with a public key cryptosystem so that only the designated user(s) can recover the content decryption key to decrypt the encrypted multimedia content. The latter encryption

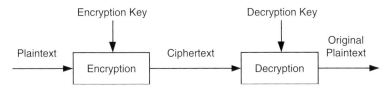

FIGURE 4.1:   A cryptosystem.

is well described in a general public key encryption textbook [2],[3]. We shall focus on symmetric encryption and its applications in multimedia encryption in this chapter.

4.2.2   Block and Stream Ciphers, Modes of Operation

Symmetric ciphers can be classified into two types, block and stream, according to the way a cipher operates. **Block ciphers** operate on blocks of plaintext and ciphertext using a fixed encryption transformation. Plaintext is partitioned into a sequence of blocks of a fixed size, padded if necessary, and a block cipher encrypts each block at a time. With the same key, the same plaintext block will always be encrypted to the same ciphertext block. The **Data Encryption Standard (DES)** and its successor, the **Advanced Encryption Standard (AES)**, are two widely used block ciphers. DES operates on 64-bit blocks with a key of 56 bits. AES operates on 128-bit blocks, and the key sizes can be 128, 192, or 256 bits. By contrast, **stream ciphers** operate on streams of plaintext and ciphertext one bit or byte at a time, using a time-varying encryption transformation. With a stream cipher, the same plaintext bit will be encrypted to a different bit every time it is encrypted. A stream cipher applies simple encryption transformations according to a keystream being used. A **keystream** is a sequence of symbols in the keyspace. It can be generated at random or by an algorithm called a **keystream generator** from a small initial keystream called a **seed** or from a seed and the previous ciphertext symbols. Many algorithms, including chaos-based methods, have been developed to generate pseudo-random keystreams. In a **self-synchronizing stream cipher**, each keystream bit is a function of a fixed number of previous ciphertext bits, while the keystream in a **synchronous stream cipher** is generated independent of the plaintext. A typical encryption transformation in a stream cipher is the exclusive-or, i.e., XOR, operation which applies on the keystream and the plaintext to produce the ciphertext. RC4 is a widely used variable-key-size synchronous stream cipher. Stream ciphers offer several advantages over block ciphers. A stream cipher is usually faster than a block cipher and uses less data buffering. A synchronous stream cipher does not produce any error propagation. This is especially useful when the encrypted multimedia is transmitted over error-prone networks such as wireless communications.

A number of different modes of operation can be used with a block cipher to encrypt a message longer than the size of a block that the block cipher operates on. Different modes offer different features and properties. Commonly used modes are the **electronic codebook (ECB) mode**, the **cipher block chaining (CBC) mode**, the **cipher feedback (CFB) mode**, and the **output feedback (OFB) mode**. In the ECB mode, each plaintext block is encrypted into a ciphertext block separately. Ciphertext blocks can be considered as codebooks of plaintext blocks. In the CBC mode, the current plaintext block is XORed with the previous ciphertext block, or with a random block called the **initialization vector** (**IV**) if there is no previous ciphertext block, before it is encrypted. The IV does not need to be secret, but should be unique for each message encrypted with the same key so that the same plaintext will be encrypted into different ciphertexts. In the CFB mode, a block cipher operates on a queue the size of a block. The queue is initialized with an IV and encrypted repetitively with the block cipher. After each encryption, the queue is shifted left by t bits, where t is the same as or smaller than the size of the queue. The left-most t bits are shifted out of the queue and XORed with the first t bits of the unprocessed plaintext. The result is fed back to the right side of the queue. The OFB mode operates in the same way as the CFB mode except the left shift is a circular shift: the left-most t bits are shifted back to the right side of the queue. A block cipher is configured into a self-synchronization stream cipher with the CFB mode and a synchronous stream cipher with the OFB mode.

4.2.3   Cryptanalysis

While cryptography is to keep confidentiality of the plaintext, cryptanalysis is the science of breaking a cryptosystem to recover the plaintext without access to the key. Kerchoff's principle that the secrecy must reside entirely in the key is a basic assumption in cryptanalysis. A cryptanalyst has complete knowledge of a cryptosystem except the key being used. This is a good assumption since details of a cryptosystem may eventually be known by a cryptanalyst. It guarantees that knowledge of how a cryptosystem works will not lead to a break of the system's security.

An attempted cryptanalysis is called an **attack**. The following attacks are frequently used to break a cryptosystem:

1. **Ciphertext-only attack**. A cryptanalyst tries to deduce the decryption key or plaintext by only observing ciphertext. A cryptosystem vulnerable to this type of attack is considered to be completely insecure.
2. **Known-plaintext attack**. A cryptanalyst has access to the ciphertext and associated plaintext for several messages and tries to deduce the key used to encrypt the messages or to develop an algorithm to decrypt any new messages encrypted with the same key.
3. **Chosen-plaintext attack**. In addition to the available information in the known-plaintext attack, a cryptanalyst chooses the plaintext that gets encrypted to yield more information about the key.
4. **Adaptive chosen-plaintext attack**. This is a chosen plaintext attack where the choice of plaintext may be modified based on the results of previous encryption.
5. **Chosen-ciphertext attack**. A cryptanalyst can choose different ciphertexts to be decrypted and has access to the corresponding decrypted plaintexts.

6. **Adaptive chosen-ciphertext attack**. This is a chosen-ciphertext attack where the choice of ciphertext may be modified based on the results of previous decryption.

Security of a modern cryptosystem relies on the complexity to break it. All these cryptosystems are breakable. A straightforward attack is to try every key in the finite keyspace one by one and check if the resulting plaintext is meaningful. This is called a **brute force** attack. A brute force attack usually has a very high complexity and may not be feasible.

4.3   THE MULTIMEDIA ENCRYPTION PARADIGM

Multimedia encryption is a special application of general encryption in which the representation of multimedia is transformed into a different representation such that the content cannot be rendered intelligibly or to an acceptable perceptual quality. Readers may ask naturally: Why do we need to study multimedia encryption? Can we treat multimedia as a general message and encrypt accordingly? Yes, we can. In fact, this is the most straightforward multimedia encryption scheme, and is generally referred to as the **naïve encryption** [4]. A variation of the naïve encryption is to encrypt the data in each packet to be transmitted over a network as if it were text encryption to provide confidentiality during transmission [5, 6]. These schemes achieve the goal to protect multimedia's confidentiality, but sacrifice many desirable features that multimedia applications may require. For example, decryption has to be applied to extract basic information such as the bitrate about the multimedia encrypted with the naïve encryption. Multimedia encryption has a number of unique issues that are not seen in text encryption. This section will discuss those issues.

In this chapter, a **bitstream** is defined as the actual sequence of bits resulting from the coding of a sequence of symbols generated from multimedia data. It may contain headers for the low-level data packetization. A **codestream** is defined as a collection of one or more bitstreams and associated information required for their decoding and expansion to multimedia data. A bitstream is often used to mean a codestream in the literature. We sometimes use it in that way too. Similar to plaintext and ciphertext used in general encryption, **plain bitstream** and **plain codestream** are defined as the unencrypted multimedia bitstream and codestream, and **cipher bitstream** and **cipher codestream** are defined as the encrypted multimedia bitstream and codestream, respectively.

4.3.1   Desirable Features and Requirements of Multimedia Encryption

As a special application, multimedia encryption shares many requirements and desirable features with general encryption. Multimedia encryption does have a number of unique requirements and desirable features that a general cryptosystem lacks. A basic requirement in multimedia encryption is that certain information such as format, bitrate, and artist should be still available to the public for an encrypted multimedia codestream. Major requirements and desirable features are listed below. It should be noted that some requirements are related to each other, while other requirements are mutually competitive. Different applications may have a different list of requirements and a different order of priorities. Trade-off and careful balance of conflicting requirements are always necessary in the design of a practical multimedia cryptosystem.

1. **Complexity**. Multimedia, especially video, contains a bulk of data to transmit or process. Multimedia data are typically compressed efficiently to reduce storage space and transmission bandwidth. Multimedia encryption and decryption require extensive computing resources and power. Many applications may require real-time playback of multimedia on inexpensive devices such as portable devices where computing resources and battery power are at a premium. Multimedia encryption and decryption may incur significant processing overhead, especially when processing a large amount of multimedia such as video data. Complexity of multimedia encryption and decryption is an important consideration in designing a multimedia cryptosystem. Low complexity is an essential requirement if the targeted application is real-time multimedia encryption or decryption at devices with limited computing resources and on battery power.

2. **Content leakage (or perceptibility)**. A unique feature of multimedia encryption is that encrypted content may be partially perceptible without access to the decryption key, i.e., some content may be allowed to leak out after encryption. Different applications require different levels of perceptibility for protected contents. For example, video encryption leading to distorted visual objects for unauthorized users is usually sufficient for home movie entertainment such as pay-per-view applications. The main purpose of multimedia encryption for this type of application is content degradation rather than secrecy. In other words, the goal of the encryption is to destroy the entertainment value of the multimedia content. Military and financial applications, on the other hand, may require the highest protection so that the adversary cannot extract any perceptible information from the protected content. The focus of multimedia encryption for this type of application is content secrecy. The different level of perceptibility usually implies different approaches and different complexity and cost. Multimedia encryption should be designed to meet the desired level of perceptibility for the application at the minimal complexity.

3. **Compression efficiency overhead**. Multimedia encryption incurs overhead on compression efficiency. The compression efficiency overhead may manifest in several ways. Multimedia encryption may lower

compression efficiency by modifying well-designed compression parameters or procedures or by modifying the statistical properties of the data to be subsequently compressed. Additional headers may be added to a compressed codestream for decryption parameters, boundary indicators of encrypted segments, etc. Compression efficiency overhead due to encryption should be minimized.

4. **Error resilience**. Multimedia applications often require multimedia data to be transmitted over networks. Networks may cause transmission errors and packet losses. Wireless networks are notorious for transmission errors. Data packets may be lost in transmission due to congestion, buffer overflow, and other network imperfections. Encryption may introduce error propagation. For example, a single erroneous bit in a ciphertext produced with a block cipher will expand to many erroneous bits in the decrypted plaintext. A well-designed multimedia cryptosystem should confine the encryption-incurred error propagation to minimize perceptual degradation and should enable quick recovery from bit errors and fast resynchronization from packet losses. Error resilience has not been taken into consideration in the design of many multimedia encryption cryptosystems proposed in the literature, where a perfect transmission environment was implicitly or explicitly assumed. These encryption algorithms might suffer a significant perceptual degradation for an extensive period of time if bit errors or packet losses occur during multimedia transmission.

5. **Adaptability and scalability**. Encrypted multimedia may be played with devices of a wide range of characteristics and processing capabilities. Post-encryption adaptation may be necessary to fit a targeted device. The bandwidth in multimedia transmission may be fluctuating, and adaptation or rate shaping may be required. It is desirable that multimedia encryption is transparent to an adaptation process so that the encrypted multimedia can still be adapted when necessary. This is especially true for encryption of scalable multimedia formats. Scalable coding has been developed to encode multimedia into a hierarchically structured and scalable bitstream which can be easily truncated, i.e., some data is dropped, to fit different application requirements. The Moving Picture Experts Group (MPEG) and the Joint Photographic Experts Group (JPEG) have recently adopted MPEG-4 Fine Granularity Scalability (FGS) [7] and JPEG 2000 [8] as their respective scalable coding standards. Encryption of scalable multimedia should preserve after encryption the scalabilities offered by the underlying scalable codec so that the desirable feature of easy adaptation is not impaired.

6. **Multi-level encryption**. A unique feature in multimedia encryption is that a single codestream can be encrypted to enable multiple accesses to the same cipher codestream. Multimedia data can be grouped and encrypted to

offer several quality levels that a user can choose from. For FGS formats, multimedia content can be encrypted into a single cipher codestream to support simultaneous accesses to multiple types such as quality, resolution, frame size, and rate and to multiple layers for each access type. This multi-level encryption enables different users to obtain different versions of the same content from a single cipher codestream that best fit into their networks and playing devices which may have a large variation of characteristics and capabilities. A user can access only the level that he or she is authorized to and cannot access the data that requires a higher privilege. Multi-level encryption is an elegant enabling technology to support the business model of what you see is what you pay with a single encrypted codestream.

7. **Syntax compliance**. A popular coding technology such as MPEG-1/2 [9,10] may have a large installation base. Many multimedia systems were designed without much consideration of encryption, so a later add-on encryption technology may not be recognized or supported by existing infrastructure and installed devices. To address this "backward" compatibility problem, it is often desirable or even mandatory that the encrypted codestream be compliant to the specific syntax of the multimedia format so that it is renderable (i.e., decodable) without decryption as if the codestream were not encrypted, although the rendered result may not be intelligible. This type of multimedia encryption is called **syntax-compliant** (or **format-compliant**) encryption. Syntax-compliant encryption is transparent. It also has the advantage of adaptability, scalability, and error resilience [11]. Syntax compliance is sought after in standardizing the protection of JPEG 2000 [12].

8. **Content-agnostic**. Multimedia has three major types: audio, image, or video. For each type of multimedia, many compression technologies can be applied. Each codec generates its own bitstreams. It is possible to package these different bitstreams into a common multimedia format. Microsoft's Advanced Systems Format (ASF) [13] is a general multimedia format that supports many multimedia types and codecs. To reduce the complexity, it is desirable that multimedia encryption for such a format be **content-agnostic**, i.e., encryption does not depend on content types or the specific coding technology used in compression. In this way, a single encryption or decryption module can be used to process a wide variety of multimedia types and encoded bitstreams. Multimedia encryption in Microsoft's Windows Media Rights Manager (WMRM) [14] and the Open Mobile Alliance (OMA)'s DRM [15] adopt the content-agnostic approach. This requirement is in direct contradiction to the requirement of syntax compliance.

In addition to the above requirements, some applications may have other requirements on an encrypted multimedia codestream, such as random access, scene change detection, content-based searching or filtering, etc., without decryption.

4.3.2   Security of Multimedia Cryptosystems

Different cryptosystems offer different levels of security. It depends on how difficult they are to break. Like a general cryptosystem, security of a multimedia cryptosystem also relies on the complexity to break it. If the cost required to break a multimedia cryptosystem is greater than the value of the encrypted multimedia, then the cryptosystem can be considered safe. The value of multimedia content decays quickly with time after its release. Figure 4.2 shows the box office revenues since the release for the movie "Star Kid." This figure indicates that the value of the movie decays exponentially with time. This is typical for a blockbuster movie. If the time required to break a cryptosystem is longer than the time the encrypted multimedia data is valuable, then the cryptosystem can also be considered safe.

Breaks can be classified into the following categories with decreasing severity:

1. **Complete break**. A cryptanalyst finds the key or an algorithm that can decrypt the encrypted multimedia to the same plain bitstream as the one obtained by an authorized user who has access to the key.

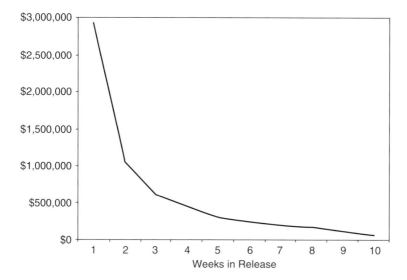

FIGURE 4.2:   The box office revenues since the release for the blockbuster movie Star Kid [16].*

---

*Reprinted by permission, Andrew Ainslie, Xavier Drèze, and Fred Zufryden, "Modeling movie life cycles and marketing share," **Marketing Science**, 24(3), 2005. Copyright 2005, the Institute for Operations Research and the Management Sciences (INFORMS), 7240 Parkway Drive, Suite 310, Hanover, MD, USA, 21076.

2. **Perceptual break**. A cryptanalyst finds an algorithm that renders without the knowledge of the key the encrypted multimedia to an acceptable level of perceptual quality or results in successful recovery of the content information that is intended to be kept secret.

3. **Local break**. A cryptanalyst deduces a local plain bitstream (i.e., a plain sub-bitstream) of a cipher bitstream and recovers some local content information.

4. **Information deduction**. A cryptanalyst gains some information about the key and the plain bitstream, but has not achieved the above more severe breaks yet.

We should emphasize that security of a multimedia cryptosystem is really application-dependent. Some high-security multimedia applications such as military applications may not allow any of the aforementioned breaks, while others such as home entertainment applications may tolerate perceptual breaks, as long as the rendered multimedia quality is significantly lower than that obtained by an authorized user. The complexity such as the time and cost to successfully break a multimedia cryptosystem, as well as the value of the protected multimedia content, should also be taken into consideration in a security evaluation. Multimedia, especially video, has a very high data rate, but the monetary value per unit data might be low in many multimedia applications. A low-cost, lightweight cryptosystem should be able to provide sufficient security for this type of applications at a reasonable cost. In the design of a multimedia system, the first consideration is to identify an appropriate level of security for the targeted application. Underprotection is obviously unacceptable, but overprotection means unnecessarily higher computational complexity and cost and is also undesirable.

4.3.3 Attacks on Multimedia Encryption

In addition to the cryptographic attacks on a cryptosystem discussed in Section 4.2.3, a cryptanalyst can exploit the unique features of multimedia data and launch additional attacks.

1. **Statistical attack** [17]. A cryptanalyst exploits the predictability of a particular data segment or predictable relationships among different data segments in a cipher codestream to deduce the plaintext without the knowledge of the decryption key or to substantially reduce the search space such that a brute force attack is feasible. There exists a strong correlation among different portions of multimedia data, either short range or long range. The correlation can be exploited to launch a statistical attack. This is particularly true for selective encryption, where only partial data is encrypted, and correlation between the unencrypted portion and the encrypted portion can help a cryptanalyst deduce information about the encrypted portion or reverse the encryption. Fortunately, multimedia data is usually compressed. Good compression is a powerful tool to reduce redundancy in multimedia.

Therefore, a substantial portion of the correlation existing in multimedia data is removed with modern compression technology, which makes a statistical attack difficult to launch.

2. **Error-concealment attack** [11, 17]. Compression does not remove all the perceptual redundancy existing in multimedia data. The remaining redundancy has been exploited to conceal perceptual quality degradation caused by bit errors or lost data. The same technologies can also be used to launch an attack on a multimedia cryptosystem to achieve a perceptual break, especially when a selective encryption scheme is used for encryption. A successful error-concealment attack usually produces an output that is inferior in quality to that which would be obtained by an authorized user. Such deducibility to obtain an inferior quality play may be considered as a break (i.e., a perceptual break) in some multimedia applications, but tolerable in other applications.

We would like to point out in particular that security against known-plaintext attacks is usually important in a practical multimedia cryptosystem, especially for encryption of audios and videos. This issue has not been given sufficient consideration in the design of many proposed multimedia cryptosystems. There are two reasons for this requirement. The first reason is that a commercial video usually starts with a known short clip such as the MGM roaring lion. The second reason is that it is usually easy to guess a local portion of multimedia data such as a silence portion in an audio, a smooth region in an image or a frame, or a static portion in a video. Selective encryption, described in Section 4.4.2, may be particularly vulnerable to known-plaintext attacks since the unencrypted portion of data may be used to deduce local plaintext which may in turn be used to launch a successful known-plaintext attack.

4.4   MULTIMEDIA ENCRYPTION SCHEMES

Multimedia contains bulky data. It is usually compressed to reduce the amount of data to be stored and transmitted. Therefore, multimedia encryption is typically combined with compression. Based on the order to apply multimedia encryption and compression, there are three ways to combine the two processes. Multimedia encryption can be applied before, in the middle of, or after the compression. Encryption introduces randomness in the output. In the first way of combination, i.e., multimedia encryption is applied before compression, encryption will destroy the strong correlation in multimedia data that compression exploits to reduce the amount of data. Therefore, multimedia encryption in the first type of combination will incur a substantial compression efficiency overhead and is strongly discouraged for a practical cryptosystem. In fact, almost all proposed multimedia encryption schemes belong to the second or the third type of combination, i.e., multimedia encryption is applied within compression or after.

We classify multimedia encryption roughly into the following categories: full encryption, selective encryption, joint compression and encryption, syntax-compliant encryption, and scalable encryption and multi-access encryption. Full encryption encrypts all the data except headers. Selective encryption encrypts partial usually important data to reduce the amount of data to be encrypted. Joint compression and encryption modify compression parameters or procedures to achieve the goal of scrambling multimedia content. Syntax-compliant encryption produces a cipher codestream which is compliant to the format syntax that an encryption-unaware decoder can still decode the encrypted codestream. Scalable encryption and multi-access encryption produce a cipher codestream that is scalable and accessible in multiple ways. Typical multimedia encryption schemes in each category are described in detail in this section. We note that such a classification is not precise. Some schemes belong to more than one category.

4.4.1 Full Encryption

Full Encryption Schemes

Full encryption is applied after compression. It is a simple and straightforward encryption scheme. Instead of encrypting a compressed codestream as a whole as in the naïve encryption, **full encryption** first partitions and packetizes the compressed bitstreams into structured data packets. Each packet consists of a header field and a data field. It then applies a cipher to encrypt the data field of each packet independently as a general message and leaves headers unencrypted. Decryption information can be inserted into headers. This multimedia encryption approach usually works with a multimedia format that supports the encryption. Microsoft's WMRM [14] and OMA's DRM [15] adopt such an approach. The format to support full encryption is ASF [13] for Microsoft and the DRM Content Format [18] for OMA. Full encryption is also proposed in Yuan et al. and Zhu et al. [19, 20] for multi-access encryption of MPEG-4 FGS, where data in each video packet is independently encrypted with a cipher. It is also used in Wee and Apostolopoulos [21, 22] for scalable encryption. Scalable encryption and multi-access encryption are described in detail in Chapters 10 and 11.

Strengths and Issues

Since the headers are not encrypted, full encryption allows a player to parse and extract basic information of the protected content from a cipher codestream without decryption. Since all the data in the data fields are encrypted, we expect that full encryption does not leak any content, i.e., the rendered multimedia, if renderable, is completely garbled without the knowledge of the decryption key. The security is also expected to be the highest among all multimedia encryption schemes. Full encryption is applied after compression. The compression efficiency is not directly affected, but full encryption does incur a small overhead on compression efficiency. An IV may be needed for independent encryption of the data in each packet. This IV may be inserted into the header field of each packet, resulting in an overhead[1] of the block size of the cipher used in encryption per packet, which is 64 bits when DES is used and 128 bits when AES is used. It is possible to reduce this overhead by generating these IVs from a "global" IV in the global space, such as a frame in a video sequence and the unique identifier of a packet, resulting in a negligibly small overhead to compression efficiency [19, 20]. A hash function can be used to generate these IVs. When a bit error occurs in the ciphertext of a packet, the whole decrypted data in the packet are usually corrupted due to encryption's error expansion. Even if a synchronous stream cipher is used in encrypting the data in each packet, which does not incur error expansion in decryption, the erroneous bit in the decrypted data may still cause decoding errors during decompression. In general, a packet with erroneous bits will be dropped. Certain adaptations without decryption are possible. What adaptation is allowed in a cipher codestream will depend on how the underlying bitstreams are packetized. With a general supporting format such as ASF or the DRM Content Format, full encryption is content-agnostic. It can be applied to different multimedia types and bitstreams compressed with different codecs.

Full encryption has a number of drawbacks. The major drawback is the complexity of the encryption and decryption process. Since all the data are encrypted and multimedia, especially video, has a very high data rate, it is expected that full encryption requires significant processing power. The scheme may not be appropriate for portable device applications, since portable devices may not have enough processing power to encrypt or decrypt in real time. In addition, portable devices usually operate on batteries. Complex computation drains batteries fast, and a portable device would have to recharge frequently to run a full encryption scheme.

4.4.2   Selective Encryption

As a contrast to full encryption, which encrypts all the data except headers, selective encryption encrypts only partial data by exploiting the compression characteristics that some data is less important than or dependent on others in a bitstream. The remaining data will be left unencrypted. Selective encryption is usually a lightweight encryption which trades content leakage and security for reduced processing complexity. Many selective encryption schemes have been proposed in the literature. Although the same principle is utilized by all these schemes, each scheme is designed to work with a specific type of bitstream to exploit the inherent properties of the codec used to generate the bitstreams.

---

[1]The overhead is usually a little larger than the cipher's block size since partition information may be needed to identify an IV in the header field.

They also differ in choosing different portions of data, different ways to encrypt, and different domains to work in. The focus of most selective encryption schemes is perceptual degradation rather than content secrecy. A partial list of selective encryption schemes has been reviewed along with their performance and security analysis in the literature [17, 23–25]. We describe representative selective encryption schemes in this section.

For an easy description, we have divided selective encryption schemes into four categories: selective encryption for images, videos, and audios, according to the multimedia types, and perceptual encryption. Readers should be aware that due to similarities between image and video compression technologies, an encryption scheme designed for one visual type may be applied to the other encoded with similar technologies with no or small modifications. For example, the similarity between JPEG and MPEG may enable an encryption scheme originally designed for MPEG to be equally applicable to JPEG images, after the parts that exploit the MPEG-specific features are dropped. Readers should be warned that extending an encryption scheme originally designed for one type to a different type without modification may cause unexpected content leakage. For example, when a secure image encryption scheme is applied to encrypt each frame of a video sequence, some content information may still leak out due to inter-frame correlation. This is evidenced in an experiment with MPEG-4 FGS reported by Zhu and co-workers [20, 26]. In the experiment, the base layer was encrypted with a full encryption scheme, and the enhancement layer was left unencrypted. When examined individually, each frame appeared like a purely random image, and no information about the content could be extracted. When the encrypted sequence was played as a video by setting all the pixel values of each frame in the base layer to a fixed value, contours and trajectories of moving objects in the video were readily visible. Viewers could easily identify those moving objects and what they were doing.

Selective Image Encryption

Selective image encryption encrypts partial image data. Depending on the compression technology it works with, these selected data can be Discrete Cosine Transform (DCT) coefficients for DCT-based compression technologies, wavelet coefficients and the quadtree structure of wavelet decomposition for wavelet-based compression technologies, or important pixel bits. These schemes are described next.

Selective Encryption on DCT Coefficients. DCT coefficients in JPEG compression can be selected for selective encryption. One method is to encrypt the bitstream of leading DCT coefficients in each DCT block [27], but it is argued in Cheng and Li [28] that such a scheme may not provide enough perceptual degradation since higher order DCT coefficients carry edge information. According to

Cheng and Li [28], even when the encrypted part is more than 50% of the total size of a JPEG compressed image, the object outlines are still visible. An opposite scheme is to encrypt all DCT coefficients except the DC coefficient or the DC coefficient plus AC coefficients of low frequencies in a block of a JPEG compressed image [29]. This is achieved by leaving the portion encoded with a variable-length code (VLC) from the Huffman table untouched and the subsequent bits specifying the sign and magnitude of a non-zero AC coefficient encrypted. The authors argued that the DC coefficients carry important visible information and are highly predictable. However, the scheme leaves substantial visible information in an encrypted JPEG image. It might be useful in an application where perceptual encryption is desired. Perceptual encryption will be described later in this section.

Selective Encryption for Wavelet Image Compression.   Selective encryption algorithms are also proposed for other image compression technologies. Wavelet compression algorithms based on zerotrees [30, 31] encode information in a hierarchical manner according to its importance. This is very suitable for selective encryption, since intrinsic dependency in a compressed bitstream enables encryption of a small amount of important data to make the remaining unencrypted data useless. A partial encryption scheme for the Set Partitioning In Hierarchical Trees (SPIHT) compression algorithm [31] is proposed in Li and co-workers [32, 33], encrypting only the bits related to the significance of pixels and sets in the two highest pyramid levels, as well as the parameter n that determines the initial threshold. Without the significance information related to the pixels and sets in the two highest pyramid levels, it is difficult for a cryptanalyst to determine the meaning of the unencrypted bits. This encryption scheme does not affect SPIHT's compression performance, but requires a deep parsing into a compressed bitstream in both encryption and decryption. The same authors have also extended the selective encryption scheme to SPIHT-based video compression [32, 33], where motion vectors, intra-frames, and residue error frames after motion compensation are encrypted. Intra-frames and residue error frames are encrypted with their SPIHT-based image encryption scheme.

Secret permutation of the wavelet coefficients in each subband of a wavelet compressed image is proposed in Uehara, Safavi-Naini, and Ogunbona [34]. This can be enhanced by encrypting the lowest subband with a cipher. An alternative scheme is proposed in Lian and Wang [35], which permutes the wavelet coefficients among the child nodes that share the same parent node for the quadtree structure of the wavelet decomposition of an image. Permutation of blocks of wavelet coefficients along with selective encryption of other data is proposed in Zeng and Lei [36, 37] for video encryption (see the Selective Video Encryption section for details). For wavelet packet image compression algorithms, the quadtree subband decomposition structure is encrypted in the schemes proposed in Uhl and co-workers [38–40]. Security of these permutation schemes is not very high due to correlation of wavelet coefficients across subbands and inhomogeneous energy distribution in a subband. For example, wavelet coefficients corresponding to a texture area have significant larger magnitudes than those corresponding to a smooth area in a high-frequency subband. This information can be used to deduce the secret permutation applied to wavelet coefficients. It is shown in Pommer and Uhl [38] that the encryption of the quadtree subband decomposition structure for wavelet packet compression algorithms is not secure enough against ciphertext-only attacks if uniform scalar quantization is used. These schemes are also vulnerable to known-plaintext attacks if such type of attacks can be launched.

Selective encryption for JPEG 2000 that maintains syntax compliance will be described in Section 4.4.4.

Selective Encryption in the Spatial Domain. Selective encryption is also applied in the spatial domain. A simple approach is to encrypt bitplanes of an image [29, 41, 42] before compression or alone without compression. Since a higher significant bitplane contains more visual information than a lower significant bitplane, it is natural for selective encryption to encrypt from the most significant bitplane to the least significant bitplane. Podesser and co-workers [41, 42] reported that for a gray-scale image of 8 bitplanes, encryption of the most significant bitplane still leaves some structural information visible, but encryption of the two most significant bitplanes renders the directly decompressed image without any visible structures and encryption of the four most significant bitplanes provides high confidentiality. Selective encryption in the reverse order, i.e., from the least significant bitplane to the most significant bitplane is proposed in Van Droogenbroeck and Benedett [29] to provide perceptual encryption.[2] These authors report that at least four or five bitplanes out of a total of eight bitplanes need to be encrypted to provide visible degradation. These schemes incur significant compression efficiency overhead if combined with compression, since encryption is applied before compression and encryption changes the statistical properties of the image data exploited by a compression algorithm.

Quadtree image compression can be considered as a spatial domain compression approach which partitions an image block recursively to form a quadtree structure, with the initial block set to the image itself [43–46]. The parameters attached to each leaf node describe the corresponding block. Quadtree compression is computationally efficient. A selective encryption scheme is proposed by Cheng and co-workers [32, 33], which encrypts only the quadtree structure and leaves the parameters attached to the leaf nodes unencrypted for the quadtree image compression where only one parameter is associated with a leaf node to describe the average intensity of the corresponding block. The unencrypted leaf node values

[2]Perceptual encryption will be described later in the Perceptual Encryption section.

have to be transmitted in some order. According to the authors, the in-order traversal of the quadtree is considered insecure since certain properties possessed in such ordering make it susceptible to cryptanalysis. It is recommended to use the ordering which encodes the leaf node values one level at a time from the highest level to the lowest level.

Selective Video Encryption

For compressed video such as MPEG video, the partial data selected for encryption can be headers, frames, macroblocks, DCT coefficients, motion vectors, etc. Since MPEG-1 and MPEG-2 are two coding standards that are widely used for video compression, most selective video encryption schemes, especially those developed at an early time, were designed for MPEG-1 and MPEG-2.

Header Encryption.   Headers are encrypted as the lowest of the four levels of encryption in SECMPEG, a modified MPEG bitstream incorporated with selective encryption and additional header information proposed by Meyer and Gadegast in 1995 [47]. On the one hand, header encryption has the advantage of low complexity, thanks to easy parsing of headers and encryption of a small fraction of data. On the other hand, the encryption prevents extraction of basic information of video from the cipher bitstream and makes adaptation impossible without decryption. Reconstruction of headers in MPEG-1 is relatively simple [17, 48] due to simple MPEG-1 headers and a limited variation of headers in a codestream. The security of header encryption is low.

Prediction-Based Selective Encryption.   In MPEG video coding, predictive coded frames (P-frames) and bidirectional coded frames (B-frames) are predicted from intra coded frames (I-frames). Without the knowledge of corresponding I-frames, P- and B-frames are not decodable and therefore are useless. This idea has been used in the selective encryption schemes proposed by Maples and Spanos [49] and Li et al. [50], where only I-frames are encrypted. Reduction of data to be encrypted in this approach depends on the frequency of I-frames. Since an I-frame contains a substantially significant number of bits than a P- or B-frame, a large fraction of data still needs to be encrypted with the scheme unless I-frames appear very infrequently, which may cause other undesirable consequences such as a long delay in switching channels or prolonged perceptual distortion when packet loss occurs.

A method to reduce the amount of data to be encrypted for an I-frame is proposed in Qiao and Nahrstedt [51, 52]. This method partitions the bytes of each I-frame in an MPEG bitstream into two halves: one half consisting of bytes at odd indices and the other half consisting of bytes at even indices. The XORing result of the two halves replaces the first half, and the second half is encrypted with a standard encryption algorithm such as DES. In effect, the DES encrypted half of the bitstream serves as a one-time pad for the other half. Low correlation between bytes in the MPEG bitstream makes this approach quite secure. MPEG compression removes effectively most correlation in a video sequence. Some correlation still remains after compression, since a practical compression scheme cannot achieve the theoretical rate-distortion limit. In addition, the headers and synchronization markers inserted into a bitstream introduce additional correlation. This approach achieves only modest reduction in complexity. The method, which is extended in Tosun and Feng [53], applies the algorithm again to the second half, resulting in a quarter of bytes being encrypted with DES. By doing so, the security is lowered since the one-time pad is no longer just one time.

Selective encryption of I-frames suffers content leakage. Agi and Gong [54] have shown that some scene content from the decoded P- and B-frames is perceptible even in the absence of I-frames, especially for a video sequence with a high degree of motion. This content leakage is partially due to inter-frame correlation and mainly from unencrypted I-blocks in the P- and B-frames. Certain multimedia applications such as pay-per-view may live with such content leakage since the perceptual quality of the reconstructed sequence is still quite low. For those applications requiring higher security, a simple remedy is to encrypt I-blocks in P- and B-frames in addition to I-frames [47, 54]. Increasing I-frame frequency may also mitigate the content leakage problem with lowered compression efficiency. Another remedy [55] is to encrypt all I-macroblocks in all frames as well as headers of all predicted macroblocks with a substantial increase in complexity. The amount of data to be encrypted is about 40–79% of the total. The complexity can be reduced by encrypting every other I-macroblock and predicted macroblock header to achieve adequate security, resulting in 18–40% of the total bits to be encrypted [56].

Selective Encryption on DCT Coefficients and Motion Vectors. DCT coefficients and motion vectors are also selected to be encrypted in selective encryption. One approach is to encrypt selected or all sign bits of DCT coefficients and motion vectors of MPEG video. The Video Encryption Algorithm (VEA) proposed in Shi and Bhargava [57] uses a secret key to randomly flip the sign bits of all the DCT coefficients. This is achieved by XORing sign bits with a keystream constructed by repeating a pseudo-randomly generated bitstream of length m. Security of this scheme is very low. It is vulnerable to known-plaintext attacks. A simple ciphertext-only attack may also break the encryption due to the repetition in the keystream. A variation is to randomly flip the sign bits of DC coefficients of I-frames and the sign bits of motion vectors of P- and B-frames [58]. The security of this variation is weaker than VEA [59]. Security is improved in the scheme proposed by Shi, Wang, and Bhargava [60]. This scheme uses a block cipher to encrypt sign bits of DCT coefficients up to 64 bits per macroblock selected from low to high frequencies. Those sign bits are extracted from each macroblock and placed back into their corresponding positions after encryption with a block cipher. These schemes have weak security. The search space is not large enough, and a brute force attack is feasible, especially for low bitrate compressed video. For example, when MPEG-4 base layer compression is applied to Quarter Common Intermediate Format (QCIF) video sequences of a frame size of 144×176 with the AC coefficient prediction turned on, "Miss America" has on average 1 non-zero AC coefficients per 8×8 block at 30 kbps, and "Coast Guard" has on average 4.3 non-zero AC coefficients per block at 100 kbps [20, 26]. This means that on average the sign bits of AC coefficients in each block can generate only 2 states for the first case and about 20 states for the latter case. They may also suffer from error-concealment-based attacks [11]. Nonetheless, these schemes may be applied to applications where degradation rather than secrecy is the main concern. Their main disadvantage is the necessity to parse fairly deeply into the compressed bit-stream at both encryption and decryption. Parsing and extraction of sign bits may take a substantial fraction of total computational time. Experiments reported in Zhu et al. [20, 26] show that with a fast cipher full encryption of all the video data in a frame is much faster, if time spent to extract data and place back is included, than the selective encryption scheme which extracts sign bits and other data, encrypts, and then places them back to their corresponding positions.

Permutation of Selected Data.   A frequently used approach is to permute randomly selected or all blocks, macroblocks, coefficients, and motion vectors. An early MPEG video encryption scheme [61] is to use a random permutation to replace the zigzag order in scanning two-dimensional (2-D) DCT coefficients into a one-dimensional (1-D) vector before run-length coding for each block. The DC coefficient is split into two halves, with the highest AC coefficient of the block being set to the higher half. This method can be combined with the aforementioned sign bit encryption of DCT coefficients [62]. In Zeng and Lei [36, 37], encryption of sign bits of DCT coefficients and motion vectors is combined with permutation of DCT coefficients at the same frequency location within each segment consisting of several 8×8 blocks or macroblocks. The permutation is controlled by a key. The same authors also describe a variation of the scheme for wavelet-based video compression that selective encryption of sign bits is combined with permutation of blocks where each subband is partitioned into a number of blocks of the same size. Rotation controlled by a key can also be applied to each block of subband coefficients. Permutation is also used in Wen et al. [11, 63] for syntax-compliant encryption, which will be described in Section 4.4.4. The security of these schemes is weak. They cannot withstand known-plaintext and chosen-plaintext attacks if the permutation table does not change frequently [51, 64, 65]. Ciphertext-only attacks can also be launched successfully against the random permutation of the scanning order of 2-D DCT coefficients by exploiting the fact that non-zero

AC coefficients are likely gathered in the upper-left corner of an I-block [51]. An additional disadvantage of the scheme of random permutation of the scanning order is a substantial penalty to compression efficiency, which can be as high as 46% [64].

Random Corruption. A completely different approach, proposed by Griwodz and co-workers [66, 67], corrupts an MPEG video bitstream randomly before distribution. The correct bytes are sent to an authorized user when the content decoding is executed. The authors reported that corruption of approximately 1% of bytes could achieve the goal of rendering the content undecodable or unwatchable. A similar approach called the Syntax Unaware Runlength-Based Selective Encryption (SURSLE) is described in Wen et al. [11]. In this approach, X consecutive bits are encrypted, followed by Y unencrypted, followed by Z encrypted, and so on. The advantage of this approach is that the scheme can be applied to any bitstreams, i.e., is content-agnostic. Unlike other selective encryption schemes that are designed to encrypt the most critical data, the encrypted bits in this approach are not necessarily the most critical bits, resulting in lowered security. Another drawback is that the approach produces format-incompatible outputs. Format-compliant encryption will be discussed in Section 4.4.4.

Selective Audio Encryption

Selective encryption has also been used to encrypt compressed audio bitstreams. A selective encryption scheme is proposed in Thorwirth et al. [68] for MPEG Audio Layer III (MP3) [9] bitstreams. MP3 bitstreams consist of frames. Each frame contains a frame header, side information, and main data from encoding 1152 raw audio samples. The portions of compressed main data associated with the most critical frequency bands are grouped into equal-size blocks and encrypted with a block cipher. The encrypted bitstream portions are then reassembled in order to preserve the MP3 format. Since encryption is applied after compression, the scheme has a very small compression efficiency overhead. The scheme requires parsing rather deeply into an MP3 bitstream.

Perceptual Encryption

Unlike typical multimedia encryption which is designed to prevent leak of content to unauthorized users or to severely distort perceptual objects to be of any entertainment value, **perceptual encryption** is designed to produce a cipher codestream that is degraded yet recognizable and playable without decryption. The original quality is fully recovered if the encrypted codestream is decrypted with the correct decryption key. Degradation is controlled by a quality factor. Syntax compliance is a basic requirement for perceptual encryption. Syntax-compliant encryption algorithms will be described in Section 4.4.4. Figure 4.3 shows the perceptual

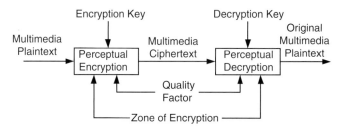

FIGURE 4.3:   Perceptual encryption and decryption process [72].

cryptosystem. In addition to encryption and decryption keys used in all multimedia encryption schemes, the perceptual cryptosystem has two more parameters at both encryption and decryption sides. The first is the quality factor which controls the level of degradation for the multimedia ciphertext. The second is the zone of encryption which specifies the visual regions that encryption should be applied to. Perpetual audio encryption does not use the second parameter in general. The selective encryption scheme to encrypt bitplanes from the least significant bitplane to the most significant bitplane described previously in the Selective Image Encryption section belongs to perceptual encryption.

A perceptual encryption scheme for MP3 audio is proposed in Torrubia and Mora [69, 70]. As we have mentioned previously, each frame in an MP3 bitstream contains a frame header, side information, and main data. The main data contain scalefactor and Huffman codeword values for each subband. The scheme encrypts the j least significant bits of the total scalefactor bits (scalefactor_bits) by XORing them with a keystream generated with a pseudo-random number generator (PRNG), where $j = floor(scalabefactor\_bits * p/100)$ is related to a quality loss parameter $p \in [0, 100]$. In addition, each Huffman codeword can be substituted with another codeword of the same size from the same codebook. The substitution is performed using a PRNG to select the new codeword.

A different perceptual encryption scheme for MP3 audio is described in Servetti, Testa, and De Martin [71]. In MP3, Modified Discrete Cosine Transform (MDCT) coefficients are partitioned into several frequency regions during Huffman encoding. Most of the spectral energy of an audio signal is concentrated in the range from 20 Hz to 14 kHz, and an MP3 encoder usually maps this segment into the big value region. This region is further subdivided into three sub-regions, called region0, region1, and region2 with increasing frequencies. Each sub-region is coded with a different Huffman table that best fits the sub-region statistics. The perceptual encryption scheme encrypts a small portion of bits in the sub-regions of higher frequencies and leaves the sub-regions of lower frequencies unencrypted. According to Servetti, Testa, and De Martin [71], if region0 is exposed without encryption, it is sufficient to encrypt 1 bit out of 20 in region1, which translates to only 1.1% of the total bitstream encrypted for a 128 kbits/s stereo bitstream at 44.1 kHz. If both region0 and region1 are exposed without encryption, 70 to 100 bits of region2 have to be encrypted. The amount of encrypted data is about 6.3-8.3% for a 128 kbits/s stereo stream at 44.1 kHz. To ensure that an MP3 player discards the encrypted sub-regions, the Huffman table index used for those encrypted sub-regions is set to "not used," and the big value number is set to its maximum. A custom header used for decryption is also inserted into the encrypted bitstream. The header is ignored by an MP3 player. These measures ensure that the encrypted MP3 bitstream can be played by an MP3 player at degraded quality. This perceptual encryption scheme produces an encrypted MP3 bitstream with one of the two possible quality levels: region0 or region0 plus region1.

A perceptual encryption scheme for JPEG, proposed in Torrubia and Mora [72], substitutes the Huffman codewords used to encode AC coefficients inside the encryption zone with alternative Huffman codewords controlled by a key. Granularity is accomplished by making a decision on performing the substitution or not based on probability p, the quality loss parameter. For wavelet-based zerotree image and video compression, a perceptual encryption scheme [73] is to encrypt the sign bits of wavelet coefficients and permute the four wavelet coefficients with the same parent node in the quadtree structure of the wavelet decomposition. The quality factor is used to control the number of wavelet coefficients to be permuted and sign-encrypted. Sign bit encryption, bit-plane permutation, and inter-block permutation are used in the perceptual encryption of JPEG 2000 code-streams proposed in Lian, Sun, and Wang [74]. For MPEG-4, the perceptual encryption scheme proposed by Lian et al. [75] encrypts Video Object Layers (VOLs) from the highest layer to the lowest layer for each video object, encrypts code blocks in each video object plane from the highest subband to the lowest sub-band, and encrypts bitplanes in each code block from the least significant bitplane to the most significant bitplane. Again, the quality factor controls how many data should be permutated or encrypted in these schemes.

Issues with Selective Encryption

The gain of less data being encrypted for selective encryption is not without any cost. The proposed selective encryption algorithms described above suffer some of the following problems [24]. Careful balance and trade-off are necessary in designing a multimedia cryptosystem for a given application.

1. **Insufficient security**. Selective encryption encrypts partial information. The focus of most selective encryption schemes is perceptual degradation rather than content secrecy. An encrypted bitstream with selective encryption usually still contains some structural information of the content. Even for perceptual degradation, many selective encryption schemes suffer from

perceptual attacks that simple signal processing technologies can recover
substantially improved perception of the content. For example, encryption
of I-frames, sign bits of DCT coefficients and motion vectors, DC and low-
frequency AC coefficients, and significant bitplanes of DCT coefficients
may be partially reversed with error concealment and other image processing technologies to recover significant structural information of the content
[11, 51, 54, 76]. For example, experiments reported in Wu and Kuo [76] show
that even if the four most significant bits[3] of all DCT coefficients are
encrypted for a JPEG compressed image, the semantic image content,
i.e., the contours of objects in an image, can still be recovered by some
simple image processing technologies. The search space of encrypted data
in some selective encryption schemes may be small enough to make a brute
force attack feasible, especially for low bitrate compression [20, 26]. Different statistical properties possessed by frequency coefficients can also
be exploited to launch ciphertext-only attacks against selective encryption
schemes. For example, low-pass property of an image can be used to dramatically narrow down the search space to launch a ciphertext-only attack
[51, 64] against the scheme which randomly permutes the zigzag order
of DCT coefficients proposed in Tang [61]. In addition, many selective
encryption schemes cannot withstand known-plaintext or chosen-plaintext
attacks. The unencrypted portion of data in selective encryption and perceptual redundancy in multimedia make known-plaintext attacks a realistic
threat.

2. **Insignificant computational reduction**. Selective encryption schemes such
   as encryption of I-frames, I-frames plus I-blocks, or selected bitplanes still
   require encrypting a substantial portion of the whole data. Other selective
   encryption schemes such as encryption of sign bits of DCT coefficients and
   motion vectors encrypt only a small portion of data, but the encryption
   and decryption need deep parsing into the compressed bitstream. The time
   needed for parsing and encryption of selected data may be even longer than
   a full encryption scheme [20, 26], especially when decryption is executed
   separately from decompression. Many selective encryption schemes may
   not gain significant computational reduction with respect to full encryption.

3. **Significant overhead on compression efficiency**. Some selective encryption schemes described above modify the statistics of the data to be
   compressed or compression parameters, which lowers the compression efficiency substantially. For example, encryption of selected bitplanes changes
   the original statistical properties of those affected bitplanes and makes them
   more difficult to compress by a compression scheme applied subsequently.

---

[3]The sign bit is considered as the most significant bit in the experiments.

Random permutation of the zigzag scan order of DCT coefficients changes the optimal design of the original JPEG and MPEG compression, resulting in lowered compression efficiency.

4. **Lack of syntax compliance**. Many selective encryption schemes such as header encryption and I-frame encryption produce outputs that are not compatible with the underlying compression syntax and cannot be decoded by encryption-unaware players such as old version or standard-compliant players. This will restrict wide adoption of the proposed selective encryption schemes.

4.4.3   Joint Compression and Encryption

Joint compression and encryption algorithms differ from other multimedia encryption algorithms in that they modify the compression procedures or parameters to achieve the goal of scrambling multimedia content. The previously described random permutation of the zigzag scan order of DCT coefficients can be considered as a joint compression and encryption scheme. Many joint schemes can also be classified as selective encryption, where compression parameters or procedures are selectively encrypted and the remaining data are left without encryption. This section will describe additional joint schemes.

A simple scheme, proposed in Vorwerk, Engel, and Meinel [77], applies secret wavelet filters selected from a pool of available wavelet filters to a wavelet-based image compression method. The wavelet filters are encrypted. It is argued that without the knowledge of the wavelet filters applied during compression, a cryptanalyst cannot correctly interpret the compressed bitstream, resulting in useless reconstructed content. The approach has also been applied to wavelet packet-based image compression [78, 79]. The approach is not sufficiently secure against ciphertext-only attacks. By exploiting the fact that the result is noisy if incorrect filters are applied in reconstruction, the following heuristic evaluation can be applied to recover the applied wavelet filters [78, 79]: starts at the first decomposition level to search for the filters, takes the ones which give the minimum entropy on the difference image obtained by measuring the difference between neighboring pixels, and then proceeds to the next decomposition level. This heuristic method reduces the attack complexity to the order of the number of wavelet filter coefficients times the number of levels of the wavelet decomposition. The scheme cannot withstand known-plaintext attacks, either. Another drawback is that the scheme uses non-optimal wavelet filters or packets in the compression, resulting in lowered compression efficiency.

Another approach is to combine encryption with adaptive arithmetic coding [80]. By arguing that the adaptive nature of the model used in adaptive arithmetic coding acts like a large size key that the intruder cannot duplicate, it is suggested in Witten and Cleary [81, 82] that an adaptive compression algorithm such as adaptive arithmetic coding can be converted into an encryption algorithm by keeping the initial model secret, with the initial model determined by the key. In addition, secret adjustments to the current interval can also be performed after each symbol is coded with an adaptive arithmetic coding [83]. An alternative method is to introduce randomness into the symbols coding probabilities by ensuring that the update time for computing the coding probabilities is performed at random intervals as specified by the output of a stream cipher in adaptive arithmetic coding [84]. These schemes encrypt a small fraction of data to achieve confidentiality. The penalty on compression efficiency is also reasonably small, about 2% worse than the original adaptive arithmetic coding described in Witten, Neal, and Cleary [80] for the scheme to secretly adjust the current interval [83]. It has been shown that encryption based on error propagation caused by the adaptive nature in adaptive arithmetic coding is vulnerable to chosen-plaintext attacks [83–87].

Using and hiding a custom Huffman table can also be used for joint compression and encryption, since decoding a Huffman coded bitstream without the knowledge of the Huffman coding table is very difficult [88]. But the scheme is vulnerable to known-plaintext and chosen-plaintext attacks. To reduce the penalty on coding efficiency, the number of Huffman tables available is limited, which makes ciphertext-only attacks also feasible [57]. Security can be enhanced by introducing randomness in using m statistical models instead of one statistical model [76, 89, 90]. One of the m statistical models is selected based on a random sequence to encode an incoming symbol. m should be large to ensure security. Although a large number of Huffman tables can be efficiently generated by the Huffman tree mutation technique [90], management of a large set of Huffman tables is complex. It is argued [90] that the scheme is secure to ciphertext-only and known-plaintext attacks, but vulnerable to chosen-plaintext attacks.

4.4.4   Syntax-Compliant Encryption

Syntax-compliant encryption ensures that the encrypted bitstream is still compliant to the syntax specifications of a specific format so that an encryption-unaware format-compliant player can play the encrypted bitstream directly without crash, although the rendered content may be unintelligible. Such encryption is transparent to decoders. Backward compatibility with the JPEG 2000 Part 1 [8] is a basic requirement in developing JPSEC [91], the security part of JPEG 2000.

A simple approach to ensure syntax compliance is to scramble multimedia data before compression is applied. This approach is proposed in Pazarci and Dipcin [92]. In this scheme, a video frame is partitioned into scrambling blocks, and a secret linear transformation is applied to the pixel values in each scrambling block which consists of one or more MPEG macroblocks. MPEG video compression is then applied to the transformed video. Such scrambling modifies the statistical properties of a video sequence that is exploited by a compression algorithm and results in a significant penalty on compression efficiency. The scheme is also vulnerable to known-plaintext attacks. Some of the previously described selective encryption algorithms are also syntax compliant. These algorithms include the permutation of the scan order of DCT coefficients, the random flipping of sign bits of DCT coefficients and motion vectors, etc. that we have described in Section 4.4.2.

Encryption of indices of VLC and fixed-length code (FLC) codewords, as well as spatial shuffling of codewords and macroblocks, is proposed in Wen et al. [11, 63, 93]. Encryption of VLC codewords is performed as follows: the VLC table is first partitioned into non-overlapping subsets, each with a number of codewords as a power of 2. Each codeword is assigned a unique index within the subset it belongs to. The indices are fixed lengths of integer bits. The VLC codewords to be encrypted in a bitstream are first mapped into their corresponding indices, concatenated, encrypted, mapped back to the codewords, and then put back into the bitstream. The same procedure is performed for FLC codewords. For syntax-compliant encryption of MPEG-4, FLC-coded DCT signs, Dquant (difference of quantization step-sizes between current and previous macroblocks), and intra-DC information are selected as the candidates for FLC encryption, and motion vectors are selected for VLC encryption in [11, 63, 93]. The scheme incurs some loss of compression efficiency since the fine-tuned MPEG codewords are replaced by non-optimal codewords during encryption. The security of the scheme may be low too, especially when the number of codewords in some subsets of the code table is small. It may also suffer from error-concealment attacks. Another drawback is that encryption and decryption require fairly deep parsing into the bitstream.

Several syntax-compliant encryption schemes have been proposed for JPEG 2000 encryption. A simple scheme is to randomly flip the bitstreams of coding passes belonging to the last layers for each code block [94]. A more sophisticated scheme is to encrypt the data in each individual packet with a cipher such as DES or AES [95, 96]. AES in CFB mode is used in Norcen and Uhl [96] to encrypt any number of bits without expansion. Note that the CFB mode converts a block cipher into a self-synchronization stream cipher. A scheme to encrypt the bitstream of each codeword segment from the coding passes of the most significant bitplane to those of the least significant bitplane for each code block is proposed in Zhu, Yang, and Li [97]. Cipher bitstreams generated by these schemes may emulate JPEG 2000 markers. Such emulation may cause erroneous parsing or synchronization, especially under error-prone transmissions or environments. Ciphers to avoid generating a byte-aligned value between $0 \times FF90$ and $0 \times FFFF$ for any two consecutive bytes and an ending byte of value $0 \times FF$ are employed in Wu and Ma, Wu, Deng and Zhu, Yang, and Li [12, 98, 99] to encrypt data in each packet, code block contribution to a packet, or codeword segments, respectively. Details of these schemes can be found in Chapter 11. A simple syntax-compliant encryption scheme is also proposed in Grosbois, Gerbelot, and Ebrahimi [94] for JPEG 2000 compression, which randomly flips the signs of the wavelet coefficients in high-frequency subbands. Encryption parameters can be inserted after the last termination marker, either implicit or explicit, of a code block to exploit the fact that bits appearing after a termination marker will not be read by a compliant JPEG 2000 entropy decoder [94, 96]. The drawback is that if the data of the last coding pass are lost along with the encryption parameters behind the termination marker during transmission, received data may not be decrypted either, resulting in error propagation.

Details of syntax-compliant encryption can be found in Chapter 9. Interested readers should refer to that chapter for further descriptions and discussions.

4.4.5   Scalable Encryption and Multi-Access Encryption

Scalable coding is a technology that encodes a multimedia signal in a scalable manner where various representations can be extracted from a single codestream to fit a wide range of applications. Early scalable coding offers layered scalability. Newer scalable coding such as MPEG-4 FGS and JPEG 2000 offers fine granularity scalability. In a similar manner, scalable encryption encrypts a multimedia signal into a single codestream so that multiple representations can be extracted from the encrypted codestream directly without decryption. A basic requirement for scalable encryption is that the encryption should be robust to allow truncations. Otherwise, a truncation may desynchronize the decryptor or remove the decryption parameters needed for decrypting the remaining data, resulting in erroneous decryption. Multi-access encryption also supports multiple representations with a single encrypted codestream. Different keys are used to encrypt different parts of a codestream to ensure that a user can only decrypt the portion of a codestream that he or she is authorized to consume. Scalable encryption and multi-access encryption generally work with a scalable coding technology. Many syntax-compliant encryption schemes described in Section 4.4.4, such as encryption schemes for JPEG 2000, are also scalable encryption schemes. Some may be truncated only at a much coarser granularity. For example, the VLC and FLC codeword indices encryption scheme [11, 63, 93] allows truncations at a level of an entire segment within which permutation occurs. If a partial segment is truncated, the remaining data of the segment may not be decryptable. If encryption parameters are inserted after the termination markers, an encryption-unaware truncation may remove the bitstream of the last coding pass along with the encryption parameters, rendering the remaining data not decryptible.

Early scalable encryption schemes [27, 100–103] support layered scalability. They partition an MPEG bitstream into several layers according to quality or spatial-temporal resolution and encrypt each layer separately. Newer scalable encryption schemes support finer granularity of scalability. In addition to the scalable encryption schemes with fine granularity of scalability for JPEG 2000 that we have mentioned above, several scalable encryption schemes have also been proposed for other scalable formats. A scalable encryption scheme, Wee and Apostolopoulos proposed in [21, 22], partitions a scalable codestream into packets and applies a block cipher in CBC mode to encrypt the data in each packet independently. A packet-level granularity of scalability with truncation of trailing data in a packet is supported with the scheme. A selective encryption scheme, proposed by Yuan et al. [26], preserves the full scalability of MPEG-4 FGS after encryption. A scheme that pseudo-randomly shuffles (RUN, EOP) symbols on a bitplane or sub-bitplane level and encrypts the sign bits of DCT coefficients is proposed in Yu [104] for MPEG-4 FGS enhancement layer encryption. The scheme supports scalability at the sub-bitplane level within which shuffling occurs. Different encryption keys are used to encrypt different parts of a codestream for multi-access encryption. An encryption scheme to support two access types with multiple layers for each type is proposed in by Yuan and co-workers [19, 20] for MPEG-4 FGS where independent encryption keys are applied. When a single encrypted codestream is required to support complex multi-accesses, such as simultaneously supporting quality, resolution, spatial, and temporal accesses, efficient key generation and management are necessary for multi-access encryption. In addition, the key scheme should be robust to collusion attacks in which a group of cryptanalysts collude to derive the decryption keys that they cannot access. Scalable encryption and multi-access encryption with efficient key schemes will be described in detail in Chapter 11. Interested readers are referred to that chapter for further studies.

4.5 CONCLUSION

Multimedia encryption provides confidentiality for multimedia content and prevents users from unauthorized access. It plays a critical role in modern digital multimedia services and applications. In this chapter, we have presented the fundamentals of multimedia encryption, including basics of modern encryption, unique issues and requirements in multimedia encryption, and typical multimedia encryption schemes. This chapter provides a basis for many remaining chapters in this book. More advanced topics and specific applications of multimedia encryption can be found in subsequent chapters. Interested readers can read Chapter 6 for key management, Chapter 9 for format-compliant encryption, Chapter 10 for streaming media encryption, Chapter 12 for broadcast encryption, and Chapter 11 for scalable encryption and multi-access control. Other multimedia security issues such as multimedia authentication can also be found in other chapters of this book.

REFERENCES

[1] B. Schneier. *Applied Cryptography: Protocols, Algorithms, and Source Code in C*, John Wiley & Sons, New York, 2nd edition, 1996.

[2] A. J. Menezes, P. C. van Oorschot, and S. A. Vanstone. *Handbook of Applied Cryptography*, CRC Press, Boca raton, FL, 1996.

[3] W. Mao. *Modern Cryptography: Theory and Practice*, Prentice Hall PTR, Upper Saddle River, NJ, 2003.

[4] I. Agi and L. Gong. An empirical study of secure MPEG video transmissions. in *Proc. Internet Soc. Symp. Network Distributed System Security*, San Diego, CA, pp. 137–144, February 1996.

[5] S. McCanne and V. Jacobson. vic: A flexible framework for packet video, in *Proc. 3rd ACM Int. Conf. Multimedia*, pp. 511–522, San Francisco, CA, 1995.

[6] P. P. Dang and P. M. Chau. Image encryption for secure internet multimedia applications, *IEEE Trans. Consumer Electronics*, 46(3):395–403, 2000.

[7] ISO/IEC. *Coding of Audio-Visual Objects, Part-2 Visual, Amendment 4: Streaming Video Profile*, ISO/IEC 14496-2/FPDAM4, July 2000.

[8] ISO/IEC. *Information Technology—JPEG 2000 Image Coding System, Part 1: Core Coding System*, ISO/IEC 15444-1:2000 (ISO/IEC JTC/SC 29/WG 1 N1646R), March 2000.

[9] ISO/IEC. *MPEG-1 Coding of Moving Pictures and Associated Audio for Digital Storage Media at Up to About 1.5 Mb/s*, ISO/IEC 11172, 1993.

[10] ISO/IEC. *Information Technology—Generic Coding of Moving Pictures and Associated Audio Information: Video*, ISO/IEC 13818-2:2000, 2000.

[11] J. Wen, M. Severa, W. Zeng, M. H. Luttrell, and W. Jin. A format-compliant configurable encryption framework for access control of video, *IEEE Trans. Circuits and Systems for Video Technology*, 12(6):545–557, June 2002.

[12] H. Wu and D. Ma. Efficient and secure encryption schemes for JPEG2000, *IEEE Int. Conf. Acoustics, Speech, and Signal Processing, 2004 (ICASSP '04)*, 5:V869–872, Montreal, Quebec, Canada, May 2004.

[13] Microsoft. Advanced Systems Format (ASF) Specifications, available from http://www.microsoft.com/windows/windowsmedia/format/asfspec.aspx.

[14] Microsoft. Architecture of Windows Media Rights Manager, http://www.microsoft.com/windows/windowsmedia/howto/articles/drmarchitecture.aspx.

[15] Open Mobile Alliance (OMA). OMA DRM Specification v2.0, March 2004, http://www.openmobilealliance.org.

[16] A. Ainslie, X. Drèze, and F. Zufryden. Modeling movie life cycles and market share, *Marketing Science*, 24(3):508–517, 2005.

[17] T. Lookabaugh, D. C. Sicker, D. M. Keaton, W. Y. Guo, and I. Vedula. Security analysis of selectively encrypted MPEG-2 streams, *SPIE Conf. Multimedia Systems and Applications VI*, 5241:10–21, Orlando, FL, 2003.

[18] Open Mobile Alliance (OMA). DRM Content Format v2.0, April 2004, http://www.openmobilealliance.org.

[19] C. Yuan, B. B. Zhu, M. Su, X. Wang, S. Li, and Y. Zhong. Layered access control for MPEG-4 FGS video, *IEEE Int. Conf. Image Processing*, 1:517–520, September 2003.

[20] B. B. Zhu, C. Yuan, Y. Wang, and S. Li. Scalable protection for MPEG-4 fine granularity scalability, *IEEE Trans. Multimedia*, 7(2):222–233, April 2005.

[21] S. J. Wee and J. G. Apostolopoulos. Secure scalable video streaming for wireless networks, *IEEE. Int. Conf. Acoustics, Speech, and Signal Processing*, 4:2049–2052, May 7–11, Salt Lake City, UT, 2001.

[22] S. J. Wee and J. G. Apostolopoulos. Secure scalable streaming enabling transcoding without decryption, *IEEE Int. Conf. Image Processing*, 1:437–440, October 2001.

[23] T. Kunkelmann, R. Reinema, R. Steinmetz, and T. Blecher. Evaluation of different video encryption methods for a secure multimedia conferencing gateway, in *Proc. 4th COST 237 Workshop*, Lisboa, Portugal, LNCS vol. 1356, pp. 75–89, December 1997.

[24] X. Liu and A. M. Eskicioglu. Selective encryption of multimedia content in distribution networks: Challenges and new directions, in *2nd Int. Conf. Communications, Internet and Information Technology*, Scottsdale, AZ, November 2003.

[25] T. Lookabaugh and D. C. Sicker. Selective encryption for consumer applications, In *Proc. First IEEE Consumer Communications and Networking Conference, 2004 (CCNC'04)*, pp. 516–521, Las Vegas, NV, Jan. 5–8, 2004.

[26] C. Yuan, B. B. Zhu, Y. Wang, S. Li, and Y. Zhong. Efficient and fully scalable encryption for MPEG-4 FGS, *IEEE Int. Symp. Circuits and Systems*, Bangkok, Thailand, 2:620–623, May 2003.

[27] T. Kunkelmann and R. Reinema. A scalable security architecture for multimedia communication standards, in *Proc. IEEE Int. Conf. Multimedia Computing and Systems*, pp. 660–661, Ottawa, Canada, 1997.

[28] H. Cheng and X. Li. On the application of image decomposition to image compression and encryption, in *Proc. IFIP TC6/TC11 Int. Conf. Communications and Multimedia Security II, Essen*, Germany, pp. 116–127, 1996.

[29] M. Van Droogenbroeck and R. Benedett. Techniques for a selective encryption of uncompressed and compressed images, in *Proc. Advanced Concepts for Intelligent Vision Systems (ACIVS'02)*, Ghent, Belgium, pp. 90–97, September 9–11, 2002.

[30] J. M. Shapiro. Embedded image coding using zerotrees of wavelet coefficients, *IEEE Trans. Signal Processing*, 41:3445–3462, December 1993.

[31] A. Said and W. A. Pearlman. A new, fast, and efficient image codec based on set partitioning in hierarchical trees, *IEEE Trans. Circuits and Systems for Video Technology*, 6:243–250, June 1996.

[32] X. Li, J. Knipe, and H. Cheng. Image compression and encryption using tree structures, *Pattern Recognition Letters*, 18(8):2439–2451, 1997.

[33] H. Cheng and X. Li. Partial encryption of compressed images and videos, *IEEE Trans. Signal Processing*, 48(8):2439–2451, August 2000.

[34] T. Uehara, R. Safavi-Naini, and P. Ogunbona. Securing wavelet compression with random permutations, in *Proc. IEEE Pacific-Rim Conf. Multimedia*, pp. 332–335, Syndney, Australia, December 13–15, 2000.

[35] S. Lian and Z. Wang. Comparison of several wavelet coefficients confusion methods applied in multimedia encryption, in *Proc. Int. Conf. Computer Networks and Mobile Computing (ICCNMC'2003)*, pp. 372–376, Shanghai, China, October 20–23, 2003.

[36] W. Zeng and S. Lei. Efficient frequency domain video scrambling for content access control, in *Proc. 7th ACM Int. Conf. Multimedia*, pp. 285–294, Orlando, FL 1999.

[37] W. Zeng and S. Lei. Efficient frequency domain selective scrambling of digital video, *IEEE Trans. Multimedia*, 5(1):118–129, 2003.

[38] A. Pommer and A. Uhl. Selective encryption of wavelet-packet encoded image data: Efficiency and security, *Multimedia Systems*, 9(3):279–287, 2003.

[39] R. Norcen and A. Uhl. Selective encryption of wavelet packet subband structures for obscured transmission of visual data, in *Proc. 3rd IEEE Benelux Signal Processing Symposium (SPS'2002)*, pp. 25–28, Leaven, Belgium, 2002.

[40] R. Norcen and A. Uhl. Selective encryption of wavelet packet subband structures for secure transmission of visual data, in *Proc. Multimedia and Security Workshop of 10th ACM Int. Conference on Multimedia*, pp. 67–70, Juan–les–Pins, France, 2002.

[41] M. Podesser, H.-P. Schmidt, and A. Uhl. Selective bitplane encryption for secure transmission of image data in mobile environments, in *Proc. 5th IEEE Nordic Signal Processing Symposium (NORSIG'2002)*, Hurtigruten, Norway 2002.

[42] R. Norcen, M. Podesser, A. Pommer, H.-P. Schmidt, and A. Uhl. Confidential storage and transmission of medical image data, *Computers in Biology and Medicine*, 33(3):277–292, 2003.

[43] P. Strobach. Tree-structured scene adaptive coder, *IEEE Trans. Communcations*, 38:477–486, April 1990.

[44] P. Strobach. Quadtree-structured recursive plane decomposition coding of images, *IEEE Trans. Signal Processing*, 39:1380–1397, June 1991.

[45] G. J. Sullivan and R. L. Baker. Efficient quadtree coding of images and video, *IEEE Trans. Image Processing*, 3:327–331, May 1994.

[46] E. Shusterman and M. Feder. Image compression via improved quadtree decomposition algorithms, *IEEE Trans. Image Processing*, 3:207–215, March 1994.

[47] J. Meyer and F. Gadegast. Security Mechanisms for Multimedia-Data with the Example MPEG-1 video, available at http://www.gadegast.de/frank/doc/secmeng.pdf, 1995.

[48] C. Griwodz, O. Merkel, J. Dittmann, and R. Steinmetz. Protecting VoD the easier way, in *Proc. ACM Multimedia 1998*, Bristol, UK, pp. 21–28, September 12–16, 1998.

[49] T. B. Maples and G. A. Spanos. Performance study of a selective encryption scheme for the security of networked, real-time video, in *Proc. 4th Int. Conf. Computer Communications & Networks*, Las Vegas, NV, September 1995.

[50] Y. Li, Z. Chen, S.-M. Tan, and R. H. Campbell. Security enhanced MPEG player, in *Proc. IEEE Int. Workshop Multimedia Software Development (MMSD'96)*, Berlin, Germany, pp. 169–175, March 1996.

[51] L. Qiao and K. Nahrstedt. Comparison of MPEG Encryption Algorithms, *Int. J. Computers & Graphics,* 22(4):pp. 437–448, 1998.

[52] L. Qiao and K. Nahrstedt. A new algorithm for MPEG video encryption, in *Proc. 1st Int. Conf. Imaging Science, Systems & Technology*, Las Vegas, NV, pp. 21–29, June 1997.

[53] A. S. Tosun and W.-C. Feng. Lightweight security mechanisms for wireless video transmission, in *Proc. Int. Conf. Information Technology: Coding and Computing*, April 2–4, pp. 157–161, Las Vegas, NV, 2001.

[54] I. Agi and L. Gong. An empirical study of secure MPEG video transmissions, in *Proc. Internet Soc. Symp. Network & Distributed System Security*, San Diego, CA, pp. 137–144, February 1996.

[55] A. M. Alattar and G. I. Al-Regib. Evaluation of selective encryption techniques for secure transmission of MPEG video bit-streams, in *Proc. IEEE Int. Symp. on Circuits and Systems (ISCAS'99)*, IV:340–343, Orlando, FL, 1999.

[56] A. M. Alattar, G. I. Al-Regib, and S. A. Al-Semari. Improved selective encryption techniques for secure transmission of MPEG video bit-streams, in *Proc. Int. Conf. Image Processing*, 4:256–260, October 24–28, Kobe, Japan, 1999.

[57] C. Shi and B. Bhargava A fast MPEG video encryption algorithm, in *Proc. ACM Int. Conf. Multimedia*, Bristol, UK, pp. 81–88, September 1998.

[58] C. Shi and B. Bhargava. An efficient MPEG video encryption algorithm, in *IEEE Proc. 17th Symp. Reliable Distributed Systems*, West Lafayette, IN, pp. 381–386, October 1998.

[59] B. Bhargava, C. Shi, and S.-Y. Wang. MPEG video encryption algorithms, *Multimedia Tools and Applications*, 24(1):57–79, 2004.

[60] C. Shi, S.-Y. Wang, and B. Bhargava. MPEG video encryption in real-time using secret key cryptography, in *Proc. Int. Conf. Parallel and Distributed Processing Techniques and Applications (PDPTA'99)*, pp. 191–201, Las Vegas, NV, 1999.

[61] L. Tang. Methods for encrypting and decrypting MPEG video data efficiently, in *Proc. ACM Int. Conf. Multimedia*, Boston, MA, pp. 219–229, November 1996.

[62] S. U. Shin, K. S. Sim, and K. H. Rhee. A secrecy scheme for MPEG video data using the joint of compression and encryption, in *Proc. Int. Workshop Information Security (ISW'99)*, Kuala Lumpur, Malaysia, M. Mambo and Y. Zheng (Eds.), LNCS vol. 1729, pp. 191–201, November 1999.

[63] J. Wen, M. Severa, W. Zeng, M. H. Luttrell, and W. Jin. A format-compliant configurable encryption framework for access control of multimedia, in *IEEE Workshop Multimedia Signal Processing*, Cannes, France, pp. 435–440, October 2001.

[64] L. Qiao and K. Nahrstedt. Is MPEG encryption by using random list instead of zigzag order secure? in *Proc. IEEE Int. Symp. Consumer Electronics*, Singapore, pp. 226–229, December 2–4, 1997.

[65] T. Uehara and R. Safavi-Naini. Chosen DCT coefficients attack on MPEG encryption scheme, in *Proc. IEEE Pacific–Rim Conf. Multimedia*, pp. 316–319, Sydney, Australia, December 2000.

[66] C. Griwodz. Video protection by partial content corruption, in *Multimedia and Security Workshop at ACM Multimedia*, pp. 37–40, Bristol, UK, September 1998.

[67] C. Griwodz, O. Merkel, J. Dittmann, and R. Steinmetz. Protecting VoD the easier way, in *ACM Int. Conf. Multimedia*, pages 21–28, Bristol, UK, 1998,

[68] N. J. Thorwirth, P. Horvatic, R. Weis, and J. Zhao. Security methods for MP3 music delivery, in *Record of the Thirty-Fourth Asilomar Conference on Signals, Systems, and Computers*, 2:1831–1835, Asilomar, CA, 2000.

[69] A. Torrubia and F. Mora. Perceptual cryptography on MPEG-1 Layer III bit-streams, in *Int. Conf. Consumer Electronics, 2002 (ICCE 2002) Digest of Technical Papers*, pp. 324–325, Los Angeles, CA, 2002.

[70] A. Torrubia and F. Mora. Perceptual cryptography on MPEG Layer III bit-streams, *IEEE Trans. Consumer Electronics*, 48(4):1046–1050, November 2002.

[71] A. Servetti, C. Testa, and J. C. De Martin. Frequency-selective partial encryption of compressed audio, in *Proc. IEEE Int. Conf. Acoustics, Speech, and Signal Processing, 2003 (ICASSP '03)*, 5:668–671, Hong Kong, 2003.

[72] A. Torrubia and F. Mora. Perceptual cryptography of JPEG compressed images on the JFIF bit-stream domain, in *Proc. IEEE Int. Conf. Consumer Electronics (ICCE'03)*, pp. 58–59, Los Angeles, CA, June 17–19, 2003.

[73] S. Lian, J. Sun, and Z. Wang. Perceptual cryptography on SPIHT compressed images or videos, in *Proc. IEEE Int. Conf. Multimedia and Expo, 2004 (ICME '04)*, 3:2195–2198, June 27–30, Taipei, Taiwan, 2004.

[74] S. Lian, J. Sun, and Z. Wang. Perceptual cryptography on JPEG2000 compressed images or videos, in *Fourth Int. Conf. Computer and Information Technology, 2004 (CIT '04)*, pp. 78–83, Wuhon, China, September 14–16, 2004.

[75] S. Lian, D. Ye, J. Sun, and Z. Wang. Perceptual MPEG-4 video encryption and its usage in video-on-demand systems, in *Proc. IEEE Int. Symp. Consumer Electronics*, pp. 83–86, Reading, UK, September 1–3, 2004.

[76] C.-P. Wu and C.-C. J. Kuo. Fast encryption methods for audiovisual data confidentiality, in *SPIE Int. Symp. Information Technologies 2000*, pp. 284–295, Boston, MA, November 2000.

[77] L. Vorwerk, T. Engel, and C. Meinel. A proposal for a combination of compression and encryption, in *Proc. SPIE Visual Communications and Image Processing 2000*, 4067:694–702, Perth, Australia, 2000.

[78] A. Pommer and A. Uhl. Multimedia soft encryption using NSMRA wavelet packet methods: Parallel attacks, in *Proc. Int. Workshop Parallel Numerics (ParNum'2000)*, pp. 179–190, Bratislava, Slovakia, 2000.

[79] A. Pommer and A. Uhl. Wavelet packet methods for multimedia compression and encryption, in *Proc. IEEE Pacific–Rim Conference on Communications, Computers and Signal Processing (PACRIM'2001)*, 1:1–4, Victoria, B.C., Canada, 2001.

[80] I. H. Witten, R. Neal, and J. G. Cleary. Arithmetic coding for data compression, *Commun. ACM*, 30(6):520–540, June 1987.

[81] D. W. Jones. Applications of splay trees to data compression, *Commun. ACM*, 31(8):996–1007, August 1988.

[82] I. H. Witten and J. G. Cleary. On the privacy offered by adaptive text compression, in *Computers and Security*, 7:397–408, 1988.

[83] X. Liu, P. G. Farrell, and C. A. Boyd. Resisting the Bergen-Hogan attack on adaptive arithmetic coding, in *Proc. 6th IMA Int. Conf. Cryptography Coding*, pp. 199–208, Cirencester, UK, 1997.

[84] A. Barbir. A methodology for performing secure data compression, in *Proc. 29th Southeastern Symp. System Theory*, pp. 266–270, Coakeville, TN, March 9–11, 1997.

[85] H. Bergen and J. Hogan. A chosen plaintext attack on an adaptive arithmetic coding compression algorithm, *Computers and Security*, 12(2):157–167, 1993.

[86] J. G. Cleary, S. A. Irvine, and. I. Rinsma-Melchert. On the insecurity of arithmetic coding, *Computers and Security*, 14(2):167–180, 1995.

[87] J. Lim, C. Boyd, and E. Dawson. Cryptanalysis of adaptive arithmetic coding encryption scheme, in *Proc. Second Australasian Conf. on Information Security and Privacy*, LNCS vol. 1270, pp. 216–227, Sydney, Australia, 1997.

[88] D. Gillman, M. Mohtashemi, and R. Rivest. On breaking a Huffman code, *IEEE Trans. Information Theory*, 42(3):972–976, May 1996.

[89] C.-P. Wu and C.-C. J. Kuo. Efficient multimedia encryption via entropy codec design, in *Proc. SPIE Security & Watermarking of Multimedia Contents III*, San Jose, CA, vol. 4314, January 2001.

[90] C.-P. Wu and C.-C. J. Kuo. Design of integrated multimedia compression and encryption systems, *IEEE Trans. Multimedia*, 7(5):828–839, October 2005.

[91] ISO/IEC. *JPSEC Commission Draft 2.0*, ISO/IEC/JTC 1/SC29/WG 1, N3397, 2004.

[92] M. Pazarci and V. Dipcin. A MPEG2-transparent scrambling technique, *IEEE Trans. Consumer Electronics*, 48(2):345–355, May 2002.

[93] W. Zeng, J. Wen, and M. Severa. Fast self-synchronous content scrambling by spatially shuffling codewords of compressed bitstreams, *IEEE Int. Conf. Image Processing*, Rochester, NY, 3:169–172, September 2002.

[94] R. Grosbois, P. Gerbelot, and T. Ebrahimi. Authentication and access control in the JPEG 2000 compressed domain, in *Proc. SPIE Appl. of Digital Image Processing XXIV*, San Diego, CA, 4472:95–104, December 2001.

[95] Y. Sadourny and V. Conan. A proposal for supporting selective encryption in JPSEC, *IEEE Trans. Consumer Electronics*, 49(4):846–849, November 2003.

[96] R. Norcen and A. Uhl. Selective encryption of the JPEG2000 bitstream, in *Proc. IFIP TC6/TC11 Sixth Joint Working Conf. Communications and Multimedia Security (CMS'03)*, Turin, Italy, A. Lioy and D. Mazzocchi (Eds.), LNCS vol. 2828, pp. 194–204, October 2003.

[97] B. B. Zhu, Y. Yang, and S. Li. JPEG 2000 encryption enabling fine granularity scalability without decryption, *IEEE Int. Symp. Circuits and Systems*, 6:6304–6307, May 2005.

[98] Y. Wu and R. H. Deng. Compliant encryption of JPEG2000 codestreams, in *IEEE. Int. Conf. Image Processing 2004 (ICIP'04)*, Singapore, pp. 3447–3450, October 2004.

[99] B. B. Zhu, Y. Yang, and S. Li. JPEG 2000 syntax-compliant encryption preserving full scalability, *IEEE Int. Conf. Image Processing 2005*, 3:636–639, Genova, Italy, September 11–14, 2005.

[100] T. Kunkelmann and U. Horn. Video encryption based on data partitioning and scalable coding—A comparison, in *Proc. 5th Int. Workshop Interactive Distributed Multimedia Systems and Telecommunication Services (IDMS'98)*, LNCS vol. 1483, pp. 95–106, Oslo, Norway, 1998.

[101] A. S. Tosun and W.-C. Feng. Efficient multi-layer coding and encryption of MPEG video streams, in *IEEE Int. Conf. Multimedia and Expo*, pp. 119–122, New York, NY, 2000.

[102] A. S. Tosun and W.-C. Feng. Lightweight security mechanisms for wireless video transmission, in *IEEE Int. Conf. Information Technology: Coding and Computing*, pp. 157–161, Las Vegas, NV, April 2001.

[103] A. M. Eskicioglu and E. J. Delp. An integrated approach to encrypting scalable video, *IEEE. Int. Conf. Multimedia and Expo*, 1:573–576, Lausanne, Switzerland, August 26–29, 2002.

[104] H. H. Yu. Scalable encryption for multimedia content access control, in *Int. Conf. Acoustics, Speech, and Signal Processing*, pp. 417–420, Hong Kong, 2003.

5

Multimedia Authentication

Dajun He and Qibin Sun

5.1   INTRODUCTION

With the development of digital technologies, alteration of multimedia data, e.g., audio, image, and video, is becoming simpler and undetectable by the human audible/visual system. Although this provides numerous new applications, it rapidly decreases the trustworthiness of multimedia data at the same time. Figure 5.1 is an example of two-party communication, in which the sender (Alice) sends multimedia data to the receiver (Bob) via an unsecured and noisy channel. Since the channel is unsecured, the adversary could easily access it and even modify the transmitted data. Therefore, the receiver may doubt whether the received data are the original data and whether the received data are really sent from the sender. Technologies of authentication aim to protect the trustworthiness of multimedia data.

Multimedia authentication is a relatively new research area, so researchers with different research backgrounds may have a different understanding of the term "authentication." For example, people in the field of multimedia watermarking usually use the term authentication for content integrity protection, while those in biometrics may use it for source identification or verification. In this chapter, both issues will be discussed. In fact, these two issues are very close to those in data authentication, which has been studied in cryptography for decades [1, 2]. Therefore, it would be a good idea to borrow some concepts and solutions from data authentication and extend them to multimedia authentication.

5.1.1   Basic Concepts in Data Authentication

- **Message**. In cryptography, a message refers to data sent by the sender to the receiver.

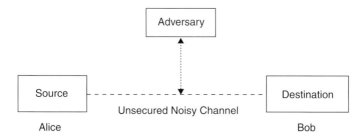

FIGURE 5.1:   General model for two-party communication.

- **Data authentication**. Data authentication is a process determined by the authorized receivers, and perhaps the arbiters, that the particular message was most probably sent by the authorized transmitter and was not subsequently altered or substituted for. In other words, data authentication is a process of integrity verification and repudiation prevention.
- **Integrity**. Integrity means that the received message has not been altered during transmission. Even with a one-bit alteration, the integrity of the message is considered to be broken. In the example shown in Figure 5.1, the message Bob received should be exactly the same as the original one sent by Alice.
- **Non-repudiation**. Non-repudiation means that the message sender (Alice in Figure 5.1) should not be able to falsely deny later that she/he sent the message.
- **Security**. The security issue comes from how to prevent an adversary from substituting a false message for a legitimate one. Two types of security solutions exist: *unconditionally secure* and *computationally secure*. A solution is unconditionally secure if there is always not enough information for the adversary to break the solution and substitute it with a false one; a solution is considered computationally secure if it cannot be broken with available resources. Cryptography, e.g., data authentication, is more concerned with the latter. Here, resources are open to interpretation, e.g., computation complexity and memory requirement.

Public key DSS (Digital Signature Scheme), together with a one-way hash function, is the typical solution for data authentication. To explain DSS, encryption should be introduced first.

- **Encryption/decryption**. As shown in Figure 5.2, encryption is a process that disguises a message, or plaintext, in such a way as to hide its substance (the encrypted message is called ciphertext); decryption is a process that turns the ciphertext back into the original plaintext. In communications through unsecured channels, an encryption scheme is usually used to achieve

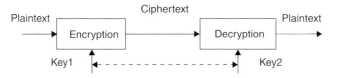

FIGURE 5.2: Encryption and decryption.

confidentiality. Therefore, if Alice wants to send the message to Bob in a secret way, Alice could encrypt the message before sending it.

- **Symmetric key/public key**: In Figure 5.2, if it is computationally "easy" to determine Key2 from Key1 and to determine Key1 from Key2, the encryption scheme is a symmetric key encryption scheme. In a public key encryption scheme, the known key is called a public key, and the unknown key is called a private key; it is computationally "infeasible" to get the private key from the public key. Symmetric key and public key encryption schemes have a number of complementary advantages. Usually, the public key scheme is efficient in signatures (especially non-repudiation) and key management, and the symmetric key scheme is efficient in encryption and data integrity applications.
- **One-way hash function**. A one-way hash function is a hash function that works in one direction. It has the properties of both a one-way function and a hash function. A good one-way hash function should fulfill the following requirements:

  - Given a variable-length input string (called a *message*), the output (called a *hash digest*) is a fixed-length string.
  - Given message m and a hash function H, it should be easy and fast to compute the hash digest $h = H(m)$.
  - Given hash digest h, it should be hard to compute message m such that $h = H(m)$.
  - Given message m, it should be hard to find another message m' such that $H(m') = H(m)$ (i.e., collision free).

These properties ensure the security of a one-way hash function against various attacks on both message and hash digest. The security is proportional to the length of the hash digest. For example, SHA-1 is a typical one-way hash function with a 160-bit output; an attacker would have to try an average of 2^{80} random messages to obtain two messages with an identical hash digest (*birthday attack*). Another property of a one-way hash function is that the hash digest is not dependent on the input message in any discernible way; even a one-bit change in the message will result in a totally different hash digest.

- **Message Authentication Code (MAC)**. MAC, also known as DAC (Data Authentication Code), is a one-way hash function with an additional secret key. The theory of MAC is exactly the same as that of a hash function, except only someone with the key can verify the hash digest.
- **Digital Signature Schemes (DSS)**. A digital signature is a bit string which associates the message with some originating entity. A DSS system, shown in Figure 5.3, consists of signature generation and signature verification. To protect the integrity of the data, a digital signature is dependent on the data to be signed. To meet the non-repudiation requirement, all digital signature algorithms are public key algorithms. The sender's private key is employed to generate the signature, and the sender's public key is used by recipients to verify the integrity of data and the sender's identity. If a dispute arises as to whether a party signed a document (caused by either a lying signer trying to repudiate a signature he did create or a fraudulent claimant), an unbiased third party can resolve the matter equitably, without accessing the signer's secret information.

Typical public key DSS include RSA (named for its creators-Rivest, Shamir and Adleman) and DSA (Digital Signature Algorithm, used as part of the Digital Signature Standard) [1, 2]. In practical implementation, since public key algorithms are too inefficient to sign large size data, a digital signature is usually generated by signing the hash digest of the original data instead of the original data. The original data associated with its digital signature are then sent to the intended recipients. At the receiving site, the recipient can verify whether (i) the received data were altered and (ii) the data were really sent from the sender by using the sender's public key to authenticate the validity of the attached signature. The authentication result is

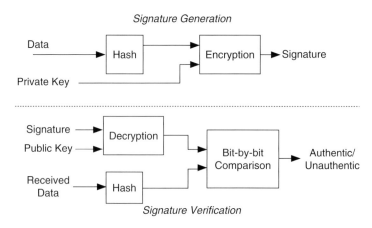

FIGURE 5.3:   Block diagram of a DSS.

based on a bit-by-bit comparison between two hash digests (one is decrypted from the signature and the other is obtained by hashing the received data) by the criterion that the received data is deemed to be unauthentic even if a one-bit difference exists.

5.1.2 Multimedia Authentication

In data authentication, a one-bit difference between the original data and the received data results in authenticity failure. In most multimedia applications, however, the received data are not an exact copy of the original data, though the meaning of the data is preserved. For example, lossy compression is often employed in video applications, e.g., MPEG-1/2/4 and H.264, to save the transmission bandwidth or storage capacity. The decompressed video is definitely different from the original video in terms of data representation; however, the meaning of the multimedia data remains unchanged so that the integrity of the multimedia content remains unbroken. Therefore, an authentication scheme which is different from the data authentication should be explored. We call this type of authentication scheme **content authentication**. In this chapter, the term *content* or *multimedia content* represents the meaning of the multimedia data, while *data* or *multimedia data* refer to its exact representation (e.g., binary bitstream). For convenience, *data* and *multimedia data*, *content* and *multimedia content* are used interchangeably in this chapter.

In content authentication, multimedia content is considered authentic as long as the meaning of the multimedia data remains unchanged, regardless of any process or transformation the multimedia data has undergone. Contrary to the content authentication, an authentication scheme which does not allow any changes in the multimedia data is defined as **complete authentication** [3]. Obviously, data authentication belongs to complete authentication.

Multimedia authentication includes both complete authentication and content authentication. In practice, the selection of complete authentication or content authentication is application-dependent. For example, complete authentication is often employed in medical or financial applications to prevent each bit of the data from being altered; content authentication is often employed in civil or domestic applications, in which only the meaning of multimedia data is concerned. The requirements for multimedia authentication are similar to those in data authentication, including integrity protection, source identification (non-repudiation), and security. However, definitions of integrity in complete authentication and content authentication are different.

In complete authentication, "integrity" refers to the whole multimedia data; even data with a one-bit alteration will be claimed as unauthentic. Therefore, no robustness is required. The main concern is the security of the authentication scheme. Such criterion motivates researchers to develop signature-based complete authentication schemes whose security level is very high and can be proven mathematically.

In content authentication, integrity refers to the content of the multimedia data; the multimedia content is considered authentic as long as the meaning of the multimedia data remains unchanged. Therefore, besides the security requirement, a certain level of robustness to distortions is required. The distortions could be classified into two classes, namely **incidental distortion** and **intentional distortion**. Incidental distortion refers to the distortions introduced from real applications which do not change the content of the multimedia data, such as a noisy transmission channel, lossy compression, or video transcoding. Intentional distortion refers to the distortions introduced by the content modifications or attacks from malicious attackers. Content authentication should tolerate all incidental distortions while detecting any intentional distortions. In other words, it should be robust to incidental distortion while being sensitive to intentional distortion.

The requirement of a certain level of robustness to distortions is the main difference between complete authentication and content authentication. This makes authenticating multimedia content much more challenging and complex [4].

In multimedia applications, defining acceptable manipulations is usually application-dependent, and different definitions of acceptable manipulations result in different incidental distortions. For example, rotating an object is not allowable in frame-based image applications, but is allowable in object-based image applications. Therefore, the distortion introduced by the object rotation is an incidental distortion in an object-based image authentication system, but an intentional distortion in a frame-based image authentication system.

Even in a specific application, it is still very hard to formalize a clear boundary between incidental distortions and intentional distortions. In other words, it is hard to define a threshold to determine whether the content of the multimedia data is authentic or unauthentic. For example, if m' represents a distorted but still authentic version of the original image m, we can always get a more distorted but still authentic version (m'') by just modifying one pixel value of m'. Thus, as shown in Figure 5.4, a fuzzy region, in which the authentication result is "not known," must exist. It means that certain false acceptance rates and false rejection rates are acceptable in the case of content authentication.

Due to its great success in data authentication, DSS has been directly applied in many multimedia authentication schemes (we denote these types of solutions as *digital signature-based multimedia authentication* solutions). However, DSS has no robustness to any distortions, and it should only be used in complete authentication. To meet the requirement of robustness in content authentication while keeping the good properties of DSS (integrity protection, source identification, and security), a content-based signature, or *media signature* [5], is proposed. A media signature is robust to content preserving manipulations and sensitive to content modification.

A media signature scheme (MSS), as shown in Figure 5.5, is an extension of DSS. The only difference between MSS and DSS is the input to the encryption block.

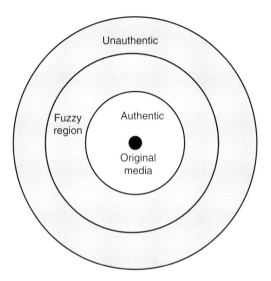

FIGURE 5.4: A fuzzy region exists in content authentication.

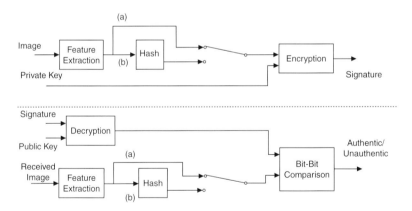

FIGURE 5.5: Block diagram of an MSS.

In MSS, the input is a feature of the multimedia data or a hash digest of the feature. In DSS, the input is the hash digest of the multimedia data. Since the mechanism of DSS is preserved in MSS, MSS also has the properties of integrity protection, source identification, and security. In MSS, the requirements of robustness to incidental distortions and sensitivity to intentional distortions are fulfilled by finding a set of features which are capable of representing the multimedia content while being robust to acceptable manipulations. Features employed in multimedia authentication are application-dependent, e.g., zero-crossing rate (ZCR) and/or pitch information in audio authentication, relationships between pixels or transformation coefficients in image and video authentication, and object descriptors in object-based authentication.

In practical applications, a media signature can be stored in the header of the compressed bitstream, e.g., "user data" in a JPEG/MPEG bitstream, or in a separate file attached to the original multimedia data, for later authentication. The disadvantages of these types of *media signature-based multimedia authentication* solutions are the size of multimedia data is inevitably increased and the signature may be lost in malicious attacks or real applications such as multi-cycle compression. To overcome these disadvantages, some researchers have proposed sending the media signature via watermarking technique, as shown in Figure 5.6. The media signature is further encoded to generate a content-based watermark, and this watermark is finally embedded into the original multimedia data to obtain a watermarked multimedia data. During authenticity verification, features of the received data are first extracted according to the same procedure as that in the signature generation. Then the embedded watermark is extracted from the received data before the media signature is obtained by decoding this watermark. The original feature can be further extracted by decrypting the media signature. Finally, features of the original and the received multimedia data are compared to determine the authenticity. Watermarking techniques are studied in Chapter 7. Here, we would like to emphasize that the requirements for watermarking algorithms in media signature-based multimedia authentication are different from the requirements for watermarking algorithms in other applications such as copyright protection. Watermarking algorithms for multimedia authentication should have a larger payload, while their robustness is required up to a certain level; that is, they should be robust to content-preserving manipulations. In addition,

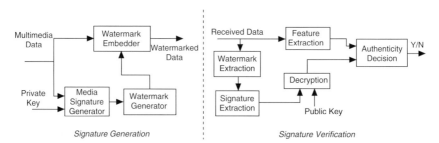

FIGURE 5.6:   MSS-based multimedia authentication where the signature is carried via watermarking technique.

a watermarking process should also be considered as a content-preserving manip-ulation in multimedia authentication; that is, the features of the original and the watermarked multimedia data should be the same.

Actually, some researchers authenticate multimedia data by directly employ-ing watermarking techniques. We denote these solutions as *watermarking-based multimedia authentication* solutions. Since watermarking techniques are stud-ied in Chapter 7, we will only briefly introduce watermarking-based multimedia authentication in the next subsection. The focus of this chapter will be media signature-based multimedia authentication.

5.1.3 Watermarking-Based Multimedia Authentication

Watermarking-based multimedia authentication solutions modify the original multimedia data to insert a watermark for later authentication. The authentic-ity verification is carried out by comparing the original watermark with the watermark extracted from the multimedia data to be authenticated. A water-mark could be a binary string, a logo, or the features of the multimedia content, and watermarking could be performed in either pixel domain or the transform domain, e.g., Discrete Cosine Transform (DCT), Discrete Wavelet Transform (DWT), or Discrete Founer Transform (DFT).

In watermarking-based multimedia authentication solutions, no additional data are required during storage or transmission. Therefore, this disadvantage of media signature-based authentication solutions has been overcome. How-ever, a new problem arises: this type of solution has no capability of source identification because a symmetric key is often employed in both watermark embedding and extraction [5]. According to the distortions caused by watermark-ing, watermarking-based authentication solutions can be classified into lossless authentication and lossy authentication. Lossy authentication can be further clas-sified into fragile authentication and semi-fragile authentication according to their robustness to acceptable manipulations.

Lossless Watermarking-Based Authentication

Lossless authentication is initially proposed for applications in which no distor-tion is allowed, e.g., military and medical applications. To achieve this objective, a hash digest or digital signature, which could detect even a one-bit change in the multimedia data, is employed as the authentication information. This authentica-tion information is inserted into the original multimedia data using a lossless data hiding technique so that the distortion caused by watermarking can be recovered at the receiving site. In lossless image authentication, usually one LSB (Least Significant Bit) [6, 7] or a specific number of LSBs [8] of the transform coef-ficients are losslessly compressed to make some space for the insertion of the authentication information. The authentication information is extracted from the image before the LSB's bitplane is decompressed.

Fridrich, Goljan, and Du further extended their image authentication solutions [6, 7] for authenticating MPEG-2 video by including a time stamp in the authentication information. To detect temporal and content attacks, two solutions, namely authentication by frame and authentication by groups of frames, are proposed in Du and Fridrich [9]. In the first solution, a watermark consisting of the frame index and hash digest of the non-zero DCT coefficients is embedded into the chrominance blocks of both intra- and non-intra-macroblocks in each frame; thus, it can detect both temporal attack and individual frame tampering. However, the distortion introduced by watermarking could become visible if the distance between two I-frames is too large. The second solution solves this problem by embedding a watermark consisting of the hash digest of all non-zero DCT coefficients from a group of frames (user defined) and the group index into the chrominance blocks of the B-frame.

The above solutions are complete authentication methods, so the watermark has no robustness. Zou et al. proposed another type of lossless image authentication in which the watermark has some robustness to content-preserving manipulations, e.g., JPEG compression[10]. In their proposed scheme, authentication information is generated from the quantized DCT coefficients and inserted into the image using their proposed lossless data hiding algorithm, namely the "Circular Histogram" algorithm.

Fragile Watermarking-Based Authentication

Like lossless authentication, fragile authentication also authenticates multimedia in a fragile way (any modification of the multimedia data is not allowed). In fragile authentication, however, the original image does not need to be recovered after the image is determined as authentic. Therefore, the distortion caused by watermarking is allowed if this distortion is imperceptible. By allowing watermarking distortion, more authentication information can be inserted in fragile authentication compared to lossless authentication. Thus, fragile authentication schemes can not only detect modifications on multimedia data, but also can locate such modifications.

Yeung and Mintzer [11] have proposed a scheme to authenticate individual pixels. In this scheme, a binary map of a watermark image is embedded into the source image to create a watermarked image. Every pixel in the source image is processed in turn as follows: for a selected pixel, apply a watermark extraction function to get an extracted value; if the extracted value is not equal to the watermark value, the selected pixel is modified until the extracted value is equal to the designed watermark value; if they are equal, the amount of modification is calculated and then propagated to the pixels not yet processed using a modified error diffusion procedure. This process is repeated until every pixel in the source image has been processed. Any alteration on the watermarked image induces an artifact on the extracted watermark, which can be visually and automatically identified.

Wong and Memon [12] proposed a public key-based fragile authentication scheme which can detect any modifications on an image and indicate the specific locations that have been modified. In their scheme, a watermark is embedded into the LSB of each pixel of the image. This watermark contains the size of the image, an approximation of the image, and block information. If the correct key is specified in the watermark extraction, then an output image is returned showing a proper watermark. Any modifications would be reflected in a corresponding error in the watermark. If the key is incorrect, or if the watermarked image is cropped, an image that resembles random noise will be returned. Since this scheme requires a user key during both the watermark embedding and the extraction, it is not possible for an unauthorized user to insert a new watermark or alter the existing one.

Besides locating modifications on image, recovering the modified image is also important in image authentication. Fridrich and Goljan proposed a fragile image authentication scheme with self-correcting capabilities [13]. In this scheme, for each 8×8 DCT block, the first 11 DCT coefficients are first quantized and then binary encoded into a 64-bit string. This binary string is then encrypted and finally inserted into the LSB of each DCT coefficient. The authors claim that the quality of a reconstructed image from this binary string is roughly half as good as that of a JPEG compressed image.

Semi-fragile Watermarking-Based Authentication

Although fragile authentication can detect or even locate modifications of multimedia data, it cannot decide whether these modifications are acceptable manipulations or malicious attacks. Semi-fragile authentication is designed to be robust to incidental distortions while being sensitive to intentional distortions.

Since the transform domain has the property of frequency localization, it is easier to design a watermarking scheme that is robust to normal manipulations in the transform domain. Most semi-fragile authentication solutions achieve such robustness by inserting watermarks into low- or middle-frequency DCT coefficients. The only differences among them are how they either generate or embed a watermark. For example, Eggers and Girod [14] took a binary sequence as a watermark and then embedded the watermark into the second through eighth DCT coefficients, in zigzag order, of an 8×8 DCT block in an image using a dither quantization rule. Lin and Chang [15] inserted a watermark using the invariant property in JPEG compression: if a DCT coefficient is modified to be an integral multiple of a quantization step that is larger than the steps used in later JPEG compressions, then this coefficient can be exactly reconstructed after these compressions. Compared with the DCT domain, the DWT domain has the property of space localization besides frequency localization. Thus, watermarking solutions performed in the DWT domain could be more robust to geometric attacks [16]. In [16], Han, Chang, and Park proposed a semi-fragile watermarking-based image authentication in the DWT domain.

As a summarization of this section, we illustrate the relationship between requirements of multimedia authentication (e.g., integrity protection, source identification, and robustness) and the main technologies employed in the multimedia authentication (e.g., digital signature, media signature, and watermarking) in Figure 5.7. Digital signature-based solutions perform well in integrity protection and source identification, but their robustness is fragile. Watermarking-based solutions can achieve integrity protection with high robustness; however, they cannot identify the source of the multimedia data. Media signature-based solutions strike a balance among these three requirements.

According to the types of multimedia, multimedia authentication could be classified into data authentication, image authentication, video authentication, and audio authentication. Speech authentication is included in audio authentication, though there are some differences between them. Since data authentication has been thoroughly studied, we will focus on image, video, and audio authentication in the following sections.

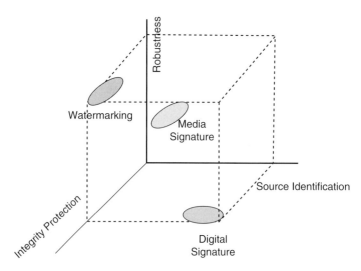

FIGURE 5.7: Relationship between the requirements of the multimedia authentication and its main techniques.

5.2 IMAGE AUTHENTICATION

As shown in Figure 5.5, image authentication solutions can be classified into two categories according to the input of the encryption module: direct feature-based image authentication (Figure 5.5(a)) and hash digest-based image authentication (Figure 5.5(b)).

5.2.1 Direct Feature

In this type of image authentication solutions, a media signature is generated by signing features of the original image using the sender's private key. During verification, an original feature is obtained by decrypting the received signature using a public key and then compared with the feature extracted from the received image to determine the authenticity. The received image can be claimed as authentic if the public key is allowable and the original and the extracted features match.

It is not easy to decide whether the original and extracted features match or not, because the two features may have some difference even if the received image has only undergone content-preserving manipulations. Usually, a threshold (Th) is employed. Let f_o and f_r represent the features of the original and the received images, respectively. The authenticity can be decided by

$$\begin{cases} |f_o - f_r| \leq Th & \text{Authentic} \\ |f_o - f_r| > Th & \text{Unauthentic} \end{cases} \tag{5.1}$$

In Queluz [17], edges are chosen as the feature of an image. The authenticity is determined by comparing the maximum connected region in an error image with a pre-defined threshold. The error image is the difference between the edges of the original and received images. In practice, this threshold is hard to determine even if a set of acceptable manipulations is defined. Ye, Sun, and Chang [18] proposed an authentication scheme for wireless channel communication in which no threshold is required; authenticity is determined by comparing two variables, namely degree of authenticity (D_Y) and degree of unauthenticity (D_N). The definitions of D_Y and D_N are based on two observed phenomena: (i) acceptable manipulations cause global distortion, while tampering operations cause local distortion; and (ii) the maximum size of the connected region in the error image caused by acceptable manipulations is small, while the one caused by tampering operations is large.

The size of a direct feature-based signature is proportional to the size of the feature, so the signature can be excessively large in some cases. This will significantly increase the computation in signature generation, and the storage or transmission of a large size signature will also be a problem.

5.2.2   Hash Digest

Two types of hash functions, content-hash and crypto-hash, are exploited in image authentication.

Content-Hash Digest

To reduce the signature size, a content-hash digest is proposed to avoid directly using the extracted features for generating the media signature. Content-hash digest, therefore, partially owns some nice characteristics of both crypto-hash-based signature and image feature-based signature. Similar to crypto-hash digest, the length of a content-hash digest is fixed independent of the image size. Similar to image feature, content-hash digests from visually similar images are similar, while content-hash digests from visually different images are different.

The concept of a content-hash was first proposed by Fridrich and Goljan [19, 20]. They call it a visual–hash or robust–hash. In their schemes, N random smooth patterns with uniform distribution in the interval [0, 1] are generated using a secret key. The image is divided into equal-size blocks, and each block is projected into these patterns to extract an N bit data string, which is robust to different types of image manipulations. Next, data strings for all blocks are concatenated into a content-hash digest. The security of this solution lies in the confidentiality of the random smooth pattern; an attacker cannot modify the projection without the knowledge of the secret key, which is similar to the crypto-hash scheme.

Arce, Xie, and Gravemen proposed another type of content-hash, Approximate Message Authentication Code (AMAC), for measuring the similarity between two different images in a short checksum [21]. AMAC is generated through a series of processes, including pseudo-random permutations, masking, and majority voting. It has a limitation: it cannot distinguish modifications caused by intentional attack from normal image manipulation such as compression. To overcome this limitation, they further extended AMAC to Approximate Image MAC (IMAC). The most significant bits of an image, which are the highest order bits of the lowest frequency coefficient in each 8 × 8 block, are extracted, followed by a parallel AMAC computation to generate the IMAC of the image [22]. The designed length of IMAC in their algorithm is 128 bits, and they claim that this type of IMAC is robust to moderate compression while being able to detect and locate intentional attacks.

To generate a small size media signature, the size of the content-hash digest should also be small. This results in a limitation of content-hash-based authentication solutions. It is very hard to differentiate incidental distortions from intentional distortions, especially when the intentional distortions are the results of attacks to only part of the image. Therefore, it is very difficult to set a proper threshold for making the authentication decision.

Crypto-Hash Digest

Most researchers prefer to employ crypto-hash in designing a media signature due to its security and wide adoption in data authentication. In this type of solution, the input of the one-way hash function (Figure 5.5) is the features of an image instead of the image data. Unlike the content-hash, in which the similarity between two hash digests is proportional to the similarity between two corresponding images, in crypto-hash a one-bit difference in the input features will result in a totally different output. Therefore, the threshold employed in content-hash-based image authentication is no longer required in crypto-hash-based image authentication. Even if only a one-bit difference between two hash digests exists, the received image will be considered as a tampered one.

However, the property of crypto-hash, that a one-bit difference in the input features will result in a totally different output, will decrease the robustness of the authentication solutions because acceptable image manipulations may cause changes to the features. Since these changes may be small compared to the changes caused by content-altering attacks, Sun et al. [23] proposed employing an Error Correcting Coding (ECC) scheme to correct these changes. A general model of this type of solution is shown in Figure 5.8.

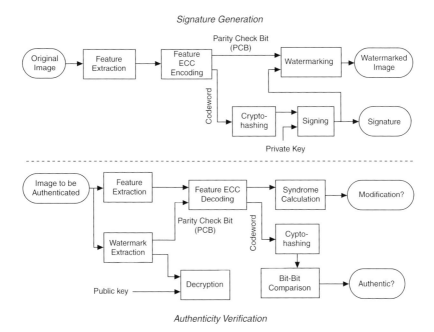

FIGURE 5.8: A semi-fragile crypto-hash-based image authentication solution.

E	E	E
E	T	E
E	E	E

FIGURE 5.9: Pattern for block labeling.

First, features of the original image are encoded using a systematic ECC scheme [24] to get an ECC codeword and Parity Check Bits (PCB). We define this EEE coding scheme as a *Feature ECC coding scheme*. A systematic ECC scheme means that after ECC encoding, a codeword can be separated into two parts: one is its original message, and the other is its PCB data. Second, the crypto-hash digest of the ECC codeword is signed using the sender's private key to generate a media signature. Third, this media signature is concatenated with the PCB data to generate authentication information, which is later embedded back into the original image to get a watermarked image. During authenticity verification, the PCB data are concatenated with the feature extracted from the received image to create a feature ECC codeword; the same Feature EEE coding scheme is employed to decode this ECC codeword. If the codeword cannot be decoded, the received image is claimed as unauthentic. Otherwise, the decoded codeword is crypto-hashed to create a hash digest; this hash digest, together with the hash digest obtained by decrypting the media signature, is employed to determine the authenticity of the received image.

Sun et al. further extended the above scheme to design a packet loss resilient image authentication system [25], in which an image is partitioned into a series of 8×8 blocks. All blocks are labeled as either **T**-block or **E**-block in a pre-defined pattern such as the one shown in Figure 5.9. An image signature is generated from the features extracted from the **T**-block and embedded back into **E**-blocks for later authentication. During authenticity verification, if the **T**-block is lost during transmission, error-concealment algorithms could be employed to reconstruct a new block T' based on the surrounding **E**-blocks; features from T' are employed to replace features of the **T**-block. Therefore, in signature generation, the **T**-block should be recursively modified until features extracted from **T** and T' are the same.

5.3 VIDEO AUTHENTICATION

Compared with image authentication, video authentication has the following special requirements:

- **Blindness**. The original video is not available during authenticity verification.

- **Temporal attack detection**. Temporal attacks are attacks in the time axis, e.g., adding, cutting, or reordering video frames in a video sequence.
- **Low computational overhead**. Authentication solutions should not be very complex since real-time authentication is often required.
- **Robustness to transcoding**. Video transcoding, e.g., requantization, frame resizing, and frame dropping, is often employed in video streaming to create a new video bitstream to adapt to various channels and terminals. In requantization, a larger quantization step is employed to requantize the DCT coefficients to reduce the bit-rate. Frame resizing means reducing the frame resolution to adapt to end-users' monitors. In frame dropping, for instance, an original video with 25 frames per second can be transcoded to a new video with 5 frames per second by dropping 20 frames.
- **Robustness to object-based video manipulations**. In object-based video applications, the corresponding authentication solutions should be robust to object-based manipulations, e.g., object-based coding and editing.

Based on applications, solutions for video authentication can be classified into frame-based and object-based solutions. The former is for MPEG-1/2-related applications, while the latter is for MPEG-4-related applications.

5.3.1   Frame-Based Video Authentication

Video can be considered as a collection of video frames, so the integrity of a video includes the integrity of each video frame and the integrity of the sequence of video frames. To authenticate each video frame, many image authentication solutions can be employed with little or even no modification. To detect the temporal attacks in the sequence of video frames, time information, such as time stamp, picture index, or GOP (Group of Picture) index in an MPEG video, could be employed.

Lin and Chang proposed two types of signatures for authenticating videos that have undergone two categories of processes [3]. In the processes in the first category, which include three transcoding approaches and one editing process, Motion Vectors (MVs) picture type, and GOP structure of a video that has undergone these processes are kept unchanged. In the second category processes, e.g., format transmission, the MVs, picture type, and GOP structure of a video may all be changed. In both types of signatures, relations between DCT coefficients in the same position of different DCT blocks are employed to detect content alteration. In the signature for authenticating videos that have undergone the first category processes, the hash digest of the GOP header, picture header, MVs, and other time and structure information is employed to detect temporal perturbation. In the second type of signature, only the picture time code is employed to detect temporal attacks, since other time information will be changed.

The above two types of signatures are generated based on each GOP. Since signature signing is much more time-consuming than signature verification, the

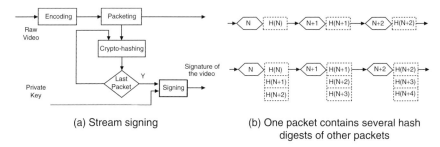

(a) Stream signing   (b) One packet contains several hash digests of other packets

FIGURE 5.10:   Stream authentication solution robust to packet loss.

computation cost of Lin and Chang's scheme [3] is high. To reduce the computation cost, a typical solution considers video as a stream of video packets and only signs the last packet (Figure 5.10(a)): the hash digest of each packet is XORed with the hash digest of its previous packet, and only the hash digest of the last packet is signed by a private key to generate a digital signature for this video. During verification, similar procedures are employed to obtain the hash digest of the received video. The whole video cannot be verified until the recipient receives the signature and the last group of video packets. Nevertheless, it is a fragile scheme; any packet loss during transmission, which is very common if the video is streamed over unreliable channels or protocols such as wireless or User Datagram Protocol (UDP), may lead to failure in authenticity verification. In order to tolerate packet loss, Park, Chong, and Siegel proposed an interesting authentication work based on the concept of ECC [26]. Their basic idea is illustrated in Figure 5.10(b). Naturally, a hash digest has to be appended to its corresponding packet for stream authentication, as shown in the upper part of Figure 5.10(b). The authentication can be executed after receiving the last packet. Such a scheme cannot deal with packet loss during the transmission because the signature was generated based on all hash digests from all packets. To overcome this problem, a straightforward solution is to append the hash digests of the current packet and several other packets to the current packet. If one packet is lost during transmission, its hash digest can still be acquired from its neighboring packets for signature generation. The basic idea behind this scheme is to reduce transmission errors by adding some redundancies.

   In Park, Chong, and Siegel's scheme [26], the importance of different packets is equal. However, in a video bitstream, the packets containing DC components are more important than those only containing AC components. Park, Chong, and Siegel's scheme is also not robust to video transcoding approaches such as frame resizing, frame dropping, and requantization. To overcome these disadvantages, Sun, He, and Tian [27] proposed a transcoding resilient video authentication system by extending Park, Chong, and Siegel's scheme. In Park, Chong, and

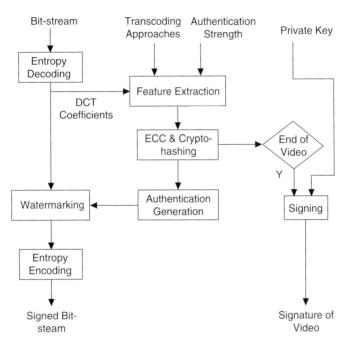

FIGURE 5.11: Diagram of the signing part of the transcoding resilient video authentication system.

Seigel's scheme, the packet is replaced by a video frame, and the hash digest of packet data is replaced by the hash digest of features of a video frame.

The brief block diagram of the signing part of Sun, He, and Tian's solution is shown in Figure 5.11. To be compatible with most video transcoding schemes and independent of video coding and transcoding approaches, the proposed solution is performed in the DCT domain by partially decoding the MPEG bitstream. The three inputs of the signing part are the video sender's private key, the authentication strength, and possible transcoding approaches. Here, the authentication strength means protecting the video content to a certain degree (i.e., the video will not be deemed as authentic if it is transcoded beyond this degree). First, frame-based invariant features are extracted from the DCT coefficients based on the given transcoding approaches and the authentication strength. Second, features are encoded using the feature ECC scheme to get a feature ECC codeword; this is to ensure that the same features can be obtained during verification in spite of the incidental distortion. Third, the feature ECC codeword is crypto-hashed to get a hash digest for every frame. Authentication information, consisting of the PCB data and the hash digests of the current video frame and other consecutive video frames, is sent to the recipient for later authentication through watermarking. In addition, the hash digest is recursively operated frame by frame until the end of the video; a signature of this video is generated by signing the final hash value using the sender's private key. This signature is also sent to the recipient through watermarking.

The robustness of the solution in Sun, He, and Tian [27] depends on how to select invariant features, how to obtain the hash digests of the dropped frames, and how to design a robust watermarking algorithm. A watermarking algorithm resilient to normal transcoding approaches has been proposed in Sun, He, and Tian [27].

To ensure a system's robustness to requantization, several quantized DCT coefficients are chosen as the feature of the video frame. The quantization step is set as the maximum quantization step that may be used in future transcoding. This is based on the invariant property discovered by Lin and Chang [15]: if a DCT coefficient is modified to be an integral multiple of a quantization step that is larger than the steps used in later JPEG compressions, then this coefficient can be exactly reconstructed after these compressions. In MPEG compression, this invariance is almost certainly preserved, except "dead-zone" quantization area in the Inter-Macroblock may cause some variance, which is however, small and could be easily eliminated [27]. To ensure a system's robustness to frame resizing (i.e., the conversion of video from the Common Intermediate Format (CIF) to the Quarter Common Intermediate Format (QCIF)), features are extracted from a QCIF video frame instead of the original CIF video frame. The issue of robustness to frame dropping is solved by embedding into the current frame (e.g., Frame N) not only its ECC check information and hash digest, but also the hash digests of other frames (e.g., Frame $N-1$, $N-2$, ? $N-m$). Therefore, even if some frames between $N-1$ and $N-m$ are dropped during transcoding, their corresponding hash digests can still be obtained from the current frame.

5.3.2   Object-Based Video Authentication

Object-based video authentication is designed for MPEG-4-related applications. In MPEG-4, a video frame is viewed as a composition of meaningful video objects with shape, motion, and texture rather than a collection of pixels with luminance and chrominance in MPEG-1/2, and video coding or editing is carried out on the Video Object Planes (VOPs).

An object-based authentication system should also be a semi-fragile authentication system. That is, it should be robust to incidental distortions while being sensitive to intentional distortions. Compared with frame-based video authentication, however, the incidental and intentional distortions in object-based video authentication are different since the acceptable video processes and intentional attacks are different. Here, some common acceptable video processes and intentional attacks are listed.

Some common acceptable video processes are

- **RST(Rotation, scaling, and translation)**. In object-based applications, the interesting video object may be rotated, scaled, and/or translated to meet the special requirements of end-users. The rotation angle could be to any degree, the translation could be in any style, and the scaling factor could be in a reasonable range.
- **Segmentation error**. Segmentation error refers to the difference between shapes of the original object at the sending site and the resegmented object at the receiving site.
- **MPEG-4 coding**. In MPEG-4 coding, processes that affect the robustness of a video authentication system can be classified into two categories. One category consists of traditional coding processes including quantization, motion estimation, and motion compensation, which are similar to those in MPEG-1/2 coding. The other category is composed of the processes that are unique for MPEG-4 coding, such as VOP formation and padding.

Common intentional attacks include traditional and object-based attacks. As shown in Figure 5.12, object-based attacks could be content modification on an object or background, object replacement, or background replacement. Note that the shape stays unchanged in the object replacement.

Not many object-based video authentication solutions have been proposed. Yin and Yu claimed that their solution for MPEG-1/2 video could be extended to MPEG-4 video [28] by expanding the locality precision to video object (VO) level, video object layer (VOL) level, video object plane (VOP) level, and group of VOP (GOV) level and/or block level and by containing shape information in the watermark besides the texture and motion information. A system-level authentication solution is proposed in He, Sun, and Tian [29]. The block diagram of this solution is shown in Figure 5.13. The procedure for signing is on the left side, while the procedure for verification is on the right side.

In the signing procedure, the input could be in either raw video format (segmentation is needed in this case) or object/background MPEG-4 compliant format, while the outputs are signed MPEG-4 bitstreams. First, robust features of the object and its associated background are extracted. Second, authentication information

(a) Original video   (b) Object replacement   (c) Background replacement   (d) Object modification

FIGURE 5.12:   Common intentional attacks.

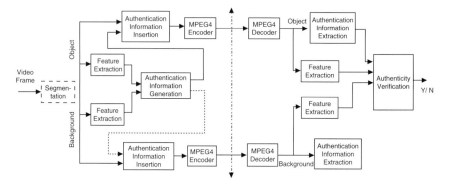

FIGURE 5.13:   Block diagram of the object-based video authentication.

is generated. The procedure for generating authentication information is similar to that in a frame-based video authentication system, in which an ECC scheme is employed to tackle feature distortions caused by acceptable video processes. The only difference is that besides the object features, features of the background are also employed to create the hash digest of the object. By including the features of the background into the authentication information, a secure link between the object and its associated background has been created. Therefore, the object is not allowed to be combined with other backgrounds. In other words, malicious attacks such as object or background replacement can be easily detected. Third, authentication information is sent using watermarking techniques. Finally, the signed object and background are compressed into MPEG-4 bitstreams. Note that a digital signature for the video could be generated by signing the hash digest using the sender's private key.

To authenticate the received video, the MPEG-4 bitstreams have to be decompressed to retrieve the object and background. Following the same procedures as in the signing part, features of the object and the background can be obtained. Meanwhile, the authentication information is extracted from the watermark. The authenticity decision comprises two steps, similar to those introduced in the semifragile crypto-hash-based image authentication solution (Figure 5.8).

The system's robustness to incidental distortions depends on how to select robust features and how to design a robust watermarking algorithm. For robust object-based watermarking schemes, refer to Chapter 7 or Reference [29]. To select robust features, the definition of Angular Radial Transformation (ART), a visual shape descriptor in MPEG-7 [30, 31], is first extended from an object mask to object content, and then the ART coefficients are selected as the features of the object and the background. ART has the following specific properties: (1) it gives a compact and efficient way to describe the object, and (2) the ART coefficients are robust to segmentation error and invariant to object rotation and shape distortions [31].

5.4 AUDIO AUTHENTICATION

Audio signals, especially speech signals, are often employed as evidence in today's courts. From the viewpoint of practical application, audio authentication plays the most important role among all types of multimedia authentication. However, solutions for audio authentication are not as abundant as those for image/video authentication. Actually, some digital audio authentication solutions are derived from solutions for image authentication.

Like image/video authentication, a natural solution for audio authentication is comparing the features of the original audio signal and the signal to be authenticated to determine the authenticity. Wu and Kuo called this type of approach a *content feature extraction approach* [32]. They proposed a speech authentication solution in which semantic features, e.g., pitch information and the changing shape of the vocal tract and energy envelope, are employed to authenticate speech signals. Compared with syntactic features such as energy function and ZCR, semantic features have a smaller size. For example, at a sampling rate of 8000 samples per second, and the syntactic feature data rate is approximately 400 bytes per second. The storage and transmission of such a large feature are impossible in audio authentication. The computation cost of extracting semantic features is high; however, it could be reduced by integrating feature extraction with Code Excited Linear Prediction (CELP) coding in Wu and Kuo's scheme.

Transcoding or D/A-A/D conversion of the speech signal may cause mis-synchronization. Therefore, synchronization between the original and received speech signals must be processed before extracting features from the received signal for authenticity verification. In Wu and Kuo's scheme, the positions of salient points, where the energy of the speech signal climbs rapidly to a peak, are employed to solve the resynchronization issue. The locations of the first 15 salient points in the original speech are encrypted and transmitted together with the authentication information. At the receiving site, salient point locations are detected from the received speech signal and compared with the decrypted data to identify the amount of time-shifting during transmission.

In Wu and Kuo [32], features and positions of salient points are transmitted to the receiving site along with speech data. As a result, the payload of data transmission in this scheme is increased. To overcome this shortcoming, Steinebach and Dittmann proposed a watermarking-based digital audio authentication system, in which authentication information is inserted back into the original audio data [33].

The system is designed to be robust to compression, dynamics, A/D-D/A conversion, and many other operations that only change the signal but not the content.

The diagram of this system is quite similar to Figure 5.6. Robust features employed in this system include RMS (root mean square), ZCR, and the spectra of the audio data. RMS provides information about the energy of a number of samples of an audio file. Muted parts or changes in an audio sequence could be detected by comparing the RMSs of the original and processed audio sequences. ZCR provides information about the amount of high frequencies in a window of sound data; the brightness of the sound data is described by it. Besides the robust features, a synchronization pattern for resynchronization is also included in the authentication information. Since the authentication information is sent to the receiver via watermarking technology and the capacity of an audio watermarking algorithm is very low, the extracted features are quantized and then employed to generate a feature checksum. The checksum could be hash digest, cyclic redundancy checks, or the result of XOR function. Therefore, the actual authentication information in this solution includes the feature checksum and synchronization pattern. Replacing features with feature checksums will not affect the robustness of the system. Since an ideal feature is robust to all acceptable manipulations, its checksum would be exactly the same after the manipulations.

Authenticity verification is a process of comparing two feature checksums after the synchronization pattern is located. One is extracted from the embedded watermark, and the other is the newly generated feature checksum from the received audio signal following the same procedure as that in signature generation.

In some high-security applications, a one-bit change in an audio track should be detected, and the original audio data should also be recovered after the watermark is detected. This is similar to lossless image authentication. However, the solutions for lossless image authentication cannot be directly employed for lossless audio authentication due to the following problems:

(i) The data size is large during a long recording. If a watermark is to be embedded in a special device, very large memory reserves would be necessary.

(ii) Integrity may not be lost even if the original data is not completely present. For example, a recording of an interview may be edited later, and the message of the interview will not be corrupted if only the introduction of the reporter is removed.

To solve these problems, Steinebach and Dittmann proposed another audio authentication solution, called invertible audio authentication [33], in which no manipulation but cutting is allowed. In this solution, a number of consecutive samples are considered as one audio frame, e.g., 44,100 samples for one second of CD-quality mono data. Since one sample is represented by 16 bits, one bit layer of this frame can be selected and compressed by a lossless compression algorithm. The difference between memory requirements of the original and the compressed bit layer is used to carry the authentication information.

The authentication information includes the necessary information for proving the integrity of the audio frame, i.e., hash digest of the audio data, synchronization header, sequence ID_s, and incremental frame ID_T. ID_s verifies that the frame belongs to a certain recording; this provides security versus exchanges from other recordings. ID_T protects the frame order in an audio sequence from being exchanged.

5.5 SUMMARY

In this chapter, we introduced a list of authentication schemes for multimedia applications. Based on the robustness to distortions, these schemes can be classified into complete authentication and content authentication. Signatures and watermarking are two important technologies employed in designing these schemes. Signatures can be further classified into digital signatures and media signatures for complete authentication and content authentication, respectively. We then focused on discussion of various media signature-based authentication techniques for multimedia applications, e.g., image, video, and audio. We argued that a good content authentication solution should be not only secure enough against malicious attacks, but also robust enough to acceptable manipulations. Such a good system should also be application-dependent.

REFERENCES

[1] A. Menezes, P. Oorschot, and S. Vanstone. *Handbook of Applied Cryptography*, CRC Press, Boca Raton, FL, 1996.

[2] B. Schneier. *Applied Cryptography*, Wiley, New York, 1996.

[3] C.-Y. Lin and S.-F. Chang. Issues and solutions for authenticating MPEG video, *SPIE Int. Conf. Security and Watermarking of Multimedia Contents*, San Jose, CA, vol. 3657, no. 06, p. 54–56, EI '99, January 1999.

[4] C.-W. Wu. On the design of content-based multimedia authentication systems, *IEEE Trans. Multimedia*, 4:385–393, 2002.

[5] Q. B. Sun and S.-F. Chang, Signature-based media authentication, in *Multimedia Security Handbook*, CRC Press, Boca Raton, FL, 2004.

[6] J. Fridrich, M. Goljan, and R. Du. Invertible authentication watermark for JPEG images, in *Proc. Int. Conf. Information Technology: Coding and Computing*, pp. 223–227, Las Vagas, NV, 2001.

[7] M. Goljan, J. Fridrich, and R. Du. Distortion-free data embedding for images, in *Proc. 4th Int. Workshop Information Hiding (IHW)*, Pittsburgh, PA, pp. 27–41, 2001.

[8] M. Awrangjeb and M.S. Kankanhall. Lossless watermarking considering the human visual system, *Digital Watermarking: Second International Workshop (IWDW)*, Seoul, Korea, pp. 581–592, October 2003

[9] R. Du and J. Fridrich. Lossless authentication of MPEG-2 video, *Proc. Int. Conf. Image Processing (ICIP)*, 2:893–896, 2002.

[10] D. K. Zou, C.-W. Wu, G. R. Xuan, and Y. Q. Shi. A content-based image authentication system with lossless data hiding, *Proc. IEEE Int. Conf. Multimedia and Expo (ICME)*, 2:213–216, 2003.

[11] M. M. Yeung and F. Mintzer. An invisible watermarking technique for image verification, *Proc. Int. Conf. Image Processing (ICIP)*, 2:680–683, 1997.

[12] P. W. Wong and N. Memon. Secret and public key image watermarking schemes for image authentication and ownership verification, *IEEE Tran. Image Processing*, 10:1593–1601, 2001.

[13] J. Fridrich and M. Goljan. Images with self-correcting capabilities, *Proc. Int. Conf. Image Processing (ICIP)*, 3:792–796, 1999.

[14] J. J. Eggers, and B. Girod. Blind watermarking applied to image authentication, *Proc. IEEE Int. Conf. Acoustics, Speech, and Signal Processing (ICASSP)*, 3:1977–1980, 2001.

[15] C-Y. Lin and S.-F. Chang. Semi-fragile watermarking for authenticating JPEG visual content, *SPIE Security and Watermarking of Multimedia Conference*, San Jose, CA, 3971:140–151, 2000.

[16] S.-J. Han, I.-S. Chang, and R.-H. Park. Semi-fragile watermarking for tamper proofing and authentication of still images, in 2nd *International Workshop on Digital Watermarking (IWDW)*, Seoul, Korea, pp. 328–339, 2003.

[17] M.P. Queluz. Towards robust, content based techniques for image authentication, in *IEEE Second Workshop Multimedia Signal Processing*, pp. 297–302, Los Angeles, CA, 1998.

[18] S. M. Ye, Q. B. Sun, and E. C. Chang. Error resilient content-based image authentication over wireless channel, in *IEEE Int. Symp. Circuits and Systems (ISCAS)*, pp. 2707–2710, Kobe, Japan, 2005.

[19] J. Fridrich. Robust bit extraction from images, *IEEE Int. Conf. Multimedia Computing and Systems*, 2:536–540, 1999.

[20] J. Fridrich and M. Goljan. Robust hash functions for digital watermarking, in *Proc. IEEE Int. Conf. Information Technology—Coding and Computing'00*, Las Vegas, pp. 178–183, 2000.

[21] G. R. Arce, L. H. Xie, and R. F. Gravemen. Approximate image authentication codes, in *Proc. 4th Annual Fedlab Symp. Advanced Telecommunications Information Distribution*, College Park, MD, vol. 1, 2000.

[22] L. H. Xie, G. R. Arce, and R. F. Graveman. Approximate image message authentication codes, *IEEE Trans. Multimedia*, 32, 242–252, 2001.

[23] Q. B. Sun, S.-F. Chang, K. Maeno, and M. Suto. A new semi-fragile image authentication framework combining ECC and PKI infrastructure, *Proc. IEEE Int. Symp. Circuits and Systems (ISCAS)*, 2:440–443, 2002.

[24] W. Wesley Peterson and E. J. Weldon, Jr. *Error-Correcting Codes*, MIT Press, Cambridge, MA, 1984.

[25] Q. B. Sun, S. M. Ye, C.-Y. Lin, and S.-F. Chang. A crypto signature scheme for image authentication over wireless channel, *Int. Image and Graphics*, 61, 1–14, 2005.

[26] J. M. Park, E. K. P. Chong, and H. J. Siegel. Efficient multicast packet authentication using signature amortization, in *Proc. the IEEE Symp. Security and Privacy*, pp. 210–223, 2002.

[27] Q. B. Sun, D. J. He, and Q. Tian. A secure and robust authentication scheme for video transcoding, *IEEE Trans. Circuits and Systems for Video Technology (CSVT)*, submitted.

[28] P. Yin and H. Yu. Semi-fragile watermarking system for MPEG video authentication, in *Proc. IEEE Int. Conf. Acoustics, Speech, and Signal Processing (ICASSP)*, 4:3461–3464, 2002.

[29] D. J. He, Q. B. Sun, and Q. Tian. A secure and robust object-based video authentication system, *EURASIP Journal on Applied Signal Processing (JASP), Special Issue on Multimedia Security and Right Management*, Vol. 2004, No. 14, p. 2185–2200, October 2004.

[30] W.-Y. Kim and Y.-S. Kim. *A New Region-Based Shape Descriptor*, ISO/IEC MPEG99/M5472, Maui, Hawaii, December 1999.

[31] M. Bober. MPEG-7 visual shape descriptors, *IEEE Trans. Circuits and Systems for Video Technology (CSVT)*, 116:716–719, 2001.

[32] C.-P. Wu and C.-C. J. Kuo. Comparison of two speech content authentication approaches, in *Photonics West 2002: Electronic Imaging, Security and Watermarking of Multimedia Contents IV*, Vol. 4675 of SPIE proceedings, pp. 158–169, San Jose, Ca, 2002.

[33] M. Steinebach and J. Dittmann. Watermarking-based digital audio data authentication, *EURASIP J. Applied Signal Processing*, 10:1001–1015, 2003.

6

Key Management for Multimedia Access and Distribution

Ahmet M. Eskicioglu

6.1 INTRODUCTION

In this chapter, we discuss standardized key management in commonly used multimedia distribution architectures. Table 6.1 shows a few applications where data needs to be protected. In some applications, such as health services or delivery of financial data, key management is privately defined. Hence, no information is available regarding the way the keys are handled.

Figure 6.1 shows five primary means of multimedia delivery to consumers: satellite, cable, terrestrial, Internet, and pre-recorded media (optical and magnetic).

In digital distribution networks, copyrighted multimedia content is protected by encryption.

- **Cable, satellite, and terrestrial distribution [1–3]**. A conditional access (CA) system provides the encryption technology to control access to digital television (TV) services. Digital content ("program") is compressed, packetized, encrypted, and multiplexed with the entitlement messages. Two types of entitlement messages are commonly used associated with each program: The Entitlement Control Messages (ECMs) and the Entitlement Management Messages (EMMs). ECMs carry the decryption keys ("control words") and a short description of the program, while EMMs specify the authorization levels related to services. Authorized users can use the appropriate decoder

Table 6.1: Protection of data in four applications.

Application	Provider	Data	What needs to be prevented?
Entertainment	Content owners (e.g., movie studios and recording companies) and service providers (e.g., cable companies and broadcasters)	Copyrighted movies and songs	Unauthorized duplication and consumption
Health services	Hospitals	Medical data for patients (e.g., X-ray pictures and history of illnesses)	Unauthorized disclosure and misuse
Finance	Investment bankers	Financial data (e.g., stocks and mutual funds)	Unauthorized use and exploitation
Military	U.S. Armed Forces	Confidential data (e.g., information about weapons, ammunition, and military personnel)	Unauthorized exposure

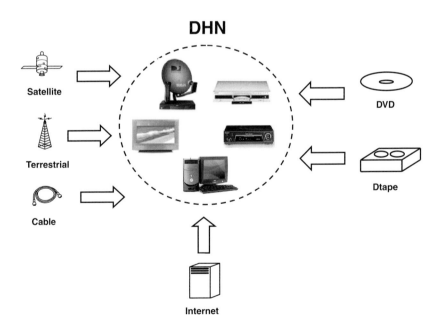

FIGURE 6.1: Multimedia distribution to consumers.

to decrypt the programs. Because of their secure features, smart cards are a good option for set-top boxes.

- **Internet distribution [3–5]**. Digital Rights Management (DRM) refers to the protection, distribution, modification, and enforcement of the rights associated with the use of digital content. The primary responsibilities of a DRM system include secure delivery of content, prevention of unauthorized access, enforcement of usage rules, and monitoring of the use of content. A customer obtains an encrypted file from a server on the Internet for viewing purposes. To be able to decrypt the file, a license, containing the usage rights and the decryption key, needs to be downloaded from a clearing house. A major responsibility of the clearing house is to authenticate the customer based on his credentials. The client device should have a player that supports the relevant DRM system to play the file according to the rights included in the license. Superdistribution is a process that allows a customer to send the encrypted file to other people. However, as licenses are not transferable, each new customer has to purchase another license for playback. Today, interoperability of DRM systems is a major problem.

- **Distribution in digital home networks [3, 6]**. A digital home network is a cluster of consumer electronics devices (e.g., DTV, DVD player, DVCR, and STB) that are interconnected. The multimedia content is encrypted in transmission across each digital interface and on storage media. The technical solutions developed in recent years are listed in Table 6.2. In a digital home network, multimedia content moves from one device to another for storage or display. These devices need to authenticate each other to make sure that they are equipped with the licensed protection technology.

Table 6.2:   Content protection solutions for digital home networks.

Media	Solution	What is protected?
	Content Scramble System (CSS) [7]	Video on DVD-ROM
	Copy Protection for Pre-Recorded	Audio on DVD-ROM
Optical media	Media (CPPM) [8]	
	Copy Protection for Recorded	Video or audio on
	Media (CPRM) [9]	DVD-R/RW/RAM
Magnetic media	High-Definition Copy Protection	Video on digital tape
	(HDCP) [10]	
Digital	Digital Transmission Copy	IEEE 1394 serial bus
interfaces	Protection (DTCP) [11]	
	HDCP [12]	Digital Visual Interface (DVI)

6.2 SECURITY OF MULTIMEDIA IN DISTRIBUTION

6.2.1 Conditional Access (CA) Systems for Satellite, Cable, and Terrestrial Distribution

A CA system [1, 2, 13–19] allows access to services based on payment or other requirements such as identification, authorization, authentication, registration, or a combination of these. Using satellite, terrestrial, or cable transmissions, the service providers deliver different types of multimedia content ranging from free access programs to services such as PayTV, Pay-Per-View, and Video-on-Demand.

CA systems are developed by companies, commonly called the CA providers, that specialize in the protection of audio/visual (A/V) signals and secure processing environments. A typical architecture of a CA system and its major components is shown in Figure 6.2. The common activities in this general model are:

1. Digital content (called an "event" or a "program") is compressed to minimize bandwidth requirements. MPEG-2 is a well-known industry standard for coding A/V streams. More recent MPEG alternatives (MPEG-4, MPEG-7, and MPEG-21) are being considered for new applications.
2. The program is sent to the CA head-end to be protected and packaged with entitlements indicating the access conditions.

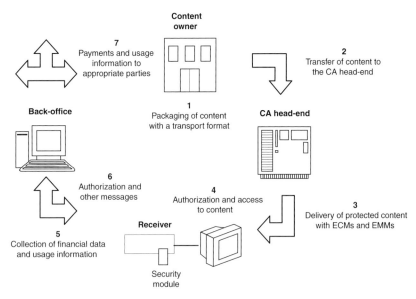

FIGURE 6.2: CA system architecture.

3. The A/V stream is encrypted and multiplexed with the entitlement messages. There are two types of entitlement messages [20] associated with each program. The ECMs carry the decryption keys (called the control words) and a short description of the program (number, title, date, time, price, rating, etc.), while the EMMs specify the authorization levels related to services. In some CA systems, the EMMs can also be sent via other means such as telephone networks. The services are usually encrypted using a symmetric cipher such as the Data Encryption Standard (DES) or any other public domain or private algorithm. The lifetime and the length of the encryption keys are two important system parameters. For security reasons, the protection of the ECMs is often privately defined by the CA providers, but public key cryptography, one-way functions [21], and secret sharing [22] are useful tools for secure key delivery.

4. If the customer has received authorization to watch the protected program, the A/V stream is decrypted by the receiver (also called a "decoder") and sent to the display unit for viewing. A removable security module (e.g., a smart card) provides a safe environment for the processing of ECMs, EMMs, and other sensitive functions such as user authorization and temporary storage of purchase records.

5. The back office is an essential component of every CA system, handling billings and payments, transmission of EMMs, and interactive TV applications. A one-to-one link is established between the back office and the decoder (or the removable security module, if it exists) using a "return channel," which is basically a telephone connection via a modem. As with other details of the CA system, the security of this channel may be privately defined by the CA providers. At certain times, the back office collects the purchase history and other usage information for processing.

6. Authorizations (e.g., EMMs) and other messages (system and security updates, etc.) are delivered to the customer's receiver.

7. Payments and usage information are sent to the appropriate parties (content providers, service operators, CA providers, etc.).

In today's CA systems, the security module is assigned the critical task of recovering the decryption keys. These keys are then passed to the receiver for decrypting the A/V streams. The workload is therefore shared between the security module and its host. Recently, two separate standards have evolved to remove all the security functionality from navigation devices. In the United States, the National Renewable Security Standard (NRSS) [23] defines a renewable and replaceable security element for use in consumer electronics devices such as digital set-top boxes and digital televisions (DTVs). In Europe, the DVB (Digital Video Broadcasting) project has specified a standard for a common interface (CI) between a host device and a security module.

The CA systems currently in operation support several purchase methods, including subscription, pay-per-view, and impulsive pay-per-view. Other models are also being considered to provide more user convenience and to facilitate payments. One such model uses pre-paid "cash cards" to store credits which may be obtained from authorized dealers or ATM-like machines.

The DVB project has envisaged two basic CA approaches: "Simulcrypt" and "Multicrypt" [17, 24].

- **Simulcrypt**. Each program is transmitted with the entitlement messages for multiple CA systems, enabling different CA decoders to receive and correctly decrypt the program.
- **Multicrypt**. Each decoder is built with a CI for multiple CA systems. Security modules from different CA system operators can be plugged into different slots in the same decoder to allow switching between CA systems.

These architectures can be used for satellite, cable, and terrestrial transmission of DTV. The ATSC [25] has adopted the Simulcrypt approach.

6.2.2 Broadcast Flag

A recent major discussion item on the agenda for content owners and broadcasters has been the broadcast flag [26]. Also known as the ATSC (Advanced Television Systems Committee) flag, the broadcast flag is a sequence of digital bits sent with a digital television program that indicates whether or not it can be recorded or if there are any restrictions on recorded content. Possible restrictions include inability to save a digital program to a hard disc or other non-volatile storage, inability to make secondary copies of recorded content (in order to share or archive), forceful reduction of quality when recording (such as reducing high-definition video to the resolution of standard TVs), and inability to skip over commercials. The suitability of the broadcast flag for protecting DTV content was evaluated by the Broadcast Protection Discussion Group (BPDG) that was comprised of a large number of content providers, TV broadcasters, consumer electronics manufacturers, Information Technology (IT) companies, interested individuals, and consumer activists. The group completed its mission with the release of the BPDG report [27].

In the United States, new TV receivers using the ATSC standard were supposed to incorporate this functionality by July 1, 2005, but the U.S. Court of Appeals for the D.C. Circuit struck down the Federal Communications Commission's (FCC) rule [28] to this effect on May 6, 2005. The stated intention of the broadcast flag is to prevent copyright infringement, but many have asserted that broadcast flags interfere with fair use rights of the viewing public. The federal court ruled that the FCC had exceeded its authority in creating this rule. The court stated that the commission could not prohibit the manufacture of computer and video hardware without copy protection technology because the FCC only has authority to regulate communications, not devices that receive communications. It is possible that a higher court may overturn this ruling or that the U.S. Congress may grant such authority to the FCC. Some of the major U.S. TV networks have stated in the past that they will stop broadcasting high-definition content if the rule does not go into effect. If the rule were to be reinstated, it is possible that non-compliant decoders would be manufactured for market in other locales, since Japan and the United States are the only countries to have such regulations.

A key U.S. Senate panel on June 23, 2005, decided not to intervene in a long-simmering dispute over the "broadcast flag." At a meeting reserved for voting on spending bills, the Senate Appropriations Committee members did not propose an amendment authorizing federal regulators to mandate the broadcast flag. The MPAA (Motion Picture Association of America) is of the opinion that the FCC rule is necessary to assure a continued supply of high-value programming to off-air DTV consumers.

6.2.3   DRM Systems for Internet Distribution

DRM refers to the protection, distribution, modification, and enforcement of the rights associated with the use of digital content. In general, the primary responsibilities of a DRM system are:

- Packaging of content
- Secure delivery and storage of content
- Prevention of unauthorized access
- Enforcement of usage rules
- Monitoring the use of content

Although such systems can, in principle, be deployed for any type of distribution media, the present discussions weigh heavily on the Internet.

The unprecedented explosion of the Internet has opened potentially limitless distribution channels for the e-commerce of content. Selling goods directly to consumers over an open and public network, without the presence of a clerk at the point of sale, has significant advantages. It allows the businesses to expand their market reach, reduce operating costs, and enhance customer satisfaction by offering personalized experience. While inspiring new business opportunities, this electronic delivery model raises challenging questions about the traditional models of ownership. The lessons learned from the MP3 phenomenon, combined with the lack of reliable payment mechanisms, have shown the need for protecting the ownership rights of copyrighted digital material.

A DRM system uses cryptography (symmetric key ciphers, public key ciphers, and digital signatures) as the centerpiece for security-related functions, which generally include secure delivery of content, secure delivery of the content key and the usage rights, and client authentication.

Figure 6.3 shows the fundamentals of an electronic delivery system with DRM: a publisher, a server (streaming or Web), a client device, and a financial

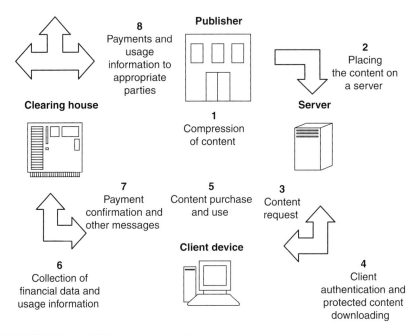

FIGURE 6.3: DRM system architecture.

clearing house. The communication between the server and the customer is assumed to be unicast, i.e., point-to-point. Although details may vary among DRM systems, the following steps summarize typical activities in a DRM-supported e-commerce system:

1. The publisher packages the media file (i.e., the content) and encrypts it with a symmetric cipher. The package may include information about the content provider, retailer, or Web address to contact for the rights.
2. The protected media file is placed on a server for download or streaming. It can be located with a search engine using the proper content index.
3. The customer requests the media file from the server.
4. The file is sent after the client device is authenticated. The customer may also be required to complete a purchase transaction. Authentication based on public key certificates is commonly used for this purpose. Depending on the DRM system, the usage rules and the key to unlock the file may either be attached to the file or need to be separately obtained (e.g., in the form of a license) from the clearing house or any other registration server. The attachment or the license is protected in such a way that only the client is able to retrieve the information. Public key ciphers are appropriately used here.

5. The customer purchases the content and uses it according to the rights and rules.
6. At certain times, the clearing house collects financial records and usage information from the clients.
7. Payment confirmation and other messages (system and security updates, etc.) are delivered to the client.
8. Payments and usage information are sent to the appropriate parties (content providers, publishers, distributors, authors, artists, etc.).

Renewability is achieved by upgrading DRM system components and preventing the compromised devices from receiving content. New security software may be released as a regular enhancement or in response to a threat or hack. Revocation lists allow the servers to refuse service to revoked clients (multimedia applications software can also be revoked if it can be authenticated by the DRM component that resides in the client).

DRM enables the content owners to specify their own business models in managing the use of content. A wide range of sales models can be supported, including subscription, pay-per-use, and superdistribution. Time-limited reading of an e-book, multiple viewings of a movie, and transfer of a song to a portable music player are all possible scenarios.

Superdistribution is a relatively new concept for redistributing content across the Internet. It is a process that allows the consumers to forward a content that they have acquired to other consumers (friends, relatives, and associates) in the market. The content forwarded to a potential buyer cannot be accessed until the new rights are obtained. This approach has important advantages and drawbacks.

1. It is an efficient way of using a DRM-supported e-commerce system, since repeated content downloads are avoided.
2. From an economic point of view, superdistribution may help widen market penetration. Once a particular content is downloaded to a client, the customer, with sufficient encouragement, can act as an agent of the retailer with minimal effort and cost.
3. From a security point of view, if the content, encrypted with a particular key, becomes available in the market in large quantities, it may increase the likelihood of the key being compromised. For increased security, different copies of a media file need to be encrypted with different keys. This, of course, requires new downloads from the server.

Interoperability of DRM Systems

Today, there are many standards that ensure the interoperability of consumer electronics devices. A consumer may buy a Toshiba TV set and connect it to a Sony DVD player, expecting that they will work together. Interoperability is also essential for content protection systems. Both the sending and receiving devices need to support the protection system for a particular media. Systems like the CSS and DTCP are available from licensing agencies for implementation in CE (Consumer Electronics) devices. Unfortunately, this is not the case for DRM systems for Internet distribution. A client device supporting the DRM system A can only download content protected by the same system.

Currently, there is no interoperability among the DRM systems for a number of important reasons, including:

- Every DRM system has secret keys/algorithms. DRM vendors are concerned about sharing secret keys/algorithms.
- Meta-data are data about data that describes the content, quality, condition, and other characteristics of data. Although Rights Expression Languages (RELs) are emerging as essential components of DRM systems, they are not standardized yet.

An alternative would be to implement several DRM systems on a client device, but this may not be feasible if the number of DRM systems is too big.

6.2.4 Copy Protection (CP) Systems in Digital Home Networks

The Copy Control Information (CCI) communicates the conditions under which a consumer is authorized to make a copy. An important subset of CCI is the two Copy Generation Management System (CGMS) bits for digital copy control: "11" (copy-never), "10" (copy-once), "01" (no-more-copies), and "00" (copy-free). The integrity of the CCI should be ensured to prevent unauthorized modification. Each solution in Table 6.2 defines a means of associating the CCI with the digital content it protects. The CCI can be associated with the content in two ways: (1) the CCI is included in a designated field in the A/V stream, and (2) the CCI is embedded as a watermark into the A/V stream.

Content Scramble System (CSS) for DVD-Video

The CSS [7] is the name of the protection system to make the content on a DVD video disc unintelligible. It prevents unauthorized duplication of movies, protecting the intellectual property of the owner. The DVD Copy Control Association (DVD CCA) is a not-for-profit corporation with the responsibility for licensing CSS to manufacturers of DVD hardware, DVDs, and related products. The CSS Specifications are provided in two sections: Procedural Specifications and Technical Specifications. The Procedural Specifications are provided only to CSS Licensees, prospective CSS Licensees, and others with a business need to know consistent with the intent and purposes of the CSS licensing process. The technical specifications for a membership category are provided to only CSS licensees in the appropriate membership category.

The CSS algorithm uses a 40-bit key and two Linear Feedback Shift Registers (LFSRs): a 17-bit LFSR and a 25-bit LFSR. The first LFSR is seeded with the first two bytes of the key, and the second LFSR is seeded with the remaining three bytes of the key. The output from the two LFSRs is combined using 8-bit addition to form the pseudo-random bitstream. This bitstream is XORed with the plaintext to generate the ciphertext. Prior to the XOR operation, bytes of the plaintext are run through a table-based S-box.

Each DVD contains a regional code that indicates the region of the world where it is intended to be played in. Motion picture studios want to control the home release of movies in different countries because theater releases are not simultaneous. Currently, eight regions have been defined, each with a unique number.

1. United States, Canada, U.S. Territories
2. Japan, Europe, South Africa, and the Middle East (including Egypt)
3. South Korea, Taiwan, Hong Kong, and parts of Southeast Asia
4. Australia, New Zealand, Pacific Islands, Central America, Mexico, South America, and the Caribbean
5. Eastern Europe (former Soviet Union), Indian subcontinent, Africa, North Korea, and Mongolia
6. China
7. Reserved
8. Special international venues (airplanes, cruise ships, etc.)

For example, while a recent film may already have played in theaters in the United States and been released to the home video market, that same film may not yet have opened in other countries. DVDs manufactured in one region will only play on players that were manufactured in that same region, implying that a DVD purchased in Japan will not play on North American players, and vice versa. On the back of each DVD package, a region number can be found.

Discs that can be played worldwide have the regional code 0. However, PAL discs must be played in a PAL-compatible unit, and NTSC discs must be played in an NTSC-compatible unit.

There are three levels of keys in the CSS: master key, disc key, and title key. Each manufacturer is assigned a distinct master key that is embedded in all of the DVD players manufactured. There are 409 master keys, and each DVD contains in a hidden sector a table that has the disc key encrypted with all 409 master keys. A player decrypts the appropriate entry in the table using its own master key. The disc key, in turn, decrypts the title key, and the title key is used for the decryption (i.e., descrambling) of the movie on the DVD. For each DVD, there is only one disc key, but there may be several titles. Hence, the disc key decrypts all the title keys on a DVD.

If a particular master key is compromised, it is replaced by a key which is used in the subsequent manufacturing of DVD players. Future releases of DVDs will have the disc key encrypted with the new master key, preventing playback on the players manufactured with the compromised key.

The CSS was hacked in late 1999 when the encryption (i.e., scrambling) algorithm and the master keys were stolen and posted on the Internet. An open-source software called DeCSS appeared on several Web sites, allowing an encrypted movie on a DVD to be copied in-the-clear to a computer disc or a blank DVD.

An additional element is needed in CSS for implementation on a PC system. Before the DVD drive sends data over the bus to the host PC, it first goes through mutual authentication with the PC. This allows each party (the DVD drive and the PC) to check if the other participant is licensed to handle CSS scrambled content. In this process, a session key is generated for encrypting the data in transition over the bus. Encryption is required, as it is possible to steal the plaintext data right off of the bus, making the prior encryption totally useless. The DVD drive decrypts the disc key using its master key. The disc key and the title key(s) are sent from the drive to the PC, using the session key for their encryption. The host is now able to decrypt the title key(s) with the disc key. The title key(s) is then used to decrypt the movie(s) on the DVD.

Content Protection for Pre-recorded Media (CPPM) for DVD-Audio

For DVD-Audio, a system similar to CSS was going to be used, but because CSS was hacked, a new system called CPPM was developed. The CPPM Specification defines a renewable method for protecting content distributed on pre-recorded (read-only) media types. The specification is organized into several "books." The "Introduction and Common Cryptographic Elements" book [29] provides a brief overview of CPPM and defines cryptographic procedures that are common among its different uses. The "DVD Book" [30] specifies additional details for using CPPM technology to protect content distributed on read-only DVD media. This document currently provides details specific to using CPPM for the DVD-Audio format only.

Common cryptographic functions used for CPPM are based on the Cryptomeria Cipher (C2) [31]. The C2 is a Feistel network-based block cipher designed for use in the area of digital entertainment content protection.

The 4C Entity, LLC [32] is responsible for licensing CPPM and CPRM technologies.

- **Media Key Block (MKB)**. CPPM uses the MKB to enable system renewability. The MKB is generated by the 4C Entity, LLC, allowing all compliant devices, each using their set of secret device keys, to calculate the same media key. If a set of device keys is compromised in a way that threatens the integrity of the system, an updated MKB can be released that causes the device with the compromised set of device keys to calculate a different media key than is computed by the remaining compliant devices. In this way, the compromised device keys are "revoked" by the new MKB.

- **Device Keys**. During manufacturing, each CPPM-compliant playback device is given a set of secret device keys. These keys are provided by the 4C Entity, LLC, and are for use in processing the MKB to calculate the media key. Key sets may either be unique per device or used commonly by multiple devices. Each device receives n device keys, which are referred to as K_{d_i}, $i = 0, 1, \ldots, n-1$. For each device key there is an associated column and row value, referred to as C_{d_i} and R_{d_i}, $i = 1, \ldots, n-1$, respectively. Column and row values start at 0. For a given device, no two device keys will have the same associated column value. It is possible for a device to have some device keys with the same associated row values.

Figure 6.4 shows a simplified example of how CPPM operates.

The steps below are followed in protecting content with CPPM.

1. The 4C Entity, LLC, provides secret device keys to the device manufacturer for inclusion into each device manufactured.
2. The media manufacturer places two pieces of information on each piece of media containing protected content: an MKB generated by the 4C Entity, LLC, and a title-specific identifier, media ID.
3. The protected content on the media is encrypted by a content key, which is derived from a one-way function of (1) the secret media key, (2) the media ID, and (3) the CCI associated with the content.
4. When media containing protected content is placed in a compliant drive or player, the device calculates the secret Media Key using its keys and the Media Key Block stored on the media. The Media Key is used to calculate the Content Key, which in turn decrypts the content.

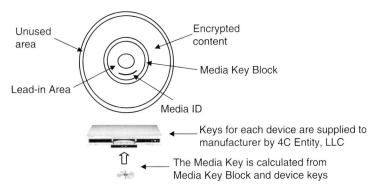

FIGURE 6.4: Content Protection For Pre-recorded Media CPPM.

Content Protection for Recordable Media (CPRM)

The CPRM Specification defines a renewable method for protecting content recorded on a number of physical media types. The specification is organized into several books. The "Introduction and Common Cryptographic Elements" book [33] provides a brief overview of CPRM and defines cryptographic procedures that are common among its different uses. Other books provide additional details specific to using CPRM protection for different applications and media types:

- "DVD Book" [34]
- "Portable ATA Storage Book"
- "Secure Digital Flash Memory Card Book"

Common cryptographic functions used for CPRM are based on the C2 block cipher. The MKB and Device Keys are similar to those for CPPM.

Figure 6.5 shows a simplified example of how CPRM operates.

The steps below are followed in protecting content with CPRM.

1. The 4C Entity, LLC provides secret Device Keys to the device manufacturer for inclusion into each device manufactured.
2. The media manufacturer places two pieces of information on each piece of compliant media: an MKB generated by the 4C Entity, LLC, and a Media ID.
3. When compliant media is placed within a compliant drive or player/recorder, the device calculates a secret Media Key using its keys and the MKB stored on the media.
4. Content stored on the media is encrypted/decrypted by a content key, which is derived from a one-way function of (1) a secret title key and (2) the CCI associated with the content. The title key is encrypted and stored on the

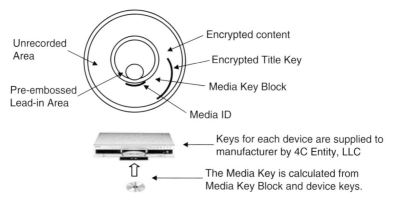

FIGURE 6.5: Content Protection For Recordable Media CPRM.

media using a key derived from a one-way function of the media key and media ID.

The CPRM components on DVD-RAM media and the CPRM components on DVD-R and DVD-RW media are similar.

Digital Transmission Content Protection (DTCP)

Five companies (Hitachi, Intel, Matsushita (MEI), Sony, and Toshiba) have developed the DTCP specification. The DTCP specification [35, 36] defines a cryptographic protocol for protecting A/V entertainment content from illegal copying, intercepting, and tampering as it traverses high-performance digital buses, such as the IEEE 1394 standard. This copy protection system protects legitimate content delivered to a source device via another approved copy protection system (such as the CSS).

The Digital Transmission Licensing Administrator (DTLA) is responsible for establishing and administering the content protection system based in part on the specification. Implementation of the DTCP specification requires a license from the DTLA.

The DTCP specification uses Hitachi's M6 as the baseline cipher. The M6 cipher is a symmetric key block cipher algorithm based on permutation-substitution.

The DTCP system addresses four fundamental layers of copy protection:

  i. Authentication and key exchange
 ii. Content encryption
iii. Copy control information
 iv. System renewability

Authentication and key exchange (AKE). The specification includes two authentication levels: full and restricted.

- Full authentication can be used with all content protected by the system and must be used for "copy-never" (11) content. The protocol employs the public key-based Digital Signature Algorithm (DSA) algorithm and the Diffie-Hellman (DH) key-exchange algorithm. Both the DSA and the Diffie-Hellman implementations for the system employ Elliptic Curve (EC) cryptography.
- Restricted authentication is an AKE method for devices with limited computing resources. It enables the protection of copy-one-generation and no-more-copies content. If a device handles either copy-one-generation or no-more-copies protection schemes, the device must support restricted authentication. Copying devices such as DV recorders or D-VHS recorders and devices communicating with them employ this kind of authentication and key exchange. No authentication is required for copy-freely content.

Both kinds of authentication involve the calculation of three encryption keys:

- An authentication key, established during authentication is used to encrypt the exchange key
- An exchange key, used to set up and manage the security of copyrighted content streams
- A content key, used to encrypt the content being exchanged

Content encryption.   To ensure interoperability, all devices must support the specific cipher specified as the baseline cipher. The channel cipher subsystem can also support additional ciphers (including the Modified Blowfish cipher and the DES cipher), the use of which are negotiated during authentication. All ciphers are used in the converted cipher block chaining mode.

Copy Control Information (CCI).   The content protection system must support transmission of encrypted data between devices, utilizing CCI. If source and sink devices do not have the same capabilities, they should follow the most restrictive CCI method(s) available, which is determined by the source device. Two methods can be used:

1. The Encryption Mode Indicator (EMI) provides easily accessible yet secure transmission of CCI via the most significant two bits of the synch field of the isochronous packet header. The encoding used for the EMI bits distinguishes the content encryption/decryption mode: "copy-freely," "copy-never," "copy-one-generation," or "no-more-copies." If the EMI bits are tampered with, the encryption and decryption modes will not match, resulting in erroneous decryption of the content.
2. Embedded CCI is carried as part of the content stream. Many content formats, including MPEG, have fields allocated for carrying the CCI associated with the stream. The integrity of embedded CCI is ensured since tampering with the content stream results in erroneous decryption of the content.

System renewability.   Devices that support full authentication can receive and process System Renewability Messages (SRMs). These SRMs are generated by the DTLA and delivered via content and new devices. System renewability provides the capability for revoking unauthorized devices. There are several mechanisms for updated SRMs to be distributed to digital home networks.

- DVD players can receive updates from newer releases of pre-recorded DVDs or other compliant devices.
- Digital set-top boxes (digital cable transmission receivers or digital satellite broadcast receivers) can receive updates from content streams or other compliant devices.

- Digital TVs can receive updates from content streams or other compliant devices.
- Recording devices can receive updates from content streams, if they are equipped with a tuner, or other compliant devices.
- PCs can receive updates from Internet servers.

High-Bandwidth Digital Content Protection (HDCP)

HDCP [37] is designed for protecting A/V content over certain high-bandwidth interfaces, referred to as HDCP-protected interfaces, from being copied. In HDCP revision 1.1, the HDCP-protected interfaces are DVI and High-Definition Multimedia Interface (HDMI). The Digital Content Protection, LLC licenses technologies for protecting commercial entertainment content.

In an HDCP system, two or more HDCP devices are interconnected through an HDCP-protected interface. The A/V content protected by HDCP, referred to as HDCP content, flows from the Upstream Content Control Function into the HDCP system at the most upstream HDCP transmitter. From there, the HDCP content, encrypted by the HDCP system, flows through a tree-shaped topology of HDCP receivers over HDCP-protected interfaces. Figure 6.6 gives an example of connection topology for HDCP devices.

The specification describes a content protection mechanism for:

i. Authentication of HDCP receivers to their immediate upstream connection (to an HDCP transmitter)

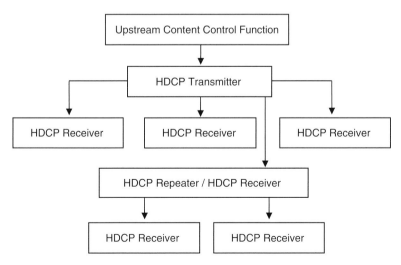

FIGURE 6.6:   Connection topology of an HDCP system.

    ii. HDCP encryption of A/V content over the HDCP-protected interfaces between HDCP transmitters and their downstream HDCP receivers

    iii. Revocation of HDCP receivers that are determined by the Digital Content Protection, LLC, to be invalid.

Authentication of HDCP receivers. The HDCP Authentication protocol is an exchange between an HDCP transmitter and an HDCP receiver that affirms to the HDCP transmitter that the HDCP receiver is authorized to receive HDCP content. This affirmation is in the form of the HDCP receiver demonstrating knowledge of a set of secret device keys. Each HDCP device is provided with a unique set of secret device keys, referred to as the Device Private Keys, from the Digital Content Protection, LLC. The communication exchange, which allows for the receiver to demonstrate knowledge of such secret device keys, also provides for both HDCP devices to generate a shared secret value that cannot be determined by eavesdroppers on this exchange. By having this shared secret formation melded into the demonstration of authorization, the shared secret can then be used as a symmetric key to encrypt HDCP content intended only for the authorized device.

Each HDCP device contains an array of 40, 56-bit secret device keys, which make up its Device Private Keys, and a corresponding identifier, received from the Digital Content Protection, LLC. This identifier is the Key Selection Vector (KSV) assigned to the device. The KSV is a 40-bit binary value.

The HDCP Authentication protocol can be considered in three parts:

- The first part establishes shared values between the two HDCP devices if both devices have a valid Device Key Set from the Digital Content Protection, LLC.
- The second part allows an HDCP repeater to report the KSVs of attached HDCP receivers.
- The third part occurs during the vertical blanking interval preceding each frame for which encryption is enabled and provides an initialization state for the HDCP cipher for encrypting the HDCP content within that frame.

HDCP encryption. The HDCP cipher is a special-purpose cipher designed for both the appropriate robustness of the authentication protocol and the high-speed streaming requirement of uncompressed video data encryption.

Figure 6.7 shows HDCP encryption and decryption processes. HDCP encryption consists of a bit-wise XOR of the HDCP content with a pseudo-random data stream produced by the HDCP cipher. The DVI uses transition-minimized differential signaling (T.M.D.S).

Renewability of HDCP. If an authorized participant in the authentication protocol becomes compromised, it may expose the Device Private Keys it possesses for misuse by unauthorized parties. Therefore, each HDCP receiver is issued a

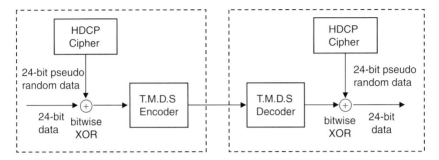

FIGURE 6.7: HDCP encryption and decryption.

unique set of Device Private Keys, matched with a non-secret identifier (the KSV), referred collectively as the Device Key Set. Through a process defined in the HDCP Adopter's License, the Digital Content Protection, LLC, may determine that a set of Device Private Keys has been compromised. It then places the corresponding KSV on a revocation list that the HDCP transmitter checks during authentication. Other authorized HDCP receivers are not affected by this revocation because they have different sets of Device Private Keys.

The HDCP transmitter is required to manage SRMs carrying the KSV revocation list. These messages are delivered with content and must be checked when available. The validity of an SRM is established by verifying the integrity of its signature with the Digital Content Protection, LLC public key, which is specified by the Digital Content Protection, LLC.

Content Protection System Architecture (CPSA)

CPSA [38] provides a framework of 11 axioms that describe how CPSA-compliant devices handle the three major areas that are critical to ensuring a comprehensive and consistent content protection scheme: content management information, access, and recording. These axioms are as follows:

Content Management Information Axioms

1. **Content Owner Selects CMI**. The content owner selects the content management information (CMI) from the supported options. The available options vary for different types of content according to agreements made between content owners and device manufacturers.

2. **Ensure Digital CMI Integrity**. While the content remains in the encrypted digital form, the CMI integrity is ensured during transmission and storage using encryption and key management protocols.

3. **Optional Watermarking**. At the content owner's option, the original content may be watermarked for the purpose of transmitting the CMI with the content, independent of its specific analog, digital, or encrypted digital representation.

Access Control Axioms

4. **Encrypt Pre-recorded Content**. All CPSA content on pre-recorded media is encrypted. Content encryption is a key facet of CPSA. It ensures that the content cannot be accessed until it is decrypted.

5. **Encrypt Authorized Copies**. All authorized copies of CPSA content are encrypted, except where specifically agreed otherwise.

6. **Playback Control**. Compliant playback modules detect the watermark CMI when present in unencrypted content and respond appropriately to prevent playback of unauthorized copies.

7. **Output Protection**. For encrypted content, compliant playback and source modules apply an approved protection scheme to all outputs, according to the digital CMI settings, except where specifically agreed otherwise.

8. **Manage Protected Output of Unencrypted Content**. Compliant source modules check the watermark CMI of unencrypted content prior to protected digital output and, if present, set the digital CMI for the output accordingly.

Recording Control Axioms

9. **Examine CCI before Copying and Respond Accordingly**. Compliant recording modules detect and respond appropriately to the CCI, if it is present, before creating a copy, if authorized to do so. Two things are examined by the recording module: digital CCI for encrypted content and watermark CCI for unencrypted content.

10. **Update CCI before Copying**. Compliant recording modules appropriately update both the digital CCI and the watermark CCI, when present, before creating a copy.

11. **Temporary Images**. Compliant recording modules do not inspect or update either the digital CCI or the watermark CCI when making an image that is both temporary and localized.

CPSA-Consistent Content Protection Technologies

A representative list of CPSA-consistent content protection technologies is given in Table 6.3.

Figure 6.8 displays the encryption-based content protection systems in Table 6.3.

Table 6.3: CPSA-consistent content protection technologies.

Technology

CSS for protecting pre-recorded DVD-Video content

CPPM for protecting pre-recorded DVD-Audio content

CPRM for protecting content stored on recordable media such as DVD or Secure
  Digital Flash Memory Card

DTCP for protecting content during digital transmission over IEEE 1394 and USB

HDCP for protecting content moving across high-bandwidth interfaces to digital displays

4C/Verance Watermark for embedding and reading watermark CMI in audio content

A video watermarking scheme to be determined by the DVD CCA

CA for protected distribution of premium content via cable or satellite

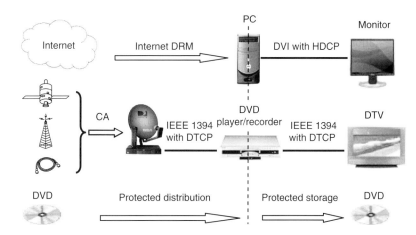

FIGURE 6.8: Encryption-based content protection systems.

6.2.5 CableCARD Copy Protection

In digital cable systems, the system operator needs to prevent unauthorized access and duplication with a CA system. An authorized CableCARD security device (previously referred to as a Point of Deployment (POD) module) decrypts the content and, depending on the CCI from the CA head-end, may re-encrypt it before sending the stream back to the receiver [39].

The Card–Host interface [40] supports the delivery of up to six independent transport streams:

- Single Stream Mode (S-Mode) is for use with or between cards and hosts capable of supporting only one MPEG program in one transport stream on

the Transport Stream interface as described in the ATSC standard [23] and the S-Mode.
- Multi-Stream Mode (M-Mode) is for use between a card and a host both implementing the Multi-stream Mode interface as specified by the M-Mode.

The copy protection system between the CableCARD and the host defines the protection of content delivered to the host as CA-encrypted MPEG programs. The encrypted content is passed to the card for CA-decryption and returned to the host across the interface. The card also delivers a CCI value to the host for all programs it CA-decrypts and applies CP-encryption to programs marked with non-zero EMI.

Card and Host Mutual Authentication

The card and host authenticate each other by a process of exchanged messages, calculations using stored secrets, and confirmations that the results meet specific criteria. The card will not CA-decrypt any content until it has successfully completed authentication of the host.

In mutual authentication, the card and host will perform the following operations to share two secrets (DHKey and AuthKey), and the binding authentication is complete.

- Calculate a DH public key from stored secrets and a generated random integer.
- Sign their DH public key with their X.509 private key (that matches the public key embedded in their X.509 device certificate).
- Send their device certificate, manufacturer certificate, DH public key, and signature of that key to the other device.
- Verify the signatures of the other device, and validate its certificate chain.
- Calculate a shared secret key, DHKey (1024 bits), that is unique to each binding.
- Calculate and exchange a long-term authentication key, AuthKey (160 bits).
- Confirm that the received AuthKey matches the internally calculated AuthKey.

XCA is the X.509 certificate authority. The device certificate is the XCA certificate unique to each card or host device, Card_DevCert and Host_DevCert. The manufacturer certificate is the XCA certificate that CHICA issues to the manufacturer of device certificates. It is used to issue device certificates and to verify them during binding. CHICA is the CableCARD–Host Interface Certificate Authority, root X.509 certificate administrator for X.509 certificates on the Card–Host interface identified under CHILA. CHILA is the CableCARD–Host Interface Licensing Agreement, formerly identified as PHILA. It covers the DFAST technology and specifies the Certificate Authority (CHICA).

Calculation of Copy Protection Key (CPKey)

The card and host each derive the CPKey based on random integers exchanged for this purpose and the binding specific secret DHKey and public AuthKey. The resulting CPKey is unique to the particular card–host pair and to the key session. Content encrypted with this key by the card will be useful only to its bound host.

The CPKey is changed/refreshed by calculating a new key based on new random integers generated by each device. The card initiates calculation of a new CPKey after its initial binding to a valid host, periodically by a refresh clock, at every power-up, on command by the CA system, and at every hard reset.

The card and host perform the following steps to generate the CPKey:

- The card checks for a valid AuthKey.
- The card generates its 64-bit random integer (N_Card).
- The card sends this N_Card and Card_ID in the clear to the host.
- The host generates its 64-bit random integer (N_Host).
- The host sends N_Host and its Host_ID in the clear to the card.
- The card shall check that the received Host_ID is equal to the previously stored Host_ID. If they are the same, the card shall proceed with the key generation process. Otherwise, the card shall CA decrypt only services with zero EMI.
- The card computes a CPKey for S-Mode and CPKeyA and CPKeyB for M-Mode, based on long-term keys and a newly exchanged random integer using the SHA-1 hash function and the DFAST algorithm.
- The host computes a CPKey for S-Mode and CPKeyA and CPKeyB for M-Mode, also based on long-term keys and a newly exchanged random integer using the SHA-1 hash function and the DFAST algorithm.

DFAST is the Dynamic Feedback Arrangement Scrambling Technique, a component of the encryption algorithm. The DFAST function accepts a 128-bit input value (Ks) and generates 56 bits of output (CPKey). SHA-1 is the Secure Hash Algorithm [41] for computing a condensed representation of a message or a data file. When a message of any length $<2^{64}$ bits is input, the SHA-1 produces a 160-bit output called a message digest.

The card operating in S-Mode and host shall each calculate the DFAST seed value, Ks, as

$$Ks = SHA\text{-}1 \, [AuthKey \mid DHKey \mid N\_Host \mid N\_Card] \, msb128.$$

The card operating in M-Mode and host shall each calculate the DFAST seed value, Ks, as

$$KsA = SHA\text{-}1 \, [AuthKey \mid DHKeylsb512 \mid N\_Host \mid N\_Card] \, msb128$$

$$KsB = SHA\text{-}1 \, [AuthKey \mid DHKeymsb512 \mid N\_Host \mid N\_Card] \, msb128$$

Truncating the 160-bit SHA-1 output to its 128 msb, left-most bits, generates a seed, Ks, with the proper 128-bit length for the input to the DFAST engine.

For S-Mode, the card and host shall apply the DFAST function to Ks to produce the CPKey:

$$CPKey = DFAST [Ks]$$

For M-Mode, the card and host shall apply the DFAST function to Ks to produce two Copy Protection Keys, CPKeyA and CPKeyB:

$$CPKeyA = DFAST [KsA] \text{ and } CPKeyB = DFAST [KsB]$$

Protection of the Interface between the card and the host

In S-Mode, the shared CPKey is used directly as $DESKey_0$ to initialize the DES processor in the card and host. In M-Mode, the card and host each generate a unique $DESKey_m$ for each current MPEG program by performing an XOR operation on the CPKey and the ECM PID | LTSID for the program to be encrypted or decrypted. The copy protection encryption algorithm shall be triple-DES in ECB (Electronic Codebook) mode. ECM PID is the Entitlement Control Message Packet Identifier, and LTSID is the Local Transport Stream ID, assigned by the host in M-Mode.

The card receives content from the host and processes it in one of the following four modes:

- **Clear**. No change of an in-the-clear, zero EMI, MPEG program. The program is returned to the host "in-the-clear."
- **Pass-through**. No change of a CA-encrypted MPEG program. The program is returned to the host unrecognizable.
- **CA-only**. CA-decrypts an MPEG program with zero EMI. The program is returned to the host "in-the-clear."
- **Rescramble**. CA-decrypts and CP-encrypts an MPEG program with non-zero EMI.

6.3 SUMMARY OF CA, DRM, AND CP SYSTEMS

We now summarize all the encryption-based protection systems for distribution and storage in Table 6.4. There are five classes of media: pre-recorded (optical or magnetic), digital interface, air (satellite and terrestrial broadcasting), cable (cable transmission), and the Internet.

Table 6.4:   CA, DRM, and CP systems.

Media protected		Secure delivery of content	Device authentication	Licensed technology	System renewability
Pre-recorded media	Video on DVD-ROM	Encryption	Mutual between DVD drive and PC	CSS	Device revocation
	Audio on DVD-ROM	Encryption	Mutual between DVD drive and PC	CPPM	Device revocation
	Video or audio on DVD-R/RW/RAM	Encryption	Mutual between DVD drive and PC	CPRM	Device revocation
Digital interface	Video on digital tape	Encryption	Transmitter authenticates receiver	HDCP	Device revocation
	IEEE 1394	Encryption	Mutual between source and sink	DTCP	Device revocation
	DVI	Encryption	Transmitter authenticates receiver	HDCP	Device revocation
	NRSS interface	Encryption	Mutual between host device and removable security device	Open standards	Service revocation
Broadcasting	Satellite	Encryption	Mutual between card and host	Conditional access system	Smartcard revocation
	Terrestrial	Encryption	Mutual between card and host	Conditional access system	Smartcard revocation
	Cable transmission	Encryption	Mutual between card and host	Conditional access system	Smartcard revocation
Internet	Unicast	Encryption	Receiver	DRM	Software update

REFERENCES

[1] R. de Bruin and J. Smits. *Digital Video Broadcasting: Technology, Standards and Regulations*, Artech House, Norwood, MA, 1999.

[2] W. Mooij. *Advances in Conditional Access Technology*, International Broadcasting Convention, IEE Conference Publication, No. 447, pp. 461–464, September 12–16, Amsterdam, Netherlands, 1997.

[3] A. M. Eskicioglu, J. Town, and E. J. Delp. Security of digital entertainment content from creation to consumption, *Signal Processing: Image Communication, Special Issue on Image Security*, 18(Issue 4):237–262, April 2003.

[4] Microsoft Windows Media DRM, available at http://www.microsoft.com/windows/windowsmedia/drm.aspx.

[5] Helix DRM, available at http://www.realnetworks.com/products/drm/index.html.

[6] Content Protection System Architecture (CPSA), available at http://www.4Centity.com.

[7] Content Scramble System, available at http://www.dvdcca.org.

[8] Content Protection for Prerecorded Media, available at http://www.4Centity.com.

[9] Content Protection for Recordable Media, available at http://www.4Centity.com.

[10] High Definition Copy Protection, available at http://www.jvc-victor.co.jp/english/products/vcr/D-security.html.

[11] Digital Transmission Content Protection, available at http://www.dtcp.com.

[12] High-Bandwidth Digital Content Protection, available at http://www.digital-CP.com.

[13] H. Benoit. Digital Television: MPEG-1, MPEG-2 and Principles of the DVB System, Arnold, Sevenoaks, 1997.

[14] L. C. Guillou and J. L. Giachetti. Encipherment and conditional access, *SMPTE J.*, 103(6):398–406, June 1994.

[15] W. Mooij. *Conditional Access Systems for Digital Television*, International Broadcasting Convention, IEE Conference Publication, No. 397, pp. 489–491, September 16–20, Amsterdam, Netherlands, 1994.

[16] B. M. Macq and J. J. Quisquater. Cryptology for digital TV broadcasting, *Proceedings of the IEEE*, Vol. 83, No. 6, p. 944–957, June 1995.

[17] G. Rossi. Conditional Access to Television Broadcast Programs: Technical Solutions, ABU Technical Review, No. 166, pp. 3–12, September–October 1996.

[18] D. Cutts. DVB conditional access, *Electronics and Communication Engineering J.*, 9(1):21–27, February 1997.

[19] A. M. Eskicioglu. A key transport protocol for conditional access systems, *Proc. SPIE Conf. Security and Watermarking of Multimedia Contents III*, San Jose, CA, pp. 139–148, January 2001.

[20] International Standard, *Information Technology—Generic Coding of Moving Pictures and Associated Audio Information: Systems, First Edition*, ISO-IEC 13818-1, 1996.

[21] J. Menezes, P. C. van Oorschot, and S. A. Vanstone. *Handbook of Applied Cryptography*, CRC Press, Boca Raton, FL, 1997.

[22] A. M. Eskicioglu and E. J. Delp. A key transport protocol based on secret sharing—applications to information security, *IEEE Trans. on Consumer Electronics*, 48(4):816–824, November 2002.

[23] EIA-679B National Renewable Security Standard, September 1998.

[24] Functional Model of a Conditional Access System, EBU Technical Review, No. 266, Winter 1995/6.

[25] ATSC Standard. Conditional Access System for Terrestrial Broadcast, Revision A, available at http://www.atsc.org/standards.html.

[26] Available at http://www.mpaa.org/Press/broadcast_flag_qa.htm.

[27] R. Perry, M. Ripley, and A. Setos. Final Report of the Co-Chairs of the Broadcast Protection Discussion Subgroup to the Copy Protection Technical Working Group, June 3, 2002.

[28] Federal Communications Commission. Report and Order and Further Notice of Proposed Rulemaking, November 4, 2003.

[29] Content Protection for Prerecorded Media Specification, "Introduction and Common Cryptographic Elements," Intel Corporation, International Business Machines Corporation, Matsushita Electric Industrial Co., Ltd., Toshiba Corporation, Revision 1.0, January 17, 2003.

[30] Content Protection for Prerecorded Media Specification, "DVD Book," Intel Corporation, International Business Machines Corporation, Matsushita Electric Industrial Co., Ltd., Toshiba Corporation, Revision 0.93, January 31, 2001.

[31] C2 Block Cipher Specification, Intel Corporation International Business Machines Corporation, Matsushita Electric Industrial Co., Ltd., Toshiba Corporation, Revision 1.0, January 17, 2003.

[32] 4C Entity, LLC, available at http://www.4centity.com.

[33] Content Protection for Recordable Media Specification, "Introduction and Common Cryptographic Elements," Intel Corporation, International Business Machines Corporation, Matsushita Electric Industrial Co., Ltd., Toshiba Corporation, Revision 1.0, January 17, 2003.

[34] Content Protection for Recordable Media Specification, "DVD Book," Intel Corporation, International Business Machines Corporation, Matsushita Electric Industrial Co., Ltd., Toshiba Corporation, Revision 0.96, January 31, 2003.

[35] 5C Digital Transmission Content Protection, White Paper, Hitachi, Ltd., Intel Corporation, Matsushita Electric Industrial, Co., Ltd., Sony Corporation, Toshiba Corporation, Revision 1.0, July 14, 1998.

[36] Digital Transmission Content Protection Specification, Volume 1 (Informational Version), Hitachi, Ltd., Intel Corporation, Matsushita Electric Industrial Co., Ltd., Sony Corporation, Toshiba Corporation, Revision 1.4, February 28, 2005.

[37] High-Bandwidth Digital Content Protection System, Revision 1.1, Digital Content Protection LLC, June 9, 2003.

[38] "Content Protection System Architecture: A Comprehensive Framework for Content Protection," Intel Corporation, International Business Machines Corporation, Matsushita Electric Industrial Co., Ltd., Toshiba Corporation, Revision 0.81, February 17, 2000.

[39] CableCARD™ Copy Protection 2.0 Specification, OC-SP-CCCP2.0-I02-050708, July 8, 2005.

[40] CableCARD™ Interface 2.0 Specification, OC-SP-CCIF2.0-I02-050708, July 8, 2005.

[41] Federal Information Processing Standards Publication 180-1, April 17, 1995.

7

An Overview of Digital Watermarking

N. Liu, P. Amin, A. Ambalavanan, and K.P. Subbalakshmi

7.1 INTRODUCTION

Data hiding (steganography) is the art of embedding data inside a host medium without substantially altering it. The art of data hiding has been used in several applications such as copyright protection, copy control, annotation, indexing, covert communications, etc. In early times, Greek messengers had messages tattooed into their shaved heads, concealing the message when their hair eventually grew back. In another example of data hiding, wax tablets were scraped down to bare wood where the message was engraved. Once the tablets were rewaxed, the hidden message was secure [1]. Over time, these primitive techniques improved, increasing the speed, capacity, and security of the transmitted message.

The general procedure for hiding a secret message in a host signal (e.g., digital image, video, audio, etc.) is as follows: a message m is embedded into a host signal c, sometimes using a key k (referred to as the stego-key), which results in the corresponding stego-object s. Clearly, to avoid detection by an adversary, the stego-object must be indistinguishable from the host c for an unauthorized interceptor. The intended receiver recovers the hidden message from the stego-object using the key k. It is assumed that the sender and the receiver exchange the key k using a secure channel. The message embedding process is shown in Figure 7.1.

Digital watermarking is a branch of digital steganography and can be used in a broad range of applications such as:

1. **Copyright protection**. A digital watermark embedded within the host signal can be retrieved later to assert the owner's copyright over the marked media.

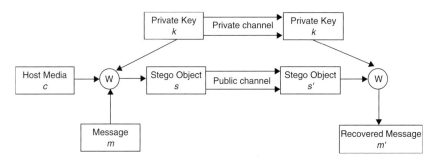

FIGURE 7.1:   Illustration of a steganographic system.

2. **Fingerprinting**. The owner of a digital content can choose to embed distinct watermarks within the content supplied to different customers. This method helps in identifying the customers that break license agreements by supplying the content illegally to unauthorized parties.

3. **Copy control**. A watermark can prevent illegal regeneration of copies of the marked data. The watermark can include a do-not-copy flag, and the watermark detector within the digital copying device detects this flag and therefore does not produce a copy of the marked media.

4. **Broadcast monitoring**. Commercial advertisements and other broadcast signals could carry tracking information in the form of hidden watermarks to monitor and verify the number of times the data has been broadcast. Hence, the customer can be charged accordingly.

5. **Unauthorized modification**. Fragile watermarks could be used to detect and highlight unauthorized modification to the protected data. These are weak watermarks and are designed to be destroyed in case of alteration of the marked data in an unauthorized manner.

6. **Annotation and indexing**. Watermarks can also be used to annotate and index digital data. These watermarks can be used by individuals as identifiers leading to the source of the marked data or by search engines to return the marked data in relevant Web searches.

7. **Medical applications**. Based on the regulations set by the Health Insurance Portability and Accountability Act [2], patient data are considered secure and are to be viewed by first-tier care providers only. The secure data can be embedded as a watermark within medical images, which can be extracted only by the authorized parties.

8. **Covert communications**. Watermarking can also be used as a means of transmitting hidden data. Since the actual evidence of hidden data transfer is missing in watermarking, this mode of covert data transfer can be

highly effective. Some researchers believe that covert communication, also known as steganography, is a branch of digital data hiding all by itself.

7.2 CLASSIFICATION OF WATERMARKING SCHEMES

Watermarking schemes can be classified into several groups, each of which serves a specific or a group of applications. We classify watermarking schemes based on watermark properties and watermarking domain.

7.2.1 Classification Based on Watermark Properties

Watermarking techniques can be classified based on several key properties such as robustness, security, complexity, imperceptibility, capacity, detection, etc.

a. Robustness is the ability of a watermark to withstand any intentional and/or unintentional attacks. Robust watermarks are designed to survive severe attacks and maintain the watermark's integrity [3–6]. Semi-fragile watermarks are designed to survive a group of selected attacks while ignoring other (mostly unintentional) attacks [7–9]. Fragile watermarks are used to identify any modification made to the host by making them sensitive to even the slightest modification to the host [10–12].

b. Security of a watermarking scheme is defined by its ability to stay undetected while in transit within a public channel. Visually secure watermarks are defined by their ability to not trigger any suspicion within an adversary following a visual inspection [13, 14]. Clearly, for visual security, the host and watermarked signals must be identical.

   Statistically secure watermarking schemes attempt to minimize the distortion induced to the probability density function (pdf) of the host signal [13, 15, 16]. Several steganalytic schemes exist that can detect the presence of a watermark by mathematical analysis of the marked host. Steganographically secure watermarking schemes belong to a group that may not be reliably detected by steganalysis [17–19].

c. The applicability of a watermarking scheme is directly dependent on its complexity. A watermarking scheme is desired to be as computationally simple as possible. Most watermarking schemes fall into this category. However, there exist some watermarking applications that necessitate the watermarking scheme to be computationally complex. At times, the applicability of a watermarking scheme is limited due to complexity [20, 21].

d. Watermarking schemes in visual media can also be classified based on whether they are visible [22–25] or invisible [26, 27]. For a number of applications such as copyright protection, copy control, illegal redistribution, etc., a watermark has to be invisible, whereas for applications such as indexing, annotation, etc., the watermark has to be embedded visibly over the host data.

e. Watermarking schemes differ in the achievable embedding capacity. A watermark can be as small as a single bit, which could be used for verification for the presence or absence of the watermark [15], although it is more common to have a much larger (more bits) watermark [28, 29]. Some watermarking schemes also employ multiple watermarking, where either the same watermark is inserted multiple times within the host to increase robustness or several watermarks are inserted within the host and, depending on the extracting party, one or more of them could be recovered. Most schemes measure capacity in terms of the number of bits that can be embedded for a given perceptual distortion criterion, where the perceptual distortion is measured as the mean squared error (MSE). However, other perceptual measure-based definitions are also possible [30, 31]. These capacity measures, however, ignore the security aspects of the hidden data. Chandramouli and Memon [32] address this drawback where they define a new capacity measure in terms of steganalysis detection probabilities.

f. Watermark schemes differ depending on the detection algorithm. A watermarking scheme that requires the presence of the unmarked host at the decoder falls into the category of a non-blind watermarking scheme. On the contrary, in a blind watermarking scheme only the marked data are required at the decoder. Based on the security requirements of the system, blind watermarking schemes can be public or private key-dependent [3–5]. In certain cases there are multiple distinct watermarks within one host, one or more of which could be decoded by one or more of the users combined.

In every watermarking scheme there exists a trade-off between the robustness, maximum allowable distortion to the host, and the embedding capacity. In the past, watermarking schemes have been proposed that use perceptually significant parts of the host to embed data in a robust manner [14, 22]. In more recent works, perceptual models have been used for adaptive watermarking [33, 34].

7.2.2 Classification Based on Watermarking Domain

Based on different types of applications of a watermark, the schemes can be classified based on the watermarking domain.

a. The earlier works in watermarking, such as least significant bit (LSB) replacement scheme [35], patchwork scheme [36], spatial quantizer scheme [37], etc., were defined in the spatial domain. Although spatial domain-based schemes have the advantage of being computationally less complex, they are generally less secure and robust.

b. Frequency domain watermarking has the potential to offer better robustness and security since it is easier to analyze the host to determine importance ordering in this domain. Several popular transforms used for this purpose are the discrete cosine transform (DCT) [22], the discrete Fourier transform (DFT) [15], the discrete wavelet transform (DWT) [8], etc. In fact, in a recent work by Amin and Subbalakshmi [6], it was shown that the Zernike moment transform can be used to increase robustness against rotation attacks.

7.3 TOOLS AND MATHEMATICAL BACKGROUND

Next, we discuss some basic mathematical tools used in the design and performance analysis of digital watermarking techniques.

7.3.1 Information Theory

Here, we introduce some basic theoretic ideas used in data hiding. We refer to Cover and Thomas [38] for more details. The entropy $H(X)$ of a discrete random variable X defined on a set $\mathcal{X}$ is given by,

$$H(X) = - \sum_{x \in \mathcal{X}} p(x) \log p(x). \tag{7.1}$$

If

$$X = \begin{cases} 1 & \text{with probability } p \\ 0 & \text{with probability } 1 - p, \end{cases} \tag{7.2}$$

then

$$H(X) = -p \log p - (1 - p) \log(1 - p) \equiv H(p). \tag{7.3}$$

The mutual information between two random variables X and Y is defined as

$$I(X; Y) = \sum_{x \in \mathcal{X}} \sum_{y \in \mathcal{Y}} p(x, y) \log \frac{p(x, y)}{p(x)p(y)}. \tag{7.4}$$

If $X \rightarrow Y \rightarrow Z$ forms a Markov chain, then $I(X; Y) \geq I(X; Z)$.

The channel capacity of a discrete memoryless channel as shown in Figure 7.2 is given by

$$C = \max_{p(x)} I(X; Y). \tag{7.5}$$

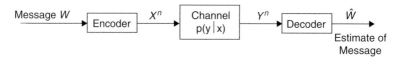

FIGURE 7.2:   A general communication system.

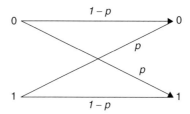

FIGURE 7.3:   Binary symmetric channel.

For a binary symmetric channel (BSC) as shown in Figure 7.3,

$$I(X; Y) = H(Y) - H(Y|X) \tag{7.6}$$

$$= H(Y) - \sum p(x)H(Y|X = x) \tag{7.7}$$

$$= H(Y) - \sum p(x)H(p) \tag{7.8}$$

$$= H(Y) - H(p) \tag{7.9}$$

$$\leq 1 - H(p). \tag{7.10}$$

Therefore, the capacity of the symmetric channel is

$$C = 1 - H(p) \text{ bits.} \tag{7.11}$$

7.3.2   Quantization

Quantization is the process of representing a large set of values with a much smaller set. In practice, the quantizer consists of two mappings: an encoder mapping and a decoder mapping. The encoder divides the range of values that the source generates into a number of intervals. Each interval is represented by a distinct codeword. The encoder represents all the source outputs that fall into a particular interval by the codeword representing that interval. Knowing the code only tells us the

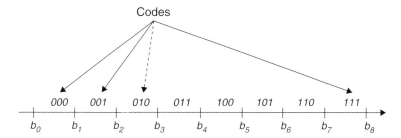

FIGURE 7.4: An example for 3-bit encoder mapping of a quantizer.

interval to which the sample value belongs; it does not tell us the actual sample value. Figure 7.4 shows an example for 3-bit encoder mapping.

For every codeword generated by the encoder, the decoder generates a reconstruction value, such as the midpoint of the interval, to represent all values in the entire interval. A decoder mapping corresponding to the 3-bit encoder in Figure 7.4 is shown in Table 7.1.

Suppose we have an input modeled by a random variable X with pdf $f_X(x)$. If we wished to quantize this source using a quantizer with M intervals we would have to specify $M + 1$ endpoints for the intervals and a representative value for each of the M intervals. The endpoints of the intervals are known as decision boundaries, while the representative values are called reconstruction points. The quantization

Table 7.1: 3-bit decoder mapping of a quantizer.

Input codes	Output
000	$\frac{b_0+b_1}{2}$
001	$\frac{b_1+b_2}{2}$
010	$\frac{b_2+b_3}{2}$
011	$\frac{b_3+b_4}{2}$
100	$\frac{b_4+b_5}{2}$
101	$\frac{b_5+b_6}{2}$
110	$\frac{b_6+b_7}{2}$
111	$\frac{b_7+b_8}{2}$

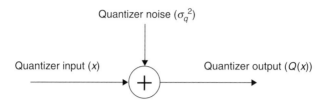

FIGURE 7.5: Additive noise model of a quantizer.

operation of x is given by

$$Q(x) = y_i \qquad if \quad b_{i-1} < x \le b_i, \tag{7.12}$$

where $\{b_i\}_{i=0}^M$ represents the decision boundaries, $\{y_i\}_{i=1}^M$ represents the reconstruction points, and $Q(\cdot)$ represents the quantization operation.

Then, the quantization distortion defined as the mean squared quantization error, σ_q^2, is given by

$$\sigma_q^2 = \int_{-\infty}^{+\infty} (x - Q(x))^2 f_X(x) dx$$

$$= \sum_{i=1}^{M} \int_{b_{i-1}}^{b_i} (x - y_i)^2 f_X(x) dx. \tag{7.13}$$

For a high-rate quantizer, the quantization error can be closely approximated as an additive noise process as shown in Figure 7.5. In this model, the quantization distortion is called *quantization noise*.

7.3.3 Frequency Domain Processing: Transforms

Frequency domain-based watermarking techniques have been well studied [14, 39–42]. Unlike spatial techniques, these provide the user with an option to embed the hidden data in certain regions of the image that are less sensitive to minor distortions and at the same time are important enough to survive general lossy compression schemes.

In this section, we use the example of the two-dimensional discrete cosine transform (2D-DCT). The DCT coefficients of digital images have interesting properties that could be exploited to obtain good hidden data imperceptibility and fidelity. The most important property of the DCT is energy compaction. It has been shown that the DCT performs as well as the Karhunen-Loeve transform (KLT) for certain images that could be statistically modeled as first-order

Markov processes [43]. The $M \times N$ DCT is an invertible transform, and the forward and inverse transforms take the following form:

$$A_{mn} = \sum_{p=0}^{M-1} \sum_{q=0}^{N-1} \alpha_p \alpha_q B_{pq} \cos\left(\frac{\pi(2m+1)p}{2M}\right) \cos\left(\frac{\pi(2n+1)q}{2N}\right), \quad (7.14)$$

where $0 < m < M - 1$ and $0 \le n \le N - 1$.

Here, α_p and α_q are defined as

$$\alpha_p = \begin{cases} 1/\sqrt{M} & \text{if} \quad p = 0 \\ \sqrt{(2/M)} & \text{if} \quad 1 \le p \le M - 1, \end{cases} \quad (7.15)$$

and

$$\alpha_q = \begin{cases} 1/\sqrt{N} & \text{if} \quad q = 0 \\ \sqrt{(2/N)} & \text{if} \quad 1 \le q \le N - 1. \end{cases} \quad (7.16)$$

Studies have shown that a good model for the DCT coefficients is the generalized Gaussian pdf, given by

$$f_x(X) = Ae^{-|\beta x|^C}, \quad (7.17)$$

where A and β can both be expressed as functions of C and the standard deviation σ as given below,

$$\beta = \frac{1}{\sigma}\left(\frac{\Gamma(3/C)}{\Gamma(1/C)}\right) \quad (7.18)$$

$$A = \left(\frac{\beta C}{2\Gamma(1/C)}\right). \quad (7.19)$$

We note that the Gaussian as well as the Laplacian distributions are special cases of the equations above with $c = 2$ and $c = 1$, respectively. The low-frequency DCT coefficients are reasonably well modeled by a generalized Gaussian distribution with $c = 1/2$. However, mid-frequency coefficients are better modeled by the Laplacian distribution. Also, it can be assumed that the samples of the DCT coefficients at the same frequency, in different blocks, are statistically independent [44]. The statistical characterization of the DCT coefficients of an image is valuable information to the decoder; however, since the original image may be unknown to the decoder, this information usually has to be estimated from the watermarked image.

7.4   DATA HIDING WITH SIDE INFORMATION

A data hiding scheme can be considered as a communication scheme and can be divided into two types: *private data hiding*, in which the host data are available at both the encoder and the decoder, and *blind data hiding*, in which the host data are available only at the encoder. We will concentrate on blind data hiding due to its wider applicability. Strictly speaking, no side information is available at the decoder for blind data hiding. However, if the side information is cryptographic key-like data independent of the host, the concerned application is still referred to as blind data hiding in the literature.

7.4.1   Information-Theoretic Analysis of Blind Data Hiding

Gelfand and Pinsker [45] derived the capacity of a fixed discrete memoryless channel with the channel state, T, known at the encoder but not at the decoder, given by

$$C = \max_{p(u,x|s)} [I(G;Y) - I(G;T)]. \tag{7.20}$$

Here, G denotes a finite alphabet auxiliary random variable, Y denotes the signal received at the decoder, and X denotes the encoded signal needed to be sent. Costa [46] proposed a special power constraint communication scheme with side information available at the encoder. The generic ideal Costa scheme is shown in Figure 7.6, where W represents the watermark; S is the Gaussian distributed $\mathcal{N}(0, QI)$ host signal; Z is Gaussian noise, $\mathcal{N}(0, N)$; $X \in R^n$ is the watermarking signal to be embedded; U is the stego-image; Y is the received stego-image; and $\hat{W}$ is the decoded watermark. X has a power constraint given by $\frac{1}{n} \sum_{i=1}^{n} X_i^2 \leq P$. Based on the result of Gelfand and Pinsker [45], Costa [46] showed that the data hiding capacity for such a scheme is

$$C^* = \frac{1}{2} \ln \left(1 + \frac{P}{N} \right), \tag{7.21}$$

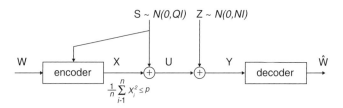

FIGURE 7.6:   The generic ideal Costa watermarking scheme.

where N is the variance of Gaussian noise. This result shows that this capacity is the same whether or not the side information is known at the decoder.

In the ideal Costa scheme, the objective is to compute the stego-image U as $U = X + \alpha \cdot S$, where X is power constrained and orthogonal to the host image S and where α is a scaling factor. Typically, in image data hiding α is chosen to lie in the interval (0,1]. Therefore, the encoder must conduct a brute force search for the sequence $X = U - \alpha \cdot S$ which is nearly orthogonal to S. According to Costa, the probability of a successful search approaches one as $n \to \infty$. In other words, there always exists some n-dimensional power constrained watermarking signal X which is nearly orthogonal to host image S. At the encoder, X is chosen such that (X, U, S) is jointly typical[1] and added to the scaled version of the host image. The scaling factor α is channel optimized. The decoder looks for the unique sequence U such that (U, Y) is jointly typical. The embedding rate $R(\alpha)$ is a function of scaling factor α and is shown to be [46]

$$R(\alpha) = \frac{1}{2} \log_2 \frac{P \cdot (P + \sigma_S^2) + \sigma_Z^2}{P \cdot \sigma_S^2 (1 - \alpha)^2 + \sigma_Z^2 \cdot (P + \alpha^2 \sigma_S^2)}, \qquad (7.22)$$

where σ_S^2 is the variance of the host image, and σ_Z^2 is the variance of the Gaussian attack. The attack optimized value of α, say, α^*, that maximizes $R(\alpha)$ is given by $\alpha^* = \frac{P}{P + \sigma_Z^2}$. We note that because of the brute force search involved in determining U, the stego-image, and the extra large size of the codebook, the ideal Costa scheme is impractical.

Moulin and O'Sullivan [47] made a comprehensive information-theoretic analysis of data hiding and showed that the achievable rate of reliable transmission is the same for private data hiding and blind information hiding. Based on the framework of the blind data hiding game in Figure 7.7, the hiding capacity was shown to be [47]

$$C_G = \frac{1}{2} \log \left(1 + \frac{[(2a^* - 1)\sigma^2 - D_2 + D_1][D_1 - (a^* - 1)^2 \sigma^2]}{[D_1 + (2a^* - 1)\sigma^2]D_2} \right), \qquad (7.23)$$

where $S = \mathcal{N}(0, \sigma^2)$, $D_2 < \left(\sigma + \sqrt{D_2}\right)^2$, and $a^* = \arg \max f(a)$, where

$$f(a) = \frac{[(2a - 1)\sigma^2 - D_2 + D_1][D_1 - (a - 1)^2 \sigma^2]}{[D_1 + (2a - 1)\sigma^2]D_2} \qquad (7.24)$$

---

[1] "The set $A_\epsilon^{(n)}$ of jointly typical sequences $\{(x^n, y^n)\}$ with respect to the distribution $p(x, y)$ is the set of n-sequences with empirical entropies ϵ-close to the true entropies." For more details, refer to Cover and Thomas [38].

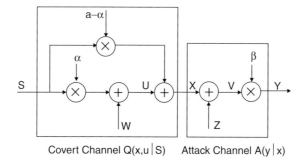

FIGURE 7.7:   The framework of a data hiding game.

in the interval $(a_{inf}, 1 + \sqrt{D_1}/\sigma)$.

$$a_{inf} = \max\left(1, \frac{\sigma^2 + D_2 - D_1}{2\sigma^2}\right). \tag{7.25}$$

Here, $X = aS + W$ and $U = \alpha S + W$, where $W \sim \mathcal{N}(0, D_1 - (a-1)^2\sigma^2)$ is independent of S. The optimal attack $A(y|x)$ is the Gaussian test channel.

$$A^*(y|x) = \mathcal{N}(\beta^{-1}x, \beta^{-1}D_2), \tag{7.26}$$

where

$$\beta = \frac{(2a-1)\sigma^2 + D_1}{(2a-1)\sigma^2 - (D_2 - D_1)} \tag{7.27}$$

$$\alpha = \frac{D_1 - (a-1)^2\sigma^2}{D_1 - (a-1)^2\sigma^2 + \beta D_2}. \tag{7.28}$$

If S is non-Gaussian with mean zero and variance σ^2, Equation 7.23 is an upper bound on the hiding capacity.

7.4.2   Classification of Blind Data Hiding

Based on the theoretical analysis above, several researchers have proposed sub-optimal, but practical schemes. For example, Chou et al. [48] proposed a practical data embedding algorithm based on the duality between distributed source coding with side information known at the decoder and channel coding with side information known at the encoder. All blind data hiding falls into two types [49]:

1. **Type I embedding.** It refers to additive schemes in which the watermark signal is added to the host signal to form the stego-signal. We can also call this type *additive embedding*, such as additive spread spectrum watermarking, which works well when channel noise is very strong. In these methods, the host signal acts as a source of interference, and since Type I schemes are not interference rejecting, this poses restrictions on attaining capacity. We discuss details in Section 7.7.2.

2. **Type II embedding.** The signal space is partitioned into intervals, each of which is mapped to the set of values taken by the data to be embedded. This type can also be called *quantization-based data hiding*. Type II embedding achieves capacity when the channel signal-to-noise ratio (SNR) is high and has the property of host image interference rejection, similar to the ideal Costa scheme (ICS).

7.5   QUANTIZATION-BASED DATA HIDING

7.5.1   Basic Quantization-Based Data Hiding Scheme

Chen and Wornell [50] proposed a quantization index modulation (QIM) method for watermarking, where the embedding algorithm essentially switches between two uniform quantizers depending upon whether a "1" or a "0" needs to be embedded. Figure 7.8 is a basic QIM scheme in the two-dimensional (2-D) case. In this figure, the numbered points represent the host image taken as a 2-D vector, the square regions represent the quantizer bins (or Voronoi regions [51]), and the unfilled circles represent the reconstruction points corresponding to the embedding of certain bit vectors. Let the distance between these reconstruction points be Δ. The arrows, along with the corresponding embedded bit vectors, are also depicted in Figure 7.8. The set of points obtained by perturbing each representation point by a given vector is called a coset. Hence, in this example, there is one coset corresponding to each of the embedded bit vectors (1,1), (1,0), (0,0), and (0,1). Therefore, we see that in the 2-D extension to QIM, the embedding region is the same as the Voronoi region. Hence, embedding a specific vector amounts to quantizing the host vector by the corresponding coset. For example, to embed the bit vector (1,1) in the host vector point marked by 1 in the inset in Figure 7.8, we would perturb the host vector to the position indicated by the thin solid arrow (perturbation vector corresponding to vector (1,1)). The distortion caused by embedding is equal to the square of the distance between these two points. The average distortion per embedded bit, D_w, of the embedding algorithm will depend on the distribution of the host vector within the embedding region.

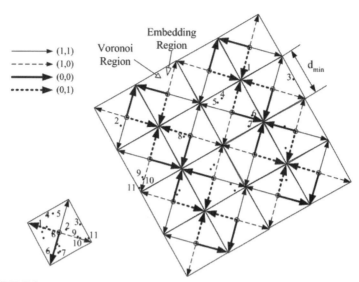

FIGURE 7.8:   The 2-D QIM scheme.

Chen and Wornell [52] define the normalized minimum distance, $d_{min-norm}$, as

$$d^2_{min-norm} \equiv \frac{d^2_{min}}{D_w}, \qquad (7.29)$$

which determines the embedding efficiency of the quantization-based scheme. Here, d_{min} is the minimum distance between cosets. This d_{min} is similar to the concept of minimum distance in classical error correcting codes.

They also prove that the embedding efficiency is

$$d^2_{min-norm-QIM} = 3 \qquad (7.30)$$

for the QIM scheme, which is greater than $d^2_{min-norm-LB}$ for the least important bit replacement (LB) technique.

7.5.2   Distortion Compensation

Inspired by Costa's idea [46], several authors of quantizer-based schemes have proposed *distortion compensation* to improve the performance of their schemes in the rate-distortion-robustness sense, which can also be called post-quantization processing. Chen and Wornell [52] proposed a distortion compensation scheme for the QIM method, where the scaling factor α was changed according to the attack variance. Ramkumar and Akansu [53] proposed thresholding type post-processing.

Hernandez et al. [54] proposed subtracting the processing distortion factor X_t from the embedded signal X. X_t is obtained by transforming X into a zero-mean Gaussian distributed random variable with a variance of σ_v^2, $X_t = -\sigma_v Q^{-1}\left(\frac{X+\frac{\Delta}{2}}{\Delta}\right)$, where $Q^{-1}(\cdot)$ is the inverse Gaussian Q-function.

The basic idea for distortion compensation is as follows. To embed one bit $m \in \{0, 1\}$ in host signal s, we need to define the embedding function $f(s, m)$:

$$f(s, m) = Q(\alpha s + (-1)^m z - d) + (1 - \alpha)s - (-1)^m z + d. \qquad (7.31)$$

Here, $Q(\cdot)$ denotes the uniform scalar quantizer with step size Δ, and $\alpha \in (0, 1]$ is the parameter to be optimized. z and d are dither values shared by the information hider and the extractor. z is bipolar in $\{\pm\frac{\Delta}{4}\}$, and d is uniformly distributed in $(0, \Delta]$, $d \sim U(0, \Delta]$. Then, based on all parameters of the data hiding scheme and the given attack, we can get the expression of the bit error rate (BER). Finally, we try to minimize the BER over α for a certain watermark-to-noise ratio (WNR).

For different attacks, the optimal solution of distortion compensation will be different. Here, we introduce three optimal solutions for Gaussian attack, JPEG attack, and optimal attack, respectively.

Gaussian Attack

Chen and Wornell [52] used the optimal α^* derived by Costa [46] in their QIM scheme:

$$\alpha_{ICS}^* = \frac{\sigma_w^2}{\sigma_w^2 + \sigma_n^2}. \qquad (7.32)$$

The ICS assumed that the watermarking signal $W \sim \mathcal{N}(0, \sigma_w^2)$. However, for the QIM scheme [52], the watermarking signal W is uniformly distributed. So α_{ICS}^* could not be optimal for uniform quantization-based schemes. Eggers et al. [55] gave a complete performance analysis of the scalar Costa scheme (SCS) and found the optimal scaling factor for uniform quantization-based schemes:

$$\alpha_{SCS}^* = \sqrt{\frac{\sigma_w^2}{\sigma_w^2 + 2.71\sigma_n^2}}. \qquad (7.33)$$

The corresponding step size of quantizer used for embedding, Δ_{SCS}, is given by

$$\Delta_{SCS}^* = \sqrt{12\sigma_w^2 + 2.71\sigma_n^2}. \qquad (7.34)$$

Experimental result showed that the SCS can achieve higher capacity than QIM.

JPEG Attack

Ramkumar and Akansu [56] estimated the hiding capacity for general compressing attacks. However, their analysis is based on additive embedding methods, so the host signal acts as a source of interference. In the future, if one can design a host-interference-rejecting algorithm optimal for a JPEG attack, the achieved capacity could be higher than the estimated capacity in Ramkumar and Akansu [56].

Optimal Attack

Goteti and Moulin [57] built up a QIM watermarking game between the Distortion Compensation (DC) factor α of DC-QIM and the pdf of attack noise p_W. Based on the Bhattacharyya bound on BER P_e, they derived the optimal α^* for worst-case p_W and the corresponding optimal *pdf* of attack, p_W^*. However, because the solution is based on the analysis of the upper bound of P_e, not P_e itself, it is not an optimal solution, but a numeric sub-optimal result.

As a matter of fact, there isn't yet any optimal solution for quantization-based schemes over an optimal attack.

7.5.3 Adaptive Embedding

There exists a gap between a non-adaptive embedding scheme and ideal theoretical capacity at the entire WNR range. Therefore, using the side information of partial host signal at the decoder, one can design an adaptive embedding scheme to achieve higher capacity. Voloshynovskiy et al. [58] proposed an estimation-subtracting (ES) approach which estimates the interference signal and subtracts it from the stego-data. Assuming a maximum a posteriori (MAP) estimate of the host data, one can derive the resulting capacity:

$$C = \frac{1}{2} \log \frac{\sigma_w^2}{\sigma_e^2 + \sigma_n^2}, \tag{7.35}$$

where $\sigma_e^2 = \frac{\sigma_x^2 \sigma_z^2}{\sigma_x^2 + \sigma_z^2}$ and $\sigma_z^2 = \sigma_w^2 + \sigma_n^2$. The ES scheme has a higher capacity for very low WNR regimes, and the difference is negligible for WNR <-10 dB. Therefore, this scheme has superior performance in comparison to the SCS in this regime. However, the ES scheme uses additive embedding, so it cannot be host interference-rejecting. In Figure 7.9, A is a representation point of the quantizer for embedding a bit 1, while B is the representation point of the quantizer for embedding a bit 0. The region between A and B is the embedding region, and C is the pixel value of the host image. Let the distance between A and B be the minimum distance between these two quantizers (d_{min}). Assume w is the bit to be embedded. Let w be uniformly distributed (i.e., $\Pr(w = 1) = \Pr(w = 0) = \frac{1}{2}$).

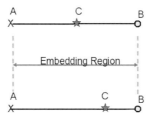

FIGURE 7.9: The embedding region in one dimension.

Let D_{w0} and D_{w1} represent the distortion caused by embedding a 0 and 1. Then the average distortion due to embedding (D_w) is

$$D_w = D_{w0} \Pr(w = 0) + D_{w1} \Pr(w = 1); \tag{7.36}$$

$$D_{w0} = \|AC\|^2, D_{w1} = \|BC\|^2. \tag{7.37}$$

From Equations 7.36 and 7.37, $D_w = \frac{1}{2} * (\|AC\|^2 + \|BC\|^2)$ for equiprobable 1 and 0 in the hidden data. Also, D_w is minimized if and only if $\|AC\| = \|BC\|$. This implies that to achieve minimum embedding-induced distortion, the host vector (one-dimensional) must lie at the center of the embedding region. If this ideal case is not possible, the host vector *pdf* must have a peak at the center of the embedding region. The maximum value of $d^2_{\min-\text{norm}}$ ($d^2_{\min-\text{norm}}{}^*$) is attained when D_w is at a minimum (D_w^*) and is given by

$$d^2_{\min-\text{norm}}{}^* = \frac{\|AB\|^2}{0.5 * \left(\frac{\|AB\|^2}{4} + \frac{\|AB\|^2}{4} \right)} = 4. \tag{7.38}$$

That means that when host vector C lies at the center of the embedding region, we get the best embedding efficiency. The efficiency of the embedding scheme for a non-uniformly distributed host vector will lie between 3 and 4. Comparing Equation 7.38 with 7.39, we can see that there exists a gap in embedding efficiency between QIM and the ideal quantization-based data hiding scheme.

Based on the analysis above, Liu and Subbalakshmi [59–61] proposed a special *pdf*-matched quantizer for embedding, which was observed experimentally to be able to have less embedding-caused distortion for the same embedding rate, while not reducing the robustness of the embedded data than that of uniform quantizer-based schemes.

7.6 LOSSLESS WATERMARKING

The watermark embedded in the host, though not perceptible to the human visual system, introduces some loss in the fidelity of the host signal. Some critical applications such as authenticating medical and military data do not allow even a small amount of loss in fidelity of the original data. To cater to such applications the watermark should be embedded in such a way that the original cover medium is restored in its entirety after the removal of the watermark. Such watermarking techniques are termed lossless, invertible, or erasable watermarking techniques. These form a category under fragile watermarking schemes, where the purpose of watermarking is for content authentication rather than copyright protection. In some cases, such as tamper detection, it is quite useful to embed a fragile watermark, as the watermarked image could be deemed as tampered if the watermark is distorted at the receiver end.

Some of the initial watermarking techniques [62] added a spatial additive watermark (w) to the original image (I) using addition modulo 256 to form the watermarked version I_w,

$$I_w = I + w \bmod 256.$$

The watermark pattern w is calculated by applying a hash function on the payload bits. The purpose of using modulo arithmetic is to combat the overflow/underflow of the digital representation of the data. The drawback of using modulo operation is that it results in visual distortions. To combat the visual distortions, Fridrich, Goljan, and Du [63] proposed a watermarking technique where less significant bitplanes were compressed using lossless data compression techniques, thereby creating space to append the watermark. These modified bitplanes are then replaced in the original image.

An improvisation of the same technique was done in Fridrich, Goljan, and Du [64], where an invertible operation $F(\cdot)$ termed flipping, with the property that $F(F(x)) = x$. If we denote small groups of adjacent pixels by G, then they can be categorized into regular, singular, and unusable as follows:

- Regular (R): $F(f(G)) > f(G)$
- Singular (S): $F(f(G)) < f(G)$
- Unusable, otherwise,

where f($\cdot$) is a discriminating function capturing the smoothness of the group. To begin with the embedding process, R and S groups are assigned a 0 or 1. The image is scanned in a pre-defined order. If the status of the group matches the bit to be embedded, it is left unaltered; otherwise, using the flipping operation they are made to match the watermark bit. To enable recovery the original status of the pixel groups are compressed and included in the embedded payload. This method of watermarking can be extended to all image formats [65]. Though we get a perfect recovery of the original image, this method also suffers from a low embedding capacity, and it is dependent on the scan order, the way the pixels are grouped, and the flipping function.

In all the RS-based embedding methods, the optimum size of the group of pixels is 4, which achieves the theoretical embedding capacity of 0.25 bits/pixel. In practice, the achievable embedding rate is less than 0.25 bits/pixel because of the overhead involved in sending the side information of the modified RS groups to the decoder.

Theoretical limits on the achievable capacity in a reversible watermarking algorithm were given by Kalker and Willems [66], where they showed that the capacity obtained from the above methods was not optimal. An improvement in embedding capacity can be achieved through a variation of the LSB embedding technique [67], where the lowest L levels of the signal sample are replaced in the space created from the compression of the signal using an L-level scalar quantizer. During extraction, the watermark data are extracted by reading the lowest L levels of the watermarked signal. The higher capacity achieved from this method is attributed to the embedding strategy employed.

Tian [68] proposed a high-capacity lossless data embedding using *difference expansion*. In this method the image is divided into pairs of neighboring pixels, and one bit is embedded in the difference of *qualified* pairs of pixels. A pair is termed qualified if the embedding operation does not result in overflow/underflow. Though this method offers high capacity, the drawbacks of this method are identifying the qualified pairs in which the message can be appended and the overhead cost involved in adding the compressed bitstream of embedded locations to the watermarked data.

7.7   FREQUENCY DOMAIN WATERMARKING

An advantage of the spatial techniques discussed above is that they can be easily applied to any image, regardless of subsequent processing (whether they survive this processing, however, is a different matter entirely). A disadvantage of the spatial domain techniques is that they do not allow subsequent processing in order to increase the robustness of the watermark. In addition to this, adaptive watermarking techniques are a bit more difficult in the spatial domain. Both the robustness and security of the watermark could be improved if the properties of the cover image could be exploited. For instance, it is generally preferable to hide watermark information in noisy regions and edges of images rather than in smoother regions. The benefit is twofold: degradation in smoother regions of an image is more noticeable to the Human Visual System (HVS) and becomes a prime target for lossy compression schemes; on the contrary, degradation in noisy regions is not as noticeable, and noisy regions are not much affected by lossy compression.

Taking these aspects into consideration, working in the frequency domain becomes very attractive. The classic and still most popular domain for image processing is that of the DCT [14]. The DCT allows an image to be broken up into different frequency bands, making it much easier to embed watermarking information into the middle frequency bands of an image. The middle frequency bands are chosen because they avoid the most visually important parts of the image (low frequencies) without overexposing themselves to removal through compression and noise attacks [69].

7.7.1   Comparison-Based Watermarking

Let us denote the low-band, mid-band, and high-band frequency coefficients of an 8×8 DCT block by F_L, F_M, and F_H, respectively, as shown in Figure 7.10. F_M is chosen as the embedding region so as to provide additional resistance to lossy compression, while avoiding significant modification of the cover image [42].

Now, two locations, $B_i(u_1, v_1)$ and $B_i(u_2, v_2)$, are chosen from the F_M region for comparison. Rather than arbitrarily choosing these locations, extra robustness to compression can be achieved if we base the choice of coefficients on the recommended JPEG quantization table shown in Table 7.2. If two locations are chosen such that they have identical quantization values, we can feel confident that any scaling of one coefficient will scale the other coefficient by the same factor, thus preserving their relative size.

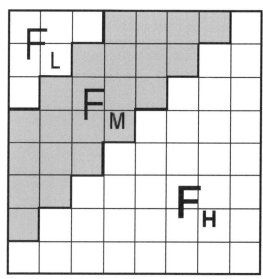

FIGURE 7.10:   DCT bands.

Table 7.2: JPEG quantization table.

16	11	10	16	24	40	51	61
12	12	14	19	26	58	60	55
14	13	16	24	40	57	69	56
14	17	22	29	51	87	80	62
18	22	37	56	68	109	103	77
24	35	55	64	81	104	113	92
49	64	78	87	103	121	120	101
72	92	95	98	112	100	103	99

Based on Table 7.2, we can observe that coefficients (4,1) and (3,2) or (1,2) and (3,0) would make suitable candidates for comparison, as their quantization values are equal. The DCT block will encode a 1 if $B_i(u_1, v_1) > B_i(u_2, v_2)$; otherwise, it will encode a 0. The coefficients are then swapped if the relative size of each coefficient does not agree with the bit that is to be encoded [70].

The swapping of such coefficients should not alter the watermarked image significantly, as it is generally observed that DCT coefficients of middle frequencies have similar magnitudes. The robustness of the watermark can be improved by introducing a watermark "strength" constant k, such that $B_i(u_1, v_1) - B_i(u_2, v_2) > k$. Coefficients that do not meet these criteria are modified through the use of random noise to satisfy the relation. Increasing k thus reduces the chance of detection errors at the expense of additional host image degradation [70].

7.7.2 Spread Spectrum-based Watermarking

Another possible technique is to embed a pseudo-random noise (PN) sequence W into the middle frequencies of the DCT block. We can modulate a given DCT block (x, y) using the following equation:

$$I_{W_{x,y}}(u, v) = \begin{cases} I_{x,y}(u, v) + kW_{x,y}(u, v), & \text{if } u, v \in F_M \\ I_{x,y}(u, v), & \text{otherwise.} \end{cases} \qquad (7.39)$$

For each 8×8 block of the image, the DCT for the block is first calculated. In that block, the middle frequency components F_M are added to a PN sequence W, multiplied by a gain factor k. Coefficients in the low and high frequencies are copied over to the transformed image unaffected. Each block is then inverse transformed to give us our final watermarked image I_W [69].

The watermarking procedure can be made somewhat more adaptive by slightly altering the embedding process as follows:

$$I_{W_{x,y}}(u, v) = \begin{cases} I_{x,y}(u, v)(1 + kW_{x,y}(u, v)), & \text{if } u, v \in F_M \\ I_{x,y}(u, v), & \text{otherwise.} \end{cases} \qquad (7.40)$$

This slight modification scales the strength of the watermarking based on the size of the particular coefficients being used. Larger k's can thus be used for coefficients of higher magnitude, hence strengthening the watermark in regions that can afford it and weakening it in those that cannot [69].

For detection, the image is broken up into those same 8×8 blocks, and a forward DCT is performed. The same PN sequence is then compared to the middle frequency values of the transformed block. If the correlation between the sequences exceeds a preset threshold T, a 1 is detected for that block; otherwise, a 0 is detected. Again, k denotes the strength of the watermarking, where increasing k increases the robustness of the watermark at the expense of added distortion to the host.

7.8   SECURITY AND ROBUSTNESS

An important property of a watermarking scheme is its robustness with respect to intentional and unintentional image distortions. This means that the watermark should be intact within the images that underwent common image processing operations, such as filtering, lossy compression, noise adding, histogram manipulation, and various geometrical transformations. Watermarks designed for copyright protection, fingerprinting, or access control must also be embedded in a secure manner. This means that an attacker who knows all the details of the embedding-extracting algorithms except the private key should not be able to detect or extract the watermark. In other applications, such as adding captions to images or subtitles to videos, there is not much motivation for intentional removal of the watermark, and the embedding/detecting key can be made public. Capacity and robustness are two important properties, and there always exists a trade-off between the two.

The robustness is directly related to the watermark extraction statistics. A majority of watermarking schemes are based on correlation between an extracted vector and a pseudo-random sequence. A preset threshold is set in order to verify detection. With decreasing threshold the probability of missed detections also decreases and the robustness increases, but at the same time, the rate of false detections will also increase. For some watermarking schemes, under simplified conditions one can actually derive the appropriate value of the threshold [71], or a set of numerical experiments can be done to estimate the probability distribution of the correlations.

Watermarking schemes that use an adaptive threshold [71] should be converted to a fixed threshold by dividing the correlation by the threshold.

The robustness is usually tested using typical image processing operations that can be divided into two groups: gray-scale manipulations (filtering, noise adding, lossy compression, gamma correction, color quantization, color truncation to a finite palette, etc.) and geometric transformations (scaling, cropping, rotation, affine transforms, and general rubber sheet deformations of StirMark [72]). It is significantly easier to achieve robustness with respect to gray-scale transformations than to geometrical transformations. The vast majority of watermarking schemes embed the watermark by modifying the gray scales while leaving the image geometry untouched. We can say that geometric transformations do not erase watermarks, but do make the detection difficult if not entirely impossible. In theory, for any combination of rotation, translation, and scale, if an extensive search is applied, the watermark can be recovered. However, this is not a practical solution due to the extensive computational complexity of the search. Watermarking schemes that are robust against geometrical transformations usually employ transformation invariants for detecting the geometrical transformations applied to the watermarked image [73]. Once the geometric transformation is estimated, an inverse transform is applied, and the actual watermark is read from the transformed image.

Another important property of data hiding is security. Currently, there are three directions in this field. The first is to encrypt the data to be embedded using a secure cipher such as the Advanced Encryption Standard (AES) and the Rivest, Shamir, Adelman public-key cryptographic system (RSA) [74]. The second approach is to provide security to feature extraction, such as deriving features through transforming coefficients into a special domain specified by a key [75]. The third approach is to provide security in the embedding mechanism itself to make it difficult for an adversary to embed a specific bit at his/her will. Traditional quantization-based data hiding schemes are not explicitly secure; rather, the main goal of these schemes is robustness against attacks. Wu [76] proposed a secure data hiding scheme based on a lookup table (LUT embedding). The encoder generates an LUT beforehand, denoted by $T(\cdot)$. To embed a 0 (or a 1), the host signal is quantized to the closest representation value that is mapped to a 0 (or a 1) as seen in Equation 7.41:

$$Y = \begin{cases} Quant(X_0), & \text{if } \quad T\left[\frac{Quant(X_0)}{q}\right] = b \\ X_0 + \delta, & \text{otherwise.} \end{cases} \qquad (7.41)$$

Here, X_0 is the original feature, Y is the marked feature, b is the bit that is to be hidden, and $Quant(\cdot)$ is the quantization operation. Conversely, the extraction is done by looking up the LUT as

$$\hat{b} = T\left[\frac{Quant(Y)}{q}\right],\tag{7.42}$$

where $\hat{b}$ is the extracted bit. From Equation 7.41, when $T(Quant(X_0)/q)$ does not correspond to the hidden bit, the encoder quantizes X_0 to the closest representation value that is mapped to the bit that is to be hidden [76]. The number of 1 and 0 mappings have to be constrained in the LUT to avoid excessive modification to the host. In order to prevent excessive modification of the host, the number of successive 1s or 0s in the LUT mapping must be limited. If "r" denotes the maximum allowable run, then the security of the scheme is given by

$$H_{LUT} = 1 - \frac{1}{2^r - 1}\text{bits.}\tag{7.43}$$

As seen from Equation 7.43, the security increases if r increases. However, increasing the security of the embedded data would inevitably lead to higher distortion to the feature values that are not mapped to the appropriate host [76]. The MSE of the LUT scheme (MSE_A) for run $r = 2$ is calculated as seen in Equation 7.44:

$$MSE_A = \frac{1}{2}\frac{q^2}{12} + \frac{1}{2}\frac{11}{12} = \frac{q^2}{2},\tag{7.44}$$

where q is the quantization step size. Note that MSE_A is greater than the distortion caused by the generic odd-even quantizer-based scheme, which is $q^2/3$.

7.9   SUMMARY

A comprehensive discussion on the different aspects of digital watermarking was presented in this chapter. State-of-the-art theoretical and practical ideas in the design, performance analysis, and applications of watermarking algorithms were given. Information-theoretic predictions of the embedding capacity were discussed using different models. The pros and cons of spatial and frequency domain watermarking algorithms were presented. Finally, security and robustness issues were also discussed.

REFERENCES

[1] Petitcolas, Fabien A.P. Introduction to information hiding, in *Information Hiding: Techniques for Steganography and Digital Watermarking*, Stephan Katzenbeisser and Fabien A.P. Petitcolas (eds.), Boston, MA, Artec House, pp.1–14, December 1999.

[2] M. Li, S. Narayanan, and R. Poovendran. Tracing medical images using multi-band watermarks, in *26th Annu. Int. Conf. Engineering in Medicine and Biology Society*, pp. 3233–3236, San Francisco, December 2004.

[3] Hwan II Kang and E. J. Delp. An image normalization based watermarking scheme robust to general affine transformation, in *Int. Conf. Image Processing (ICIP'04)*, Singapore, October 2004.

[4] S. Lin and C. Chen. A robust DCT-based watermarking for copyright protection, *IEEE Trans. Consumer Electronics*, 46:415–421, 2000.

[5] D. Simitopoulos, D. Koutsonanos, and M. G. Strintzis. Robust image watermarking based on generalized radon transformations, *IEEE Trans. Circuits and Systems for Video Technology*, 13:732–745, 2003.

[6] P. Amin and K. Subbalakshmi. Rotation and cropping resilient data hiding with zernike moments, in *Int. Conf. Image Processing (ICIP'04)*, Singapore, October 2004.

[7] T. Chen, C. Huang, T. Chen, and C. Liu. Authentication of lossy compressed video data by semi-fragile watermarking, in *Int. Conf. Image Processing (ICIP'04)*, Singapore, October 2004.

[8] Q. Qin, W. Wang, S. Chen, D. Chen, and W. Fu. Research of digital semi-fragile watermarking of remote sensing image based on wavelet analysis, in *IEEE Int. Symp. Geosciences and Remote Sensing (IGARSS'04)*, pp. 2542–2545, Anchorage, AK, September 2004.

[9] Z. Lu, C. Liu, D. Xu, and S. Sun. Semi-fragile image watermarking method based on index constrained vector quantization, *IEEE Electronics Letters*, 39:35–36, 2003.

[10] F. Shih and Y. Wu. A novel fragile watermarking technique, in *Int. Conf. Multimedia and Expo (ICME'04)*, pp. 875–878, Sorrento, Italy, June 2004.

[11] C. Li. Digital fragile watermarking scheme for authentication of JPEG images, *IEE Vision, Image and Signal Processing*, IEE proceedings, 151:460–466, 2004.

[12] H. Lu, R. Shen, and F. Chung. Fragile watermarking scheme for image authentication, *IEEE Electronics Letters*, 39:898–900, 2003.

[13] F. Alturki and R. Mersereau. Secure fragile digital watermarking technique for image authentication, in *Int. Conf. Image Processing (ICIP'01)*, pp. 7–10, Thessaloniki, Greece, October 2001.

[14] I. J. Cox, J. Kilian, T. Leighton, and T. Shamoon. Secure spread spectrum watermarking for multimedia, *IEEE Trans. Image Processing*, 6(1):1673–1687, 1997.

[15] P. Moulin and A. Briassouli. A stochastic QIM algorithm for robust, undetectable image watermarking, in *Int. Conf. Image Processing*, pp. 1173–1176, Singapore, October 2004.

[16] M. Cheng, K. Lay, and C. Sun. A trellis-enhanced secure spread watermarking scheme and its performance analysis, in *Asia-Pacific Conf. Circuits and Systems*, pp. 593–596, Tainan, Taiwan, December 2004.

[17] Y. Seo, M. Kim, H. Park, H. Jung, H. Chung, Y. Huh, and J. Lee. A secure watermarking for JPEG-2000, in *Int. Conf. Image Processing*, pp. 530–533, Thessaloniki, Greece, October 2001.

[18] S. Ei-Din and M. Moniri. Multiple secure image dependent watermarks for copyright protection, in *Int. Conf. Visual Information Engineering*, pp. 321–324, Surrey, UK, July 2003.

[19] P. Bareto, H. Kim, and V. Rijmen. Toward secure public-key blockwise fragile authentication watermarking, *IEE Vision, Image and Signal Processing*, IEE Proceedings, 149:57–62, 2002.

[20] P. Doets, I. Setyawan, and R. Lagendijk. Complexity-scalable compensation of geometrical distortions in image watermarking, in *Int. Conf. Image Processing*, pp. 14–17, Barcelona, Spain, September 2003.

[21] Y. Seong, Y. Choi, and T. Choi. Scene-based watermarking method for copy protection using image complexity and motion vector amplitude, in *Int. Conf. Acoustics, Speech, and Signal Processing*, pp. 409–412, Montreal, Quebec, Cannada, May 2004.

[22] I. Cox, T. Leighton, and T. Shamoon. Secure spread spectrum watermarking for images, audio and video, in *Int. Conf. Image Processing (ICIP'96)*, pp. 16–19, Chicago, IL, September 1996.

[23] P. Amin, N. Liu, and K. Subbalakshmi. Statistically secure digital image data hiding, in *IEEE Multimedia Signal Processing (MMSP05)*, China, October 2005.

[24] N. Liu, P. Amin, and K. Subbalakshmi. Secure quantizer based data embedding, in *IEEE Multimedia Signal Processing (MMSP05)*, China, October 2005.

[25] H. Oh, J. Seok, J. Hong, and D. Youn. New echo embedding technique for robust and imperceptible audio watermarking, in *Int. Conf. Acoustics, Speech, and Signal Processing*, pp. 1341–1344, Salt Lake City, UT, May 2001.

[26] Y. Hu and S. Kwong. An image fusion based visible watermarking algorithm, in *Proc. 2003 Int. Symp. Circuits and Systems, 2003 (ISCAS'03)*, pp. 794–797, China, May 2003.

[27] A. Lumini and D. Maio. Adaptive positioning of a visible watermark in a digital image, in *2004 IEEE Int. Conf. Multimedia and Expo, 2004 (ICME'04)*, pp. 947–970, Italy, June 2004.

[28] S. Thiemert, T. Vogel, J. Dittmann, and M. Steinebach. A high-capacity block based video watermark, in *30th Euromicro Conference*, pp. 457–460, Rennes, France, May 2004.

[29] C. Serdean, M. Ambroze, A. Tomlinson, and J. Wade. DWT-based high-capacity blind video watermarking, invariant to geometrical attacks, *IEE Proc. Vision, Image and Signal Processing*, 150:51–58, 2003.

[30] H. Wu, D. Tan, B. Qui, and Z. Yu. Adaptation of vision model based distortion metrics to perceptual image coding, *14th Int. Conf. Digital Signal Processing*, 1:181–184, 2002.

[31] S. Winkler. A perceptual distortion metric for digital color images, *Proc. 1998 Int. Conf. Image Processing, 1998 (ICIP 98)* 3:399–403, 2003.

[32] R. Chandramouli and N. Memon. Steganography capacity: A steganalysis perspective, in *Proc. SPIE Security and Watermarking of Multimedia Contents*, 5022:173–177, 2003.

[33] C. Podilchuk and W. Zeng. Image-adaptive watermarking using visual models, in *IEEE J. Selected Areas in Communications*, 16:525–539, May 1998.

[34] C. Podilchuk and W. Zeng. Perceptual watermarking of still images, in *IEEE First Workshop Multimedia Signal Processing*, pp. 363–368, Princeton, NJ, June 1997.

[35] E. Delp and R. Wolfgang. A watermark for digital images, in *Int. Conf. Image Processing*, pp. 219–222, Lausanne, Switzerland, September 1996.

[36] J. Bruyndockx, J. Quisquater, and B. Macq. Spatial method for copyright labeling of digital images, in *IEEE Workshop Image Processing*, pp. 456–459, Neos Marmaras, Greece, September 1995.

[37] H. Lu, A. Kot, and J. Cheng. Secure data hiding in binary document images for authentication, in *2003 Int. Symp. Circuits and Systems*, pp. II-806–II-809, Bangkok, Thailand, May 2003.

[38] T. M. Cover and J. A. Thomas. *Elements of Information Theory*, John Wiley & Sons, New York, 1991.

[39] M. Mansour and A. Tewfik. Techniques for data embedding in images using wavelet extrema, in *SPIE Conf. Security and Watermarking of Multimedia Contents*, pp. 329–335, California, October 2001.

[40] D. Zheng, J. Zhao, and A. Saddik. RST invariant digital image watermarking based on log-polar mapping and phase correlation, *IEEE Trans. Circuits and Systems for Video Technology*, 13(8):753–765, 2003.

[41] V. Fotopoulos and A. N. Skodras. A subband DCT approach to image watermarking, in *Tenth European Signal Processing Conference*, Tampere, Finland, September 2000.

[42] J. Hernandez, M. Amado, and F. Perez-Gonzalez. DCT-domain watermarking techniques for still images: Detector performance analysis and a new structure, *IEEE Trans. Image Processing*, 9(1):55–68, 2000.

[43] R. R. Clarke. Relation between karhunen-loeve and cosine transforms, *Proc. Instrumentation and Electrical Engineering*, 128:359–360, 1981.

[44] R. Clarke. *Transform Coding of Images*, Academic Press, San Diego, CA, 1986.

[45] S. Gelfand and M. Pinsker. Coding for channel with random parameters, *Problems of Control and Information Theory*, 9(1):19–31, 1980.

[46] M. Costa. Writing on dirty paper, *IEEE Trans. Information Theory*, IT-29:439–441, 1983.

[47] P. Moulin and J. O'Sullivan. Information-theoretic analysis of information hiding, *IEEE Trans. Information Theory*, 49:563–593, Mar. 2003.

[48] J. Chou, S. Pradhan, L. Ghaoui, and K. Ramchandran. On the duality between data hiding and distributed source coding, in *Proc. 33rd Annu. Asilomar Conf. Signals, Systems, and Computers*, 2:1503–1507, Pacific Grove, CA, 1999.

[49] M. Wu. Data hiding in image and video: Part I–fundamental issues and solutions, *IEEE Trans. Image Processing*, 12:685–695, June 2003.

[50] B. Chen and G. W. Wornell. Digital watermarking and information embedding using dither modulation, in *Proc. IEEE Second Workshop Multimedia Signal Processing*, pp. 273–278, Redondo Beach, CA, 1998.

[51] Y. Linde, A. Buzo, and R. Gray. An algorithm for vector quantizer design, *IEEE Trans. Communication*, COM-28:84–95, 1980.

[52] B. Chen and G. W. Wornell. Quantization index modulation: A class of probably good methods for digital watermarking and information embedding, *IEEE Trans. Information Theory*, 47(4):1423–1443, 2001.

[53] M. Ramkumar and A. Akansu. Self-noise suppression schemes for blind image steganography, in *Proc. SPIE International Workshop Voice, Video and Data Communication, Multimedia Applications'99*, 3845: pp. 55–56, September 1999.

[54] J. Hernandez, F. Perez-Gonzalez, J. Rodriguez, and G. Nieto. Performance analysis of a 2-D multipulse amplitude modulation scheme for data hiding and watermarking of still images, *IEEE J. Selected Areas in Communications*, 16(4):510–524, 1998.

[55] J. Eggers, R. Bäuml, R. Tzschoppe, and B. Girod. Scalar costa scheme for information embedding, *IEEE Trans. Signal Processing*, 51:1003–1019, 2003.

[56] M. Ramkumar and A. N. Akansu. Capacity estimates for data hiding in compressed images, *IEEE Trans. Image Processing*, 10:1252–1263, August 2001.

[57] A. K. Goteti and P. Moulin. QIM watermarking games, in *IEEE Int. Conf. Image Processing*, Singapore, October 2004.

[58] S. Voloshynovskiy, A. Herrigel, N. Baumgartner, and T. Pun. A stochastic approach to content adaptive digital image watermarking, in *Int. Workshop Information Hiding*, Dresden, Germany, pp. 211–236, September 1999.

[59] N. Liu and K. Subbalakshmi. Non-uniform quantizer design for image data hiding, in *IEEE Int. Conf. Image Processing*, Singapore, October 2004.

[60] N. Liu and K. Subbalakshmi. Vector quantization based scheme for data hiding for images, in *Proc. SPIE Int. Conf. Electronic Images'04*, pp. 548–559, San Jose, CA, January 2004.

[61] N. Liu and K. Subbalakshmi. TCQ-based quantizer design for data hiding in images, in *Proc. SPIE Int. Conf. Electronic Images'05*, pp. 185–193, San Jose, CA, January 2005.

[62] C. W. Honsinger, P. W. Jones, M. Rabbani, and J. C. Stoffel. Lossless Recovery of an Original Image Containing Embedded Data, *U.S. Patent No. 6278791*, August 2001.

[63] J. Fridrich, M. Goljan, and R. Du. Invertible authentication, *SPIE1*, pp. 197–208, January 2001.

[64] J. Fridrich, M. Goljan. and R. Du. Lossless data embedding — A new paradigm in digital watermarking, *EURASIP J. Applied signal Processing*, 53:185–196, February 2002.

[65] J. Fridrich, M. Goljan, and R. Du. Lossless data embedding — A new paradigm in digital watermarking, *Proc. SPIE Photonics West, Electronic Imaging*, 4675:572–583, January 2002.

[66] T. Kalker and F. M. J. Willems. Capacity bounds and constructions for reversible data hiding, *Security and Watermarking of Multimedia Contents*, 5020:pp. 604–611, 2003.

[67] M. Celik, G. Sharma, A. Teklap, and E. Saber. Lossless generalized LSB data embedding, *IEEE Trans. Image Processing*, 14:2:pp. 253–266, February 2005.

[68] J. Tian. Reversible data embedding using difference expansion, *IEEE Trans. Circuits and Systems for Video Technology*, 14:pp. 890–896, August 2003.

[69] G. Langelaar, I. Setyawan, and R. Lagendijk. Watermarking digital image and video data, *IEEE Signal Processing Magazine*, 17:20–43, 2000.

[70] N. Johnson. *A survey of steganographic techniques*, in *Information Hiding: Techniques for Steganography and Digital Watermarking*, Artec House, Boston, MA, 1999.

[71] A. Piva, M. Barni, F. Bartolini, and V. Cappellini. Threshold selection for correlation-based watermark detection, in *Proc. COST 254 Workshop Intelligent Communications*, pp. II-806–II-809, L'Aquila, Italy, June 1998.

[72] F. Petitcolas, R. Anderson, and M. Kuhn. Attacks on copyright marking systems, *Lecture Notes in Computer Science*, 1525:219–239, 1998.

[73] A. Piva, M. Barni, F. Bartolini, and V. Cappellini. DCT-based watermark recovering without resorting to the uncorrupted original image, in *Proc. ICIP'97*, 1:pp. 520–523, Atlanta, GA, October 1997.

[74] W. Trappe and L. C. Washington. *Introduction to Cryptography With Coding Theory*, Prentice-Hall, Englewood Cliffs, NJ, 2001.

[75] M. Alghoniemy and A. H. Tewfik. Self-synchronizing watermarking techniques, in *Proc. Symp. Content Security and Data Hiding in Digital Media*, (NJ Center for Multimedia Research and IEEE), Newark, NJ, September 1999.

[76] M. Wu. Joint security and robustness enhancement for quantization based data embedding, *IEEE Trans. Circuits and Systems and Video Technology*, 13:831–841, August 2003.

8

Biometrics in Digital Rights Management

Anil Jain and Umut Uludag

8.1 INTRODUCTION

The use of digital techniques for creation and distribution of copyrighted content (e.g., audio, video, image, and electronic book) has brought many advantages compared to analog domain processing. For example, (i) the digital content can be delivered quickly using high-speed computer networks, (ii) it can be accessed via a multitude of consumer devices (e.g., servers, notebook computers, PDAs, and cell phones), and (iii) effective search strategies can facilitate access to content (e.g., finding audio files of a specific singer). Further, digital techniques allow additional value-added functionalities such as efficient filtering and compression.

All of these advantages have played a key role in increasing the number of customers and associated revenues/profits for content owners (henceforth, "owner" will be used to denote authors, artists, copyright holders, licensees, distributors, and the like, as a whole). Ironically, digital content has also made its unauthorized duplication/distribution feasible and, as such, underscores the problem of Digital Rights Management (DRM): how to control access to content in a way that content owners and customers can enjoy the aforementioned benefits of digital infrastructure, while still respecting each other's rights (basically, the owners' right to be compensated fairly and the customers' right to access content easily). This problem is becoming more important every day [1], as

i. The number of people with access to high-speed Internet is increasing (naturally, so does the number of people willing to violate the copyright laws).

ii. The skills needed to illegally duplicate/distribute content are becoming simpler.

iii. Content owners are spending increasing amounts of money for creation of their content, and they want to be fairly compensated for this.

User (consumer) authentication is an important part of any DRM system. However, it should be noted that there are many other issues involved in this realm (e.g., legal, privacy-related concerns, as discussed elsewhere in this book). They make the problem increasingly complex, and they should be taken into account, along with user authentication, when designing and operating a DRM system.

In this chapter we focus on the following problem: how can the users be reliably authenticated so that only "legitimate" ones access the content? User authentication (which also arises in many contexts other than DRM) can be accomplished in one (or as a combination) of the following three schemes [2]: (i) token-based (e.g., ID cards, RFID tags) authentication, (ii) knowledge-based (e.g., password) authentication, and (iii) biometrics-based authentication. The so-called *traditional* authentication schemes, (i) and (ii), are known to be ineffective in solving the DRM problem. From the content owner's point of view, these schemes can be fooled relatively easily (e.g., by sharing the critical token/knowledge with unauthorized parties), thus allowing illegitimate access to content. From the content user's point of view, these schemes can force the users to carry/remember many tokens/passwords and, as such, can be impractical to use. The final scheme, which is based on biometric traits (e.g., fingerprint, face, iris, and voice) of individuals for authentication, has the potential to either replace or augment the traditional schemes in arriving at an authentication system for DRM.

The need for biometrics-based DRM schemes has been mentioned in the literature. For example, in his work on analyzing requirements of DRM systems (such as interoperability and ease of use) Barlow [3] stated,

> "... furthermore, emerging technologies such as smart cards and biometrics are set to play an increasingly important role in the trust domain. DRM should work alongside these technologies, providing content providers and consumers alike with the secure environment they require to maximize the business benefit of digital commerce ...."

Along the same lines, even though biometrics-based authentication is not cited specifically, MPEG-21 Multimedia Framework's Rights Expression Language [4] mentioned an extensible authentication mechanism as

> "... a principal denotes the party that it identifies by information unique to that individual. Usefully, this is information that has some associated authentication mechanism by which the principal can prove its identity. The Principal type supports the following identification technologies: - a principal that must present multiple credentials, all of

which must be simultaneously valid, to be authenticated, ... , - other identification technologies that may be invented by others ...."

Howells et al. [5] also proposed a multimedia document framework for their representation and manipulation and stated,

"... the following are desirable features for an autonomous multimedia document: ... - provision for whole or selective encryption (and data compression), possibly multi-layered encryption schemes and support for authentication measures and biometric identification schemes ...."

Finally, The European Union's report [6] that includes possible scenarios for the usage of biometrics in everyday life in year 2015 mentions:

"... biometrics might be useful for digital rights management (DRM) to replace code and/or password protected files ...."

The outline of this chapter is as follows. In Section 8.2 we introduce biometric systems and elaborate on their applicability to the DRM problem. We summarize several commercial and academic studies that combine biometrics with DRM in Section 8.3. Finally, we conclude the chapter and provide future directions for this important and emerging field in Section 8.4.

8.2 BIOMETRICS

8.2.1 Basic Characteristics

A generic biometric authentication system is composed of several modules (Figure 8.1). The sensor (e.g., fingerprint sensor) captures the biometric trait F and transfers its digital representation F_s to the host device. The feature extractor creates a *template* F_t, a concise representation of the raw biometric signal (e.g., fingerprint image), corresponding to the identity I. The matcher judges the similarity between two or more templates. If this similarity is high, the biometric system implies that the associated templates are likely to originate from the same user and access should be granted to the back-end application protected by biometrics. The database (which can be *remote*, such as a server connected to the Internet, or *local*, such as a smart card issued to the user) holds the templates to be used whenever an authentication need arises. These modules are used in three interrelated tasks: (i) *enrollment*, the user's biometric is converted to a template and stored in the database; (ii) *verification*, the user's template obtained online (e.g., at the point of transaction), $F_{v,s}$, is compared to the stored template associated with the claimed identity (e.g., "John Doe") to output a binary decision (accept versus reject); and (iii) *identification*, the user does not claim an identity; instead the biometric system tries to find the identity I of the user by comparing

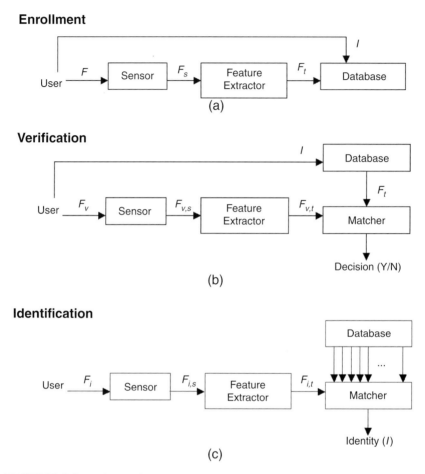

FIGURE 8.1: Biometric system processes: (a) enrollment, (b) verification, and (c) identification.

the online template, $F_{i,s}$, with all the templates stored in the database. The term *authentication* encompasses both verification and identification.

Within this biometric system, a number of different traits can be utilized (Figure 8.2). Each one of these traits has its strengths and weaknesses, and the choice depends on the requirements of the specific application (e.g., accessing bank accounts, health care records, copyrighted content, or international border crossing) into which biometric authentication is incorporated. None of the biometric traits is "optimal" for all applications. In addition to these traits, there are other biometric characteristics (e.g., retina, gait, odor, ear shape, and DNA) currently

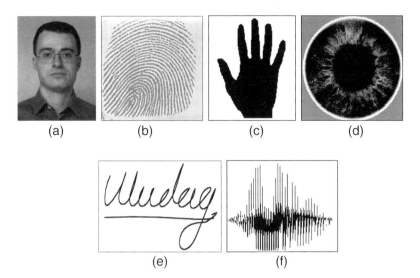

FIGURE 8.2: Examples of biometric traits: (a) face, (b) fingerprint, (c) hand geometry, (d) iris, (e) signature, and (f) voice.

Table 8.1: Comparison of various biometric traits.

Biometric identifier	Universality	Distinctiveness	Permanence	Collectability	Performance	Acceptability	Circumvention
Face	H	L	M	H	L	H	H
Fingerprint	M	H	H	M	H	M	M
Hand geometry	M	M	M	H	M	M	M
Iris	H	H	H	M	H	L	L
Signature	L	L	L	H	L	H	H
Voice	M	L	L	M	L	H	H

Note: High, medium, and low are denoted by H, M, and L, respectively.

being investigated for their applicability to various authentication tasks. A brief comparison of some of the biometric traits based on the following seven factors is provided in Table 8.1 [7]:

- **Universality**. Do all users have this biometric trait?
- **Distinctiveness**. Can all the users be distinguished based on this trait?

- **Permanence**. How permanent is this trait?
- **Collectability**. Is it feasible to capture and quantify this trait?
- **Performance**. Does this trait allow accurate and fast authentication?
- **Acceptability**. Are users willing to use this trait for authentication?
- **Circumvention**. Is it easy to fool the authentication system?

Let us analyze these seven factors considering our specific application at hand; namely, accessing copyrighted content.

i. **Universality**. DRM systems should be operational for a large portion of the population. If many people in the target population do not possess a particular biometric trait, its applicability will reduce dramatically. For example, fingerprints of manual workers may not be usable due to accumulated wear of this trait, and considering that authentication for DRM systems should work in "stand-alone" mode (e.g., there will be no human attendant to manually check the ID card in lieu of biometric), this can decrease the applicability of the biometric trait in a DRM application.

ii. **Distinctiveness**. As seen in Table 8.1, different traits differ in the level of distinctiveness. Again, considering that DRM systems need to deal with a very large population, the selected trait should offer an appropriate level of distinctiveness so that the probability of user A's biometric trait matching that of user B is extremely small.

iii. **Permanence**. Biometric traits may change over time either permanently or temporarily. For example, voice features may change drastically during puberty, or they can change temporarily due to a cold, etc. DRM systems may need to be operational for a relatively long period of time. In a biometrics-based DRM system, a user may want to access copyrighted content that she acquired years ago. Hence, if the trait changes significantly during this period, it will create inconvenience for the users. The system may need to have the capability to perform a template update on a regular basis.

iv. **Collectability**. In the realm of the DRM applications, several traits may not be feasible due to the associated sensor characteristics. For example, hand geometry systems are large and heavy, and naturally, they are not appropriate for mobile content access devices (e.g., PDAs and cellular phones).

v. **Performance**. Authentication accuracy requirements for DRM systems may be less stringent compared to, say, high-security access control. However, considering the highly networked nature of the society, even if a small number of people manage to bypass the biometric authentication system (see Section 8.2.4), they will have the means to distribute the unprotected content (that they can access) to scores of other users. Authentication speed is also important, as many users of multimedia devices will require near-real-time access.

vi. **Acceptability**. Aside from the technical aspects of biometric authentication systems, the public perception may play an important role in choosing a trait for DRM systems. For example, fingerprint-based systems may be perceived as associated with criminal/law enforcement applications, and some users may not feel comfortable using this trait for routine tasks like accessing copyrighted content.

vii. **Circumvention**. Considering that DRM systems are likely to operate in unattended mode, the means to detect circumvention attempts may be limited. Therefore, choosing a biometric system that can withstand such attempts is desirable.

Many of the above requirements are contradictory, and that is why the choice of a biometric for a given application is a difficult task. Further, for DRM applications, the cost of biometric sensors is very important, as the mobile devices themselves are relatively cheap and the device manufacturers will not be willing to add a sensor that increases the price of their product considerably. Similarly, the computational resources (processor speed and memory) of such devices may prevent execution of very complex biometric matching algorithms. However, decreasing the computational resources of associated biometric modules, either by devising new algorithms or by simplifying complex algorithms (at the expense of decreased authentication accuracy), can remedy this problem.

8.2.2 Fingerprint-Based Biometric System

To gain more insight into the operation of biometrics-based authentication systems, let us consider fingerprint matching as an example. The most widely used features for fingerprint templates are based on *minutia* points, where the fingerprint ridges end or bifurcate (Figure 8.3). The minutiae pattern forms a compact and robust (e.g., relative to using the fingerprint image itself) representation of

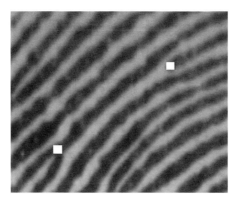

FIGURE 8.3: Fingerprint minutiae: a ridge bifurcation (left) and a ridge ending (right) are shown.

the fingerprint. The simplest of the minutiae-based representation constitutes a list of triplets (x, y, θ), where (x, y) represents the spatial coordinates in a fixed coordinate system, and θ represents the orientation of the ridge at that minutia. Typically, a good quality live-scan fingerprint image has 20–70 minutiae.

Only in the highly constrained fingerprint systems could one assume that the input and template fingerprints depict the same portion of the finger and both are aligned (in terms of displacement from the origin of the coordinate system and of their orientations) with each other. So, given two (input and template) fingerprint representations, the matching module typically aligns the input and template minutiae and determines whether the prints are impressions of the same finger by identifying *corresponding* minutiae within an acceptable spatial neighborhood of the aligned minutiae. The number of corresponding minutiae is an effective measure of similarity (*matching score*) between the matched prints. Figure 8.4 illustrates a typical matching process.

An important advantage of fingerprint-based biometric systems is the compact size and low cost of fingerprint sensors. These characteristics allow their incorporation into devices such as PDAs and memory sticks (Figure 8.5).

8.2.3   Biometric Trait Variability

Traditional token or knowledge-based authentication schemes do not involve complex matching algorithms. In the former, the token (e.g., an ID card with a specific RFID tag) is either present or not. In the latter, the provided password is either correct or incorrect. However, a biometric matcher has to consider the variability of biometric data, as two acquisitions of an identical biometric trait (e.g., user A's right index finger) are rarely identical (intra-class variability). Instead, both the raw biometric data and the templates extracted from them exhibit differences due to alignment, missing/spurious features, and differences in the values of features that are present in both acquisitions (Figure 8.6). Further, large inter-class similarity (i.e., the similarity between the biometric data of users A and B) complicates the feature extraction and matching problem. Minimizing the effect of intra-class variability and inter-class similarity requires relatively complex pattern representation and matching algorithms, and this may not be feasible in some consumer devices with limited resources that are used for accessing copyrighted content (e.g., MP3 players).

8.2.4   Biometric System Performance

A biometric authentication system makes two types of errors: (i) mistaking biometric measurements from two different persons to be from the same person (called *false match*) and (ii) mistaking two biometric measurements from the same person to be from two different persons (called *false non-match*). These two types of errors are often termed as *false accept* and *false reject*, respectively. There is a

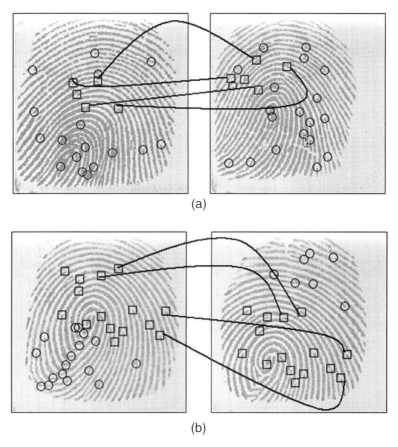

(a)

(b)

FIGURE 8.4: Fingerprint matching consists of feature (minutiae) extraction followed by alignment and determination of *corresponding* minutiae (four correspondences are shown via lines): (a) matching two impressions of different fingers, matching score = 33, number of corresponding minutiae = 5; and (b) matching fingerprints from the same finger, matching score = 80, number of corresponding minutiae = 15. The normalized maximum possible score is 100.

trade-off between the false match rate (FMR) and false non-match rate (FNMR) in every biometric system. In fact, both FMR (False Accept Rate, FAR) and FNMR (False Reject Rate, FRR) are functions of the system threshold (against which the similarity score between two templates is compared and an accept/reject decision is output). On the one hand, if the threshold is decreased to make the system more tolerant to biometric intra-class variability (hence, decreasing FNMR),

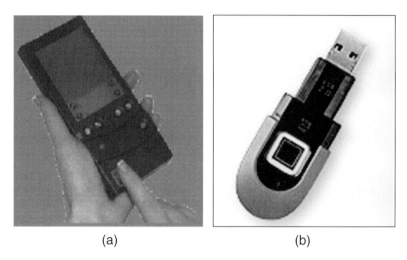

(a)   (b)

FIGURE 8.5:   Embedded fingerprint sensors: (a) PDA and (b) memory stick.

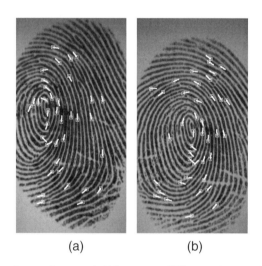

(a)   (b)

FIGURE 8.6:   Intra-class variability: two different fingerprint images of a finger with overlaid minutiae.

FMR increases. On the other hand, if the threshold is increased to make the system more secure (hence, decreasing FMR), FNMR increases. The point at which FNMR = FMR is called the Equal Error Rate (EER). The Genuine Accept Rate (GAR) is directly related to FNMR as GAR = 1 − FNMR. A plot of GAR versus FAR for various system thresholds is called a Receiver Operating Characteristics

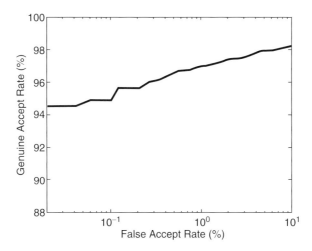

FIGURE 8.7:   The ROC curve of a fingerprint verification system.

(ROC) curve. The ROC curve for database DB1 of the Fingerprint Verification Competition FVC2002 is shown in Figure 8.7 [8].

The actual operating point for a DRM system can be chosen based on the security/usability characteristics of the content to be secured. For example, for the advance screening of yet-to-be-released movies, a higher security setting may be appropriate. For the distribution of sample audio segments with the aim of promoting a particular music group, a lower security (but higher user convenience) setting can be chosen.

8.3   INTEGRATING BIOMETRICS WITH DRM SYSTEMS

Biometrics-based authentication can be incorporated into DRM systems in several different scenarios. In this section, we review these scenarios and highlight their advantages and disadvantages.

8.3.1   Securing the Multimedia Delivery

Here, the aim is to *deliver* the copyrighted content only to legitimate users, e.g., users who pay their regular (e.g., monthly) or access-based (e.g., per song) fees. Biometrics-based authentication can verify the identity of the user (and back-end applications can check whether this specific user is entitled to receive the content) before the content is sent to her over a secure communication channel. Note that this scenario does not address the problems that arise when these otherwise legitimate users distribute the content to other illegitimate users. It inherently relies on *trusted* users, which may not always be the case.

8.3.2   Securing the Multimedia Player

Here, the multimedia player (e.g., mobile phone, PDA, or desktop computer) is secured using biometric authentication. Only the users that are *authorized* are allowed to *play* the multimedia content. The system relies on the assumption that without appropriate playing mechanisms, the multimedia data are *useless* to consumers. If *every* player that is in use today had this biometric authentication capability, this scenario would be successful. However, this is not the case; very few players currently possess biometric-based matching. So, illegitimate users can easily play (*use*) the copyrighted content. Example systems include fingerprint matching for PDAs [9] and voice recognition for mobile phones [10]. As a sample system, Figure 8.8 shows a mobile phone equipped with a fingerprint sensor,

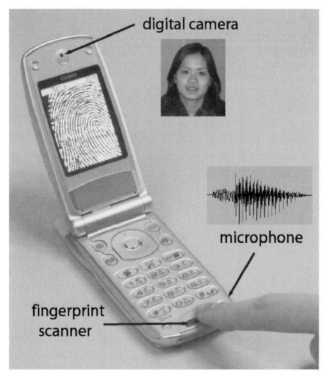

FIGURE 8.8: Mobile phone with fingerprint sensor, camera, and micro-phone.

a camera, and a microphone that can benefit from matching of multiple biometric traits (*multimodal biometrics*).

8.3.3 Securing the Multimedia Content

Here, the multimedia content *itself* is secured using biometrics. Traditionally, digital data are secured using encryption/decryption schemes. The data are converted to essentially a sequence of random bits (*encryption step*) using secret encryption keys. Only with the knowledge of the correct decrypting keys can the data be converted back to useful data (*decryption step*) that can be played.

The problem with this scenario is that it still relies on *trusted* users, i.e., users who will not distribute the supposedly secret keys along with encrypted content to illegitimate users. This key management problem can be remedied by incorporating biometric authentication into the associated cryptographic framework. This can be done either by (i) using traditional encryption schemes with biometric data or by (ii) using biometric data to release/generate keys (*biometric cryptosystems*) that can, *in turn*, be used in such content protection frameworks. In this section we review both of these approaches.

Encryption Using Biometrics

Uludag and Jain [11] use fingerprint minutiae data in layered encryption of multimedia content. After exchanging information about user identity and access status (e.g., based on payment information), the server and the user's device exchange encryption/decryption keys that are based on fingerprint minutiae and traditional entities such as passwords. The layered encryption, which encrypts the content successively using different keys, uses the Data Encryption Standard (DES) algorithm [12]. For addressing the biometric intra-class variability, the authors propose local storage of the fingerprint minutiae template *within* the encrypted content that, in turn, is used as encryption/decryption keys after hashing it with the MD5 (Message-Digest algorithm 5) algorithm [12]. Utilization of the widely available DES (Data Encryption Standard) and MD5 algorithms as the building blocks increases the applicability of the proposed framework. However, the authors also mention that false accept and false reject errors will always be observed with any biometric-based system and propose to use multiple biometric traits together (multimodal biometrics) to decrease the effect of this problem.

A commercial product, wireless iVue Personal Media Player by VeriTouch [13], is said to encompass fingerprint-based encryption/decryption of multimedia content. A specialized network using the HDTV spectrum accessible to selected retailers (access points) will relay the encrypted content to the wireless players. No details about the underlying encryption scheme are available.

Biometric Cryptosystems

Biometric cryptosystems [14] are not specifically designed for multimedia content protection per se, but for the more general aim of combining the advantages of biometrics-based authentication with the theoretical and practical security of cryptographic systems. These systems merge the biometrics and cryptography at a more fundamental level; keys are either released or generated using novel cryptographic constructs that are implicitly designed with the variability of biometric data in mind (Figure 8.9).

In biometrics-based key release, the biometric matching is decoupled from the cryptographic part. Biometric matching operates on the traditional biometric templates: if they match, the cryptographic key is released from its secure location, e.g., a smart card or a server. Here, biometrics effectively acts as a *wrapper* mechanism in the cryptographic domain. In biometrics-based key generation, biometrics and cryptography are merged together at a much deeper level. Biometric matching can effectively take place *within* the cryptographic domain, and it extracts the secret key from the conglomerate (key/biometric template) data.

Soutar et al. [15–17] proposed a key-binding algorithm in a correlation-based fingerprint matching system. This algorithm binds a cryptographic key with the user's fingerprint images at the time of enrollment. The key is then retrieved only

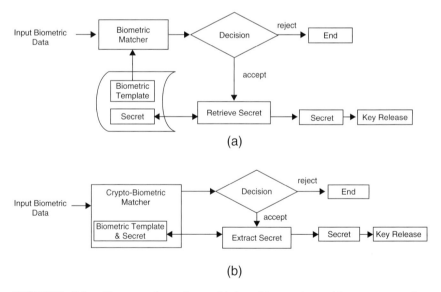

FIGURE 8.9: Two modes of combining biometrics with cryptography: (a) key release and (b) key generation.

upon a successful authentication. By using several (training) fingerprint images of a finger (typically five), the algorithm first creates a correlation filter function $H(u)$ which has both the magnitude, $|H(u)|$, and phase, $e^{i\varphi(H(u))}$, components. The design criteria for this function include both distortion tolerance (in order to minimize FNMR) and discriminability (in order to minimize FMR). The algorithm also computes an output, $c_0(x)$, which is obtained by convolution/correlation of the training fingerprint images with $H(u)$. Then, the complex conjugate of the phase component of $H(u)$, $e^{-i\varphi(H(u))}$, is multiplied with a randomly generated phase-only array of the same size, resulting in $H_{stored}(u)$, and the magnitude $|H(u)|$ of $H(u)$ is discarded. This process eliminates reverse engineering of the user's fingerprint image from $H(u)$. A given or randomly generated N-bit (typically 128-bit) cryptographic key, k_0, is then linked with binarized correlation output c_0 by using an error correcting code (in order to tolerate some expected variation in the biometric signal during authentication), resulting in a lookup table, LT. The cryptographic key, k_0, is also used as an encryption key to encrypt S bits of $H_{stored}(u)$, and the resultant encrypted message is hashed (using a standard hashing function such as SHA-1 or Triple-DES [12]) to form an identification code id_0. Finally, $H_{stored}(u)$, LT, and id_0 are stored in the database as the biometric template for the user (called *Bioscrypt* by the authors).

During authentication, the user inputs one or more (typically five) fingerprint images of her finger. The $H_{stored}(u)$ for this user is retrieved from her stored *Bioscrypt* and combined with the input fingerprint images to produce a correlation output $c_1(x)$. A cryptographic key retrieval algorithm then uses the LT for the user (stored in her *Bioscrypt*) to extract a key k_1 from the correlation output $c_1(x)$. The retrieved key, k_1, is used to create a new identification code id_1 in exactly the same way as was done during enrollment. If $id_1 = id_0$, then k_1 is released into the system; otherwise an "authentication failed" message is returned. Thus, the system never releases any (wrong) key into the system if the biometric authentication fails. The main criticism of Soutar et al.'s work in the literature [18, 19] is that the method does not carry rigorous security guarantees. Further, the resulting FMR and FNMR values are unknown. The authors also assume that the input and database templates are completely aligned.

Davida et al. [18, 20] proposed an algorithm based on iris biometric. They consider binary representation of iris texture, called IrisCode [21], which is 2048 bits in length. The biometric matcher computes the Hamming distance between the input and database template representations and compares it with a threshold to determine whether the two biometric samples are from the same person or not. The authors assume that the IrisCodes from different samplings of the same iris can have up to 10% of the 2048 bits (204 bits) different from the same iris's template IrisCode. The authors also assume that the IrisCodes of different irises differ in as many as 45% of the 2048 bits (922 bits).

During enrollment, multiple scans of the iris of a person are collected and K-bit IrisCodes are generated for each scan. The multiple IrisCodes are then combined (through a majority decoder) to arrive at a canonical IrisCode, T, of the same length. An $[N, K, D]$ bounded distance decoding error correcting code [22] is then constructed by adding C check bits to the K-bit IrisCode (C is determined such that 10% of K bits can be corrected), resulting in an N-bit codeword, denoted by $T \| C$. The codeword, $T \| C$, is hashed and digitally signed, denoted by $Sig(Hash(T \| C))$, and, together with the check bits C, is stored as the database template for the user. At the time of authentication, again, multiple samples of the iris of a person are collected, and T' is estimated. The check bits C from the database template are used to perform error correction on the codeword $T' \| C$, and the corrected IrisCode T'' is produced. Then $T'' \| C$ is hashed and signed (just like during enrollment), resulting in $Sig(Hash(T'' \| C))$. If $Sig(Hash(T'' \| C))$ is exactly the same as the $Sig(Hash(T \| C))$ stored in the database template, authentication succeeds. Davida et al. [18, 20] argue that the database template of a user itself can be used as a cryptographic key. Their algorithm is fast and has provable security. However, they propose to store error correcting bits C in the database, and this leads to some leakage of information about the user's biometric data. Further, the error tolerance of their scheme is rather small. The authors' assumption that only 10% of the bits at the k-bit IrisCode change among different presentations of the iris of a person is too restrictive. Finally, the authors assume that the input and database template IrisCodes are completely aligned. Although constrained iris image acquisition systems can limit the misalignment among different acquisitions of the same iris, some degree of misalignment is natural.

Monrose, Reiter, and Wetzel [23] proposed a method to make passwords more secure by combining keystroke biometrics with passwords. Their technique was inspired by password "salting," where a user's password (pwd) is salted by prepending it with an s-bit random number (the "salt"), resulting in a hardened password ($hpwd$). During enrollment, the following information is stored in the user's database template: (i) a randomly chosen k-bit (typically 160) number, r; (ii) an "instruction table" encrypted with pwd (the instruction table is created as follows: first, the user's keystroke features, typically 15 in number, are thresholded to generate a binary feature descriptor, then the binary feature descriptor and r are used to create the instruction table using Shamir's secret sharing scheme [12]; the instruction table essentially contains instructions on how to generate $hpwd$ from the feature descriptor, r, and pwd); and (iii) a "history file" encrypted with $hpwd$. At the time of authentication, the algorithm uses the r and the instruction table from the user's template and the authentication password pwd' and keystroke features acquired during the authentication to compute $hpwd'$. The $hpwd'$ is then used to decrypt the encrypted history file. If the decryption is successful, the authentication is successful, and the number r and history file of the user are modified in the template. If the authentication is unsuccessful, another instance of $hpwd'$ is generated from the instruction table in a similar way but with some error correction, and the authentication is tried again. If the authentication does not succeed within a fixed number of error correction iterations, the authentication finally fails. The authors claim that the hardened password itself can be used as an encryption key. A weakness of this work is that it only adds about 15 bits of entropy to the passwords, thus making them only marginally more secure. However, in their subsequent publications [24–26], Monrose et al. made some minor modifications to their original scheme, applied it to voice biometrics (which is more distinctive than keystroke biometrics), and were eventually able to generate cryptographic keys of up to 60 bits, which although much higher than the 15 bits achieved in their earlier work, is still quite low for most security applications.

Linnartz and Tuyls [27] assume that a noise-free template X of a biometric identifier is available at the enrollment time and use this to enroll a secret S to generate a helper data W. Assume that each dimension (of a multi-dimensional template) is quantized to q resolution levels. In each dimension, the process of obtaining W is akin to finding residuals that must be added to X to fit to odd or even grid quantum depending upon whether the corresponding S bit is 0 or 1. At decryption time, the (noise-prone) biometric template Y is used to decrypt W to obtain a decrypted message S' which is approximately the same as S. In each dimension, the process of decryption guesses whether a particular bit of secret S is 0 or 1 depending upon whether the sum of Y and W resides in even or odd quantum of the corresponding dimension. It is hoped that the relatively few errors in S' can be corrected using error correction techniques. The proposed technique assumes that the biometric representations are completely aligned and that noise in each dimension is relatively small compared to the quantization Q. Due to the intra-class variability in the biometric identifier, different W may be generated for the same message S. The authors prove that very little information is revealed from W by appropriately tuning the quantization scheme with respect to the measurement noise.

In their "fuzzy commitment" scheme [28], Juels and Wattenberg generalized and significantly improved Davida et al.'s methods [18, 20] to tolerate more variation in the biometric characteristics and to provide stronger security. At the enrollment time, the user selects a secret message C. Let d denote the difference vector between the user biometric keys X and C. The encrypted message (which is considered as a *fuzzy commitment*) then consists of d and $y = hash(C)$, where *hash* is a one-way hash function such as SHA-1 [12]. At the decrypting end, with biometric representation Y, $Y + d$ is used to decode the nearest codeword C'. Again, with the help of error correcting techniques, it is hoped that the error in C' can be corrected to obtain the original message C. The authors acknowledge that one of the major shortcomings of the fuzzy commitment scheme is that it requires the biometric representations X and Y to be ordered so that their correspondence is obvious.

In order to overcome the correspondence problem of the fuzzy commitment scheme, Juels and Sudan [19] proposed a *fuzzy vault* scheme. Let us consider what happens at enrollment time in the fuzzy vault scheme. In this scheme, the secret message C to be transmitted is embedded (in a (say, single variable x) polynomial $P(x)$ as its coefficients). The polynomial value $y = P(x)$ can be computed for different values of x. Each value of x can be chosen such that it represents a component of biometric representation, A. Let us call the set of pairs of values (x, y) lying on $P(x)$ as the genuine set G. Let us introduce a set of extraneous points (x', y') called N. The union of G and N constitutes the encrypted message. At the decrypting end, it is hoped that a biometric representation B which substantially matches A can help determine most of the genuine points G with little contamination from N. The recovered set of points R is then used to fit a polynomial to recover C'. With the help of error correction schemes, it is hoped that the errors in C' can be corrected to obtain the transmitted message C. Juels and Sudan [19] prove the security of the fuzzy vault scheme in an information-theoretic sense. Although the authors specifically mention application of their scheme to biometric keys, it is not clear how robust the algorithm is to typical variations in the biometric signal. Further, although this scheme takes into account unordered feature representations, it is not obvious how this algorithm will handle the alignment requirements.

Clancy, Kiyavash, and Lin [29], Uludag, Pankanti, and Jain [30], and Yang and Verbauwhede [31] proposed implementations of this construct either by assuming that fingerprint representations are pre-aligned [29, 30] or by using reference points extracted from multiple minutiae locations for pre-alignment [31]. Encryption keys of 128-bit (that can be used for encryption/decryption of multimedia content) were successfully secured with no false accepts and between 20–30% FRR. Increasing the number of genuine points utilized during fuzzy vault enrollment decreases this FRR value at the expense of increased false accepts.

Dodis, Reyzin, and Smith [32] proposed theoretical foundations for generating keys from the "key material" that is not exactly reproducible (e.g., pass phrases, answers to questionnaires, and biometric data that changes between enrollment and verification). Similar to the notion of helper data of Linnartz and Tuyls [27], Dodis, Reyzin, and Smith [32] define *fuzzy extractors* (FE) that create variable R from the key material w and generate public (helper) data P. FE again generates R from w', if w' is "close" to w, given the variable P. For three distance metrics (Hamming distance, set difference, and edit distance), the authors calculate the information revealed by P and elaborate on the existence of possible algorithms for FE construction. They also propose a modification of Juels and Sudan's fuzzy vault scheme [19]: instead of adding chaff points to the projections of the polynomial p, Dodis, Reyzin, and Smith [32] propose using a polynomial p' (of degree higher than p) which overlaps with p *only* for the points from the genuine set A.

The security of the scheme is based on the degree of this new polynomial p', which replaces the final point set R of Juels and Sudan's scheme [19].

Note that these biometric cryptosystems (which are not designed for the copyright protection per se) fit into the multimedia content protection framework described previously; the secret keys (that secure the content using traditional encryption schemes) are themselves tied to the biometric data. This increases both user convenience (no need to remember long and random keys) and authentication accuracy (a system can be designed to accept *only* the keys originating from biometric cryptosystem; hence, the illegal key sharing problem is eliminated).

8.4 CONCLUSION

As the digital computing infrastructure becomes the preferred platform for copyrighted content processing (e.g., creation, editing, distribution, and utilization), the problem of assuring only legitimate access to content is becoming critical. An important component of this problem is related to accurate personal authentication.

Personal authentication has been traditionally performed via knowledge- (e.g., password) and token- (e.g., ID card) based schemes. Biometrics can eliminate the problems associated with these schemes (e.g., illegal key sharing).

In this chapter, we introduced biometric authentication, specifically highlighting its characteristics that come into play when our target application of DRM is considered. Several scenarios that aim to secure disjoint portions of the overall system, namely delivery, player, and content, are summarized. Securing the content is generally superior to the others in terms of the security it provides, but it is computationally more demanding.

This content security (that is supported by the widely available encryption/decryption framework) can be accomplished either by simply augmenting it to use biometric data or by using dedicated cryptographic constructs (biometric cryptosystems) to act as *gatekeepers* for the framework. The former has increased applicability due to the widespread availability of associated computational modules. However, the latter can provide increased security as the characteristics of the biometric data (e.g., intra-class variability) are considered much more elaborately in the system design.

Even though biometric-based personal authentication is in its infancy in security applications that are generally not perceived as "critical" (compared to, e.g., border control), we are beginning to see the introduction of commercial products that integrate biometrics with multimedia access in the market. However, biometrics-based authentication will never completely replace all of the competing authentication mechanisms; it will possibly augment them to result in a system that can support the very complex nature of the DRM problem. Further, when biometric authentication is incorporated into the next generation of standardized computing architectures (such as TCPA [33] and Palladium [34]), its applicability to copyright protection will increase even more.

REFERENCES

[1] IDG News Service. U.S. Global Piracy Losses Estimated at $9.2B in 2002, February 14, 2003. Available at http://www.computerworld.com/securitytopics/ security/cybercrime/story/0,10801,78545,00.html?from=story_picks.

[2] J. Wayman, A. Jain, D. Maltoni, and D. Maio (Eds.). *Biometric Systems: Technology, Design and Performance Evaluation*, Springer-Verlag, Berlin/New York, 2005.

[3] A. Barlow. Position paper on digital rights management, in *Proc. Workshop Digital Rights Management for the Web 2001*, http://www.w3.org/2000/12/drm-ws/ pp/phocis-barlow.html.

[4] MPEG-21 Overview v.5, ISO/IEC JTC1/SC29/WG11/N5231, http://www. chiariglione.org/mpeg/standards/mpeg-21/mpeg-21.htm.

[5] W. G. J. Howells, H. Selim, S. Hoque, M. C. Fairhurst, and F. Deravi. The Autonomous Document Object (ADO) model, in *Proc. Int. Conf. Document Analysis and Recognition*, pp. 977–981, Seattle, WA, September 2001.

[6] European Commission, Joint Research Centre. Biometrics at the Frontiers: Assessing the Impact on Society, Technical Report EUR 21585 EN, http://europa.eu.int/ comm/justice_home/doc_centre/freetravel/doc/biometrics_eur21585_en.pdf.

[7] D. Maltoni, D. Maio, A. Jain, and S. Prabhakar. *Handbook of Fingerprint Recognition*, Springer-Verlag, Berlin/New York, 2003.

[8] D. Maio, D. Maltoni, R. Cappelli, J. L. Wayman, and A. K. Jain. FVC2002: Second fingerprint verification competition, in *Proc. Int. Conf. Pattern Recognition*, pp. 811–814, Quebec City, Canada, August 2002.

[9] K. Uchida. Fingerprint-based user-friendly interface and pocket-PID for mobile authentication, in *Proc. Int. Conf. Pattern Recognition*, pp. 4205–4209, Barcelona, Spain, September 2000.

[10] S. Narayanaswamy, J. Hu, and R. Kashi. User interface for a PCS smart phone, in *Proc. Int. Conf. Multimedia Computing and Systems*, pp. 777–781, Florence, Italy, June 1999.

[11] U. Uludag and A. K. Jain. Multimedia content protection via biometrics-based encryption, *Proc. Int. Conf. Multimedia & Expo*, III:237–240, 2003.

[12] W. Stallings. *Cryptography and Network Security: Principles and Practices*, Third Edition, Prentice Hall, New York, 2003.

[13] The Digital Network and VeriTouch Announce Wireless Entertainment Network, http://www.veritouch.com/news/100104.html, 2004.

[14] U. Uludag, S. Pankanti, S. Prabhakar, and A. K. Jain. Biometric cryptosystems: Issues and challenges, *Proc. IEEE, Special Issue on Multimedia Security for Digital Rights Management*, 92(6):948–960, 2004.

[15] C. Soutar, D. Roberge, S. A. Stojanov, R. Gilroy, and B. V. K. Vijaya Kumar. Biometric encryption using image processing, *Proc. SPIE, Optical Pattern Recognition IX*, 3314:178–188, 1998.

[16] C. Soutar, D. Roberge, S. A. Stojanov, R. Gilroy, and B. V. K. Vijaya Kumar. Biometric encryption — Enrollment and verification procedures, *Proc. SPIE, Optical Pattern Recognition IX*, 3386:24–35, 1998.

[17] C. Soutar, D. Roberge, S. A. Stojanov, R. Gilroy, and B. V. K. Vijaya Kumar. Biometric encryption, *ICSA Guide to Cryptography*, R. K. Nichols (Ed.), McGraw-Hill, New York, 1999.

[18] G. I. Davida, Y. Frankel, and B. J. Matt. On enabling secure applications through off-line biometric identification, in *Proc. 1998 IEEE Symp. Privacy and Security*, pp. 148–157, 1998.

[19] A. Juels and M. Sudan. A fuzzy vault scheme, in *Proc. IEEE Int. Symp. Information Theory*, A. Lapidoth and E. Teletar (Eds.), p. 408, Lausanne, Switzerland, June 2002.

[20] G. I. Davida, Y. Frankel, B. J. Matt, and R. Peralta. On the relation of error correction and cryptography to an offline biometric based identification scheme, *Workshop Coding and Cryptography*, pp. 129–138, Paris, France, January 1999.

[21] J. G. Daugman. High confidence visual recognition of persons by a test of statistical independence, *IEEE Trans. Pattern Analysis and Machine Intelligence*, 15:1148–1161, 1993.

[22] W. W. Peterson and E. J. Weldon. *Error Correcting Codes*, MIT Press, Cambridge, MA, 1988.

[23] F. Monrose, M. K. Reiter, and S. Wetzel. Password hardening based on keystroke dynamics, in *Proc. 6th ACM Conf. Computer and Communications Security*, pp. 73–82, Singapore, November 1999.

[24] F. Monrose, M. K. Reiter, Q. Li, and S. Wetzel. Using voice to generate cryptographic keys, in *Proc. 2001: A Speaker Odyssey, The Speaker Recognition Workshop*, pp. 237–242, Crete, Greece, June 2001.

[25] F. Monrose, M. K. Reiter, Q. Li, and S. Wetzel. Cryptographic key generation from voice, in *Proc. 2001 IEEE Symp. Security and Privacy*, pp. 202–213, Oakland, CA, May 2001.

[26] F. Monrose, M. K. Reiter, Q. Li, D. P. Lopresti, and C. Shih. Towards speech-generated cryptographic keys on resource constrained devices, in *Proc. 11th USENIX Security Symposium*, pp. 283–296, San Francisco, CA, August 2002.

[27] J.-P. Linnartz and P. Tuyls. New shielding functions to enhance privacy and prevent misuse of biometric templates, in *Proc. 4th Int. Conf. Audio- and Video-based Biometric Person Authentication*, pp. 393–402, Guildford, UK, June 2003.

[28] A. Juels and M. Wattenberg. A fuzzy commitment scheme, in *Proc. Sixth ACM Conf. Computer and Communications Security*, pp. 28–36, Singapore, November 1999.

[29] T. C. Clancy, N. Kiyavash, and D. J. Lin. Secure smartcard-based fingerprint authentication, in *Proc. ACM SIGMM 2003 Multimedia, Biometrics Methods and Applications Workshop*, pp. 45–52, Berkeley, CA, November 2003.

[30] U. Uludag, S. Pankanti, and A. Jain. Fuzzy vault for fingerprints, in *Proc. 5. Int. Conf. Audio- and Video-Based Biometric Person Authentication*, pp. 310–319, Rye Brook, NY, July 2005.

[31] S. Yang and I. Verbauwhede. Automatic secure fingerprint verification system using fuzzy vault scheme, in *Proc. IEEE Int. Conf. Acoustics, Speech, and Signal Processing*, pp. 609–612, Philadelphia, PA, March 2005.

[32] Y. Dodis, L. Reyzin, and A. Smith. Fuzzy extractors: How to generate strong keys from biometrics and other noisy data, in *Proc. Int. Conf. Theory and Applications of Cryptographic Techniques*, pp. 523–540, Jeju Island, Korea, December 2004.

[33] Trusted Computing Group. https://www.trustedcomputinggroup.org/home.

[34] Microsoft. Microsoft Seeks Industry-Wide Collaboration for Palladium Initiative, January 25, 2003, http://www.microsoft.com/presspass/features/2002/jul02/07-01palladium.mspx.

PART C

ADVANCED TOPICS

Format-Compliant Content Protection

Wenjun Zeng

9.1 INTRODUCTION

Recent advances in networking and digital media technologies have created a large number of distributed networked multimedia applications and services that are vulnerable to piracy and malicious attacks. The security concerns, if not addressed appropriately, may potentially prevent or delay the wide dissemination of multimedia applications.

Traditionally, cryptographic techniques such as encryption, authentication, integrity check, and key management have been used to protect data communication and storage by preventing an unauthorized party from having access to clear data and making sure the authorized party receives authentic information. In recent years, the digital watermarking technique has also been proposed as an effective tool to protect the intellectual property rights of the multimedia content, often complementing other security technologies. By securely embedding invisible information into multimedia data, digital watermarks can be used to identify the rightful owner of the content as well as the buyers of the content, to convey copyright information, to facilitate copyright monitoring over the Internet, and to prevent unauthorized copy/playback on compliant devices, etc. [1].

Multimedia data, unlike traditional textual data, exhibit several unique characteristics, including high data rate, power hungry, delay constrained (including real-time constraint), synchronous, loss tolerant, having components of different importance, highly adaptable, and sometimes relatively low valued. Some of the characteristics such as loss tolerance, prioritized components, and adaptability can, in fact, be exploited in a real-time multimedia communication system. Accordingly, advanced digital signal processing and networking technologies have been designed specifically for the efficient delivery of multimedia data. For example, in order for end-users with different access networks, client devices, and/or user profiles to access the same information source and interoperate with each other, using potentially different distribution models (e.g., client-server, download, streaming, Peer-to-Peer (P2P), and broadcast), *content adaptation*, through, for example, media transcoding, has been introduced to tailor the same media content to different derived user contexts characterized by a set of real-world constraints such as bandwidth, channel error rate, power, user access control, etc. [2, 3]. Other examples include error resilient techniques, scalability, bandwidth adaptation, ITU-T Recommendation H.323 for IP (Internet Protocol)-based video conferencing applications [4], Real-Time Streaming protocol (RTSP) [5], Real-time Transport protocol (RTP) [6], etc. These unique properties of multimedia data and its distribution mechanisms have posed significant challenges to conventional security technologies that were mainly designed for general data communication. Direct application of conventional security technologies to multimedia applications may render many of the advanced technologies difficult, if not impossible, to function, resulting in performance degradation of the applications.

In general, a few important factors need to be considered in providing add-on security services, as discussed in Reference 7. First, security measures may reduce the convenience and usability of the applications they protect. Security functions that are not transparent to the user and automatically applied are likely to be perceived by the user as costs that interfere with his/her ability to get work done. Second, in some cases, the use of certain security measures can detract from the compatibility of networked applications that may have interoperated in the absence of those measures. Loss of interoperability and compatibility may be too high a price to pay for adding security measures. Third, security measures often consume computational resources such as execution time or memory. This is especially a concern for multimedia applications that typically have real-time constraints. To provide sufficient security while minimizing the negative impact on the Quality of Service (QoS) performance and cost of the multimedia applications, media security technologies have to be carefully designed, preferably by explicitly considering the interplay between cryptographic, signal processing, and networking technologies. Accordingly, content protection is typically applied at the application layer so as to facilitate the exploitation of the characteristics of multimedia data and to address the specific requirements of multimedia applications.

Among others, one general approach to address the above issues is *format-compliant content protection*, in which security protection is applied without requiring a change in the format of the original unprotected content. The term "format compliant" for content protection was probably first introduced in Wen et al. [8, 9], where a format-compliant encryption framework was proposed to address several issues in access control of multimedia data, especially for multimedia applications over lossy networks with dynamic bandwidth. Nevertheless, the general concept of format compliance for content protection had been implicitly used in the past. One notable example is the digital watermarking technique [1]. By securely embedding invisible information directly into multimedia data, digital watermarking keeps the format of the media under protection intact. In fact, the embedded watermarks can typically survive various forms of format conversion that may subsequently be applied to the protected media. In a more general sense, robust digital watermarking is a *format-agnostic* content protection technique. Format-agnostic may be a more desirable property for content protection, but is typically more difficult to achieve. A subset of format-compliant content protection solutions can achieve a full or certain degree of format-agnostic protection.

Format compliant is sometimes also referred to as syntax compliant, as typically a format is defined by syntax and the associated semantics. This implies that format compliant is defined only loosely in the sense that it does not guarantee that the semantics of the syntax is compliant. Format compliant can be extended to semi-format compliant by relaxing the constraint of full compliance of syntax in exchange for greater flexibility in security protection.

In the rest of this chapter, we first discuss the security architectures for content protection and the rationales for format-compliant content protection. We then present a few general approaches to achieve this goal, together with some discussion on the implications and trade-offs introduced by such approaches.

9.2 SECURITY ARCHITECTURES FOR CONTENT PROTECTION

Before we discuss the rationales behind format-compliant content protection, it is worthwhile to first take a look at the security architectures that have been studied for data communication. This provides a basis for addressing the specific security requirements of multimedia applications [10].

9.2.1 Placement of Security Functions

One of the most important issues to be considered in secure networked multimedia applications is where to place the security functions. This is especially important in the context of potential content adaptation along the delivery path. The placement of security functions determines what kinds of data they can protect against what kinds of attacks. It also has significant implications on what kinds of content adaptation can be performed directly on the *protected* content. Traditionally, the placement of security functions has been discussed for *general data* communication [11]. It was pointed out that there are two basic degrees of freedom concerning the placement of security functions, i.e., horizontal degree of freedom (choices among different distributed components along the communication path) and vertical degree of freedom (choices among different layers of the network protocol stack). Three classes of security functionality were defined in Sailer, Federrath, and Pfitzmann [11], i.e., end-to-end security, point-to-point security, and link-by-link security. The advantages and disadvantages of these three security approaches were discussed in Sailer, Federrath, and Pfitzmann [11]. Among others, one general consideration in adding the security service to a communication system is that the security functions should influence existing architectures as little as possible to save the huge amount of investment in the existing network infrastructure. These principles are equally applicable to the design of a multimedia content security system. In addition, the potential negative impact of the security service on content adaptation and QoS performance should be minimized.

9.2.2   Link-by-Link Security Architecture

Link-by-link security is implemented by adjacent nodes and is related to a single physical transmission link of the communication network. From the layering perspective, link-by-link security is performed at lower layers. For example, it is implemented by the IEEE 802.10 secure data exchange sub-layer [12]. The advantages of this architecture include more efficient data transmission by handling packet loss in lower layers, protection of upper layer data transparently, etc. In multimedia content adaptation, adaptation points would have full access to the clear content at upper layers, and all adaptation techniques can be applied as usual. However, trust is required in all intermediate nodes that are most probably not supervised by the end-users. In addition, extra complexity is introduced to every node. Another problem is that since clear data surfaces at upper layers of every intermediate node, eavesdropping on compromised intermediate nodes could significantly affect the security of many applications.

9.2.3   Point-to-Point Security Architecture

Point-to-point security refers to the implementation of the distributed security functions in some (but not all) components along the communication path. The Point-to-Point protocol (PPP) [13] is an example where the security mechanisms span local exchanges and some other intermediate nodes between terminals and Internet service providers. Figure 9.1 shows a point-to-point security architecture where content adaptation is implemented in the intermediate node (the adaptation point). In this architecture, the adaptation point will unprotect the incoming content using the original key, perform content adaptation, and then reprotect the adapted content using the original key or a new key prior to further distribution to the downlink clients. The advantage of this model is that any adaptation techniques that are designed to work on the unprotected content can be applied at the adaptation point above the layer where the security functions operate. It is very flexible and may be attractive for offline content adaptation scenarios where real-time performance is not a significant concern.

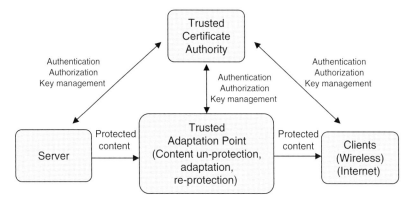

FIGURE 9.1: Point-to-point security architecture for content adaptation. (Adapted from Zeng, Lan, and Zhuang [10].)

This point-to-point security architecture would require the adaptation point to be trusted by both the end-users involved, to have access to the original key, to be able to access/generate/distribute the new key if necessary, and to be capable of supporting various cryptographic protection mechanisms. This may not only introduce significant cryptographic processing overhead and delay at the adaptation points, but also may impose significant challenges to the cryptographic system, especially the key management system. Another potential problem is that this model may require that the content be reliably transmitted between the server/client and the adaptation point in order for the protection mechanisms to function correctly, just like any traditional data. This may not be very suitable for real-time multimedia applications where the delay is very sensitive but loss is tolerable.

More significantly, relying on security mechanisms at the intermediate adaptation points may pose significant threats to end-to-end security [8, 9, 14]. Clear content and the cryptographic keys will surface in the adaptation point. The adaptation point becomes a point of potential attack. A compromised adaptation point will result in significant impact on a large number of applications. In some cases, the adaptation points may not be trusted by the end-users, in which cases content adaptation is difficult to function, and QoS performance may suffer.

9.2.4   End-to-End Media Security Architecture

The link-by-link and point-to-point security architectures are very generic and are applicable to other general data as well. However, they do not fully take into account the unique characteristics of real-time multimedia distribution.

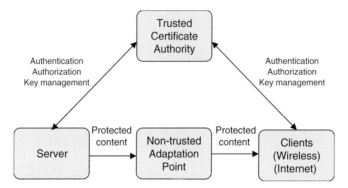

FIGURE 9.2:   End-to-end media security architecture. (Adapted from Zeng, Lan, and Zhuang [10].)

End-to-end security refers to the implementation of the distributed security functions only within the endpoints of a communication. The Secure Sockets Layer (SSL) protocol [15] is an example which runs above TCP/IP for reliable data communication between two endpoints. Figure 9.2 presents an end-to-end media security architecture for applications where content adaptation is implemented in the intermediate nodes. In this architecture, the adaptation point is not required to perform the security functions. Instead, the content is protected in such a way that content adaptation can be performed in transparency to the content protection mechanisms. As a result, no trust is assumed on the adaptation point. Furthermore, the media security solution is designed in a network-friendly fashion such that it works well with existing and future multimedia networking technologies to reduce the deployment cost of the security service.

Format-compliant content protection is one of the approaches that falls under this architecture. We discuss the rationales behind format-compliant content protection in the next section.

9.3   RATIONALES FOR FORMAT-COMPLIANT
CONTENT PROTECTION

For many multimedia applications, maintaining bitstream compliance after content protection is very important. For example, due to several unique characteristics of the wireless networks and the relatively low processing power and memory of mobile terminals, content encryption for wireless multimedia applications has a number of unique challenges and is one of the applications to which syntax compliance after content protection is of importance. Several motivations behind format-compliant content protection are analyzed here.

- **Resource-constrained networks/devices**. For wireless multimedia content protection, especially for consumption on mobile terminals, low processing overhead and delay becomes an extremely critical requirement. Due to the small amount of data that could be protected given the tight processing power and memory budget, it becomes important to "select" only the most critical bits to protect, with possibly the trade-off of security level. Format/syntax compliance makes it easier to locate protected fields in the protected content without side information and is therefore desirable [9].
- **Error resiliency for lossy networks**. Today's Internet and most wireless networks provide only the best-effort services. This makes secure transmission of real-time multimedia data even more challenging. Many standard cryptographic methods require all bits to be received correctly, at the cost of increased latency or bit overhead for channel protection. This overlooks the fact that many multimedia applications have real-time constraints, but can tolerate data loss that is perceptually less important. Traditional cryptographic algorithms do not cope well with lossy networks and the loss-tolerant nature of the multimedia data. In fact, great efforts have been dedicated to the design of digital content compression standards to provide some level of error resiliency. It is desirable that most of these existing tools can be readily applied to the transmission of a protected media bitstream. Format-compliant content protection makes this possible by preserving the error resiliency property of the original unprotected compressed bitstream.
- **Protocol friendliness**. Efficient and quality multimedia delivery often requires specially designed communication protocols such as transport packetization, unequal error protection, and random access. Most of these protocols, however, have been designed to work with *unprotected* compressed contents. For example, transport packetization using standard RTP requires understanding the syntactical structures of the compressed bitstreams [16]. Efficient content delivery over heterogeneous networks (including both packet-switched networks and circuit-switched networks) may also require using different transport protocols for networks of different characteristics in the course of the delivery. The media security technologies should be designed to cope well with many existing and future network protocols. Format-compliant content protection preserves the syntactical structures of the compressed bitstreams and thus works with existing communication and networking protocols.
- **Content adaptation and scalability**. To achieve a certain level of end-to-end QoS, application layer adaptation techniques such as rate/congestion control and media transcoding performed by proxy servers located at gateways between heterogeneous networks, or performed by the intermediate

nodes in an overlay network, have been developed [2, 3]. Most of these existing content adaptation techniques work only on the *unprotected* bitstreams. Format-compliant content protection would allow many of these techniques to be directly applied to the protected bitstream.

- **Seamless protection in both storage and transit**. In some applications, it is desirable that contents be protected and pre-packaged into some format for both storage and delivery to potential consumers without the need to do repackaging, as evidenced in the superdistribution business model where pre-packaged protected contents are redistributed/streamed from some users to other potential consumers separately from the delivery of the protection key and consumption license. This requires application layer security protection, and format-compliant content protection would allow existing content delivery protocols such as RTP [16] that were designed for unprotected content to work directly with the protected content.

- **End-to-end security implication**. More importantly, requiring cryptographic processing at the intermediate nodes may compromise the end-to-end security. The conventional point-to-point approach requires the intermediate nodes to be trusted and secure, which in some cases (e.g., in the emerging fully distributed P2P networks) may not be feasible. In fact, for some applications the content providers may prefer to securely manage their contents independent of the streaming servers that are under the control of the service providers. Thus, sharing keys between the content providers, who encrypt the contents, and the service providers, who deliver the contents and need the key to decrypt the contents for content adaptation, e.g., transport packetization using RTP, may not be desirable.

- **Ease of deployment**. In general, the security functions should influence existing communication and networking architectures as little as possible to save the huge investment in the existing infrastructure and to ease the deployment of multimedia applications. In addition, many popular existing multimedia systems such as a multimedia player were designed without much consideration of content protection so that an add-on content protection technology introduced later may not be recognized or supported by these legacy devices. This "backward" compatibility issue needs to be addressed.

In summary, the direct application of traditional security technologies may potentially render many of the existing adaptation and other enabling technologies in a content delivery food chain difficult to function. It is desirable to minimize the need to perform intermediate cryptographic processing on the protected content along the food chain of content delivery. One significant advantage of such an approach is that many existing network infrastructures and standard techniques will be left intact, facilitating the deployment and adoption of the system. This would require that the content protection techniques be designed in such a way that various content and network adaptations can be performed directly on the protected bitstreams, without cryptographic operations.

The ability of a content protection scheme to maintain format compliance provides one satisfactory solution to all of the requirements discussed above. Syntax compliance inherits many carefully designed and desirable properties of the unprotected compressed bitstream, such as error resiliency, scalability, and protocol friendliness, and provides the possibility of performing various types of signal processing directly on the protected bitstream. There will be no marker emulation problem. A standard player that is not aware of the protection will not crash when playing the protected content, so a legacy system where no Digital Rights Management (DRM) solution was incorporated can deal with the secured content gracefully [9].

There have been quite a few recently developed format-compliant content protection solutions that address various network-friendly end-to-end security issues for multimedia delivery. We categorize them into three categories, i.e., format-compliant content encryption, format-agnostic content protection, and semi-format-compliant content protection, and discuss them in the following sections.

9.4   FORMAT-COMPLIANT CONTENT ENCRYPTION

In this section, we describe two general approaches for format-compliant content encryption: joint encryption and compression, and format-compliant selective encryption/scrambling.

9.4.1   Integrated Encryption and Compression

While most conventional approaches separate encryption from compression, a joint approach, as illustrated in Figure 9.3, would generally lead to an improved system performance in terms of speed and flexibility that would allow many requirements of multimedia applications to be addressed. More importantly, this joint approach would result in an encrypted compressed bitstream that is compliant with the compression format, a desired property we discussed above.

It is important to address the mutual impact between encryption and compression in the integrated encryption/compression approach. In general, encryption should not be applied in the spatial/temporal domain as encryption results in

FIGURE 9.3:   A joint encryption/compression architecture.

redundancy-free ciphertext that renders compression helpless. To integrate encryption with compression, two general approaches have been studied in the literature. One is to apply encryption to the transformed coefficients in the transform domain. The other is to integrate encryption with the entropy coding process. We discuss these two general approaches in the following subsections.

Transform Domain Encryption

It is well-understood that typical transformations will result in so-called transform coding gain [17]. Applying encryption in the transform domain judicially can preserve the transform coding gain, therefore reducing the potential negative impact on the compression efficiency. Nevertheless, applying encryption in the transform domain will still have an impact on the performance of the subsequent entropy coding typically employed in a compression system, as advanced entropy coding techniques rely on exploiting the redundancy/dependency of the transformed coefficients. Encryption may potentially destroy/reduce such redundancy/dependency. A general idea to address such a problem is to ensure that encryption and compression operate in two orthogonal or near-orthogonal spaces so as to reduce their interference [20].

The Zigzag-Permutation algorithm [18] is one of the earliest scrambling algorithms designed for joint MPEG video encryption/compression. The technique applies permutation to the Discrete Cosine Transform (DCT) coefficients of an 8×8 image block so that they are encoded using an order different from the standard zigzag order, thus generating a scrambled MPEG compressed bitstream. The algorithm, however, could result in a significantly lower compression ratio (as much as 50% bit overhead) since the permutation destroys the statistics relied upon by the runlength coder. It also has some security problems since the DC (direct current) coefficients can be easily recovered, and the spatial energy distribution of the image remains largely unchanged due to the *local* permutation operation [20]. See Figure 9.4(c) for an example of the scrambled frames.

A joint encryption/compression framework was proposed in Zeng and Lei [19, 20], where the transform coefficients are divided into blocks and are subject to selective scrambling which includes random sign change, block shuffling, block rotation, spatial coefficient shuffling within a subband segment, etc. The Motion Vectors (MVs), if any, are also subject to random sign change and spatial shuffling. The scrambled coefficients and MVs are then subject to normal entropy coding and compressed bitstream formation. In this approach, the block-based spatial shuffling process (a high-level *global* operation) and the compression process (typically, a low-level *local* operation) intend to work in two near-orthogonal spaces, thus achieving a good compromise between security and compression efficiency. The resultant encrypted bitstream conforms to the compression format.

(a) Unscrambled frame   (b) Scrambled frame using [20] (c) Scrambled frame using [18]

FIGURE 9.4: Scrambled P-frame using the joint encryption/compression techniques.

Figure 9.4 shows that for an 8×8 DCT-based system, encrypting the signs of all coefficients and signs of all MVs and only shuffling along the slice (i.e., Group of Macroblocks) for I (Intra)-frames/blocks, denoted as I(sign+slice) + P(sign+MV_sign) in Zeng and Lei [20], provides a very good compromise between security and coding efficiency. It only increases the bitrate by 4.8% on average [20], while the video sequence is completely indiscernible. The scrambled compressed video sequence can be decoded and played by a standard video decoder that is unaware of the scrambling, as shown in Figure 9.4(b), just like an ordinary unencrypted compressed video bitstream. Content adaptation can be performed directly on the scrambled content. For example, to perform requantization-based transcoding, one can simply decode the scrambled compressed bitstream into *spatially* shuffled DCT coefficients, perform requantization, and then re-encode the requantized shuffled coefficients. No cryptographic key is necessary at the transcoding point. This approach is very flexible and attractive, as it allows most transcoding techniques that are designed to work in both the original transform domain and the compressed domain to function directly on the scrambled content. The format-compliant property of this approach also allows all lower layer protocols to work directly with the scrambled content.

Random permutation-based encryption/scrambling techniques are generally vulnerable to known plaintext attacks, if the permutation table is fixed over time. To increase the security, the permutation table needs to be updated frequently using a cryptographically secure process [20].

Integrated Encryption and Entropy Coding

Another general approach for joint encryption/compression is to integrate encryption into the entropy coding process. As discussed above, encrypting/scrambling transformed coefficients will have some impact on the coding efficiency, despite some great efforts that have been made to reduce that impact. By introducing randomness in the entropy coding process, it is possible to turn an entropy coder into an engine that can do both entropy coding and encryption, where security is achieved without necessarily sacrificing the compression efficiency and increasing the computational load.

Early work in this area focused on adaptive arithmetic coding using higher order models [21–23]. The entropy coder was converted into a cipher by hiding the initial statistical model. As the statistical model changes constantly and the model space is enormous, attack by a brute-force exhaustive search is prohibited. It is generally believed that this scheme is very secure against ciphertext-only and known-plaintext attacks, but vulnerable to chosen-plaintext attacks [21–23]. The coder is slow, though, and not very suitable for compressing large amounts of multimedia data.

An integrated multimedia compression and encryption approach is proposed in Wu and Kuo [24] that turns the entropy coder into a cipher by employing multiple statistical models alternately in a secret order. The hiding of the statistical model information in the decoding process is used to completely prevent correct decoding of the compressed bitstream. Two specific encryption schemes are discussed by applying this approach to the Huffman coder using multiple coding tables and to the QM coder using multiple state indices, respectively. The basic structures of these coders are maintained, but the space of the statistical models is increased, e.g., through a process called Huffman tree mutation, to provide sufficient security. Security enhancement techniques, e.g., changing the keystream frequently, are also proposed to enhance the security against known-plaintext and chosen-plaintext attacks.

Strictly speaking, this approach results in encrypted bitstreams that are not fully format compliant. For example, in the case of using Huffman coders, the standard decoder that is unaware of the encryption will encounter invalid codewords in the decoding process using the standard coding table. Nevertheless, the major syntactical structures including the synchronization codewords will be preserved to be exploited by the decoder and other content and network adaptation techniques. For example, a decoder implementation that is resilient to transmission error should be able to handle those "invalid" decoded codewords and continue the decoding process by searching for the next synchronization point. This approach, however, may not accommodate the application of some content adaptation techniques such as requantization-based transcoding on the protected content.

9.4.2   Format-Compliant Selective Encryption/Scrambling

A format-compliant selective encryption/scrambling framework [9] has been developed and adopted by the MPEG-4 Intellectual Property Management and Protection (IPMP) Extension standard [25, 26]. The MPEG-4 IPMP Extension defines a messaging framework that allows different IPMP tools, potentially from different vendors, to be easily plugged into the terminal and to interoperate with

FIGURE 9.5:   Format-compliant selective encryption/scrambling architecture.

each other and with the terminal in a secure way. One of the messages, i.e., the IPMP_SelectiveDecryptionInit message defined in Annex A of the MPEG-4 IPMP Extension, allows a terminal to configure a selective decryption tool (e.g., the ones proposed by Zeng and colleagues [9, 27]). It tells how the bitstream is encrypted, whether all bits are encrypted or only portions of it, what portions/fields of the received bitstream are encrypted [9] or shuffled [27] and therefore need to be decrypted or deshuffled, etc.

In this format-compliant selective encryption/scrambling framework, as shown in Figure 9.5, encryption operations are executed intelligently on the compressed bitstream, and full bit-level compliance to the compression syntax can be maintained. One tool developed in this framework, as reported by Wen and colleagues [8, 9], is to extract some fixed-length and Variable-Length Codewords (VLC), map them to fixed-length index, and then encrypt the fixed-length index using standard encryption algorithms such as the Data Encryption Standard (DES) [28]. The encrypted fixed-length index is then mapped back to a codeword which is then inserted back into the bitstream to generate a fully format-compliant encrypted bitstream. This process is illustrated in Figure 9.6. A primary concern of encrypting the VLCs using this tool is the potential bitrate overhead (e.g., from 1% to over 20%, depending on the content and bitrate, when only VLC coded MVs are encrypted [9]), as the mapping/encryption/remapping processes eliminate the benefit of variable-length coding. A generalized index mapping scheme that can be applied directly to any symbols that take values from a finite set is discussed in Wu and Mao [29].

Another tool developed within this framework is to "spatially" (i.e., across a group of spatial blocks) shuffle codewords of the compressed bitstream in a way that the resultant bitstream would preserve the syntactical structure of, and achieve nearly full bit-level compliance to, the compression format [9, 27]. It introduces no bit overhead, as it is simply a cryptographic key-based reorganization of the already compressed bitstream, whereas the coefficient block shuffling process proposed in Zeng and Lei [19, 20] is done in the transform domain prior to compression and therefore would reduce the compression efficiency.

Subsequently, several syntax-compliant encryption schemes have been proposed for JPSEC [30], the security part of the latest international still image compression standard JPEG 2000, to ensure the backward compatibility with the JPEG 2000 Part 1 [31] so that important properties of JPEG 2000 such as scalability

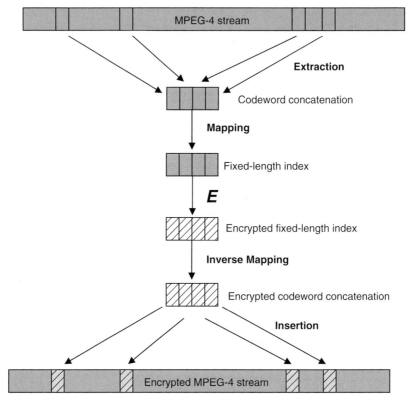

FIGURE 9.6:   Format-compliant selective encryption of MPEG-4 bitstream.

and error resiliency will be maintained. These include encrypting the sign bits of selected high-frequency wavelet coefficients or randomly flipping the bits of the coding passes codewords belonging to the last layers of each code block [32], encrypting the data in each individual packet [33, 34, 37], code block contribution to a packet [36, 37] or codeword segments [35, 37], with mechanisms to prevent marker emulation, i.e., to prevent any two consecutive bytes of the encrypted bitstream to assume a value in the interval of $[0 \times FF90, 0 \times FFFF]$ which are reserved for use by JPEG 2000 markers [36, 37].

Compared to the transform domain joint compression/encryption approach [20] discussed above, format-compliant selective encryption is a little bit less flexible as it may not allow some content adaptation schemes that work in the frequency domain to function in transparency to encryption. However, any content adaptation schemes (e.g., rate shaping by coefficient dropping without drift compensation) or network processing (e.g., transport packetization) that work with the compressed bitstream should be able to function directly on the scrambled compressed bitstream.

9.5   FORMAT-AGNOSTIC CONTENT PROTECTION

For content protection techniques other than encryption, it may be feasible to introduce the protection regardless of the format in which the media is packaged. More importantly, the protection can usually survive various types of format conversions. We refer to this type of content protection as *format-agnostic content protection*. We briefly discuss two general types of such an approach in this section. More detailed discussions about these two topics are presented in Chapters 5 and 7 of this book.

9.5.1   Robust Digital Watermarking

Perhaps the best example of format-agnostic content protection is digital watermarking [1]. Digital watermarks are robustly integrated with the content and require no additional storage or new format standards. Robust digital watermarks are robust to many intentional/unintentional attacks such as cropping, low-pass filtering, compression, requantization, transcoding, compression format conversion, scaling, digital-to-analog conversion, analog-to-digital conversion, etc. As a result, content adaptation can be performed directly on the watermark-protected content. In fact, all adapted contents may still be securely protected by the original robust watermarks.

9.5.2   Content-Based Media Authentication

Traditional cryptographic authentication schemes using digital signatures or message authentication codes are designed to ensure that no single-bit alteration is allowed. However, in many multimedia applications, it is desirable for an authentication system to tolerate some content-preserving operations such as compression and content adaptation, while being capable of detecting other malicious attacks. Such an authentication system is referred to as a *content integrity system*. Among others, a semi-fragile digital watermark [38] has been proposed to detect, measure, and locate malicious modifications to the host media while surviving content-preserving adaptation. Other content-based image authentication systems have also been studied [39–41]. For example, the system proposed in Queluz [40] relies on image edges and tries to tackle the problem of image/video integrity from a semantic, high-level point of view. It extracts essential image characteristics that should survive the whole processing and transmission chain, which are then encrypted and authenticated and conveyed as additional information to the receiver for content-based authentication of the received image.

An *approximate* Image Message Authentication Code (IMAC) is proposed in Xie, Arce, and Graveman [41] for soft image authentication. The approximate IMAC can successfully tolerate JPEG compression, but preserves the capability to detect and locate image tampering.

One of the most significant advantages of the content-based media authentication schemes is that the protection is introduced largely independent of the actual format in which the content is presented, which provides the greatest flexibility for subsequent content processing and adaptation.

9.6 SEMI-FORMAT-COMPLIANT CONTENT PROTECTION

As discussed above, fully format-compliant content protection schemes are most friendly to existing modules in an end-to-end communication system. However, a fully format-compliant solution could be overrestrictive for some applications, thus sacrificing some performance (e.g., in terms of bitrate overhead and/or security level). In fact, in many applications, the preservation of *some* important syntactical structures of the compression format that are required for content adaptation and network processing would be sufficient. We refer to this property as *semi-format compliance*. For example, for RTP packetization of MPEG-4 video, only syntactical structures above the video packet level are required. Accordingly, it might be more efficient to design some compromised solutions where only some of the most desirable properties (e.g., transport protocol compatibility, scalability, and error resiliency) are preserved [14, 27, 29]. For example, the "spatially" shuffling codeword approach reported in Zeng, Wen, and Severa [27] and discussed in Section 9.4.2 is, in fact, only near fully format compliant in the sense that it preserves all the syntactical structures of the compressed video, but the actual decoding of the scrambled video may result in more than 64 coefficients in one 8×8 DCT block (therefore, not fully compliant *semantically*). In exchange, no bit overhead due to encryption is incurred in this approach.

When multimedia content is layered or scalable coded, layered/scalable content protection is feasible that would allow some content adaptation without violating the end-to-end security requirement. One way to deal with end-to-end security of content adaptation is to divide the content into several layers with different importance during content creation and to protect different layers separately, with clear-text metadata annotation, to preserve the layered structure of the content. When content adaptation is required, one can simply drop those less important layers based on the clear-text metadata [42–44]. This is especially suitable when the multimedia content consists of multiple modalities, e.g., text, audio, and video information, which can be protected separately and be selectively dropped depending on the bandwidth/resource constraint. It is also applicable to a layered coded single media as reported in Yuan et al. [43] for layered coded MPEG-4 video and in Gibson et al. [44] for layered coded MPEG-4 scalable speech bitstreams.

The trade-off here is that within each layer, the syntactical structures of the compression format are not preserved. The granularity of content adaptation is limited to only the layer level.

When the compressed media is created using fine granularity scalable coding, scalable protection becomes feasible [14, 45]. An example is shown in Wee and Apostolopoulos [14] for Motion JPEG 2000 and MPEG-4 Fine Granularity Scalable bitstream using a non-fully format-compliant secure scalable streaming architecture (please refer to Chapter 10 of this book for a detailed discussion of this architecture) that enables low-complexity and high-quality transcoding to be performed at intermediate, possibly untrusted, network nodes without compromising the end-to-end security. With the joint design of scalable coding and progressive encryption techniques, secure scalable packets are created with unencrypted headers providing hints such as priority information and optimal truncation points to the transcoder which can then perform near-rate-distortion optimal transcoding for fine-grain bitrate reduction. A few percents of bitrate overhead is reported in Wee and Apostolopoulos [14] for achieving such functionality.

9.7 CONCLUSION

In this chapter, we analyze the security requirements and architectures in a multimedia communication system, discuss the motivations behind format-compliant content protection, and describe a few popular approaches to achieve format-compliant content protection. We show that format-compliant content protection can maintain the end-to-end security, ease of deployment, backward compatibility to legacy systems, and QoS performance of multimedia applications, albeit at the cost of potentially sacrificing certain content adaptation functionality and granularity, depending on where and how the security functions are implemented.

Despite recent progress in network-friendly end-to-end security technologies, there are still many open issues, especially regarding how to quantify the trade-offs between complexity, security level, QoS performance, and ease of deployment. Some potential topics for further research include semi-format-compliant content protection that preserves only *some* important syntactical structures of the compression format to reduce the potential negative impact on bitrate overhead and security level, co-design and standardization of media compression, security protection, and transport, co-design of *fully* scalable video coding and protection, etc.

Acknowledgements

Many viewpoints and material presented in this chapter are the results of previous collaborative work with Jiangtao Wen, Mike Severa, Max Luttrell, Shawmin Lei, Junqiang Lan, and Xinhua Zhuang. The author would like to thank them for many insightful discussions in the past few years.

REFERENCES

[1] I. Cox, M. Miller, and J. Bloom. *Digital Watermarking*, ISBN: 1558607145, Elsevier, Amsterdam/New York, 2001.

[2] R. Han and J. Smith. Transcoding of the Internet's multimedia content for universal access, *Multimedia Communications: Directions and Innovations*, Academic Press, San Diego, Chapter 15, 2000.

[3] A. Vetro, C. Christopoulos, and H. Sun. Video transcoding architectures and techniques, an overview, *IEEE Signal Processing Magazine*, 20:2: pp. 18–29, March 2003.

[4] ITU-T Recommendation H.323, Packet-based multimedia communications systems.

[5] Schulzrinne et al. [IETF RFC 2326] RTSP: Real Time Streaming Protocol, April 1998.

[6] Schulzrinne et al. [IETF RFC 3550] RTP: A Transport Protocol for Real-Time Applications, July, 2003.

[7] Committee on Information Systems Trustworthiness, National Research Council, Trust in Cyberspace, http://www7.nationalacademies.org/cstb/pub_trust.html. 1999.

[8] J. Wen, M. Severa, W. Zeng, M. H. Luttrell, and W. Jin. A format-compliant configurable encryption framework for access control of multimedia, in *Proc. IEEE Workshop Multimedia Signal Processing*, Cannes, France, pp. 435–440, October 2001.

[9] J. Wen, M. Severa, W. Zeng, M. Luttrell, and W. Jin. A format compliant configurable encryption framework for access control of video, *IEEE Tran. Circuits and Systems for Video Technology*, 12(6):545–557, June 2002.

[10] W. Zeng, J. Lan, and X. Zhuang. Security architectures and analysis for content adaptation, in *Conf. Security, Steganography, and Watermarking of Multimedia Contents VII, IS&T/SPIE Symp. Electronic Imaging*, pp. 84–95, San Jose, CA, January 2005.

[11] R. Sailer, H. Federrath, and A. Pfitzmann. Security functions in telecommunications—Placement & achievable security, in *Multilateral Security in Communications*, G. Müller and K. Rannenberg (Eds.), Addison–Wesley–Longman, Reading, MA, pp. 323–348, 1999.

[12] IEEE 802.10: Interoperable LAN/MAN Security. IEEE Standards for Local and Metropolitan Area Networks, http://grouper.ieee.org/groups/802/101/1992.

[13] [IETF RFC 1661] The Point-to-Point Protocol (PPP). W. Simpson (Ed.), July 1994.

[14] S. Wee and J. Apostolopoulos. Secure scalable streaming enabling transcoding without decryption, *IEEE Int. Conf. Image Processing*, 1:437–440, 2001.

[15] Freier, Alano, Karlton, Philip, and Kocher, Paul C. The SSL Protocol—Version 3.0. Netscape Communications Corporation, 1996, available at http://home.netscape.com/eng/ssl3.

[16] Y. Kikuchi, et al. RTP payload format for MPEG-4 audio/visual streams, IETF RFC 3016, November 2000.

[17] A. Gersho and R. M. Gray. *Vector Quantization and Signal Compression*, Kluwer Academic, Dordrecht, Norwell, MA, 1992.

[18] L. Tang. Methods for encrypting and decrypting MPEG video data efficiently, *Proc. ACM Int. Multimedia Conference*, pp. 219–229, Boston, MA, 1996.

[19] W. Zeng and S. Lei. Efficient frequency domain video scrambling for content access control, *Proc. 7th ACM Int. Conf. Multimedia*, pp. 285–294, Orlando, FL, 1999.

[20] W. Zeng and S. Lei. Efficient frequency domain selective scrambling of digital video, *IEEE Tran. Multimedia*, 5(1):118–129, March 2003.

[21] A. Barbir. A methodology for performing secure data compression, in *Proc. 29th Southeastern Symp. System Theory*, 266, Cookeville, TN, March 1997.

[22] H. Bergen and J. Hogan. A chosen plaintext attack on an adaptive arithmetic coding compression algorithm, *Computer Security*, 12:157, 1993.

[23] J. Lim, C. Boyd, and E. Dawson. Cryptanalysis of adaptive arithmetic coding encryption scheme, in *Proc. Australasian Conf. on Information Security and Privacy (ACISP)*, pp. 216–227, Sydney, Australia, 1997.

[24] C.-P. Wu and C.-C. J. Kuo. Design of integrated multimedia compression and encryption systems, *IEEE Trans. Multimedia*, 7(5):828–839, October 2005.

[25] ISO/IEC. Information Technology—Coding of Audio-Visual Objects—Part 13: Intellectuals Property Management and Protection (IPMP) extension, Shanghai, ISO/IEC JTC1/SC29/WG11 MPEG, N5284, October 2002.

[26] M. Ji, S. Shen, W. Zeng, et al. MPEG-4 IPMP extension—For interoperable protection of multimedia content, *EURASIP J. Applied Signal Processing*, *Special Issue on Multimedia Security and Rights Management*, 14:2201–2213, 2004.

[27] W. Zeng, J. Wen, and M. Severa. Fast self-synchronous content scrambling by spatially shuffling codewords of compressed bitstreams, in *Proc. IEEE Int. Conf. Image Processing*, Rochester, pp. 169–172, September, 2002.

[28] Data Encryption Standard (DES), FIPS PU 46-3, Reaffirmed October 25, 1999. Available at http://csrc.nist.gov/publications/fips/fips46-3/fips46-3.pdf.

[29] M. Wu and Y. Mao. Communication-friendly encryption of multimedia, *IEEE Workshop of Multimedia Signal Processing*, pp. 292–295, St. Thomas, US Virgin Islands, 2002.

[30] JPSEC Final Committee Draft—Version 1.0, ISO/IEC/JTC1/SC29/WG1/N3480, November 2004.

[31] ISO/IEC. Information Technology – JPEG 2000 Image Coding System, Part 1: Core Coding System, ISO/IEC 15444-1:2000 (ISO/IEC JTC/SC 29/WG 1 N1646R), March 2000.

[32] R. Grosbois, P. Gerbelot, and T. Ebrahimi. Authentication and access control in the JPEG 2000 compressed domain, in *Proc. SPIE Applications of Digital Image Processing XXIV*, 4472:95–104, December 2001.

[33] Y. Sadourny and V. Conan. A proposal for supporting selective encryption in JPSEC, in *IEEE Trans. Consumer Electronics*, 49(4):846–849, November 2003.

[34] R. Norcen and A. Uhl. Selective encryption of the JPEG 2000 bitstream, in *Proc. IFIP TC6/TC11 Sixth Joint Working Conf. Communications and Multimedia Security*, A. Lioy and D. Mazzocchi (Ed.), *Lecture Notes in Computer Science*, 2828:194–204, Turin, Italy, October. 2003, Springer-Verlag.

[35] B. Zhu, Y. Yang, and S. Li. JPEG 2000 encryption enabling fine granularity scalability without decryption, in *IEEE Int. Symp. Circuits and Systems*, 6:6304–6307, May 2005.

[36] Y. Wu and R. H. Deng. Compliant encryption of JPEG2000 codestreams, in *Proc. IEEE Int. Conf. Image Processing*, Singapore, pp. 3447–3450, October 2004.

[37] B. Zhu, Y. Yang, and S. Li. JPEG 2000 syntax-compliant encryption preserving full scalability, in *Proc. IEEE Int. Conf. Image Processing*, 3:636–639, September, 2005.

[38] C. Lin and S. Chang. Semi fragile watermarking for authentication of JPEG visual content, *Proc. SPIE Int. Conf. Security and Watermarking of Multimedia Contents*, 3971: pp. 140–151, January 2000.

[39] M. Schneider and S.-F. Chang. A robust content based digital signature for image authentication, in *Proc. IEEE Int. Conf. Image Processing*, 3: pp. 227–230, 1996.

[40] M. P. Queluz. Towards robust, content based techniques for image authentication, *IEEE Workshop Multimedia Signal Processing*, pp. 297–302, Los Angeles, CA, December 1998.

[41] L. Xie, G. Arce, and R. Graveman. Approximate image message authentication codes, *IEEE Trans. Multimedia*, 3(2):pp. 242–252, June 2001.

[42] Y. Chang, R. Han, C. Li, and J. Smith. Secure transcoding of Internet content, in *Int. Workshop Intelligent Multimedia Computing and Networking (IMMCN)*, pp. 940–948, Durham, NC, 2002.

[43] C. Yuan, B. Zhu, M. Su, S. Li, X. Wang, and Y. Zhong. Layered access control for MPEG-4 FGS video, in *Proc. IEEE Int. Conf. Image Processing*, pp. 517–520, 2003.

[44] J. D. Gibson, et al. Selective encryption and scalable speech coding for voice communications over multi-hop wireless links, in *Proc. IEEE Military Communications Conference*, Monterey, CA, October 31–November 3, 2004.

[45] C. Yuan, B. B. Zhu, Y. Wang, S. Li, and Y. Zhong. Efficient and fully scalable encryption for MPEG-4 FGS, *Proc. IEEE Int. Symp. Circuits and Systems*, 2:620–623, May 2003.

10

Secure Media Streaming and Secure Transcoding

John G. Apostolopoulos and Susie Wee

10.1 INTRODUCTION

Technology advancements are allowing new media applications and services to be delivered over the Internet and third-generation (3G) or fourth-generation (4G) cellular networks. Many of these applications and services require a flexible media distribution infrastructure and security mechanisms that can protect the confidentiality of media content and ensure its authenticity; however, achieving flexibility and security traditionally are conflicting goals. For example, most media distribution systems are designed to allow flexible media processing and handling at various stages in the distribution chain. In contrast, most secure media distribution systems are designed to deny access to the content during distribution as shown in Figure 10.1. This prohibits media processing and handling during distribution. If an entity did want to process the protected stream during distribution, it would require decrypting the protected content to perform the processing, creating a potential security hole in the system.

The reason that security and flexible handling are typically conflicting goals is because security is usually incorporated in a media distribution system in a media-unaware manner. For example, media is often encrypted as if it were a block of data and then stored as an encrypted file or transported as a sequence of encrypted bits. While this protects the media content itself by completely hiding the bits, it also hides valuable information, including metadata contained in the media bits which facilitate handling and processing. Thus, when end-to-end security is

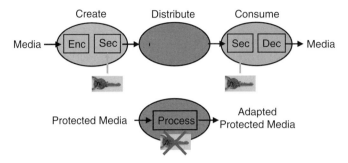

FIGURE 10.1:   Traditionally, media distributions systems are designed to allow flexible processing and handling during distribution, while secure media systems are designed to prevent access during distribution. This chapter describes technologies that simultaneously enable end-to-end security and allow flexible processing and handling during media distribution without requiring access to the content.

a requirement, using traditional (media-unaware) protection methods prevents the protected media from being flexibly handled and processed in the middle of the value delivery chain.

In this chapter, we show that media-aware protection can be used to simultaneously achieve end-to-end security and flexible mid-network handling and processing of the protected content. We focus on the security services of confidentiality and authentication, and we describe the technologies that make this possible. Our approach draws parallels to application-layer framing which uses media-aware transport to achieve improved error resilience to packet losses in a network [1].

This chapter continues by examining three basic problems: (1) *secure streaming* from a sender to a receiver, (2) *secure transcoding* at an untrustworthy node in the middle of the network, and (3) *secure adaptive streaming* of pre-stored content at an untrustworthy sender. We refer to a node as untrustworthy to denote that the node should not have access to the unencrypted media, or, equivalently, to the security keys.

10.1.1   Secure Media Streaming from Sender to Receiver

There are a variety of practically very important data security techniques which may be straightforwardly applied for secure media streaming. We briefly discuss these approaches to highlight their advantages and disadvantages.

Figure 10.2 shows a secure media streaming system that uses conventional application-level encryption. The media is first encoded into a compressed

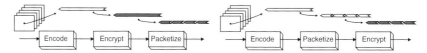

FIGURE 10.2: Examples of conventional application-layer encryption (left) and network-layer encryption (right).

bitstream, and the bitstream is then encrypted. The encrypted bitstream is then split into packets and transmitted over the network using a transport protocol such as UDP. The difficulty with this approach occurs when a packet is lost. Specifically, without the data from the missing packet, decryption and decoding of the remaining data may be very difficult, if not practically impossible. Note that if the encrypted media was delivered via file download, where a reliable delivery mechanism is used, then this problem would not occur since all packets would be reliably delivered to the receiver. However, streaming applications typically prohibit the use of reliable delivery mechanisms since each media packet must be delivered by its appropriate delivery deadline so that it can be decoded and played out in time.

An alternative method is to use media-aware packetization and packet-by-packet encryption, as shown in Figure 10.2. In this case the same compression algorithm is used as in the previous system. However, in this system the packetization is performed in a manner that considers the content of the coded media, a concept referred to as application-level framing. Specifically, each packet payload can be designed so that it can be independently decodable even if the surrounding packets are not received, thereby leading to much better loss recovery. For example, a common approach is to use Moving Picture Experts Group (MPEG) compression with the Real-time Transport Protocol (RTP) on top of User Datagram Protocol (UDP). RTP provides streaming parameters such as time stamps and suggests methods for packetizing MPEG payload data to ease error recovery in the case of lost or delayed packets. In this case each packet can be independently encrypted and authenticated, and then even if packet loss occurs the receiver can decrypt, authenticate, and decode all of the received packets.

Security of RTP flows is practically very important. Therefore, an extension of RTP, referred to as Secure RTP (SRTP), was developed which provides confidentiality, message authentication, and replay protection for the RTP traffic, as well as for its associated control traffic Real-time Transfer Control Protocol (RTCP) [2].

SRTP and similar approaches (e.g., see Reference 3) provide the basic security services required for secure streaming between a sender and a receiver. In the remainder of this chapter we examine techniques that not only provide secure streaming, but in addition the ability to securely adapt the protected content.

10.1.2   Secure Transcoding at a Mid-Network Node

A basic and important functionality for media streaming is the ability to adapt the media to clients with diverse device capabilities and delivery over heterogeneous and time-varying communication links. For example, clients can have different display sizes, communication, power, and computational capabilities. In addition, wired and wireless networks have different maximum bandwidths, quality levels, and time-varying characteristics. This may require mid-network nodes, or proxies, to perform stream adaptation, or transcoding, to adapt streams for downstream client capabilities and time-varying network conditions. This is illustrated in Figure 10.3, where streaming media content is delivered to three devices with different capabilities, each connected by a network which supports a different bandwidth. The mid-network node or proxy transcodes the incoming media stream to match the specific characteristics of each client and network connection.

Another important property is security to protect content from eavesdroppers. This makes it necessary to transport streams in encrypted form. The problem of adapting to downstream conditions while also providing security is particularly acute for mobile wireless clients, since the available bandwidth can be highly dynamic and the wireless communication makes the transmission highly susceptible to eavesdropping.

The challenge is to perform transcoding in the middle of the network while preserving end-to-end security. To provide end-to-end security, the media should be encrypted at the sender and decrypted only at the receiver—everywhere in-between the sender and receiver, the media should remain in encrypted form.

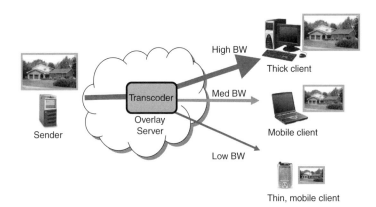

FIGURE 10.3:   The high-resolution high-bitrate coded content on the left is transcoded at a mid-network node to best match the three receiver display sizes and associated access networks on the right.

FIGURE 10.4: The conventional approach for transcoding encrypted streams involves decryption, transcoding, and re-encryption.

The conventional approach for transcoding encrypted streams poses a serious security threat because it requires (1) decrypting the stream, (2) transcoding the decrypted stream, and (3) re-encrypting the result, as shown in Figure 10.4. Since every transcoder must decrypt the stream, each network transcoding node presents a possible breach to the security of the entire system. This is not an acceptable solution in situations that require end-to-end security. This situation has two basic vulnerabilities: (1) the content is in the clear at the transcoding node, and (2) the transcoding node requires the decryption key, leading to key distribution and associated problems. Furthermore, in many situations it is desirable to perform transcoding at mid-network nodes or servers that are untrustworthy and therefore should not have access to the key. Thus, what is desired is a method that enables transcoding to be performed without requiring the key. However, this task of simultaneously achieving the conflicting goals of (1) transcoding at intermediate, possibly untrusted network nodes, while (2) preserving end-to-end security, leads to a paradox because, intuitively, to transcode in the middle of the network you want to know what the bits are, but the goal of end-to-end security is to prevent any intermediate node from knowing what the bits are.

In Section 10.2 we show that by careful co-design of the compression, security, and packetization, in a framework referred to as Secure Scalable Streaming (SSS), we can solve this problem. This approach allows for the end-to-end delivery of encrypted media content, while enabling mid-network adaptation to be performed without decryption, as shown in Figure 10.5. We refer to this capability as *Secure Transcoding* in order to stress that the transcoding is performed without requiring decryption (without requiring the key), therefore preserving the end-to-end security. Note that with this approach the media content is protected throughout the delivery chain from the content creator to each receiving client, so the encryption keys are only available to these entities and not to the mid-network nodes which perform the secure transcoding.

10.1.3 Secure Adaptive Streaming at an Untrustworthy Sender

In addition to securely adapting the content at an untrustworthy mid-network node, another important and related capability is to enable a (potentially) untrustworthy sender to stream and adapt the streaming of encrypted content without knowing what the content is. For example, content creators typically prefer to protect

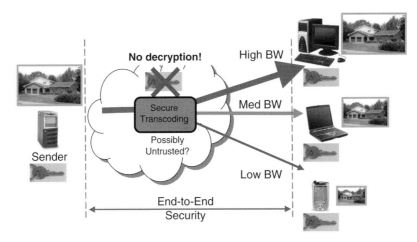

FIGURE 10.5:   Secure scalable streaming technology allows a media distribution system to achieve the seemingly conflicting goals of end-to-end security and allowing mid-network transcoding.

the content themselves and would like the media distributors to appropriately distribute the content without unprotecting it. Similarly, the media distributors would also prefer, if possible, to be able to adapt the delivery of the content without having access to the keys or unprotecting it, as then they are not liable for any breaches.

10.1.4   Chapter Outline

This chapter continues in Section 10.2 by describing the Secure Scalable Streaming framework which enables secure streaming and secure transcoding at mid-network nodes. This framework is applicable to both scalably coded media (Section 10.2) and, to a more limited extent, to non-scalably coded media (Section 10.3). Important themes throughout this chapter include the co-design of the coding, encryption, and packetization to facilitate adaptation; and the creation of "hints," such as rate-distortion (R-D) hints, which can be used to intelligently direct the adaptation. These hints can be placed in the unencrypted packet headers of Secure Scalable Packets, as described in Section 10.2.2, to enable R-D optimized secure transcoding at untrustworthy mid-network nodes. These hints can also be placed as unencrypted hints in the Secure R-D Hint Tracks, as described in Section 10.3.3, to enable secure R-D optimized adaptation at untrustworthy senders. Section 10.4 highlights the basic design principles behind these systems and describes how they can be applied to different types of media including speech, audio, image, and video. The application to imagery is examined in more detail since the associated JPEG 2000 Security (JPSEC) standard is the first standard to apply these techniques to media. Finally, we conclude with a summary of the chapter.

10.2   SECURE STREAMING AND SECURE TRANSCODING FOR SCALABLE CODERS

This section describes a basic framework that enables secure streaming and secure transcoding, where this framework is referred to as Secure Scalable Streaming (SSS). This section begins by giving an overview of SSS given the entire compressed media data and continues by describing the additional issues related to the packet-based processing required for streaming. The concept of secure packets with unencrypted packet headers is then described and how they enable secure R-D optimized transcoding to be performed. The relative benefits of layered versus packet versus sub-packet granularity are highlighted. Additional details are given in regard to how security services are provided using popular cryptographic primitives, followed by a brief summary.

10.2.1   Basic Overview of SSS

SSS, and the capability to perform Secure Transcoding, are based on a careful co-design of the compression, encryption, and packetization operations used in media delivery. Specifically, these operations are combined in a manner that allows secure transcoding to be performed by intelligent truncation or discarding of packets, and thereby without requiring decryption.

SSS is particularly well-matched to scalable coders, which are also referred to as layered or progressive coders. Scalable coding methods encode media into scalable data with prioritized importance in a manner that allows the bitrate, resolution, spatial extent, frame rate, audio bandwidth, and/or quality of the decoded media to depend on the amount of decoded data. For example, if an image is scalably coded by resolution, then a small portion of the data can be used to decode a low-resolution image, a larger portion of the data can be used to decode a medium-resolution image, and all the data can be used to decode the full resolution, as shown in Figure 10.6. The following example considers the conceptually simple case where scalable coding is used to produce a bitstream where the bits are ordered in terms of importance. This is often referred to as an embedded or progressive bitstream.

We define the term *progressive encryption* to represent encryption methods that encrypt plaintext into ciphertext in a sequential or beginning-to-end manner [4, 5]. Block ciphers in various modes (e.g., electronic code book (ECB), cipher block chaining (CBC), counter (CTR), output feedback (OFB)) as shown in Figure 10.6, and stream ciphers all satisfy this property [6, 7]. Progressive encryption results in ciphertext that also can be decrypted progressively from beginning to end. It is

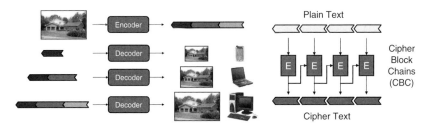

FIGURE 10.6:   Left: Example of scalable image coding where the image is coded into three layers corresponding to three spatial resolutions. Right: The practically important cipher block chains (CBC) mode of encryption is an example of a progressive encryption algorithm, where the earlier portion of the encrypted bitstream may still be decrypted even if the later portion is not available.

important to note that progressive encryption algorithms correspond to a large class of conventional encryption methods, e.g., Advanced Encryption Standard (AES) in CBC or CTR modes. A well-known design rule, which nevertheless we want to stress, is that the design of SSS systems should be performed using existing, highly studied cryptographic primitives, as opposed to designing new primitives, since any new primitives are likely to have subtle, hidden flaws. The novelty in SSS is that these well-known and well-studied cryptographic primitives are used in a different manner than how they are typically used. The term progressive encryption is used to emphasize a key attribute of the encryption that is analogous to scalable coding. Specifically, by combining scalable coding and progressive encryption, SSS creates secure scalable data. The secure scalable data have two key properties. First, because of the use of progressive encryption, the receiver can decrypt an earlier portion of the encrypted bitstream even if the later portion is not available. Second, because of the use of scalable coding, the receiver can decode the earlier portion of the bitstream even if the later portion is not available. These two properties enable transcoding to be performed by simple truncation of the encrypted bitstream, as shown in Figure 10.7. Since the truncation is performed without requiring decryption, it preserves the end-to-end security. Note that in this simple example the quality of the transcoded content is a function of its length; the less data that is truncated the higher the quality.

   The above discussion focuses on the conceptually simple case of creating a single secure scalable bitstream, which may be transcoded by a simple truncation operation. However, this situation assumes that the entire bitstream is available for performing the processing. In many applications, such as media streaming, only a subset of the bitstream is available. We next examine the additional steps required to perform secure streaming and secure transforming.

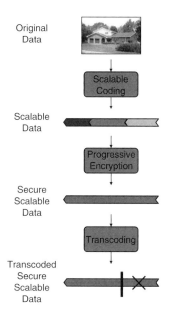

FIGURE 10.7: The combination of scalable coding and progressive encryption produce secure scalable data, which may be transcoded by a simple truncation operation.

10.2.2   Secure Scalable Packets

In streaming applications, a mid-network transcoder typically has access to a number of packets corresponding to only a portion of the coded and encrypted media. Specifically, in contrast to the prior simple example, where the transcoder had access to the entire encrypted bitstream, in the streaming context the transcoder typically only has access to a small portion of the entire stream. Furthermore, the transcoder must operate on packets instead of the entire bitstream, and the available packets correspond to only a small portion of the entire bitstream.

The technique of SSS and secure transcoding can be extended to streaming over packet networks through a concept called *secure scalable packets*. Secure scalable packets are created by deliberately placing the scalable data into packets in a prioritized manner so that transcoding can be performed via a packet truncation or discard operation, without decrypting the data. Packet truncation is facilitated by placing higher priority data in earlier portions of packets and lower priority data in later portions. As is discussed in Section 10.2.5, the capability to perform packet truncation provides much finer granularity than operations such as packet select/discard or the much coarser select/discard of scalable layers. For example, consider the case when a transcoder has access to only two packets and must reduce the bitrate by 10%. Clearly, the ability to truncate a packet could lead to better performance than being forced to discard a packet.

Figure 10.8 illustrates how to create secure scalable packets from original scalable bitstreams. The original scalable bitstreams are first parsed to extract the scalable data according to priority. These different priority data segments are then concatenated to form scalable packet data. This packet data is then encrypted using a progressive encryption method to form secure scalable packet data. Depending on the particular encryption method that is used, an initialization vector and/or padding may be added to the packet data. While the discussion focuses on the operation of packet truncation because of its conceptual and practical simplicity, we should stress that one can discard the head of the packet payload or arbitrary ranges of bytes in the interior of the packet payload. The preferred form of

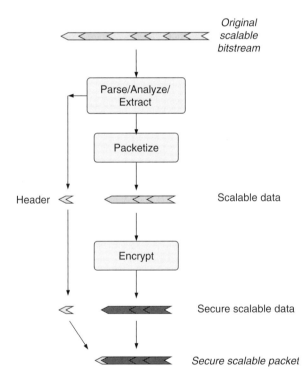

FIGURE 10.8:   Creating secure scalable packets from scalably coded media. Each packet includes an unencrypted header followed by encrypted scalably coded data.

discarding of data depends on a variety of issues including the compression algorithm, encryption algorithm, network packet size, and granularity required for the
transcoding.

A very important aspect of the creation of SSS packets is that an *unencrypted
header* is added to each packet. These unencrypted headers contain information
that is used to direct the subsequent SSS transcoding and decoding operations.
This information may include a series of recommended truncation points for
each packet, or hints to guide downstream transcoders to perform transcoding
operations such as resolution reduction or R-D optimized bitrate reduction. These
properties are examined in more detail in Section 10.2.4. In addition, the header
may include authentication information which enables the receiver to authenticate
the received content.

These secure scalable packets provide a number of properties: they are scalable to enable downstream transcoding by operations such as packet truncation or
packet discarding, are encrypted to provide end-to-end security, provide hints to
optimally guide the transcoding operation (as discussed next), are authenticatable
to ensure only valid content and permissible changes have been performed, and
are independently decodable to provide resilience to errors such as packet loss.

10.2.3   Secure Transcoding

The secure transcoding operation is illustrated in Figure 10.9. The transcoder
simply reads the unencrypted packet header and then uses the information in the
header to intelligently perform a packet truncation or packet discard operation as
appropriate. For example, if a secure scalable packet contains low-, medium-, and

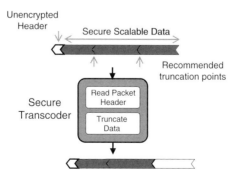

FIGURE 10.9:   In the Secure transcoding operation, the transcoder reads
each unencrypted packet header and then truncates or discards the packet as
appropriate. In this example the packet is truncated at the third recommended
truncation point.

high-resolution data segments, but is being transmitted to a medium-resolution client, then the secure transcoder simply reads the header, truncates the high-resolution data segment, and then transmits the resulting transcoded secure scalable packet to the client. As another example, if the transcoder is trying to meet a down-stream bitrate constraint, it can read the unencrypted header of each packet and then truncate each packet appropriately to achieve the necessary bitrate reduction. This capability is examined in more detail in Section 10.2.4.

This operation is referred to as *secure transcoding* to emphasize that it does not require decryption and therefore preserves the end-to-end security. The key idea once again is that transcoding is performed by an intelligent discarding of data, without requiring knowledge of what the data actually is. We next discuss how to perform this discarding of data in an intelligent manner to maximize the performance.

10.2.4   R-D Optimized Streaming and Transcoding

A highly desirable feature of a media system is the ability to stream or transcode the compressed stream in a manner which maximizes the quality (minimizes the distortion) subject to the available bitrate. This is referred to as R-D optimized processing [8] and is an active area of research with significant practical importance. In the following, R refers to the rate expressed in bits, and D refers to the distortion expressed as total squared-error distortion or mean squared-error distortion.

R-D optimized media encoding has been important for many years, where access to the original media makes R-D optimized coding possible. R-D optimized transcoding is also possible for unencrypted content, since significant information can be derived from the compressed data to appropriately direct the transcoding operation. However, when the data is encrypted, the situation is much more complex, and the conventional solution is to decrypt the data to access the compressed bitstream for transcoding. However, this compromises the end-to-end security.

The key idea behind R-D optimized secure transcoding is that the necessary information to perform the R-D optimized processing can often be distilled into a small amount of data and made available with the unencrypted hints. For example, this information can be placed in the unencrypted packet headers or the unencrypted hint tracks (as discussed in Section 10.3.3).

A simple example may help illustrate the situation. Consider the case of encoding an image, where the image is split into two portions which are coded independently (while this example considers encoding, the same concepts are applied for transcoding and adaptive streaming). The problem is how to code each segment to minimize the total distortion subject to a total bitrate constraint. Observe that since the segments are coded independently this means that both the total distortion and the required bitrate are additive across the segments, i.e., the total distortion for both segments is equal to the sum of the distortions for each segment and the total bitrate is equal to the sum of the bitrates for each segment. In this case, the R-D optimal coding is achieved by generating an operational R-D curve for each segment (i.e., list of achievable R-D points with the given coder) and then coding each image segment at the same operating point (slope λ) that generates the desired total bitrate. The intuition why this provides the optimal solution is discussed here. Note that the slope at a specific point on the R-D curve describes the trade-off between distortion reduction and increase in bitrate at that operating point. Therefore, by operating each segment at the same slope λ, the marginal return for an extra bit is the same for both segments. If this was not true (i.e., if giving an extra bit to segment 1 would lead to a larger reduction in distortion than the increase in distortion from taking a bit away from segment 2), then one could divert bits from one segment to the other to further reduce the total distortion. By operating both segments at the same slope, we have the same marginal return for each, and there is no reallocation of the available bits which would lead to a smaller total distortion. Therefore, a basic principle for R-D optimized coding, transcoding, and streaming is to operate each segment or coding unit at the same slope on their R-D curves.

Given that we want to operate at the same slope, the next question is how to determine what is the appropriate slope to meet the desired total bitrate constraint. There are a number of approaches to achieve this, including performing a binary search across slopes to find the slope which meets the desired total bitrate constraint, as well as parallel packet truncation as discussed next. An excellent review of R-D optimized techniques is given in Ortega and Ramchandran [8].

For SSS, the R-D information associated with media data contained in each packet is placed in the unencrypted header of the packet. This information corresponds to R-D hints that can be used by a sender or mid-network node to perform R-D optimized secure streaming or secure transcoding without decrypting the data.

For example, Figure 10.10 shows an example where a mid-network transcoder receives two packets and has a transmission bitrate constraint where the output rate

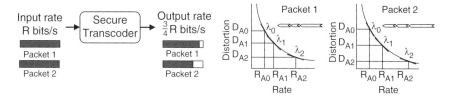

FIGURE 10.10: R-D optimal secure transcoding across two packets is achieved by appropriately truncating each packet so that they operate at the same slope λ on their R-D curves.

must be less than 3/4 of the input rate. A conventional node in the network would meet this bitrate constraint by discarding one of the two packets. However, with the unencrypted packet headers which contain R-D information for the two packets, the transcoder can estimate the R-D curves for each packet and then truncate each packet so that it is operating at the same slope on the R-D curve for each packet while satisfying the bitrate constraint. Intuitively, one way to achieve this is by truncating, in parallel, across the packets based on the slopes of their R-D curves until the desired rate reduction is achieved. The resulting transcoded secure scalable packets can be decrypted and decoded by the receiver with a reconstructed quality that depends on the received data [4, 5, 9].

There are some important trade-offs that occur between packet header size and transcoding performance. The more information contained in the packet header, the more accurate the transcoder's estimate of the packet's R-D curves, and the more accurate the transcoding performance. On the other hand, the larger the header the greater the overhead. A useful approach is to include a small number of R-D data points in the header, and the transcoder can interpolate (estimate) the R-D curve in between. Careful header design is therefore necessary and depends on, for example, whether the encrypted packet payload is fully embedded with bit or byte granularity or whether it has coarser granularity. There is also an issue of potential leakage of information, since the unencrypted header describes some attributes of the coded media. This is discussed in Section 10.4.1.

10.2.5   Granularity: Layer Verses Packet Versus Truncated Packet

This section examines the important issue of the granularity that can be achieved with secure streaming and secure transcoding. Scalable coding creates multiple layers of compressed data that are prioritized in terms of importance. These layers can be independently encrypted and sent in separate packet flows, allowing a secure transcoder to discard a flow containing low-priority data while forwarding the flows containing high-priority data which are then received, decrypted, and decoded at the receiver. This can be straightforwardly achieved using SSS, and it is a fine solution in certain contexts. However, the granularity with which the transcoding can be performed is limited by the granularity of the layers, which is not sufficient in certain contexts. Fortunately, SSS enables much finer granularity.

Packet networks operate with a packet granularity, so the operation of select/discard for each packet is natural in this context. However, sometimes even finer granularity can be beneficial.

As discussed in Sections 10.2.3 and 10.2.4, the capability to perform packet truncation provides much finer granularity and improved performance as compared to operations such as packet select/discard or the much coarser select/discard of layers. For example, consider the case when a transcoder has access to only two packets and must reduce the bitrate by 10%. In this case, select/discard of layers, or even of packets, is intuitively inefficient. Furthermore, when only one packet is available and a reduction in bitrate of 10% is required, then the inefficiency is even more apparent—if limited to packet select/discard then no data will be delivered. These simple examples illustrate how the capability to truncate packets can be quite valuable.

SSS can provide secure, coarse-grain to fine-grained (layer to packet to sub-packet) transcoding capabilities. The choice of granularity depends on the desired flexibility and the media type, compression algorithm, encryption algorithm, etc. Furthermore, and perhaps somewhat surprising, fine-grained secure transcoding can be performed in an R-D optimized manner by using the information contained in the unencrypted packet headers.

10.2.6 Security Services and Associated Protection Methods

For simplicity, our discussion has focused on providing the security service of confidentiality via encryption. The SSS framework also supports additional basic security services, including authentication, data integrity, access control, etc. A very important design rule, which we strongly recommend to follow, is to design SSS-based systems using existing, highly studied, cryptographic primitives, as opposed to designing new primitives, since any new primitives are likely to have subtle, hidden flaws. In addition, there is no need to create new cryptographic primitives. The innovation with SSS is in using well-known and well-studied cryptographic primitives in a different manner from how they are conventionally used. For example, SSS can be used with a variety of standard encryption methods, including block ciphers such as the Data Encryption Standard (DES), Triple-DES (3DES), and AES, as well as stream ciphers such as RC4, or stream ciphers created out of blockciphers (e.g., OFB or CTR). Similarly, authentication may be provided using a number of popular and well-studied authentication tools. Proto-types of SSS systems have been tested using the AES block cipher in CBC and Counter (CTR) modes and authentication using the keyed-hash message authen-tication code (HMAC) with Secure Hash Algorithm-1 (SHA-1). The compressed media payload of each packet is encrypted using CBC or CTR mode and is placed in a packet following the unencrypted header. Note that other cipher or authentica-tion methods can be used, as well as digital signature techniques, for example, the techniques specified in Figure 10.15. Many important details are not covered here because of the limited space, see, e.g., References 10 and 4 for more information. In addition, a number of different types of authentication may be employed which provide different services, e.g., see Sun et al. [11, 12]. Of course, the desired security services should be designed while carefully considering the associated Digital Rights Management (DRM) system, as described in other chapters of this book and in the literature [13, 14].

10.2.7   Summary

This section describes Secure Scalable Streaming and Secure Transcoding, which are based on careful co-design of scalable coding, encryption, and packetization. This results in secure scalable packets which can be transcoded with a simple truncation or select/discard operation. SSS allows streaming media systems to simultaneously achieve two seemingly conflicting properties: network-node transcoding and end-to-end security. Specifically, since the transcoding operation corresponds to simply truncating or discarding packets—without requiring decryption—it preserves the end-to-end security of the system and allows the operation to be performed at untrustworthy nodes in the network. Furthermore, the unencrypted packet headers enable secure transcoding to be performed in an R-D optimized manner.

An important point to emphasize is that the transcoder does not require knowledge of the specific compression algorithm, encryption algorithm, or even the type of media being transcoded. This is by design since the goal is for the transcoder to be able to manipulate the (encrypted) content without requiring knowledge about the content. All the transcoder needs is to be able to understand the unencrypted packet header. SSS can, in principle, be used with any scalably coded media, and this is examined in more depth in Section 10.4. In addition, the SSS framework can also be used with non-scalable coders, as discussed next.

10.3   SECURE STREAMING AND ADAPTATION FOR NON-SCALABLE CODERS

The prior section examines secure streaming and secure transcoding for scalably coded content. While it is evident that the SSS framework is applicable to any scalable coder, in this section we show its applicability to non-scalable coders. Clearly, non-scalable coded media cannot be scaled to the same extent as scalable coded media. However, perhaps surprisingly, a limited amount of scalability is possible, and this capability may be quite useful in various contexts. This perhaps non-intuitive capability essentially results because all (lossy) media coders inherently produce compressed bits where some bits are more important than other bits. This suggests the idea of reducing the bitrate by deliberately dropping the less important bits. This idea can be extended to dropping the less important video frames, speech frames, etc.

To examine SSS with a non-scalable coder, we consider the recent video compression standard H.264/MPEG-4 Part 10 Advanced Video Coding (AVC). Specifically, we consider when the video is coded with an initial I-frame followed by all P-frames and no B-frames. Since the coded video consists of all P-frames, it does not suggest a natural prioritization of frames (besides for the earlier P-frames being more important than the later ones). Nonetheless, we can prioritize different

P-frames in a surprisingly beneficial manner. We examine two specific examples of SSS with non-scalable H.264 [15]: (1) the use of a Secure Media R-D Hint Track (SM-RDHT) for secure adaptive streaming and (2) the use of Secure Scalable Packets for secure mid-network adaptation. In each case the R-D information for each frame or packet is derived and left unencrypted to enable efficient R-D optimized streaming and adaptation, while the coded media data is encrypted. As we will see, the R-D information is placed in the SM-RDHT, thereby enabling efficient R-D optimized streaming and adaptation at the sender, and then placed in the packet header, enabling that adaptation at a mid-network node or proxy.

An alternative approach to adapt the content is instead of trying to adapt a single compressed/encrypted stream, the original video may be coded at multiple different bitrates and encrypted copies of each may be stored at the server [16]. The server can then switch between the different copies at appropriate switch points in what is referred to as multiple file switching. While this approach enables adaptation at the sender with a granularity depending on the number and type of pre-encoded files, it requires multiple files, and it does not enable adapting a single compressed and encrypted stream or adapting the stream at a mid-network node.

The two basic questions in regard to scaling non-scalable video are: (1) How do we scale non-scalable video? and (2) How do we do it securely? Scaling in this context corresponds to reducing the bitrate or reducing the packet rate or frame rate. Clearly, non-scalable media cannot be scaled to the same extent as scalable media. However, it is important to understand to what extent it can be scaled.

10.3.1 Scaling of Non-Scalable H.264 Video: Not All P-frames Are Equal

A basic property of compressed video that has been exploited over the years is that different coded frames, and associated transport packets, may have different importance, e.g., I-frames are more important than P-frames, which are more important than B-frames, where importance in our context is in terms of the total squared-error distortion that is incurred if that frame is lost. This property of IPB frame coding, and also of scalable coding, is widely used to provide unequal (prioritized) treatment to the coded data and thereby to provide improved performance. In particular, this property is exploited in R-D optimized streaming.

To examine the use of SSS with non-scalable H.264 video, we consider when the video is coded with an initial I-frame followed by all P-frames and no B-frames (note that if we have conventional I-, P-, and B-frames, then we have a form of scalably coded video). It is known that different P-frames have different importance, where, for example, the later P-frames in an MPEG Group of Pictures (GOP) typically are less important than the earlier P-frames in the GOP. However, a somewhat surprising observation is that P-frames can also differ in importance by a very significant amount. This observation is practically important since various applications primarily use P-frames with very few I-frames, no B-frames, and

no scalable coding (e.g., low-latency applications such as conversational applications do not use B-frames and constant bitrate constraints may limit the use
of I-frames). Therefore, by identifying and exploiting the varying importance of
different P-frames in a sequence, we can achieve improved performance. This
approach extends straightforwardly to include I- and B-frames, as well as other
forms of scalability, such as those being standardized in MPEG's Scalable Video
Coding (SVC) effort.

The following illustrative experiments are performed using the H.264/MPEG-4
AVC video compression standard. Four standard test sequences in Quarter
Common Intermediate Format (QCIF) are used: *Carphone, Foreman, Mother
& Daughter (MthrDhter)*, and *Salesman*. Each is coded at a constant quantization level for an average Peak Signal-to-Noise Ratio (PSNR) of about 36 dB, at
30 fps, and has at least 350 frames. The first frame of each sequence is intra-coded,
followed by all P-frames. Every four frames, a slice is intra-updated to improve
error resilience by reducing error propagation, corresponding to an intra-update
period of $N = 4 \times 9 = 36$ frames. Every P-frame fits within a single 1500 byte
packet; hence, in these experiments the loss of one packet corresponds to the loss
of one P-frame. Every lost frame is replaced by the last correctly received frame,
and distortion is measured after decoder error concealment.

The importance of each P-frame is estimated by the total distortion that results
from the loss of that frame (assuming all other frames are correctly received),
including error propagation to all subsequent frames. Further comments on our
motivation for this simple model are given later in this section. An important
observation is that in all four test sequences there are some P-frames which are two
orders of magnitude more important than other P-frames in the same sequence.
This large difference in the max-to-min total distortions for P-frames within a
sequence signifies that considerable gain can be achieved by identifying and
exploiting the unequal importance of different P-frames and their associated
packets.

10.3.2   R-D Optimized Processing of P-frames

The great diversity in importance of different P-frames can be exploited by placing
the R-D information for each P-frame into an unencrypted packet header [4, 5] or
in an R-D Hint Track (RDHT) associated with the coded video (and the additional storage available may support more information and sophisticated R-D
optimization techniques [17]).

The prior discussion focused on the total distortion produced by a single
lost/dropped packet, including the effects of all error propagation. The total distortion produced by simultaneously dropping multiple packets may be approximated
as the sum of the distortions that result for losing each packet alone. This additive
model for distortion ignores the important interdependencies that result from the

loss of multiple packets within an intra-refresh period (e.g., a burst loss generally leads to more distortion than an equal number of isolated losses [18]). However, the additive distortion model is a reasonable first-order approximation (note that this additive model explicitly accounts for the great diversity in importance of different P-frames, in contrast to some prior additive models which implicitly assume a homogeneous model of the video). This approach also requires significantly less R-D information, which is an important consideration when placing R-D hints in each packet (but of lesser importance for R-D hints stored on a server). Furthermore, this simple model of additive distortion has the important benefit that it is generally applicable for a variety of different types of coders and types of media.

Assuming the additive model for total distortion, the optimal method for selecting among packets can be determined by associating for every packet j a corresponding utility measured in terms of distortion per bit, defined as $\lambda_j = D(j)/R(j)$. For example, if the total available bitrate is less than the video rate, a decision must be made as to which packets to transmit and which to drop in order to minimize the total distortion while simultaneously satisfying the rate constraint. This problem is straightforwardly solved by rank ordering the packets based on their utility and transmitting those with higher utility while dropping those with lower utility.

10.3.3 Secure Adaptive Streaming Using an SM-RDHT

This section describes a technique based on an SM-RDHT for designing and operating media streaming systems that can perform R-D optimized streaming with low complexity, while preserving the content security.

As background, the popular MPEG-4 File Format (MP4) incorporates a "hint track" which contains information about media type, packet framing, and timing information. This MP4 hint track provides "hints" to the streaming system that greatly simplifies the streaming. This is because the streamer no longer needs to (1) understand the compressed media syntax and (2) analyze the media data in real time for packet framing and timing information.

The SM-RDHT provides two important extensions of conventional MP4 hint tracks [15]: (1) the R-D attributes for the media are derived and summarized in the hint track to enable low-complexity R-D optimized streaming [17], and (2) the RDHT is stored unencrypted (analogous to the unencrypted headers in the secure scalable packets), while the media itself is encrypted. The SM-RDHT therefore enables a sender to read the unencrypted R-D hints and perform low-complexity R-D optimized streaming of the media without having knowledge of the actual media. The R-D hints can also be placed in unencrypted packet headers to enable down-stream transcoder nodes to securely adapt the rate of the encrypted streams. We next consider illustrative examples of the performance which can be achieved at the sender and at a mid-network node.

10.3.4   Secure Rate-Adaptive Streaming Using SM-RDHT

The performance of an SM-RDHT system is shown in Figure 10.11, where the transmitted bitrate for the Foreman sequence is reduced below the original coded bitrate. The conventional system does not distinguish between P-frames and therefore randomly selects packets to drop, while the SM-RDHT system intelligently determines which packets to drop to maximize the quality while meeting the available bandwidth constraint. Note that non-scalable H.264 provides limited ability to scale the bitrate as compared to a scalable coder. However, it is also clear that the SM-RDHT system provides dramatic improvements in quality over a conventional system when scaling is necessary.

10.3.5   Secure Transcoding at Mid-network Node Using Secure Scalable Packets

In this example, non-scalable H.264 video is packetized into secure scalable packets with unencrypted packet headers that provide R-D information about the importance of each packet. This information provides hints for the downstream transcoders. Specifically, the rate of each packet is given by the packet length, and only the importance, e.g., total distortion associated with the (loss) of the packet, needs to be signaled in the unencrypted header. Typically, one or two bytes of information in the unencrypted packet header are sufficient to provide adequate differentiation between the importance of different packets. However, this depends on the specific capabilities desired. Mid-network transcoders read

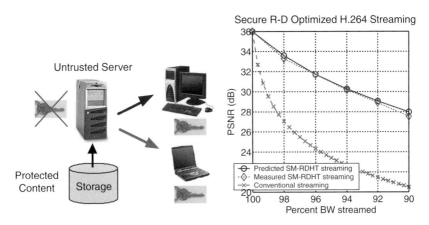

FIGURE 10.11:   An untrustworthy sender can use an SM-RDHT to securely stream and adapt encrypted content for the available bandwidth without knowing what the content is (© 2004 IEEE) [15].

the unencrypted headers of each packet and select or discard each packet based on its importance and the network constraints. An important attribute of this approach is that the mid-network transcoder can perform R-D optimized adaptation across multiple packets of a single stream or across multiple packets of multiple different streams. Furthermore, some of the streams may be encrypted and some may not, but as long as every packet includes transcoding hints, then both encrypted and unencrypted streams can be processed using the same low-complexity R-D optimization techniques.

The performance of this system is illustrated in Figure 10.12, where a large number of streams simultaneously pass through a node with limited output bandwidth, requiring the node to transcode the streams. The transcoder examines all packets from all sequences within a time window and selects which packets to transmit and which to discard based on the importance of each packet and the output bandwidth constraint. This is achieved by reading the unencrypted header of each packet in the window, sorting the results (a partial sort is sufficient), and selecting/discarding based on the priority. This example provides an estimated upper bound on achievable performance for the four sequences, where all four test sequences are simulated to be streamed at all possible phases relative to each other; see Apostolopoulos [15] for details.

The performance in Figure 10.12 is better than that in Figure 10.11, as evident by the smaller drop in PSNR. This is due to the diversity gain from processing

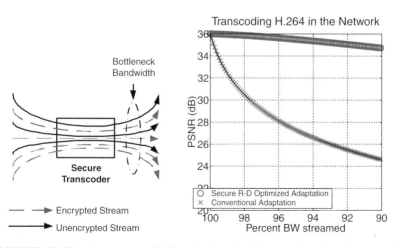

FIGURE 10.12:   In a secure R-D optimized mid-network adaptation, a mid-network transcoder can securely adapt across a large number of streams to satisfy an output bandwidth constraint. The diversity gain from processing across multiple streams is evident. (© 2004 IEEE) [15].

across streams. Specifically, by transcoding across streams we can exploit the fact that many frames of MthrDthr and Salesman are of lesser importance than those of Foreman and hence can be preferentially dropped. Therefore, the secure transcoder is attempting to maximize the quality (minimize the total distortion) across all of the streams. Of course, the streaming server in Section 10.3.4 can also exploit the diversity across multiple streams if it is faced with an output bottleneck.

10.3.6   Summary

This section describes how encrypted non-scalably coded media can be efficiently streamed and adapted, while preserving end-to-end security. In particular, the SSS framework can be applied to non-scalable H.264 coded video by identifying and intelligently distinguishing the importance of different P-frames. Specifically, we can exploit the fact that the P-frames within a single sequence may differ in importance by over two orders of magnitude, and may differ by even larger amounts between multiple sequences. By encrypting the media and placing the associated R-D information in the SM-RDHT and in unencrypted packet headers, we enable efficient R-D optimized streaming and adaptation at the sender, or at a mid-network node or proxy, for non-scalable H.264 video. Furthermore, this approach for R-D optimized streaming and adaptation can be used for streaming both encrypted and unencrypted content, as well as other forms of non-scalably coded media. Finally, in the prior section and in this section we have seen that the SSS framework can be applied to both scalably coded and non-scalably coded media. This is discussed further in Section 10.4.1.

10.4   SECURE MEDIA SYSTEMS

The goal of our secure media system is to simultaneously provide end-to-end security while allowing flexible media handling and processing throughout the media distribution value chain. These systems have *creators* that protect media data in a manner that allows it to be decrypted and authenticated by allowable *consumers*. They also have secure *streamers* and *transcoders* that can flexibly stream and transcode the protected media during distribution without requiring decryption or access to the protected content itself.

A critical element is the creation process itself, which must create protected content that can be securely streamed and transcoded, and the consumption process, which must authenticate that the received stream was handled appropriately during distribution. This is discussed further in Section 10.4.1. Section 10.4.2 describes JPSEC, a standard for secure digital imaging with JPEG 2000, which is the first standard that supports SSS and secure transcoding.

10.4.1   Basic Design Principles

An important capability of the creator is that it should protect the media content in a manner that allows streamers and downstream transcoders to perform their functions without requiring them to unprotect the content.

In SSS, adaptation is performed while preserving the end-to-end security by viewing the adaptation operation as an intelligent (R-D optimized) select/discard/truncate operation. In addition to avoiding decryption, this approach has the additional benefit of low-complexity streaming and transcoding. The key steps in performing secure streaming and secure transcoding or adaptation are:

1. Understand/analyze the coded media.
2. Create (unencrypted) R-D information (hints) for maximizing the streaming and transcoding quality of the encrypted media.
3. Encrypt the media in a media-aware manner to facilitate easy access.
4. Organize/packetize the (protected) media in a media- and security-aware manner to enable easy access.
5. Adaptively stream or transcode the (protected) media using the R-D hints.

This approach is equally applicable for encrypted or unencrypted content, which is quite useful. For unencrypted content, the third step (encryption) is not performed. For unencrypted content, it provides the benefits of low-complexity R-D optimized streaming and adaptation. The R-D information may be produced during encoding, or it can be derived from pre-encoded content.

An example consumer is shown in Figure 10.13 for a secure media system that uses SSS and secure transcoding technologies discussed in Section 10.2. The protected stream can be securely transcoded during media distribution. The consumer first decrypts the received transcoded stream with the key. Then, each component of the received scalable data can be authenticated with the appropriate key and Message Authentication Code (MAC) value to verify that the transcoding was performed in a valid and permissible manner. If it was, then the decrypted, authenticated data can be decoded to appropriately render the content.

When designing a secure media system, it is important to consider the level of security needed for the application. Specifically, when deciding how to protect the media data, its attributes (e.g., encrypted packet sizes), and its hints (e.g., R-D information), it is necessary to consider the potential leakage of information. For example, it may be important for an application to encrypt the media data during distribution, but not the hints. This would allow any distribution system to use the hints to optimize streaming and transcoding. Alternatively, for another application this leakage of information may not be allowable. In this case, it may be appropriate to encrypt the media content with a set of keys that is understood by legal consumers, while encrypting the hints with another set of keys that is understood by legal transcoders and streamers during distribution.

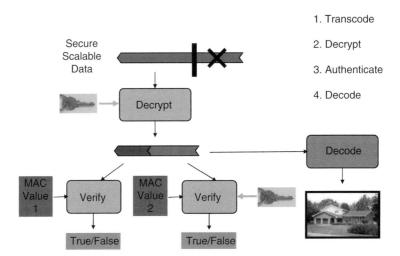

FIGURE 10.13:   When using the SSS and secure transcoding technologies discussed in Section 10.2, allowable consumers can decrypt the received transcoded streams and use authentication to verify that the transcoding occurred in a legal manner.

Another design consideration is the trade-off between the R-D optimized streaming/transcoding performance and the size of the R-D information/hints. The size of the R-D information increases when it is provided at finer granularities, but this would lead to the best streaming and transcoding performance. Furthermore, in systems where the hints are left unencrypted, this also leads to the greatest leakage of information.

10.4.2   Secure Imaging: JPEG-2000 Security (JPSEC) Standard

JPSEC is a media security standard for protecting JPEG-2000 digital images. The JPSEC standard was designed to support the following six security services [19]:

1. Confidentiality via encryption and selective encryption
2. Integrity verification (including data and image content integrity, using fragile and semi-fragile verification)
3. Source authentication
4. Conditional access and general access control
5. Registered content identification
6. SSS and secure transcoding

The sixth service is a non-traditional security service that arises for media. This section provides a brief overview of JPSEC, with an emphasis on the aspects that are relevant for supporting secure streaming and secure transcoding.

JPSEC Architecture

The JPSEC standard was designed to allow significant flexiblity and a high level of security through the use of protection tools and associated signaling that are applied to JPEG-2000 coded images. The JPSEC architecture allows interlayer interaction between the coding, security, file format, and packetization to provide the above-desired attributes. Note that the addition of the secure transcoding requirement into the JPSEC standard led to significant design changes to the standard since it brought forth a need for interlayer awareness, as highlighted in various parts of this chapter.

JPSEC provides security services for JPEG-2000 by defining a number of protection tools, including decryption templates for confidentiality and conditional access services and authentication templates for integrity verification and source and message authentication services. A JPSEC system consists of a JPSEC creator, JPSEC bitstream, and JPSEC consumer. The JPSEC creator can apply one or more protection tools to an image. The resulting JPSEC bitstream shown in Figure 10.14 contains signaling information for the protection tools and the modified data that may have resulted from their application. The signaling information is placed in an SEC (security) marker segment that is added to the JPEG-2000 header, and it includes the parameters that a JPSEC consumer needs to interpret and process the protected stream. The JPSEC bitstream contains three general types of information to describe to the JPSEC consumer the what, where, and how of the applied security services.

What Security Service Is Provided?

A JPSEC consumer needs to know what security service is provided or what protection tool it should use to process and render the protected JPSEC bitstream. This is accomplished by specifying a tool type and ID for each tool that is to be applied.

The JPSEC syntax has three types of protection tools: template tools, registration authority tools, and user-defined tools. The *template tools* are defined by the normative part of the JPSEC standard. They have an identifier that specifies which protection method template is used. JPSEC provides templates for decryption, authentication, and hashing. The *registration authority tools* are registered with and defined by a JPSEC registration authority and have a registration authority ID number that is specified in the syntax. The *user-defined tools* are defined by a user or application. JPSEC reserves a set of ID numbers that can be used by private applications. However, ID collisions may occur if the same ID number is used by

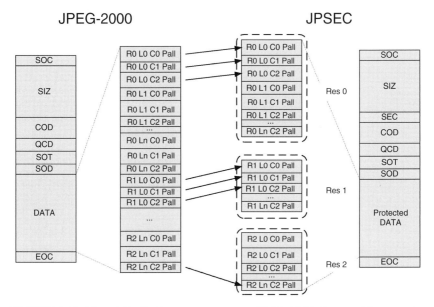

FIGURE 10.14:   A JPSEC creator protects JPEG-2000 data and inserts signaling information into the JPEG-2000 header. JPSEC consumers use the signaling information to determine which protection tools to apply to the protected JPSEC content.

different JPSEC applications, so the user must be careful in defining the use and scope of these bitstreams.

Both the registration authority and user-defined tools allow proprietary protection methods to be applied; for example, new techniques or classified government security techniques can be applied in this fashion. The remainder of this discussion focuses on the JPSEC template tools that are defined by the normative part of the standard.

Where Is the Security Tool Applied?

JPSEC uses a Zone of Influence (ZOI) to describe where the protection tool is applied to the data. The ZOI functionally describes the coverage area of the tool, and it may also include valuable metadata about the coded data and protected image itself. The coverage area can be described by image-related or non-image-related parameters. Image-related parameters can specify parameters such as resolution, image area, tile index, quality layer, or color component. For example, the ZOI can specify that the lowest resolution component of the image is encrypted.

Non-image-related parameters can specify areas such as byte ranges or packet. For example, the ZOI can specify that the JPSEC stream is encrypted from bytes 198 through 1368. In addition, the ZOI can use image-related parameters and non-image-related parameters together to specify the correspondence between these areas. For example, the ZOI can be used to indicate that the resolutions and image area specified by the image-related parameters correspond to the byte ranges specified by the non-image-related parameters. This correspondence feature allows the ZOI to be used as metadata that signals where certain parts of the image are located in the JPSEC bitstream. This is especially useful when encryption is used because the image data is no longer accessible in the protected JPSEC stream. Thus, it may be impossible to determine where the various image data boundaries lie in the encrypted JPSEC stream.

The ZOI can also include distortion information in the metadata. The distortion information and the size of the protected data together provide the R-D information of the stream that can be used as hints by a secure streamer or secure transcoder as discussed in earlier sections.

How Is the Security Tool Applied?

While the identifier describes what security services are used, and the ZOI describes where the security tool is applied, further details are needed to instruct a JPSEC consumer on how to consume the protected stream. JPSEC uses template and processing parameters for this task. The template parameters describe the detailed parameters of the template tool. For example, while the IDs indicate that decryption and authentication are to be applied, the template parameters indicate that the JPSEC consumer should use AES decryption in counter mode for decryption and HMAC with SHA-1 for authentication. The decryption and authentication protection templates and their parameters are shown in Figure 10.15.

In addition to specifying the template parameters, JPSEC also specifies the processing parameters, including the processing domain and granularity, that describe how the tools are applied. For example, the processing parameters can instruct a JPSEC consumer to apply the specified decryption method with a granularity of a resolution layer and to the domain of JPEG-2000 packet bodies only. With this information and the access keys, a JPSEC consumer can correctly decrypt and decode the portions of the data that it is allowed to access.

Putting It All Together

Figure 10.16 shows the parameters that would appear in an SEC header for two JPSEC security tools that would be used by the consumer shown in Figure 10.13. This shows the ZOI, protection template, processing domain, and granularity for the decryption tool and authentication tool. The decryption tool uses both

Decryption Template	
Block cipher	
Cipher	DES, 3DES, AES
Block cipher mode	ECB, CBC, CFB, OFB, CTR
Padding mode	Ciphertext stealing, PKCS#7
Block size	Cipher dependent
Key template	Application dependent
Intiliazation vector	Variable
Stream Cipher	
Cipher	RC4
Key template	Application dependent
Intiliazation vector	Variable
Asymmetric Cipher	
Cipher	RSA
Key template	Application dependent

Authentication Template	
Hash-based authentication	
Method	HMAC
Hash function	SHA-1, RIPEMD-160, SHA256
Key template	Application dependent
Size of MAC	Variable
MAC value	Signal dependent
Cipher-based Authentication	
Method	CBC-MAC
Block cipher	Cipher ID
Key template	Application dependent
Size of MAC	Variable
MAC value	Signal dependent
Digital Signature	
Method	RSA, Rabin, DSA, ECDSA
Hash function	Hash ID
Key template	Application dependent
Digital signature	Signal dependent

FIGURE 10.15: Example parameters for decryption (left) and authentication (right) templates.

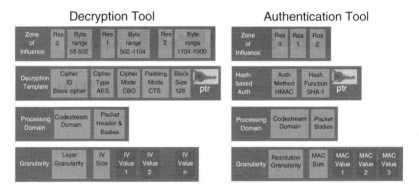

FIGURE 10.16: The SEC header includes parameters for the decryption tool (left) and the authentication tool (right). A JPSEC consumer uses the parameters in the ZOI, protection template, processing domain, and granularity to process and render the protected JPSEC bitstream.

image- and bitstream-related parameters to describe each resolution that was protected and the location or byte range of the protected data. It specifies using AES
decryption in CBC mode and includes a pointer to access the appropriate decryption key. It specifies that the codestream itself is protected, including the JPEG
2000 packet headers and bodies. It also specifies that a new initialization value is
used for each layer, and it includes the initialization values. The SEC header also
specifies that MAC values are provided for each resolution using HMAC authentication with SHA-1. It specifies that the MAC values were computed only on the
packet bodies (not on the packet headers). It also contains the MAC values and a
pointer to access the key.

In the example shown in Figure 10.17, a portion of the JPEG-2000 coded
image is selectively left unencrypted, while the remaining portions are encrypted.
An end-user without the key can still see part of the image contents and therefore
decide whether to purchase it or not. An important note here is that these encrypted
JPEG-2000 bitstreams were decoded using a JPEG-2000 decoder and not a JPSEC
decoder, i.e., the encrypted bitstreams in these examples were designed to be use-
fully decoded by a JPEG-2000 decoder which does not have the key or even know
that the content was encrypted.

Zone B

FIGURE 10.17: Selected spatial regions are left unencrypted, while the
remaining regions are encrypted. A JPEG decoder (w/o the key) decodes the
left image, while a JPSEC decoder with the key recovers the right image. This
can be specified by dividing the image into two zones. The decryption tool's
ZOI specifies that Zone A is protected.

Security protection tools may be applied to an image using one key or multiple keys. The advantage of using multiple keys is that they can provide multiple levels of access control. For example, different access rights may be provided to different individuals by providing each individual with an appropriate key. These access rights may correspond to different qualities of the image, e.g., given JPEG 2000's various forms of scalability, one can provide access to different resolutions, quality levels (pixel fidelity), spatial regions or regions of interest, etc. [20–22].

The multiple keys may be independent of each other, but this can lead to the requirement for a large number of keys complicating key distribution, etc. Another common approach is for the keys to be related in a structured manner, e.g., they may be recursively computed from a master key using a hash tree. Given a master key k, a sequence of keys may be computed by applying a one-way hash function $H()$, where $k_{i+1} = H(k_i)$. For example, with a two-level wavelet decomposition, three resolution levels are available {low, medium, high}. By encrypting these three levels with the three keys k_2, k_1, k_0, where $k_1 = H(k_0)$ and $k_2 = H(k_1) = H(H(k_0))$, a user with k_0 can generate k_1 and k_2 and thereby decrypt all three resolution layers to get the high-resolution image, a user with k_1 can generate k_2 and thereby decrypt two resolution layers to get the medium resolution, and a user with k_2 can only decrypt one resolution layer to get the low-resolution version of the image, as illustrated in Figure 10.18. Note that while this brief discussion

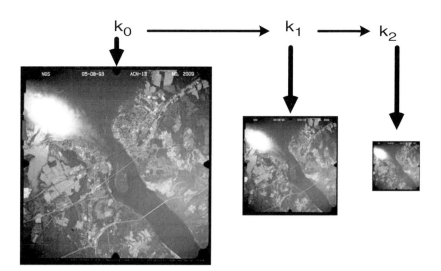

FIGURE 10.18:   Multi-level access control: given one encrypted image, the user with key k_0 can access the high-, medium-, or low-resolution images; the user with key k_1 can access medium or low resolution; while the user with key k_2 can only access the lowest resolution.

for simplicity focuses on a one-dimensional (1-D) hash chain for key generation, general tree structures (including non-binary, unbalanced, and multi-dimensional (M-D) trees) are straightforward extensions and provide very valuable flexibility and richness for access control. In this manner, one copy of encrypted media content provides multiple levels of access control where the access depends on the accessor's key.

10.4.3 General Application to Speech, Audio, Image, Video, and Graphics

SSS can be used with any scalable coding algorithm or standard. Prominent examples include scalable speech coders such as the MPEG-4 Natural Speech Coding Tools (HVXC and CELP); audio coders such as MPEG-4 scalable Advanced Audio Coding (AAC) and the Scalable Lossless (SLS) extension of AAC; image coders including JPEG-2000; and video coders including Motion JPEG-2000, three-dimensional (3-D) subband coding, MPEG-4 Fine Granular Scalability (FGS), and the spatial, temporal, and SNR scalable versions of MPEG-2, MPEG-4, H.263, and MPEG-4 AVC/H.264, as well as the emerging MPEG-4 Scalable Video Coding (SVC) standard. SSS may also be incorporated as an extension of MPEG-21 Digital Item Adaptation (DIA), which was designed to adapt scalably coded data, in order to support security. Scalable graphics descriptions and coding are currently a popular research topic and may also be secured in a similar manner to how conventional scalably coded media signals are protected. As illustrated in Section 10.3, non-scalably coded media can also be processed using the SSS framework, although the degree of scalability is, of course, much less than that for scalably coded media. Finally, while the above discussion is intended to convey to the reader how the SSS framework can be applied generically, a successful design involves careful consideration of the specific application, media type, codec, protection services required, and so forth. Hopefully, this chapter has provided the reader with sufficient background to consider the trade-offs necessary for a successful secure media system design.

10.5 SUMMARY

Conventional approaches for securing media are media unaware in that they treat media as if it were a block of data. For example, media can be encrypted at the application layer as a file and then packetized and transported over the network, or the media can be packetized and then encrypted at the network packet layer using network-layer encryption. While these approaches do provide end-to-end security, they disallow flexible mid-network streaming and transcoding because all of the structure of the original media is lost. If one wished to optimally stream or transcode the protected media, it would not be possible with these conventional approaches.

This chapter describes Secure Scalable Streaming and Secure Transcoding, where by co-designing the scalable coding, encryption, and packetization operations one can enable streaming and mid-network transcoding to be performed without requiring decryption. Specifically, the scalable data dependencies are matched up with the encryption dependencies in a manner that allows the resulting secure scalable data to be transcoded by truncating or discarding packets. It also adds unencrypted header information to the secure scalable data that can contain recommended truncation points and distortion information for different segments of data. In other words, this can convey the R-D information of the various segments of the protected data. A mid-network entity can use this information to perform R-D optimized streaming and transcoding of the protected data without requiring to unprotect the content.

We also show how this approach can be applied to non-scalable coders by recognizing that the different data segments of non-scalably coded data also have different degrees of importance, and this leads to a prioritization of data segments for streaming and transcoding. Once again, by applying the encryption in a manner that respects this importance and by conveying this R-D information in an unencrypted header, a mid-network entity can also perform R-D optimized streaming and transcoding of the protected data without requiring decryption.

We show how these approaches can be used in secure media systems, and we discuss some basic design principles for these systems. Finally, we describe the JPSEC standard, which is the first standard which supports SSS and secure transcoding, and we show how JPSEC is designed to achieve this. The SSS framework can also be extended to create standards for securing other types of media data, including speech, audio, video, and graphics.

Finally, in regard to the security of the SSS framework, the design of SSS systems use existing, highly studied cryptographic primitives, such as AES for encryption or HMAC with SHA-1 for authentication. The novelty in SSS is that these well-known and well-studied cryptographic primitives are used in a different manner than how they are typically used. Also, note that the untrustworthy sender or transcoder does not require knowledge of the specific compression algorithm, encryption algorithm, or even the type of media being streamed or transcoded. This is by design since the goal is to be able to manipulate the encrypted content without requiring knowledge about the content. All the sender or transcoder needs is the ability to understand the unencrypted hint track or packet header. This is sufficient to enable the sender or transcoder to perform secure R-D optimized streaming or transcoding without knowledge of the protected content.

REFERENCES

[1] D. Clark and D. Tennenhouse. Architectural considerations for a new generation of protocols, *ACM SIGCOMM*, September 1990.

[2] M. Baugher, D. McGrew, M. Naslund, E. Carrara, and K. Norrman. The secure real-time transport protocol (SRTP), *IETF RFC 3711*, 2004.

[3] ISMA. *ISMA Implementation Specification: Encryption and Authentication Specification, Version 1.0*, Internet Streaming Media Alliance (ISMA), www.isma.tv, February 2004.

[4] S. Wee and J. Apostolopoulos. Secure scalable video streaming for wireless networks, *IEEE ICASSP*, May 2001.

[5] ——, Secure scalable streaming enabling transcoding without decryption, *IEEE ICIP*, October 2001.

[6] B. Schneier. *Applied Cryptography*, 2nd ed., John Wiley & Sons, New York, 1995.

[7] W. Stallings. *Cryptography and Network Security: Principles and Practices*, 3rd ed., Prentice Hall, New York, 2003.

[8] A. Ortega and K. Ramchandran. Rate-distortion techniques in image and video compression, *IEEE Signal Processing Magazine*, 15(6): November 1998.

[9] S. Wee and J. Apostolopoulos. Secure scalable streaming and secure transcoding with JPEG-2000, *IEEE ICIP*, September 2003.

[10] ——, Secure transcoding with JPSEC confidentiality and authentication, *IEEE ICIP*, October 2004.

[11] Q. Sun, D. He, Q. Tian, and Z. Zhang. A secure and robust approach to scalable video authentication, *IEEE ICME*, July 2003.

[12] Z. Zhang, Q. Sun, G. Qiu, Y. Shi, and Z. Ni. A unified authentication framework for JPEG2000, *IEEE ICME*, 2004.

[13] D. Kundur, C.-Y. Lin, B. Macq, and H. Yu. (Eds.). Special issue on enabling security technologies for digital rights management, *Proc. IEEE*, June 2004.

[14] M. Ji, S. Shen, W. Zeng, T. Senoh, and T. Ueno. Mpeg-4 IPMP extension — For interoperable protection of multimedia content, *EURASIP J. Applied Signal Processing*, 2004.

[15] J. Apostolopoulos. Secure media streaming & secure adaptation for non-scalable video, *IEEE ICIP*, October 2004.

[16] C. Venkatramani, P. Westerink, O. Verscheure, and P. Frossard. Secure media for adaptive streaming, *ACM Multimedia*, pp. 307–310, November 2003.

[17] J. Chakareski, J. Apostolopoulos, S. Wee, W. Tan, and B. Girod. R-D hint tracks for low complexity R-D optimized video streaming, *IEEE ICME*, June 2004.

[18] Y. Liang, J. Apostolopoulos, and B. Girod. Analysis of packet loss for compressed video: Does burst-length matter? *IEEE ICASSP*, April 2003.

[19] ISO/IEC. ISO/IEC JPEG-2000 Security (JPSEC) Final Committee Draft, T. Ebrahimi, C. Rollin, and S. Wee (Eds.), November 2004.

[20] D. Taubman and M. Marcellin. *JPEG 2000: Image Compression Fundamentals, Standards, and Practice*, Kluwer Academic, Boston, MA, 2002.

[21] A. Skodras, C. Christopoulos, and T. Ebrahimi. The JPEG 2000 still image compression standard, *IEEE Signal Processing Magazine*, September 2001.

[22] Y. Wu, D. Ma, and R. Deng. Progressive protection of JPEG 2000 code-streams, *IEEE ICIP*, October 2004.

11

Scalable Encryption and Multi-Access Control for Multimedia

Bin B. Zhu

11.1 INTRODUCTION

A major effort in recent years has been directed to developing technologies to enable users to enjoy multimedia anywhere, anytime, and with any device (A^3). Networks may have different capacities and characteristics. Devices may have different display sizes and computing capabilities. To deliver the A^3 experience in multimedia entertainment, a traditional approach is to compress a multimedia content into multiple copies, with each copy targeted at a specific application scenario such as a PC with wideband Internet access, a 3G cellular phone, etc. These multiple copies are all stored in a server to make them available for each individual user to select a copy that best fits his or her need. Another approach is to apply a transcoder at some edge server en route to the destination to generate a lower resolution or quality bitstream to fit the targeted network condition or device capability. Both approaches may need to be combined since multiple copies of a multimedia content can only address a given number of preset client capabilities and network conditions.

A more elegant solution is to encode a multimedia content with a scalable codec. Scalable codecs have attracted increasing interests and attention in recent years in both industry and academia due to their flexibility and easy adaptation to a wide range of applications. A scalable codec encodes a signal into a single codestream which is partitioned and organized in hierarchical structures according to certain scalable parameters such as quality, resolution, etc. Based on scalabilities offered by a codestream, each individual user can extract from the same codestream the best representation that fits the specific application. Different scalable codecs offer different scalabilities. Possible scalabilities include quality, spatial and temporal resolution, rate, color space, etc. Early scalable codecs provide layered scalability [1, 2], i.e., scalability at a small number of discrete levels. Later scalable codecs provide Fine Granularity Scalability (FGS) [3, 4]. An FGS scalable codec offers a near-continuous optimal trade-off between quality and rates in a large range. Unlike the traditional approaches, a single scalable codestream is stored and used for all different applications, with possible simple adaptation manipulations such as truncation on the codestream. Scalable coding saves significant storage space and adapts to varying transmission bandwidths and playing devices. This capability of "one-compression-to-meet-the-needs-of-all-applications" is very desirable in many multimedia applications.

Several Discrete Cosine Transform (DCT)-based or wavelet-based scalable codecs have been developed or are under active development. The Moving Picture Experts Group (MPEG) has recently adopted a new scalable video coding format called *Fine Granularity Scalability* to its MPEG-4 standard [3]. The Joint Photographic Experts Group (JPEG) has also adopted a wavelet-based scalable image coding format called *JPEG 2000* [4]. MPEG/JVT (Joint Video Team) is also actively developing a new scalable video coding standard [5]. In addition to standardizations, other scalable codecs are also proposed [6, 7]. All these scalable codecs offer FGS. In MPEG-4 FGS, a video sequence is compressed into a single stream consisting of two layers: a base layer and an enhancement layer. The base layer is a non-scalable coding of a video sequence at the lower bound of a bitrate range. The enhancement layer encodes the difference between the original sequence and the reconstructed sequence from the base layer in a scalable manner to offer a range of bitrates for the sequence. In JPEG 2000, a codestream is organized hierarchically into different structural elements: tiles, components, resolution levels, precincts, layers, and packets. The packet is the most fundamental building block in a JPEG 2000 codestream. The *video packet* is the counterpart of an MPEG-4 FGS codestream. We would like to point out that although a granularity of scalability at the fundamental building block level may be enough for many applications, some applications may need to exploit the finest scalable granularity offered in a scalable codestream. Both MPEG-4 FGS and JPEG 2000 offer much finer scalable granularity than their respective fundamental building blocks. For example, an MPEG-4 FGS codestream can be truncated at any (RUN, EOP) symbol of a bitplane in an 8×8 DCT block.

Multimedia Digital Rights Management (DRM), as described in detail in Chapter 2, manages all rights for multimedia from creation to consumption. DRM technologies are widely used in protecting valuable digital assets. A typical DRM system encrypts multimedia content and controls consumption of multimedia content through a license which contains the decryption key along with specifications on how the content can be used by a user. A license is usually individualized, typically encrypted with a key that binds to the hardware of a user's player, so that the license cannot be illegally shared with others. Control of content consumption rather than distribution is much more efficient in protecting digital assets in the

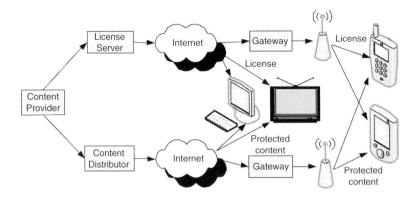

FIGURE 11.1:   Flow of protected content and license in a DRM system.

digital world since modern networks, storage, and compression technologies have made it trivial to transfer digital content from one device or person to another. Figure 11.1 shows the flow of protected contents and licenses in a DRM system. As shown in the figure, the content distributor is, in general, different from the content publisher and the license server (or clearing house) and does not know the encryption or decryption keys.

Multimedia encryption was introduced in Chapter 4. A natural question arises: Can we apply those encryption technologies developed for non-scalable multi-media formats to the newly developed scalable coding formats such as MPEG-4 FGS or JPEG 2000? An encryption technology developed for the traditional non-scalable coding may not be appropriate for scalable coding. A scalable codec is designed to compress multimedia content once, and a single codestream can be easily adapted to fit different applications. Applying an encryption scheme designed for non-scalable to a scalable codestream may destroy the scalability offered by the unencrypted scalable codestream. In DRM and many other multi-media applications, multimedia content is encrypted by the content publisher who is usually different from the content distributor. En route to the destination, content may be processed by edge servers to best fit the targeted devices and network con-ditions. These edge servers may be untrusted and may not be aware of the specific encryption scheme applied to a codestream. If encryption destroys the scalability of the scalable coding, these edge servers will not be able to perform simple adap-tations to select the best fitting codestream, and the advantages and benefits offered by scalable coding are neutralized. Readers are referred to Chapter 10 for further discussion on the necessity to preserve scalability after encryption. In addition, a scalable codestream can be encrypted to enable new services that cannot be offered effectively or efficiently by non-scalable coding. One example is the multi-access encryption to support "what you see is what you pay" with a single encrypted codestream. Different users can consume only the representations extracted from a single cipher codestream that they have acquired the rights to.

Scalability, especially FGS, offered by scalable coding poses great new challenges to the design of a cryptosystem for scalable codestreams. The scalable granularity to be supported in scalable media encryption is an important factor to consider in designing an encryption scheme for a scalable codec. A unique requirement for encryption of scalable multimedia formats is to minimize the adverse impact on the adaptation capability offered by the scalable coding technology so that edge servers can directly process the encrypted codestream without decryption. After arbitrary allowed truncations of an encrypted codestream, the result should be decryptable and decompressable. These design goals may be difficult to achieve, especially if the full original scalability is required to be preserved after encryption for FGS scalable coding. Multi-access encryption allows different users to access different access types and levels of a single encrypted codestream. Access to a higher privileged level should allow access to all the lower privileged levels of the same type. A user can access only those types and levels that he or she is authorized to. This implies that a different portion of data in multi-access encryption is encrypted with different keys. Key generation and management play an important role in multi-access encryption.

In this chapter, we present an overview of scalable encryption and multi-access encryption technologies for DRM and other multimedia applications. We first present briefly MPEG-4 FGS and JPEG 2000 scalable coding standards in Section 11.2. Scalable encryption technologies are reviewed in Section 11.3. Multi-access encryption and corresponding key schemes are presented in Section 11.4. The chapter concludes with Section 11.5.

11.2   SCALABLE CODING

Many scalable coding technologies have been proposed in the literature. Two recently adopted scalable coding technologies by standard bodies are the MPEG-4 FGS [3] for scalable video coding and JPEG 2000 [4] for scalable image coding. Both coding technologies offer FGS and are superior to old scalable coding technologies [1, 2] with layered scalability. Encryption for FGS scalable coding is more challenging than that for layered scalable coding since the FGS may need to be preserved in an encrypted scalable codestream. In addition, modern FGS scalable coding technologies also offer very flexible multiple accesses to a single codestream. Multi-access encryption for FGS scalable coding may require a complex key scheme. In the next two subsections, we shall briefly describe the two FGS coding standards.

11.2.1 MPEG-4 FGS Video Coding

This subsection provides a brief introduction to MPEG-4 FGS so that readers can better understand the encryption technologies for MPEG-4 FGS described in this chapter. More details can be found in Reference 3. In MPEG-4, the Video Object (VO) corresponds to entities in the codestream that can be accessed and manipulated. An instance of VO at a given time is called a *Video Object Plane* (VOP) [8]. MPEG-4 FGS encodes a video sequence into two layers: a non-scalable base layer which offers the lowest quality and bitrate for the scalable codestream and a scalable enhancement layer which offers enhancement in a large range of Signal-to-Noise Ratios (SNRs) and bitrates to the base layer. The MPEG-4 Advanced Simple Profile (ASP) provides a subset of non-scalable video coding tools to achieve high-efficiency coding for the base layer. The base layer is typically encoded at a very low bitrate. The FGS profile is used to obtain the enhancement layer to achieve an optimized video quality with a single codestream for a wide range of bitrates. More precisely, each frame's residue, i.e., the difference between the original frame and the corresponding frame reconstructed from the base layer, is encoded for the enhancement layer in a scalable manner: the DCT coefficients of the residue are compressed bitplane-wise from the most significant bit to the least significant bit. DCT coefficients in each 8×8 block are zigzag ordered. For each bitplane of a block, (RUN, EOP) symbols are formed and variable-length coded to produce the enhancement layer codestream, where RUN is the number of consecutive zeros before a non-zero value and EOP indicates if there are any non-zero values left on the current bitplane for the block. For a temporal enhancement frame which does not have a corresponding frame in the base layer, the bitplane coding is applied to the entire DCT coefficients of the frame. This is called *FGS temporal scalability* (FGST). FGST can be encoded using either forward or bi-directional prediction from the base layer. MPEG-4 FGS provides very fine grain scalability to allow near-rate-distortion (RD) optimal bitrate reduction.

In MPEG-4 FGS, video data is grouped into video packets, which are separated by the resynchronization marker. The bitplane start code, *fgs_bp_start_code*, in the enhancement layer also serves as a resynchronization marker for error resilience purposes. Video packets are aligned with macroblocks. In MPEG-4 FGS, video packets are determined at the time of compression, but can be changed later by modifying the resynchronization marker positions.

Due to the different roles they play, the base layer and the enhancement layer are typically unequally protected against network imperfection in transmission in practical applications. The base layer is usually well protected against bit errors or packet losses. The enhancement layer, on the other hand, is lightly or not protected against network imperfection. We would like to emphasize that scalability in MPEG-4 FGS is offered by the enhancement layer. The base layer does not provide any scalability. This implies that encryption of the base layer does not affect the scalability of the resulting codestream. In other words, traditional multimedia encryption technologies developed for non-scalable coding can be applied directly to the base layer.

11.2.2   JPEG 2000 Image Coding

JPEG 2000 is a wavelet-based image coding standard [4]. In JPEG 2000, an image can be partitioned into smaller rectangular regions called *tiles*. Each tile is encoded independently. Data in a tile are divided into one or more components in a color space. A wavelet transform is applied to each tile component to decompose it into different resolution levels. The lowest frequency subband is referred to as the resolution level 0 subband, which is also resolution 0. The image at resolution $r(r > 0)$ consists of the data of the image at resolution $(r - 1)$ and the subbands at resolution level r. The wavelet coefficients are quantized by a scalar quantization to reduce the precision of the coefficients, except in the case of lossless compression. Each subband is partitioned into smaller non-overlapping rectangular blocks called *code blocks*. Each code block is independently entropy encoded. The coefficients in a code block are encoded from the most significant bitplane to the least significant bitplane to generate an embedded bitstream. Each bitplane is encoded within three sub-bitplane passes. In each coding pass, the bitplane data and the contextual information are sent to an adaptive arithmetic encoder for encoding. By default, arithmetic coding is terminated at the end of the last bitplane encoding, and a codeblock's embedded bitstream forms a single *Arithmetic Codeword Segment* (ACS). JPEG 2000 also allows termination at the end of each sub-bitplane coding pass such that the bitstream from each coding pass forms an ACS. Context probabilities can also be reinitialized at the end of each coding pass to enable independent decoding of the bitstream from each coding pass. The optional arithmetic coding bypass puts raw bits into bitstream for certain coding passes. In this case, the boundary between arithmetic coding passes and raw passes must be terminated. Both ACS and the raw codeword segment are referred to as *Codeword Segment* (CS) in this chapter.

A code block's bitstream is distributed across one or more layers in the codestream. Each higher layer represents a quality increment. A layer consists of a number of consecutive bitplane coding passes from each code block in the tile, including all subbands of all components for that tile. JPEG 2000 also provides an intermediate space-frequency structure known as a *precinct*. A precinct is a collection of spatially contiguous code blocks from all subbands at a particular resolution level. The fundamental building block in a JPEG 2000 codestream is called a *packet*, which is simply a continuous segment in the compressed codestream that consists of a number of bitplane coding passes from each code block in a precinct. The data length of each Codeblock Contribution to a Packet (CCP) is indicated in the packet header. In the case of multiple codeword segments, the length of each CS in a CCP is indicated in the packer header. Each ACS or CCP does not allow byte-aligned values between 0xFF90 and 0xFFFF for any two consecutive bytes or ending with a byte of value 0xFF. A raw codeword segment when arithmetic coding bypass is enabled does not allow any byte-aligned nine consecutive bits of 1 or ending with a byte of value 0xFF. JPEG 2000 uses the unattainable range of two consecutive bytes to represent unique markers to facilitate organization and parsing of the bitstream and to improve error resilience.

The canvas coordinate system is used in JPEG 2000. An image is bounded by its upper left corner of coordinates (a_x, a_y) and its bottom right corner of coordinates (b_x, b_y). Let (P_x, P_y) be the coordinates of the top left corner of the first tile on the high-resolution grid, then JPEG 2000 requires that P_x, $P_y \geq 0$; $P_x \leq a_x$, $p_y \leq a_y$; and $P_x + T_x > a_x$, $P_y + T_y > a_y$, where $T_y \times T_y$ is the size of a tile at the high-resolution grid. Once the coordinates of the first tile are known, the coordinates of the remaining tiles can be derived. Coordinates for precincts are similarly defined. Those of the lower resolution grid can be derived. Details on JPEG 2000 can be found in Reference 4.

Each packet in a tile can be uniquely identified by the four parameters: component, resolution level, layer, and precinct. Each code block can be uniquely identified by the following parameters: tile, component, resolution level, precinct, subband, and the canvas coordinates of the upper left point of the code block on the reference grid. Packets for a tile can be ordered with different hierarchical ordering in a JPEG 2000 codestream by varying the ordering of parameters in nested "for loops," where each for loop is for one of the parameters uniquely specifying a packet in a tile.

JPSEC [9], the security part of JPEG 2000, introduces two new marker segments. One is SEC in the main header which is used to carry overall information about the security tools and parameters applied to the image. The other is INSEC placed in the bitstream to provide information of localized security tools and parameters. Details on JPSEC can be found in Reference 9.

11.3 SCALABLE ENCRYPTION

Many encryption algorithms have been proposed for multimedia encryption, as described in Chapter 4. There are two typical approaches in scalable encryption: full encryption and selective encryption. Full encryption partitions a scalable codestream into data blocks and applies a cipher to encrypt the data in each block with the block headers unencrypted to yield block-level scalability [10–13]. Selective encryption encrypts only partial data. Some selective encryption schemes developed with non-scalable compression in mind can be applied equally well to scalable coding and can preserve the original or a coarser scalable granularity in the encrypted codestream. One example is the format-compliant encryption schemes such as those proposed in Wen et al. [15, 16] that are discussed in detail in Chapter 9. Selective encryption usually leaks some content information and is often less secure than full encryption in trading for less data to be encrypted and finer scalable granularity. Due to deep parsing and other operations typically used in selective encryption, the processing speed advantage of selective encryption may be largely neutralized when a fast cipher such as the Chain & Sum (C&S) cipher proposed in Jakubowski and Venkatesan [14] is used in full encryption [12, 13].

We shall focus in this section on proposed technologies that were specially designed for encrypting scalable codestreams to enable certain levels of scalability in the encrypted codestream. This type of multimedia encryption is referred to as *scalable encryption* in this chapter. Some of the proposed scalable encryption schemes have been reviewed in Yu [17] and Zhu, Swanson, and Li [18].

Early scalable encryption schemes [19–23] are based on partitioning transform coefficients in a non-scalable coding, such as DCT coefficients in the MPEG-2 video coding, into a number of layers according to the importance of the coefficients. For example, the scheme proposed in Tosun and Feng [21] partitions DCT coefficients into three layers: base, middle, and enhancement layers. This rough data partition provides layered scalability in the resulting codestream. The base layer is encrypted to provide minimum protection to the codestream. If higher protection is desired, the middle layer or even the enhancement layer can be encrypted. Each layer is encrypted independently with the same key or a different key [23]. The encrypted codestream provides layered scalability that higher layers can be truncated if necessary.

FGS scaling coding such as MPEG-4 FGS or JPEG 2000 offers much finer granularity scalability than the scalability offered by the aforementioned layered scalable coding schemes. Researchers have proposed encryption schemes designed specifically to work with FGS scalable coding to preserve a certain level of scalability after encryption [10–13, 24–36]. Almost all of them were designed for the two standard scalable codecs. Scalable encryption schemes for JPEG 2000 are presented in Section 11.3.1, and those for MPEG-4 FGS are in Section 11.3.2.

11.3.1   Scalable Encryption for JPEG 2000

Grosbois, Gerbelot, and Ebrahimi [24] proposed two selective encryption schemes for JPEG 2000 to provide access control on resolutions or on layers. To provide access control on resolutions, the signs of the wavelet coefficients in high-frequency subbands are pseudo-randomly flipped. The output of a pseudo-random sequence generator is used to determine if the sign of a coefficient is inverted or not. A different seed to the generator is used for each code block. A seed for a code block is encrypted and inserted into the codestream right after the last termination marker, either implicit or explicit, of the code block by exploiting the fact that any byte appearing behind a termination marker is skipped by a JPEG 2000 standard compliant decoder. The resulting encrypted codestream is syntax compliant. Security of sign bit encryption is low in general. To provide access control on JPEG 2000 layers, the second scheme flips the bitstreams generated by the coding passes belonging to the last layers pseudo-randomly in the same way as in the first scheme. The resulting codestream is not syntax compliant since a flipped bitstream may emulate JPEG 2000 markers. Since a seed has to be inserted into the codestream for each code block, the encrypted codestream for both encryption schemes should have a noticeable overhead on compression efficiency, especially at a low bitrate coding. A potential problem of the schemes is that an edge server unaware of the proposed schemes may remove the inserted seeds for some code blocks in performing adaptation manipulations such as truncating bitstreams corresponding to lower significant bitplanes of a code block. Without a seed, the whole data of the corresponding code block cannot be decrypted.

More sophisticated schemes have been also proposed for scalable encryption of JPEG 2000. A straightforward method is to encrypt the data in each individual packet with a cipher such as Data Encryption Standard (DES) or Advanced Encryption Standard (AES) [25, 26]. AES in the Cipher FeedBack (CFB) mode is used in Norcen and Uhl [26] to encrypt any number of bits without size expansion. Another scheme proposed in Zhu, Yang, and Li [27] is to encrypt the bitstream of each codeword segment from the coding passes of the most significant bitplane to those of the least significant bitplane for each code block. The encrypted bitstreams are then partitioned and distributed into different layers. Cipher bitstreams generated by these schemes may emulate JPEG 2000 markers. Such emulation may cause erroneous parsing or synchronization, especially under error-prone transmissions or environments. Ciphers to avoid generating byte-aligned values between 0xFF90 and 0xFFFF for any two consecutive bytes and an ending byte of value 0xFF are employed in the schemes proposed in Wu and Ma [28], Wu and Deng [29], and Zhu, Yang, and Li [30]. These schemes encrypt the data in each packet, CCP, or codeword segment, respectively. The resulting cipher codestream is syntax compliant. While different syntax compliant ciphers are used in those schemes, a simple syntax-compliant cipher used in Wu and Ma [28], and Wu and Deng [29] is to iteratively encrypt until the output is syntax compliant. A block cipher can be applied without any modification. When a stream cipher is used, the operation to exclusive-or, i.e., XOR, the plaintext with a keystream is replaced by modular addition. The plaintext and the keystream are added modulo two's power of n, where n is the number of bits in the plaintext. This may expand an error in ciphertext to the whole decrypted plaintext since the error may produce a wrong iteration in decryption. An improved syntax-compliant cipher, called locally iterative encryption, is used in Zhu, Yang, and Li [30] to confine error propagation within a small block. In the scheme proposed in Zhu, Yang, and Li [30], the bitstream in each codeword segment is independently encrypted with a syntax-compliant cipher and partitioned and distributed into individual layers. The Initialization Vector (IV) for each independent encryption is generated from a global IV and a unique identifier to the codeword segment. There is no need to store the IVs except the global one. Recall that a code block can be uniquely identified by its tile, component, resolution level, precinct, subband, and the canvas coordinates of the upper left point of the code block on the reference grid. The canvas coordinates of the upper right point on the reference grid are used to identify each tile and precinct in generating an IV so that the code block identifier is invariant after truncations allowed by JPEG 2000. In addition to syntax compliance, the scheme produces an encrypted codestream with the same fine scalable granularity and error resilience as the unencrypted case. The overhead on compression efficiency is basically one global IV and therefore negligible. An alternative scheme is to encrypt the intersection of a CCP with a codeword segment instead of a codeword segment with a syntax compliant cipher [30].

11.3.2 Scalable Encryption for MPEG-4 FGS

Unlike a JPEG 2000 codestream which is entirely scalable, an MPEG-4 FGS codestream contains a non-scalable base layer and a scalable enhancement layer. Since an enhancement layer VOP depends on the base layer VOP(s) in decompression, it is natural to encrypt the base layer to protect the content. Any encryption scheme designed to encrypt non-scalable MPEG video can be used to encrypt the base layer. For example, the base layer can be fully encrypted such as the scheme proposed by Zhu and co-workers [13, 31] where the video data inside each video packet is independently encrypted with the C&S cipher [14], or selectively encrypted such as the scheme proposed by Yuan and co-workers [31], where the DC values with known number of bits (i.e., *intra_dc_coefficient* and *dct_dc_differential*), the sign bits of DCT coefficients, and the sign bits of Motion Vectors (MVs) (i.e., the sign bits of *horizontal_mv_data* and *vertical_mv_data*), as well as the MV residues (*horizontal_mv_residual* and *vertical_mv_residual*), are encrypted to provide syntax compliant encryption. The C&S cipher is selected in Yuan et al. [31] since it has low complexity, and, more importantly, any difference as small as a single bit in the plaintext results in completely different ciphertext if encrypted with the C&S cipher. This property is much desired in multimedia encryption because extra encryption parameters such as the IV are not needed in independently encrypting each data segment. Extra encryption parameters, if used, may have to be inserted into the codestream to send to the decryptor to decrypt the encrypted data properly, resulting in lowered compression efficiency. This advantage is clearly shown by the scalable encryption schemes proposed in Yuan et al. [12, 13, 31] which use the C&S cipher and in which the encrypted codestream has incurred a negligible overhead on the compression efficiency, as compared to other schemes which have noticeable compression efficiency overhead. In addition, these scalable encryption schemes are also robust to known-plaintext attacks [13]. A drawback of using the C&S cipher rather than a stream cipher or a block cipher in the Cipher Block Chaining (CBC) mode is that trailing truncations of an independent encryption block are not allowed when the C&S cipher is used, but are allowed when either of the two types of ciphers is used.

Encryption of the base layer alone in MPEG-4 FGS seems to render the resulting video frames random since an enhancement layer VOP is the residue of the difference between original VOP and the corresponding reconstructed VOP from the base layer. This may be true if each frame is viewed individually. When these frames are viewed together as a video sequence, the outlines and trajectories of the moving objects are readily visible. The nature of these objects and their actions can be easily identified [13, 31]. Leakage of such content information may not be acceptable in some applications. If that is the case, the enhancement layer should also be encrypted.

A lightweight, syntax compliant selective encryption scheme is proposed in Zhu et al. [13, 31] to encrypt an MPEG-4 FGS codestream that preserves the full scalability of MPGE-4 FGS. Different encryption schemes are used to encrypt the base layer and the enhancement layer so that each scheme can be designed to fully exploit the features of each layer. The base layer can be either fully or selectively encrypted, as described above. To encrypt an enhancement VOP, the encryption key and a hashed version of the base layer VOP that the enhancement VOP depends on are used jointly to generate a random bitmap of fixed size that matches the frame size. Each random bit in the bitmap is used to XOR the sign bit of the DCT coefficient at the corresponding position to ensure correct recovery of all the sign bits of any received enhancement data even under packet losses. The MV sign bits and the MV residues in an FGST VOP are scrambled in a similar manner. In addition to preserving the original scalability, the resulting encrypted codestream has exactly the same error resilience performance as the unencrypted case. Figure 11.2 shows the visual effect of the encryption scheme when the base layer is either selectively or fully encrypted. There exists content leakage when the base layer is selectively encrypted, especially when the motion is small. Some outlines of the speaker in Akyio are still partially visible with the selective encryption. The encrypted MPEG-4 FGS codestream in this mode is syntax compliant. The encryption is completely transparent to an application. An encrypted codestream can be processed as if it were not encrypted. When the base layer is fully encrypted, the resulting video appears very random. In this mode, the encrypted codestream as a whole is not syntax compliant, but the encrypted enhancement layer is syntax compliant. The security with the base layer fully encrypted is also much higher than that with the base layer selectively encrypted. In both cases, the aforementioned content leakage problem associated with encryption of the base layer alone disappears.

FIGURE 11.2:   Visual effect for video encrypted with the scheme proposed in Zhu et al. [13, 31]: (left column) original *Akyio* (top) and *Foreman* (bottom); (middle) base layer is selectively encrypted; (right) base layer is fully encrypted. (©2005 IEEE)

Wu and Mao [32] apply the scrambling scheme for Variable-Length Codewords (VLCs) proposed in Wen et al. [15, 16] to scramble each (RUN, EOP) symbol in the MPEG-4 FGS enhancement layer. More specifically, each possible (RUN, EOP) symbol is assigned with a fixed-length index. The (RUN EOP) symbols are first converted into the corresponding indexes. These indexes are then encrypted with a conventional cipher. The encrypted indexes are partitioned into indexes, and each index is mapped back to the codeword domain. The overhead on compression efficiency is about 7.0% for the Quarter Common Intermediate Format (QCIF) "Foreman" sequence [32]. The DCT transform compacts energy of a frame to low-frequency coefficients. This means that (RUN, EOP) symbols in an 8×8 block of an enhancement VOP may show much skewed distribution, especially in high bit-planes. In other words, some symbols appear more frequently than others. This fact can be exploited to break the encryption scheme just described. This scheme is also vulnerable to known-plaintext attacks when the mapping of (RUN, EOP) symbols to indexes does not change frequently enough. Frequent changes of the mapping will increase the overhead on compression efficiency significantly. We conclude that the security of the scheme should not be very high. An alternative encryption scheme is proposed in Yu [33], and Yu and Yu [34] to encrypt the MPEG-4 FGS enhancement layer, where the (RUN, EOP) symbols are pseudo-randomly shuffled on a bitplane or sub-bitplane level and the sign bits of DCT coefficients are scrambled for each enhancement VOP. Both schemes are syntax compliant for an error resilient decoder. The scalable granularity of an encrypted enhancement layer is reduced to a segment in which indexes are encrypted independently for the first scheme and to a bitplane or sub-bitplane level, depending on the level that (RUN, EOP) symbols are scrambled for the second scheme. Both encryption schemes also introduce error propagation since a wrong bit in a VLC encoded (RUN EOP) symbol renders the VLC decoding for the current and subsequent (RUN, EOP) symbols wrong, which in turn causes the encryption of indexes for the first scheme and the scrambling of (RUN, EOP) symbols for a whole bitplane in the second scheme irreversible. Whether that error propagation translates into perceptual degradation as compared to the unencrypted case or not depends on how encryption or shuffling is aligned with video packets and how a decoder behaves when errors occur. If the range of encryption or shuffling does not cross video packets, and if a decoder drops a whole video packet when an error occurs in it, then encryption does not incur any adverse impact on the error resilience. Otherwise, encryption introduces perceptual degradation.

An encryption scheme called *Secure Scalable Streaming* is proposed to work with scalable coding such as MPEG-4 FGS [10] and JPEG 2000 [11]. The scheme partitions a scalable codestream into packets and applies a block cipher in CBC mode to encrypt the data in each packet. The supported adaptations are to drop an entire packet or to truncate trailing data in a packet. Details of the scheme can be found in Chapter 10.

A full encryption scheme proposed in Yuan et al. [12, 13] applies the C&S cipher to encrypt the video data in each Video Packet (VP) independently for MPEG-4 FGS. The scalable granularity is reduced to a VP level after encryption. In other words, an entire VP is either dropped or maintained in an adaptation manipulation on an encrypted codestream. Any ciphertext error in an encrypted VP renders the whole decrypted VP unusable, no matter where the error occurs in a VP. This is due to the dependency on the whole ciphertext in decryption with the C&S cipher. An improved version with scalable granularity smaller than a VP and better error resilience proposed in Zhu et al. [36] operates in two modes: the Video Packet Encryption mode (VPE) and the Block Encryption mode (BE). In the VPE mode, compressed data in each VP are independently encrypted with a syntax-compliant cipher which produces ciphertext that neither emulates the VP delimiters or increases the length. In the BE mode, the compressed enhancement data of each 8×8 block or macroblock (MB) are independently encrypted with a stream cipher or a block cipher operating in the Output FeedBack (OFB) mode bitplane-wise from the Most Significant Bit (MSB) to the Least Significant Bit (LSB). The ciphertext is partitioned and allocated to each VP, with stuffing bits possibly inserted to avoid VP delimiter emulation. The IV for each independent encryption of the data in a frame is generated in both modes by hashing a random "frame" IV for the frame and the identifier of a VP or a block unique within the frame. For a VP, the bitplane ID and the index of the first MB in the VP right after the VP's resynchronization marker as well as layer ID (e.g., base layer or enhancement layer) are used as the unique identifier. For a block or MB, the index of the block or MB as well as the layer ID is used as the unique identifier. The frame IV is inserted into the base VOP or FGST VOP. The IVs actually used in both encryption and decryption are generated on the fly. In this way, the overhead on compression efficiency is small, about 960 bps for a video with a frame rate at 30 frames per second. The scheme provides a decent solution to typically competitive requirements of fine scalable granularity and minimal impact on compression efficiency. The VPE mode enables truncations at a VP or trailing VP level, and the BE mode preserves the full scalability of a scalable bitstream[1] at the cost of much higher complexity. For the BE mode, decryption and decompression have to be executed in an interleaving manner to allocate data correctly to each independently encrypted segment. Both modes have an error resilience performance virtually the same as the unencrypted case, thanks to the careful design of the scheme which makes the error propagation behavior of the encryption the same as that of the decompression. The base layer which does not provide any scalability is always encrypted with the VPE mode.

11.4   MULTI-ACCESS ENCRYPTION AND KEY SCHEMES

A modern scalable codec supports multiple access types in addition to FGS with a single scalable codestream. JPEG 2000 [4] supports five scalable types: tile, resolution, layer (i.e., quality), color component, and precinct. MPEG-4 FGS [3] supports both temporal and quality scalabilities. The universal scalable video coding proposed in Wu et al. [6] supports temporal, spatial, and quality scalabilities. The embedded audio coding proposed in Li [7] supports quality, sampling rate, and channel scalabilities. Encryption for these scalable codecs should support multiple accesses after encryption so that different applications can still extract a best-fit representation from a single encrypted codestream. Most scalable encryption schemes use a single key to encrypt an entire scalable codestream (if rekeying is not considered). This may be undesirable in many applications. For example, it may be desirable to charge different accesses at different prices. A mobile phone playing video at a reduced resolution with lowered quality should pay less than a PC playing at the full resolution with the highest quality. A business model that a consumer pays according to the quality of the service he or she receives makes more sense. In other words, a DRM-protected scalable codestream should

---

[1]Truncations at a block or MB level may need auxiliary information on the possible truncation points.

support "what you see is what you pay," which implies that multiple keys are needed to encrypt a scalable codestream. Multi-access encryption and corresponding key schemes will be discussed in this section. We describe a general multi-access encryption framework in Section 11.4.1 and key schemes to support multi-access encryption in Section 11.4.2.

11.4.1 Multi-Access Encryption

A general framework of multi-access encryption for scalable coding is proposed in Zhu, Li, and Feng [37, 38]. A scalable codestream is organized on some fundamental building blocks, denoted in general as *Scalable Building Blocks* (SBBs) in this chapter. Each SBB can be uniquely identified. For example, the SBB for JPEG 2000 is the packet which can be uniquely identified by its tile, component, resolution level, precinct, and layer. Based on the supported scalabilities, SBBs can be extracted from a codestream to form a best-fit representation for an application. An SBB may also be truncated or rate shaped. For multi-access encryption, a single encrypted codestream may support multiple access types, and each access type may be divided into discrete levels. The most fundamental building block in the multi-access encryption framework is called a *Scalable Access Building Block* (SABB), which is the smallest unit of data to be encrypted with the same content encryption key in multi-access encryption. Each SABB is uniquely identified by the set of levels of the supported access types. For each scalable type, an empty level denoted by ϕ is added. The empty level is used when the scalable type has no contribution to a SABB. One SABB usually contains one or more SBBs, depending on the supported multi-access granularity. Encryption of each SABB can be any of the encryption schemes described in Section 11.3, which determine the scalable granularity for each SABB after encryption.

11.4.2 Key Schemes for Multi-Access Encryption

Scalable multi-access encryption allows different users to access different access types and levels of a single encrypted codestream. A key scheme for multi-access encryption must ensure that a user can access only the data of those types and levels that he or she is authorized to. An access to a higher privileged level should allow accesses to all the lower privileged levels of the same type. In addition, the key scheme should be robust to collusion attacks. When a group of cryptanalysts with different access rights collude, they cannot derive any keys that they have no right to access. An additional requirement in DRM applications is that a multi-access key scheme should minimize the number of keys sent to a user in a license.

The key scheme for a layered scalable codestream is simple. Each layer is encrypted independently with a different key [23]. These keys can be related to each other with a hash function. Recall that a higher layer contains enhancement data to lower layers in a layered scalable codestream. The encryption key for a lower layer is derived from the key of the next higher layer by a cryptographic hash function. The hash function guarantees that a higher layer can derive the keys of lower layers, but it is practically impossible vice versa. For an FGS scalable codestream which supports simultaneously multiple access types with multiple access layers for each type, the design of a key scheme for multi-access encryption is much more challenging.

A simple key scheme for multi-access encryption of MPEG-4 FGS is used in Yuan et al. [12, 13], where each SABB in a VOP is encrypted with an independent key. All the keys associated with the encryption of SABBs that a specific access is entitled to consume have to be sent to a client. The key scheme is secure and robust to collusion attacks, but not efficient in the key distribution since multiple keys may need to be sent to a client in a license. A tree-based key scheme is proposed in Deng, Wu, and Ma [39] for the multi-access control of JPEG 2000 codestreams. One or more keys may need to be sent to a user. An efficient key scheme based on the Diffie-Hellman (DH) key agreement is proposed in Zhu, Feng, and Li [40] for multi-access encryption described in Yuan et al. [12, 13] which supports two access types with an arbitrary number of levels for each type. Only a single key is needed to send to a user in a license. The scheme is generalized in Zhu, Li, and Feng [37] to support an arbitrary number of access types. In this generalized scheme, a cryptographic hash function is used to derive the level key for each level from its next higher level of the same type, and an encryption key is derived with the Group Diffie-Hellman (GDH) key agreement [41] from the level keys of those type levels that uniquely specify the SABB to be encrypted. The scheme is efficient in terms of the amount of formation needed in generating the keys: only a single key and a simple description of the access types and level partitions are needed in generating all the keys. But the key transmission is not efficient in general. For an access specified by multiple types, multiple-level keys have to be sent to a user. In this case, the GDH exponentials may need to be guarded securely and sent to users when needed instead of published in the protected content that everybody can access. Otherwise, the available level keys can be used to derive encryption keys that a user may not be entitled to access. The key scheme is also vulnerable to collusion attacks.

A key scheme for general multi-access encryption is proposed in Zhu, Feng, and Li [38], where multi-access control is shown to be equivalent to the hierarchical access control for a partially ordered set (poset) first studied by Akl and Taylor [42]. Many key schemes developed for poset can be used for multi-access encryption. In the following, we first describe how a multi-access control is equivalent to a poset. We then present two key schemes for multi-access control in the subsection Efficient Key Schemes for Multi-Access Encryption. JPEG 2000 is used as an example to show the detail, but the two schemes are applicable to general scalable codestreams.

Multi-Access Control Is Equivalent to Poset

By examining the relationship of different values for a scalable type of JPEG 2000, it is clear that there are two different scalable types. Different values of the first scalable type, such as resolutions, form a fully ordered hierarchy, i.e., given any two distinct values, one is fully included in the other or vice versa. Different values of the second scalable type, on the other hand, are independent of each other, and a set of those parameters must be specified for a scalable access. Tiles and precincts are of the second type. A tile or a precinct specifies a unique spatial or frequency-spatial block. A tile or a precinct is disjoint with other tiles or precincts. If a user wants to view the whole image, then all the tiles and precincts have to be selected. A user can also select a group of tiles or precincts to view a portion of an image. From a user's perspective, different values of the second type can be organized according to different combinations of the values, i.e., different ways a user may access the scalable feature specified by a scalable parameter of the type. These combinations form either an inclusive or a non-inclusive relationship and, therefore, form a poset. For this reason, the second scalable type is called a *Partially Ordered Hierarchy* (POH) type, while the first type is called a *Fully Ordered Hierarchy* (FOH) type. Other scalable coding has similar properties.

A poset is denoted as $(P, \leq)$, where "$\leq$" is a binary relation, and P is a finite set. $a \leq b$ for $a, b \in P$ means b can access a, i.e., b's key can derive a's key, but not vice versa. A poset $(P, \leq)$ can be uniquely described by a Hasse diagram, where each vertex is an element in P, and an edge is a relation $\leq$ that an upper (parent) vertex has an access priority. Due to this correspondence, we use vertex, node, and element interchangeably.

It is clear that the empty level (or empty element) ϕ is the minimal element in a fully or partially ordered set. The poset of a POH type such as JPEG 2000's tiles or precincts is constructed in the following way. The top level has a single vertex including all non-empty elements. The number of non-empty elements is denoted as n. The next level consists of vertices with one element dropped. There are $C_n^{n-1} = n$ vertices at this level. If all the elements of a vertex at this level are completely included in a vertex at the next higher level, then an edge is drawn between the two vertices. The vertices at the next lower level are the vertices with $n - 2$ elements. There are $C_n^{n-2} = n(n - 1)/2$ vertices at this level. Edges for the vertices at this level are drawn in the same way as described for the second level. This process continues until reaching the bottom level which consists of a single vertex ϕ connecting to all the vertices at the next higher level where each vertex contains a single element. The total number of vertices including the empty vertex is 2^n.

Example 1:   Suppose we want to control accesses to tiles, resolutions, and layers for a JPEG 2000 codestream. Suppose a JPEG 2000 codestream

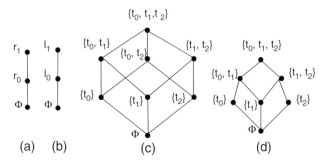

FIGURE 11.3:   Hasse diagrams for the fully ordered sets of two resolutions (a) and two layers (b) and the poset of three tiles (c) for JPEG 2000. The simplified Hasse diagram for the poset of three tiles arranged in a row if disconnected regions are inaccessible is shown in (d).

is partitioned into two resolutions r_0, r_1; two layers l_0, l_1; and three tiles t_0, t_1, t_2 arranged in one row. Then the two resolutions and two layers form fully ordered sets, while the three tiles form a poset. The corresponding Hasse diagrams are shown in Figure 11.3. Each diagram includes an empty element ϕ.

In most applications, a user's request is continuous spatial regions. If that is the case, the Hasse diagram of the poset of three tiles shown in Figure 11.3(c) can be simplified by removing the inaccessible combination $\{t_0, t_2\}$ since we have assumed that the three tiles are arranged in a row and the tiles t_0 and t_2 are separated by a tile t_1 and not continuous. The resulting Hasse diagram is shown in Figure 11.3(d).

The poset $(P, \leq)$ of the scalable access control is just the product of the fully and partially ordered sets $(P_i, \leq)$ of all scalable types: $(P, \leq) = \times_i (P_i, \leq)$. The number of vertices in the product is equal to the product of the numbers of vertices in scalable types: $|P| = \prod_i |P_i|$, where $|X|$ is the cardinality of a set X. The number of edges in the product's Hasse diagram is $\sum_i e_i \cdot |P|/|P_i|$, where e_i is the number of edges in the Hasse diagram of ith scalable type. The Hasse diagram of the product can be constructed by first laying out all the vertices of the product, checking each set of vertices obtained by fixing all the component parameters except one, and drawing edges according to the running component's Hasse diagram as if the fixed components did not exist.

Example 2:   The product of the Hasse diagrams of Figure 11.3(a) and (d) is shown in Figure 11.4.

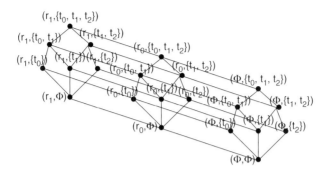

FIGURE 11.4: The product of the Hasse diagrams of (a) and (d) shown in Figure 11.3.

We note that not every key in a multi-access control poset is used as a content encryption key to encrypt an SABB. Some keys are used for the pure purpose of deriving the keys of descendent vertices. This occurs when there exists a POH scalable type, such as tile or precinct in JPEG 2000. In this case, only the vertices with a single parameter corresponding to a POH type are associated with content encryption keys. For the case given in Example 1, if the supported scalable access is only resolutions and tiles, then the Hasse diagram shown in Figure 11.4 is the multi-access poset. The keys associated with the vertices containing more than one tile are not associated with any content encryption keys. They are simply used to derive other keys with access permission according to the access hierarchy.

If each SABB must be specified by a non-empty element of a scalable parameter, then the empty element is not needed for that scalable type, and any nodes containing the empty element of that scalable type can be removed. For JPEG 2000, each packet is uniquely identified by the five scalable parameters: tile, resolution, layer, color component, and precinct. None of the scalable types is empty. Therefore, all vertices containing one or more empty components ϕ can be removed from the posets and Hasse diagrams for JPEG 2000. The actual poset associated with the scalable access control for JPEG 2000 given in Example 1 is shown in Figure 11.5, where no empty element is used. There are 24 vertices and 48 edges in this Hasse diagram. The empty element ϕ is included in Figures 11.3 and 11.4 to show a general case.

Efficient Key Schemes for Multi-Access Encryption

For DRM applications, content encryption is executed once. The key generation information and allowed access rights by the publisher are uploaded to a license

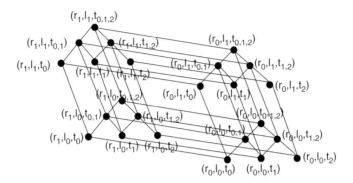

FIGURE 11.5: Poset of the scalable access control for JPEG 2000 given in Example 1, where $t_0, \ldots, i$ means $\{t_0, \ldots, t_i\}$. We have assumed that disconnected tiles are inaccessible.

server for users to download after certain conditions such as payment are met. Therefore, the DRM application of scalable codestreams is a static hierarchic access control problem. There is no need to consider adding or removing vertices in the key management, which greatly simplifies the key management problem. All hierarchic key schemes developed for poset can be used with the resulting scalable access control poset $(P, \le)$, especially those that are efficient for static key management. In this section, we describe two key schemes for DRM applications of multi-access encryption. The first key scheme [38] is a modification of the GDH-based key scheme described in Zhu, Li, and Feng [37] to fit into the scalable access hierarchic structure described in the subsection Multi-Access Control Is Equivalent to Poset. The second key scheme [43] is an application of the hash-based key scheme for a poset proposed in Zhong [44] and Frikken, Atallah, and Bykova [45] to the multi-access control.

GDH-Based Key Scheme for Scalable Multi-Access Control

a. **Preparation and Key Generation**. A content publisher of a scalable code-stream first picks up an appropriate prime p and a generator $\alpha \in Z_p^*$, $2 \le \alpha \le p - 2$ and then makes a decision on which scalable access types to support and how many levels for each access type. A poset $(P, \le)$ is then constructed with the method described in the subsection Multi-Access Control Is Equivalent to Poset. Each vertex $v_i \in (P, \le)$ is assigned a random number $r_i \in Z_p^*$. For a root vertex v_r, i.e., a vertex with no parent, the random number r_r is its key $k_r = r_r$. In the multi-access control of JPEG 2000, there is only one root vertex. For example, the vertex $(r_1, l_1, t_{0,1,2})$ shown in

Figure 11.5 is the root vertex for the poset. The key k_i of a non-root vertex v_i is calculated from the keys of its parents and the random number r_i of the vertex with GDH. Let $K(v_i)$ be the set of keys of all the parents of a vertex v_i, then $k_i = \alpha^{r_i \cdot R_i} \mod p$, where $R_i = \prod_{k \in K(v_i)} k$, which is the product of the keys of v_i's parents.

As we mentioned previously, some vertices may not be associated with content encryption of SABBs, due to partially ordered scalable types such as tiles and precincts in JPEG 2000. For example, only the vertices containing a single tile in Figure 11.5 correspond to encryption of the packets specified by the three scalable parameters of the vertices (the other two JPEG 2000 scalable parameters not used for access control in this example can be of any values). The content encryption key $k^c_{r_i,l_j,t_k}$ for the packets specified by (r_i, l_j, t_k) is generated by hashing the corresponding vertex key: $k^c_{r_i,l_j,t_k} = H(k_{r_i,l_j,t_k})$, where H is a cryptographic hash function, or by a modular operation: $k^c_{r_i,l_j,t_k} = k_{r_i,l_j,t_k} \mod \rho$, where ρ is a proper integer. The purpose of this hashing process is to generate the content encryption key with the desired size. The content is then encrypted with the generated content encryption keys and a proper symmetric encryption. The key generation information (see below) along with allowed access rights is uploaded to a server, and the protected content is released to distribute to users.

b. **Public Information and Key Derivation**. When a client acquires a right to access a certain representation of an encrypted scalable codestream, i.e., to access a certain vertex $v_i \in (P, \leq)$, the vertex's key is sent to the client. Then the client has to derive the keys of all the descendent vertices of that vertex. The client first derives the keys of v_i's children and then the keys of v_i's children's children. This iterative process keeps running until all the needed keys are derived. The content encryption keys are then derived with the hash function or the modular operation and are used to decrypt the content a user is entitled to access.

In order to achieve the aforementioned key derivation, the following public information is packed into an unencrypted header of the protected content for every client to access: $(P, \leq)$ (or its description so the poset can be derived), p, α, and $\{\alpha^{r_i \cdot R_i/k} \mod p | k \in K(v_i)\}$ for each non-root vertex v_i. A parent vertex v_i can derive its child vertex v_j by using its key k_i and the public information $\alpha^{r_j \cdot R_j/k_i} \mod p$ of the vertex v_j: $k_j = (\alpha^{r_j \cdot R_j/k_i})^{k_i} \mod p$.

Hash-Based Key Scheme for Scalable Multi-Access Control. One of the most efficient key schemes for a poset is the hash-based key scheme proposed in Zhong [44] and Frikken, Atallah, and Bykova [45]. In this scheme, each node n_i is assigned a unique label l_i and a secret key k_i. Suppose that there is an edge e_{12} linking a node n_i to another node n_2, where $n_1 > n_2$. Then the edge is assigned a value $v_{12} = k_2 - H(k_1, l_2)$, where H is a secure cryptographic hash function.

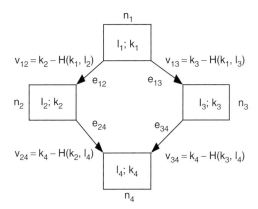

FIGURE 11.6: Node and edge values for a poset. All arithmetic is modulo ρ, a proper integer.

The labels l_i and edge values $v_{i,j}$ are public information which can be packed into the encrypted codestream. Figure 11.6 shows an example of a poset with four nodes. To derive the key of a child node, the label of the child node and the edge linking from the current node to the child node is used. For example, if the key k_1 of the node n_1 in Figure 11.6 is known, then the key k_3 for a child node n_3 can be derived with the following equation:

$$k_3 = v_{1,3} + H(k_1, l_3),$$

from key k_1 of node n_1 and public edge value $v_{1,3}$ and label l_3. Both $v_{1,3}$ and l_3 are public information.

This scheme uses hash functions rather than exponential operations of large integers and is therefore much faster than the previous GDH-based key scheme. The hash-based key scheme has to store both the edge values and the unique labels in generating node keys. They are public information packed into a protected content in DRM applications. For a complex multi-access control like JPEG 2000, the additional storage, i.e., the overhead on compression efficiency, might be significant. Is there a way to reduce the overhead? A natural approach to reduce the overhead is to use the unique identifiers of the SABBs associated with each node. The key issue in doing so is to ensure that those labels remain the same after truncations so that the keys of descendents can still be derived correctly. For a JPEG 2000 codestream, tiles are indexed with a unique integer starting from the upper left tile. If some tiles are truncated, say, the surrounding tiles are truncated to convert an image or frame of aspect 16:9 to 4:3, the tiles in the resulting JPEG 2000 codestream will be indexed differently from the original indexes.

Therefore, the tile indexes used in JPEG 2000 codestreams cannot be used as the unique labels l_i in the key generation; otherwise, the keys generated from truncated codestreams will be different from the actual decryption keys. The canvas coordinates are used in generating unique labels l_i as described in detail next. The resulting labels are invariant when truncations occur. Therefore, the values of labels and edges are preserved even if an encrypted codestream undergoes truncations. The poset structure can be derived from the information carried in a JPEG 2000 codestream. Only the edge values are required to be packed into an encrypted codestream with the scheme. The additional overhead due to the storage of unique node labels is therefore removed.

To exploit the invariance of canvas coordinates and yet satisfy the requirements set by JPEG 2000 on tiles, as described in Section 11.2.2, a truncation-invariant virtual coordinate system to uniquely identify each tile is presented. To generate this virtual coordinate system, an image and its tiles are extended upward and leftward in the following way until it cannot move any further: each time the coordinates (a'_x, a'_y) of the top left corner of the extended image and the coordinates (P'_x, P'_y) of the extended first tile are moved upward and leftward stepwise. Each move reduces the coordinates of both points (a'_x, a'_y) and (P'_x, P'_y) in either x or y direction by subtracting the corresponding T_x or T_y, where $T_x \times T_y$ is the size of a tile at the high-resolution grid. For the resulting virtual coordinate system, we have $P'_x, P'_y \geq 0$, $a'_x, a'_y \geq 0$, $P'_x < T_x, P'_y < T_y$, $P'_x \leq a'_x, P'_y \leq a'_y$, and $P'_x + T'_x > a'_x, P'_y + T'_y > a'_y$. Figure 11.7 shows an example of the actual image, its tiles (solid lines), the extended image, and the extended tiles (dotted lines indicating virtual tiles and virtual image areas).

After the aforementioned extension and generation of the virtual coordinate system, tiles are indexed, with both virtual and real tiles counted, starting from

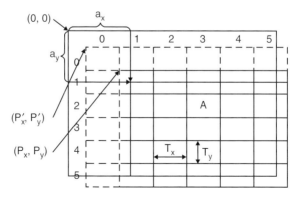

FIGURE 11.7:   A virtual coordinate system for extended image and tiles.

0 on both x and y directions, from top to bottom and from left to right. We use two binary arrays to index a tile in an image. Each array is associated with a direction, and the ith bit in the binary array is associated with the tile of index i in the corresponding direction. For example, the tile "A" shown in Figure 11.7 is indicated by the two binary arrays 00010... and 00100.... It is clear to see that in this tile indexing system, a combination of tiles can be simply represented by setting the corresponding bits in the two binary arrays. Therefore, the component associated with the tile access for each node of the poset representing a multi-access control of JPEG 2000 can be represented by the two binary arrays. We note that such a tile indexing system does not change even if a JPEG 2000 codestream undergoes truncations.

Having presented an invariant indexing system for tiles, let us turn our attention to other scalable types. It is easy to see that the indexes used in JPEG 2000 to represent resolution levels, layers, and components do not change after truncations. The index for precincts does not change either, even if some precincts can be truncated. This is because indexes of precincts are generated against the coordinates of the corresponding bands, which in turn are generated against the coordinates of the corresponding tiles and, therefore, are invariant after truncations.

The aforementioned truncation-invariant indexing system is used to indicate each node in a poset representing a multi-access control of JPEG 2000. The index for each node is unique and, therefore, can be used as the labels $\{l_i\}$ in the hash-based poset key scheme. We note that these indexes can be generated from the information contained in the headers of a JPEG 2000 codestream and, therefore, are not needed to be packed into a codestream. The poset corresponding to a multi-access control can also be derived from the headers in a codestream, and is not packed into a codestream. The only public information that has to be packed into a codestream is the edge values of the poset. The same scheme can be used for motion JPEG 2000, where the keys are reused for each frame unless they are rekeyed. Similar approaches can be used for other scalable formats.

Figure 11.8 shows an image of aspect ratio 16:9 cropped to 4:3 by truncating the surrounding tiles directly from an encrypted JPEG 2000 codestream. This type of truncation is widely applied to show a movie content of aspect ratio 16:9 on a TV of aspect ratio 4:3.

11.5 CONCLUSION

We present an overview of scalable encryption and multi-access encryption for DRM applications in this chapter. Both work with scalable multimedia coding. Scalable encryption ensures that the encrypted codestream still maintains a certain level of scalability. Scalable granularity after encryption is a key consideration in the design. Some scalable encryption schemes are syntax compliant to make the

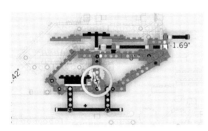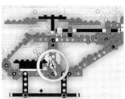

FIGURE 11.8: Cropping an encrypted JPEG 2000 codestream from aspect ratio 16:9 (1280 × 720 pixels) to 4:3 (792 × 594 pixels).

encryption transparent to an application. Scalable multi-access encryption, on the other hand, ensures that different users can extract different representations from a single encrypted codestream to fit their respective applications and that a user can consume only the particular representations he or she is authorized to. Designing a secure yet efficient key scheme is a critical issue in multi-access encryption. A key scheme should guarantee that a user can only access the decryption keys that he or she is entitled to access. In addition, a key scheme should withstand collusion attacks, where a group of cryptanalysts collude to derive keys that they have no rights to access. The proposed technologies have addressed these issues. As a new research area, many issues still remain to be further studied and optimized in future research endeavors.

REFERENCES

[1] R. Aravind, M. R. Civanlar, and A. R. Reibman. Packet loss resilience of MPEG-2 scalable video coding algorithm, *IEEE Trans. Circuits and Systems for Video Technology*, 6(10):426–435, 1996.

[2] H. Gharavi and H. Partovi. Multilevel video coding and distribution architectures for emerging broadband digital networks, *IEEE Trans. Circuits and Systems for Video Technology*, 6(5):459–469, 1996.

[3] ISO/IEC. Coding of Audio-Visual Objects, Part-2 Visual, Amendment 4: Streaming Video Profile, ISO/IEC 14496-2/FPDAM4, July 2000.

[4] ISO/IEC. Information Technology — JPEG 2000 Image Coding System, Part 1: Core Coding System, ISO/IEC 15444-1:2000 (ISO/IEC JTC/SC 29/WG 1 N1646R, March 2000.

[5] ISO/IEC. Working Draft 4 of ISO/IEC 14496-10:2005/AMD3 Scalable Video Coding, ISO/IEC JTC 1/SC 29/WG 11N 7555, October 2005.

[6] F. Wu, S. Li, R. Yan, X. Sun, and Y. Zhang. Efficient and universal scalable video coding, in *IEEE Int. Conf. Image Processing*, 2:37–40, Rochester, NY, September 2002.

[7] J. Li. Embedded audio coding (EAC) with implicit auditory masking, in *Proc. 10th ACM Int. Conf. Multimedia*, pp. 592–601, Juan les Pins, France, December 2002.

[8] ISO/IEC. MPEG-4 Video Verification Model Version 17.0, ISO/IEC JTC1/SC29/WG11 N3515, Beijing, China, July 2000.

[9] ISO/IEC. JPSEC Commission Draft 2.0, ISO/IEC/JTC 1/SC29/WG 1, N3397, 2004.

[10] S. J. Wee and J. G. Apostolopoulos. Secure scalable video streaming for wireless networks, *IEEE. Int. Conf. Acoustics, Speech, and Signal Processing*, 4:2049–2052, Salt Lake City, UT, May 7–11, 2001.

[11] S. J. Wee and J. G. Apostolopoulos. Secure scalable streaming and secure transcoding with JPEG-2000, *IEEE Int. Image Processing*, 1:I-205–208, Barcelona, Spain, September 14–17, 2003.

[12] C. Yuan, B. B. Zhu, M. Su, X. Wang, S. Li, and Y. Zhong. Layered access control for MPEG-4 FGS video, *IEEE Int. Conf. Image Processing*, 1:517–520, September 2003.

[13] B. B. Zhu, C. Yuan, Y. Wang, and S. Li. Scalable protection for MPEG-4 fine granularity scalability, *IEEE Trans. Multimedia*, 7(2):222–233, April 2005.

[14] M. H. Jakubowski and R. Venkatesan. The chain & sum primitive and its applications to MACs and stream ciphers, in *EUROCRYPT'98*, pp. 281–293, Helsinki, Finland, 1998. Also available from http://www.research.microsoft.com/~mariuszj/pubs.htm.

[15] J. Wen, M. Severa, W. Zeng, M. H. Luttrell, and W. Jin. A format-compliant configurable encryption framework for access control of multimedia, in *IEEE Workshop Multimedia Signal Processing*, Cannes, France, pp. 435–440, October 2001.

[16] J. Wen, M. Severa, W. Zeng, M. H. Luttrell, and W. Jin. A format-compliant configurable encryption framework for access control of video, *IEEE Trans. Circuits and Systems for Video Technology*, 12(6):545–557, June 2002.

[17] H. H. Yu. An overview on scalable encryption for wireless multimedia access, *Proc. SPIE, Internet Quality of Service*, 5245:24–34, Orlando, FL, August 2003.

[18] B. B. Zhu, M. D. Swanson, and S. Li. Encryption and authentication for scalable multimedia: Current state of the art and challenges, *Proc. SPIE Internet Multimedia Management Systems V*, 5601:157–170, October 2004.

[19] T. Kunkelmann and R. Reinema. A scalable security architecture for multimedia communication standards, in *IEEE Int. Conf. Multimedia Computing and Systems*, pp. 660–661, Ottawa, Canada, June 3–6, 1997.

[20] T. Kunkelmann and U. Horn. Video encryption based on data partitioning and scalable coding – A comparison, in *Proc. 5th Int. Workshop Interactive Distributed Multimedia Systems and Telecommunication Services, IDMS'98*, Oslo, Norway, LNCS, 1483:95–106, September 1998.

[21] A. S. Tosun and W.-C. Feng. Efficient multi-layer coding and encryption of MPEG video streams, *IEEE Int. Conf. Multimedia and Expo*, 1:119–122, New York, NY, July 30–August 2, 2000.

[22] A. S. Tosun and W.-C. Feng. Lightweight security mechanisms for wireless video transmission, in *IEEE Int. Conf. Information Technology: Coding and Computing*, pp. 157–161, Las Vegas, NV, April 2001.

[23] A. M. Eskicioglu and E. J. Delp. An integrated approach to encrypting scalable video, *IEEE. Int. Conf. Multimedia and Expo*, 1:573–576, Lausanne, Switzerland, August 26–29, 2002.

[24] R. Grosbois, P. Gerbelot, and T. Ebrahimi. Authentication and access control in the JPEG 2000 compressed domain, *Proc. SPIE 46th Annual Meeting, Applications of Digital Image Processing XXIV*, 4472:95–104, 2001.

[25] Y. Sadourny and V. Conan. A proposal for supporting selective encryption in JPSEC, *IEEE Trans. Consumer Electronics*, 49(4):846–849, November 2003.

[26] R. Norcen and A. Uhl. Selective encryption of the JPEG 2000 bitstream, in *Proc. IFIP TC6/TC11 Sixth Joint Working Conf. Communications and Multimedia Security (CMS'03)*, A. Lioy and D. Mazzocchi (Ed.), Turin, Italy, LNCS 2828:194–204, October 2003.

[27] B. B. Zhu, Y. Yang, and S. Li. JPEG 2000 encryption enabling fine granularity scalability without decryption, *IEEE Int. Symp. Circuits and Systems 2005*, 6:6304–6307, Kobe, Japan, May 2005.

[28] H. Wu and D. Ma. Efficient and secure encryption schemes for JPEG 2000, *IEEE Int. Conf. Acoustics, Speech, and Signal Processing 2004 (ICASSP'04)*, 5:V869–872, Montreal, Quebec, Canada, May 2004.

[29] Y. Wu and R. H. Deng. Compliant encryption of JPEG 2000 codestreams, in *IEEE. Int. Conf. Image Processing 2004 (ICIP'04)*, Singapore, pp. 3447–3450, October 2004.

[30] B. B. Zhu, Y. Yang, and S. Li. JPEG 2000 Syntax-compliant Encryption Preserving Full Scalability, *IEEE Int. Conf. Image Processing 2005*, 3:636–639, Genova, Italy, September 2005.

[31] C. Yuan, B. B. Zhu, Y. Wang, S. Li, and Y. Zhong. Efficient and fully scalable encryption for MPEG-4 FGS, *IEEE Int. Symp. Circuits and Systems*, 2:620–623, May 2003.

[32] M. Wu and Y. Mao. Communication-friendly encryption of multimedia, in *IEEE Workshop Multimedia Signal Processing*, pp. 292–295, St. Thomas, US Virgin Islands, December 9–11, 2002.

[33] H. H. Yu. Scalable encryption for multimedia content access control, *IEEE Int. Conf. Acoustics, Speech, and Signal Processing*, 2:II-417–420, Hong Kong, April 6–10, 2003.

[34] H. H. Yu and X. Yu. Progressive and scalable encryption for multimedia content access control, *IEEE Int. Conf. Communications*, 1:547–551, Anchorage, AK, May 11–15, 2003.

[35] H. H. Yu. On scalable encryption for mobile consumer multimedia applications, *IEEE Int. Conf. Communications*, 1:63–67, Paris, France, June 20–24, 2004.

[36] B. B. Zhu, Y. Yang, C. W. Chen, and S. Li. Fine granularity scalability encryption of MPEG-4 FGS bitstreams, in *IEEE Int. Workshop Multimedia Signal Processing 2005 (MMSP 2005)*, Shanghai, China, October 30–November 2, 2005.

[37] B. B. Zhu, S. Li, and M. Feng. A framework of scalable layered access control for multimedia, in *IEEE Int. Symp. Circuits and Systems 2005*, 3:2703–2706, Kobe, Japan, May 2005.

[38] B. B. Zhu, M. Feng, and S. Li. Secure key management for flexible digital rights management of scalable codestreams, in *IEEE Int. Workshop Multimedia Signal Processing 2005 (MMSP 2005)*, pp. 465–468, Shanghai, China, October 30–November 2, 2005.

[39] R. H. Deng, Y. Wu, and D. Ma. Securing JPEG 2000 code-streams, in *Int. Workshop Advanced Developments in Software & Systems Security*, http://www.i2r.a-star.edu.sg/icsd/staff/madi/papers/WADIS2003.pdf., December 2003.

[40] B. B. Zhu, M. Feng, and S. Li. An efficient key scheme for layered access control of MPEG-4 FGS video, in *IEEE Int. Conf. Multimedia and Expo*, pp. 443–446, Taiwan, June 27–30, 2004.

[41] M. Steiner, G. Tsudik, and M. Waidner. Diffie-Hellman key distribution extended to group communication, in *Proc. ACM Conf. Computer & Communications Security*, New Delhi, India, pp. 31–37, March 1996.

[42] S. G. Akl and P. D. Taylor. Cryptographic solution to a problem of access control in a hierarchy, *ACM Trans. Computers Systems*, 1(3):239–248, August 1983.

[43] B. B. Zhu, Y. Yang, and S. Li. An efficient key scheme for multiple access of JPEG 2000 and motion JPEG 2000 enabling truncations, in *IEEE Consumer Communications & Networking Conf.*, 2:1124–1128, Las Vegas, NV, January 2006.

[44] S. Zhong. A practical key management scheme for access control in a user hierarchy, *Computer & Security*, 21(8):750–759, 2002.

[45] K. Frikken, M. Atallah, and M. Bykova. Hash-Based Access Control in an Arbitrary Hierarchy, CERIAS Technical Report 2004-49, Purdue University, http://www.cerias.purdue.edu/tools_and_resources/bibtex_archieve/2004-49.pdf., November 2004.

12

Broadcast Encryption

Jeffrey Lotspiech

12.1 INTRODUCTION

I have to begin this chapter on broadcast encryption by admitting that the term "broadcast encryption" is a bit of a misnomer. It is not encryption, at least not in the sense of being about a particular cipher, and among the hundreds of millions of devices that have been manufactured to date that use broadcast encryption, not one has been designed for a traditional broadcast application. Instead, broadcast encryption is a key management scheme. It is an alternative to public key cryptography. Unlike public key cryptography, broadcast encryption allows two parties to agree upon a key without ever having a two-way conversation. It is this one-way nature of the interaction that gives "broadcast" encryption its name.

Because the calculations needed in deriving a key in a broadcast encryption system are substantially less involved ($>100\times$ less) than the calculations in public key systems, many have assumed that a broadcast encryption system is somehow less secure than a public key system. This is not true. Broadcast encryption-based keys are equally intractable to exhaustive search. More to the point, the latest broadcast encryption schemes are as powerful and accurate in revoking compromised keys as are public key schemes. Effective revocation is usually the most important tool in keeping a system secure.

This is not to say that public key and broadcast encryption are equivalent. Each have their own interesting advantages and disadvantages. Before we get into that, however, I would like to give the reader a sense of how broadcast encryption works.

Broadcast encryption works by the originator sending a special block of data to the recipient. In the original 1993 Amos Fiat and Moni Naor paper [1], which launched the whole area of broadcast encryption, this block of data was called a *session key block*. However, all practical systems to date have been concerned with physical media, and their system designers have chosen to call the block a *media key block*. These are just different names for the same thing. I will follow the media key block terminology in this chapter. The media key block allows participating devices to calculate a key, called the *media key*. Each device has a set of *device keys* which allows it to perform this calculation. Each device does the calculation in a different way, so if a device's keys are compromised, new media key blocks can be produced where those compromised keys can no longer be used to calculate the media key.

In general, media key blocks are produced by a single trusted agency that also assigns every device its keys. (There is a proposed scheme that works in another way, and I will return to that later.) The media key blocks are distributed to every device in the system that might want to send a message. To actually send the message, the originator takes a media key block and processes it, obtaining the media key. It encrypts the message using the media key and sends *both* the encrypted message and the media key block to the recipient. The recipient, in turn, processes the media key block in its own way, obtains the media key, and decrypts the message. The secure communication is achieved without requiring a two-way handshake between the devices.

Of course, not only can the intended recipient read the message, but *any* device with a set of device keys can also read it. Broadcast encryption is certainly not well suited to private communication between two parties. In contrast, in a public key system, the originator would simply encrypt the message in the public key of the recipient. On the surface, that appears to also require only a one-way transfer; however, the originator has to first learn the public key of the recipient. This requires the recipient (or somebody) to send the public key to the originator. In most systems, this is done by the recipient transmitting a certificate that both communicates its public key and contains a digitally signed confirmation by a trusted third party that the public key does, in fact, correspond to the recipient. Furthermore, the originator should check that the certificate does not belong to the list of devices whose private keys have been compromised. Note that in the broadcast encryption approach, the originator never needed anything from the recipient. In fact, if the message was intended to be recorded for later playback, the final recipient might not even have existed at the time the message was created. This is the major advantage of broadcast encryption.

12.2 PUBLIC KEY CRYPTOGRAPHY VERSUS BROADCAST ENCRYPTION

Public key systems are based on *identity*. A device proves who it is by doing something with its private key. Furthermore, usually, the private key must correspond to the public key in a non-revoked certificate. In contrast, broadcast encryption systems are based on *membership*. A device, by correctly processing the media key block, proves it is a member in good standing in the club, but does not in any way reveal which member it happens to be. As you can imagine, this inherent anonymity is excellent in some applications and a disaster in others. Anonymity is not a particularly good property to have in a banking system, for example. However, in the application of content protection, broadcast encryption shines. A recorder that is making an allowed recording of a video, for example, does not need to know—may not even be able to know—the identity of the player that finally ends up playing it back. However, if the recording is marked "no more copies," the recorder wants to know that the final player is not going to make further copies of the video. In other words, it wants to know that the player is playing by the rules. If the player can process the media key block, it must be a member in good standing of the club, meaning it plays by the rules.

To carry this example further, imagine how this would be done in a public key system. Even if the recorder could find the identity of the intended player in order to encrypt the recording with its public key, that is not enough. The recorder must also verify that that identity is not on the list of devices that have been circumvented. In other words, what the broadcast encryption system establishes directly, namely that the player is not a circumvention device, the public key system establishes indirectly, as a side effect of establishing the player's identity. Note that there is nothing in a broadcast encryption system (or public key system, for that matter) that technically prevents the player from making a copy, given that it has a key allowing it to decrypt the recording. Instead, there would have been a license that the player manufacturer would have signed before being given the necessary keys. In a content protection scheme, it is not the cryptography, but the legal structure that is set up by the licenses that fundamentally restricts the copies being made.

Without an effective revocation mechanism, any cryptographic system degenerates into a global secret scheme, in which the first attack breaks the system. In a public key system, the revocation list is a separate element. In a broadcast encryption system, the revocation information is implicit in the media key block. In theory, that difference is just a detail. In practice, however, it can be important. No designer of a broadcast encryption system would ever be accused of leaving out the media key block—the system would not work without it. On the other hand, some designers of public key systems have been guilty of being too cavalier about the revocation list; they have allowed attacks where the attackers simply block new revocation information from getting to the target devices. Again, this is a case where broadcast encryption is well suited to the content protection application. Because new media key blocks are inherently tied to new content, it becomes impossible for the attackers to receive new content and still prevent new revocation information from reaching the same device.

A public key system, simply by the nature of public key cryptography, provides the capability of generating digital signatures on an item. A digital signature is a proof that only a device with access to the private part of a public key could have certified the item. This is not possible in a broadcast encryption system. Instead, the broadcast encryption system has a different way to certify an item, using the media key and a Message Authentication Code (MAC). MACs are easier to calculate and verify than signatures, but a MAC can be produced by any device that knows the media key. This is another example of identity versus membership: the public key signature was made by an individual device, while a broadcast encryption MAC was made by some member in good standing in the club.

Actually, the difference is not quite as crisp as all that. To carry on with our analogy, one of the bylaws of the club might be that the members must include their identity in the item being attested with the MAC. So there can be a cryptographic guarantee that the device attesting for an item with the broadcast encryption MAC is, at least, not a habitual liar—then he would have been revoked and not have been able to process the media key block. This can be quite effective in some applications, if the only economically significant attacks require large-scale and systematic false attestations. Again, the content protection application comes to mind as an example of this.

12.3   A TUTORIAL EXAMPLE

The following scheme is spectacularly inefficient, at least in terms of the size of the media key block, but it does serve to illustrate some broadcast encryption principles. Imagine you have a system with a large number of devices, and each device has a unique secret key. A media key block is created which has a number of cells (encryptions) equal to the total number of devices in the system, with each device associated with a single cell. Each cell is simply the encryption of the media key with the device key at that cell.[1] A device receiving this media key block looks at its particular cell, decrypts it using its secret key, and thereby knows the media key. If any devices are compromised, the licensing agency starts producing new media key blocks where the cells associated with the compromised devices have garbage values.

---

[1]Well, it is not quite that simple. Cryptographers would recognize that encrypting the same value over and over again with different keys exposes a weakness that can be attacked. So, instead, it is better to encrypt a different value in each cell; for example, the media key exclusive-or'ed with the cell number. This detail is true for all broadcast encryption schemes, so I will ignore it from this point on.

Most cryptographers would not call this scheme broadcast encryption, although it certainly has the one-way property. To be a true broadcast encryption scheme, the scheme should contain some technique for reducing the size of the media key block so it is not just equal to the number of devices in the system. The real-life broadcast encryption systems I discuss in the next section were typically designed for one billion devices or more over the life of the system, which would imply that this "naive" media key block would have size one billion cells and take many gigabytes.

But now suppose we imagine a billion-device system where each device has two keys: its unique device key as before and a "high key" or a "low key." Devices whose cells are in the range of 1 to 500,000,000 are given the low key; devices whose cells are in the range of 500,000,001 to 1,000,000,000 are given the high key. Now, if there are no compromised devices, the media key block's size is only two cells: an encryption of the media key with the low key and an encryption of the media key with the high key. If a single device is compromised, the media key block requires 500,000,001 cells: 1 cell for the uncompromised high/low key and 500,000,000 cells for the devices that also have the compromised key, to keep them in the system using their unique device keys. Of course, one of these 500,000,000 cells contains garbage data, namely the cell that corresponds to the compromised device. As soon as a device is compromised that has the other high/low key, this system degenerates into the original system with one billion cells in the media key block.

Obviously, this system is not very practical, but it does illustrate the basic trick that all designers of broadcast encryption schemes use: the device is given more than one key, and the media key block is organized to give all non-revoked devices the media key in a "small" media key block. There are various ways to organize the keys. I will explain some of these schemes in the next section.

12.4   SOME PRACTICAL SYSTEMS

In 1995, the consumer electronics industry and the movie industry were poised to release a new technology for movies, Digital Versatile Discs or DVDs. This was a digital technology which brought with it both obvious advantages and obvious concerns about piracy, since digital copies are perfect copies. It was decided to encrypt the data on the discs. The real problem was how to distribute the keys. Using a public key system was out of the question because it would require all the players be connected. Although the pioneering Fiat and Naor theoretical work on broadcast encryption [1] had been published a year or so earlier, it was unknown among the content protection community. So, instead of using broadcast encryption, the DVD protection scheme, called the Content Scrambling System (CSS), was based on shared secrets between the player manufacturers and the

DVD replicators. In 1999, a 16-year-old Norwegian[2] found one of the shared secrets and effectively defeated the system, since revocation was not possible. It turns out that the actual CSS cryptography was remarkably weak, and others soon found the remaining shared secrets with cryptanalysis. These additional attacks were superfluous, since the possession of even one secret was all that was needed to copy a DVD.

12.4.1   Content Protection for Recordable Media

In 1997, Brendan Traw from Intel, inspired in part by a simple matrix-based broadcast encryption scheme devised by Kevin McCurley and myself at IBM, made the vital connection between broadcast encryption and protection of content on physical media. This insight was too late to protect DVD movies, but it has been the basis of all new protection schemes for physical media. Intel and IBM filed a joint patent on this fundamental idea. They were later joined by Matsushita and Toshiba to commercialize this scheme. The four companies called themselves "4C" (for "four companies") and called the technology they developed *Content Protection for Recordable Media* (CPRM) [2]. CPRM is used today on DVD-Recordable discs, on DVD-Audio discs (where it is called Content Protection for *Pre*-recorded Media), and on the Secure Digital (SD) flash memory card.

Broadcast encryption's one-way property is essential to provide adequate revocation on the recordable DVDs; it is impossible to have a two-way conversation with a piece of media that is nothing more than a lump of plastic. In the CPRM system, participating DVD blank-disc replicators are given media key blocks from the CPRM licensing agency. The replicators emboss a media key block in the lead-in area of the blank recordable disc. Due to the economy of optical disc replication, it is necessary that a single media key block has to be embossed on roughly one million discs. If the media key were used directly to encrypt the content, CPRM would not be a very effective content protection scheme; attackers could simply make a bit-for-bit copy from one disc to another, and the copy would play as long as the two discs had the same media key block.

Intead, the CPRM does not use the media key directly. The players and recorders produce a transformation of the media key called the media *unique* key, which is used for encryption. This key is a one-way function of the media key and the unique serial number of the disc, called the *media ID*. The media ID is put in a special place on the disc in the manufacturing process. This place is called the burst cut area. Now, if an attacker makes a bit-for-bit copy of content from one

---

[2]This story is partly apochrypal. There certainly was a 16-year-old in Norway who did some part of the work. However, other important information necessary to breaking the CSS system had been made available by insiders, apparently unhappy that the CSS seemed to be at odds with open-source operating systems such as Linux.

disc to another, the copy is unreadable because the media unique keys encrypting the content will be different. It is also important that both the burst cut area and the lead-in area, where the media key block resides, are not writable by normal consumer equipment, so the attackers cannot easily copy the media ID or media key block from one disc to another.

This is how the SD flash memory card works as well. However, it was not absolutely essential to use broadcast encryption on a flash memory card. The card contains a control unit, and the host can, in theory, have a two-way public key conversation with the control unit in order to establish a key to protect stored content. However, the large-integer math calculations required for public key protocols would severely tax the limited processing power in these very small control units. The simple symmetric key calculations needed in broadcast encryption are a much better match. In fact, the SD card does have a two-way conversation with the host for certain operations. This two-way conversation is nonetheless secured with broadcast encryption, simply because the overhead is so much less.

As shown in Figure 12.1, the CPRM media key block is based on a matrix of keys. The matrix contains 16 columns and many more rows. The actual number of rows differs based on the type of physical media. Each device has one key in each column. Therefore, it has 16 keys in total. The keys for one device are shown in Figure 12.1. Although two devices may share one or more keys, no two devices will have exactly the same set of 16 keys. The media key block is basically the encryption of the media key with the matrix of device keys. Of course, any compromised device keys cannot calculate the media key correctly; their positions in the matrix contain invalid values rather than the encrypted media key. Now consider the case of an innocent device that, by bad luck, might have one or more compromised keys. If the device finds that the first device key it tries does not decrypt the media key correctly, it simply tries another. It has 15 more chances to

eD0,0(Km)	eD0,1(Km)	eD0,2(Km)	. . .	eD0,c-1(Km)	eD0,c(Km)
eD1,0(Km)	eD1,1(Km)	eD1,2(Km)	. . .	eD1,c-1(Km)	eD1,c(Km)
eD2,0(Km)	eD2,1(Km)	eD2,2(Km)	. . .	eD2,c-1(Km)	eD2,c(Km)
eD3,0(Km)	eD3,1(Km)	eD3,2(Km)	. . .	eD3,c-1(Km)	eD3,c(Km)
. . .	. . .	. . .	. . .	. . .	. . .
eDr-1,0(Km)	eDr-1,1(Km)	eDr-1,2(Km)	. . .	eDr-1,c-1,(Km)	eDr-1,c(Km)
eDr,0(Km)	eDr,1(Km)	eDr,2(Km)	. . .	eDr,c-1(Km)	eDr,c(Km)

FIGURE 12.1: The CPRM key matrix, illustrating the example keys given to a single device.

find a key that has not been compromised. With high probability, it will find such a key.

For example, suppose one quarter of all the keys in the system has been compromised. If the keys are randomly assigned to devices, the probablity that a particular innocent device will have all compromised keys is $(\frac{1}{4})^{16}$ or roughly one in four billion. On the other hand, the compromised devices will have all their keys invalidated with probability 1.0. This example assumes that the 4C licensing agency assigns keys randomly. In fact, the agency has a systematic code for assigning keys that makes the probabilities of having to revoke an innocent device even less.

The CPRM matrix has an interesting feature that can also serve to give it more revocation capability against certain types of attacks. Instead of the media key block being a flat encryption of the entire matrix, the media key block works column by column. Subsequent columns need the key derived from a previous column. In other words, devices needing subsequent columns to find the media key (because their key in the first column was compromised) need both their device key for the subsequent column and a key they have calculated from a previous column; the cells in subsequent columns are doubly encrypted.

Let us see how this might work in practice. Suppose CPRM is beset by two attackers, A and B, but for various reasons they are not colluding and are not sharing their keys. The CPRM licensing agency picks a column in which the keys the two attackers know are disjoint. The agency uses that column as the first column. All uncompromised cells in that column get the encrypted media key; the compromised cells each get one of two other encrypted keys, k_A and k_B, depending on whether the cell's key is known by attacker A or attacker B. Then, the second column comes in two versions, one encrypted with k_A and one encrypted with k_B (in addition to being encrypted by the device keys for that column). Attacker A cannot use the column encrypted with k_B, and vice versa. Thus, a key known to attacker A does not have to be invalidated in the column encrypted by k_B. In effect, the number of compromised keys has been cut in half in the subsequent columns, with an exponential reduction in the chance that an innocent device would have to be revoked because all its keys were compromised.

CPRM is a practical system. As of January 2005, roughly 300 million devices have incorporated the technology. Nonetheless, those of us who developed the CPRM technology recognized it had some limitations. First and foremost, the size of the matrix pre-defines the amount of revocation that the system can support. If too large a fraction of the matrix is compromised, then too many innocent devices have to be revoked as part of revoking the compromised keys. If this happens, the system has been irrecoverably defeated. This is somewhat mitigated by the way the CPRM media key block was designed. It is possible to increase the matrix "in the field." In other words, the first-generation devices are designed to ignore additional rows and columns in the matrix if they encounter them. However, this is not a completely satisfactory solution. If the attackers are able to focus their attacks entirely on the first-generation devices, the initial matrix defines the total revocation.

The second limitation in CPRM is what we have called the "Evil Manufacturer Problem." If a manufacturer cynically signs the CPRM license with no intention of playing by the rules and instead builds circumvention devices, he does substantially more damage to the system than a single attacker does. If the device keys were randomly assigned, in fact, the evil manufacturer could get almost the entire matrix before it became apparent what he was doing. Anticipating this, the CPRM key assignment algorithm restricts the fraction of keys that any single manufacturer receives. Nonetheless, the problem is serious. For obvious anti-trust reasons, the CPRM license must be available to everyone. It is not possible to restrict the licensees, for example, to well-established consumer electronics companies.

Both of these limitations in CPRM were solved by the scheme described in the next section.

12.4.2 Logical Key Hierarchy

In 1998, two independent groups, one led by Debbie Wallner [3] and one led by C.K. Wong [4], developed a broadcast encryption scheme that has come to be called the *Logical Key Hierarchy* (LKH). Instead of being based on a matrix of keys like CPRM, LKH is based on a tree of keys. The easiest way to understand this is to go back to my tutorial example. In LKH, each device also has either a high key or a low key. However, LKH goes on from there. The devices that have the low key, for example, are further divided in half into devices that have a "low-low" key or a "low-high" key. Likewise, the devices that have the high key are further divided into devices that have a "high-low" key and a "high-high" key. The subdivisions continue; devices that have the low-low key have either the "low-low-low" key or the "low-low-high" key. Eventually, the subdivision process ends when the groups contain single devices.

The subdivision process defines a tree structure of keys. As shown in Figure 12.2, each device is associated with a single leaf of the tree and possesses all the keys on the path from this leaf to the root of the tree. Assuming one billion devices, the tree will be height 30, and each device will store 30 keys. So the device has to store more keys than it did in the CPRM case, but the LKH structure gives the licensing agency the ability to do precise revocation, with zero probability of revoking an innocent device.

To understand how the revocation works, consider the case of a single compromised device. The licensing agency creates a media key block that encrypts the media key using the keys of all the *siblings* of the compromised keys' nodes. By "siblings," I mean the nodes that are at the same level and have the same parents as the compromised keys' nodes. Looking at Figure 12.2 again, if the nodes

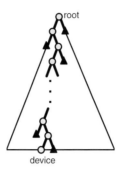

FIGURE 12.2:   An LKH tree.

represented as circles have the compromised keys, then the nodes shown as tri-angles are the sibling nodes. Although it is not immediately obvious, every other device in the system has exactly one of the sibling nodes' keys. Look at the sibling key at the top of the figure. It is our old friend, the high key, and half of all the devices have that. One level down, the low-low key, another one quarter of the devices has that key. By the time we reach the bottom of the tree, all the innocent devices will be accounted for.

It is also straightforward to revoke multiple devices. The rule is the same: encrypt the media key with the sibling keys of the compromised keys. However, at some point the paths to the root of two compromised devices join. Right below that point, both keys are compromised—each keys' node is the sibling of the other. The licensing agency does not have to encrypt anything at that point. The licensing agency's simple rule is only to encrypt using *uncompromised* sibling keys.

If the licensing agency is careful to lump each manufacturer's devices contigu-ously in the tree, the Evil Manufacturer Problem is almost non-existent. It takes fewer encryptions in the media key block to exclude an entire subtree than it does to exclude a single device. Also, in LKH, the size of the media key block is pro-portional to the number of devices that need to be excluded and does not have any fixed limit like the matrix does.

However, for an equivalent amount of revocation, the LKH system offers no advantage in space over the CPRM system. Compared to a public key system, this space is significant. A CPRM or LKH media key block is roughly 40× larger than an equivalent public key certificate revocation list. Anecdotally, when those of us working on CPRM were very close to the start of licensing, Gene Itkis, then of NDS, alerted us to the newly invented LKH scheme. The timing was unfortunate, but the size of the LKH media key block was even more significant to us. Although theoretically the LKH system has unlimited revocation, all the CPRM applications had an inherent fixed size for the media key block. For example, the DVD media key block had to fit within the DVD lead-in area. We kept the matrix scheme for CPRM.

The scheme described in the next section solved the media key block size problem.

12.4.3   Subset-Difference and the Advanced Access Content System

In 2000, Dalit Naor, Moni Naor, and I developed a broadcast encryption scheme called *subset difference* SD [5].[3] The basic insight came from the two Naors, husband and wife, who had the "out-of-the-box" idea to invert the normal sense of the LKH tree. In an LKH tree, the device has every key on the path between its leaf node and the root. In an SD tree, the device has every key *except* those on the path between its leaf node and the root. I characterize the SD tree as the photographic negative of the LKH tree. In Figure 12.3, the device at the leaf has all the keys in the shaded area of the tree, but none of the keys along the path from the leaf to the root.

The result is that it is easy to find a single key that can be used to give many devices the media key. For example, if there is a single device that needs to be revoked, every other device in the system knows the key associated with that device's leaf node. The compromised device does not know that key because it is on its path to the root. The media key block takes only a single encryption—this is the great space efficiency of the SD scheme.

It has probably not escaped the reader's attention that a device in an SD scheme has to know billions of keys. That is true, but it is not as bad as it sounds. The keys in the SD tree are not truly independent. The keys lower in the tree are one-way functions of the keys higher in the tree. A device with one key can calculate every

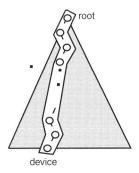

FIGURE 12.3:   An SD tree contrasted with an LKH tree.

---

[3]Not to be confused with the SD flash memory card.

key below it in the tree. This trick substantially reduces the number of keys that a single device needs to store. If there were only a single tree in an SD scheme, the number of keys that the device needs to store would be identical to LKH. Unfortunately, however, an SD scheme needs more than one tree.

A single tree does not suffice because of the problem of revoking multiple devices. LKH revokes multiple devices in a completely straightforward way. SD's revocation mechanism is more involved. For example, suppose the licensing agency needs to revoke two devices, A and B. A knows B's leaf node key, and B knows A's leaf key, so what key can be used in the media key block? The answer is that every subtree in the SD tree must have *a complete, independent system of keys*. Devices must have a different set of keys in every subtree that they belong to. The licensing agency performs revocation by finding the largest subtrees (the "subsets") that contain a single revocation (the "difference"). This is how the "subset-difference" scheme got its name.

It is best to understand this by example. In Figure 12.4, we have a simple 16-device system, and we need to revoke device 2 and device 4. The largest subtree that can revoke device 2 alone is labeled "A" in the figure and covers unrevoked devices 0, 1, and 3. Those devices know the leaf key for 2 in the A subtree and device 2 does not, nor do the other devices 4–15 because they are not in subtree A. So the media key block contains an encryption of the media key in the 2 leaf key in subtree A. That is not enough, of course. The subtree labeled "B" contains the revoked device 4. Thus, the media key block must also contain an encryption of the media key in the 4 leaf key in subtree B.

At this point, the unrevoked devices in the range 0:7 have a way to calculate the media key. The devices in the range 8:15 do not yet have a way to calculate the media key, however, since they do not have keys in either the A or B subtree.

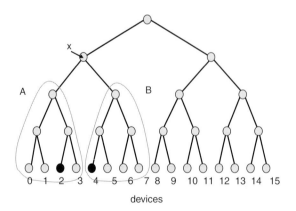

FIGURE 12.4: An SD tree with two revocations.

Fortunately[4], there is a key those devices have, but none of the 0:7 devices have. It is the key at the node labeled "x" in the master tree. It is on the path to the root for all the devices 0:7, but not on the path for devices 8:15. By additionally encrypting the media key in the x key in the master tree, the devices 8:15 are given a way to calculate the media key, but the compromised devices 2 and 4 are still kept in the dark.

In general, the SD media key block needs an encryption for each revoked device and occasionally needs other encryptions, as shown in the example, to cover devices that would not otherwise be part of single-revocation subtrees. On average, if the revocations are random, the number of encryptions is $1.28\times$ the number of revoked devices. Unlike in the LKH scheme, the number of encryptions (that is, the size of the media key block) is independent of the total number of devices in the system. In this respect, the SD system is identical to a public key system with its certificate revocation list.

The downside of the SD system is that the devices are required to store more keys. If the height of the tree is H, the number of keys the device must store is $\frac{H(H+1)}{2}$. In a one-billion-device system, the device must store 465 keys. On the other hand, the SD scheme is the most concise broadcast encryption scheme known in terms of the size of the media key block. In most applications, the cost of increasing the device key storage is more than offset by the advantage of reducing the size of the media key block. In 2004, eight companies, Disney, IBM, Intel, Matsushita, Microsoft, Sony, Toshiba, and Warners Bros., announced they had come together and were developing a content protection technology for the new generation of high-definition DVDs. Their technology is called the *Advanced Access Content System* (AACS), and its key management is based on the SD tree.

The new high-definition optical discs use blue lasers for reading and have enormous capacity—25 gigabytes or more. It would appear, on the surface, that the size of the media key block is irrelevant. It turns out, though, that in a system as large and complex as AACS, the media key block gets used in more places then just the actual media. For example, recorders must have non-volatile storage to keep the most recent media key block, in order to place it on new blank media. Also, the new players will be able to take advantage of an online connection to enrich the consumer's experience in interacting with the movie. The server may demand that the player process a new media key block in case the movie disc is old and contains an old media key block that now can be processed by many circumvention devices. In cases like these, the small size SD media key block is an advantage to AACS.

---

[4]Of course, this is not dumb luck. The SD scheme has been designed so there will always be such a key.

Layered SD

In 2001, Dani Halevy and Avi Shamir came up with a way to reduce the number of keys required in a device in an SD system [6]. They called their scheme *layered subset difference*, which has inevitably taken on the shorthand notation LSD. Halevy and Shamir observed that in an SD tree, most of the keys that the device stores are the keys in the larger subtree. This makes sense. In any subtree, the device stores the keys associated with the siblings of the nodes on the path between it and the root of the subtree. The longer that path, the more keys that need to be stored.

For example, take the AACS technology. It is based on a 32-bit tree. By a "32-bit tree," I mean that the nodes in the tree can be represented with 32-bit integers. That means that the height of the binary tree is 31, and the number of leaves (devices) is 2^{31}, or over two billion devices. Shamir and Halevy's idea can be understood by imagining dividing the tree in half, with the upper 16-bit layer of the tree being one complete SD system and the lower 16-bit layer being divided into 2^{15} independent SD systems, as shown in Figure 12.5. Devices need only to store keys in two 16-bit SD systems: the keys in the upper system and the keys in whatever lower system they belong to. This takes 240 (120×2) keys, instead of the 496 keys that a full 32-bit SD system needs.

Now imagine we want to revoke a single device. Let us say that device belongs to subtree T. In the upper layer, we encrypt the media key in the leaf key associate with subtree T. All the devices that are not in that subtree know that leaf key. Now we need to use the SD system based on the T subtree to give the uncompromised devices in that subtree the correct media key. That is done using the leaf key of the compromised device in the T subtree.

Note, however, that this revocation took two encryptions, and this is one of the drawbacks of LSD. Although the number of encryptions is still proportional

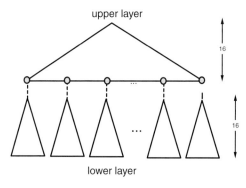

FIGURE 12.5:   A layered SD tree.

to the number of revocations r, so the size of the SD and LSD media key blocks are both $O(r)$, the constant is different. In a two-layer LSD system, the constant is $1.60\times$ versus the $1.28\times$ for SD. Also, the LSD need not be restricted to two layers. Dividing the master tree into additional layers reduces the number of device keys, while increasing the constant size factor of the media key block.

It turns out that there is another trick that can be played to reduce the number of keys that need to be stored in the device. This trick was developed at IBM soon after we started on practical SD applications in earnest in 2001, but was not published until AACS released their specifications in 2005. The trick is simply not to populate the keys in the larger subtrees. This means that the minimum media key block is larger: it needs as many encryptions as the number of maximum-height populated subtrees. In AACS's 32-bit tree, the maximum sized populated subtrees have size 22, so the minimum media key block always looks as if it had 512 revocations. However, the device needs only to store 253 keys, and new revocations are added at the 1.28 rate. Thus, the number of revocations that can fit into a fixed-area media key block, an important question in physical media, is maximal.[5]

To a certain extent, also, the first true revocations in AACS will come for free, in the sense that the revocation encryption just replaces the encryption that was already necessary due to the subtree. This is only completely true, however, if revocations are truly random across the tree. In real life, revocations tend to be clumped. Some manufacturers are better than others in making robust device implementations that successfully hide their keys, and the less robust devices are attacked proportionally more often. Of course, because of the Evil Manufacturer Problem, it is important to cluster a manufacturer's devices into a few subtrees.

In general, because a system designer can always play the AACS "trick," LSD seems more useful for truly large trees, larger than 32 bits.

12.4.4 Tracing the Device Keys—the Forensic Media Key Block

Now that I have covered several practical broadcast encryption schemes and explained how in each case the licensing agency generates a media key block to revoke keys that have been compromised, it is perhaps time to explain how the licensing agency determines exactly *which* keys have been compromised. This is never a problem in a public key system; the system is based on the identity of the devices, and the licensing agency knows which keys have been compromised simply by observing the identity the compromised devices are purporting to have. A broadcast encryption system is inherently anonymous. It is a problem,

---

[5]There is another AACS trick, but it is a real detail. In AACS, the left-most device in each maximal subtree is never assigned, so there is always something to revoke in the subtree. That way, the devices do not need to store one more key: the key for the "subtree minus nil" subset difference.

although not an insurmountable problem, to determine which keys are in use in the compromised device.

It is typical for real-life circumvention devices to use anti-reverse engineering techniques to hide their keys. Instead of reverse engineering, the licensing agency has a better approach, using what is called a *forensic* media key block. The agency, having obtained a copy of the circumvention device, keeps feeding it test media key blocks, in which some of the keys give invalid results, and, for each block, determines if the device is able to use it. It is a divide-and-conquer strategy, a binary search on the key space.

For matrix-based media key blocks, the binary search is straightforward. It is normal for innocent devices to have one or more of their keys revoked, so it is practically impossible for the circumvention device to tell the difference between a forensic media key block and an operational media key block. This is not so in the tree-based schemes. Imagine you have a media key block that revokes half of a large subtree. The circumvention device might reasonably conclude that this tree could not possibly be an operational media key block—because there is too much revocation. The circumvention device simply refuses to use that media key block, even if they have keys in the unrevoked half. The licensing agency learns nothing. Note that it is not obvious by looking at a matrix media key block how much revocation is present, whereas in a tree media key block, that is inherent in the structure.

Instead, in a tree-based scheme, the forensic media key blocks have to be more subtle. In this case, the forensic media key block is designed to produce two (or more) media keys, and the licensing agency needs a way to determine which one the device is using. For example, in a content protection scheme, only one of the keys would allow the content to be decrypted. Now, the difficulty is that the circumvention device, unlike a legitimate device, could have more than one set of device keys. If such a device detects that one set of keys is calculating one media key and another set of keys is calculating a different media key, such a media key block cannot possibly be an operational media key block. The device knows it is being tested with a forensic media key block.

How does the circumvention device respond when it detects it is being tested? For example, it could self-destruct. If circumvention devices are hardware devices, the testing process could become expensive for the licensing agency. Fortunately, in most applications, the attacking devices are actually software and can be sandboxed so that they cannot permanently disable the platform they are running on. The original SD paper contained a proof that no matter what strategy the attackers use, the keys they are using can eventually be determined.[6] We felt that the

---

[6]To be more precise, the proof is that the licensing agency can always determine a revocation that prevents the circumvention device from working. After all, the device can be designed to stop working

most effective strategy for the attackers was to act randomly when the circumvention devise knows it is under attack, although the proof did not make any such assumption.

12.5 SOME EXTENSIONS TO BROADCAST ENCRYPTION

12.5.1 "Public" Broadcast Encryption

Because public keys are such a popular concept in cryptography, it seems inevitable that cryptographers would have asked the question, Is it possible to combine public key cryptography and broadcast encryption? They did, and the simple answer is "yes." In the CPRM and LKH schemes, if you were to simply replace the normal symmetric keys used in the media key blocks with public keys, and give the devices the private keys of those public keys, you would have achieved a "public-broadcast-encryption" system. The answer in the SD or LSD schemes is not so obvious, however. Remember, in an SD-based system the device must be able to derive keys lower in the tree using keys higher in the tree using a one-way function. What kind of one-way function generates a good private key from another private key? Well, in 2002, Yevgeniy Dodis and Nelly Fazio found a way to do that [7], so now even SD can have a public key version.

What is the advantage of a public key-based broadcast encryption system? In such a system, the licensing agency needs to no longer produce the media key blocks. Instead, it produces a media key block template, which contains the public keys. At the same time, following the normal key assignment method required in each scheme, it gives device manufacturers the private keys associated with those public keys. Anyone can now generate a correct media key block using the public keys in the template. In fact, this anonymous media key block creator can even decide on the revocation himself, without the help of the licensing agency. On the surface this seems quite useful, but in my favorite broadcast encryption application, content protection, this turns out to be a negative, not a positive.

Content protection systems are the result of delicate and sometimes painfully reached compromises between different commercial entities, with the content owners and the player/recorder manufacturers generally being on the two poles. While both parties agree that unlimited unauthorized copying is a bad thing and limited personally copying for the convenience of the consumer is a good thing, content owners are understandably more conservative and recorder manufacturers are more liberal in the gray areas between those two extremes. It does not help that a given copy is usually an infringement or not based on the *intent* of the user

---

if the subtree it is in gets too small, evidence that the licensing agency is getting close to the device's leaf node(s). However, all the licensing agency has to do is prevent the device from working so that the media key block is as effective as one that revokes the leaves.

making the copy. No technological solution is going to be able to read the mind of the user.

So, when the compromise is reached, it is equally important that the content owners play by the rules as it is that the equipment manufacturers do. It is not a good thing, then, if the content owners are able to generate media key blocks themselves, without the assistance of a licensing agency. Unilateral revocation is an especially bad thing, also. In a phenomenon well known to any printer manufacturer, consumers blame the device, not the software, when something does not work. For example, if a new Disney movie does not play on your brand-new DVD player, do you call Disney or do you call the DVD player manufacturer? It is inevitable that the cost of revocation is paid entirely by the device manufacturers. To put the power of revocation unilaterally into another party is one of those "compromises" that is unlikely to ever be accepted.

So the idea of combining public key cryptography and broadcast encryption languishes as an intriguing idea that has yet to identify its compelling application.

12.5.2   Two-Way Broadcast Encryption

As I alluded to in the section on CPRM and the Secure Digital card, it is possible to use broadcast encryption in a two-way application. This is straightforward. A media key block provides a common key that the two parties can use to carry on the secure conversation. MACs can provide attestation of data items. With the advent of the SD scheme, so that there is no longer any significant difference in the amount of data that needs to be passed in a broadcast encryption scheme versus a public key scheme (media key block versus certificate revocation list), many of us wondered if broadcast encryption could be applied in a traditional public key application. In 2001, Florian Pestoni, Dalit Naor, and I experimented with using broadcast encryption to protect content on a home entertainment network, an experiment we called the xCP (for Extensible Content Protection) Cluster protocol [8].

In a network system, of course, all protocols can be two way, and all other proposed solutions to home network content protection have used public key cryptography. Our broadcast encryption-based solution ceased to be an academic exercise when we realized that all of the broadcast encryption advantages still applied: the low-overhead cryptography in the devices, the easy way in which revocation can be tied to content, and the inherent way that consumer privacy can be maintained. Our original xCP idea has been improved by many others at IBM, who have gone on to implement and demonstrate this technology at many trade shows.

We found that one of the major difficulties with using broadcast encryption in this application was the problem of determining which of two media key blocks might be the more recent. This problem has also arisen in the AACS technology. The simple idea of putting a version number in the media key block and certifying it with a MAC does not work. If the attackers have once cracked a single media key block so that they know the media key, they can modify the version number in this block and correctly MAC it with the media key. Of course, the licensing agency could digitally sign the media key block, but to those of us who are true believers in the broadcast encryption religion, this seems like heretical backsliding to public key cryptography.

It turns out there is a way to keep a secure version number in the media key block and remain pure to the broadcast encryption principles. If the media key in each cell in the media key block is first exclusive-or'ed with a hash of the cell location and the media key block version number before encrypting, the integrity of the version number is guaranteed. If an attacker modifies the version number, the devices will no longer calculate the correct media key. In fact, each cell will imply a different incorrect media key.

There is a curious "denial-of-service" style attack that can come about if the attacker also has some unrevoked device keys. In that case, the attacker can convincingly modify the cells that it has device keys for. Devices that are using other cells remain unconvinced about the tampered-with version number. Such a media key block is basically unusable, but some legitimate devices might begin using it, thinking it was the most recent. This attack can be thwarted over time in the SD tree scheme if the devices follow the following rule: if they find themselves in a smaller subtree in one media key block than in another media key block, they assume that the block with the smaller subtree is more recent, regardless of what the version number says. That way, if a device has locked in to a denial-of-service media key block with a maximal version number, the licensing agency has a way to produce a media key block that the device would accept as more recent. Even if the attackers continue with the attack, the subtrees get smaller and smaller, fewer devices are affected each time, and eventually all the actual keys known to the attacker are revealed and can be revoked.

12.6   CONCLUSION

In this chapter I have tried to give the reader a sense of the relatively recent area of cryptography called broadcast encryption. Broadcast encryption is an alternative to public key cryptography, but not in the sense that it makes public key cryptography obsolete. Instead, the reader should understand that broadcast encryption has interesting advantages in some, but not all, applications—the "poster child" application being content protection. Broadcast encryption probably deserves more attention from designers of cryptographic systems than it gets today, but it will never completely replace public key systems.

I have also explained several different broadcast encryption schemes, both matrix-based and tree-based. Some of them, such as CPRM, are in widespread use today. Others, such as AACS, are likely to become even more ubiquitous if the new generation of DVDs turns out to be as popular as the original technology.

Finally, I ended the chapter with some advances people have made by combining the basic broadcast encryption concept with other ideas from cryptography.

REFERENCES

[1] A. Fiat and M. Naor. Broadcast encryption. In *Advances in Cryptology (Crypto 93), Lecture Notes in Computer Science*, 480–491, 1993.

[2] C. Entity. Cprm: Introduction and common cryptographic elements, 1999. Available at http://www.4Centity.com.

[3] D. Wallner, E. Harder, and R. Agee. Key management for multicast: Issues and architectures. RFC 2627 (informational), July 1999. Available at ftp://ftp.isi.edu/in-notes/rfc2627.txt.

[4] C. Wong, M. Gouda, and S. Lam. Secure group communications using key graphs, in *Proc. SIGCOMM*, ACM Press, pp. 68–79, Vancouver, Canada 1998.

[5] D. Naor, M. Naor, and J. Lotspiech, Revocation and tracing routines for stateless receivers, in *Advances in Cryptology (Crypto 2001), Lecture Notes in Computer Science*, 41–62, 2001.

[6] D. Halevy and A. Shamir, The lsd broadcast encryption scheme. In *Advances in Cryptology (Crypto 2002), Lecture Notes in Computer Science*, 47–60, 2002.

[7] Y. Dodis and N. Fazio. Public key broadcast encryption for stateless receivers, in *ACM Workshop Digital Rights Management*, pp. 61–80, Washington, DC, November 2002.

[8] IBM. xcp cluster protocol. IBM White Paper, 2002. Available at http://www-03.ibm.com/solutions/digitalmedia/doc/content/bin/xCPWhitepaper_final_1.pdf.

13

Practical "Traitor Tracing"

Hongxia Jin and Jeffrey Lotspiech

13.1 INTRODUCTION

Tracing traitors is a term from the cryptographic literature referring to a particular way to trace the source of unauthorized copies when the system is broadcast based; in other words, when it is impossible to mark each copy individually for each recipient. Instead, the system broadcasts limited variations at certain points, and a recipient device has the cryptographic keys that allow it to decrypt only one of the variations at each point. The variations are logically equivalent, but can be distinguished back at the source. For example, they might be differently watermarked. Each recipient would follow a different path through the variations, and, over time, it may be possible to detect the devices in a copyright attack by the variations recovered in the unauthorized copies. The authors have been involved in what we believe is the first large-scale deployment of the tracing traitors approach. Along the way, we had to solve both practical and theoretical problems that had not been apparent in the literature to date.

In July 2004, eight companies, Disney, IBM, Intel, Matsushita, Microsoft, Sony, Toshiba, and Warner Bros., announced that they had come together to work on content protection for the new generation of high-definition DVD optical discs. The technology they are developing is called the *Advanced Access Content System* (AACS). The fundamental protection of the AACS system is based on broadcast encryption with a subset-difference tree using device keys and a media key block (see Chapter 12 in this book). It allows unlimited, precise revocation without danger of collateral damage to innocent devices. The mechanism is designed to exclude clones or compromised devices, such as the infamous "DeCSS" application used for copying "protected" DVD-Video discs. Once the attacker has been detected, newly released content incorporates new media key blocks which exclude the keys known to the attackers. To identify which keys have been used in the compromised devices, a forensic media key block, a type of carefully crafted test media key block, is fed into the device. The observed results determine the keys used in the device.

However, the AACS founders do not believe that this level of renewability solves the piracy problem completely. In fact, because of the inherent power of the revocation of the AACS system, it is possible that the attackers may forgo building clones or non-compliant devices and instead devote themselves to server-based attacks where they try to hide the underlying compromised device(s). This is progress, because these server attacks are inherently more expensive for the attackers. However, the AACS found it desirable to be able to respond to even these types of attacks. In one particular attack, you could imagine the attackers building a server that distributes per-movie keys. Of course, the attackers would have to compromise the tamper resistance of one or more players to extract these keys. With a compromised player, it is also possible to get an exact in-the-clear digital copy of the movie, with all of its extra navigation and features, and distribute it. In these cases, the only forensic evidence availability is the per-movie keys or the actual copy of the content. To help defend against these types of attacks, the AACS system uses tracing traitors technology.

One of the first thing the AACS founders did was change the name of the tracing traitors technology. Compared to the previous DVD Content Scrambling System (CSS) system, which is a flat "do-not-copy" technology, the AACS is an enabling technology, allowing consumers to make authorized copies of purchased movie discs and potentially enriching the experience of the movie with an online connection. In this environment, no one thought of the consumer as a potential "traitor" who needed tracing. Instead, since attacks against the AACS are more or less forced to be server based, the attackers are likely to be professional, funded pirates, not end-users. The AACS uses the term *sequence keys* to refer to its tracing traitors technology. The suitability of the term will become apparent.

However, to be consistent with the cryptographic literature, we are going to stick to the terminology of tracing traitors in this chapter. The device used in an attack will be called equivalently either a *traitor* or a *colluder*. A traitor tracing scheme allows the identification of at least one of the traitors. The AACS scheme allows us to apply the watermark early on in the content publishing process and can still provide traceability down to the individual content recipient.

The traitor tracing problem was first defined by Fiat and Naor in a broadcast encryption system [1]. This system allows encrypted contents to be distributed to a privileged group of receivers (decoder boxes). Each decoder box is assigned a unique set of decryption keys that allows it to decrypt the encrypted content.

The security threat in that system, which is different from the one we are dealing in this chapter, is that a group of colluders can construct a clone pirate decoder that can decrypt the broadcast content. The traitor tracing scheme proposed by Chor and co-workers [2, 3] randomly assigns the decryption keys to users before the content is broadcast. The main goal of their scheme in their context is to make the probability of exposing an innocent user negligible under as many real traitors in the coalition as possible.

The threat model that this chapter is concerned with is what AACS has called the "anonymous attack." Attackers can construct a pirate copy of the content (content attack) and try to resell the pirate copy over the Internet. Or the attackers reverse engineer the devices and extract the decryption keys (key attack). They can then set up a server and sell decryption keys on demand, or they can build a circumvention device and put the decryption keys into the device. A content attack requires good watermarking schemes that embed different information for every variation. There are two well-known models for how a pirated copy (be it the content or the key) can be generated:

1. Given two variants v_1 and v_2 of a segment, the pirate can only use either v_1 or v_2, not any other valid variant.
2. Given two variants v_1 and v_2 of a movie segment ($v_1 \neq v_2$), the pirate can generate any variant out of v_1 and v_2.

The second model, of course, assumes that the attackers have more power. However, in this chapter, we will be assuming that the attackers are restricted to the first model. This is not an unreasonable assumption in the AACS application: in a practical watermarking scheme, when given some variants of a movie segment, it would be infeasible for the colluders to come up with another valid variant because they do not have the essential information to generate such a variant. As discussed in Cox et al. [4], there are methods that make it very difficult for colluders to remove the marks. Another important point to note is that building a different variation is a media format-specific problem. Watermarking is only one of the solutions. For example, in a DVD format using Blue Laser, the variation can be simply a different playlist. In this case, it may have nothing to do with the watermark. Thus, it is not restricted by the watermark robustness requirement.

Also, for the key attack, the traitors will need to redistribute at least one set of keys for each segment. For cryptographic keys, it is impossible to generate a valid third key from combining two other valid keys. This is equivalent to the first model.

A tracing scheme is static if it pre-determines the assignment of the decryption keys for the decoder or the watermarked variations of the content before the content is broadcast. The traitor tracing schemes in Chor and co-workers [2, 3] are static and probabilistic. Tassa and Fiat introduced a dynamic traitor tracing scheme [5] to combat the same piracy under the same business scenario considered in this chapter.

In their scheme, each user gets one of the q variations for each segment. However, the assignment of the variation of each segment to a user is dynamically decided based on the observed feedback from the previous segment. The scheme can detect up to m traitors. It involves real-time computational overhead. Avoiding this drawback, sequential traitor tracing is presented in Safani-Naini and Wang [7], and more formal analyses are shown in Staddor, Stinson, and Wei [8] and Stinson and Wei [9].

The AACS uses a similar model as Safani-Naini and Wang [7] that requires no real-time computation/feedback. However, the AACS scheme is more suited toward the real-world requirement, as shown below. The AACS has designed a traitor tracing scheme that attempts to meet all the practical requirements. In the existing traitor tracing schemes, either more bandwidth is needed than the content provider can economically afford, or the number of players their schemes can accommodate is too few to be practical, or the number of colluding traitors under which their schemes can handle is too few. Bringing the long-standing theoretical work to practice was the major effort we undertook in the AACS system.

In the rest of this chapter we will discuss the practical problems we have encountered in implementing the AACS tracing traitors scheme. The AACS has been a collaborative effort among the eight companies involved. Although the authors were the individuals primarily involved in this aspect of AACS, we benefited extensively from discussions, reviews, and proposals from the other companies. We would like to especially acknowledge Toru Kambayashi from the Toshiba Corporation, who worked out the details of mapping the technology to the HD-DVD disc format, and Tateo Oishi from the Sony Corporation, who worked out the details of mapping the technology to the Blue Ray disc format.

13.2   PROBLEM: OVERHEAD

The first problem to be solved is the problem of the overhead that a tracing traitors scheme might require. While it is perfectly reasonable in a theoretical context to talk about schemes that increased the space required by 200 or 300%, no movie studio would have accepted this. Although the new generation of DVDs has substantially more capacity, the studios want to use that capacity to provide a high-definition picture and to offer increased features on the disc, not to provide better forensics. Most studios were willing, however, to accept some overhead for forensics, if it could be kept below 10%. As a nominal figure, we began to design, assuming we had roughly 8 additional minutes (480 seconds) of video strictly for forensic purposes.

The cryptographic literature implied that we should use our 480 seconds to produce the most variations possible. For example, at one particular point in the movie, we could have produced 960 variations of a 1/2-second duration. This clearly would not work. The attackers could simply omit that 1/2 second in the unauthorized copy without significantly diminishing the value of that copy. Instead, we settled on a model where there were on the order of 15 carefully picked points of variation in the movie, each of a 2-second duration and each having 16 variations. Even then, you could argue that the attackers can avoid these 30 or so seconds of the movie. Our studios' colleagues have studied whether these parameters are sufficient, and their answer is, frankly, "it depends." As a result, when we mapped our scheme to the actual disc format, we made sure that the duration of the variations was not pre-determined. Of course, longer durations require more overhead. This is a trade-off studios can make. We should also mention that whether or not a given movie uses tracing traitors technology is always the studio's choice. In the absence of attacks, they would never use it, and the discs would have zero overhead for this purpose.

So, in the AACS model, we assume that each movie is divided into multiple segments, among which n segments are chosen to have differently marked variations. Each of these n segments has q possible variations. Each playing device receives the same disc with all the small variations at chosen points in the content. However, each device plays back the movie through a different path, which effectively creates a different movie version. Each version of the content contains one variation for each segment. Each version can be denoted as an n-tuple $(x_0, x_1, \ldots, x_{n-1})$, where $0 \leq x_i \leq q - 1$ for each $0 \leq i \leq n - 1$. A coalition could try to create a pirated copy based on all the variations broadcast to them. For example, suppose there are m colluders. Colluder j receives a content copy $t_{-j} = (t_{j,0}, t_{j,1}, \ldots, t_{j,n-1})$. The m colluders can build a pirated copy $(y_0, y_1, \ldots, y_{n-1})$, where the ith segment comes from a colluder t_{-k}; in other words, $y_i = t_{k,i}$, where $1 \leq k \leq m$ and $0 \leq i \leq n - 1$. It would be nice to be able to trace back the colluders (traitors) who have constructed a pirated copy once such pirated copy is found. Unfortunately, the variations $(y_0, y_1, \ldots, y_{n-1})$ associated with the pirated copy could happen to belong to an innocent device. A weak traitor tracing scheme wants to prevent a group of colluders from thus "framing" an innocent user. A strong traitor tracing scheme allows at least one of the colluders to be identified. In the AACS scheme we deal only with strong traitor tracing schemes, so when we say "traitor tracing scheme," we mean strong traitor tracing scheme.

The AACS traitor tracing scheme, called sequence keys hereafter, is a static scheme. Like all tracing schemes in this category, it consists of two basic steps:

1. Assign a variation for each segment to devices.
2. Based on the observed rebroadcast keys or contents, trace back the traitors.

13.2.1 Basic Key Assignment

For the first step, the AACS systematically allocates the variations based on an error correcting code. Assume that each segment has q variations and that there are n segments. We represent the assignment of segments for each user using a *codeword* $(x_0, x_1, \ldots, x_{n-1})$, where $0 \le x_i \le q - 1$ for each $0 \le i \le n - 1$.

A practical scheme needs to have small extra disc space overhead, accommodate a large number of devices in the system, and be able to trace devices under as large a coalition as possible. It is not hard to see that these requirements are inherently conflicting. Let us show some intuition on the conflicts between these parameters. Take a look at a code $[n, k, d]$, where n is the length of the codewords, k is the source symbol size, and d is the Hamming distance of the code, namely the minimum number of symbols by which any two codewords differ. q is the number of variations. Mathematically, these parameters are connected to each other. The number of codewords is q^k, and the Hamming distance has the property that $d <= n - k + 1$. q is also related to n, for example, for a "Maximal Difference Separable" (MDS) code, $n <= q$. We know the number of variations q decides the extra bandwidth needed for distributing the content. Without variations, $q = 1$. The extra bandwidth needed for the content is $(q - 1) * length\_of\_each\_variation * n$. The Hamming distance d decides its traceability. To defend against a collusion attack, intuitively we would like the variant assignment to be as far apart as possible. In other words, the larger the Hamming distance is, the better traceability of the scheme. On the other hand, to accommodate a large number of devices, e.g., billions, intuitively either q or k or both have to be relatively big. Unfortunately, a big q means big bandwidth overhead, and a big k means smaller Hamming distance and thus weaker traceability. It is inherently difficult to defend against collusions.

In order to yield a practical scheme to meet all the requirements, the AACS concatenates codes [6]. The number of variations in each segment are assigned following a *code*, namely the inner code, which are then encoded using another *code*, namely the outer code. We call the nested code the *supercode*. The inner code effectively creates multiple movie versions for any movie, and the outer code assigns different movie versions to the user over a sequence of movies, hence the term "sequence keys." This supercode avoids the overhead problem by having a small number of variations at any single point. For example, both inner and outer codes can be Reed-Solomon (RS) codes [6]. In an RS code, if q is the alphabet size, $n \le q - 1$ is the length of the code. If k is its source symbol size, then its Hamming distance is $d = n - k + 1$, and the number of codewords is q^k. For example, for our inner code we can choose $q_1 = 16$, $n_1 = 15$, and $k_1 = 2$, thus $d_1 = 14$. For the outer code we can choose $q_2 = 256$, $n_2 = 255$, and $k_2 = 4$, thus $d_2 = 252$. The number of codewords in the outer code is 256^4, which means that this example can accommodate more than four billion devices. For the supercode, which is the concatenation of the inner and outer codes, $q = 16, n = n_1 \cdot n_2 = 15 \cdot 255 = 3825$, $k = k_1 \cdot k_2 = 6$, and $d = d_1 \cdot d_2 = 14 \cdot 252 = 3528$. Suppose each segment is a 2-second clip; the extra video needed in this example is 450 seconds, within the 10% contraint being placed on us by the studios. So, both q, the extra bandwidth needed, and q^k, the number of devices our scheme can accommodate, fit. The actual choices of these parameters used in the scheme depend on the requirements and are also constrained by the inherent mathematical relationship between the parameters $q, n, k,$ and d. In fact, there does not exist a single MDS code that can satisfy all the practical requirements. For an MDS code, $n <= q$, and $d = n - k + 1$. An MDS code is, in general, too short.

The second step of any tracing traitors scheme, that of actually tracing the traitors during an attack, quite naturally leads to the next problem we encountered. We will discuss this in the next section.

13.3   PROBLEM: INEFFICIENT TRACING

Although the scheme we designed for assigning variations was as good as any in the literature, it did not appear to be good enough, in the sense that it could be defeated by too small a coalition. So, for a couple of years, we put our sequence key approach on the shelf as an interesting idea, but one that was not yet practical. Then, in late 2004, we had an insight that seemed to substantially increase the traceability of our basic scheme. This insight had nothing to do with how we assign the keys; it had to do with how we actually perform the tracing.

It appears that the tracing traitors literature has focused strictly on the former problem. The assumption is that tracing is simple: you take your sequence of recovered movies and simply score all the devices based on how many segments each device could have produced. High-scoring devices are likely to be traitors. Of course, you have to have confidence, based on your key assignment scheme, that a high-scoring device is not just an unlucky innocent device that just happened to have many segments in common with the attackers. Of course, the attackers want just the opposite.

Using this tracing algorithm in the literature, the traceability of our scheme can be formally analyzed based on the combinatorial properties of the codes used in the first step. While our focus is on the practical aspects of the design and not on the formal analysis, we refer readers to [7] Safani-Naini and Wang and Staddon, Stinson, and Wei [8] for the formal traceability analysis. The formal analysis tells us the largest collusion under which the scheme can still deterministically identify at least one traitor. When the collusion is larger than that, the identification of the traitor will have to be probabilistic.

For concreteness, let us assume we have a population of one billion DVD players and we are using our 255 movie supercode we described above. In this case, no two players follow identical paths in more than three movies. Now consider a coalition of T players being used in an attack and an innocent player P that, by bad luck,[1] has maximal overlap with each player. P's score (the number of movies P has in common with the recovered movies) is $3T$. At least one traitor must have a

---

[1]We are assuming the attackers do not know the codes of any innocent player to deliberately incriminate it. In the AACS, the codes remain secret, and this is a reasonable assumption.

score greater than or equal to $255/T$. This analysis reveals that T cannot be greater than 9 to have a deterministic certainty that the highest scoring player is a traitor rather than innocent.

It was an analysis like this that caused us to despair. Also, the reader may have observed that this analysis was assuming a movie-by-movie attack. If the attackers were going to mix-and-match, in other words, to pick segments from different movies, the maximum number of traitors would be 3. On the other hand, countless simulations showed, in practice, the numbers were much better. We wondered if we could prove anything about the probabilistic analysis. We think we made progress, which we will explain. But first, let us develop the reader's intuition about this.

For each movie there are 256 encodings. Any two players use the same encoding for at most 3 movies out of the 256. For any given movie, $\frac{1}{256}$ of the players (about 4 million players) encode the movie the same way. For a given 3 movies, only $\left(\frac{1}{256}\right)^3$ of the players (about 60 players) encode those movies the same way. For a given 4 movies, exactly 0 of the players encode the movies the same way. That is the essential property of the outer code.

Imagine a licensing agency has purchased a subscription to an illegal key server. By the variations used in the keys, the agency is trying to deduce which of the players were used to make the copies. A significant real-life problem is that the license agency doing the tracing rarely knows exactly how many players are involved in the attack. As a result, the answers it gets are always qualified. For example, an answer might be as follows: "If N players are involved, it must be exactly this N. However, different innocent coalitions of $N + M$ players may have produced the same result."

Let us take the case of an attack where only a single player **X** is being used. After recovering a single movie, the license agency has four million players that are potential candidates, including **X**. After the second or third movie, the number of candidates is reduced, but it is not until the fourth movie is recovered that the guilty player **X** is positively identified, but only if it is known that only a single player is involved. Millions of pairs of players could also have produced the four movies.

By the time nine movies have been recovered, the license agency knows there are no possible innocent pairs of players. (By "innocent," we mean a pair that does not include the actual guilty player **X**.) An innocent pair could have produced, at most, six of the movies. However, an innocent triplet could have produced all nine movies, with each member of the triplet having three movies in common with the guilty player. It is instructive to calculate the probability that an innocent triplet picked at random could have produced those nine movies.

The number of such triplets are:

$$\binom{9}{3} * 60 * \binom{6}{3} * 60 * \binom{3}{3} * 60.$$

That is a relatively large number, but, of course, there are $\binom{1,000,000,000}{3}$ total triplets. Thus, the probability that a triplet picked at random is in the set is roughly 2 in 10^{18}. If the licensing agency is willing to assign a priori probabilities to the different numbers of attackers, and assuming that the attackers cannot deduce the code and therefore must act randomly, the license agency can perform a Bayesian analysis and conclude, based on the observed result, what the probability is that the indicated player **X** is, in fact, guilty.

There are some caveats. Although it is highly unlikely that an innocent triplet is involved, the number of partially innocent triplets (triplets that include the guilty player plus two innocent players) abound. Likewise, the larger the coalition is, the more likely a coalition picked at random could have produced the observed result. By the time you reach a coalition of size 60 players, which between them probably know every variation of every movie, no coalition can be deterministically disproved by any observed result.

The first caveat is traditionally addressed by defining the tracing problem to be finding a single member of the coalition, not finding the exact membership of the coalition. So the Bayesian analysis really reveals the probability that player **X** is an attacker, not that he is the sole attacker. The second caveat reveals the fundamental limitation of tracing traitors: it stops working once the coalition gets too large. Table 13.1 summarizes the above results when only a single player is involved.

Moving on to another example, let us assume that a coalition of five players has combined to release unauthorized copies of movies. Let us assume that the attackers are using players in a round-robin way: player 1 is used for movie 1, player 2 is used for movie 2, and so on, with player 1 used again for movie 6. We pick this strategy not because we think it is a good strategy, but because we can calculate the scores of each guilty player after every movie is recovered.

After the first three movies, as far as the license agency can determine, there is only a single player being used. It has a list of about 60 players that are potential culprits. It turns out they are all innocent.

After the fourth movie, there is a $\frac{60}{256}$ chance that the coalition has picked an encoding that is consistent with a single player. Otherwise, the licensing agency deduces that there are at least two players involved in the attack.

Table 13.1:

Number of movies detected	Possible traitors
1	About 4 million players
2	About 16,000 players
3	60 players
4	Single player **X**

After the sixth movie, it is unlikely that the license agency still thinks it is a single player. However, there are roughly 2^{17} possible pairs that could have produced this sequence of six movies. How did we estimate that? The chance that a given pair could have encoded those six movies is roughly $\left(\frac{2}{256}\right)^6$. However, there are 2^{59} possible pairs among the one billion players. Potential pairs are being eliminated at the rate of $\frac{254}{256}$ per movie (roughly).

After the ninth movie, it likely that all the suspect pairs have been eliminated, and the licensing agency can deduce that there are at least three players involved. There are $1.5 * 2^{88}$ total triplets being eliminated, roughly, at the rate of $\frac{253}{256}$ per movie.

The 13th movie is the likely point at which the licensing agency will have eliminated all triplets and will be able to deduce that there are at least four players involved, and after the 19th movie is the likely point at which the licensing agency will deduce that there are at least five players involved.

The 29th movie is the likely point at which the licensing agency would have deduced that there are at least six players involved, had there been six players. Instead, the licensing agency continues to think that there are only five players involved, and, by the same probabilistic argument, has narrowed it down to a single five-tuple. These are, in fact, the guilty players; however, the licensing agency only knows this at this point if it knows that there are exactly five players involved. For example, at this point there should be a handful of *completely innocent* six-tuples. And the number of partially innocent six-tuples are in the millions. Imagine replacing the guilty player that encoded 5 of the 29th movies with two innocent players, one encoding three and the other encoding two. There are over 800,000 of those.

The next interesting point is the 80th movie. We call this the *deterministic threshold*. At this point, all the guilty players have encoded 16 movies. No innocent player could have possibly encoded that many, because they would have had to overlap by more than three movies with one of the players in the coalition, an impossibility in the code. In other words, there is no possible code assignment, or possible choice of a coalition of five with an innocent player, that could have conceivably incriminated the innocent player. Observe that in the average case, with a random choice of a coalition of five, the licensing agency would have settled on the five after the 29th movie. The worst case, however, is 80 movies. That is quite a discrepancy, and we conjecture that the worst case is not achievable with a final population of players.

What has happened between the 29th and 80th movie is that the completely innocent coalitions of six, seven, and eight have fallen by the wayside. However, small, partially innocent coalitions are much harder to rule out, but during this entire period the minimum number of attackers in the coalition continues to be five. The licensing agency might be justified in concluding that there are, in fact, five players in the attack.

As shown above, a hard real-life fact is that the licensing agency rarely knows the coalition size, which makes it rarely possible to deterministically identify a traitor in real practice. To really bring the theoretical work to practice, we need a more practical and efficient tracing scheme than the above straightforward count-and-compare approach used in the literature.

So, the classic method for detecting a traitor is to score each individual player. Based on the examples we just went through, a new method immediately suggests itself: should not the problem be finding *every* member of the coalition? Although this second method seems more useful, the classic method has some obvious advantages.

1. It seems easier.
2. The number of coalitions is exponential compared to the number of individuals. For example, if there are a 1 billion participants in the world, there are roughly 500 quadrillion pairs of participants.
3. It seems essential against the "scapegoat" strategy. In this strategy, the coalition sacrifices a few devices and uses them heavily while using the others lightly, to keep some in reserve. Note that even without the scapegoat strategy, simulation results usually show some unlucky innocent devices intermixed with guilty players when the devices are scored in the classic way.

It may seem anti-intuitive, but we believe it is easier to find the entire coalition than the individual traitor. The problem of finding a coalition of players that covers a sequence of movies is equivalent to a well-known problem in computer science called Set Cover. It is NP-complete. But in reality, the calculation time is still reasonable for the parameters that the AACS is concerned with.

Our new tracing algorithm (use Set Cover) performs better than the approach used in the state-of-the-art in terms of successful detection. Finding the entire coalition has clear advantages over the traditional detection of finding individual traitors one by one. To illustrate where the advantage comes from, for example, look at a random sequence of 20 movies. Assuming that each movie has 256 variations of which a given player has only 1, how many players in a population of 1 billion players would have 5 variations in common with the sequence? The answer is roughly 15. On the other hand, what is the chance that a coalition of size four might have all the variations in the sequence? The answer is roughly 1 in 25. In other words, there are plenty of players that can explain 5 movies, but it is unlikely that any 4 of them can "cover" all 20 movies. If we find four players that do cover the sequence, it is unlikely that this could have happened by chance. It is more likely that that is the guilty coalition.

Also, the coalition approach makes it no longer obvious that the best strategy for the attackers is to mix-and-match segments within movies. The same algorithm that can trace a coalition of players can trace a "coalition" of paths through the movie. For example, the licensing agency might be able to deduce with high probability that exactly three players were involved in playing a given movie and precisely which paths they had. From the point of view of the outer code, it is as if the licensing agency has recovered three movies for the price of one. Of course, at some point, the attackers can overwhelm the inner code and thereby defeat the system. We do not know exactly where that point is. If we did, it is likely that we would keep it an AACS trade secret.

With the new tracing algorithm, our rule of thumb is that it takes six recovered movies (or "effective movies" if the attack is mix-and-match) for each traitor in the coalition. Although this was quite a bit better than what we started with, some studios, especially Twentieth Century Fox, wondered whether we had still reached the level of practicality. Of course, nobody knows; we will await some real-life attacks, which, with luck, may never come. However, our colleagues Chris Cookson, Spencer Stephens, and Alan Bell from Warner Bros. pointed out something that was obvious only in retrospect: it should be possible to divide a single logical movie into multiple movies for the purpose of tracing. For example, the first third of the movie could use one sequence key, the second third of the movie could use a second sequence key, and the last third of the movie could use a third sequence key. As a result, recovering the movie from a single disc would be like recovering three movies, even if the attackers were not doing a mix-and-match attack. Of course, this would triple the amount of overhead, from roughly 10% to roughly 30%, but in some attack scenarios with some movies, this might be an option the studios would choose. In fact, the AACS scheme does allow the studios this flexibility, but only after some careful design by our consumer electronics colleagues to make sure that this arbitrary division would not cause consumer problems due to hiccups during "trick play" (fast forward and rewind).

13.4   PROBLEM: REDUCE THE NUMBER OF KEYS STORED IN THE DEVICE

As shown above, each variation for the segment is differently watermarked and encrypted. Therefore, each device basically needs to know all the variant keys in order to play back the movie. In the example shown above, each device needs to store 15×55 keys for the purpose of traitor tracing. If each key is 8 bytes, the storage requirement is 30.6 KB. Needing to store 30.6 KB securely and uniquely for each device turned out to be a significant concern for the device manufacturer. It was not the absolute size; it was the fact that the data had to be different for each device and kept secure during the manufacturing process that argued for a smaller number.

In a solution that is again more obvious in retrospect, we added a level of indirection, such that each device only needs to store 255 keys. By using this 255 keys, it can get the 15 keys (or more) that it needs for each movie. So the space requirement now is only $\frac{1}{15}$ of what was needed before.

The assignment of these keys will be based on the outer code of the super-code, corresponding to the sequence of 255 movies; these are the sequence keys. Nominally, each key comes with 256 versions in the world, corresponding to the 256 movie versions for each movie decided by the inner code. A single device will have only one version for each sequence key. Each sequence key is responsible for one movie.

For a given movie, the device can use its sequence key to decrypt a table associated with the content that gives it the 15 (or more) keys used for the individual segments. This means that the content needs to store 256 tables, one for each sequence key value (movie version). Although this slightly increases the storage associated with the content, it substantially reduces the storage required in the device (from 30 KB to 2 KB), which is much more expensive storage. It does not change the basic strength of the code against a coalition of attackers. For more details, refer to Jin and Lotspiech [11].

13.5   PROBLEM: LACK OF FLEXIBILITY

In the previous section, we said that, nominally, each movie in the sequence has 256 versions of the sequence key. But what about movies which have unused space on the disc? They could use the extra space for more variations.

We improved our scheme by extending the variations of each key. We think of the sequence keys as being organized in a matrix with 255 columns for the 255 movie sequence and 256 rows for the variations within each sequence. What if, for example, each sequence key comes with 1024 versions in the world even though there are only 256 versions per movie created from the inner code? In this case, there would be 1024 variant encrypting key tables. Although there would only be 256 unique inner code tables, each table would be duplicated 4 times and separably encrypted with 4 different sequence keys. With this extension, we improved the flexibility of the inner code. It now can accommodate an inner code that creates more than 256 versions. The extension also achieves better traceability for key tracing with little added cost. Each device continues to store only 255 keys. The only additional overhead is the 1024 tables, which is negligible compared to storage of a high-definition movie.

Another important benefit of the extension is that the length of the movie sequence is, in effect, increased without increasing the number of keys in each device. The attackers know which sequence key (which column) is used for each movie. After 255 movies in our example, the movies unavoidably start reusing columns. The attackers, noticing this, should use the same variation in a new movie that they previously used in an older movie at the same point in the sequence (column). In the nominal scheme, this tactic would have guaranteed the tracing agency no new information from the new movie. In this new extension, the grouping of four sequence keys to each variation (for example) can be reshuffled in a new sequence of movies. Even if the attackers are careful to use the same sequence key in the same column in the new sequence, some tracing information is revealed; in particular, which of the possible four sequence keys the attackers must have had in the first sequence.

Yet another important benefit of the extension is the improvement of the scheme's overall resistance to attacks. Every time the attacker redistributes keys, fewer keys remained in the system to be useful for the future. When the number of exposed keys is big enough, the system is broken. Suppose the movies are randomly being attacked, then the event can be modeled as a Bernoulli trial. A simple combinatorial analysis tells us that it takes $q \log q$ movies to expose all the q versions of keys in each column in the key matrix with high probability. The extended scheme with a larger number of key versions can survive longer.

13.6   PROBLEM: TRACING TO MODELS INSTEAD OF TO INDIVIDUAL DEVICES

Under certain attacks the AACS licensing agency only wants to trace to the manufacturer/model of a particular leak, instead of revoking an individual device. Why is this? Certain attacks are what have been called *class attacks*. A manufacturer may have made a mistake that makes it easy for people to extract the keys from the device. In this case, the key revocation mechanism might be overwhelmed by the sheer volume of the number of compromised keys. A more effective response might be to cooperate with the manufacturer to distribute firmware updates along with the content. Alternatively, code might be distributed with the content that "sniffs"; that is, it checks to see if it is running in the legitimate environment or in a circumvention platform and refuses to play in the latter. We believe it is desirable to have a hybrid approach that flexibly allows either tracing to manufacturer/model or to individual device, depending on the different needs at different times. The AACS has designed a practical and systematic key management approach to assign the variation/keys to devices so that it is possible to switch on and off the ability to trace to models or to individuals.

In order to trace to models, one can always trace to devices first and then find out their models. However, a class attack might be so severe that the size of the coalition overwhelms the tracing. If they are all in the same model, however, they are in a coalition of size 1 for that type of tracing. Also, since there are many fewer models than there are individual devices, model tracing is inherently faster. Clearly, it is desirable to have an approach to flexibly allow both types of tracing to work in some attacks and in other attacks to only allow detection of the manufacturer/model and disable the detection of individual traitors.

Note that there are two naive ways to enable both tracings to work. One way is to store 2 sets of 255 keys in the player. One set of 255 keys is used in a scheme for tracing only to manufacturer/model, and the other set of 255 keys is used in the scheme for tracing to devices. Of course, the drawback of this is that it doubles the storage requirement, which is a cost for the device manufacturers.

The second naive way is to put in 256×256 tables instead of 256 tables on the disc. We know that each player stores 255 movie keys that can be assigned based on the outer code. However, note that the outer code specified above is based on tracing to individuals. As mentioned above, when tracing down to an individual, the scheme needs 256 tables on the disc (although, as explained in the last section, we actually use more), and each table is encrypted by its corresponding movie key version for that movie. For example, for movie #44, the table #i is encrypted by movie key version #i for movie #44. Remember, nominally, each sequence key comes with 256 versions. When tracing only to manufacturer/model, for any movie, the individuals within the same manufacturer/model should get the same movie version assignment. However, when the sequence keys are assigned on the outer code specified above, they are based on tracing to individuals. As a consequence, most individuals are not assigned the same movie key version for a movie. In order for the players to be able to play back, each table needs to be duplicated 256 times, and each of these 256 tables needs to be encrypted using all 256 movie key versions. This results in 256×256 tables per movie (or much more if you are using the flexible scheme in the previous section). Clearly, the drawback of doing this is the amount of space required on the disc, which is a cost to the content owner/distributor.

In order to have a practical scheme, we must reduce the cost for the storage requirement both in the device and on the disc. Accordingly, the AACS has designed an efficient key assignment that enables one to perform hybrid tracing without incurring any additional storage cost on the device and the disc.

13.6.1   Key Assignment for Hybrid Tracing

As mentioned above, the sequence keys are assigned based on the outer code. The outer code is assigned from a key matrix as shown in Figure 13.1. Columns correspond to movie sequences, and each column corresponds to one movie. Rows correspond to movie key versions. Each column contains many, even thousands, rows. For example, if there are 1024 movie key versions for each movie and there are 255 movies in the entire sequence, then the key matrix has 255 columns and 1024 rows. Each device is assigned a single key from each column.

In order to enable hybrid tracing, we introduce a new concept called a "slot," which is similar to a method for assigning encryption keys [10]. Now the rows

	movie #1	movie #2	movie #3	movie #4
key version #1	X			
key version #3				X
key version #9		X		
		X		
key version #16				

player A: (1,9,15,3)

FIGURE 13.1:   Key matrix.

in the key matrix are grouped into clusters. A slot is defined as an assignment of row clusters, with one cluster for each column. At any given column, two slots are either identical or completely disjoint. Slots can be assigned to individual manufacturers, and the keys within the clusters are assigned to the devices made by the manufacturer. In effect, the outer code is now itself a two-level code. The entire system is now a three-level code.

Figure 13.2 shows a toy example. The first-level codes assign clusters to the manufacturer/models X and Y, and the second-level codes assign keys to players A, B within model X and players C, D within model Y. Model X gets the slot (1,3,4,1), which means it is assigned cluster #1 for movie #1, cluster #3 for movie #2, etc.

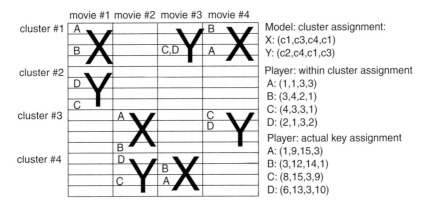

Model: cluster assignment:
X: (c1,c3,c4,c1)
Y: (c2,c4,c1,c3)

Player: within cluster assignment
A: (1,1,3,3)
B: (3,4,2,1)
C: (4,3,3,1)
D: (2,1,3,2)

Player: actual key assignment
A: (1,9,15,3)
B: (3,12,14,1)
C: (8,15,3,9)
D: (6,13,3,10)

FIGURE 13.2:   Key assignment using "slots."

Note that the second-level code is the assignment inside the cluster. For example, player A gets $(1,1,3,3)$ within the clusters assigned to model X, which makes its actual key assignment $(1,9,15,3)$ from the key matrix.

As a more real example, suppose each sequence key comes with 512 versions. So the key matrix has 512 rows and 255 columns. We divide all 512 rows into 32 clusters, and each cluster contains 16 rows. The first-level code is about the cluster assignment throughout the 255 movie sequence. Each codeword is a slot. So the code has $q = 32$ and $n = 255$. Each slot is given to one manufacturer/model, and a given manufacturer/model may get multiple slot assignments if it is producing a lot of devices. The second-level code is about the sequence key assignment within a slot. So the code has $q = 16$, and $n = 255$. Each player gets the sequence key assignment based on this code.

Of course, the choices of the parameters when using the slots also depend on how many manufacturers/models and how many devices the system needs to support. Just by way of example, we assume each movie key comes with 512 versions in this world and there are 512 movie versions created from inner code. Suppose the system needs to accommodate at least 16,000 models and at least 1 billion devices. A $q = 32, k = 3, n = 255$ code for the slot assignment accommodates about 32,000 (precisely 32^3) manufacturer models. Another $q = 16$, $k = 4$, $n = 255$ code can be used to assign movie sequence keys to about 65,536 (precisely 16^4) devices within each manufacturer model. The total number of devices the scheme can accommodate is 2 billion. If each movie key comes with 256 versions in this world, and there are only 256 movie versions created from the inner code, we can also divide all 256 rows at each column into 16 clusters. In this case we have to use a $q = 16, k = 4$ code to assign slots to manufacturers, accommodating 65k manufacturers. The same $q = 16, k = 4$ and $n = 255$ code can be used to assign sequence keys to the devices with the model. As a result, the scheme can totally accommodate 4 billion devices.

13.6.2 Hybrid tracing

After the sequence keys are assigned based on slots, the sequence keys can be stored inside the players. On the disc there will be multiple tables. Note that we can choose to have more key versions per each sequence key than the number of movie versions actually created from the inner code. But for the sake of simplicity, we will assume that the number of movie versions created from the inner code is equal to the number of key versions for each movie key. In our scheme, unlike the naive approach shown earlier, even when we allow both tracing to models and to devices, we do so without increasing the number of tables on the disc. For example, if the inner code creates 256 movie versions, and each movie key comes with 256 versions, there will be 256 different tables on the disc, each encrypted with one different movie key.

In the case of tracing only to manufacturer, the capability of tracing to devices can be disabled. This can be done by sending the same movie version to the individual devices of the same model. Basically, you can choose a movie version from the cluster, and its corresponding table can be duplicated to the number of times equal to the number of keys within each cluster. Each duplicated table is encrypted with one of the sequence keys within the cluster. In the example shown above, the 512 rows are divided into 32 clusters, and there are 16 rows in each cluster. Instead of having 512 different tables, as is the case when allowed to trace to devices, there will be only 32 different tables, but each of the 32 tables is duplicated 16 times. All the devices that have those 16 keys within the same cluster will use their own sequence keys to encrypt the 16 identical tables for the cluster. But some of the movie versions are not used; only 32 versions are used. Of course, when doing this, there is no way for the tracing agency to trace down to devices. After all, every device within the same model gets the same movie version. Note that, when doing this, the number of total tables for the movie on the disc is still 512, the same as when tracing to devices. Because the different tables are equal to the number of clusters, in reality, when the number of rows is large, we can add another level of indirection to keep the number of tables at the number of clusters. For example, we can randomly choose one key k_i to encrypt table i. We can then add an index array to map the sequence keys to the actual key k_i that is used to encrypt the table.

This scheme allows the detection of the pirate manufacturer/model using less recovered movies than that needed for tracing to devices. The reason for this is not hard to understand. Following the sequence key assignment shown above, the outer code used for manufacturer/model tracing would simply be the first-level code used for slot assignment. However, the outer code used for individual tracing would be the combination of the two levels of the assignment shown above. In the example shown above, the outer code used for tracing models is $q = 32, n = 255$ and Hamming distance $d1$, namely, the $[255, k1, d1]$ code. The outer code used for tracing devices will be the combination of $q = 32$, $[255, k1, d1]$ code and $q = 16$, $[255, k2, d2]$ code. Therefore, the actual outer code is $q = 512$, $[n = 255, k1 \times k2, d1 \times d2]$ for tracing devices. The property of the codes determines that it is more efficient for tracing only to models than tracing to devices. The exact traceability of the scheme can be derived in the same way as we did for the basic scheme used for tracing to individual devices alone [7, 8]. The only differences are the parameters. For example, using the parameters shown in the above example, when there is a single traitor, it takes four movies to deterministically identify the traitor. It only takes two movies to deterministically know which manufacturer/model the traitor belongs to. In fact, after the pirate model is detected, with more recovered movies, the individual traitor can also be detected.

The AACS's hybrid tracing scheme allows detection of collusion between manufacturers/models as well as collusion between devices. The traceability against collusion between models depends on the first-level outer code, and the traceability against collusion between devices depends on the combination of the two-level outer code.

We know this scheme allows the content owner to tune the parameters for the inner code differently for different movies. Also, whether the content owner chooses to prepare the movie for the purpose of tracing individual players or tracing the manufacturer/model is transparent to the players and can also be a movie-by-movie decision. The number of tables does not change based on the inner code decision. If the actual number of movie versions created for a movie is less than the movie key versions, each movie version will be encrypted by multiple versions of the movie key for that movie.

This scheme keeps the space requirement small both on the disc and in the player. In fact, the storage requirement on the player and the number of tables on the disc for hybrid tracing are kept the same as when the scheme is used only for individual tracing.

13.7   PROBLEM: EVIL MANUFACTURERS

The AACS was also motivated by the need to defend against the so-called "evil manufacturer attack," where a licensed manufacturer misuses all the keys assigned to him. When this attack happens, it is desirable to take action against that manufacturer without harming other innocent manufacturers' devices. Interestingly enough, our key management approach can be highly resilient to the attack that many devices within the same model line are compromised.

There are two general types of attacks: one is the random individual hacking events, and the other is the evil or sloppy manufacturers who misuse all the keys assigned to them and cause all those keys be exposed. To a lesser extent, attackers reverse engineer multiple devices from the same manufacturer/model and compromise many keys assigned to the particular manufacturer/model. In fact, if the sequence keys are assigned randomly from the entire key matrix, an evil manufacturer could quickly learn all the keys in the matrix and break the system. On the other hand, when an evil manufacturer attack occurs, all those keys can be exposed, and it can be equivalent to multiple random individual attacks. It turns out that the slot idea explained in the previous section is also a very good way to defend against the evil manufacturer problem.

It is interesting that the AACS's scheme can defend effectively against both evil manufacturers' attacks and random individual attacks. Intuitively, we want to minimize the overlap between slots. Our systematic assignment of the keys to the devices provides a deterministic guarantee of the Hamming distance, thus the maximum overlap between slots. The Hamming distance can be so big that a collusion up to certain number (for example, m, decided by the Hamming distance) of evil manufacturer models cannot completely cover any given innocent device's sequence keys. In other words, the probability that a given device's sequence keys are covered by m manufacturer models is zero. On the other hand, with random assignment, suppose there are q clusters, a given device's sequence key can be entirely covered by a device in another manufacturer model with probability $(1/q)^n$, where n is the number of sequence keys each device gets. This probability is small, but not zero. Similarly, the probabilities that it can be covered by multiple manufacturers are not zero. The systematic assignment is a better option than random assignment.

13.8   PROBLEM: WHAT TO DO AFTER YOU TRACE

In the original tracing traitors scheme, Chor, Fiat, and Naor [2] carefully defined the problem so that the system only had to trace once; presumably, if more tracing is required, the devices would be provisioned with new keys for that purpose. Obviously, this solution was unacceptable to the AACS; the sequence keys that are put in the device at manufacturing time have to last for the life of the system. Imagine the following attack scenario: a server-based attack is foiled by using sequence keys to determine the compromised players, and then the standard broadcast encryption-based revocation using device keys is employed to make sure those players no longer work with new movies. But now suppose the attackers, in a fit of pique, publish their players' sequence keys on the Internet. Suppose further a new attack comes along with new players and new sets of device keys. Finally, suppose they have compromised their players to such an extent that they can use the old, published sequence keys. The license agency can learn nothing about the new attack because the tracing will keep pointing back to the players from the original attack.

Of course, not all attacks are of this nature. For example, attacks in which the players are only minimally compromised to extract the in-the-clear movies would not be like this but the attack is plausible enough to be a serious concern. Disturbingly, this issue is not discussed in the tracing traitors literature. It was clear to us that we had to design a scheme where the sequence keys could be revoked, in the sense that the attackers would be forced to use new, uncompromised sequence keys in their attacks. We called the scheme we designed to solve this problem *renewable* traitor tracing, and we call the actual mechanism *Sequence Key Blocks* (SKBs).

The main idea is to combine traitor tracing with broadcast encryption technologies as described earlier in this book. Sets of sequence keys are assigned to individual devices out of a matrix of keys, very similar to 4C Entity's Content Protection for Recordable Media (CPRM) technology. The license agency also assigns SKB to be used on the pre-recorded media, similar to CPRM's MKB (Media Key Block).

For example, say the matrix has 256 columns and not more than 65,536 rows.[2] Each cell is a different sequence key. A single device has one key in each column. Thus, each device has 256 sequence keys. Attackers would prefer to use already-compromised sequence keys if they could so that no new forensic information could be deduced by the licensing agency. Therefore, it is important that compromised keys no longer be usable by the attackers. The problem is that there are many thousands of devices that will have a single compromised key. Therefore, revocation of a single key is impossible. On the other hand, since no two devices have that many keys in common, even if the system has been heavily attacked and a significant fraction of the sequence keys is compromised, all innocent devices will have many columns in which they have uncompromised keys. Thus, it is possible to revoke a set of compromised keys rather than a single key. It is the purpose of the SKB to give all innocent devices a column they can use to calculate the correct answer, while at the same time preventing compromised devices (who have compromised keys in all columns) from getting to the same answer. In an SKB there are actually many correct answers, one for each variation in the content. For the purpose of explanation, however, it is helpful to imagine that a single SKB is producing a single answer. We will call that answer the *output key*. Then the SKB mechanism is completely identical to the CPRM mechanism.

As shown in Figure 13.3, the SKB begins with a first column, called the "unconditional" column. This column will have an encryption of the output key (denoted 'K' in the figure) in every uncompromised sequence key. Devices that do not have compromised keys in that column immediately decrypt the output key, and they are done. Devices, both innocent and otherwise, that do have compromised keys instead decrypt a key called a link key that allows them to process a further column in the SKB. To process the further column they need both the link key and their sequence key in that column. Thus, the subsequent columns are called "conditional" columns because they can only be processed by the device if it were given the necessary link key in a previous column. The subsequent additional conditional columns are produced in the same way as the first column; they will have an encryption of the output key in every uncompromised sequence key. Devices with a compromised key will get a further link key instead of the output key. However, after some number of columns depending on the compromised keys, the AACS licensing agency will know that only compromised devices are getting the link key; all innocent devices would have found the output key in this column or a previous column. At this point, rather than encrypting a link key, the agency encrypts a 0, and the SKB is complete.

---

[2] If the reader is frustrated that we keep choosing different sizes for the sequence key matrix, we apologize. The actual AACS matrix size is confidential, and we are choosing different examples to illustrate the different problems we encountered.

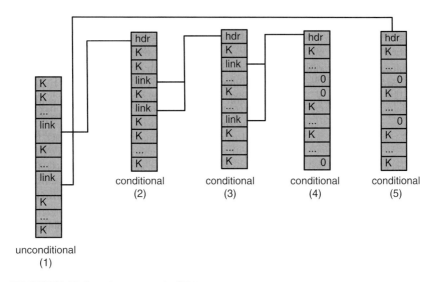

FIGURE 13.3:   An example SKB.

How do the devices know they have a link key versus the output key? The short answer is they do not, at least not at first. Each conditional column has a header of known data (DEADBEEF in hexadecimal) encrypted in the link key for that column. The device decrypts the header with the key it currently has. If the header decrypts correctly, the device knows it has a link key and processes the column. If it does not decrypt correctly, the device knows it has either the output key or a link key for a further column. When it reaches the end of the SKB, it knows it must have an output key. Note that this device logic allows the licensing agency to send different populations of devices to different columns by having more than one link key output from a single column. For example, in Figure 13.3, column (1) links to both column (2) and column (5). This flexibility can help against certain types of attacks. This is basically how the SKB works, with the exception that there is not a single output key, but multiple output keys called *variant keys*. The variant keys are actually used by a device to decrypt the variant tables, which in turn allows it to decrypt its particular path through the variations in the movie.

13.9   PROBLEM: WHEN TO APPLY THE TRACING TECHNOLOGY

All the other problems we discussed in this chapter are technical ones. This problem is legal/social and is the authors' personal opinion and not necessarily the opinion of any of the AACS founders. Basically, the problem is that it is not clear legally whether or not the licensing agency is entitled to revoke a player if its owner has used it to make unauthorized copies of the content without compromising the player. For example, the user might have digitized the movie from the player's analog output. On the other hand, if the attackers have compromised the player in order to get the movie in the clear, it is reasonable to argue that by compromising it, they have broken the player, and revocation is a reasonable action. However, there are some application scenarios where revocation is an acceptable remedy even in the analog redigitization case. It is certainly natural to use it in a subscription-based model where the player itself is free of charge and the movies are pay-per-view. Upon identification, the content owner should not have the obligation to continue to provide movies to a user who is proven to be pirating them. There are other business models, as well. Generally speaking, they are when the content distributor's business model not only relies on selling physical media, but also on an accompanying service agreement with the customer. The service agreement can specify the consequences of the user engaging in piracy. Those business models include but are not limited to:

1. **Business-to-business applications** target a specific end-user population usually under a subscription agreement. This is the case for the distribution of pre-release movies to screeners in the movie industry or the delivery of professional videos to a limited subscriber base, such as training material in a commercial or military setting.

2. **Download of content to recordable media** is an innovative business model where the end-user separately obtains empty recordable media in a physical store and content through Internet download. This scheme allows online distribution of content using an eCommerce model and gives the end-user access to a more extensive library than a conventional retailer.

3. **Rental business models** are where the end-user has access to the content for a limited time under a specific rental agreement. Well-known distribution models in this category are the ones used by the Blockbuster video rental stores or NetFlix.

4. **eCommerce features of pre-packaged media** include all functionality of pre-packaged content, which allows the end-user to purchase additional related material in an online fashion. This essentially requires an independent transaction with a separate contractual agreement.

13.10   CONCLUSION

In this chapter, we study the problem of tracing the users (traitors) who instrument their devices and illegally resell the pirated copies by redistributing the content or the decryption keys on the Internet. We have listed some of the application areas in which this technology can be useful.

We have presented a complete and practical solution to defend against the anonymous attacks. The AACS's sequence key technology attempts to meet practical restrictions on a traitor tracing scheme. A traitor tracing scheme consists of two steps, namely the assignment of the variations and the traitor detection. The first step is restricted by the extra bandwidth and the large number of devices that need to be supported. The second step is demanded by the large coalition that needs to be defended against. The first step in the AACS's sequence key scheme is made practical by a systematic key assignment approach using classic error correcting codes and two levels of the codes in the construction. The second step, traitor detection, is improved significantly by employing an efficient tracing algorithm to detect the entire coaltion rather than the traitors one by one. This brand new algorithm can detect much larger coalitions to make a traitor tracing scheme useful in practice.

As the AACS sequence key scheme was brought to practice, we overcame several barriers. We allowed the scheme to be flexible during deployment. We designed an efficient key management system to make the space requirement in the player substantially reduced without impacting the tracing strength. We further improved our key assignment to accommodate the need to flexibly trace to manufacturer/model only and/or individual device. The advantage of the scheme is that the capability of tracing to the individual device can be switched on and off based on a particular application requirement. It allows faster tracing to models and protects the user's privacy in case devices can be tied back to users. It also defends well against attacks that compromise many devices within the same manufacturer/model or, in the extreme case, that evil manufacturers misuse and compromise all the keys assigned to them.

The last, but also very important, piece that fills in the puzzle is, for the first time, to add renewability into a traitor tracing scheme. We use SKBs. This allows the traitor device's sequence keys to be revoked and excluded from new attacks. Although the solution is complete, there is continued research that needs to be done to make the technology more practical and useful; for example, improve the tracing capability and revocation capability to trace and survive an even larger collusion.

REFERENCES

[1] A. Fiat and M. Naor. Broadcast encryption, *Crypto'93, Lecture Notes in Computer Science*, 773:480–491, 1993.
[2] B. Chor, A. Fiat, and M. Naor. Tracing traitors, *Crypto'94, Lecture Notes in Computer Science*, 839:257–270, 1994.
[3] B. Chor, A. Fiat, M. Naor, and B. Pinkas. Tracing traitors, *IEEE Trans. Information Theory*, 46:893–910, 2000.
[4] I. Cox, J. Killian, T. Leighton, and T. Shamoon. Secure spread spectrum watermarking for multimedia, *IEEE Trans. Image Processing*, 6(12):1673–1687, 1997.

[5] A. Fiat and T. Tassa. Dynamic traitor tracing, *Crypto'99, Lecture Notes in Computer Science*, 1666:354–371, 1999.

[6] S. Lin and D. J. Costello. *Error Control Coding: Fundamentals and Applications*, Prentice Hall, New Yark, 1983.

[7] R. Safani-Naini and Y. Wang. Sequential traitor tracing, *IEEE Trans. Information Theory*, 49:1319–1326, 2003.

[8] J. N. Staddon, D. R. Stinson, and R. Wei. Combinatorial properties of frameproof and traceability codes, *IEEE Trans. on Information Theory*, 47:1042–1049, 2001.

[9] D. R. Stinson and R. Wei. Combinatorial properties and constructions of traceability schemes and frameproof codes, *SIAM J. Discrete Mathematics*, 11:41–53, 1998.

[10] R. Fagin, F. B. Lotspiech, D. Naor, and S. Naor, U.S. Patent application 6,947,563 B2, Method for Assigning Encryption Keys, 2005.

[11] H. Jin and J. Lotspiech. Traitor tracing for prerecorded and recordable media, *ACM DRM Workshop*, pp. 83–90, Washington, D.C., October 2004.

14

Steganalysis

Jessica Fridrich

14.1 BASIC CONCEPTS

Steganography is the art of stealth communication. Its purpose is to make communication undetectable—to hide the very presence of communication. By contrast, in cryptography messages are made unintelligible for those not possessing the decryption key, but the fact that encrypted information is being sent is not hidden or masked in any way. Thus, cryptographic communication can be secure, but is obvious.

The steganography problem is also known as the prisoners' dilemma formulated for the first time by Simmons [62]. Alice and Bob are imprisoned and want to hatch an escape plan. They are allowed to communicate via a channel monitored by a warden. If the warden finds out that they are communicating secretly, he will throw them into solitary confinement. Thus, the prisoners need to design a method to exchange messages without raising the warden's suspicion.

The field of steganography is old. An excellent historical narrative about cryptography and steganography is given by Kahn [38]. Today, digital objects, such as digital images, audio files, video, and other forms of digital data, are ideal carriers for hidden data. Multimedia files are suitable objects for steganography because they consist of a large number of samples of real physical quantities, such as voltages or currents. Thus, by their very nature, the samples contain noise and offer redundancy necessary for data hiding. In this text, we will be primarily dealing with digital images because this is where the majority of work in steganography and steganalysis has focused so far.

At the first International Information Hiding Workshop in 1996 [55], researchers agreed on the following terminology. The original object before any data is hidden in it is called the *cover* object. After embedding, the modified object is called the *stego*-object. The embedding process is usually driven by a stego-key, which is a secret shared between Alice and Bob. It is typically used to select a subset of the cover object and the order in which the samples are visited for embedding. The secret message may also be encrypted using a separate encryption key. By combining encryption with steganography, new concepts such as public key steganography [2] can be developed.

Originally, the term steganography was used as a synonym for data hiding. As the field diversified and expanded in the last ten years, the meaning of steganography shifted as well. Today, it is used for *undetectable* data hiding, meaning no one, except for the intended recipient, should be able to detect the presence of hidden data. The embedded message is usually unrelated to the cover object, which only plays the role of a decoy. Because steganography is about the exchange of information, practical steganographic systems should provide enough capacity to communicate long messages.

Under the passive warden scenario [53], the communication channel that the sender and recipient use is free of distortion, which means that the secret message does not have to be embedded robustly. If the communication channel is subject to distortion, such as white noise or lossy compression, we speak of an active warden [13]. When the warden intentionally tampers with the messages to prevent any attempts to use steganography, we speak of a malicious warden. This chapter focuses on the passive warden case.

At this point, it is proper to contrast steganography with digital watermarking—another major research stream in data hiding. A digital watermark [11] usually supplies additional data about the cover object (e.g., the authorship, intended recipient, authentication code, meta-data, date and place of origin, etc.). Depending on the application, the watermark may be robust to withstand distortion or fragile (designed to break easily) to enable detection and localization of manipulation/distortion. In most cases, digital watermarks do not have to be embedded in an undetectable manner. In fact, the presence of watermarks may be public knowledge or even advertised beforehand, for example, to discourage illegal redistribution. Watermarks must be usually perceptually transparently designed to preserve the fidelity of the watermarked object. In some applications, however, visible yet hard-to-remove watermarks are required [59].

The process of steganographic embedding can be formalized as a mapping E that assigns a stego-object Y to every possible triple consisting of the cover object X, message M, and stego/encryption key K. The extraction function D is a mapping from Y to the message space

$$E(X, M, K) = Y, D(Y, K) = M \text{ for each } X, M, \text{ and } K. \qquad (14.1)$$

The requirement of undetectability means that Y must be free of visible artifacts. Thus, the embedding distortion is usually further constrained using an appropriately defined distance function (metric) in the space of cover/stego-objects

$$d(X, Y) < \delta. \qquad (14.2)$$

Under the Kerckhoffs' principle, the cover objects are drawn from a known source X, and the embedding function is publicly known as well. As long as the probabilistic distribution of covers over X is identical (or ε-close in Kullback-Leibler norm), the stego-system is called secure (ε-secure). This information-theoretic definition of steganographic security has been put forward by Cachin [7]. An alternative approach to steganographic security from the point of view of complexity is due to Katzenbeisser and Petitcolas [40].

The Kerckhoffs' principle is sometimes viewed as too idealistic because in real life we may not always know all the necessary details of the source X or the embedding mapping E. This underlies the need for steganalytic schemes that are "blind" and can detect suspicious objects without assuming the detailed knowledge of the embedding algorithm and the cover object source. Nevertheless, over a long time span it is a reasonable assumption that the source of the cover objects, as well as the embedding scheme, will be found out.

Steganalysis is the counterpart of steganography, as its goal is to detect the presence of hidden data. Even if the hidden data cannot be extracted, it is still very useful to know that a certain object contains hidden data with high probability as this knowledge may pinpoint one or both communicating parties. For example, imagine the situation when Alice communicates with Bob by posting images on a public Internet bulletin board. By monitoring the board traffic using a steganalytic tool and identifying images that repeatedly raise the red flag as posted by Alice, we know that Alice is communicating secretly, but we do not know with whom she is communicating as the images are viewed by a potentially very large number of people who regularly visit the board.

In the wide sense, steganalysis belongs to forensic analysis. The job of a forensic steganalyst does not end by stating that certain objects are stego-objects. In fact, it starts with this finding and continues with an effort to first identify the embedding mechanism (e.g., least significant bit (LSB) embedding, additive noise embedding, etc.) and the steganographic program. If a known, publicly available program was used, the steganalyst can attempt to identify the stego-key and extract the embedded message bits. If these message bits are encrypted, cryptanalysis can be used to recover the embedded message. In this process, depending on the circumstances, there are many places when the analysis simply cannot proceed further or when some information becomes available essentially "for free." For example, the analyst may have a computer seized from a suspect and on the computer he finds a steganographic program or its traces.[1] In this case, we already know what type of embedded signal we are looking for, which greatly simplifies the process of identifying potential stego-objects. A brute force password cracking[2] with dictionary search [58] or methods described in Fridrich et al. [23] and by Chandramouli and co-workers [9, 64] can be used to recover the embedded data from a stego-object.

In some cases, the analyst will have the cover and the stego-object available, which further simplifies the task. In fact, forensic steganalysis, similar to cryptanalysis, recognizes similar categories of attacks, such as known cover attack, chosen cover attack, etc. [37]. At the other extreme, having a few candidate stego-objects without any additional information (e.g., "JPEG in the wild") is the hardest case for steganalysis. If an unknown hiding program has been used, there is little hope that the hidden message can be recovered.

The steganalyst might also use other obvious fingerprints left over by amateur and professional steganographic tools, such as the presence of specific markers, comments, choice of JPEG compressor, and other artifacts unintentionally introduced by software creators. This valuable and easily accessible information may significantly help narrow down the possibilities about the origin of the file. For example, as pointed out by Niels Provos, the early release of the F5 algorithm [69] had the following JPEG compressor comment header "JPEG Encoder Copyright 1998, James R. Weeks and BioElectroMech," which is rarely present in JPEG images and can be used as a reliable indicator of F5 processed images. Other interesting unintentional fingerprints of some stego-products have been pointed out by Johnson [36, 37].

Although such clues are undoubtedly useful in practice, the research community (and this chapter) is primarily concerned with statistical analysis of the individual sample values forming the image file, assuming that the stego-program can be made free of such obvious artifacts.

14.2 STEGANOGRAPHY—HISTORICAL PERSPECTIVE

Before studying steganalytic methods, we explain the basic embedding principles of steganography. The early approach to steganography appears a little naïve from the point of view of what we know today. The least impact of embedding on the cover data file is flipping the Least Significant Bit (LSB) of a given

---

[1] WetStones' Gargoyle © tool can be used for this purpose (http://www.wetstonestech.com).

[2] StegoSuite © by WetStones, Inc. has password crackers for more than 300 stego-programs.

sample value, e.g., flipping the LSB of a gray-scale value or a quantized Discrete Cosine Transform (DCT) coefficient in a JPEG file. Since the LSB plane of most images looks "random," or at least without any visible structure, it seems that replacing the LSBs with message bits cannot be detected. Indeed, fueled by this (quite wrong) belief, the early steganographic methods frequently employed this simplistic embedding mechanism. Although LSB embedding was proven to be easily detectable in all image formats even at low embedding rates, it is still used today in a surprisingly large number of stego-products available on the Internet [76].

A trivial modification of LSB embedding can make it significantly more difficult to detect. If, instead of flipping the LSB, we add or subtract 1 from the sample value, the majority of steganalytic methods designed for detection of LSB embedding will be ineffective. This embedding method has been termed LSB matching [42, 43] or ±1 embedding [63, 71] in the research community and has been incorporated for steganography in the spatial domain [61] as well as the DCT domain for JPEG images [69].

In the spatial domain, ±1 embedding is a special case of additive noise embedding [1, 29, 51]. Stochastic Modulation [29] is a general methodology to embed message bits at high embedding ratios (up to 0.8 bpp) by superimposing independent, identically distributed (iid) noise with an arbitrary probability distribution on the cover image. Although this approach may sound similar to spread spectrum methods used in robust watermarking, it is, in fact, fundamentally different because the message bits are embedded in a fragile manner and extracted from individual pixels rather than by using correlation. At this point, we remark that using the newly proposed concept of wet paper coding [21], it is possible to drop the requirement that the noise in Stochastic Modulation be identically distributed, thus opening up doors to various versions of *adaptive* additive noise steganography in which the noise probability density function (pdf) is determined by the (local) content of the cover image itself.

It is still an open question whether or not adaptive steganography [20, 39] generally provides better steganographic security. It seems intuitive that embedding in highly textured segments while avoiding changing relatively flat areas (e.g., blue sky) should be more secure than randomly scattering the message bits over the whole image. However, the adaptivity may give some advantage to the attacker [67] as well because he can approximately determine the same embedding areas and focus on them while using the unmodified areas for calibrating certain parameters of the cover image.

Steganalysis is essentially a critical feedback to steganographers. The moral provided by the first steganalytic methods was that care needs to be taken to preserve certain important statistics to avoid being detected. This realization triggered a number of steganographic methods, all claiming undetectability with respect to some existing steganalytic attack, e.g., OutGuess [57], Statistics Preserving LSB embedding [20], Model-Based Steganography [60],

Steghide (http://steghide.sourceforge.net/), and many others. As of the day of writing this text (May 2005), all of these methods have been successfully attacked in Fridrich et al. [28]; Westfeld and Böhme [67]; Böhme and Westfeld [6], Fridrich and Pevny [22], and Fridrich [24], respectively. This is because, while it is certainly possible to preserve a small set of certain statistics used by steganalysts, it is impossible to preserve them all or at least preserve all "canonical" statistics that exhaust the space of all cover objects in some sense. All that an attacker needs to do is to take a look at other, "orthogonal," statistics that may not be preserved. With the great advancements of blind steganalysis based on higher order statistics [3, 4, 8, 19, 22, 24, 32, 33, 50, 72], efforts that aim to preserve specific quantities seem to be futile.

Does this mean that secure steganography is impossible? Indeed perhaps it is. In another round of this never-ending cat and mouse game that is played on higher and higher levels, steganographers turned their attention to the very process of data acquisition. When a digital object, such as digital image, is acquired in its final form, there already are too many complex dependencies built in among the samples that make the task of identifying a space where one can embed a message extremely difficult. The situation may be somewhat alleviated if the sender uses available side information.

For example, the sender may have a raw, never compressed image and wish to embed into its JPEG compressed form. During compression, the real values of DCT coefficients are scaled by quantization steps and then rounded to integers to be further processed using a Huffman coder and finally stored in the JPEG file. Before the rounding occurs, the sender can identify those real-valued DCT coefficients (changeable coefficients) that are close to the middle of the quantization intervals and round them up or down at his will to embed a message. This embedding methodology is called Perturbed Quantization [26], and it requires codes for memories with stuck cells (wet paper codes [21]). Perturbing the rounding of only the changeable coefficients introduces the smallest combined distortion. Of course, small distortion does not imply steganographic security, and additional rules for selection of embedding changes may have to be applied. Perturbed Quantization can be carried out whenever an image is subjected to an information-reducing operation that includes rounding. Another example is the process of converting a 14-bit signal to an 8-bit signal at the end of the image processing sequence applied to a digital camera image.

Of course, in the ideal case, we should avoid modifying the cover image altogether. But then, how would one embed? A bold idea was recently proposed by Petrowski et al. [54] in which the authors take many pictures of the same scene and then construct a new image as a mosaic (or patchwork) of blocks from individual images, with each block selected so that its (shortened) hash matches a set of message bits. This method has a few underlying assumptions that must be satisfied in order for this approach to lead to undetectable steganography. First, it is not an easy task to obtain two samplings of the exact same scene. The camera shutter may cause small spatial shifts between the images, the shutter speed may be subject to variations, and the outside light conditions may change. Second, even when these technical problems are resolved, the small variations between individual pixels may be dependent, thus potentially leading to detectable artifacts at the block borders. A practical problem with studying this method is that it is difficult to verify the claims as they are strongly dependent on the experimental conditions and the particular piece of hardware. Nevertheless, this approach seems promising, and more papers can be expected to be published on this topic in the future.

One of the most important findings for future development of steganography was the realization that the type of the cover image influences steganographic security in a major manner [44, 45]. JPEG compatibility steganalysis [31] showed that decompressed JPEG images should not be used for spatial domain steganography because decompressed and embedded JPEGs still contain a strong fingerprint of previous JPEG compression, yet their 8×8 pixel blocks can be proven to be incompatible with all 8×8 matrices of quantized DCT coefficients. Thus, even a single pixel change can be detected with high certainty. Moreover, decompressed JPEG images have a lower level of noise, which makes their steganalysis much easier, as witnessed by recent studies by Ker [42–45] and others [34].

Never compressed images obtained using digital cameras with the raw format setting are much more challenging for detection of steganography. The most difficult classes of images from the point of view of detection of steganographic content are scans of analog photographs or films. Scanning at high dpi resolves the grain structure of the film or photographic paper, which makes scans appear rather noisy with a characteristic superimposed grain structure.

Another rule of thumb is that steganalysis of color images is easier than for gray scales. This is because color histograms are, in general, sparser than gray-scale histograms and thus react more sensitively to embedding. Moreover, steganographic embedding may decrease the correlations between channels and create a large number of new colors (embedding has a tendency to equalize the color distribution in the RGB color space).

The influence of image content and other image attributes on the accuracy of LSB message length estimators was recently studied by Böhme [5] using multiple regression models.

14.3   TARGETED STEGANALYSIS

Steganalytic methods can be roughly divided into targeted and blind. Targeted methods address a specific embedding paradigm, e.g., LSB embedding, while blind methods do not assume the knowledge of the embedding mechanism. Instead, blind methods start by characterizing natural images in some high-dimensional feature space and training a classifier to distinguish between cover and stego-images. The advantage of blind schemes is that they can be used to detect unknown steganography, but are usually less reliable than targeted approaches and may require a lot of computing power to train. On the other hand, some targeted steganalysis may be too narrow and not extensible to other embedding types. For example, the most reliable detectors of LSB embedding cannot be extended to detect ± 1 embedding. On the other hand, targeted steganalysis can, in many cases, estimate the number of embedding changes and thus the embedded message length, which is an important piece of knowledge for a forensic steganalyst.

Having pointed out the dissimilarities between targeted and blind methods, I will now play the devil's advocate and claim that the boundary between targeted and blind approaches is somewhat fuzzy. Targeted approaches typically use certain statistics that indicate the presence of hidden data. These statistics can always be added to a blind scheme and improve its performance. On the other hand, certain features in a blind scheme may turn out to be the most influential quantities to attack specific steganographic methods and even estimate the number of embedding changes.

The boundary between targeted and blind methods has recently been further blurred by the latest spatial domain steganalytic methods [32, 34, 42, 43, 72]. These methods suggest the existence of a general methodology applicable to detection of additive noise steganography, which forms quite a large class of steganographic techniques. Is this approach targeted or blind?

14.3.1   Chi-Square Attack

From historical reasons, we first describe the chi-square attack by Westfeld and Pfitzmann [70]. This attack can be applied to any steganographic technique in which a fixed set of disjoint groups of values are changed into each other to embed message bits. For example, the mechanism of LSB embedding creates Pairs of Values (PoVs) that differ in the LSB. Before embedding, in the cover image the two values from each pair are distributed unevenly. After message embedding, the occurrences of the values in each pair will have a tendency to become equal (this depends on the message length). Since swapping one value into another does not change the sum of occurrences of both values in the image, we can test for the statistical significance of the fact that the occurrences of both values in each pair are the same using a chi-square test.

For example, for a palette image there are at most 256 colors c_i in the palette, which means at most 128 PoVs. For the ith pair, $i = 1, \ldots, k$, let $n'_i = 1/2$ (number of indices in the set $\{c_{2i}, c_{2i+1}\}$), and $n_i =$ (number of indices equal to c_{2i}). The value n'_i is the theoretically expected frequency if a random message has been embedded, and n_i is the actual number of occurrences of color c_{2i}. We can now perform a chi-square test for the equality of n'_i and n_i. The chi-square statistics are calculated as

$$\chi_{k-1}^2 = \sum_{i=1}^{k} \frac{(n_i - n_i')^2}{n_i'} \tag{14.3}$$

with $k–1$ degrees of freedom. The p-value

$$p = 1 - \frac{1}{2^{\frac{k-1}{2}} \Gamma\left(\frac{k-1}{2}\right)} \int_0^{\chi_{k-1}^2} e^{-\frac{x}{2}} x^{\frac{k-1}{2}-1} dx \tag{14.4}$$

expresses the probability that the distributions n_i' and n_i are equal.

For a sequentially embedded message, one can scan the image in the same order in which the message has been embedded and evaluate p for the set of all already visited pixels. The p-value will at first be close to 1 and then it suddenly drops to 0 when we arrive at the end of the message. It will stay at zero until we get to the lower right corner. Thus, this test determines with a very high probability that a message has been embedded and also estimates the size of the secret message.

If the message-carrying pixels in the image are selected randomly rather than sequentially, this test becomes less effective unless a majority of pixels have been used for embedding. Provos and Honeyman [58] noted that if this technique is applied to different smaller areas in the image, the chi-square statistics will fluctuate with a decreasing degree of fluctuation as the message length increases (the generalized chi-square attack). This is because a randomly spread message, due to chance, will be more concentrated in some areas than in others. Westfeld [68] later extended his attack to randomly spread messages by inspecting small groups of pixels (color channels). The extended method is able to detect random LSB embedding up to approximately 0.3 bpp.

14.3.2 Steganalysis of LSB Embedding

Statistical methods that start with sample counts neglect very important information: the placement of pixels in the stego-image. It is intuitively clear that by utilizing the spatial correlations in images, one should be able to build much more reliable and accurate detection. The approach described below (Sample Pairs Analysis) is due to Dumitrescu, Wu, and Memon [16] and is based on the first method of this kind proposed in Fridrich, Goljan, and Du [30].

Let us assume that we have a gray-scale cover image I with n pixels and with pixel values from the set $\{0, \ldots, 255\}$. Denote by P the set of all horizontally adjacent pixel pairs in the image. We partition P into three disjoint subsets X, Y, and Z:

- X is the set of pairs $(u, v) \in P$ such that v is even and $u < v$, or v is odd and $u > v$.
- Y is the set of pairs $(u, v) \in P$ such that v is even and $u > v$, or v is odd and $u < v$.
- Z is the set of pairs $(u, v) \in P$ such that $u = v$.

Furthermore, partition the set Y into two subsets W and V, with W being the set of pairs in P of the form $(2k, 2k + 1)$ or $(2k + 1, 2k)$, and $V = Y - W$. Note that $P = X \cup W \cup V \cup Z$. The sets X, Y, W, V, and Z are called primary sets.

It will become clear later why this partitioning should be useful for detection of LSB embedding by analyzing what happens to a given pixel pair (u, v) under LSB embedding. There are four possibilities:

a. Both u and v stay unmodified   (modification pattern 00).
b. Only u is modified   (modification pattern 10).
c. Only v is modified   (modification pattern 01).
d. Both u and v are modified   (modification pattern 11).

LSB embedding causes a given pixel pair to change its membership to one of the four primary sets. The arrows pointing from set A to set B in Figure 14.1 are labeled by the modification pattern, meaning that a pixel pair originally in A becomes a member of B if modified by the specified pattern during LSB embedding.

For each modification pattern $\pi \in \{00,10,01,11\}$ and any subset $A \subset P$, let $\rho(\pi, A)$ be the fraction of pixel pairs in A modified with pattern π. Assuming that the message bits are randomly spread over the image and are thus independent of the image content (non-adaptive embedding), we must have for each modification pattern $\pi \in \{00,10,01,11\}$ and each primary set $A \subset P, A \in \{X, V, W, Z\}$

$$\rho(\pi, A) = \rho(\pi, P). \tag{14.5}$$

If p is the relative message length in bits per pixel (the number of message bits divided by the number of pixels), then the number of modified pixels is $p/2$.

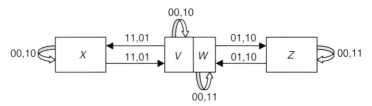

FIGURE 14.1:   Transitions between primary sets.

Here, we assume that the embedded message is a random bitstream independent of the LSBs. Using Equation (14.5), we thus have

$$\rho(00,\,P) = (1 - p/2)^2$$
$$\rho(01,P) = \rho(10,P) = p/2(1 - p/2)$$
$$\rho(11,P) = (p/2)^2.$$

These transition probabilities and the set migration relationship from Figure 14.1 allow us to express the cardinalities of the primary sets after the embedding as functions of p and the cardinalities before the embedding. Denoting the primary sets after embedding with a prime, we obtain

$$|X'| = |X|(1 - p/2) + |V|p/2 \tag{14.6}$$
$$|V'| = |V|(1 - p/2) + |X|p/2 \tag{14.7}$$
$$|W'| = |W|(1 - p + p^2/2) + |Z|p(1 - p/2). \tag{14.8}$$

Our goal now is to derive an equation for the unknown quantity p using only the cardinalities of primed sets as they can be calculated from the stego-image. Equations (14.6) and (14.7) imply that

$$|X'| - |V'| = (|X| - |V|)(1 - p). \tag{14.9}$$

We now note that on average

$$|X| = |Y|. \tag{14.10}$$

This assumption is true for natural images that typically contain a certain amount of noise. This is because the horizontal gradient is equally likely to be positive or negative independently of the fact whether one of the pixels is even or odd. Additionally, note that the roles of X and Y reverse after adding 1 to I.

Thus, since $|X| = |Y|$, we have $|X| = |V| + |W|$, and from Equation (14.9)

$$|X'| - |V'| = |W|(1 - p). \tag{14.11}$$

It can be seen from Figure 14.1 that the embedding process does not modify the set $W \cup Z$. Denoting $\gamma = |W| + |Z| = |W'| + |Z'|$, by replacing $|Z|$ with $\gamma - |W|$, the expression in Equation (14.8) for $|W'|$ becomes

$$|W'| = |W|(1 - p)^2 + \gamma p(1 - p/2). \tag{14.12}$$

Eliminating $|W|$ from Equations (14.11) and (14.12) leads to

$$|W'| = (|X'| - |V'|)(1 - p) + \gamma p(1 - p/2). \qquad (14.13)$$

Since $|X'| + |Y'| + |Z'| = |X'| + |V'| + |W'| + |Z'| = |P|$, Equation (14.13) is equivalent to

$$\tfrac{1}{2}\gamma p^2 + (2|X'| - |P|)p + |Y'| - |X'| = 0.$$

All quantities in this equation can be calculated from the stego-image (recall that $\gamma = |W'| + |Z'|$). The unknown message length p is obtained as the smaller root of this quadratic equation. Note that $\gamma = 0$ implies $|X'| = |X| = |Y| = |Y'| = |P|/2$. The quadratic equation becomes an identity, and we cannot calculate p. However, since γ is the number of pixel pairs that only differ in their LSBs, this will happen with very small probability for natural images.

Figure 14.2(a) shows the estimated value of p for cover images $(p=0)$ and stego-images embedded with $p=0.05$, 0.2, and 0.5 for 955 gray-scale never compressed images of natural scenes obtained by three different digital cameras (Canon G2, Canon S40, and Kodak DC 290). The images were used in their native resolution, 2272×1704, for both Canons and in 1792×1200 for Kodak, but were converted to gray-scale. Figure 14.2(b) is the Receiver Operating Characteristic (ROC) showing the separation between cover images and stego-images embedded with $p=0.05$ (5% of capacity).

Sample Pairs Analysis (SPA) was later further improved [15, 44, 45, 48] and extended to groups of more than two pixels [14, 41], giving an even more astonishingly accurate and reliable performance.

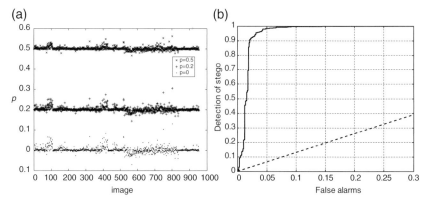

FIGURE 14.2:   Performance of SPA tested on 955 raw gray-scale images.

Other related approaches to the detection of LSB embedding in the spatial domain that are based on statistics of differences between pairs of neighboring pixels are discussed in Fridrich, Goljan, and Soukal [27] and Zhang and Ping [74]. One of the first approaches based on cover image estimation is found in Chandramouli and Memon [10]. A qualitatively different approach called the Weighted Stego-image (WS) method that uses local image estimators is found in Fridrich and Goljan [25]. Methods for the detection of LSB embedding in the JPEG domain (J-steg) are described in Yu, Wang, and Tan [66] and Zhang and Ping [73].

14.3.3   Attacking the F5 Algorithm

The F5 algorithm [69] played a major role in the development of steganographic methods for JPEG images because its embedding mechanism contained several important novel design principles. The challenge to break F5 initiated a surge in JPEG steganalysis, eventually resulting in new concepts, such as that of calibration, which turned out to be essential for reliable JPEG steganalysis.

The F5 algorithm embeds message bits as the LSBs of coefficients along a key-dependent random walk through all DCT coefficients of the cover image while skipping the DC coefficients and all coefficients that are zeros. If the coefficient's LSB does not match the message bit, the absolute value of the coefficient is always *decremented*. If the subtraction leads to a zero coefficient (shrinkage), the same message bit must be embedded at the next coefficient because at the receiving end the message is extracted only from non-zero coefficients. Additionally, the F5 algorithm employs matrix embedding [12] to minimize the necessary number of changes when embedding short messages.

Because the embedding is not based on bit replacement or exchanging any fixed PoVs, the F5 algorithm cannot be detected using the chi-square attack or its variants. On the other hand, the F5 algorithm does modify the histogram of DCT coefficients in a predictable manner.

Let us denote by $h(d)$, $d = 0, 1, \ldots$ the total number of AC DCT coefficients in the cover image with absolute value equal to d. In a similar manner, $h_{kl}(d)$ will be the total number of AC coefficients corresponding to the frequency (k, l), $1 \leq k$, $l \leq 8$, whose absolute value is equal to d. The corresponding histogram values for the stego-image will be denoted using the capital letters H and H_{kl}.

Assuming the embedding process changes n AC coefficients, the probability that a given non-zero AC coefficient was modified is $\beta = n/N_0$, where N_0 is the total number of non-zero AC coefficients, $N_0 = h(1) + h(2) + \ldots$. Because the selection of coefficients is pseudo-random in F5, assuming a random bitstream is embedded, it follows from the F5 embedding mechanism that the expected values of the histograms H_{kl} of the stego-image are

$$H_{kl}(d) = (1 - \beta)h_{kl}(d) + \beta h_{kl}(d + 1), \text{ for } d > 0,$$

$$H_{kl}(0) = h_{kl}(0) + \beta h_{kl}(1), \text{ for } d = 0. \tag{14.14}$$

Having an estimate $\hat{h}_{kl}(d)$ of the cover image histogram, we can solve Equation (14.14) for β because $H_{kl}(d)$ is known. Since the first two values in the histogram ($d = 0$ and $d = 1$) experience the largest change during embedding (see Figure 14.3), only these two values are used to calculate an estimate β_{kl} of β:

$$\beta_{kl} = \arg\min_{\beta}[H_{kl}(0) - \hat{h}_{kl}(0) - \beta\hat{h}_{kl}(1)]^2 + [H_{kl}(1) - (1-\beta)\hat{h}_{kl}(1) - \beta\hat{h}_{kl}(2)]^2. \tag{14.15}$$

The least square approximation in Equation (14.15) leads to the following formula for β_{kl}:

$$\beta_{kl} = \frac{\hat{h}_{kl}(1)[H_{kl}(0) - \hat{h}_{kl}(0)] + [H_{kl}(1) - \hat{h}_{kl}(1)][(\hat{h}_{kl}(2) - \hat{h}_{kl}(1))]}{\hat{h}_{kl}^2(1) + [\hat{h}_{kl}(2) - \hat{h}_{kl}(1)]^2} \tag{14.16}$$

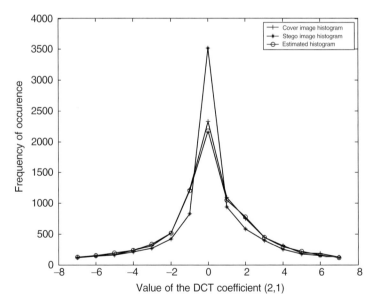

FIGURE 14.3: The effect of F5 embedding on the histogram of the DCT coefficient (2,1).

The final value of β is obtained as an average over selected low-frequency[3] DCT coefficients $(k, l) \in \{(1,2),(2,1),(2,2)\}$.

We now explain how one can obtain the estimate $\hat{h}_{kl}$ of the cover image histogram. The method is called calibration, and it is an important concept in steganalysis, enabling attacks on other JPEG steganographic techniques (e.g., OutGuess [57]) as well as on the development of a blind steganalysis for JPEG images [24] (Section 14.4.2).

The stego-image is decompressed to the spatial domain, cropped by four columns, and recompressed again using the same quantization matrix as that of the stego-image. The resulting DCT coefficients are the estimates $\hat{h}_{kl}(d)$. We note that other geometrical transformations would work here, such as slight rotation, resizing, or global random bending (e.g., Stirmark).

We give a heuristic explanation of why this works. Unless the quality factor of the JPEG compression is too low (e.g., lower than 60), the stego-image produced by F5 is still very close to the cover image, both visually and using measures such as the Peak Signal to Noise Ratio (PSNR). The spatial shift by 4 pixels effectively breaks the structure of quantized DCT coefficients. Thus, it is not surprising that certain macroscopic properties, such as the statistics of DCT coefficients, are similar to the ones of the cover image.

Figure 14.3 shows a typical example of how good the histogram estimate is when compared to the cover image histogram. The graph shows the cover image histogram values $h_{21}(d)$ (crosses), histogram values after applying the F5 algorithm with maximal possible message or $\beta = 0.5$ (stars), and the estimate of the cover image histogram (circles).

Figure 14.4 shows the performance of the estimator in Equation (14.16) for 670 test JPEG images embedded with messages of different relative lengths with β in the range [0.3, 0.5].

Last but not least, we comment on a very important phenomenon that is characteristic of some JPEG steganographic methods, such as the F5 or OutGuess, one that substantially complicates the steganalysis. When F5 is presented with a JPEG image with quality factor Q_1, it decompresses it to the spatial domain and recompresses (and embeds) again with a default quality factor Q_2. Unless both factors are the same, this leads to double compression, which must be compensated for; otherwise, Equation (14.16) may give completely misleading results. The remedy is to estimate Q_1 and adjust the calibration process accordingly (after cropping compress with Q_1, decompress, and recompress with Q_2). Fridrich et al. [28] mentioned a simple procedure to estimate Q_1, but better methods can be found in Fan and de Queiroz [18] and [49].

---

[3]Coefficients corresponding to medium or high frequencies may not provide enough statistics (most of them are zeros) for accurate estimation.

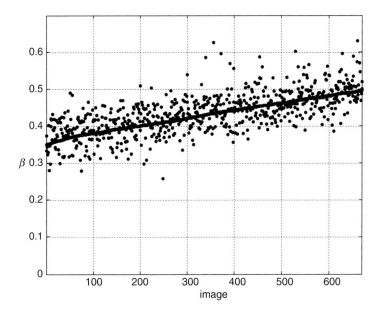

FIGURE 14.4: The true value of β (thick line) versus the estimated β for 670 gray scale images of natural scenes embedded with messages corresponding to $\beta \in [0.3, 0.5]$ with quality factor 80. The images were originally larger and stored as JPEGs. They were all resized to 800×600 pixels to avoid double compression by F5.

14.4 BLIND STEGANALYSIS

Blind steganalysis is a meta-detection method in the sense that it can potentially detect any steganographic method as long as one has sufficiently many examples of cover and stego-images on which a classifier can be trained. The trick is to find an appropriate set of statistical quantities (features) sensitive to embedding modifications, but insensitive to the image content. We also desire to have independent features that exhaust the space of covers as much as possible, hoping to eliminate the space in which a message can be hidden. Neural networks, clustering algorithms, support vector machines, and other tools of soft computing can then be used to construct the detection engine from the training set of cover and stego-image features.

An important advantage of blind detectors is their ability to classify embedding techniques by their position in the feature space and thus give a starting point to the forensic analysts whose aim is to extract the secret embedded message. An example of this method classification for JPEG images is given in Section 14.4.2.

For the design of features, most authors use heuristic and intuitive principles, sometimes borrowing concepts from targeted steganalysis. Different blind steganalyzers are compared by testing them on the same database of images [33, 46].

As already mentioned in Section 14.2, the performance of blind classifiers heavily depends on the type, format, and source of the cover objects on which the classifier is trained and tested. For example, it is significantly easier to detect embedding in the spatial domain if the images have been previously JPEG compressed than in never compressed raw images. This underlies the importance of reliable pre-classification for constructing a blind classifier universal across different image formats.

Historically, the first blind detection algorithm was described by Avcibas, Memon and Sankur [3], in which the authors used various image quality metrics as features. This and later work by the same authors [4] proved that analysis using classifiers trained on features obtained from cover and stego-images is a viable approach to detect embedded data.

14.4.1 Farid's Universal Blind Detector

One of the most popular blind steganalyzers today was proposed by Farid and Lyu [19]. It is universal in the sense that the detection is designed to work for steganography in any domain (e.g., both JPEG and spatial domains). This approach starts with the nth level Quadrature Mirror Filter (QMF) wavelet decomposition ($n = 4$) of the stego-image with $V_i(x, y)$, $H_i(x, y)$, and $D_i(x, y)$ denoting the vertical, horizontal, and diagonal subbands at scale i. Then, the first four moments for all three subbands are calculated for all levels $i = 1, \ldots, n - 1$. This gives the total of $12(n - 1)$ features. Additional features are calculated using an optimal linear predictor of coefficients from their spatial, orientation, and scale neighbors (total of seven neighbors). For example, the vertical wavelet coefficients are predicted using the following linear predictor: $V_i(x,y) = w_1 V_i(x - 1, y) + w_2 V_i(x + 1, y) + w_3 V_i(x, y - 1) + w_4 V_i(x, y + 1) + w_5 V_{i+1}(x/2, y/2) + w_6 D_i(x, y) + w_7 D_{i+1}(x/2, y/2)$. The weights $w_1, \ldots, w_7$ that minimize the squared prediction error are calculated using the standard least square approach. Denoting the linear prediction for $V_i(x,y)$ as $\tilde{V}_i(x,y)$, the log error of the prediction is defined as $E_v(i) = \log_2(|V_i|) - \log_2(|\tilde{V}_i|)$. The first four moments of $E_v(i)$ are taken as additional features. The whole process is repeated for all $n - 1$ scales with horizontal and diagonal subbands. Thus, the final length of the feature vector is $12(n - 1) + 4 \times 3(n - 1) = 24(n - 1) = 72$ for $n = 4$. For color images, the same features are calculated for each channel, giving a total of 216 features [50].

Once the features are selected, the standard procedure in blind steganalysis is to calculate the feature vector for a large database of cover images and stego-images. In their original work, Farid and Lyu [19] used the Fisher Linear Discriminant,

Table 14.1:   Performance of Farid and Lyu's blind detector.

Embedding	Messsage	1% false alarm			0% false alarms		
		JPEG	GIF	TIFF	JPEG	GIF	TIFF
Jsteg	256×256	99.0	—	—	98.5	—	—
Jsteg	128×128	99.3	—	—	99.0	—	—
Jsteg	64×64	99.1	—	—	98.7	—	—
Jsteg	32×32	86.0	—	—	74.5	—	—
OutGuess–	256×256	98.9	—	—	97.1	—	—
OutGuess–	128×128	93.8	—	—	85.8	—	—
OutGuess–	64×64	72.6	—	—	53.1	—	—
OutGuess–	32×32	33.2	—	—	14.4	—	—
OutGuess+	256×256	95.6	—	—	89.5	—	—
OutGuess+	128×128	82.2	—	—	63.7	—	—
OutGuess+	64×64	54.7	—	—	32.1	—	—
OutGuess+	32×32	21.4	—	—	7.2	—	—
EzStego	194×194	—	77.2	—	—	76.9	—
EzStego	128×128	—	39.2	—	—	36.6	—
EzStego	64×64	—	6.5	—	—	4.6	—
EzStego	32×32	—	2.7	—	—	1.5	—
LSB	194×194	—	—	78.0	—	—	77.0
LSB	128×128	—	—	44.7	—	—	40.5
LSB	64×64	—	—	6.2	—	—	4.2
LSB	32×32	—	—	1.9	—	—	1.3

Source: From H. Farid and S. Lyu. *Information Hiding, 5th Int. Workshop*, LNCS vol. 2578, pp: 340–354, 2002, with permission.

but later showed that the performance could be noticeably improved by replacing the linear classifier with non-linear Support Vector Machines (SVMs).

An example of the performance of Farid and Lyu's blind steganalyzer is in Table 14.1. It shows the detection accuracy of stego-images (percent) with 1 and 0% false positives for varying message sizes (the maximum message size for EzStego and LSB is 194×194). For each image, the embedded message was a center crop of the specified size from the same cover image stored in the same format as the cover image. The test database was the Greenspun database (philip.greenspun.com) consisting of 1800 images cropped to their central 640×480 section. All images were converted to gray scale before steganalysis. OutGuess– and + correspond to versions 0.1 and 0.2. J-steg is a JPEG steganography program, and EzStego is a Graphics Interchange Format (GIF) steganography program; both are available from http://www.stegoarchive.com/ [76]. LSB denotes generic LSB embedding with random scatter.

Introducing blind detectors prompted further research in steganography. Based on the previous work of Eggers, Bäuml, and Girod [17], Tzschoppe et al. [65] constructed a JPEG steganographic scheme Histogram Preserving Data Mapping (HPDM) that is undetectable using Farid and Lyu's scheme. However, the same scheme turned out to be easily detectable using a single scalar feature—the spatial blockiness also previously used to attack OutGuess version 0.2 [28].

The differences between embedding mechanisms in the JPEG and spatial domains suggest that much can be gained by designing separate blind steganalyzers for both domains capitalizing on specific properties of embedding schemes in each embedding domain. This is the subject of the following two sections.

14.4.2 DCT Features for Blind JPEG Steganalysis

If we constrain ourselves to the JPEG format, it makes sense to calculate the features directly in the JPEG domain rather than from the spatial representation, because the embedding changes are lumped in this domain. Moreover, such features would enable more straightforward interpretation of the influence of individual features on detection, as well as easier formulation of design principles for more secure JPEG steganography. The process of calibration described in Section 14.3.3 can be used to decrease features' image-to-image variations. The feature description is taken from Fridrich [24], and the experimental results are from Fridrich and Pevny [22].

The construction of calibrated features proceeds in the following manner (follow Figure 14.5). A vector functional F is applied to the stego JPEG image J_1. This functional could be the global DCT coefficient histogram, a co-occurrence matrix, spatial blockiness, etc. The stego-image J_1 is decompressed to the spatial domain, cropped by 4 pixels in each direction, and recompressed with the same quantization

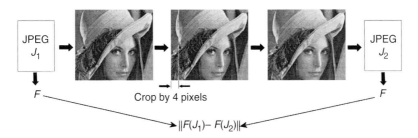

FIGURE 14.5:   Calibrated features are obtained from (vector) functionals F.

table as J_1 to obtain J_2. The same vector functional F is then applied to J_2. The calibrated feature f is obtained as an L_1 norm of the difference

$$f = \|F(J_1) - F(J_2)\|_{L_1}. \tag{14.17}$$

The first set of functionals is formed by the global DCT histogram, histograms of individual DCT modes, and dual histograms. Suppose the stego JPEG file is represented with a DCT coefficient array $d_k(i, j)$ and the quantization matrix $Q(i, j)$, $i, j = 1, \ldots, 8$. The calibration process is quite sensitive to double compression. Thus, for double compressed images, an estimation of the previously used quantization table must be incorporated in the calibration as discussed at the end of Section 14.3.3.

The first set of functionals is formed by the global DCT histogram and histograms of individual DCT modes. Suppose the stego JPEG file is represented with a DCT coefficient array $d_k(i, j)$ and the quantization matrix $Q(i, j)$, $i, j = 1, \ldots, 8$, $k = 1, \ldots, B$, where $d_k(i, j)$ denotes the (i, j)th quantized DCT coefficient in the kth block (there are total of B-blocks). The global histogram of all $64k$ DCT coefficients will be denoted as H_r, where $r = L, \ldots, R$, $L = \min_{k,i,j} d_k(i, j)$ and $R = \max_{k,i,j} d_k(i, j)$. For a fixed DCT mode (i, j), let $h_r^{ij}, r = L, \ldots, R$, denote the individual histogram of values $d_k(i, j)$, $k = 1, \ldots, B$.

For a fixed coefficient value d, the dual histogram for d is an 8×8 matrix g_{ij}^d:

$$g_{ij}^d = \sum_{k=1}^{B} \delta(d, d_k(i,j)), \tag{14.18}$$

where $\delta(u,v) = 1$ if $u = v$ and 0 otherwise. In other words, g_{ij}^d is the number of how many times the value d occurs as the (i, j)th DCT coefficient over all B-blocks. The dual histogram captures the distribution of a given coefficient value d among different DCT modes. Note that if a steganographic method preserves all individual histograms, it also preserves all dual histograms and vice versa.

If the DCT coefficients from different blocks were independent, then any embedding scheme that preserves their first order statistic would be undetectable by Cachin's definition of steganographic security. However, because natural images can exhibit higher order correlations over distances larger than 8 pixels, individual DCT modes from neighboring blocks are not independent. Thus, we add features that capture inter-block dependencies because they will likely be violated by most steganographic algorithms.

Let I_r and I_c denote the vectors of block indexes while scanning the image "by rows" and "by columns," respectively. The first functional capturing inter-block dependency is the "variation" V defined as

$$V = \frac{\sum_{i,j=1}^{8} \sum_{k=1}^{|I_r|-1} |d_{I_r(k)}(i,j) - d_{I_r(k+1)}(i,j)| + \sum_{i,j=1}^{8} \sum_{k=1}^{|I_c|-1} |d_{I_c(k)}(i,j) - d_{I_c(k+1)}(i,j)|}{|I_r| + |I_c|}$$

(14.19)

Because most steganographic techniques in some sense add entropy to the array of quantized DCT coefficients, the variation V is more likely to increase than decrease.

Embedding changes are also likely to increase the discontinuities along the 8×8 block boundaries. Because this observation has proven very useful in steganalysis in the past [57], two blockiness measures $B_\alpha, \alpha = 1, 2$, are added to the set of functionals. The blockiness is calculated from the decompressed JPEG image and thus represents an "integral measure" of inter-block dependency over all DCT modes over the whole image:

$$B_\alpha = \frac{\sum_{i=1}^{\lfloor(M-1)/8\rfloor} \sum_{j=1}^{N} |x_{8i,j} - x_{8i+1,j}|^\alpha + \sum_{j=1}^{\lfloor(N-1)/8\rfloor} \sum_{i=1}^{M} |x_{i,8j} - x_{i,8j+1}|^\alpha}{N \lfloor(M-1)/8\rfloor + M \lfloor(N-1)/8\rfloor}$$

(14.20)

In Franz (20), M and N are image dimensions, and x_{ij} are gray-scale values of the decompressed JPEG image.

The final three functionals are calculated from the co-occurrence matrix of neighboring DCT coefficients. Recalling that $L \le d_k(i, j) \le R$, the co-occurrence matrix C is a square $D \times D$ matrix, $D = R - L + 1$, defined as follows:

$$C_{st} = \frac{\sum_{k=1}^{|I_r|-1} \sum_{i,j=1}^{8} \delta\left(s, d_{I_r(k)}(i,j)\right) \delta\left(t, d_{I_r(k+1)}(i,j)\right)}{|I_r| + |I_c|}$$
$$+ \frac{\sum_{k=1}^{|I_c|-1} \sum_{i,j=1}^{8} \delta\left(s, d_{I_c(k)}(i,j)\right) \delta\left(t, d_{I_c(k+1)}(i,j)\right)}{|I_r| + |I_c|}$$

(14.21)

The co-occurrence matrix describes the distribution of pairs of neighboring DCT coefficients. It usually has a sharp peak at $(0,0)$ and then quickly falls off. Let $C(J_1)$ and $C(J_2)$ be the co-occurrence matrices for the JPEG image J_1 and its calibrated version J_2, respectively. Due to the approximate symmetry of C_{st} around $(s, t) = (0, 0)$, the differences $C_{st}(J_1) - C_{st}(J_2)$ for $(s, t) \epsilon \{(0,1), (1,0), (-1,0), (0,-1)\}$

are strongly positively correlated. The same is true for the group $(s, t) \epsilon \{(1,1), (-1,1), (1,-1), (-1,-1)\}$. For practically all steganographic schemes, the embedding changes to DCT coefficients are essentially perturbations by some small value. Thus, the co-occurrence matrix for the embedded image can be obtained as a convolution $C * P(p)$, where P is the probability distribution of the embedding distortion, which depends on the relative message length p. This means that the values of the co-occurrence matrix $C * P(p)$ will be more "spread out." To quantify this spreading, the following three quantities are taken as *features*:

$$N_{00} = C_{0,0}(J_1) - C_{0,0}(J_2)$$

$$N_{01} = C_{0,1}(J_1) - C_{0,1}(J_2) + C_{1,0}(J_1) - C_{1,0}(J_2) + C_{-1,0}(J_1) - C_{-1,0}(J_2)$$
$$+ C_{0,-1}(J_1) - C_{0,-1}(J_2) \tag{14.22}$$

$$N_{11} = C_{1,1}(J_1) - C_{1,1}(J_2) + C_{1,-1}(J_1) - C_{1,-1}(J_2) + C_{-1,1}(J_1)$$
$$- C_{-1,1}(J_2) + C_{-1,-1}(J_1) - C_{-1,-1}(J_2).$$

The final set of 23 functionals (the last three are directly features) is summarized in Table 14.2.

To show the performance of these features for detection of individual stego-algorithms, separate support vector machine classifiers were built to distinguish between cover images and stego-images for F5, OutGuess version 0.2, Model-Based Steganography (MB1) [60], Model-Based Steganography with deblocking (MB2), Steghide (http://steghide.sourceforge.net/), and JP Hide & Seek (http://linux01.gwdg.de/%7Ealatham/stego.html) (see Table 14.3). The SVM was trained on 2700 cover images and 2700 stego-images (all images were obtained in the raw format using various digital cameras). For each algorithm with the

Table 14.2: List of 23 calibrated DCT features.

Functional/feature name	Functional F
Global histogram	$H/\|\|H\|\|_{L_1}$
Individual histograms for 5 DCT modes	$\dfrac{h^{21}}{\|\|h^{21}\|\|_{L_1}}, \dfrac{h^{31}}{\|\|h^{31}\|\|_{L_1}}, \dfrac{h^{12}}{\|\|h^{12}\|\|_{L_1}}, \dfrac{h^{22}}{\|\|h^{22}\|\|_{L_1}}, \dfrac{h^{13}}{\|\|h^{13}\|\|_{L_1}}$
Dual histograms for 11 DCT values $(-5, \ldots, 5)$	$\dfrac{g^{-5}}{\|\|g^{-5}\|\|_{L_1}}, \dfrac{g^{-4}}{\|\|g^{-4}\|\|_{L_1}}, \ldots, \dfrac{g^{4}}{\|\|g^{4}\|\|_{L_1}}, \dfrac{g^{5}}{\|\|g^{5}\|\|_{L_1}}$
Variation	V
L_1 and L_2 blockiness	B_1, B_2
Co-occurrences	N_{00}, N_{01}, N_{11} (features, not functionals)

Table 14.3:   Detection of stego-images and false alarms for DCT features for six JPEG stego-algorithms.

Classifier	Detection %	False positives %
Cover vs. F5	98.2	1.8
Cover vs. OutGuess 0.2	99.0	0.2
Cover vs. MB1	98.4	1.4
Cover vs. MB2	98.2	3.8
Cover vs. Steghide	97.4	2.2
Cover vs. JP Hide & Seek	98.2	1.8

exception of MB2, 3×900 images were embedded with 100, 50, and 25%, respectively, of the maximum capacity for each image. When testing MB2, all stego-images were embedded at 30% of the capacity of MB1 as for higher pay-loads the algorithm experienced a high failure to correct blockiness. The width of the Gaussian kernel γ and the penalty parameter C were determined for each method by search on a multiplicative grid $(\gamma, C) \in \{(2^i, 2^j)| \ i = -5, \ldots, 3, \ j = -2, \ldots, 9\}$ using five-fold cross-validation. The decision threshold for the SVM was fixed at the default value of zero. The DCT features were calculated only from the luminance. The embedding was done for a fixed quality factor 75%.

We now use the 23 DCT features to classify stego-images to $c = 5$ classes Cover, F5, OutGuess, MB1, MB2. First, $c(c–1)/2$ two-class SVMs are built that distinguish between each pair of classes. Then, a given image is presented to each two-class SVM, and a histogram of answers is built. The most frequent answer determines the final class. The results of this "Max-Wins" multi-class SVM [56] are shown in Table 14.4. We note that all four cover versus stego-SVMs had their threshold adjusted to give less than 1% of false positives.

14.4.3   Blind Steganalysis in the Spatial Domain

Stego-signals in the spatial domain are, in general, much weaker than in the DCT domain. This translates into a much less favorable Signal-to-Noise Ratio (SNR) for successful detection. Recently, several new approaches to steganalysis of additive noise embedding based on classifiers [32], signal estimation methods [63], and their combinations [34] were proposed by various researchers. In this chapter, we very briefly explain two recent approaches.

We follow the exposition by Ker [43], whose work is based on the approach originally proposed by Harmsen and Pearlman [32]. Let $h_c(i)$ be a fraction of pixels with gray-scale value i (h_c is a normalized histogram). It can be easily shown that assuming the stego signal added to the image is a random signal independent of

Table 14.4: Confusion matrix for the "Max Wins" multi-classifier trained on four steganographic algorithms.

Embedded		% of classified as				
	Message	Cover	F5	MB1	MB2	OG
F5	100%	0.75	99.1	0.19	0	0
MB1	100%	0.94	0	98.3	0.19	0.56
OutGuess	100%	0.37	0	0	0	99.63
F5	50%	0.75	97.6	1.31	0.19	0.19
MB1	50%	0.56	1.31	94.9	2.6	0.94
OutGuess	50%	0.56	0.19	0.56	0	98.7
MB2	30%	5.4	2.1	2.6	89.5	0.38
F5	25%	12	79.8	3.8	4.1	0.37
MB1	25%	15.6	3.8	67.2	12.2	0.94
OutGuess	25%	0.94	1.1	3	4.1	90.8
Cover	0%	98.3	0.19	0.56	0.94	1.1

the image with probability mass function $f(j) \geq 0$, $\Sigma_j f(j) = 1$, the histogram of the stego-image is a convolution $h_s = h_c * f$. Thus, for the corresponding Fourier transformed quantities (capital letters),

$$H_s(k) = H_c(k)F(k) \text{ for each } k. \qquad (14.23)$$

The function H_s is called the Histogram Characteristic Function (HCF) of the stego-image. The Center of Mass (COM) of $|H|$,

$$C(H) = \frac{\sum_k k|H(k)|}{\sum_k |H(k)|}, \qquad (14.24)$$

is taken as the feature for blind steganalysis. In Harmsen and Pearlman [32], it is shown that $C(H_s) \leq C(H_c)$, which is intuitive because the stego-image histogram $h_s (= h_c * f)$ is smoother than h_c and thus its Fourier transform has less energy in higher frequencies, which translates into more "mass" concentrated in low frequencies.

For color images, the normalized histogram $h_c(r,g,b)$ is a function of three variables and so is the HCF. Correspondingly, a three-dimensional (3-D) Fourier transform must be used in Fridrich et al. (23).

Harmsen and Pearlman uses the COM (14.24) directly to build a one-dimensional (1-D) feature space for gray-scale images or a 3-D feature space for color images. Recently, Xuan et al. [72] showed that it is beneficial to use several absolute moments of $|H_s|$ instead of just the COM. Ker [42, 43] noticed that the performance of Harmsen and Pearlman's classifier can be markedly improved by further removing the influence of the image content on the COM by calibrating it. They estimate the COM of the cover image from the stego-image resized to half its size by averaging values of 2×2 pixels. It turns out that the resizing produces just the right amount of blurring that enables approximate estimation of the cover image COM of HCF.

Let us denote by $\hat{H}$ and $C(\hat{H})$ the HCF and its COM of the resized image, respectively. The ratio $C(H)/C(\hat{H})$ is taken as the distinguishing feature. The benefit of calibration lies in the fact that the quantities $C(H_s)/C(\hat{H}_s)$ and $C(H_c)/C(\hat{H}_c)$ are better separated than $C(H_s)$ and $C(H_c)$, because for typical cover images $C(H_c) \approx C(\hat{H}_c)$ while $C(H_s) < C(\hat{H}_s)$ for the stego-images.

To further improve the performance of this method for gray-scale images, Ker [42] proposed to work with the color adjacency histogram, which is sparser than the histogram of gray-scale values and thus more sensitive to embedding. The adjacency histogram $h(i,j)$ is defined as the number of horizontal neighboring pixel pairs with gray-scales i and j. This quantity is also sometimes called the co-occurrence matrix [20, 24]. Because of local correlations present in natural images, the adjacency histogram has the largest values on the diagonal and then it quickly falls off. The HCF of the adjacency histogram is now a two-dimensional (2-D) $H(k,l)$, and the COM is defined as

$$C(H) = \frac{\sum_{k,l}(k+l)|H(k,l)|}{\sum_{k,l}|H(k,l)|} \tag{14.25}$$

By comparing the performance of this scheme for ± 1 embedding (LSB matching) to Harmsen and Pearlman's original scheme, Ker showed that using the calibrated COM leads to quite a significant performance improvement, enabling even detection of embedding in gray-scale scans of films. More details and results can be found in Ken [42, 43].

Using a different approach, Holotyak, Fridrich, and Voloshynovskii [34] report results that are quantitatively similar and for some image classes even better. This method works with a noise *residual*, which is an estimate of the stego-signal obtained by denoising [52] the stego-image, rather than with the stego-image itself. This has the advantage of decreasing the influence of the cover image and thus improving the SNR between the stego-signal and the cover image, which enables construction of more sensitive features. Also, instead of the HCF, Holotyak and co-workers use higher order moments of the residual's probability mass function as features.

Holotyak and co-workers report results for several different image databases. The first test was done for 2567 raw, never compressed color images of different dimensions (all larger than 1 megapixel), some stored in the 48-bit TIFF format and some in the 24-bit BMP format acquired by 22 different digital cameras ranging from low-cost cameras to semi-professional cameras. Part of this database was downloaded from the Digital Forensic Image Library (DFIL) (http://www.cs.dartmouth.edu/cgi-bin/cgiwrap/isg/imagedb.py). All images were converted to gray scale, and, when needed, their color depth was decreased to 8 bits.

The second test was performed on 2375 high-resolution, never compressed 1500×2100 scans of films in the 32-bit CMYK TIFF format from the NRCS (Natural Resources Conservation Service) Photo Gallery (http://photogallery.nrcs.usda.gov). Similar to Ker [43], all color images were converted to gray scale and downsampled to 640×480 using bicubic resampling. The results of both tests are shown in Table 14.5 and Figure 14.6.

14.5 THE FUTURE

Blind steganalytic methods are getting increasingly more powerful and sensitive. In my opinion, we will see substantial advancements in this direction in the near future. The biggest advantage I see is the *extensibility* and *modularity* of this approach. Future blind steganalyzers will be quite complex systems consisting of a hierarchy of modules capable of making specialized individual conclusions. For example, given the fact that the reliability of steganalysis substantially depends on the source of the image, it seems natural to add a pre-classification module to the steganalyzer that will first investigate the likely source of the tested image and then forward it to an appropriate set of modules. Feature sets proposed by different authors can be merged, together with statistics derived from targeted analysis, to build a better classifier with superior performance. Advancements in machine learning will also have a direct and immediate positive influence. Moreover,

Table 14.5: False positives at 50% correct detection of stego-images for different message lengths.

Image source	Embedding ratio (bpp)			
	0.25	0.5	0.75	1.0
Digital camera images	16.24%	3.12%	1.17%	0.58%
Scans	28.63%	13.98%	6.57%	3.45%

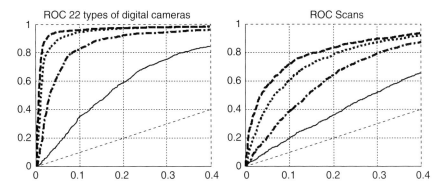

FIGURE 14.6: ROCs showing the percentage of successful detection of stego-objects versus false alarms for ± 1 embedding detection for raw digital camera images (left) and raw scans (right) with different embedding capacities: solid = 0.25 bpp, dash-dotted = 0.5 bpp, dotted = 0.75 bbp, and dashed = 1 bpp.

it seems that the very young field of digital forensics will play an increasingly important role in developing the next generation of steganalyzers because it can provide technology for pre-classification of images into separate sources or identify and estimate the previous processing history of the image (e.g., classes of scans of photographs or films, raw digital camera images, decompressed JPEGs, double compressed images, gamma adjusted images, etc.).

Progress in steganalysis will provide estimates of the steganographic capacity of each image (maximal number of random bits embeddable without causing detectable artifacts). Currently, practical steganalytic methods give upper bounds on steganographic capacity, but so far no lower bounds are known even for fairly simple embedding schemes. Development of more accurate and realistic stochastic models for images will undoubtedly help with solving these problems.

As most steganographic methods are statistical tests, they are subject to fundamental limitations when the available statistics is insufficient, such as small, overcompressed, or extremely noisy images.

Certain concepts, originally developed for a specific embedding method or format, are likely to be extendable to future formats. For example, calibration as used for steganalysis of JPEG images can likely be used for other lossy formats, such as JPEG 2000. This is because any lossy compression must represent images with quantities that exhibit a certain level of "robustness" to small distortion. As long as these quantities are calculated in some fixed coordinate domain, a small perturbation of coordinates and subsequent recompression will provide data for calibration.

Recent advances in JPEG steganalysis made steganography for this format a very challenging task. It is my estimate that all steganographic techniques that start with a JPEG and modify the coefficients to embed more than 2 bits per 8×8 block (in a gray-scale image with medium quality factor) will eventually be broken. This would mean that JPEG images provide a relatively small capacity for communication. A possible way to increase the capacity is to select the DCT coefficients for embedding using side information, such as a high-resolution uncompressed version of an image as in Perturbed Quantization [26].

As the bandwidth on the Internet continues to grow, the ability to communicate large quantities of covert data through audio/video streaming channels will likely increase in importance and thus create a much bigger threat than distribution of relatively small messages through JPEG images. Steganalysts should prepare by directing their attention to large compressed and uncompressed cover objects that include WAV and MP3 audio files or MPEG/AVI video formats. The popularity of the exchange of these files over the Internet and their size make such cover objects ideal for steganographic communication of very large amounts of data. Another emerging environment for steganography is the network traffic and network protocols, such as TCP/IP. It is possible to hide data by slightly varying timings between individual packets or by using redundancy in existing network protocols.

In Section 14.2, a few emerging promising research directions in steganography are listed. One of them is embedding in the unprocessed raw data domain where data samples are independent and contain physical randomness, such as photonic noise due to quantum properties of light or circuit noise [35]. The principle to embed in this domain (at signal acquisition) has a higher chance to succeed than modifying the processed signal (e.g., the JPEG coefficients or 24-bit pixels values in a TIFF file) that already contains many complex dependencies between individual samples.

The second direction is based on interleaving multiple different samplings of the same signal [54]. If the practical problems with acquiring such samplings can be solved, this approach may present the ultimate challenge to steganalysis. Most likely than not, however, it will be just another cycle of a never-ending competition of creative minds on both sides of the fence.

Acknowledgment

The author would like to thank Chet Hosmer for his valuable comments.

REFERENCES

[1] F. Alturki and R. Mersereau. A novel approach for increasing security and data embedding capacity in images for data hiding applications, in *Proc. ITCC*, Las Vegas, pp. 228–233, April 2–4, 2001.

[2] R. J. Anderson and F. A. P. Petitcolas. On the limits of steganography, *IEEE J. Selected Areas in Communications*, Special Issue on Copyright and Privacy Protection, 16(4):474–481, 1998.

[3] I. Avcibas, N. D. Memon, and B. Sankur. Image steganalysis with binary similarity measures, *Proc. ICIP*, 3:645–648, 2002.

[4] I. Avcibas, N. D. Memon, and B. Sankur. Steganalysis using image quality metrics, *Proc. SPIE, Electronic Imaging, Security and Watermarking of Multimedia Contents III*, 4314:523–531, 2001.

[5] R. Böhme. Assessment of steganalytic methods using multiple regression models, in M. Barni et al. (Eds.), Information Hiding, 6th Int. Workshop, LNCS vol. 3727, pp. 278–295.

[6] R. Böhme and A. Westfeld. Breaking Cauchy model-based JPEG steganography with first order statistics, in P. Samarati, P. Ryan, D. Gollmann, and R. Molva (Eds.), *Computer Security—ESORICS 2004. Proc. 9th European Symp. Research in Computer Security*, Sophia Antipolis, France, LNCS vol. 3193, pp. 125–140, 2004.

[7] C. Cachin. An information-theoretic model for steganography, in D. Aucsmith (Ed.), *Information Hiding, 2nd Int. Workshop*, LNCS vol. 1525, pp. 306–318, 1998.

[8] M. U. Celik and G. Sharma. Universal image steganalysis using rate-distortion curves, *Proc. SPIE, Electronic Imaging, Security, Steganography, and Watermarking of Multimedia Contents VI*, 5306:467–476, 2004.

[9] R. Chandramouli and N. D. Memon. On sequential watermark detection, *IEEE Trans. on Signal Processing*, Special Issue on Signal Processing for Data Hiding in Digital Media and Secure Content Delivery, 51(4):1034–1044, 2003.

[10] R. Chandramouli and N. D. Memon. Analysis of LSB based image steganography techniques, in *Proc. ICIP*, Thessaloniki, Greece, October 7–10, 2001.

[11] I. Cox, J. A. Bloom, and M. L. Miller. *Digital Watermarking*, Morgan Kaufman, San Francisco, CA, 2001.

[12] R. Crandall. Some Notes on Steganography, posted on Steganography Mailing List, 1998. Available at http://os.inf.tu-dresden.de/~westfeld/crandall.pdf.

[13] S. Craver. On Public-Key Steganography in the Presence of Active Warden, Technical Report RC 20931, IBM, 1997.

[14] S. Dumitrescu and X. Wu. LSB steganalysis based on higher-order statistics, in *Proc. ACM Multimedia and Security Workshop*, pp. 25–32, New York City, August 1–2, 2005.

[15] S. Dumitrescu, X. Wu, and Z. Wang. Detection of LSB steganography via sample pair analysis, in F.A.P. Petitcolas (Ed.), *Information Hiding, 5th Int. Workshop*, LNCS vol. 2578, pp. 355–372, 2003.

[16] S. Dumitrescu, X. Wu, and N. Memon. On steganalysis of random embedding in continuous-tone images, in *Proc. ICIP*, Rochester, NY, pp. 324–339, September 22–25, 2002.

[17] J. Eggers, R. Bäuml, and B. Girod. A communications approach to steganography, *Proc. SPIE, Electronic Imaging, Security and Watermarking of Multimedia Contents IV*, Santa Clara, CA, pp. 26–49, January 21–24, 2002.

[18] Z. Fan and R.L. de Queiroz. Identification of bitmap compression history: JPEG detection and quantizer estimation, *IEEE Trans. Image Processing*, 12(2):230–235, 2003.

[19] H. Farid and S. Lyu. Detecting hidden messages using higher-order statistics and support vector machines, in F.A.P. Petitcolas (Ed.), *Information Hiding, 5th Int. Workshop*, LNCS vol. 2578, pp. 340–354, 2002.

[20] E. Franz. Steganography preserving statistical properties, in F.A.P. Petitcolas (Ed.), *Information Hiding. 5th Int. Workshop*, LNCS vol. 2578, pp. 278–294, 2002.

[21] J. Fridrich, M. Goljan, and D. Soukal. Efficient wet paper codes, in M. Barni et al. (Eds.), Information Hiding, 6th Int.Workshop, LNCS vol. 3727, pp. 204–218.

[22] J. Fridrich and T. Pevny. Towards multi-class blind steganalyzer for JPEG images, IWDW, 2005, LNCS vol. 3710, Springer-verlag, New York, pp. 39–53, 2005.

[23] J. Fridrich, M. Goljan, D. Soukal, and T. Holotyak. Forensic steganalysis: Determining the stego key in spatial domain steganography, *Proc. SPIE, Electronic Imaging, Security, Steganography, and Watermarking of Multimedia Contents VII*, 5681:631–642, 2005.

[24] J. Fridrich. Feature-based steganalysis for JPEG images and its implications for future design of steganographic schemes, in J. Fridrich (Ed.), *Information Hiding, 6th Int. Workshop*, LNCS vol. 3200, pp. 67–81, 2004.

[25] J. Fridrich and M. Goljan. On estimation of secret message length in LSB steganography in spatial domain, *Proc. SPIE, Electronic Imaging, Security, Steganography, and Watermarking of Multimedia Contents VI*, 5306:23–34, 2004.

[26] J. Fridrich, M. Goljan, and D. Soukal. Perturbed quantization steganography with wet paper codes, in *Proc. ACM Multimedia Security Workshop*, Magdeburg, Germany, pp. 4–15, September 20–21, 2004.

[27] J. Fridrich, M. Goljan, and D. Soukal. Higher order statistical steganalysis of palette images, in *Proc. SPIE, Electronic Imaging, Security, Steganography, and Watermarking of Multimedia Contents V*, Santa Clara, CA, pp. 178–190, January 21–24, 2003.

[28] J. Fridrich, M. Goljan, D. Hogea, and D. Soukal. Quantitative steganalysis of digital images: Estimating the secret message length, *ACM Multimedia Systems J.*, Special issue on Multimedia Security, 9(3):288–302, 2003.

[29] J. Fridrich and M. Goljan. Secure digital image steganography using stochastic modulation, *Proc. SPIE, Electronic Imaging, Security, Steganography, and Watermarking of Multimedia Contents V*, 5020:191–202, 2003.

[30] J. Fridrich, M. Goljan, and R. Du. Detecting LSB steganography in color and grayscale images, *Magazine of IEEE Multimedia, Special Issue on Security*, October-November:22–28, 2001.

[31] J. Fridrich, M. Goljan, and R. Du. Steganalysis based on JPEG compatibility, in *Proc. SPIE Multimedia Systems and Applications IV*, Denver, CO, 4518:275–280, August 21–22, 2001.

[32] J.J. Harmsen and W.A. Pearlman. Steganalysis of additive noise modelable information hiding, in *Proc. SPIE, Electronic Imaging, Security, Steganography, and Watermarking of Multimedia Contents V*, Santa Clara, CA, 5020:131–142, January 21–24, 2003.

[33] M.T. Hogan, G.C.M. Silvestre, and N.J. Hurley. Performance evaluation of blind steganalysis classifiers, *Proc. SPIE, Electronic Imaging, Security, Steganography, and Watermarking of Multimedia Contents VI*, 5306:58–69, 2004.

[34] T. Holotyak, J. Fridrich, and S. Voloshynovskii. Blind statistical steganalysis of additive steganography using wavelet higher order statistics, in *9th IFIP*

TC-6 TC-11 Conf. Communications and Multimedia Security, Salzburg, Austria, September 19–21, 2005.

[35] J.R. Janesick, *Scientific Charge-Coupled Devices*, SPIE PRESS Monograph vol. PM83, SPIE–The International Society for Optical Engineering, January 2001.

[36] N.F. Johnson and S. Jajodia. Steganography: Seeing the unseen, *IEEE Computer*, February:26–34, 1998.

[37] N.F. Johnson and S. Jajodia. Steganalysis of images created using current steganography software, in D. Aucsmith (Ed.), *Information Hiding. 2nd Int. Workshop*, LNCS vol. 1525, pp. 273−289, 1998.

[38] D. Kahn, *The Codebreakers: The Comprehensive History of Secret Communication from Ancient Times to the Internet*, Revised Edition, Scribners, New York, 1996.

[39] M. Karahan, U. Topkara, M. Atallah, C. Taskiran, E. Lin, and E. Delp. A hierarchical protocol for increasing the stealthiness of steganographic methods, in *Proc. ACM Multimedia and Security Workshop*, Magdeburg, Germany, pp. 16–24, September 20–21, 2004.

[40] S. Katzenbeisser and F.A.P. Petitcolas. Defining security in steganographic systems, *Proc. SPIE, Electronic Imaging, Security and Watermarking of Multimedia Contents IV*, 4675:50–56, 2002.

[41] A. Ker. A general framework for structural analysis of LSB replacement, in M. Barni et al. (Eds.), Information Hiding, 6th Int.Workshop, LNCS vol. 3727, pp. 296–311.

[42] A. Ker. Resampling and the detection of LSB matching in color bitmaps, *Proc. SPIE, Electronic Imaging, Security, Steganography, and Watermarking of Multimedia Contents VII*, 5681:1–15, 2005.

[43] A. Ker. Steganalysis of LSB matching in gray-scale images, *IEEE Signal Processing Letters*, 12(6):441–444, June 2005.

[44] A. Ker. Quantitative evaluation of pairs and RS steganalysis, *Proc. SPIE, Electronic Imaging, Security, Steganography, and Watermarking of Multimedia Contents VI*, 5306:83–97, 2004.

[45] A. Ker. Improved detection of LSB steganography in gray-scale images, in J. Fridrich (Ed.), *Information Hiding, 6th Int. Workshop*, LNCS vol. 3200, pp. 97–115, 2004.

[46] M. Kharrazi, H. T. Sencar, and N. D. Memon. Benchmarking steganographic and steganalytic techniques, *Proc. SPIE, Electronic Imaging, Security, Steganography, and Watermarking of Multimedia Contents VII*, 5681:252–263, 2005.

[47] K. Lee, C. Jung, S. Lee, and J. Lim. New distribution model and its application for steganalysis, in M. Barni et al. (Eds.), Information Hiding, 6th Int.Workshop, LNCS vol. 3727.

[48] P. Lu, X. Luo, Q. Tang, and L. Shen. An improved sample pairs method for detection of LSB embedding, in J. Fridrich (Ed.), *Information Hiding, 6th Int. Workshop*, LNCS vol. 3200, pp. 116–127, 2004.

[49] J. Lukáš and J. Fridrich. Estimation of primary quantization matrix in double compressed JPEG images, *Proc. DFRWS 2003*, Cleveland, OH, August 5–8, 2003.

[50] S. Lyu and H. Farid. Steganalysis using color wavelet statistics and one-class support vector machines, *Proc. SPIE, Electronic Imaging, Security, Steganography, and Watermarking of Multimedia Contents VI*, 5306:35–45, 2004.

[51] L.M. Marvel, C.G. Boncelet, and C.T. Retter. Reliable blind information hiding for images, in D. Aucsmith (Ed.), *Information Hiding, 2nd Int. Workshop*, LNCS vol. 1525, pp. 48–61, 1998.

[52] M.K. Mihcak, I. Kozintsev, K. Ramchandran, and P. Moulin. Low-complexity image denoising based on statistical modeling of wavelet coefficients, *IEEE Signal Processing Letters*, 6(12):300–303, 1999.

[53] F.A.P. Petitcolas and S. Katzenbeisser (eds.). *Information Hiding Techniques for Steganography and Digital Watermarking*, Artech House, Norwood, MA, 2000.

[54] K. Petrowski, M. Kharrazi, H.T. Sencar, and N.D. Memon. Psteg: Steganographic embedding through patching, *Proc. ICASSP* 2005, Philadelphia, March 18–23, 2005.

[55] B. Pfitzmann. Information hiding terminology, in R.J. Anderson (Ed.), *Information Hiding, 1st Int. Workshop*, LNCS vol. 1174, pp. 347–350, 1996.

[56] J. Platt, N. Cristianini, and J. Shawe-Taylor. Large margin DAGs for multiclass classification, in S.A. Solla, T.K. Leen, and K.-R. Mueller (Eds), *Proc. Advances in Neural Information Processing Systems*, 12:547–553, 2000.

[57] N. Provos. Defending against statistical steganalysis, *10th USENIX Security Symposium*, Washington, DC, 2001. http://www.usenix.org/events/secϕ1/index.html.

[58] N. Provos and P. Honeyman. Detecting steganographic content on the internet, CITI Technical Report 01-11, August 2001.

[59] A.R. Rao, G.W. Braudaway, and F.C. Mintzer. Automatic visible watermarking of images, *Proc. SPIE, Electronic Imaging*, 3314:110–121, 1998.

[60] P. Sallee. Model based steganography, in T. Kalker, I.J. Cox, and Yong Man Ro (Eds.), *Int. Workshop Digital Watermarking*, LNCS vol. 2939, pp. 154–167, 2004.

[61] T. Sharp. An implementation of key-based digital signal steganography, in I. S. Moskowitz (Ed.), *Information Hiding, 4th Int. Workshop*, LNCS vol. 2137, pp. 13–26, 2001.

[62] G.J. Simmons. The prisoners' problem and the subliminal channel, in D. Chaum (Ed.), *Advances in Cryptology: Proceedings of Crypto 83*, Plenum Press, New York, pp. 51–67, 1984.

[63] D. Soukal, J. Fridrich, and M. Goljan. Maximum likelihood estimation of secret message length embedded using PMK steganography in spatial domain, *Proc. SPIE, Electronic Imaging, Security, Steganography, and Watermarking of Multimedia Contents VII*, 5681:595–606, 2005.

[64] S. Trivedi and R. Chandramouli. Secret key estimation in sequential steganography, *IEEE Trans. Signal Processing*, Supplement on Secure Media, 53(2):746–757, February 2005.

[65] R. Tzschoppe, R. Bäuml, J.B. Huber, and A. Kaup. Steganographic system based on higher-order statistics, in *Proc. SPIE, Electronic Imaging, Security and Watermarking of Multimedia Contents V*, Santa Clara, CA, 5020:156–166, January 21–24, 2003.

[66] X. Yu, Y. Wang, and T. Tan. On estimation of secret message length in J-steg-like steganography, *Proc. Int. Conf. Pattern Recognition*, 4:673–676, 2004.

[67] A. Westfeld and R. Böhme. Exploiting preserved statistics for steganalysis, in J. Fridrich (Ed.), *Information Hiding, 6th Int. Workshop*, LNCS vol. 3200, pp. 82–96, 2005.

[68] A. Westfeld. Detecting low embedding rates, in F.A.P. Petitcolas (Ed.), *Information Hiding, 5th Int. Workshop*, LNCS vol. 2578, pp. 324–339, 2002.

[69] A. Westfeld. High capacity despite better steganalysis (F5–A Steganographic Algorithm), in I. S. Moskowitz (Ed.), *Information Hiding, 4th Int. Workshop*. LNCS vol. 2137, pp. 289–302, 2001.

[70] A. Westfeld and A. Pfitzmann. Attacks on steganographic systems, in A. Pfitzmann (Ed.), *Information Hiding, 3rd Int. Workshop*, LNCS vol. 1768, pp. 61–75, 2000.

[71] P.W. Wong, H. Chen, and Z. Tang. On steganalysis of plus-minus one embedding in continuous-tone images, *Proc. SPIE, Electronic Imaging, Security, Steganography, and Watermarking of Multimedia Contents VII*, 5681:643–652, 2005.

[72] G. Xuan, Y.Q. Shi, J. Gao, D. Zou, C. Yang, Z. Zhang, P. Chai, C. Chen, and W. Chen. Steganalysis based on multiple features formed by statistical moments of wavelet characteristic functions, in M. Barni et al. (Eds.), Information Hiding, 6th Workshop, LNCS vol. 3727.

[73] T. Zhang and X. Ping. A fast and effective steganalytic technique against JSteg-like algorithms, in *Proc. Symposium on Applied Computing*, Melbourne, FL, pp. 307–311, 2003.

[74] T. Zhang and X. Ping. A new approach to reliable detection of LSB steganography in natural images, *Signal Processing*, 83(10):2085–2094, 2003.

[75] J. Zöllner, H. Federrath, H. Klimant, A. Pfitzmann, R. Piotraschke, A. Westfeld, G. Wicke, and G. Wolf. Modeling the security of steganographic systems, in D. Aucsmith (Ed.), *Information Hiding, 2nd Int. Workshop*, LNCS vol. 1525, pp. 344–354, 1998.

[76] Steganography software for Windows, http://www.stegoarchive.com/.

15

Passive-blind Image Forensics

Tian-Tsong Ng, Shih-Fu Chang, Ching-Yung Lin, and Qibin Sun

15.1 INTRODUCTION

One of the key characteristics of digital images with a discrete representation is its pliability to manipulation. Therefore, even back in 1989, the sesquicentennial year for photography when digital images were gaining popularity, 10% of all color photographs published in United States were actually digitally altered and retouched, according to *The Wall Street Journal* [1]. The recent well-known tampered images are the Iraq soldier picture of *The Los Angeles Times* (March 2004) and the Internet image showing Jane Fonda and John Kerry sharing the same speaker platform (February 2004).[1] The advanced digital image processing techniques provided by image editing software such as Adobe Photoshop are the catalyst for the prevalence of the manipulated digital images in the public domain, which is evident in Web sites such as www.worth1000.com, which is a creative competition and Photoshop contest sites hosting as many as 178,582 Photoshop-created images as of October 2005. Besides image compositing, computer graphics nowadays

---

[1]The L.A.Times image can be found at http://www.sree.net/teaching/lateditors.html, and the John Kerry image can be found at http://www.camerairaq.com/2003/02/john_kerry_and_.html.

can also produce image forgery of high photorealism. To showcase the high photorealism of computer graphics which rivals that of real camera images, a three-dimensional (3-D) graphics company has set up a web site, www.fakeorfoto.com, for challenging viewers to distinguish computer graphics and camera images.

Traditionally, a photograph implies truth. However, a similar faith on digital images is diminished due to the ease of manipulation. Unlike text, images provide an effective and natural communication media for humans, as humans often need no special training to understand the image content. Therefore, being able to verify the credibility of digital images and perform image forensics can protect the truthfulness of digital images. Today, digital images have already been heavily used for news reporting, insurance claim investigation, forensic or criminal investigation, legal proceeding, and national intelligence analysis. As such, image forensics would have a great impact in the above-mentioned application domain.

The main function of image forensics is to assess the authenticity and the origin of images. Therefore, a trustworthy digital image is a main concern for image forensics. Back in 1993, the idea of a trustworthy camera [2] was proposed as a way to make the trustworthiness of digital images accountable. A trustworthy camera embeds a digital watermark on an image at the instant of its acquisition, and any later tampering of the image can be detected based on the changes on the digital watermark. However, the realization of the trustworthy camera idea requires the camera manufacturers to concur on a common standard protocol, while the consumers need to accept the reduced image quality due to the embedding of a digital watermark. Apart from that, the most basic worry lies on the fundamental security of digital watermarks, as evident from the Secure Digital Music Initiative (SDMI) fiasco [3], where the proposed audio watermarking system was swiftly hacked by a coalition of cryptography and watermarking researchers from Princeton University, Xerox PARC, and Rice University. Digital watermarking is considered as an active approach, as it requires a known signal to be embedded onto an image for image forensics to be possible. In contrast, *Passive-Blind Image Forensics* (PBIF) was proposed [4, 5, 6, 7, 8, 9, 10], with a goal of detecting image alteration or identifying the image source without any prior measurement and registration of the image including the availability of the original reference image. At this time when the digital image alteration techniques have become so versatile, the burgeoning of PBIF research is indeed timely.

We begin with an overview of PBIF in Section 15.2, where the two main functions of PBIF, i.e., passive-blind image forgery detection and passive-blind image source identification, are identified. The overview also covers a brief history and a general description of image forgery creation. Then, in Section 15.3, we provide a detailed review of the work in image forgery detection and image source identification. Before concluding, we describe the resources and the challenges for PBIF.

15.2 OVERVIEW OF PBIF

In general, PBIF is concerned with the following two main problems:

1. Image forgery (alteration) detection (Section 15.3.1)
2. Image source identification (Section 15.3.3)

As most of the image forgery detection techniques are associated to the specific image forgery creation techniques, we begin with a short history of image forgery creation in Subsection 15.2.1, followed by a brief description of the image forgery creation process in Subsection 15.2.2. (more details are in the Appendix)

15.2.1 The History of Image Forgery Creation

Just within a few decades from the birth of photography, various methods had already been invented for altering images. The combination print was one of the earliest forms of image forgery creation techniques, where darkroom skills are used to print multiple fragments of an image onto a single sheet of photographic paper. One of the earliest well-known combination prints was Oscar G. Reijlander's *The Two Ways of Life* (1857), which used up to 30 images.[2] Later, in the early twentieth century, photomontage, a cut-and-paste composite of image fragments, gained popularity, mainly for surreal art, political satires, and many other purposes. Both combination print and photomontage are technically demanding and time consuming, and their application is often detectable.

15.2.2 Image Forgery Creation in Modern Times

With the wide availability of the powerful image editing tool, such as Adobe Photoshop, the similar image alteration functions described in the previous section can be performed in the digital domain with a much easier process while resulting in a much higher verisimilitude. In general, the image forgery creation process involves selection, transformation, composition of the image fragments, and retouching of the final image as shown in Figure 15.1. The process often begins with extracting a fragment or a 3-D object model from an image. The forgery creators can then fuse the transformed image fragment or the image portion generated from the transformed 3D model into another image using techniques such as matting for coherent-looking composition. Finally, the composite image is retouched to remove the remaining artifacts. This stage may involve the removal of certain objects from the image, which is sometimes known as *reverse cropping*. The Appendix provides a glimpse of the state-of-the-art image editing techniques.

---

[2] The image of the combination print *The Two Ways of Life* by Oscar G. Reijlander can be found at http://www.bradley.edu/exhibit96/about/twoways.html.

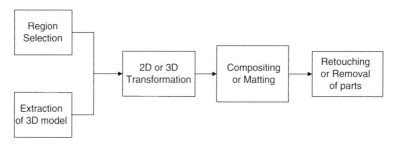

FIGURE 15.1:   The process for image forgery creation.

15.3   FORGERY DETECTION AND SOURCE IDENTIFICATION

In this section, we provide a detailed description of the two main problems in PBIF, i.e., image forgery detection and source identification.

15.3.1   Passive-blind Image Forgery Detection

Just like the adversarial roles of the spy and the counter-intelligence agent in an espionage game, the forgery creators and the forgery detectors are opponents, as shown in Figure 15.2. The goal of the forgery creators is to create image forgery as a fabrication of the truth, while the forgery detectors try to uncover any possible act of fabrication by assessing the *authenticity* of a given image. Examples of image forgery are the digital photomontage and the images with removed objects.

The concept of image authenticity is essentially based on the image characteristic. It is meaningless to talk about the authenticity of a random pixel image, as it has no meaningful characteristic. In contrast, natural-scene images occupy a highly regularized subspace in the entire image space; if one tries to generate images using

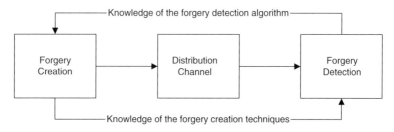

FIGURE 15.2:   The setting for the passive-blind image forgery detection problem.

a random pixel generator, the chance of getting a natural-scene image is very small. Therefore, an authentic characteristic can be defined on natural-scene images. As the authenticity of natural-scene images is related to the natural scenes and the imaging process, we can define its authenticity based on two distinct qualities, i.e., the *imaging process quality* and the *natural-scene quality*.

The imaging process quality is due to the image acquisition devices. For instance, a typical Charge Coupled Device (CCD) digital camera imposes effects of lens distortion, demosaicing, white balancing, non-linear gamma correction, and sensor noise on the images it produces. One can estimate the above-mentioned effects on an image in order to verify the authenticity of a camera image and distinguish it from a computer graphic image which has not undergone the camera acquisition process [11].

The natural-scene quality is entailed by the physics of the real-world light transport involved in the image formation process. An image is essentially a snapshot of the light field resulting from the complex interaction between the illumination sources and the objects. The physical process, for instance, imposes a relationship between the orientation of the shadow and the direction of the illumination sources. Therefore, by checking the consistency of the lighting directions estimated independently from the surface shading at two different locations, one can verify whether an image is produced by a composition [12].

The adversarial game between image forgery creators and image forgery detectors is made possible by the probabilistic nature of the natural-scene image authentic characteristic as well as the limited knowledge of its distribution. If the distribution of the natural-scene images is deterministic and fully known, then an image forgery creator can always produce perfect image forgery which is indistinguishable from an authentic natural-scene image. To construct a complete description of natural-scene images, one needs to have a large amount of images to form an empirical distribution in the high-dimensional image space, and this is difficult to achieve. As an approximation, one can model the marginal distribution or low-order joint distribution of the transformed images as the natural image statistics [13]. The resulting statistical image model is partial and incomplete. This is good news for image forgery detectors, as it is hard for the opponent to check whether an image forgery is totally free of the forgery telltale signs. On the other hand, it makes passive-blind image forgery detection difficult. Without a complete model for the natural-scene images, the knowledge of the opponent's modus operandi would become a great advantage, as shown in Figure 15.2. This implies that image forgery detectors should prevent image forgery creators from having full knowledge of the detection algorithm and, at the same time, should understand the image forgery creation process well.

Although the above discussion focuses on natural-scene images, the same principle can be applied to other types of images, such as aerial, X-ray, and microscopic images.

15.3.2   Passive-blind Image Forgery Detection Techniques

From the formulation of image forgery detection in Section 15.3.1, two approaches are possible for image forgery detection, i.e., detecting the authentic characteristics of images and detecting the telltale characteristics specific to the image forgery creation techniques.

Detecting Image Authenticity Quality

The authentic imaging process quality is a characteristic of the imaging devices, such as digital cameras and scanners, and this quality can be different for various devices. We hereupon focus on the CCD digital camera, which is the most popular device for producing digital images. A CCD digital camera can be considered as a pipeline process, as shown in Figure 15.3. The following subsections review the work on image forgery detection using different characteristics of the digital camera, as well as the natural-scene authentic characteristics.

Optical Low-pass of the Camera Lens

Ng, Chang, and Sun [7] detected the presence of abrupt discontinuities in an image or, conversely, the absence of the optical low-pass property as a telltale sign for identifying spliced images. The spliced images are produced by a simple cut-and-paste operation without any sophisticated matting or blending (refer to the Appendix) in the compositing step. For detecting the abrupt splicing discontinuity, a higher order moment spectrum, bicoherence, is used. Bicoherence is a normalized third-order moment spectrum, and its mathematical form for a

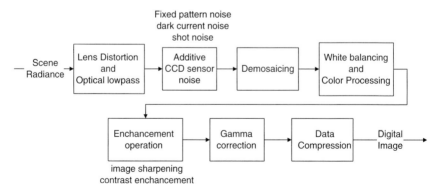

FIGURE 15.3:   CCD camera imaging pipeline.

one-dimensional (1-D) signal with a Fourier spectrum $X(\omega)$ is given by

$$b(\omega_1, \omega_2) = \frac{E\left[X(\omega_1)X(\omega_2)X^*(\omega_1 + \omega_2)\right]}{\sqrt{E\left[|X(\omega_1)X(\omega_2)|^2\right] E\left[|X(\omega_1 + \omega_2)|^2\right]}}. \tag{15.1}$$

Note that the normalization factor is the upper bound for the Cauchy-Schwartz inequality; therefore, $|b(\omega_1, \omega_2)|$ is between 0 and 1. Another important property of bicoherence is its sensitivity to a phenomena called *Quadratic Phase Coupling* (QPC), i.e., the simultaneous presence of three frequency harmonics at ω_1, ω_2, and $\omega_1 + \omega_2$, respectively, with a phase ϕ_1, ϕ_2, and $\phi_1 + \phi_2$ (the phases are coupled and hence not random). Note that at (ω_1, ω_2), which corresponds to a harmonic triplet with QPC, the bicoherence has a zero phase. However, it is shown in Ng and Chang [6] that the bicoherence is sensitive to the splicing discontinuity due to a variant of QPC which induces a $\pm\frac{\pi}{2}$ phase for the bicoherence instead of the zero phase. This theoretical result is validated experimentally.

When only the bicoherence features are used for spliced image detection, the detection accuracy evaluated on the "Columbia Image Splicing Detection Evaluation Dataset" [14] is only 62% (50% for a random guess). To improve the detection performance, a functional texture decomposition method is used to decompose an image into a gross-structure component and a fine-texture component. The gross-structure component is used to approximate the authentic reference of an image (the hypothetically authentic image). By incorporating the discrepancy between an image and its authentic reference, the detection rate improves from 62% to 71%.

Demosaicing

Apart from the optical effect, the correlation between the image pixel values can also be useful for image forgery detection. The consumer CCD digital camera captures spectral energy corresponding to the red (R), blue (B), and green (G) colors at the same time with a single CCD sensor array by distributing the sensors in the array among the RGB color channels. The allocation of the sensors results in a partial sampling of the color signal in the sensor array. The process of designing the sensor allocation is likened to mosaicing, and the most common sensor allocation pattern is the Bayer pattern as shown in Figure 15.4. To obtain a full array of pixel values for the RGB color channels, the missing samples are interpolated from the available samples, and this operation is called demosaicing. The interpolation process will inevitably introduce a statistical correlation between the interpolated pixels and the original pixels.

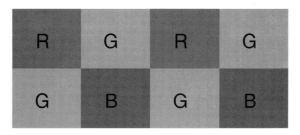

FIGURE 15.4: Bayer pattern for the camera sensor array.

In Popescu and Farid [15], the demosaicing operation is modeled by a linear interpolation as shown below:

$$I(x, y) = \sum_{u,v \in \Omega} \alpha_{u,v} I(x + u, y + v), \qquad (15.2)$$

where Ω is a set of relative indexes of a neighborhood, α's are the interpolation coefficients, and the $I(x, y)$ is a two-dimensional (2-D) image. To evaluate the probability of a pixel as being an original pixel (or an interpolated one), an Expectation-Maximization (EM) algorithm is formulated, where the pixels' type is the hidden variable and the linear interpolation coefficients are the model parameters. As the EM algorithm converges, a 2-D probability map of the hidden variables is obtained, and it shows the interpolation pattern of the image. The correctly estimated interpolation pattern of an authentic image would have a periodic pattern corresponding to the sensor allocation pattern. The periodicity of the probability map leads to a set of the dominant frequency harmonics in the Fourier domain. As image compositing can disrupt the regular interpolation pattern, the estimated interpolation pattern can be used for detecting composite images. The experiments are conducted on the artificially generated demosaiced images, as well as on images from three commercial cameras.

Camera Response Function

There are works which consider the camera response function for image forgery detection. The image irradiance (light energy incident on the image sensors) r is related to the image intensity (the final output image) R by a non-linear Camera Response Function (CRF) f as in $R = f(r)$. This non-linear function is a characteristic of an image, which can be estimated from a single image [16, 17, 18]. The inconsistency in the estimated CRF over an image is a telltale sign for a composite image.

Popescu and Farid [19] perform blind estimation of the CRF based on a gamma curve model, $f(r) = r^\gamma$, where γ is the gamma parameter. The estimation method is founded on the observation that the non-linear transform on the image irradiance introduces frequency harmonics with quadratically coupled phases. This effect is due to the observation that a non-linear function can be approximated by the power series of a Taylor expansion as shown below:

$$f(r) = f(0) + \frac{r}{1!}f'(0) + \frac{r^2}{2!}f''(0) + \cdots \tag{15.3}$$

for the expansion of a function f at $r = 0$. The power series has a linear-quadratic function term (the linear combination of a linear and a quadratic term). The effect of a linear-quadratic function on a signal can be illustrated using a simple 1-D signal with two frequency harmonics:

$$r(x) = a_1 \cos(\omega_1 x + \theta_1) + a_2 \cos(\omega_2 x + \theta_2). \tag{15.4}$$

The quadratic phase coupling phenomena is induced when $r(x)$ passes through a linear-quadratic operation:

$$
\begin{aligned}
r(x) + \alpha r(x)^2 \ = \ & a_1 \cos(\omega_1 x + \theta_1) + a_2 \cos(\omega_2 x + \theta_2) \tag{15.5} \\
& + \frac{1}{2}\alpha a_1^2 \cos(2\omega_1 x + 2\theta_1) + \frac{1}{2}\alpha a_2^2 \cos(2\omega_2 x + 2\theta_2) \\
& + a_1 a_2 \cos((\omega_1 + \omega_2)x + (\theta_1 + \theta_2)) \\
& + a_1 a_2 \cos((\omega_1 - \omega_2)x + (\theta_1 - \theta_2)) + \frac{1}{2}\alpha a_1^2 + \frac{1}{2}\alpha a_2^2,
\end{aligned}
$$

where α is an arbitrary constant. Note that there exist harmonics at ω_1, ω_2, and $\omega_1 + \omega_2$, respectively, with a phase θ_1, θ_2, and $\theta_1 + \theta_2$. As QPC induces a (non-random) zero phase in bicoherence, the magnitude of bicoherence at the corresponding (ω_1, ω_2) takes a large value as an expectation of a constant phase random variable. Therefore, bicoherence can be used to measure the amount of the QPC effect. As non-linear transformation of an image increases the amount of QPC effect, it is reasonable to assume that the inverse transform of the image intensity by a correct gamma curve would correspond to a minimum for the bicoherence magnitude. As a result, the CRF can be estimated by searching for a curve which minimizes the bicoherence magnitude. In Popescu and Farid [19], this idea is demonstrated using a simple image where the upper and the lower halves of the image are separately transformed with gamma curves of a different gamma parameter.

A more realistic scenario for image forgery detection by the CRF characteristic is demonstrated in Lin et al. [9], where the CRF is estimated using the method

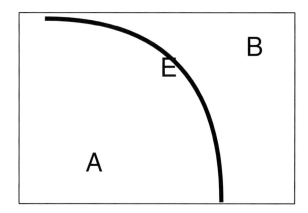

FIGURE 15.5:   The curved line represents an image edge. There are three points at a local edge region: A and B are points at the homogenous intensity regions separated by the edge. E is the edge point.

proposed in Lin et al. [16]. This single-image CRF estimation method is based on the linear pixel blending property for the image irradiance at the edge pixels:

$$r_E = \alpha r_A + (1 - \alpha) r_B, \tag{15.6}$$

where α is the blending factor, and r_E, r_A, and r_B are the image irradiance at the corresponding points E, A, and B in Figure 15.5.

When the pixel blending factors α of an edge are uniform over the RGB color channels, there exists a co-linear relationship between the values of the edge pixel and the values of the pixels in the adjacent homogenous regions (which are separated by the edge) in the RGB color space:

$$\begin{pmatrix} r_E^R \\ r_E^G \\ r_E^B \end{pmatrix} = \alpha \begin{pmatrix} r_A^R \\ r_A^G \\ r_A^B \end{pmatrix} + (1 - \alpha) \begin{pmatrix} r_B^R \\ r_B^G \\ r_B^B \end{pmatrix}, \tag{15.7}$$

where the upper index for r corresponds to the RGB color channels. As a non-linear transform distorts the co-linearity relationship, the CRF can be estimated from the form of the distortion.

Lighting Consistency

The work described above utilizes the camera authenticity quantity. However, Johnson and Farid [12] demonstrate the novel idea of image forgery detection by the natural-scene authenticity quality. The authors estimate the 2-D lighting directions (in the image plane) from the occlusion edge. At the occlusion edge, the surface normal has a zero z-component, while the (x, y)-component is just the normal of the occlusion contour, which can be easily estimated. Under the assumption of the Lambertian surface, a constant reflectance, and a single distant point light source, the image intensity (linear to the image irradiance) R is given by

$$R(x, y) = \rho \mathbf{N}(x, y) \cdot \mathbf{L} + A, \tag{15.8}$$

where $\mathbf{N}$ is the surface normal, $\mathbf{L}$ is the point light source direction, A is the constant ambient light, and ρ is the reflectance. As the surface normal at the occlusion edge is known, the light source direction in the x and y directions and the ambient light A can be recovered by the linear least square method when the surface normal and the image intensity at more than three points are available. When the 2-D lighting directions are independently estimated at the occlusion edges of different objects, consistency checking of the lighting directions can be performed to verify whether an image is composite.

Johnson and Farid [12] further relax the above assumption by considering the case of locally constant reflectance and multiple local point light sources. However, the algorithm requires manually extracted edge points. Experiments using the real-world images and the synthetic images are shown and achieve promising results. In another ongoing work [20], it is shown that the lighting consistency can be examined without explicitly estimating the lighting. This preliminary theoretical result is based on the spherical frequency invariants and is currently assuming known object geometry.

Detecting Image Forgery Creation Artifact

Geometry transformation of a digital image potentially involves resampling or interpolation of some image pixels. To estimate the probability map of interpolation, the same EM algorithm explained previously is used [21]. In one scenario, during the process of image composition, an image fragment may undergo resampling as it is resized, before being spliced onto another image. The resampled region can be detected from the probability map if the host image is not similarly resampled. Figure 15.6[3] illustrates this scenario with a simple example. Note that the periodicity of the probability map at the spliced region manifests as peaks in its Fourier spectrum.

Apart from this, the presence of duplicate regions and the discrepancy in the Signal-to-Noise Ratio (SNR) at different image regions can also be considered as

---

[3] From A. Popescu and H. Farid. *IEEE Trans. Signal Processing*, 52(2):758–767, 2005. Courtesy of Hany Farid.

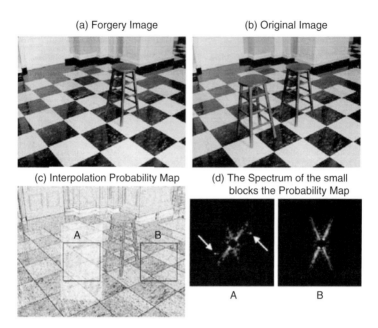

FIGURE 15.6:   Image (a) is the forgery image created from image (b) by removing a stool from the image. The removed region is covered by the resized patch of the same background. Image (c) is the probability map output from the EM algorithm, and image (d) is the Fourier spectrum of the small blocks A and B. Dominant peaks in the Fourier spectrum indicate the periodicity of the probability map at the block region at a specific frequency. (Figure courtesy of Hany Farid.)

telltale signs for image compositing, and techniques are proposed to detect these artifacts [19, 22]. When an object is removed from an image, one way to fill in the removed region is by example-based texture synthesis, i.e., cover up the removed region using similar background patches. This method is especially effective for covering up the homogenous background region. The work in [22] proposes an effective way to detect duplicate image blocks (8×8 pixels) in a single image. The image blocks are reduced in dimension by using Principal Component Analysis (PCA), and a lexicographic sort is applied to the PCA vectors for efficiently detecting the duplicate image blocks. The PCA vectors corresponding to the duplicate image blocks will be adjacent to each other in the lexicographically sorted list. The experiments show that the method is not only computationally efficient, but it also works well even when the image is highly compressed and when there is additive noise in the image.

On the other hand, if the assumption that image noise is uniform over an image, then the discrepancy of the noise variance at different regions of a same image would be a telltale sign for a composite image. A method for estimating noise variance, with the assumption of known signal kurtosis, is used to demonstrate the above image using a toy example.

Apart from the approaches that directly detect the artifacts closely linked to image forgery, there are approaches that detect the indirect evidence for image forgery. Popescu and Farid [19] propose considering Joint Photographic Experts Group (JPEG) double compression as indirect evidence for image forgery. In the process of producing image forgery using the image editing software, it is likely that a JPEG image may be compressed once again at the end of the process with a different quality factor than the original one. Such JPEG double compression introduces a periodicity in the histogram of a JPEG Discrete Cosine Transform (DCT) coefficient. Figure 15.7[4] illustrates the effect of double JPEG compression using a sample sequence. Note that for both cases when the quantization step is increased or decreased at the second quantization, the histogram displays a periodic pattern. When such a periodic pattern is observed for the DCT coefficients of a JPEG image, it indicates the act of JPEG double compression and calls for further examination on the image.

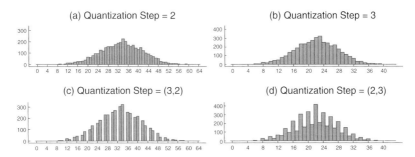

FIGURE 15.7:   The double JPEG compression introduces an effect on the JPEG DCT coefficients as a result of the double quantization. This figure illustrates the double quantization effect on a sample sequence. (a) The histogram of a sample sequence quantized with a quantization step 2, (b) The histogram of the same sequence quantized with a quantization step 3, (c) The histogram from a double quantization with a quantization step 3 followed by step 2. (d) The histogram from a double quantization with quantization step 2 followed by step 3. (Figure courtesy of Hany Farid.)

---

[4]From A. Popescu and H. Farid. *IEEE trans. Signal Processing*, 52(2):758–767, 2005. Courtesy of Hany Farid.

On the other hand, Lukas, Fridrich, and Goljan [54] present a method to detect the presence of camera pattern noise in an image for the purpose of image integrity verification or image forgery detection. The pattern noise is due to the non-uniform property of the individual camera sensors in terms of the dark current and the pixel responsivity. The absence of camera pattern noise in an image region may be a telltale sign of an image forgery. However, this method requires either the camera with which the image was produced or a set of images produced by the same camera.

Another type of indirect evidence for image forgery is the distortion resulting from the common post-processing operations on a composite image such as brightness adjustment, contrast adjustment, and so on. A reference-free image quality/distortion measure is proposed for quantifying the quality of images. This objective image quality measure is used as features for training an image forgery detector [8], which achieves a detection rate of 69.2% for brightness adjustment, 74.2% for contrast adjustment, and 80% for mixed processing (i.e., a sequence of operations including scaling, rotation, brightness adjustment, and contrast enhancement).

15.3.3   Passive-Blind Image Source Identification

There are various devices from which digital images can be produced. Examples are cameras, scanners, medical imaging devices, and so on. Besides that, images can also be generated by computer graphic techniques. The goal of the passive-blind image source identification is to identify the type of image source, as shown in Figure 15.8. In a more complicated scenario, an image may be composed of fragments from multiple different sources.

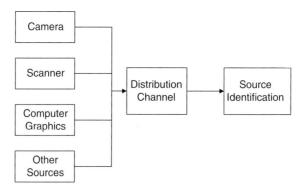

FIGURE 15.8:   The setting for the passive-blind image source identification problem.

Identification of the image source can help us in the decision of whether an image is acceptable for a specific application. For example, a computer graphic image is definitely unacceptable for news reporting, and a human face image shown to a face biometric security system should not be mistaken by the authentication system as the actual presence of the person in front of the system.

15.3.4   Passive-Blind Image Source Identification Techniques

One problem of concern in image source identification is the classification of Photographic Images (PIMs) and PhotoRealistic Computer Graphics (PRCGs). Despite the fact that the classification which involves general computer graphics images (including drawings and cartoons) has already been applied for the purpose of improving the image and video retrieval performance [23, 24], the classification which involves PRCGs is a new problem. Lyu and Harid [25] use the wavelet-based natural image statistics for PIM and PRCG classification. The method extracts the first four order statistics (mean, variance, skewness, and kurtosis) of the in-subband wavelet coefficients and also computes the first four order statistics of the linear prediction error for the wavelet coefficients using the coefficients of the neighboring location, scale, orientation from the other color channels, as illustrated in Figure 15.9. The statistical features are used for classifying PIMs and PRCGs and achieve a PIM detection accuracy of 67% with a 1% false alarm rate. As this technique is purely statistical, it provides little insight into the physical differences between PIM and PRCG.

In Ng et al. [11], the problem is approached by analyzing the physical differences between the image generative process for PIMs and PRCGs. This approach provides a physical explanation for the actual differences between PIMs and PRCGs, while the geometry features from this approach outperform the features in the prior work.

Specifically, the difference between PIMs and PRCGs can be briefly summarized below.

1. **Object Model Difference**. The surface of real-world objects, except for man-made objects, is rarely smooth or of simple geometry. Mandelbrot [26] showed the abundance of fractals in nature and also related the formation of fractal surfaces to basic physical processes such as erosion, aggregation, and fluid turbulence. Furthermore, a surface such as human skin is full of subtleties and a result of the natural biological process. However, the computer graphics 3-D objects are often represented by the polygonal models. Although the polygonal models can be arbitrarily fine grained, it comes with a higher cost of memory and computational load. Furthermore, such a polygonal model is not a natural representation for fractal surfaces [27]. A coarse-grained polygonal model may be used at the perceptually insignificant area for saving computational resources.

FIGURE 15.9:   An illustration on how the linear prediction error of a wavelet coefficient is computed using the wavelet coefficients in the neighboring spatial location, orientation, and scale for a gray-scale image case. For a color image, the wavelet coefficents of other color channels can also be used for computing the prediction error.

2. **Light Transport Difference** [28]. The physical light field captured by a camera is a result of the physical light transport from the illumination source reflected to the image acquisition device by an object. The precise modeling of this physical light transport involves an eight-dimensional (8-D) function of the object's reflectance property, hence its simulation requires substantial computational resources. Therefore, a simplified model based on the assumption of isotropy, spectral independence, and parametric representation is often used.

3. **Acquisition Difference**. PIMs carry the characteristics of the imaging process, while PRCGs may undergo different types of post-processing after the rasterizer stage. There is no standard set of post-processing techniques, but a few possible ones are the simulation of the camera effect, such as the depth of field, gamma correction, addition of noise, and retouching.

The above differences are captured using the geometry features derived from the differential geometry, the fractal geometry, and the local patch statistics. Specifically, the authors propose a two-scale image description framework, as shown in Figure 15.10. At the finest scale of the linear Gaussian scale-space, the geometry can be characterized by the local fractal dimension and also by the "non-parametric" local patches [29]. At an intermediate scale, when the

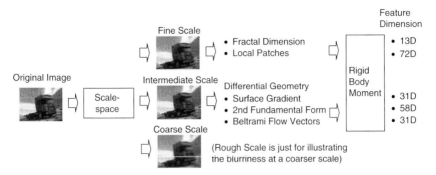

FIGURE 15.10:   The geometry-based image description framework.[5]

fine-grained details give way to a smoother and differentiable structure, the geometry can be best described in the language of differential geometry, where the surface gradient, the second fundamental form, and the Beltrami flow vectors are computed. While these features are motivated by the physical properties of the image generative process, it provides a better classification performance compared to the techniques in prior work by at least 3%.

The image source identification problem includes the identification of the model of a camera which is useful for image forensics. Mehdi, Sencar, and Memon [30] exploit the characteristics of the in-camera color processing module to identify different models of digital cameras. The features related to the color processing module are the average pixel value (motivated by the gray world assumption in white balancing), the pairwise correlation of the RGB color channels, the center of mass for the neighbor pixel distribution at different intensity values (related to the sensitivity of the camera at different intensity values), and the pairwise energy ratio for the RGB color channels (related to the white point correction). They also use the mean of the wavelet subbands as additional features. Their experiment on the Sony DCS-P51, Nikon E-2100, and Canon Powershot S100, S110, and S200 obtains a classification accuracy of 88%.

On the other hand, a scanned image of a printed document can be analyzed for identifying the printer from which the printed document was produced. In Mikkilineni et al. [31], the quasi-periodic banding artifacts in the process direction are used as the intrinsic printer signatures for identifying the laser printers. The banding artifacts often manifest as the non-uniform light and dark lines as the paper scrolls during the printing. The effect is due to the non-uniform movement of the optical photoconductor in the print mechanism, see Figure 15.11. Mikkilineni et al. [31] detect the effect by analyzing the pixel intensity co-occurrence

---

[5]The track image is from http://www.realsoft.fi/gallery/vehicles/scania/jpg.

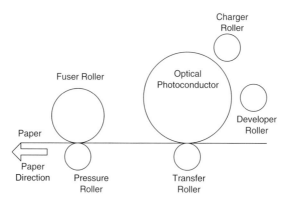

FIGURE 15.11: The cross-section view of a typical laser printer. The non-uniform movement of the optical photoconductor due to the variations at the gear train results in the banding artifact on a printout.

matrix computed on the interior region of a specific printed character. The paper demonstrates the idea using the character "e" due to its high frequency of appearance. For printer classification, 22 features including the marginal mean, marginal variance, entropy, energy, and so on are extracted from the co-occurrence matrix. Then, a 5-nearest neighbor classifier is trained to classify each feature vector corresponding to a single character "e." The printer model is identified through the majority vote from all the characters "e". The experiment involves ten printers of different models, and the test documents are generated as random text. A promising result is obtained as the test documents from nine out of ten printer models are correctly classified.

15.4 CHALLENGES AND RESOURCES FOR PBIF

PBIF is still a burgeoning research field, and its advances depend on the carefully identified research directions and the availability of the required resources such as the experimental data set. The general architecture of an image forensic engine, be it for image forgery detection or image source identification, is shown in Figure 15.12. In reference to the architecture, the elements for advancing the PBIF research are discussed in the following subsections.

15.4.1 Image Modeling and Parameter Estimation

Image modeling is important for image forensics. Three types of image models relevant to image forensics are the natural image statistics, the physical image model based on the camera parameters, and the model based on the scene constraints.

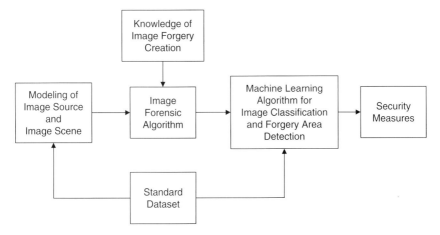

FIGURE 15.12: The basic architecture of an image forensic engine.

A good review for natural image statistics can be found in Srivastava et al. [13]. Natural image statistics represent the statistical regularity in natural-scene images. The well-known natural image statistics are the power law of the natural image power spectrum, the sparse marginal distribution for wavelet coefficients, the non-trivial joint distribution of the wavelet coefficients, and the higher order statistics of images. For a physical model, images can be characterized by the parameters of the camera, such as the geometric lens distortion, the CCD sensor noise statistics, the camera response function, the demosaicing pattern, and so on; whereas at the scene level, a physical model can be based on scene constraints such as the relationship between the shadow and the lighting, the consistency between the shading and the lighting, the consistency between the inter-reflection of light and the surface properties, and so on.

Once there is a good image model, the next concern would be the possibility to estimate the model parameters from a single image. Estimating the natural image statistics from a single image is not a problem, but it is a very difficult challenge for the physical model. The main reason is that an image is the combined effect of the various scene and camera factors. When attempting to factorize this combined effect or jointly estimate the multiple parameters, there exist multiple solutions because it has no unique solution. For instance, there is an inherent ambiguity in the estimation of the lighting, the reflectance property, and the surface geometry from a single image, without any specific assumptions.

However, some progress has been seen in the estimation of the camera parameters, such as the camera response function from a single image [16, 17, 18]. Besides that, there are also some new semi-automatic methods for estimating the scene parameters such as the shadow [32]. Once the scene parameters are estimated, the consistency checking for the scene parameters is possible.

Interestingly, a parallel can be drawn between image forensics and face recognition in terms of the general approach toward image modeling in order to attain some kinds of invariance. As the image authenticity and the image source characteristics for image forensics are essentially independent of image content (e.g., lighting, the presence of objects, and so on), the above-mentioned image model for image forensics is image content invariant. In face recognition, the face image model has to be pose and illumination invariant. The two general approaches to achieve pose and illumination invariance are the subspace-based model approach [33] and the physical geometric model-based approach [34]. These two general approaches correspond exactly to the natural image statistics approach and the physical model-based approach in image forensics.

15.4.2   Knowledge of Image Forgery Creation

For the image forgery detection techniques reviewed in Section 15.3.1, their evaluation on the state-of-the-art image forgery creation techniques (see Appendix) is still uncommon. For instance, the method of photomontage detection in Ng, Charg, and Sun [7] addresses only the simplest form of image composition which is image splicing, the simple cut-and-paste of image fragments, without sophisticated matting or blending. The composite image detection method using the camera gamma curve in Popescu and Farid [19] demonstrates the idea only using a toy example. The main reason could be that the current detection techniques have not attained a level of sophistication which matches that of the image forgery creation techniques. However, if having no access to the image forgery creation system is one of the causes, a collaboration between the image forgery creation and image forgery detection research would be a good idea.

15.4.3   Full Automation and Fine-Grained Analysis

An ideal image forensic system is one which is fully automated (i.e., requiring no human intervention) and provides a fine-grained analysis (e.g., at a local region). However, in most of the work discussed in Section 15.3.1, the proposed techniques are still either semi-automated or for a coarse-grained analysis (e.g., at the level of a large size region or on the entire image). To replace the role of a human in the system, certain non-trivial tasks such as the detection of the object boundary in a composite image detection system need to be automated. To refine the analysis granularity, one needs to devise image forensic methods that rely on a smaller amount of data, while ensuring that the analysis remains reliable.

Despite the benefit of full automation, devising a fully automated yet sophisticated image forgery detection system is not always possible because of some fundamental limitations. For instance, as explained in Section 15.4.1, the estimation of the physical model parameters from a single image without any user intervention is inherently impossible. If the level of automation has a trade-off relationship with the detection accuracy and resolution, then a good system would have a simple but fully automatic module as a front end for pre-filtering the potential image forgery and a semi-automatic but more comprehensive detection module as the back end for the final detailed analysis of the images.

15.4.4   Data Set

A Data Set is important for image modeling and the evaluation of a proposed algorithm. Furthermore, a common data set provides a common platform for the research community to compare various algorithms, thereby facilitating communications among researchers. To address this concern, the "Columbia Image Splicing Detection Evaluation Dataset" [14] and the "Columbia Photographic Images and Photorealistic Computer Graphics Dataset" [35] are made available to the research community. These two data sets can be downloaded from http://www.ee.columbia.edu/trustfoto.

The "Columbia Image Splicing Detection Evaluation Dataset" is for the image splicing detection experiments. It contains 933 authentic and 912 spliced image blocks of size 128×128 pixels. These image blocks are mainly extracted from the Calphoto image set [36]. For image blocks of both classes, there are subcategories of the homogenous textured and smooth image blocks. There are also subcategories of image blocks with an edge or a splicing boundary which separates two textured, two smooth, and a textured with a smooth regions. Examples of the data set are shown in Figure 15.13.

The "Columbia Photographic Images and Photorealistic Computer Graphics Dataset" is for the PIM and PRCG classification experiments. There are four categories of images in the data set, as described below and shown in Figure 15.14.

1. **800 PRCGs from the Internet**. These images are categorized by content into architecture, game, nature, object, and life. The PRCGs are mainly collected from various 3-D artists (more than 100) and about 40 3-D graphics Web sites, such as www.softimage.com, www.3ddart.org, www.3d-ring.com, and so on. The rendering software used includes 3ds MAX, softimage-xsi, Maya, Terragen, and so on. The geometry modeling tools used include AutoCAD, Rhinoceros, softimage-3D, and so on. High-end rendering techniques used include global illumination with ray tracing or radiosity, simulation of the camera depth-of-field effect, soft-shadow, caustics effect, and so on.

2. **800 PIMs from a few photographers**. Four hundred of them are from the personal collection of Philip Greenspun. They are mainly travel images with content such as indoor, outdoor, people, objects, buildings, and so

(a) Authentic Blocks

| Textured | Smooth | Textured Smooth | Smooth Smooth | Textured Textured |

(b) Spliced Blocks

FIGURE 15.13: Examples from the "Columbia Image Splicing Detection Evaluation Dataset." The data set has five subcategories with the textured, smooth, textured-smooth, smooth-smooth, and textured-textured image blocks. (Image block courtesy of Cal Photos from the University of California at Berkeley and the individual photographers of the images.)

personal   Google   CG   recaptured CG

FIGURE 15.14: Examples from the dataset of photographic and computer graphic images. Note the photorealism of all images.[6]

on. The other 400 were acquired in a data collection project [35] using the professional single-len-reflex (SLR) Canon 10D and Nikon D70. It has content diversity in terms of indoor or outdoor scenes, natural or artificial objects, and lighting conditions of daytime, dusk, or nighttime.

---

[6]The personal image at the second row is by the courtesy of Philip Greenspun. The Google images are from http://www.geocities.com/nowarski7/ta/02110602.jpg (first row) and http://associate.com/photos/Samples-n-Things/fruit-bowl.jpg (second row). The CG images are from http://www.realsoft.fi/gallery/vehicles/scania.jpg (first row) and http://www.marlinstudios .com/gallery/cgallery/summerfun/sunshine.htm (second row).

3. **800 PIMs from Google Image Search**. These images are the search results based on keywords that match the computer graphics categories. The keywords are architecture, people, scenery, indoor, forest, statue, and so on.

4. **800 rephotographed PRCGs**. These are the photographs of the screen display of the mentioned 800 computer graphics. Computer graphics are displayed on a 17-inch (gamma linearized) LCD monitor screen with a display resolution of 1280 × 1024 and photographed by a Canon G3 digital camera. The acquisition is conducted in a darkened room in order to reduce the reflections from the ambient scene.

Despite the two data sets, there are many problems that also call for a benchmark data set. For instance, the experiments involving the physical image model based on the camera characteristics require a data set of images acquired by diverse models of cameras at various acquisition settings. Furthermore, in order to facilitate the evaluation of the image forgery detection techniques using the images produced by the state-of-the-art image forgery creation techniques, a data set of these images would be necessary. Therefore, further effort on producing and standardizing the additional benchmark data set is needed.

15.4.5 Security Measure

Once a forgery creator has an unlimited access to the forgery detector, an oracle attack can be launched, where the forgery creator incrementally modifies the created forgery according to the detection results from the detector until it passes the detector. Such an attack is also a serious threat to the public watermarking system. For the incremental modification to be efficient and have a minimum distortion on the image, the attacker needs to identify the shortest path to the decision boundary of the detector. This is possible when the decision boundary is known to the attacker.

With unlimited access to the detector, a parametric decision boundary can be estimated by the following procedure. The attacker first locates the sample points on the decision boundary by incrementally modifying some sample images until it just crosses the boundary. Then, the parameters of the decision boundary can be estimated by using the boundary points, so long as the number of the boundary points is equal or greater than the number of the parameters. In most cases, the number of the parameters is not too large, and the estimation is feasible. To make the estimation more challenging, Tewfik and Mansour [37] propose a method of converting the parametric decision boundary of a detector into a fractal (non-parametric) one, so that an accuracy estimation of the boundary requires a much larger number of sample points on the decision boundary. However, there is a trade-off where the fractal boundary should not be very well approximated by the original parametric decision boundary (ensuring high security), while the excessive deviation for the original boundary should be avoided (minimizing image distortion).

Venturini [38] addresses the oracle attack issue by modifying the temporal behavior of the detector such that the duration for returning a decision is lengthened when an oracle attack is suspected based on the sequence of input images. The hallmark of an oracle attack is the sequential input images with a similar content. The delay strategy for the lazy detector with memory can be designed so that the total time duration needed for an oracle attack to succeed is painfully long.

15.5   SUMMARY AND CONCLUSION

In this chapter, we review PBIF, beginning with an overview and following with a detailed review on the two main problems of image forensics, i.e., image forgery detection and image source identification. We also provide a description of our thoughts on the resources and the challenges concerning PBIF.

PBIF is still a research area in its infancy. There are fundamental issues related to the physical model parameter estimation, the practical system design issues, and the system security issues, which remain to be addressed. For an effective solution to these issues, expertise from various domains such as computer vision, signal processing, computer graphics, machine learning, imaging sensors, and even mechanical systems is needed. On the other hand, it is reasonable to envision that the digital watermarking techniques could be used in conjunction with the PBIF methods. Therefore, the combined active and passive approach may be another future research direction.

15.6   FORGERY CREATION TECHNIQUES

This section provides a review of the automatic or the semi-automatic computer techniques for image forgery creation. The following subsections are according to the image forgery creation model shown in Figure 15.1.

15.6.1   Region Selection

While automatic image segmentation still leaves much to be desired, various interactive foreground-background image segmentation techniques have been invented. From the operational perspective, these techniques can be categorized into boundary-based methods [39, 40] and region-based methods [41, 42]. For boundary-based methods, users approximately trace the object boundary and the algorithm interactively refines the traced contour so that the background and the foreground are well segmented; whereas in region-based methods, users mark the background and the foreground region, and then the algorithm finds a contour to separate the two regions. The well-known Magic Wand and

Intelligent Scissor in Photoshop are, respectively, a region-based method and a boundary-based method. There are techniques, such as Lazy Snapping [43], which combine the benefits of the two methods.

15.6.2   3D Model Extraction

Humans have a good capability of extracting a three-dimensional (3-D) scene structure from a single image, even under the condition of mono-vision. Mimicking such a human capability has been one of the focuses in computer vision research. A 3-D morphable human face model [34] was used to extract the 3-D human face model from a single image with some user's intervention for matching the correspondence points in the image. Once the 3-D face model has been extracted, manipulation of the face features such as changing the facial expression and altering the fullness and the gender characteristics of the face, is possible. There are various other algorithms being proposed for the single-view 3-D model reconstruction from a more generic scene with planar or other simple geometric primitives [44], such as a scene with buildings. For images of a more complex scene structure, a semi-automatic method for reconstructing the 3-D structure of an arbitrary free-form curved surface from a single image using the sparse surface normals supplied by the user is demonstrated in [45] and shown in Figure 15.15.[7]

15.6.3   Geometric Transformation

The common geometric transformation applied to an image fragment before being pasted onto another image includes translation, Euclidean transformation (translation and rotation), similarity transform (scaled rotation and translation), affine transform (a transform that preserves parallel lines), and projective transform (a transform that preserves straight lines). Mathematically, these transformations can be represented by a linear transform with possibly constrained 3×3 matrices operating on two-dimensional (2-D) homogenous coordinate vectors [46]. These transformations take the perspective projection of the camera into account. Interestingly, in his 1917 book *On Growth and Form*, biologist D'Arcy Thompson showed that different species of fish can be related by a simple geometric transformation, as shown in Figure 15.16.[8] This similar type of transformation is also possible for a human skull.

15.6.4   Compositing

Direct pasting of an image fragment onto another image would introduce visually perceptible seams. To produce a natural-looking composite image, matting or

---

[7]The image is extracted from http://grail.cs.washington.edu/projects/svm/CGW/single_view_ modeling.htm, courtesy of Li Zhang et al.

[8]The image is extracted from http://www.bio.umass.edu/biology/kunkel/shape.html.

FIGURE 15.15:   An example of single view modeling. (Figure courtesy of Li Zhang et al.)

blending is usually performed. Matting is to mix the pixels near the fragment boundary by the weighted sum of the pixels of the fragments and those of the original image. The weight is given by the matte which needs to be estimated. There are various ways to estimate the matte given a user-supplied *trimap*, which is a tri-region partitioning for "definitely foreground," "definitely background," and "unknown" regions. The examples for the matting methods are Bayesian matting [47], coherence matting [48], and poisson matting [49]. The blending technique is more than just blending of near-boundary pixels; it has the capability of realigning the exposure differences and other misalignments between the pasted image fragments and the host image. This form of blending can be done by directly compositing the multi-resolution version of the image fragments in a Laplacian pyramid [50], and the final image is recovered from the composite Laplacian pyramid. In another technique, direct compositing is performed in the gradient domain, and the final composite image is recovered by solving a partial differential equation [51].

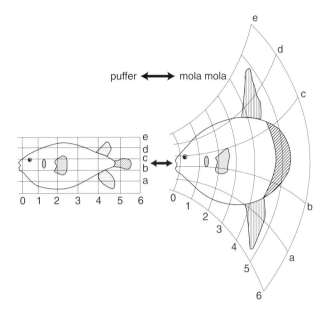

FIGURE 15.16: An example showed by D'Arcy Thompson for transforming a type of fish called puffer to another type called mola mola.

15.6.5 Retouch and Object Removal

At the final stage of the image editing pipeline, the composite image may be retouched by airbrushing to remove the remaining artifact or the minor/narrow objects like the overhead electrical wiring. However, removal of a larger size foreground object is also possible, and this practice is sometimes known as *reverse cropping*. After an object is removed, the resulted void needs to be filled in with the background pixels. This filling-in process is known as *image inpainting*. The simple image inpainting technique would be to synthesize the background texture to fill in the empty region [52]. This technique works well for homogenous textured backgrounds. The more complex image inpainting algorithm takes the geometric structure at the surrounding of the void into account. One method employs the classical Navier-Stokes equation in fluid dynamics to propagate the geometric structure from the surrounding region into the void [53] and achieves promising inpainting results.

REFERENCES

[1] C. Amsberry, Alterations of photos raise host of legal, ethical issues, *The Wall Street Journal*, January 1989.

[2] G. Friedman, The trustworthy digital camera: Restoring credibility to the photographic image, *IEEE Trans. Consumer Electronics*, 39(4):905–910, November 1993.

[3] S. Craver, M. Wu, B. Liu, A. Stubblefield, B. Swartzlander, D. Dean, and E. Felten. Reading between the lines: Lessons learned from the sdmi challenge, in *Usenix Security Symposium*, Washington D.C., pp. 353–363, August 2001.

[4] H. Farid. Detecting digital forgeries using bispectral analysis, MIT, MIT AI Memo AIM-1657, 1999. Available at ftp://publications.ai.mit.edu/ai-publications/pdf/AIM-1657.pdf.

[5] H. Farid and S. Lyu. Higher-order wavelet statistics and their application to digital forensics, in *IEEE Workshop Statistical Analysis in Computer Vision*, Madison, WI, 2003.

[6] T.-T. Ng and S.-F. Chang. A model for image splicing, in *IEEE Int. Conf. Image Processing*, 2:1169–1172, Singapore, 2004.

[7] T.-T. Ng, S.-F. Chang, and Q. Sun. Blind detection of photomontage using higher order statistics, in *IEEE International Symposium on Circuits and Systems*, 5:v-688–v-691, Vancouver, Canada, May 23–26, 2004.

[8] I. Avcibas, S. Bayram, N. Memon, M. Ramkumar, and B. Sankur. A classifier design for detecting image manipulations, in *IEEE Int. Conf. Image Processing*, 4:2645–2648, October 2004.

[9] Z. Lin, R. Wang, X. Tang, and H.-Y. Shum. Detecting doctored images using camera response normality and consistency, *IEEE Computer Society Conference on Computer Vision and Pattern Recognition*, 1:1087–1092, June 2005.

[10] G. N. Ali, P.-J. Chiang, A. K. Mikkilineni, J. P. Allebach, G. T.-C. Chiu, and E. J. Delp. Intrinsic and extrinsic signatures for information hiding and secure printing with electrophotographic devices, in *IS&T Int. Conf. Digital Printing Technologies*, pp. 511–515, New Orleans, LA, 2003.

[11] T.-T. Ng, S.-F. Chang, J. Hsu, L. Xie, and M.-P. Tsui. Physics-motivated features for distinguishing photographic images and computer graphics, in *ACM Multimedia*, pp. 239–248, Singapore, November 2005.

[12] M. Johnson and H. Farid. Exposing digital forgeries by detecting inconsistencies in lighting, in *ACM Multimedia and Security Workshop*, pp. 1-10, New York, NY, August 1–2, 2005.

[13] A. Srivastava, A. B. Lee, E. P. Simoncelli, and S.-C. Zhu. On advances in statistical modeling of natural images, *J. Mathematical Imaging and Vision*, 18(1):17–33, 2003.

[14] T.-T. Ng and S.-F. Chang. A data set of authentic and spliced image blocks, Columbia University, ADVENT Technical Report 203-2004-3, June 2004. Available at http://www.ee.columbia.edu/trustfoto

[15] A. Popescu and H. Farid. Exposing digital forgeries in color filter array interpolated images, *IEEE Tran. Signal Processing*, 53(10):3948–3959, 2005.

[16] S. Lin, J. Gu, S. Yamazaki, and H.-Y. Shum. Radiometric calibration from a single image, *IEEE Computer Society Conference on Computer Vision and Pattern Recognition*, 2:938–945, June 2004.

[17] S. Lin and L. Zhang. Determining the radiometric response function from a single grayscale image, in *IEEE Computer Society Conference on Computer Vision and Pattern Recognition*, 2:66–73, June 2005.

[18] T.-T. Ng, S.-F. Chang, and M.-P. Tsui. Camera response function estimation from a single-channel image using differential invariants, ADVENT Technical Report 216-2006-2, Columbia University, March 2006.

[19] A. Popescu and H. Farid. Statistical tools for digital forensics, in *6th Int. Workshop Information Hiding*, Toronto, Canada, May 23–25, 2004.

[20] D. Mahajan, R. Ramamoorthi, and B. Curless. Spherical harmonic convolution for inverse rendering, BRDF/lighting transfer and image consistency checking, European Conference on Computer Vision, Eraz, Austria, May 7–13, 2006.

[21] A. Popescu and H. Farid. Exposing digital forgeries by detecting traces of re-sampling, *IEEE Trans. Signal Processing*, 52(2):758–767, 2005.

[22] A. Popescu and H. Farid. Exposing digital forgeries by detecting duplicated image regions, Computer Science, Dartmouth College, Technical Report TR2004-515, 2004. Available at http://www.cs.dartmouth.edu/ farid/publications/tr04.pdf.

[23] T. Ianeva, A. de Vries, and H. Rohrig. Detecting cartoons: A case study in automatic video-genre classification, *IEEE Int. Conf. Multimedia and Expo*, 1:449–452, 2003.

[24] J. R. Smith and S.-F. Chang. Visually searching the web for content, *IEEE Multimedia*, 4(3):12–20, 1997.

[25] S. Lyu and H. Farid. How realistic is photorealistic? *IEEE Trans. Signal Processing*, 53(2):845–850, February 2005.

[26] B. B. Mandelbrot. *The Fractal Geometry of Nature*, W.H. Freeman, San Francisco, 1983.

[27] A. Pentland. On describing complex surface shapes, *Image and Vision Computing*, 3(4):153–162, November 1985.

[28] T. Akenine-Moller, T. Moller, and E. Haines. *Real-Time Rendering*, A. K. Peters, Ltd., MA, 2002.

[29] A. B. Lee, K. S. Pedersen, and D. Mumford. The nonlinear statistics of high-contrast patches in natural images, *Int. J. Computer Vision*, 54(1):83–103, 2003.

[30] K. Mehdi, H. Sencar, and N. Memon. Blind source camera identification, *IEEE Int. Conf. Image Processing*, 1:709–712, October 2004.

[31] A. K. Mikkilineni, P.-J. Chiang, G. N. Ali, G. T.-C. Chiu, J. P. Allebach, and E. J. Delp. Printer identification based on texture features, in *IS&T Int. Conf. Digital Printing Technologies*, Salt lake City, UT, October 3–November 5, 2004. pp. 306–312, 2004.

[32] T.-P. Wu and C.-K. Tang. A bayesian approach for shadow extraction from a single image, in *IEEE Int. Conf. Computer Vision*, 1:480–487, Beijing, China, October 15–21, 2005.

[33] P. N. Belhumeur and D. J. Kriegman. What is the set of images of an object under all possible lighting conditions?, in *IEEE Computer Vision and Pattern Recognition*, Washington, DC, p. 270, June 18–20, 1996.

[34] V. Blanz and T. Vetter. A morphable model for the synthesis of 3d faces, in *ACM SIGGRAPH*, pp. 187–194, Los Angeles, CA, August 8–13, 1999.

[35] T.-T. Ng, S.-F. Chang, J. Hsu, and M. Pepeljugoski. Columbia photographic images and photorealistic computer graphics dataset, Columbia University, ADVENT Technical Report 205-2004-5, Feb 2005. Available at http://www.ee.columbia.edu/trustfoto.

[36] Calphoto. A database of photos of plants, animals, habitats and other natural history subjects, University of Berkeley, 2000. Available at http://elib.cs.berkeley.edu/photos/.

[37] A. Tewfik and M. Mansour. Secure watermark detection with non-parametric decision boundaries, in *IEEE Int. Conf. Acoustics, Speech, and Signal Processing*, pp. 2089–2092, Orlando, FL, May 13–17, 2002.

[38] I. Venturini. Counteracting oracle attacks, in *ACM Multimedia and Security Workshop on Multimedia and Security*, Magdeburg, Germany, pp. 187–192, September 20–21 2004.

[39] E. N. Mortensen and W. A. Barrett. Intelligent scissors for image composition, in *ACM SIGGRAPH*, pp. 191–198, Los Angeles, CA, August 6–11, 1995.

[40] M. Gleicher. Image snapping, in *ACM SIGGRAPH*, pp. 183–190, 1995.

[41] J. Reese and W. Barrett. Image editing with intelligent paint, in *Eurographics*, 21(3):714–723, Los Angeles, CA, August 6–11, 2002.

[42] Y. Boykov and M.-P. Jolly. Interactive graph cuts for optimal boundary & region segmentation of objects in n-d images, *IEEE Int. Conf. Computer Vision*, I:105–112, 2001.

[43] Y. Li, J. Sun, C.-K. Tang, and H.-Y. Shum. Lazy snapping, *ACM SIGGRAPH*, 23(3):303–308, 2004.

[44] P. E. Debevec, C. J. Taylor, and J. Malik. Modeling and rendering architecture from photographs: a hybrid geometry and image-based approach, in *ACM SIGGRAPH*, pp. 11–20, August 4–9, 1996.

[45] L. Zhang, G. Dugas-Phocion, J.-S. Samson, and S. M. Seitz. Single view modeling of free-form scenes, in *IEEE Conf. Computer Vision and Pattern Recognition*, 1:I-990-I-997, Kauai, Hawaii, December 9–14, 2001.

[46] R. I. Hartley and A. Zisserman. *Multiple View Geometry in Computer Vision*, 2nd ed., Cambridge University Press, Cambridge, UK, 2004.

[47] Y.-Y. Chuang, B. Curless, D. Salesin, and R. Szeliski. A bayesian approach to digital matting, in *IEEE Conference on Computer Vision and Pattern Recognition*, 2:II-264–II-271, Kauai, Hawaii, December 9–14, 2001.

[48] H.-Y. Shum, J. Sun, S. Yamazaki, Y. Li, and C.-K. Tang. Pop-up lightfield, *ACM Trans. Graphics*, 23(2):143–162, 2004.

[49] J. Sun, J. Jia, C.-K. Tang, and H.-Y. Shum. Poisson matting, *ACM Trans. Graphics*, 23(3):315–321, 2004.

[50] P. J. Burt and E. H. Adelson. A multiresolution spline with application to image mosaics, *ACM Trans. Graphics*, 2(4):217–236, 1983.

[51] P. Perez, M. Gangnet, and A. Blake. Poisson image editing, *ACM Trans. Graphics*, 22(3):313–318, 2003.

[52] A. A. Efros and T. K. Leung. Texture synthesis by non-parametric sampling, in *IEEE Int. Conf. Computer Vision*, pp. 1033–1038, Kerkyra, Corfu, Greece, September 20–25, 1999.

[53] M. Bertalmio, A. Bertozi, and G. Sapiro. Navier-stokes, fluid dynamics, and image and video inpainting, in *IEEE Conference on Computer Vision and Pattern Recognition*, 1:I-355–I-362, Kauai, Hawaii, December 9–14, 2001.

[54] J. Lukas, J. Fridrich, and M. Goljan. Detecting digital image forgeries using sensor pattern noise, in *SPIE Electronic Imaging, Photonics West*, San Jose, CA, January 15–19, 2006.

16

Security in Digital Cinema

Jeffrey A. Bloom

16.1 INTRODUCTION

The Era of Digital Cinema began in June of 1999 with the first public demonstrations of high-resolution digital projection of motion picture content in a theater. George Lucas' "Star Wars: Episode I—The Phantom Menace" was exhibited in four theaters in Los Angeles and New Jersey. On two of the screens the movie was exhibited on projectors based on Texas Instruments' Digital Light Processing (DLP) technology. The other two screens used a Hughes/JVC ILA projector based on JVC's Direct Drive Image Light Amplifier (D-ILA) technology. The same month saw the exhibition of the Mirimax film "An Ideal Husband" on two digital screens.

Since then, there have been advances in technology and corresponding demonstrations, a number of seminars and conferences bringing together industry and government, and activity within standards bodies. One of the areas where we have seen significant advancement in technology demonstrations is that of content security. Those first demonstrations did not employ any content security, while a digital version of the movie "Star Wars: Episode II—Attack of the Clones" (the first major motion picture produced entirely in digital format) was encrypted with Texas Instruments' "Local Link" encryption prior to distribution to 94 screens in May of 2002.

The Society of Motion Picture and Television Engineers (SMPTE) and the University of Southern California held a seminar entitled "The Future of the Cinema" in May of 1999, and the National Institute of Standards and Technology (NIST) sponsored a conference on digital cinema in January of 2001. Both of these meetings stressed the need for content security.

The need for standards has been widely accepted. SMPTE formed the Digital Cinema Technology Committee (DC28) in January of 2000, and MPEG-DC was formed in January of 2001. In 2002, the seven major Hollywood studios formed the Digital Cinema Initiative, LLC (DCI), which spent three years creating a Digital Cinema Specification, the first proposed guidelines in the field. Readers interested in learning more about digital cinema are referred to Swartz's [2] professional handbook describing all aspects of digital cinema from mastering to projection.

This chapter focuses on content security in digital cinema. We use the term *content security* to mean the prevention of unauthorized use of the motion picture content. This includes the prevention of piracy and the prevention of illegitimate exhibition. Note that not all legitimate exhibition decisions can be authorized by the rights owner in advance, so a content security system would also encompass a mechanism of secure audit reporting of content usage.

Next, we look at some of the standardization efforts around digital cinema. We then discuss the goals of a security system for digital cinema and some of the available tools. We conclude this chapter with a description of the security system proposed in the DCI Digital Cinema Specification.

16.2   DIGITAL CINEMA STANDARDIZATION EFFORTS

In order for digital cinema to be successful, many people in the industry believe that standards for interoperability are necessary. Along these lines, there have been two major efforts in the United States: SMPTE and DCI. In the meantime, a number of digital cinema demonstrations since July of 2001 have used the MPEG-2 compression standard for representation of the motion picture. Not surprising, MPEG has also been active in considering standards for digital cinema. For a more detailed list of worldwide standardization efforts, the reader is referred to the opening chapter of Swartz [2].

16.2.1   SMPTE DC28

In 1999, SMPTE, along with the University of Southern California, held a one-day seminar titled "The Future of the Cinema." The seminar occurred just as "Star Wars: Episode 1—The Phantom Menace" and "An Ideal Husband" became the first public demonstrations of digital cinema. The seminar concentrated on demonstrations of various projection technologies and discussed the need for better compression and good security. These are the two issues that most clearly call out for the need for the establishment of industry-wide standards.

This meeting was followed in January of 2000 with the formation of the SMPTE DC28 Digital Cinema Technology Committee. The committee was divided into seven study groups with DC28.4, Conditional Access, tasked with discussing the security requirements of a deployed digital cinema system. The early focus of this study group was an overall security system utilizing strong encryption, link encryption, watermarking, tamper-resistant hardware, and access to a certificate authority and time server. These ideas were generalized and formalized, resulting in the release of a set of recommendations, known as the Interim Report, to SMPTE at the end of 2001 [3]. Under this study group, an ad hoc discussion group called Key Management Ad Hoc (KMAH) was established. This group continues to be active under the DC28.30 Exhibition Working Group for Digital Cinema.

16.2.2   NIST

In early 2001, the U.S. government got involved to help spur on the efforts. The NIST of the U.S. Commerce Department held a two-day conference to:

- Articulate a vision for digital cinema
- Identify technological and business issue barriers to achieving that vision
- Develop strategies for breaching the barriers, including needed standards, technology development, and research

At this conference were speakers from NIST, representatives of the Motion Picture Association of America (MPAA) and the National Association of Theater Owners (NATO), industry scientists and technologists, representatives from SMPTE DC28 and MPEG, and representatives from commercial companies involved in, or hoping to get involved in, the business of digital cinema.

A major theme of the NIST conference was the need for security and, as importantly, standardization of security technologies. The catch phrase was "DRM."

16.2.3   DCI

The seven major Hollywood studios, Disney, Fox, MGM, Paramount, Sony, Universal, and Warner Bros., got together in early 2002 and formed a collective called Digital Cinema Initiatives, LLC (DCI). The purpose of DCI was to establish a uniform specification to ensure interoperability between equipment manufactured by different vendors.

After three and a half years of effort, DCI released its "Digital Cinema System Specification V1.0" in mid-2005 [4]. This document provides interoperability specifications for the digital cinema distribution master, compression, packaging, transport, theater systems, projection, and security. While all seven of these topics are important, it is interesting to note that the section that defines the security requirements is by far the longest and most detailed section in the specification. In the final section of this chapter, we provide a description of the security system proposed in that specification.

16.3   GOALS OF THE DIGITAL CINEMA SECURITY SYSTEM

Motion picture content is distributed from one party to another in the context of a business agreement. The recipient agrees to pay a certain price in exchange for the authorization to use the content in a certain way. For example, a theater may be authorized to show a motion picture up to 15 times per week for 5 weeks. They are expected to return the film after 5 weeks. They are not supposed to show the film more than the agreed upon 15 times in a given week. Of course, depending on the success of the film, these terms can often be modified during the run. There may be other conditions of the business agreement as well. The theater is not authorized to make copies of the film and is held responsible for assuring that no copies are made and that the physical film reels are not stolen. It is not authorized to modify the film. The theater may be required to show the film in its entirety, uninterrupted. In other words, they are not permitted to insert commercials or intermissions or to show the movie in multiple parts. The business arrangement may require that a movie be shown a minimum number of times or may dictate the days of the week or hours of the day that a movie should be shown. Since this is a business agreement between two parties, one offering certain rights to exhibit their intellectual property and one agreeing to pay for those rights, the terms of that arrangement can be as strict or as loose as the two parties negotiate.

Traditionally, these business agreements have been protected by legal and social mechanisms. The legal protections include both contract law enforcing the business agreement and copyright law protecting any profits lost due to copyright breaches. The primary social protection mechanism is trust. Theaters are trusted to abide by the contractual relationship. Breaches of this trust will diminish the theater's trustworthiness and may lead to exclusion from future business deals.

Technology has played a role in protecting the business agreements only in that it would require access to expensive equipment in order to make a copy of a 35-mm motion picture. Possession of such a copy would permit the theater to show the film on multiple screens simultaneously or to continue exhibiting the film after the contract had expired and the original copy had been returned to the distributor. If a copy is removed from the theater, it could be exhibited at another venue that is not contractually obligated to compensate the owner or it could be converted to a consumer format (e.g., VHS or DVD) and distributed to consumers, again without the permission of the content owner or compensation to that owner.

The transition to digital cinema does not change the legal or social mechanisms in place to enforce the business agreements; however, it significantly changes the impact of technology in two important ways. First, it removes the technological barrier to copying and redistribution of a movie. Assuming that the movie is stored in a standard file system as a file or set of files, the computer skills necessary to copy the movie are available to a very large percentage of the population and the equipment necessary has become a commodity. With the ready availability of high-bandwidth connections to a worldwide information network, the Internet, the copied movie can be easily, and in many cases anonymously, redistributed. The second impact is the opportunity to use technology to enforce some of the business terms. The remainder of this chapter describes the technology available and suggested for use in enforcing the terms of the contractual relationships between the content owners, content distributors, theater operators, and other stakeholders in the context of digital cinema.

16.4   TOOLS OF DIGITAL CINEMA CONTENT SECURITY

There are a number of technologies that can be employed to help prevent unauthorized use of digital cinema content. These include cryptographic tools to secure the digital content during transportation and to insure its integrity upon receipt, physical security technologies to help keep critical secrets, optical techniques to prevent the recording of a movie via camcorder, and forensic tools to track the source of the piracy that manages to circumvent all other protection measures.

16.4.1   Conditional Access

The basic tool for protecting a digital movie from unauthorized use is encryption. Encryption of multimedia files is discussed in detail in Chapter 4. The digital file or files containing the movie are encrypted prior to distribution and are stored in their encrypted state at the theater. Due to the relatively large sizes of the movie content files, symmetric key encryption is typically recommended. This avoids the need for the movie to be individually encrypted for each theater, but it rests the security of the movie with a small set of symmetric keys which must be distributed to the theaters. These keys are delivered with an explicit or implicit set of conditions that must be satisfied before use of the keys is justified. Explicit conditions may include a time window during which the movie can be played. Implicit conditions may include the ability of the exhibition equipment to demonstrate that it is certified and has not been tampered with. Careful management of the keys can insure that the movie is not available to would-be copiers while it is in the clear.

Any copies made and possibly redistributed would be neither valuable to the copier nor damaging to the content owner without the ability to decrypt. While the conditional access mechanism described above will prevent unauthorized access during transmission and storage, it does not protect the content from unauthorized access after it has been decrypted. A number of technologies can be employed here including link encryption, tamper-resistant hardware, and forensic marking. More on these topics can be found later in Sections 16.4.4, 16.4.5, and 16.4.7.

16.4.2   Key Management

"Careful management of keys" is a difficult challenge, as discussed in Chapter 6. Note that the security of the movie is now dependent on the security of the keys protecting it. The encryption technique should use keys that are long enough that a brute force attack of exhaustively trying all possible keys would be computationally infeasible. The long key length would also mean that the likelihood of randomly guessing a valid key would be extremely small. The actual selection of valid keys should maintain this resistance to attack by avoiding any learnable pattern in the valid key sequence.

The valid keys, once securely generated, must themselves be protected with encryption. This is necessary to protect the keys, as they are distributed to the theaters and stored for use there. Then a key management system must provide certain authorized modules the ability to access the keys and use them to access the content. A number of technologies are relevant here. First, public key cryptography allows the key management system to encrypt the keys in such a way as to insure that only the authorized target module can extract the keys. For this to be secure, the authorized module must make sure that its private key remains a secret. This is often accomplished with the help of tamper-resistant hardware. In addition, the key management system must be sure that the receiving module is authorized. This leads to the use of authentication protocols and enables the "de-authorization" of modules through the use of revocation lists. Authentication is typically accomplished through the use of digital certificates.

16.4.3   Digital Rights Management

Traditional Digital Rights Management (DRM), as discussed throughout this book, involves the representation of specific rights within the context of a system that can accommodate content with widely varying rights or entitlements. Previous chapters discuss the construction of languages to express and represent the rights associated with the content. The DRM client is then responsible for insuring that use of the content does not violate those rights. SMPTE DC28 has considered the use of a number of different rights expression languages for digital cinema.

One cost for this flexibility is a complexity that typically exceeds that of a conditional access system. Thus, before selecting a DRM technology, the diversity of rights that might accompany a motion picture needs first to be examined. Motion pictures from Hollywood are currently delivered to theaters with a very consistent set of rights. The theater has the rights to store the movie and exhibit the movie after a certain date. These rights expire at a later date, at which time the physical film is removed from the theater. Because of this modest need for a flexible rights management system, DCI has selected a conditional access system as discussed later in Section 16.5.

16.4.4   Link Encryption

A security system for digital cinema may be composed of a number of different components, each of which may be individually secured with various hardware mechanisms. While the content may be assumed to be protected when in the physical security perimeter of each component, steps must be taken to protect the content as it passes from one component to another. The typical tool for this type of protection is encryption.

As mentioned above, public key cryptography is not efficient for very large data sets, such as is the case with a digital motion picture. Instead, symmetric key ciphers are preferred. Standard methods exist for two devices or processes to securely establish a single symmetric key (often called a session key) using digital certificates and public key cryptography. One example of such a standard method is IETF RFC 3447 [7].

16.4.5   Physical Security

In general, it is very hard to keep a secret when you have to provide your adversary with a hardware device or software process that contains and uses that secret. Software can be disassembled, and hardware can be taken apart and reverse engineered. There are a number of items that must remain secret in a digital cinema system, including the cleartext content, the primary decryption keys, any link encryption session keys, and the private keys associated with any of the components of the security system.

There are many applications where cryptography is used to provide security to computer and communications systems. All of these applications run into this same problem of maintaining their secrets. In response to this need, a number of approaches have emerged to create systems that resist tampering, detect tampering, or even react to tampering by destroying the secret data (e.g., see Dyer et al. [8]). Security requirements for implementation of cryptographic modules were standardized by NIST in FIPS 140-2 [9]. This standard also provides relevant requirements for secure operating systems and key generation and management. See Anderson [25] for a good discussion of security in general, and see Chapter 14 of that text for a discussion of tamper resistance in particular.

16.4.6   Camcorder Jamming

Cryptographic systems can potentially protect digital content while in transit and while in storage, but at some point the motion picture must be deciphered, decompressed, and converted to light and sound for human consumption. This leaves the content vulnerable to recording on a camcorder.

Camcorder capture is a significant source of pirated motion pictures. In a recent study, 16% of movies available on a peer-to-peer (P2P) network were found to be captured via camcorder [5]. These pirated copies were first available, on average, nine days after theatrical release. In some cases, the capture is performed *after hours* when the theater is closed. The projectionist can run the film with a camcorder set up on a tripod in the back of the theater. This results in a high-quality capture. In addition, the audio can be recorded directly off of the theater sound system. In other cases, the capture is performed during a normal exhibition with an audience in the theater. Even in these cases, high-quality audio can be recorded using the hearing impaired headsets available in many theaters.

There are a number of approaches to defeating camcorder piracy, including temporal modulation, color fusion, CCD sensor saturation using infrared, and temporal aliasing generation. As of this writing, there are a number of companies that are working on technologies to defeat camcorder piracy. These include Thomson, Cinea, Sarnoff, Eastman Kodak, Sony, Sitrick & Sitrick, and Hughes Electronics. Although a number of U.S. and European patents have emerged, there are very few publications in the research literature in this area.

16.4.7   Forensic Tracking

It will not always be possible to prevent the creation of a pirated copy of a motion picture. An expert adversary may discover a way to circumvent the anti-camcorder technology and find success capturing the movie. An untrustworthy theater employee may discover a weakness that can be exploited to disable or bypass a security function. A security device may fail in an unpredicted mode. A tampered security device may be accidentally dropped from a revocation list. A thorough threat analysis will help minimize these events, but we cannot assume that they will be eliminated.

When a pirated copy of a movie is discovered by the rights owner, mechanisms should be in place to allow that copy to be traced back to its source. Thus, the pirated movie itself should expose the tampered hardware or untrustworthy employee. In the case of camcorder capture, the pirated copy should identify the theater and screen from which the movie was captured and the time and date of the capture. This will, in turn, identify the specific security equipment used and the theater operators on duty. Not only will this allow tampered equipment and untrustworthy employees to be identified and removed from the system, but it will also serve as a deterrent and, as such, reduce the incidence of piracy.

A combination of two technologies can be used to address this situation. First, a digital watermark can be added to the movie during exhibition. The water-mark makes imperceptible changes to the content to uniquely identify the location and show time. This information should be recoverable from a pirated copy of the movie even if that copy is significantly degraded as compared to the exhibited motion picture. Two good examples of appropriate watermarking tech-nology for digital cinema can be found in Lubin, Bloom, and Cheng [10] and

Haitsma and Kalker [11]. A more detailed discussion of the requirements and watermarking technologies for this application can be found in Bloom and Polyzois [12] and Bloom [13]. Watermarking is a field that is advancing quickly, and it is likely that, upon reading this book, new watermarking technologies will be available.

The second technology used to help analyze the security breach that led to an incident of piracy is the secure log or audit. A secure log is a mechanism to record all theater operations, including playback events. The mechanism is secure against deletion, modification, or forgery of log records. Rights holders can require theaters to periodically provide a copy of the log, and they can cryptographically confirm its integrity and continuity. The log will indicate how many times the movie was exhibited and when. This would be expected to be consistent with the agreed upon business arrangements. The log can also identify the specific set of exhibition equipment used for each showing and the identity of the operators of that set of equipment (as learned, for example, from smart cards or biometric identifiers necessary to use the equipment).

16.5　DCI DIGITAL CINEMA SPECIFICATION

As previously mentioned, the DCI released its Digital Cinema Specification during the summer of 2005. In this section we describe the basic security mechanisms described in that specification. As the reader might expect from the previous discussions, it involves strong encryption of the content, methods for securely delivering decryption keys only to authorized recipients, forensic marking, and secure logging. The implementation makes use of many well-accepted security standards, including those for implementation of secure silicon devices. Finally, a disclaimer: This description is the author's high-level presentation of the published specification. It is not a complete presentation and does not necessarily use the same language as that used in the specification. The interested reader is encouraged to refer directly to the specification for actual details [4].

16.5.1　Some Non-Security Specifications

Before diving into the security aspects of the specification, we present some imagery and audio representation specification details that may be helpful in understanding the context in which the security system operates.

The imagery is represented in JPEG 2000 [14]. While this standard was developed for still images, it can be applied, with high quality, to each frame of a motion sequence [15]. The compression ratios are not as great as those obtainable from compression methods that exploit interframe redundancies, such as MPEG-2 or H.264, but in this case, the demands for very high fidelity outweigh the need for compression.

DCI-compliant decoders are required to support two different image resolutions: 2K (2048 × 1080) and 4K (4096 × 2160) at frame rates of 24 fps for either resolution and 48 fps for the 2K resolution. Each pixel is represented with 36 bits: 12 bits in each of 3 color dimensions. This leads to uncompressed bitrates of 228 MB/sec (2K @ 24 fps), 456 MB/s (2K @ 48 fps), or 911 MB/s (4K @ 24 fps).

The DCI specification supports both 48 and 96 kHz audio at 24 bits per sample. The Digital Cinema Package (the packaged content as delivered to the theater) will have 16 channels of audio, although currently only two channel mappings are defined: a 6-channel configuration and an 8-channel configuration. The audio is not compressed. It is represented in a Pulse-Code Modulation (PCM) format and stored as a WAV file. During the decoding phase, this PCM audio will be converted to AES3 for playback.

16.5.2   Transport Encryption

The motion picture content is encrypted for transport from the distributor to the theater. In fact, it must remain encrypted in the theater and may only be decrypted at show time. The imagery, sound, and subtitles are all encrypted separately with different encryption keys. For transport of the motion picture content, a symmetric key cipher is used. More specifically, the specification designates that AES will be used in the Cipher Block Chaining (CBC) mode with a key size of 128 bits. As discussed in Chapter 4, AES is the Federal Information Processing Standard (FIPS) for the Advanced Encryption Standard [16] and is based on the symmetric block cipher known as Rijndael [17, 18].

Symmetric block cipher algorithms can be operated in a number of different modes. NIST has defined five modes [19] for use with FIPS-approved symmetric block ciphers. The CBC mode involves the chaining of each plaintext block of data with the ciphertext of the previous block prior to application of the forward block cipher. The chaining process is an exclusive-or (XOR) operation. More details on this can be found in Schneier [20].

By encrypting the content with such a strong cipher, the Digital Cinema Package can then be transported over insecure networks without the risk of exposing the cleartext content. This means that the actual transport network is not relevant to the security of digital cinema as long as the transport is successful. DCI, in fact, makes a point of stating that "content security is transport agnostic, and can be accomplished by either electronic or physical means." This means that the current distribution network of couriers could continue to exist. Instead of transporting film reels, they could be transporting hard drives or optical discs. It also allows for a sophisticated satellite delivery network or delivery via fiber optic cable or even over the public Internet.

As with most encryption-based security systems, this one transfers the security challenge from secure content delivery to secure key delivery. The gain is that the size of the critical payload has been drastically decreased.

16.5.3   Key Transport

The Digital Cinema Package is delivered to the theater with its three major components—imagery, audio, and subtitles—encrypted. Also delivered to the theater, perhaps over a separate channel and at a different time, is a special construct called the Key Delivery Message (KDM). This KDM carries a number of important items with it, but primary among them is the set of content keys necessary to decipher the movie content.

This payload of keys is itself encrypted so that interception of the KDM does not compromise the security of the motion picture. In order to insure that only the intended recipient can recover the keys, a public key cipher is used. This means that, although the distributor can multicast the same encrypted movie content to many theaters, each KDM will be uniquely created for its intended receiver. In fact, each projector will receive a unique KDM: the payload encrypted with the public key of the projector's controlling *Security Manager*. More on Security Managers will be discussed in the next section.

DCI specifies that the RSA public key cipher will be used with a 2048-bit key for encrypting the payload of the KDM. The RSA algorithm is the most widely used public key cryptosystem, and with such a long key length, it is considered extremely secure [21].

Once the Security Manager has successfully deciphered the payload of the KDM and has obtained the content decryption keys, it must insure that those keys remain unobtainable by any other device or adversary. This typically means maintaining them in secure hardware. Should the Security Manager have the need to cache the keys temporarily in an off-chip store, it must protect them with a symmetric key cipher. DCI-compliant Security Managers can choose between AES with a 128-bit key or Triple-DES (TDES) with a 112-bit key. These techniques for securely transporting content and associated keys from a distributor to a security manager in a theater are illustrated in figure 16.1.

16.5.4   Security Manager

The DCI specification identifies a number of security devices that will exist in a theater security system, but the most important of these is the Security Manager. The Security Manager coordinates all of the security devices within the security system. It is responsible for identifying the other security devices and authenticating them. It establishes a secure communications channel with each of the other security devices. Finally, the Security Manager confirms the authorization of each security device. These three topics are discussed in the subsections below.

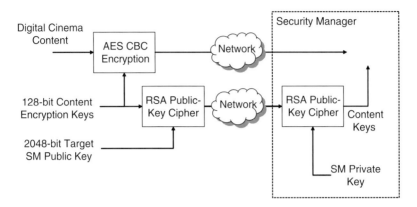

FIGURE 16.1: The digital cinema content is encrypted using AES and sent over an arbitrary network to the theater. The content keys that are used to encrypt this content are needed at the theater for decryption. These content keys are delivered to the theater with the RSA public key cipher using the public key of the receiving Security Manager (SM) to insure that only SM will be able to recover the content keys.

Security Device Authentication

The Security Manager is responsible for insuring that only DCI-compliant security devices participate in security operations. It does this by examining a digital certificate offered by the device. The certificate, issued by the device vendor and encrypted with that vendor's private key, contains the public key associated with the device and a set of identifying data including the make, model, device Universal Unique ID (UUID), and serial number of the certificate. The certificate also contains information defining the specific role or roles that the device can play within the context of a digital cinema security system.

By decrypting the certificate with the vendor's public key, the Security Manager can verify that the certificate was issued by that vendor, obtain the device's public key, and retrieve the device identity details. The certificate represents the vendor's declaration that the device is compliant with the DCI specification for the specified roles.

Rather than having the vendor encrypt the entire certificate with his private key, an alternative approach has the vendor applying a digital signature to the certificate. A number of different digital signature algorithms are available, but in all cases, the vendor calculates a cryptographic hash, or digest, of the certificate and encrypts that digest with his private key. Upon receipt of the digital certificate, the digital signature can be decrypted with the vendor's public key and the digest contained within compared to a calculated digest of the certificate. This verifies the originator of the signature as well as the integrity of the certificate.

This use of digital certificates is consistent with common usage for presenting the assurance of a third party (usually a *Certificate Authority* or CA) regarding one's identity. As such, the format used is based on the commonly used Internet Engineering Task Force (IETF) format, X.509 version 3 [22]. The digital signature algorithm for a digital cinema digital certificate must use the RSA public key cipher to encrypt a SHA-256 digest of the certificate [23].

Secure Communications Channel

The Security Manager is responsible for establishing secure communications channels between itself and each of the authenticated security devices in the digital cinema security system. The process of establishing such a channel involves a cryptographic protocol in which a session key is generated and then exchanged using the private/public key pairs of the two participating devices. This process insures that no eavesdropper observing the communication between the two devices would be able to learn the key that was exchanged. This session key is then used to encrypt the communications between those two devices.

The process described above is commonly used for secure Internet communications, and DCI has adopted the well-known Transport Layer Security (TLS) protocol [24]. In fact, since the TLS protocol requires an exchange of digital certificates and an authentication of those certificates, establishment of a TLS session encompasses the device authentication step described in the previous section. In other words, while device authentication and creation of secure communications have been presented as two separate steps, they are, in fact, performed simultaneously during the establishment of a TLS session.

Device Authorization

Once the TLS sessions have been established, the Security Manager knows the identity of each of the other security devices in the security system. It does not, however, know if those devices are trustworthy. In a DCI digital cinema environment, the Security Manager will trust only those specific devices that the rights owner trusts. The rights owner maintains a list of trusted devices for each and every theater and each and every projection suite within each theater. When composing the KDM containing the decryption keys for a specific Security Manager, the rights owner will include a list of trusted devices within that projection suite or theater. This list is called the Trusted Device List (TDL).

Because the TDL is sent in the KDM, it can be different for each projection environment and for each composition. It identifies the specific security devices authorized to participate in playback of the particular composition with which it is associated and specifies the roles for which each device is approved. Rights owners can "revoke" the trust of a device or family of devices by simply removing them from all TDLs.

16.5.5 Physical Security

The Security Manager and other security devices that participate in security operations in the digital cinema system must be implemented in secure hardware. Secure hardware could be enclosures without access doors. Enclosures with access doors may need to be equipped with mechanisms to detect the opening of those enclosures. The Security Manager and a number of other security devices, however, must be implemented in secure silicon.

The physical security requirements for digital cinema components are based on those specified by NIST for secure cryptographic modules (FIPS 140-2 [9]). This standard describes the operating system requirements as well as the requirements for physical perimeter protection for four different levels of security. Most digital cinema security components, including the SM, are required to meet the Level 3 requirements. Among other things, this requires that devices be able to detect tampering attempts and react to those attempts by zeroing out all sensitive data including all cryptographic keys. The digital cinema security system further requires that all security chips report tampering attempts in the secure audit log (see Section 16.5.7).

16.5.6 Link Encryption

Decrypted content may need to pass from one security device to another (e.g., Image Media Block to projector), and this content must be protected with link encryption. The DCI specification states that the link encryption can be either AES with a 128-bit key or TDES with a 112-bit key. The symmetric AES key used for this session is generated by the Security Manager. This key generation process itself must be secure and thus must follow the process specified in IETF RFC 3447 [7].

16.5.7 Forensics: Logging

One theme of the DCI specification is the notion *"Control Lightly/Audit Tightly."* The light control means that the rights owners will not attempt to control how and when the movie can be exhibited beyond specifying the engagement window, location, and the list of authorized devices. However, the rights owners will expect a cryptographically secure audit log of how and when the movie was exhibited. They also expect to see log entries indicating the status of the security system.

To create this log, all security devices are required to record security events. Examples of security events are power-up and power-down, the establishment and termination of TLS sessions, and the beginning and ending of a decryption or decoding or forensic marking process. In addition, all tamper detections and maintenance on security components are logged.

Log entries are sequentially numbered and signed by the device that creates them. This provides non-repudability and protection against deletion or modification of log entries. Upon request, each security device will transmit their audit log to the Security Manager. This communication is done within the context of a TLS session to further maintain the integrity of the log.

Log entries are stored in a pre-defined XML format that contains a header, content, and signature. The header contains the sequencing information, the type of log entry, a time stamp, and a hash of the content. The signature authenticates the header.

Once all log entries are collected from the various security devices, the Security Manager can pass the log up to management processes. The structure of the log messages allows a filtering operation to be applied while maintaining the continuity guarantees. Filtering is necessary to create reports that can be sent to the rights owners. Only information relevant to that party and the exhibition of compositions that belong to that party need to be shared.

A filtering operation will remove the content of log entries that are not relevant to the query (e.g., specifying the time window, entry type or class, and the device that created the entry). However, the headers and signatures will remain. The signatures of the removed entries will still authenticate the headers, and examination of these headers can confirm that no entries have been deleted and that the filtered log entry contents fell outside of the query.

16.5.8   Forensics: Watermarking

DCI has specified that a compliant digital cinema exhibition system will have the capability to embed digital watermarks into both the audio and the imagery, but it has not specified which watermarking technology should be used. It has specified a minimum payload and fidelity requirement, but has not specified any meaningful robustness requirements. Furthermore, the DCI specification does not address the *security* of the watermark, i.e., its ability to resist unauthorized embedding, detection, or removal (see Chapter 9 of Cox, Miller, and Bloom [6] for a discussion of these aspects of watermark security). The one exception is the statement that the imagery watermark is required to survive collusion attacks. All of these issues are left to the market as various watermark technology vendors compete to supply the most robust and secure watermark that meets the fidelity and payload requirements.

One of the most important devices in a digital cinema projection system is the Image Media Block (IMB). This is the device that performs image decryption and decoding. This device must also have the ability to add a forensic watermark to the imagery. Thus, since the IMB must be implemented in secure silicon, decrypted and unwatermarked imagery will never be available.

Another important device is the Audio Media Block. This device performs audio decryption and formatting to synchronize the audio and convert it to AES3. It also must have the ability to add a forensic watermark to the audio content within the secure physical perimeter of the secure silicon.

These two primary devices, the IMB and the Audio Media Block, may need to transfer the content to a subsequent device via a link encrypted channel. The receiving device will first apply the corresponding link decryption. The DCI specification states that any device that performs link decryption may optionally have the ability to follow the decryption with the addition of a secondary forensic watermark.

Watermarking is typically seen as a trade-off between fidelity, robustness, and payload. One can typically improve the performance along one of these axes at the expense of the others. Regarding fidelity, DCI says that both the audio and imagery watermarks must be imperceptible to the critical viewer/listener. It specifies that imagery be evaluated in butterfly tests and that audio be evaluated in A/B tests.

The watermark must be able to indicate the time of exhibition to within 15 minutes. Each hour of the day is thus partitioned into four 15-minute blocks. This results in 96 blocks per day and 35,136 blocks per year (assuming 366 days). Representation of time, therefore, requires 16 bits. The watermark must also be able to identify the location of the exhibition. Nineteen bits have been reserved for this purpose. Thus, the minimum watermark payload is 35 bits. This payload must be embedded into every 5 minutes of content.

The watermark is "required to survive" a number of different processes and transformations. Among these, an imagery watermark is required to survive the following: digital-to-analog-to-digital conversion, resampling, requantization, dithering, contrast and color enhancement, scaling, letterbox, aperture control, low-pass filtering, anti-aliasing filtering, brick wall filtering, noise reduction, frame swapping, compression, scaling, cropping, additive noise, format conversion, change in frame rate, shifting, change in aspect ratio, etc. In addition, the imagery watermark is required to survive recording on a camcorder followed by low bitrate compression (e.g., H.264 @ 500 Kbps).

Examples of the kind of processing that audio watermarks are required to survive include digital-to-analog-to-digital conversion, radio-frequency (RF) and infrared (IR) transmission, channel combination, resampling, pitch change, pitch preserving time scaling, data reduction coding, amplitude compression, additive and multiplicative noise, equalization, echo addition, band-pass filtering, wow and flutter, etc.

Note that the phrase "required to survive" is subject to interpretation. For example, an imagery watermark is required to survive cropping. But does this mean the removal of the rightmost column or could it mean extraction of a 10% by 10% window from the field? Both are different extreme examples of cropping. Each watermarking technology can be evaluated as to its *degree of survival* to each of the listed processes. This then provides a means of comparison of different watermarking technologies that meet the minimum fidelity and payload requirements and compete against each other with regard to robustness.

16.5.9   Image Media Block

As briefly mentioned in the previous section, the primary security device in a theater security system is the IMB. This device performs decryption of the imagery as well as decoding and watermarking. Optionally, if the output imagery is to be passed to another security device, the IMB can contain a link encryption component as well. Finally, the IMB must include the Security Manager.

The DCI specification does allow a number of Security Managers to co-exist in a theater security system, but the Security Manager that resides in the IMB will be the one responsible for coordinating all of the other security devices. It is this Security Manager that is the intended recipient of the KDM. This Security Manager can be associated with only one projector.

The entire IMB, including the media decryptor, forensic marker, image decoder, Security Manager, and optional link encryptor, must be implemented in secure silicon as described in Section 16.5.5. This secure device can also hold other components as well. For example, the IMB could include a media decryptor for the audio and its corresponding forensic marker: components which are together referred to as the Audio Media Block. The IMB can also be integrated into the projection system.

16.5.10   Example

Figure 16.2 illustrates some of the security devices discussed in this chapter. This figure shows the IMB, Audio Media Block, and projection system as three separate components. In practice, these three may be implemented as one secure device, thus eliminating the need for link encryption and secondary (optional) forensic marking.

The content is AES encrypted and stored in the theater. The encrypted imagery is sent to the IMB and the encrypted audio is sent to the Audio Media Block. The IMB, which contains the Security Manager, receives the KDM containing the AES keys, information describing the authorized engagement window and location, and the TDL. This KDM is received via RSA public key encryption.

The Security Manager authenticates the other security devices via their digital certificates and establishes TLS sessions with each. It then verifies that all of these devices are found on the TDL. The Security Manager then provides the Audio Media Block with the AES key necessary to decrypt the audio and the link encryptors and corresponding link decryptors exchange session keys.

Now, the IMB can begin decrypting the imagery and marking and decoding that imagery. Note that while figure 16.2 shows the marking occurring prior to the decoding, this is not specified by DCI. The marking could potentially be

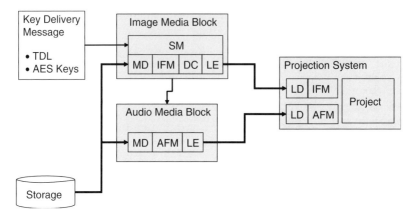

FIGURE 16.2:   An example of a set of theater security devices with optional components included. This figure shows the KDM containing a TDL and the AES keys. The IMB contains an SM, a media decryptor (MD), an image forensic marker (IFM), a decoder (DC), and a link encryptor (LE). The Audio Media Block has an MD, an audio forensic marker (AFM), and a link encryptor. Finally, the projection system has link decryptors (LD) and audio and image forensic markers. The IMB communicates with the other two devices over TLS-secured communication channels.

placed after the decoding. The Audio Media Block decrypts and marks the audio, synchronizes it, and codes it in AES3 audio. Both the Audio Media Block and the IMB encrypt their outputs for delivery to the projection system. The projection system decrypts the audio and imagery and (optionally) marks both. At this point, both the imagery and the audio will leave the protection of secure silicon, but will remain within the physical protection of tamper-detecting hardware as it is sent to the theater audio system and the projection mechanism of the projector.

16.6   SUMMARY

Digital cinema has been developing for the past five years. We have seen the evolution of the technology and the evolution of the business models, both of which are critically necessary for a successful, wide-scale deployment. In this chapter we have focused on the technology for content security.

An important milestone in the technology development is the emergence of standards. This indicates the relative maturity of the technologies and the willingness of technology providers to agree on architectures and interfaces. Standards are required to insure interoperability and to encourage vendors to invest in the development of compliant equipment.

SMPTE has played a critical role in this process by establishing an early strawman architecture for security and by providing a forum for rights owners and technology vendors to discuss the security issues. The DCI specification builds upon these discussions and represents a first attempt by the rights owners themselves at recommending standard digital cinema specifications.

In this chapter we have presented a discussion of some of the components that make up a security system for digital cinema. We then illustrated these components through a high-level presentation of the security aspects of the DCI Digital Cinema Specification of July 2005.

REFERENCES

[1] J. A. Bloom, I. J. Cox, T. Kalker, J. P. Linnartz, M. L. Miller, and B. Traw, Copy protection for DVD Video, *Proc. IEEE*, 87(7):1267–1276, 1999.

[2] C. S. Swartz. *Understanding Digital Cinema: A Professional Handbook*, Elsevier, Amsterdam/New York, 2005.

[3] SMPTE DC28.4 Study Group. SMPTE Digital Cinema Study Group DC28.4 on Encryption and Conditional Access: Interim Report, Release Version 1.0, September 10, 2001.

[4] Digital Cinema Initiatives, LLC. Digital Cinema System Specification V1.0, July 20, 2005.

[5] S. Byers, L. Cranor, D. Kormann, P. McDaniel, and E. Cronin. Analysis of security vulnerabilities in the movie production and distribution process, in *Proc. 2003 ACM Workshop on Digital Rights Management*, Washington, DC, October 27, 2003.

[6] I. J. Cox, M. L. Miller, and J. A. Bloom. *Digital Watermarking*, Morgan Kaufmann, San Mateo, CA, 2001.

[7] J. Jonsson and B. Kaliski. IETF RFC 3447, Public-Key Cryptography Standards (PKCS) #1: RSA Cryptography Specifications Version 2.1, The Internet Society, February 2003, http://www.ietf.org/rfc/rfc3447.txt.

[8] J. G. Dyer, M. Lindemann, R. Perez, R. Sailer, L. van Doorn, S. W. Smith, and S. Weingart. Building the IBM 4758 secure coprocessor, *Computer*, 34(10): 57–66, 2001.

[9] National Institute of Standards and Technology. Security Requirements for Cryptographic Modules, FIPS 140-2, 2002, http://csrc.nist.gov/publications/fips/fips140-2/fips1402.pdf.

[10] J. Lubin, J. A. Bloom, and H. Cheng, Robust, content-dependent, high-fidelity watermark for tracking in digital cinema, security and watermarking of multimedia contents V, *Proc. SPIE* 5020:536–545, 2003.

[11] J. Haitsma and T. Kalker. A watermarking scheme for digital cinema, in *Int. Conf. Image Processing*, pp. 487–489, Thessalaniki, Greece, October 7–10, 2001.

[12] J. A. Bloom and C. Polyzois. Watermarking to track motion picture theft, in *Proc. Thirty-Eighth Asilomar Conf. Signals, Systems, and Computers*, Pacific Grove, CA, pp. 363–367, 2004.

[13] J. A. Bloom. Security and rights management in digital cinema, in *Proc. IEEE Int. Conf. Multimedia and Expo, ICME'03*, 1:621–624, Baltimore, MD, July 2003.

[14] D. S. Taubman and M. W. Marcellin. *JPEG 2000: Image Compression Fundamentals, Standards and Practice*, Kluwer Academic, Dordrecht, Norwell, MA, 2002.

[15] W. Yu, R. Qui, and J. Fritts. Advantages of motion-JPEG 2000 in video processing, *Visual Communications and Image Processing, Proc. SPIE*, 4671:635–645, 2002.

[16] National Institute of Standards and Technology. Advanced Encryption Standard, FIPS 197, 2001, http://csrc.nist.gov/publications/fips/fips197/fips-197.pdf.

[17] J. Daemen and V. Rijmen. The block cipher Rijndael, in *Proc. Int Conf. Smart Card Research and Applications*, LNCS vol.1820, pp. 288–296, 1998.

[18] J. Daemen and V. Rijmen. *The Design of Rijndael: AES — The Advanced Encryption Standard*, Springer-Verlag, Berlin/New York, 2002.

[19] Dworkin, M. Recommendation for Block Cipher Modes of Operation: Methods and Techniques, NIST Special Publication 800-38A, December 2001. http://csrc.nist.gov/publications/nistpubs/800-38a/sp800-38a.pdf.

[20] B. Schneier. *Applied Cryptography Second Edition*, John Wiley & Sons, New York, 1995.

[21] R. Rivest, A. Shamir, and L. Adleman. A method for obtaining digital signatures and public-key cryptosystems, *Communications of the ACM*, 21(2):120–126, 1978.

[22] R. Housley, W. Ford, W. Polk, and D. Solo. Internet X.509 Public Key Infrastructure Certificate and CRL Profile, IETF RFC 2459, 1999.

[23] National Institute of Standards and Technology. Secure Hash Standard, FIPS 180-2, 2002, http://csrc.nist.gov/publications/fips/fips180-2/fips-180-2.pdf.

[24] T. Dierks and C. Allen. The TLS Protocol Version 1.0, IETF RFC 2246, 1999.

[25] R. Anderson. *Security Engineering: A Guide to Building Dependable Distributed Systems*, John Wiley & Sons, New York, 2001.

PART **D**

STANDARDS AND LEGAL ISSUES

17

DRM Standard Activities

Xin Wang

Zhongyang Huang and Shengmei Shen

17.1 INTRODUCTION

With the advent of digital technologies, many new market opportunities have emerged for content owners, content distributors, and consumer electronics/information technology industries. An essential requirement for developing a thriving marketplace is the protection of copyrighted content in digital form. Digital Rights Management (DRM), or Intellectual Property Management and Protection (IPMP), is a collection of hardware, software, services, and technologies that have been developed for persistently governing authorized distribution and use of content and services according to their associated rights and managing consequences of that distribution and use throughout their entire lifecycle or workflow. As DRM-enabled content, products, and services start to emerge in the consumer market, there are some problems that remain to be solved.

The first problem is the lack of interoperability among the existing DRM system offerings. Fundamentally, these systems work by encrypting content in some manner and binding the content with a set of usage rules that are used to govern the distribution and use of the content. Largely because of business arrangements, different content providers tend to use different formats and different DRM systems to protect and distribute the content. For instance, the bloom of online music distribution services, such as iTunes from Apple, Rhapsody from Real Networks, Napster and Yahoo using Microsoft products, and Vodafone Live! from Vodafone, offers legitimate audio content and provides an attractive value proposition to the consumers. However, songs purchased using one service cannot be played using other players, due to the incompatibility of the DRM-enabled content formats, the licenses for usage rules, and DRM capability requirements on the player applications and devices. This situation is expected to become worse as other major players like Sony, Microsoft, and even Wal-Mart and Coca-Cola prepare to enter this online music distribution business.

The second problem of the existing DRM market is the poor renewability of DRM products. Many existing DRM systems are likely to be broken, due to the rapidly growing computer science and technology and the high interests in content of high value or popularity. This is one of the serious problems encountered in the digital content delivery business. It is therefore desirable to design and deploy robust and flexible DRM systems, where one can effectively renew broken DRM systems.

Whereas solving the renewability problem relies on the advance and evolution of DRM technologies and systems themselves, solving the interoperability problem demands open, international standardization efforts so that content can be delivered anytime, and to anywhere in the world, and consumed anytime and on any device the consumer wants.

This chapter lists a number of DRM standard activities that thrive at designing robust DRM technologies and DRM systems. It starts with describing in detail the activities in the Moving Picture Experts Group (MPEG) and Open Mobile Alliance (OMA). MPEG provides a general interoperable multimedia framework and component technologies, whereas OMA focuses on a mobile industry-specific DRM system. Next, this chapter introduces briefly a few standards organizations such as the Digital Media Project (DMP), Internet Streaming Media Alliance (ISMA), Advanced Access Content System (AACS), Coral Consortium, and Digital Video Broadcasting (DVB) Project. Finally, this chapter compiles a quick reference list of DRM-related standards and consortiums, many of which are not discussed in this chapter due to space limitation.

17.2   MPEG

MPEG is a working group of ISO/IEC in charge of the development of standards for coded representation of digital audio and video. Established in 1988, the group has produced MPEG-1, the standard on which such products as video CD and MP3 are based; MPEG-2, the standard on which such products as digital television set-top boxes and DVD are based; MPEG-4, the standard for multimedia for the fixed and mobile Web; MPEG-7, the standard for description and search of audio and visual content; and MPEG-21, the multimedia framework for end-to-end content delivery and consumption.

To ensure secure content delivery and legitimate content consumption, MPEG has been devoting significant efforts, for the last seven years, to achieving the goal of developing DRM standards that enable the functionalities of renewability and interoperability [1]. The MPEG specific term for DRM is "Intellectual Property Management and Protection," (IPMP). The latest IPMP standard for the MPEG-4 system is the MPEG-4 IPMP Extension (IPMPX) [2], the latest IPMP standard for MPEG-2 system is MPEG-2 IPMP [3, 4] (using MPEG-4 IPMP Extension Framework), and the latest IPMP efforts in MPEG-21 multimedia framework [5, 6] are IPMP Components [7], Rights Expression Language (REL) [8], and Rights Data Dictionary (RDD) [9].

The rest of this section first provides some background information for the DRM/IPMP works conducted at MPEG and then provides overviews of the MPEG extension architectures for MPEG-4/2 and the MPEG-21 IPMP Components, and the MPEG-21 REL.

17.2.1 The Need for a Flexible and Interoperable MPEG IPMP Framework

MPEG started its IPMP effort in the development of MPEG-4. The first attempt is often referred to as the "hooks" approach, where normative syntax is defined in the MPEG-4 system to allow the bitstream to carry information that informs the terminal which (of possibly multiple) IPMP system should be used to process the governed content objects in compliance with the rules declared by the content provider. The respective IPMP systems themselves were not specified within MPEG-4 [10]. MPEG-4 integrates the hooks tightly with the MPEG-4 system layer, which makes it possible to build secure MPEG-4 delivery chains in very smart and efficient ways.

This hooks model, however, appears to have many significant problems. For example, IPMP systems can be "hooked" into the MPEG-4 terminal, but it can only be done on a proprietary basis. Since the protection is normally required to be associated with some elements of the MPEG-4 terminal, and its behavior cannot be independent of other parts of the MPEG-4 terminal, if the IPMP system is not interoperable, the MPEG-4 terminal with IPMP protection would also become non-interoperable.

In the year 2000, MPEG began to address this issue of interoperability between different products, often for similar services, as developed within the IPMP framework of the MPEG-4 standard. In addition, with convergence becoming a reality, e.g., through the deployment of broadband Internet access and the start of new services on mobile channels, MPEG further put up a requirement that different types of devices and services should be able to work together to play secure digital

MPEG-4 content from multiple sources in a simple way, e.g., without the need to change the devices. This effort resulted in an extension to the MPEG-4 systems standard published in October 2002 [2].

During the progress of the MPEG-4 IPMPX, most of its architecture and concepts were applied and adopted to the MPEG-2 system. This work led to the MPEG-2 IPMP, published in March 2003 in the forms of an amendment to the MPEG-2 system [3] and a new part 11 of the MPEG-2 standard [4].

The reason for creating the MPEG-2 IPMP part is the following. The old MPEG-2 system provides hooks to proprietary Conditional Access (CA) systems for the protection of content carried in transport streams and program streams. It provides the following functionalities: (i) signaling whether particular packets have been scrambled: elementary stream or transport stream packets; (ii) sending messages to be used in (proprietary) CA systems: the Entitlement Control Message (ECM) and the Entitlement Management Message (EMM); and (iii) identifying the CA system used (under the assumption that registration authorities outside of MPEG take care that no collisions between identifiers occur).While proprietary CA systems can be integrated with the MPEG-2 audio/video technology, there are no provisions for achieving interoperability between different CA systems. The Simulcrypt system, providing a limited form of interoperability in digital television, was integrated in using these hooks with some further semantics defined in the European Digital Video Broadcast (DVB) project. It is also known that MPEG-2's provision for CA systems is not flexible, has no support for CA systems to perform watermarking and rights management, and has no support for multiple CA systems to perform on a same stream simultaneously. Moreover, the provision is not secure enough, as it does not provide good renewability of CA systems. Finally, the lack of syntax for the ECM and EMM also results in less interoperability. The MPEG-2 IPMP is designed to address the above problems, especially, the renewability and interoperability ones.

Recently, a new standardization effort has been put in MPEG to make it possible to deliver content in more interoperable, secure, and global manners. The vision for a new collection of MPEG-21 standards is to define a multimedia framework that will enable transparent and augmented use of multimedia resources across a wide range of networks and devices used by different industries and communities [5, 6]. The intent is that the framework will cover the entire multimedia content delivery chain encompassing content creation, production, delivery, and trade. The MPEG-21 standard specifications describe how these existing components can be used together and provide new models to distribute and trade digital content electronically. Naturally, DRM is a major concern in the MPEG-21 framework. As such, MPEG-21 developed its REL [8] and RDD [9], both published in April 2004, and IPMP Components [7], published in October 2005. These standards, together with others in the MPEG-21 collection such as the Digital Item Declaration, Digital Item Identification, Digital Item Adaptation, and Digital Item Processing and

Event Reporting, provide a suite of DRM components technologies that enable development of robust, flexible, interoperable, and renewable DRM systems and products.

17.2.2   Architectures for MPEG-4; IPMPX and MPEG-2 IPMP

Key Concepts

It is important to achieve robustness and flexibility in the interoperable framework provided by a standard. To achieve robustness, the IPMPX provides tool renewability, which protects against security breakdown. It also provides flexibility by allowing use of various cipher tools as well as decoding tools according to system designer's choice. The IPMPX defines the following five key elements:

- **IPMP Tools**. IPMP Tools are modules that perform (one or more) IPMP functions such as authentication, decryption, watermarking, etc. A given IPMP Tool may coordinate with other IPMP Tools. Each IPMP Tool has a unique IPMP Tool ID that identifies the Tool in an unambiguous way, either at a presentation level or at a universal level.

  It is realized that it is not possible to standardize all IPMP Tools, mainly due to two reasons. The first is that different content providers may have different preferences on what IPMP Tools to use. The second reason is that there are some tools that are difficult to standardize. For example, it's not possible to standardize a video watermarking tool, as there is no watermarking algorithm that has been proven to be robust yet. With these considerations, the IPMPX is designed to differ from many prior approaches in that it intelligently provides an open secure framework allowing tools from different vendors to cooperate with each other.

- **IPMP Descriptors**. Originated from MPEG-4 Object Descriptors (OD), IPMP Descriptors describe how an object can be accessed and decoded. These IPMP Descriptors are used to denote an IPMP Tool that is used to protect the object. An independent Registration Authority (RA) is used so any party can register its own IPMP tools and identify them without collisions.

- **IPMP Elementary Streams**. IPMP-specific data such as key data and rights data are carried by IPMP elementary streams. All MPEG objects are represented by elementary streams, which can reference each other. These special IPMP elementary streams can be used to convey IPMP-specific data.

- **IPMP Tool Lists**. An IPMP tool list carries the information of IPMP tools required by the terminal to consume the content. It is carried in the Initial Object Descriptor (IOD) of the MPEG-4 system stream or in the IPMP control information table in the Program-Specific Information (PSI) of the MPEG-2 system stream. This mechanism enables the terminal to select, manage the tools, or retrieve them when the tools are missing.

- **Secure Messaging Framework**. The IPMPX framework does not follow the conventional approach to define functional interfaces; instead, it is based on secure message communication. This is one of the most important concepts in the IPMPX. Interaction between the terminal and IPMP Tools is realized through messages via a conceptual entity called "message router." The syntax and semantics of the messages are clearly defined in order to facilitate full interoperability. Mutual authentication and secure messages are also introduced to define a secure framework.

  The message-based architecture has three advantages over functional interface-based architectures. Note that the normal functional interfaces are unlikely to cover various kinds of interfaces for different algorithms, even for the same encryption function. Furthermore, the normal functional interfaces are highly dependent on the operating system and the implementation. The first advantage is that security can be more easily maintained, as messages are easier to protect in an open framework than the parameters in a function parameter list. The second is that the only entities that need to be concerned with a given message's definition are those that need to generate or act upon a given message, so additional functionality can be created and supported simply through the addition of the required messages. The third is that full interoperability with IPMP Tools can be easily achieved by registering the messaging application programming interface(API) to an RA and carrying the registered API ID within in the IPMP descriptor or by defining a single messaging API by a third party forum which adopts the IPMPX. Note that MPEG does not undertake the role of defining a single messaging API, since MPEG standards are mainly developed for a large number of industrial domains. Individual industrial domains should take the IPMPX as a base and fill in the gap in order to make the IPMPX truly interoperable.

MPEG-4 IPMPX Architecture

The terminal architecture within the MPEG-4 IPMPX framework is shown in Figure 17.1. The original MPEG-4 system without IPMP protection is shown at the upper half of the diagram (above the dotted line). The incoming MPEG-4 content stream is de-multiplexed in the Delivery Multimedia Integration Framework (DMIF). Audio, Video, OD, and Binary Format for Scenes (BIFS) bitstream are supplied to the Decoding Buffers (DBS) and then decoded. The decoded audio and video data are fed to the audio composition Buffer (CB) and the Video CB, respectively, and then are composed in the compositor together with the decoded ODs and the decoded BIFS tree or scene graph.

  The lower half of the figure (below the dotted line) shows the modules provided by the IPMPX. The Tool List is included in the IOD of the MPEG-4 system stream to identify the IPMP tools required to consume the protected content. IPMP stream

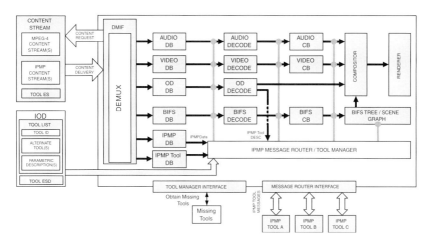

FIGURE 17.1: The MPEG-4 IPMPX terminal architecture.

arrives as an elementary stream multiplexed in the MPEG-4 system stream. Note that the Tool list and the IPMP stream are constructed during the content authoring process. The Tool Manager (a conceptual entity) manages IPMP Tools within the terminal (e.g., downloading a missing tool from a remote location), while the message router routes messages among the terminal and the IPMP tools using a secure messaging framework to ensure that different IPMP Tools from different vendors can work together. IPMP tools can act on several control points, which are positions along the dataflow where the IPMP tool functions by taking over the protected content bitstream, processing it, and returning it back to the control point for subsequent processing of the content by the MPEG-4 terminal. The supported control points are dictated by the gray circles in the architecture diagram. For example, an encrypted MPEG-4 video stream needs to be decrypted by an IPMP tool (decryptor) at the control point right before the video decoder, and a watermark reader may need to be applied to the watermarked audio stream at the control point right after the audio decoder. If necessary, an IPMP tool can be applied to the control points right before the compositor to control the rendering process.

MPEG-2 IPMP Architecture

The new MPEG-2 IPMP framework is depicted in Figure 17.2. The tool list, tool container, and rights container are included in the IPMP control information table which is part of the PSI. An IPMP stream arrives as an elementary stream multiplexed in an MPEG-2 transport or program stream. The tool manager manages IPMP tools within the terminal, while the message router routes messages among the terminal and IPMP tools. The incoming content is de-multiplexed by the MPEG-2 system DeMux. Audio and video bitstreams are supplied to the DB

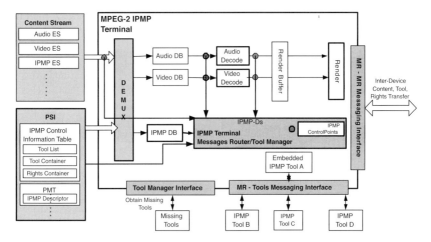

FIGURE 17.2: The MPEG-2 IPMP terminal architecture.

and then decoded and rendered. IPMP tools can act on several control points as dictated by gray circles.

17.2.3   Features of the IPMPX Architecture

The IPMPX architecture has several important features:

- **Interoperability**. The IPMP extension standardizes IPMP messages and the process of message routing. By using a common set of IPMP messages, together with some industry defined messaging API and messages extension, different IPMP Tools can be easily plugged into the terminal and can interact with each other.
- **Renewability**. Through the usage of the tool list and IPMP descriptor, one can easily renew a tool for better IPMP protection by, e.g., indicating to the terminal that a new tool is needed, carrying the new tool in the tool elementary stream in the content stream, or downloading the new tool from somewhere. Note that tool downloading is not mandatory in IPMP; rather, IPMP provides the architecture to facilitate tool downloading.
- **Flexibility**. The IPMPX does not standardize IPMP tools. With the support of independent registration authorities, the ability to carry tools inside the content stream, and the terminal's potential capability to download required IPMP Tools from a remote location, one can choose whatever tools to perform decryption, watermarking, user authentication, or integrity checking.
- **Dynamic Operation**. Various IPMP tools can be signaled in the content with the help of the IPMP descriptor, control point, and sequence code. Different

tools can operate at the same or different control points, acting on the same or different streams.

• **Tool Security**. The terminal and tools can choose to perform mutual authentication using the IPMP authentication messages to achieve a secure communication framework.

17.2.4   MPEG-21 IPMP Components

Without standardizing a specific system used to deliver the multimedia content like the MPEG-2/4 systems, the MPEG-21 multimedia framework covers the entire multimedia content delivery chain encompassing content creation production, delivery, and trade. The MPEG-21 IPMP Components specification describes the technologies for effectively managing and protecting the digital content. It specifies how protection is applied to content captured as Digital Items in the MPEG-21 Digital Item Declaration Language (DIDL) [11] and facilitates the exchange of governed content between MPEG-21 peers. The basic concepts such as tool list, IPMP tools, and IPMP Descriptor defined in the MPEG-2/4 IPMPX framework are utilized to retain the features of the IPMPX architecture mentioned in Section 17.2.3, but without defining the messaging infrastructure in the MPEG-2/4 IPMPX.

Figure 17.3 illustrates how content is described and protected using the MPEG-21 IPMP within the multimedia content delivery chain.

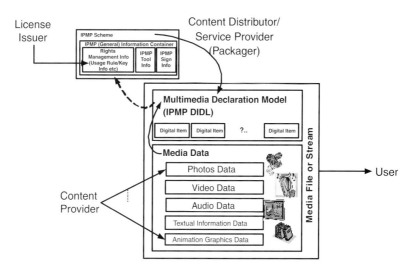

FIGURE 17.3:   Block diagram of content creation, distribution, and protection using the MPEG-21 IPMP.

During the digital content creation stage, the content provider supplies the valuable media data which may include all kinds of digital media resources (photos, video, audio, text, animation, graphics, etc.) to the content distributor or service provider. The structure and content of the media data are unambiguously expressed as a Digital Item. As the Digital Item expressed in the DIDL is a clear XML document, the information of the Digital Item represented in the DIDL is all exposed. The MPEG-21 IPMP provides an alternative representation for parts of a Digital Item that require protection and governance. The language for defining this representation is termed as the IPMP DIDL. The language defines governed XML elements in correspondence to entities in the model of digital items. Each of these IPMP DIDL elements is indented to link a corresponding DIDL element (which may be encrypted) with IPMP information about the governance so that the Digital item hierarchy thus represented is used in accordance with the Digital Item author's wishes.

The model provided by the IPMP DIDL can be used to package content together with its associated actual media data to form the digital representation of a work (for example, a digital music album, an e-book, or a piece of software including setup and configuration information). The two most useful and prominent application forms of such a digital work are file and stream that are to be received by the user.

At the same time, the content owner, provider, or distributor can create the scheme description data, IPMP Scheme, that is related to security, protection, and governance of the content. The IPMP Scheme is an IPMP information container and includes not only IPMP tool (capability) information and IPMP signature information, but also the rights management information (e.g., usage rule and key information) that is created by a license issuer and carried inside the IPMP scheme. The description of the IPMP governance and tools is required to satisfy intellectual property management and protection for the Digital Item or its parts to be accessed. The IPMP Scheme can either be placed directly inside the IPMP DID model or be indirectly referred to the declaration model by some means such as Universal Resource Identifier (URI). It is noted that the media data input to a file or stream can be in different forms (in encrypted, watermarked, or other formats) as long as the IPMP scheme is associated. Based on the extracted IPMP scheme, the MPEG-21 terminal should convert the protected media data into the clear forms for content consumption or further distribution, if all rights conditions are fulfilled and all required data (e.g., keys) are available.

17.2.5   MPEG-21 REL

In order to develop effective and efficient DRM systems, the capability of specifying and communicating rights information among the participants is certainly required at each step of content delivery and consumption. A content user needs to know what rights are associated with a piece of content. A content distributor needs not only to communicate the rights that are available for consuming the content, but also to understand the rights that pertain for distributing the content. More importantly, a content provider in the upstream of the supply-distribution-consumption value-chain needs to ensure that both usage and distribution rights are granted precisely as intended for every participant in the content delivery chain. With rights properly specified, DRM systems can then correctly interpret them and effectively enforce them.

The MPEG-21 REL [8, 12], published in April 2004 together with the MPEG-21 RDD [9], is an XML-based developed from the ContentGuard's eXtensible rights Markup Language (XrML) version 2.0 [13] that can be used to declare rights and conditions using the action terms as defined in the RDD, as the RDD is developed to ensure that the semantic interpretation of each right be precise and unambiguous in order to promote interoperability at the rights level. Using the REL, anyone owning or distributing content can identify some principals (such as users, groups, devices, and systems) allowed to use the content, the rights available to those principals, and the terms and conditions under which those rights may be exercised.

For example, consider a movie, Ocean Wild, distributed by a studio, Acme Studio, to the owner of a DVD player, called Alice. A typical MPEG-21 REL expression might make the statement, Under the authority of Acme Studio, Alice is granted the right to play "Ocean Wild during the month of November 2003." In the MPEG-21 REL terminology, Alice is considered as a "principal," play is a "right," the movie "Ocean Wild" is a "resource," "during November 2003" is a "condition," and Acme Studio is an "issuer" of the right. While the example is simple, it captures the essence of every MPEG-21 REL expression, as shown in the REL data model in Figure 17.4. The right-granting portion of this statement ("Alice is granted with the right to play 'Ocean Wild' in the month of November 2003") is called a "grant," and the entire statement is called a "license," which in this case consists of the grant and the issuer, Acme Studio.

MPEG has developed its REL to meet the requirements it defined, especially those on unambiguous semantics and comprehensiveness in supporting identified business models. Nevertheless, MPEG recognizes that several industries and communities will need to modify the language to better meet their specific needs. To facilitate easy mapping of the REL to these industry-specific applications, the MPEG REL has been designed in a way that can be profiled as well as extended. Profiling the REL allows selection of only the parts of the language applicable to a target application. This enables optimizing the payload of digital items and computation requirements of MPEG terminals. On the other hand, extending the REL allows the introduction of new types and elements to the language based on particular application needs. This includes the development of new verbs and schematic elements to improve efficiency in a specific domain. It is important to note that profiling and extending can be used concurrently to optimize the applicability of

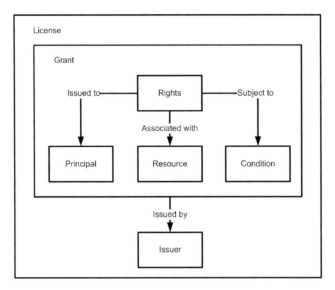

FIGURE 17.4:   The MPEG REL data model.

the REL to one specific application. Currently, MPEG is developing a number of
REL profiles and extensions for application domains like mobile, optical media,
and broadcasting. Some of the resulting profile specification will be published in
mid-2006 or early 2007.

17.3   OMA

OMA is an industry standard organization for developing mobile service enabler
specification work, in order to stimulate and contribute to the creation of interoperable services. The organization goals of OMA include (1) delivering quality, open
technical specifications based upon market requirements that drive modularity,
extensibility, and consistency, and (2) enabling interoperability across different
devices, geographies, service providers, operators, and networks [14].

   Clearly, downloading content to a mobile phone or receiving content by
messaging services has become one of the most popular mobile data services.
The typical content consumed by a mobile device today includes limited value
content types such as ringtones, screensavers, and background images. As new
smartphones and other smart devices penetrate the market, and mobile network
capacities increase, a demand for a wider range of new and higher value content types (music, game, movies, etc.) is emerging and expanding the digital

content market. OMA began working on mobile DRM specifications in late 2001 in response to the clear market demand.

DRM systems must play different roles depending on the time value of information. Some simple digital resources are primarily considered for protection in the OMA release 1.0 DRM solution. Some valued digital resources are also considered to use separate delivery (superdistribution) to protect in some simple cases. The OMA DRM technology release 1.0 finalized in December 2002 is an initial protection system that can be extended into a more comprehensive and secure DRM system. From a security point of view, the OMA DRM release 1.0 is quite lightweight. The rights object or the Content Encryption Key (CEK) carried within is not protected. The device or the DRM agent is not authenticated prior to issuing rights. All this makes it relatively easy to circumvent the DRM protection. OMA continued its effort to work on its 2.0 release, which is trying to include a more sophisticated trust and security model. The latest OMA DRM release 2.0 was issued in March 2006, and recently, the OMA DRM group is also working on the solution for mobile broadcasting content protection.

17.3.1   OMA DRM V1.0

OMA DRM version 1.0 Enabler Release was created as a solution that was timely and inexpensive to deploy, could be implemented in mass market mobile devices, and should not require costly infrastructure to be rolled out. The scope of this standard is to enable the controlled consumption of digital media objects by allowing content providers to express usage rights, e.g., the ability to preview DRM content, to prevent downloaded DRM content from being illegally forwarded to other users, and to enable superdistribution of DRM content.

OMA DRM v1.0 includes three levels of functionality:

- Forward-lock: preventing content from leaving device. The purpose of forward-lock is to prevent peer-to-peer distribution of low-value content. This applies often to subscription-based services such as news, and sports clips. The plaintext content is packaged inside a DRM message that is delivered to the terminal. The device is allowed to play, display, or execute the content, but it is not allowed to forward the content.
- Combined delivery: adding rights definition. Combined delivery equally prevents peer-to-peer distribution, but it also controls the content usage. In combined delivery, the DRM message contains two objects: the content and a rights object. The rights object defines permissions and constraints for the use of the content. These can be, for example, a permission to play a tune only once or to use the content only for x number of days. Neither content nor the rights object is allowed to be forwarded from the target device.
- Separate Delivery: providing content encryption and supports superdistribution. The purpose of Separate Delivery is to protect higher value content.

It enables the so called superdistribution, which allows the device to forward the content, but not the usage rights. This is achieved by delivering the media and usage rights via separate channels. The content is encrypted into DRM Content Format (DCF) using symmetric encryption; the DCF provides plaintext headers describing content type, encryption algorithm, and other useful information. The rights object holds the symmetric CEK, which is used by the DRM user agent in the device for decryption. The rights object is defined using OMA REL.

Superdistribution is an application of separate delivery that also requires a rights refresh mechanism that allows additional rights for the media. Recipients of superdistributed content must contact the content retailer to obtain rights to either preview or purchase the media. Thus, the separate delivery method enables viral distribution of media, maximizing the number of potential customers while retaining control for the content provider through centralized rights acquisition.

17.3.2   OMA DRM V2.0

OMA DRM version 2.0 enabler release [15] was created to meet the new requirements to support more valuable content (e.g., video, music, games, etc.), which requires a more complicated key management infrastructure to provide more security. The scope of this release is to enable the controlled consumption of digital media objects by allowing content providers the ability, for example, to manage previews of protected content, to enable superdistribution of protected content, and to enable transfer of content between DRM agents. The OMA DRM 2.0 specifications provide mechanisms for secure authentication of trusted DRM agents and for secure packaging and transfer of usage rights and DRM-protected content to trusted DRM agents.

OMA DRM v2.0 includes three main technical parts in its specification [15]:

- **OMA DCF**. This part is to define the content format for DRM-protected encrypted media objects and associated meta-data. The DCF can be delivered separately from an associated rights object, which contains the encryption key used to encrypt the media object. There are two DCF profiles. One is used for discrete media (such as still images), and one is used for continuous media (such as music or video). The profiles share some data structures. Both profiles are based on a widely accepted and deployed standard format, the ISO base media file format. But the discrete media profile is meant to be an all-purpose format, not aiming for full compatibility with ISO media files.
- **OMA DRM system**. The OMA DRM system enables content issuers to distribute protected content and rights issuers to issue rights objects for the protected content. The DRM system is independent of media object formats, operating systems, and runtime environments. In order to consume

the content, users acquire permissions to protected content by contacting rights issuers. Rights issuers grant appropriate permissions, in the form of rights objects, for the protected content to user devices. The content is cryptographically protected when distributed; hence, protected content will not be usable without an associated rights object issued for the user's device.

The protected content can be delivered to the device by any means (over the air, LAN/WLAN, local connectivity, removable media, etc.). But the rights objects are tightly controlled and distributed by the rights issuer in a controlled manner. The protected content and rights objects can be delivered to the device together, or separately.

This part defines an end-to-end system for protected content distribution. The Rights Object Acquisition Protocol (ROAP), the key management schemes utilized, and the domain-related functionalities in OMA DRM are described in detail in different sections of this part.

- **OMA REL**. Rights are used to specify the access a consuming device is granted to DRM-governed content. The REL defined in this part specifies the syntax and semantics of rights governing the usage of DRM content. It is based on a subset of the Open Digital Rights Language (ODRL) [16] version 1.1, together with a data dictionary defining additional permissions and constraints beyond those provided by ODRL. DRM-governed content is consumed according to the specified rights. Therefore, the value is in the rights and not in the content itself. Rights objects are specified so that they only become usable on authorized devices.

17.4   CORAL

Founded in late 2004, Coral Consortium is an industry consortium chartered to promote interoperability between DRM technologies for consumer devices and services, so digital music and video can be easily accessed and enjoyed, regardless of the service provider or the device. Coral recognizes the fact that, while recent innovations in digital media distribution provide consumers with new channels to acquire music and video, proprietary differences still exist and will probably continue to exist in underlying DRM or content protection technology that prevent consumers from playing content packaged and distributed using one DRM technology on a device that supports a different DRM technology. Its focus is to define a service provider architecture that allows existing DRM systems to co-exist, and it provides necessary protocols and interfaces to bridge these DRM systems to enable interoperability between different content formats, devices, and content distribution services. Though Coral announced availability of the consortium's 1.0 interoperability specification in March 2005, a full Coral specification is still under development.

Closely related to Coral Consortium is another consortium called the Marlin Joint Development Association (or Marlin JDA), which was formed in early 2005. Unlike Coral, Marlin's objective is to provide a DRM technology toolkit to enable device makers to build DRM functions into their portable digital media devices. The connection between the two consortiums is that the Marlin JDA's specifications are intended to be compatible with the Coral Consortium's services-based specifications in a way that Marlin-based devices will be able to interoperate with Coral-enabled DRM systems even if those systems do not use Marlin DRM components.

17.5   DMP

DMP is a non-profit association, launched in mid-2003, to develop technical specifications for promoting the development, deployment, and use of digital media. The Interoperable DRM Platform, phase I (IDP-1) specification was published in May 2005, enabling the implementation of digital media services based on portable audio and video devices. The phase II specification is currently under development.

The DMP specifications are designed to provide interoperability between value-chain players of governed (i.e., DRM protected) digital media within and between value-chains that exist as well as those expected in the future. To support interoperability in such a dynamic environment, DMP considers that the only practical solution is to provide standardized DRM technologies that value-chain users can configure to suit their needs. The interoperable DRM Platform (IDP) is the assembly of standardized technologies that DMP calls tools. These tools are grouped into the following seven major categories.

- Represent. Tools to represent content, keys, and rights expressions (or licenses).
- Identify. Tools to identify content, licenses, devices, and domains.
- Package. Tools to package content in files or streams.
- Authenticate. Tools to recognize and enable trust between devices and users using certificates, identification data, and certificate proxies.
- Manage. Tools to manage domains for domain establishment, membership management, and content usage control.
- Access. Tools to access and update content and licenses.
- Process. Tools to transform XML documents to their binary format version before transmission or storage and to perform encryption and decryption functions.

The standardized DRM technologies promoted by DMP are mainly from MPEG-21 [5, 6], including the Digital Item Declaration (DID), Digital Item Identification (DII), IPMP components, REL, RDD, and file format.

DMP just released, in February 2006, its IDP phase-II (IDP-II) technical specifications and references designed to support the implementation of value chain
centered around stationary audio and video devices, i.e. devices with network
access.

17.6 ISMA

Founded in 2000, the ISMA is an industry alliance dedicated to the adoption and
deployment of open standards for streaming rich media such as video, audio, and
associated data over Internet protocols.

The technical requirements of ISMA DRM can be understood in the context
of the archetypal server-client-based DRM architecture shown in Figure 17.5.
The MASTERING entity is where a content work is prepared for dissemination.
It may be encrypted and associated with a rights specification that is formatted
according to an REL (e.g., [8, 15]). The KEY/LICENSE MGT entity associates
a rights specification and cryptographic keys with an ISMA content work. It
translates the rights specification into a license. The license authorizes particular types of access to the work, possibly according to a set of "business rules."
The access may be at a highly granular level of access such as to view/hear the
content, write to a DVD, or send to a friend. The SENDER entity manages the
requests from receivers (labeled "CONTROL") and disseminates content works
("MEDIA") to receivers; both CONTROL and MEDIA flows may use encryption, authentication, and integrity services. The RECEIVER entity decrypts and
authenticates content works contained in the MEDIA flow and may decrypt and

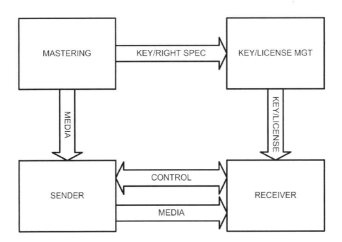

FIGURE 17.5:   ISMA DRM architecture.

authenticate CONTROL flows. Depending on the nature of the key/license management protocol in use, the RECEIVER may perform mutual authentication with the KEY/LICENSE MGT entity to prove that the receiver is an authorized platform. This process is controlled by the license, which specifies the terms and conditions under which a key is provided to an ISMACryp device [8, 15]. The license determines what authenticating information is exchanged, such as information about the RECEIVER's hardware, software, or human user.

The latest ISMA DRM specification is officially named Internet Streaming Media Alliance Encryption and Authentication (ISMACryp), Version 1.1. It includes the following features:

- Payload encryption and message authentication for ISMA 1.0 and ISMA 2.0 streams, including AVC/HE-AAC
- Encryption of ISMA 1.0- and 2.0-based files
- Extensible framework allowing combinations of various DRM systems
- Guidelines for combination with OMA DRM version 2 systems

The ISMACryp is being recommended by DVB-H (Digital Video Broadcasting for Handhelds), which is a standard for mobile TV devices embraced by the international European Telecommunication Standards Institute (ETSI) body. Future ISMA specifications will build on ISMACryp and define a complete DRM system that is possibly integratable with multiple key/license management systems.

17.7 AACS

AACS is an industry standard consortium aimed at developing a set of specifications for managing content stored on the next generation of pre-recorded and recorded optical media for consumer use with PCs and CE devices. AACS specifications complement the next generation of high-definition optical discs such as HD-DVD and Blu-Ray.

AACS utilizes advanced cryptography and flexible usage rules to protect and authorize the use of digital media. AACS-protected content is encrypted, via a broadcast encryption scheme [17], under one or more title keys using the Advanced Encryption Standard (AES) [18]. Title keys are derived from a combination of a media key and several elements, including the volume ID of the media (e.g., a physical serial number embedded on a DVD) and a cryptographic hash of the title usage rules. The AACS broadcast encryption-based approach provides a much more effective mechanism for device revocation than earlier content protection systems such as the Content Srambling Systems (CSS) used in the DVD protection [19].

By specification of title usage rules, AACS is flexible to support new distribution and business models for content and service providers, as well as to improving functionality and interactivity for the consumer. For example, AACS supports the ability to grant the users rights, to the extent authorized by title usage rules, to save licensed, protected copies of pre-recorded movie titles onto, for example, a portable player, a desktop PC, or authorized media, while preventing unauthorized reproduction and distribution of next-generation optical media.

17.8   LIST OF DRM STANDARD ORGANIZATIONS AND CONSORTIUMS

Due to the space limitation of this chapter, many DRM-related standard activities have not been discussed. This section, nevertheless, provides a quick reference list of DRM standard organizations and consortiums in addition to those discussed in the previous sections. It should be pointed out that this list is by no means a complete one. This is partially because the limited standards participation and personal views of DRM from the authors and the DRM technologies and applications are still evolving and expanding.

- 4C Entity (4C)
    - URL: http://www.4centity.com
    - Scope: Recordable and Removable Media
    - Work: Content Protection
- Advanced Access Content System (AACS)
    - URL: http://www.aacsla.com
    - Scope: Pre-Recorded and Recordable High-Definition Media
    - Work: Content Protection and Usage Rules-Based Control
- ATIS IPTV Interoperability Forum (ATIS/IIF)
    - URL: http://www.atis.org/iif/index.asp
    - Scope: IPTV Interoperability
    - Work: Requirements and DRM systems
- Audio Video Coding Standard Workgroup of China (AVS)
    - URL: http://www.avs.org.cn/
    - Scope: Audio-Video Technologies and Systems
    - Work: DRM Framework, Rights Expression Language, and Communication Protocols
- ChinaDRM
    - URL: http://www.chinadrm.org.cn
    - Scope: Broadcasting
    - Work: DRM Requirements, Testing Platform, and Technologies

- Copy Protection Technical Working Group (CPTWG)
    - URL: http://www.cptwg.org
    - Scope: Consumer Electronics
    - Work: Copy Protection
- Coral Consortium
    - URL: http://www.coral-interop.org
    - Scope: Consumer Electronics
    - Work: Service-based Architecture and Implementations
- Digital Media Project (DMP)
    - URL: http://www.chiariglione.org
    - Scope: Interoperability Framework
    - Work: Interoperable DRM Platform
- Digital Transmission Content Protection (DTCP, 5C)
    - URL: http://www.dtcp.com
    - Scope: Digital Transmission
    - Work: Content Protection
- Digital Video Broadcasting (DVB) Project
    - URL: http://www.dvb.org
    - Scope: Video Broadcasting
    - Work: Content Protection and Content Management, Usage State Information
- IEEE Learning Technology Standards Committee
    - URL: http://ltsc.ieee.org/wg4/
    - Scope: Electronic Learning
    - Work: Use Cases and Requirements for Rights Expression Languages
- International Digital Publishing Forum (IDPF, formerly OeBF)
    - URL: http://www.idpf.org/
    - Scope: Electronic Publications
    - Work: Rights Expression Language, Publication Specification, Metadata, and Container
- Internet Streaming Media Alliance (ISMA)
    - URL: http://www.isma.tv/
    - Scope: Internet Streaming
    - Work: Authentication and Encryption, Integrated DRM System

- ISO/IEC Moving Picture Experts Group (MPEG)
  - URL: http://www.chiariglione.org/mpeg/
  - Scope: Multimedia Framework and Supporting Component Technologies
  - Work: Intellectual Property Protection and Management, Rights Expression Language, Rights Data Dictionary, Digital Item Declaration, Digital Item Identification, Digital Item Adaptation, Digital Item Processing, Digital Item Streaming, File Format, and Event Reporting
- Open Mobile Alliance (OMA)
  - URL: http://www.openmobilealliance.org
  - Scope: Mobile Communication
  - Work: Mobile DRM System, Protocols, and Rights Expression Language
- Secure Video Processor (SVP) Alliance
  - URL: http://www.svpalliance.org
  - Scope: Digital Home Networks and Portable Devices
  - Work: Content Protection Technology
- Society of Motion Picture and Television Engineers (SMPTE)
  - URL: http://www.smpte.org
  - Scope: Digital Cinema
  - Work: Security and Rights
- TV-Anytime Forum
  - URL: http://www.tv-anytime.org
  - Scope: Audio-Visual Services
  - Work: Rights Management and Protection Information

REFERENCES

[1] L. Chiariglione. Intellectual property in the multimedia framework, in *Management of Digital Rights*, October 2000, Berlin.
[2] ISO/IEC. MPEG-4 system on IPMP extension, *Amendment 3*, Shanghai, China, October 2002.
[3] ISO/IEC. MPEG-2 system: Support of IPMP on MPEG-2 systems, *Amendment 2*, Pattaya, Thailand, March 2003.
[4] ISO/IEC. IPMP on MPEG-2 systems, First Edition, Pattaya, Thailand, March 2003.
[5] J. Gelissen, J. Bormans, and A. Perkis. Mpeg-21: The 21st century multimedia framework, *IEEE Signal Processing Magazine*, 20:53–62, March 2003.
[6] I. Burnett, R. Van de Walle, K. Hill, J. Bormans, and F. Pereira. MPEG-21: Goals and achievements, *IEEE Multimedia*,10:60–70, October – December 2003.

 [7] ISO/IEC. Information technology—multimedia framework—Part 4: Intellectual property management and protection components, First Edition, Busan, Korea, April 2005.

 [8] ISO/IEC. Information technology—multimedia framework—Part 5: Rights expression language, First Edition, Munich. Germany, April 2004.

 [9] ISO/IEC. Information technology—multimedia framework—Part 6: Rights data dictionary, First Edition, Munich, Germany, April 2004.

[10] ISO/IEC. MPEG-4 intellectual property management and protection (IPMP) overview and applications, First Edition, Rome, Italy, December 1998.

[11] ISO/IEC. Information technology—Multimedia framework—Part 2: Digital Item Declaration, Second Edition, Hong Kong, China, January 2005.

[12] X. Wang, T. DeMartini, B. Wragg, M. Paramasivam, and C. Barlas. The MPEG-21 rights expression language and rights data dictionary, *IEEE Trans. Multimedia*, 7: 408–417, June 2005.

[13] ContentGuard, Inc. eXtensible rights Markup Language (XrML), Version 2.0, http://www.xrml.org, November 2001.

[14] OMA. OMA DRM Short Paper, http://www.openmobilealliance.org, 2003.

[15] OMA. OMA DRM release 2.0 enabler package, http://www.openmobilealliance.org, March 2006.

[16] ODRL Initiative. Open Digital Rights Language (ODRL), Version 1.1, http://www.odrl.net, August 2002.

[17] A. Fiat and M. Naor. Broadcast encryption, *Lecture Notes in Computer Science*, 773:480–491, 1994.

[18] National Institute of Standard and Technology. Advanced Encryption Standard (AES), *FIPS*, 197:2001.

[19] J. A. Bloom, I. J. Cox, T. Kalker, J.-P. M. G. Linnartz, M. L. Miller, and C. B. S. Traw. Copy protection for DVD video, *Proc. IEEE*, 89:1267–1276, July 1999.

18

The Digital Millennium Copyright Act

Gregory Stobbs

Harness, Dickey and Pierce, P.L.C.

18.1 DIGITAL MEDIA AND SIX-TOED CATS

Ernest Hemingway wrote many of his famous novels at his home in Key West, FL, in the company of a six-toed cat that had been given to him by a ship's captain. While Hemingway was busy writing, it seems his six-toed cat managed to keep busy at other endeavors; for today there are approximately 60 cats living on Hemingway's estate and about half of them have six toes. The genetic code, it would seem, is a highly efficient instrument with which to write one's legacy, especially if you happen to be a six-toed cat. Hemingway wrote his legacy with a decidedly more crude instrument, the typewriter.

Creation in Hemingway's time was a very organic, earthy, non-digital process. Perhaps that is still true today. Artists still daub and drip paint onto canvas in fits of inspiration. Poets still pour words from their soul. Guitarists still stretch, pluck, and torture the E-strings of their guitars with fingers and picks and matchbook covers. All use the same human, analog touch that our ancestors exploited 32,000 years ago when they decorated their limestone cave walls with paintings of bears, lions, horses, and oxen.

Yet something has changed. In Hemingway's day his words were set by a mechanical process onto paper and bound into books. Properly cared for, those books could last for centuries, but sooner or later, they would turn yellow and then brown and then crumble into flaky dust no longer capable of holding Hemingway's words. The prehistoric cave painters, it seems, employed a more durable medium, although even their works are slowly deteriorating through exposure to the elements.

Digital technology has changed all of that. Now Hemingway's words are set by an electronic process into digital storage media. Embodied now in digital form, his words may be copied in a flash to other digital storage media, communicated electronically to any location where human-generated electromagnetic waves will reach, and even printed onto paper if that is one's desire.

In one sense, digital technology has made it far easier to make an exact copy of Hemingway's original words and thus propagate those words far into the future. In theory, Hemingway's words are now less at risk of being lost forever in a pile of crumbled, flaky dust. Yet digital technology carries a hidden flaw. Digital storage media have their own way of crumbling into flaky dust. Sooner or later, digital memories begin to forget. The digital synapses of even the finest archival storage media have a simple flaw: they are man-made. They will fail.

Proponents of digital technology will, of course, argue that there is no need to ever lose information to such digital Alzheimer's disease. Many copies upon copies upon copies can be made, reducing the probability of losing Hemingway's words to nil. All of this is true, provided there is someone interested in and capable of making the copies. Certainly, Hemingway has no need to fear as long as students of American literature occupy this planet. However, there is a new wrinkle. The U.S. Congress has passed a law, called the Digital Millennium Copyright Act, designed to stop the making of copies upon copies upon copies of digital works by making it illegal to do so under certain circumstances. That law is the subject of this chapter.

As you will learn in the remainder of this chapter, Hemingway will be with us for centuries. However, the way you will be permitted to enjoy Hemingway (or any other book, movie, song, photograph, Web site, software program, map, or even instruction manual) has changed. Pay-per-view is about to take on a whole new meaning; Congress has made sure of that.

18.2   SPECIAL INTEREST GROUPS, A TREATY, AND THE DIGITAL MILLENNIUM COPYRIGHT ACT IS BORN

Politics is the engine that powers the congressional lawmaking machine. Powered by politics, Congress enacts some laws in response to broad popular demand or to address an urgent need of a majority of the citizens. However, Congress enacts countless other laws that ordinary people never really hear about. These are laws sponsored by special interest groups who employ skilled lobbyists to whisper words in their congressmen's ears, trading influence for favors and favors for influence. The best special interest lobbyists cut deals by manipulating influence and by skillfully exploiting nuances of our complex legal system that many do not see coming. Such was the case with the Digital Millennium Copyright Act.

The Digital Millennium Copyright Act traces its roots to a task force created by President Clinton in February 1993 to assist his administration in formulating a vision for a national information infrastructure. The World Wide Web, or "information superhighway" as Vice President Gore liked to call it, was all the buzz in the early 1990s, and the Clinton administration wanted to lead instead of merely react. Thus, President Clinton created the Information Infrastructure Task Force (IITF) and charged it to conduct a study of how the federal government could advance the development and application of information technologies. President Clinton selected Bruce A. Lehman, whom he had also appointed to be the Commissioner of the U.S. Patent and Trademark Office, to chair the task force. Commissioner Lehman was no ordinary civil service appointee, however. Prior to his appointment as leader of the Patent and Trademark Office, Lehman had served as a copyright lobbyist representing the special interests of powerful copyright holders, most notably Hollywood and several large software companies, including Lotus and Microsoft.

Under Lehman's close supervision, the IITF formed committees, took testimony of interested parties in public hearings, and then authored and distributed a preliminary draft report known as the "Green Paper," which the public was invited to comment upon. The Green Paper, published on July 7, 1994, was thereafter reworked and published in final form as the "White Paper" in September 1995. The White Paper became the roadmap that the Clinton administration used to radically revamp the U.S. copyright law, giving large copyright holders far more power than they had ever had.

The White Paper characterized intellectual property law (which includes patent law, trademark law, trade secret law, and copyright law) as something that must evolve in response to technological change:

> Intellectual property is a subtle and esoteric area of the law that evolves in response to technological change. Advances in technology particularly affect the operation and effectiveness of copyright law. Changes in technology generate new industries and new methods for reproduction and dissemination of works of authorship, which may present new opportunities for authors, but also create additional challenges. Copyright law has had to respond to those challenges, from Gutenberg's moveable type printing press to digital audio recorders and everything in between — photocopiers, radio, television, videocassette recorders, cable television and satellites.[1]

Although the need to evolve in the face of heady new digital technologies made for an appealing political argument, the real motive behind the prescribed change was almost certainly something else. In 1984, Hollywood had suffered a major setback when the U.S. Supreme Court ruled in the Sony Betamax case that taping a television program for time-shifting purposes in the privacy of one's own home was "fair use." The White Paper now concluded that recent "advances in technology"

---

[1] Intellectual Property and the National Information Infrastructure. The Report of the Working Group on Intellectual Property Rights, Bruce A. Lehman, chair, September 1995.

required major changes if the "authors" rights were to be adequately protected. Betamax was about to change.

The White Paper did have one thing right. Intellectual property is a subtle and esoteric area of the law. Thus, it should not come as a surprise that the major changes proposed in the White Paper were themselves enacted by Congress in a subtle and esoteric way. Initially, the White Paper formed the basis of a bill known as the National Information Infrastructure Copyright Protection Act of 1995. The bill was introduced to the 104th Congress and met with great resistance from both end-users and the industry. The bill eventually failed, but that was not the end of the White Paper. It was later submitted to the World Intellectual Property Organization (WIPO), a multi-national body that is currently trying to unify intellectual property laws throughout the world. This time the White Paper was successful. WIPO drafted a treaty, based on the White Paper, which the United States ultimately ratified. Significantly, the treaty *required* its signing members to enact laws in their respective countries to put the terms of the treaty into effect. Interestingly, the U.S. delegation to WIPO was none other than Bruce Lehman.

Thus, to comply with the treaty requirements and to overhaul other aspects of the copyright law, in 1998 Congress this time passed a massive addition to the copyright law, known as the "Digital Millennium Copyright Act." The act was signed into law by President Clinton. The law took effect on October 28, 1998, and many of the substantive provisions took effect two years thereafter.

18.3   THE DIGITAL MILLENNIUM COPYRIGHT ACT
IN A NUTSHELL

In a nutshell, the new law did two things. First, it made it illegal to circumvent a technological measure that controls access to a work. Second, it made it illegal to remove someone's copyright "management information," which was broadly defined to cover all sorts of things, ranging from the title and author of the work to the licensing terms offered by the copyright owner. The new law defined both civil and criminal penalties, including statutory damages of up to $2500 per act of circumvention and up to $25,000 for removing someone's management information. If criminal charges were brought, the act called for fines of up to $500,000 or imprisonment for up to 5 years or both.

Thus, after October 28, 2000, the student caught converting copy protected digital music files into standard MP3 files, so that he could share them with his girlfriend, could be subject to damages of up to $2500 per act of circumvention. A converted playlist of, say, 100 songs could cost him up to $250,000 in statutory damages. Similarly, after October 28, 2000, the artist who downloaded a digital photograph from a Web site for use in her PowerPoint presentation could be subject to damages of up to $25,000 because she "cleaned up" the image by removing the original photographer's name at the bottom of the image. Ouch! Moreover, if the FBI managed to get involved and the federal prosecutor decided to press criminal charges, our law-violating friends could be looking at massive fines and some serious jail time. What is this world coming to?

The Digital Millennium Copyright message could not be more clear. What your powerful digital media manipulation tools giveth, Congress taketh away. Of course, as with any law there are exceptions, but those exceptions involve many legal twists and turns that one should not try to navigate without the aid of an attorney. Experienced attorneys don't come cheap; thus, the best advice is to give the Digital Millennium Copyright Act a wide berth. Don't succumb to temptation and use your powerful digital media manipulation tools to mess with things that others put into their works to protect their rights and to prevent unauthorized use.

As a user of digital media, the simple advice offered above should keep the copyright police from gracing your door. However, as a developer of digital media, there is quite a bit more you should probably know about the Digital Millennium Copyright Act. The next sections will explore the act in more detail.

18.4 CIRCUMVENTING A TECHNOLOGICAL MEASURE—A DMCA VIOLATION OF THE FIRST KIND

The Digital Millennium Copyright Act addresses two basic topics: (1) unauthorized circumvention of technological measures and (2) maintaining integrity of copyright management information. Let us begin with the first topic, circumvention. It can be a bit mind-numbing to read the copyright statutes, so we will break things down into more accessible chunks. The act begins by defining certain violations regarding circumvention of technological measures:

(1) (A) No person shall circumvent a technological measure that effectively controls access to a work protected under this title. The prohibition contained in the preceding sentence shall take effect at the end of the 2-year period beginning on the date of the enactment of this chapter [enacted Oct. 28, 1998].

So, what exactly is a "technological measure" and how "effectively" must it control access to a work protected under this title? While we are at it, what exactly is a "work protected under this title"? Those are precisely the questions that a lawyer would ask when construing this provision. Knowing that such questions would undoubtedly arise, Congress put the following definitions into the act:

As used in this subsection—

(A) to 'circumvent a technological measure' means to descramble a scrambled work, to decrypt an encrypted work, or otherwise to avoid, bypass, remove, deactivate, or impair a technological measure, without the authority of the copyright owner; and

(B) a technological measure 'effectively controls access to a work' if the measure, in the ordinary course of its operation, requires the application of information, or a process or a treatment, with the authority of the copyright owner, to gain access to the work.

These definitions may answer some of your questions. However, the basic work protected under this title is not defined here. The term "title" in that phrase refers broadly to the copyright law. Thus, the Digital Millennium Copyright Act applies to works that are protected under the U.S. copyright laws. Such works include:

(1) Literary works
(2) Musical works, including any accompanying words
(3) Dramatic works, including any accompanying music
(4) Pantomimes and choreographic works
(5) Pictorial, graphic, and sculptural works
(6) Motion pictures and other audiovisual works
(7) Sound recordings
(8) Architectural works[2]

Although not expressly stated in the above list, computer software is considered a form of literary work that may be protected by copyright law.

There are limits to what the copyright law may protect. Indeed, the copyright law expressly states certain things, such as ideas, concepts, methods of operation, and the like, are off limits:

In no case does copyright protection for an original work of authorship extend to any idea, procedure, process, system, method of operation, concept, principle, or discovery, regardless of the form in which it is described, explained, illustrated, or embodied in such work.[3]

In simple terms this means that you can protect how an idea is expressed, but not the underlying idea itself. Thus, Microsoft can protect its Word word processing program code by copyright, but that copyright does not prevent others from using the "idea" of making a what-you-see-is-what-you-get word processing program that can perform spell-checking, change fonts, and embed spreadsheets and graphics within the text document.

Perhaps you are looking at the above list of protected works and thinking that this is all fine, but how does it apply to me? Think again. The next time you create a document on your word processor (an original work of authorship) and

---

[2]Amended Dec. 1, 1990, Publ. L. No. 1001-650, Title VII, Sec. 703, 104 Stat. 5133; codified at 17 USC § 102(a).

[3]Amended Dec. 1, 1990, Publ. L. No. 1001-650, Title VII, Sec. 703, 104 Stat. 5133; codified at 17 USC § 102(b).

then save that document with password protection, you have just applied a technological measure that effectively controls access to a work protected under the copyright act. Yes, even your word-processed document, assuming you wrote it yourself, is a protected work under the copyright act. If someone thereafter hacks your password and gains access to your encrypted document, they have "circumvented a technological measure" and probably violated the Digital Millennium Copyright Act.

Because the piracy of digital works is such a vexing problem, it is quite natural for the technologically minded person, such as yourself, to seek out increasingly more sophisticated ways of encrypting works so that they cannot be readily pirated. If you are a developer of such ways, please keep up the good work. Your innovation is sorely needed. However, for whatever comfort it may bring, the Digital Millennium Copyright Act has you covered should someone eventually figure out how to hack your anti-piracy technological measures. How is that, you may ask? Take another look at how Congress defined what it takes for your anti-piracy technological measure's capability to "effectively control access to a work."

> [A] technological measure 'effectively controls access to a work' if the measure, in the ordinary course of its operation, requires the application of information, or a process or a treatment, with the authority of the copyright owner, to gain access to the work.

If you think about what Congress is saying here, even a simple password, if required in the ordinary course of operation, would suffice to effectively control access to a work. This means that even anti-piracy schemes that today's pirates would consider "lame" may still allow the copyright owner's lawyer to successfully invoke the Digital Millennium Copyright Act. In other words, while it is still desirable to seek out new and better forms of encryption, the simple ones we rely on today are enough to trigger the provisions of the Digital Millennium Copyright Act.

From a legal standpoint, the hard part is not making the encryption scheme impossible to break. The hard part is catching the person who was actually responsible for "circumventing" the technological measure designed to control access. To see why this is so, consider how the issue would play out in court.

> Lawyer A (representing the copyright owner): 'Your Honor, we have shown, through the testimony of FBI agent Efrem Zimbalist, Jr. that the defendant was caught, red-handed, with 1,500 MP3 files on his computer. These files were exact digital copies of our client's copyrighted music recordings. We have further shown that in at least 975 instances there was direct evidence that our client's anti-piracy protection measures had been removed using the Napper-Zapper copy-protection-removal software.'
>
> Judge: 'Counselor, for the record, would you please clarify for the Court, how is it that you can tell that the Napper-Zapper program was used to remove your client's technological measures to control access to these works?'

Lawyer A: 'Yes your Honor. As our agent Zimbalist's testimony has established, the Napper-Zapper program changes the 53rd encryption bit from a 1 to a 0, and that change is enough to allow breaking our client's copy protection scheme. However, Napper-Zapper does not change the 56th bit, which is set to 1 on all protected works and set to 0 on all non-protected works. Thus, we have established that at least 975 of the works found on the defendant's computer were stolen from our client by hacking the copy-protection system.'

Judge: 'Thank you Counselor A. Counselor B, do you have any rebuttal?'

Counselor B (representing the accused defendant): 'Yes your Honor. My client is accused of violating the Digital Millennium Copyright act. If proven, this is a very serious offense; one for which he could be subjected to very harsh penalties. However, as your Honor knows, our legal system places the burden on the copyright owner to show that the *defendant* was the one responsible for circumventing the technological measures put in place by the copyright owners to control access to their copyrighted works.

'The problem with plaintiff's case is simply this: while they have offered testimony that 975 files were possibly hacked using the Napper-Zapper program, there is absolutely no evidence that my client was the one who changed the encryption bit from 1 to 0.'

Judge: 'But your client's computer had 975 files on it, showing clear evidence of hacking, when it was seized by the FBI.'

Counselor B: 'We do not dispute that my client's computer had 975 files in which the encryption bit had been changed from 1 to 0. However, there is absolutely no evidence that my client was responsible for changing the encryption bit on those files from 1 to 0. If the Court believes that it is more likely than not that my client's son, a five-year-old cub scout, changed those files, after he downloaded them from the Free Music For All web site, then we have a serious problem here. I agree. However, I would submit that it is far more likely that the encryption bit on those files had been changed from 1 to 0 long before my client's son downloaded those files onto his parent's computer.'

Judge: 'I am inclined to agree. Counselor A, unless you can show me evidence tending to show that the defendant, or his son, ran the Napper-Zapper program—or whatever—to change these 975 files, I have no choice but to dismiss this case.'

Counselor A: 'We have no further evidence to offer, your Honor.'

Judge: 'Then the Court finds that the plaintiff has not met its burden of proving that defendant was the one responsible for circumventing the technological measures. I therefore find in favor of defendant. Case dismissed.'

From a technical standpoint, it can be very difficult to establish that a given person was the one who circumvented a technological measure. In most cases, a court will thus rely on inferences which, if not refuted, tend to show that a given person was responsible. In the preceding example, Counselor A might have introduced evidence that the Napper-Zapper program was installed on the defendant's computer (or had recently been deleted from defendant's computer). Such evidence would establish that the defendant had access to the tools needed to circumvent the plaintiff's technical measures and would give rise to the inference that defendant used those tools to perform the circumvention. Had Counselor A done this, the burden would have shifted to Counselor B to refute the inference. Failing to refute the inference in such a case could be fatal for the defendant, as the court would have a legal basis to rule in the plaintiff's favor. Such a rebuttal might go like this.

> Counselor B: 'Your Honor, while it is true that my client's computer had the Napper-Zapper program installed on it, our computer expert, Dr. Balmer, who has tested my client's computer, has conclusively established that the Napper-Zapper program on my client's computer could not have performed the circumventing operation. Recall Dr. Balmer testified that Napper-Zapper would require at least 512 Mbytes of RAM and 100 Mbytes of free hard disk memory to actually complete the circumvention operation. My client's computer has only 256 Mbytes of RAM and 2 Mbytes of free hard disk memory. Moreover, Dr. Balmer has shown that all of the files on my client's computer bear creation dates *before* the Napper-Zapper program was installed. This shows that my client's hard disk was nearly full when Napper-Zapper was installed. At no time after Napper-Zapper was installed did it have the requisite 100 Mbytes of free space.
>
> 'So quite simply, your Honor, there is no way my client's computer would have been capable of running Napper-Zapper.'

18.5 OVERSEEING THE PROCESS SHALL BE TWO COMPETING GOVERNMENT AGENCIES

Congress most certainly recognized that the sweeping prohibitions of the Digital Millennium Copyright Act could produce unwanted side effects. If broadly construed and enforced, the Digital Millennium Copyright Act might slam the door on the free discourse of ideas, as increasing numbers of copyright holders placed digital locks on their digital content. To address this concern, Congress provided a loophole, of sorts, whereby Congress made arrangements to designate certain classes of copyrighted works as being okay to "unlock" under certain circumstances without the copyright holder's permission. Congress created this loophole cautiously and required that it be subject to careful periodic review.

Congress knew itself better than to actually commit its members to undertake this periodic task. So Congress delegated that responsibility to the Librarian of Congress, with input from the Assistant Secretary for Communications and Information of the Department of Commerce. The Library of Congress is the nation's oldest federal cultural institution and serves as the research arm of Congress. The U.S. Copyright Office forms part of the Library of Congress. The Department of Commerce is part of the executive branch of the U.S. government. The U.S.

Patent and Trademark Office forms part of the Department of Commerce. Thus, essentially, Congress delegated to the U.S. Copyright and Patent offices the task of assessing which works might be eligible for a waiver of the prohibition to circumvent a technological measure.

Before we take a look at exactly how the loophole works, it may be interesting to reflect a moment upon the decision to involve both the Library of Congress and the Department of Commerce in the review process. In short, Congress officially opened the door to allow the Department of Commerce (read U.S. Patent and Trademark Office) to involve itself in what would otherwise have been the exclusive turf of the Library of Congress (read U.S. Copyright Office). These two offices were conceived by the founding fathers, primarily by Thomas Jefferson, to serve the common purpose of promoting science and the useful arts. If you search the U.S. Constitution, you will find at Article I, Section 8, Clause 8, these words: "Congress shall have the power to promote the progress of science and useful arts." However, for political reasons, science and the useful arts were separated at birth into separate branches within the federal government. Copyrights in literary, audiovisual, motion picture works, and the like became the charge of the Library of Congress in the legislative branch of government, whereas patents for inventions became the charge of the Department of Commerce in the executive branch of government.

Given that technical measures to control access to a work involve technology that may be more familiar to the technically minded patent examiners of the Department of Commerce, you might think that Congress included the Assistant Secretary for Communications and Information of the Department of Commerce to get this viewpoint. More likely, it was because the main proponent of the Digital Millennium Copyright Act was Bruce A. Lehman, a former copyright lobbyist who had been appointed by President Clinton to serve as the Commissioner of Patents. During his tenure as boss of the U.S. Patent and Trademark Office, he spearheaded, along with Senator Hatch, an unsuccessful attempt to merge the Copyright Office into the Patent Office.[4]

18.6   LOOPHOLES ONLY A LAWYER COULD LOVE

Every law has loopholes of one sort or another. Sometimes they are intended, and sometimes they are inadvertent. The Digital Millennium Copyright Act is no exception. Indeed, Congress placed certain loopholes into the law to expressly permit certain behavior that would otherwise violate its terms. For example, Congress decreed that there may be a certain class of works for which the prohibition

---

[4] Omnibus Patent Act of 1996 (S. 1961), sponsored by Sen. Hatch.

against technical measure circumvention shall not apply. In the words of the statute:

> (B) The prohibition contained in subparagraph (A) shall not apply to persons who are users of a copyrighted work which is in a particular class of works, if such persons are, or are likely to be in the succeeding 3-year period, adversely affected by virtue of such prohibition in their ability to make noninfringing uses of that particular class of works under this title, as determined under subparagraph (C) [subparagraph C, which we shall visit momentarily explains how the particular 'class of works' is to be arrived at].

The loophole says, basically, that there will be a "class of works" for which the prohibition against circumvention does not apply. Perhaps we might call this the "loophole class." The loophole provision says that if you are making a *non-infringing* use of a work in the loophole class, then the prohibition against circumvention does not apply. The key here is the use must be a *non-infringing* use. For example, the copyright law permits you to make an archival backup copy of a computer program. You can't let someone else use that archival backup copy, or it no longer would be deemed an archival backup. You could use it, lawfully, to restore the software to your computer after your original copy was lost during a hard disc crash. If word processing software packages are among the loophole class, then you would be permitted to remove a circumventing technical measure to make an archival backup copy of the word processing software program. On the other hand, if DVD movies are not among the loophole class, then you could not remove a circumventing technical measure to make an archival backup copy of the DVD movie.

Congress was fairly specific in what the Librarian of Congress could and could not put in the loophole class. It's a bit long-winded, but here is what the statute provides (our so-called loophole class is identified in paragraph (D) below):

> (C) During the 2-year period described in subparagraph (A), and during each succeeding 3-year period, the Librarian of Congress, upon the recommendation of the Register of Copyrights, who shall consult with the Assistant Secretary for Communications and Information of the Department of Commerce and report and comment on his or her views in making such recommendation, shall make the determination in a rulemaking proceeding for purposes of subparagraph (B) of whether persons who are users of a copyrighted work are, or are likely to be in the succeeding 3-year period, adversely affected by the prohibition under subparagraph (A) in their ability to make noninfringing uses under this title of a particular class of copyrighted works. In conducting such rulemaking, the Librarian shall examine—
>
> (i) the availability for use of copyrighted works;
>
> (ii) the availability for use of works for nonprofit archival, preservation, and educational purposes;

  (iii) the impact that the prohibition on the circumvention of technological mea-
         sures applied to copyrighted works has on criticism, comment, news reporting,
         teaching, scholarship, or research;

  (iv)   the effect of circumvention of technological measures on the market for or
         value of copyrighted works; and

  (v)   such other factors as the Librarian considers appropriate.

(D) The Librarian shall publish any class of copyrighted works for which the Librarian
has determined, pursuant to the rulemaking conducted under subparagraph (C), that
noninfringing uses by persons who are users of a copyrighted work are, or are likely
to be, adversely affected, and the prohibition contained in subparagraph (A) shall not
apply to such users with respect to such class of works for the ensuing 3-year period.

What is all this business about the ensuing three-year period? Basically, this is
Congress's way of limiting the loophole for any given class of works to three-year
chunks. If word processing software is placed on the loophole list in 2005, you
need to know that it *could* evaporate from the list after 2008 if the Librarian of
Congress makes such a rule.

In general, the factors (i)–(v) that the Librarian of Congress must consider all
relate to the concept of *fair use*. This is a traditional notion in copyright law
that certain types of uses should be permitted, even if they technically amount
to copyright infringement. For example, a journalist who excerpts portions of
President Bill Clinton's memoirs, in order to provide a critical commentary, would
be making *fair use* of the quoted portions. Likewise, the den mother who passes
out pages copied from a picture magazine so that the cub scouts can cut them
up to make posters would be making *fair use* of the copied pages. As you would
expect, however, *fair use* often lurks in the shadows where it can be quite difficult
to make generalizations about what is fair or not. To be safe, if you find yourself
in a *commercial context* where you think something must be fair use, think again.

The *fair use* topics that Congress enumerated for the Librarian of Congress to
consider should not be taken as a sign that one can use *fair use* as a carte blanche
defense to any act prohibited by the Digital Millennium Copyright Act. The statute
makes it quite clear that the fair use defenses enumerated do not apply outside that
one aspect of the act dealing with circumventing a technological measure:

  (E) Neither the exception under subparagraph (B) from the applicability of the prohibition contained in subparagraph (A), nor any determination made in a rulemaking
  conducted under subparagraph (C), may be used as a defense in any action to enforce
  any provision of this title other than this paragraph.

So what is this really saying? As we shall see in a moment, the Digital
Millennium Copyright Act contains other prohibitions (other than circumvention
of a technological measure). The fair use defenses do not apply to those other
prohibitions.

Okay. So far we know that circumventing a technological measure is now against the law. Congress went further than this, however. Congress no doubt recognized that kids will be kids and that it is practically impossible (not to mention undesirable) to bring suit against every cub scout who uses the Napper-Zapper copy-protection-breaking program that his older brother downloaded from the Internet, thereby infringing the anti-circumvention provisions of the Digital Millennium Copyright Act. Thus, Congress added another provision to the act that was specifically directed to those who manufacture and distribute the Napper-Zapper copy-protection-breaking program. If you have a friend (whose name shall remain anonymous) who finds breaking copy protection schemes to be an irresistible challenge, here is the section of the Digital Millennium Copyright Act your friend needs to know about:

(2) No person shall manufacture, import, offer to the public, provide, or otherwise traffic in any technology, product, service, device, component, or part thereof, that—

   (A) is primarily designed or produced for the purpose of circumventing a technological measure that effectively controls access to a work protected under this title;

   (B) has only limited commercially significant purpose or use other than to circumvent a technological measure that effectively controls access to a work protected under this title; or

   (C) is marketed by that person or another acting in concert with that person with that person's knowledge for use in circumventing a technological measure that effectively controls access to a work protected under this title.

Note that the above language has an "or" between clauses (B) and (C). Thus, any one of these described acts can result in liability. Thus, if you make a software product that will unlock someone else's copy protection measure, that product would give rise to liability under the act.

Would writing an article describing how to break someone's copy protection scheme be construed as a "product [or service]...produced for the purpose of circumventing a technological measure..."? That is an interesting question. The answer seems to boil down to this. Can a written article be construed as a "product," or does its author provide a "service" that is "primarily designed...for the purpose of circumventing a technological measure"? It is not an easy question. On the one hand, the nefarious, child-molesting crook who purposefully teaches children how to hack the copy protection on their digital music should expect to find himself in serious trouble if the copyright police come knocking. On the other hand, what about the computer scientist who publishes an article showing how a technological measure can be compromised, as a way of alerting the software community to a previously unrecognized security risk?

Congress didn't provide explicit answers to questions like these. That is where the federal courts come in. When a question of statutory interpretation arises, it is the job of a federal judge to decide. However, you can't simply call up your local federal judge on the telephone and ask, "If I write an article explaining how to remove the copy protection on my cable's premium channels, is that a product or service?" Judges have a long-standing rule that they will not answer questions like these unless there is an actual case or controversy between two or more parties. Thus, you would have to write the article first, get sued by your cable company, and only then would a federal judge be willing to answer the question. This long-standing rule would seem to promote controversy, rather than prevent it. While arguably that is true, the real reason for the rule is to protect judges from being inundated with all sorts of half-baked questions, asked in a vacuum without presenting all of the facts. Our legal system thus places the initial risk upon the author to determine if he thinks his actions are worth the risk of retribution. Thus, the would-be author must ask himself, "If I publish this article, is my cable company likely to do something unpleasant to me?"

If you were a federal judge deciding this issue, how would you rule? Child molester: guilty; computer scientist: innocent, right? Unfortunately, these simple cases are typically not the ones that end up in court. More likely, the issue would arise in a case that lurks in the shadowy region between good and evil. That case would involve a Web site that attracts children to share and enjoy free music and then provides "helpful" informative links to the computer scientist's article as well as links to other articles further "explaining" the implications of the computer scientist's article. Any 12-year-old kid would get the message, loud and clear; yet in court it could be very difficult to refute the Web purveyor's argument that he was merely exercising his constitutional rights of freedom of speech and freedom of the press to express his views and provide information about the free music movement.

Although Congress did not define what is meant by product and service, Congress did provide explicit definitions of other terms used in this section of the statute:

(2) As used in this subsection—

    (A)   to 'circumvent protection afforded by a technological measure' means avoiding, bypassing, removing, deactivating, or otherwise impairing a technological measure; and

    (B)   a technological measure 'effectively protects a right of a copyright owner under this title' if the measure, in the ordinary course of its operation, prevents, restricts, or otherwise limits the exercise of a right of a copyright owner under this title.

After reading these definitions you may think, wait a minute; weren't these definitions already presented earlier in the statute? Actually, not quite.

The definitions presented earlier were for the part of the statute prohibiting one from circumventing a technological measure (unlocking the copy protection mechanism, for example). The definitions provided here are for the part of the statute that prohibits one from manufacturing, importing, offering, or providing a product or service for the purpose of circumventing protection (distributing Napper-Zapper, for example). The fact that Congress chose to put these definitions in the statute twice can mean only one thing. The definitions are different. The question is, how are they different? Let us examine the respective definitions side by side:

§1201(a)(3)(A): 'circumvent a technological measure' means to descramble a scrambled work, to decrypt an encrypted work, or otherwise to avoid, bypass, remove, deactivate, or impair a technological measure, without the authority of the copyright owner.

§1201(b)(2)(A): 'circumvent protection afforded by a technological measure' means avoiding, bypassing, removing, deactivating, or otherwise impairing a technological measure.

A careful inspection shows that, first, these two definitions are written in slightly different ways because they apply to different prohibited acts. The former definition applies to the act of circumventing; the latter definition applies to the act of providing something (to someone else) that circumvents. However, there are other differences. The former definition gives two explicit examples of circumvention; namely, descrambling a scrambled work and decrypting an encrypted work. The latter definition does not contain these explicit examples. Does that mean it is okay to offer a product that descrambles a scrambled work or that decrypts an encrypted work? In a word, no. These explicit acts are most certainly covered by the general prohibition against bypassing, removing, deactivating, or impairing a technological measure.

One wonders why Congress chose to put explicit examples (descrambling and decrypting) in the former definition, but left those out of the latter definition. Perhaps an answer to this riddle will appear as we continue to study the other aspects of the Digital Millennium Copyright Act.

If you have been following along so far, you know that the Digital Millennium Copyright Act contains at least two major prohibitions: (1) a prohibition against circumventing a technological measure designed to control access to a work and (2) a prohibition against distributing a product or offering a service designed to circumvent such a technological measure. Actually, there are more prohibitions than these, which we will cover below. Before we do, let us pause to reflect on how the Digital Millennium Copyright Act changed the status quo.

Consider this. Prior to the Digital Millennium Copyright Act, when you bought a DVD, the DVD likely came shrink-wrapped with some insidiously difficult to remove tape, designed to prevent in-store theft. Having lawfully purchased the DVD, you take it home and pick at the anti-theft tape until you finally remove it. Indeed, you can't watch the DVD until you do. The DVD is now your property.

You have the right to remove that tape. Having picked through the first line of anti-theft measures, you next find that someone has placed an encryption lock on "your property," which prevents you from being able to make an archival backup copy onto your VCR.

Ever since you lost your record collection in a basement flood during college, it has been your solemn practice to make backup copies of all your media, which you keep offsite, just to be safe. The encryption system is preventing you from doing this. So you read professor Torvold's article on defeating encryption systems, learn how to edit certain bits in the media headers using your personal computer, and with a little effort you finally manage to unlock the encryption system. Now, using the unlocked version of your DVD, you then transfer the movie to videotape for archival purposes should the original DVD become lost, damaged, or stolen.

Prior to the Digital Millennium Copyright Act, there was nothing wrong with unlocking the encryption lock for this purpose. Making copies for archival backup purposes had long stood as one of the permitted *fair uses* of a copyrighted work. Unfortunately, that had to change. Congress and everyone else knew that for every one person who makes a lawful archival backup, there are a thousand who share those backups with friends, thereby violating the copyright laws. So the Digital Millennium Copyright Act was inevitable. The problem Congress faced, however, was to make that act fit within the framework of existing copyright laws, which law-abiding persons had come to enjoy.

18.7   A COLLECTION OF SAFETY VALVES

In passing the Digital Millennium Copyright Act, Congress undoubtedly knew that it was tinkering with the status quo. To minimize damage to the existing framework, Congress added quite a long list of extra provisions to explain how the existing laws would not be affected. The list is broken into six categories, which we will now take a look at.

The first category Congress did not want the act to tinker with addresses a broad spectrum of rights and practical considerations:

(c) Other rights, etc., not affected.

  (1) Nothing in this section shall affect rights, remedies, limitations, or defenses to copyright infringement, including fair use, under this title.

  (2) Nothing in this section shall enlarge or diminish vicarious or contributory liability for copyright infringement in connection with any technology, product, service, device, component, or part thereof.

  (3) Nothing in this section shall require that the design of, or design and selection of parts and components for, a consumer electronics, telecommunications,

or computing product provide for a response to any particular technological measure, so long as such part or component, or the product in which such part or component is integrated, does not otherwise fall within the prohibitions of subsection (a)(2) or (b)(1).

(4) Nothing in this section shall enlarge or diminish any rights of free speech or the press for activities using consumer electronics, telecommunications, or computing products.

The first two items listed in the statutory language above explain that the existing copyright laws remain intact. What was a copyright infringement before remains a copyright infringement. What was fair use before remains fair use. In essence, the Digital Millennium Copyright Act created new laws against picking the digital lock (and against selling digital lock picking tools). That law did not change the existing laws against stealing what was now protected by those digital locks. Thus, Congress placed the first two items in the list to assure everyone that the basic copyright laws were not being tinkered with.

The third item listed is undoubtedly placed there to satisfy consumer electronics, telecommunications, and computer product manufacturers that their existing and future products would not be tinkered with. While such products might be designed to take part in an electronic challenge-response dialog, Congress did not want to create a requirement that they do so. In effect, Congress wanted to assure manufacturers that Congress did not intend to meddle in the design of electronic products.

The fourth item addresses important constitutional rights of free speech and free press. Constitutional rights represent a particularly touchy subject for this reason. In general, Congress can pass just about any law that the majority will support. However, if that law violates a constitutional right, the Supreme Court can toss the entire law out by declaring it unconstitutional. Congress undoubtedly put a lot of effort into passing the Digital Millennium Copyright Act, and it certainly did not want to see that effort wasted through a successful accusation that the law violated a citizen's right to free speech or free press. So Congress placed the fourth item in the act to reduce the chance of having the entire act thrown out as being unconstitutional. The fourth item thus represents an expression of congressional intent that the act should not be construed in a way that will violate the Constitution.

The second category of rights that Congress saw fit to clarify in the Digital Millennium Copyright Act involves libraries and schools:

(d) Exemption for nonprofit libraries, archives, and educational institutions.

(1) A nonprofit library, archives, or educational institution which gains access to a commercially exploited copyrighted work solely in order to make a good faith determination of whether to acquire a copy of that work for the sole purpose of engaging in conduct permitted under this title shall not be in violation of

subsection (a)(1)(A). A copy of a work to which access has been gained under this paragraph—

    (A) may not be retained longer than necessary to make such good faith determination; and

    (B) may not be used for any other purpose.

(2) The exemption made available under paragraph (1) shall only apply with respect to a work when an identical copy of that work is not reasonably available in another form.

(3) A nonprofit library, archives, or educational institution that willfully for the purpose of commercial advantage or financial gain violates paragraph (1)—

    (A) shall, for the first offense, be subject to the civil remedies under section 1203 *[17 USCS § 1203]*; and

    (B) shall, for repeated or subsequent offenses, in addition to the civil remedies under section 1203 *[17 USCS § 1203]*, forfeit the exemption provided under paragraph (1).

(4) This subsection may not be used as a defense to a claim under subsection (a)(2) or (b), nor may this subsection permit a nonprofit library, archives, or educational institution to manufacture, import, offer to the public, provide, or otherwise traffic in any technology, product, service, component, or part thereof, which circumvents a technological measure.

(5) In order for a library or archives to qualify for the exemption under this subsection, the collections of that library or archives shall be—

    (A) open to the public; or

    (B) available not only to researchers affiliated with the library or archives or with the institution of which it is a part, but also to other persons doing research in a specialized field.

As you can see, Congress gave non-profit libraries and schools the right to obtain a "commercially exploited" copy of a work, but only for the limited purpose of allowing it to decide whether to purchase it or not. Under the current practice of offering a try-before-you-buy demo, this statutory concession to non-profit libraries and schools seems a bit trifling. Perhaps the lobbyists for non-profit libraries and educational institutions were tending to other business when the Digital Millennium Copyright Act was being debated in Congress.

If lobbyists for libraries and schools may have missed the party, the same cannot be said for the lobbyists representing law enforcement. Congress made it clear that agencies like the FBI, the CIA, the Office of Homeland Security, and other "government activities" will not be impeded from any lawful investigation:

(e) Law enforcement, intelligence, and other government activities. This section does not prohibit any lawfully authorized investigative, protective, information security, or intelligence activity of an officer, agent, or employee of the United States, a State, or a political subdivision of a State, or a person acting pursuant to a contract with the United States, a State, or a political subdivision of a State. For purposes of this subsection, the term 'information security' means activities carried out in order to identify and address the vulnerabilities of a government computer, computer system, or computer network.

18.8   A CHILLING EFFECT UPON REVERSE ENGINEERING

So far, the categories of extra provisions have dealt with fairly mundane details that only a lawyer could love. However, that is certainly not true of the next category: reverse engineering. As many readers of this book well appreciate, reverse engineering is a time-honored practice that is often necessary if one is to design products that will communicate with and integrate with the products of others. Broad information sharing systems, such the Internet, would not exist without reverse engineering. Yet, reverse engineering also has a black eye, especially in the American culture where reverse engineering often implies copying, which is considered lazy and undignified. Some Asian cultures find this attitude strange, as copying offers a quick way to learn and promotes efficient improvement of existing technology. Regardless of which side of the ocean your sentiments lie, reverse engineering is a staple of technological development. Thus, Congress had no choice but to address it.

(f) Reverse engineering.

(1)   Notwithstanding the provisions of subsection (a)(1)(A), a person who has lawfully obtained the right to use a copy of a computer program may circumvent a technological measure that effectively controls access to a particular portion of that program for the sole purpose of identifying and analyzing those elements of the program that are necessary to achieve interoperability of an independently created computer program with other programs, and that have not previously been readily available to the person engaging in the circumvention, to the extent any such acts of identification and analysis do not constitute infringement under this title.

(2)   Notwithstanding the provisions of subsections (a)(2) and (b), a person may develop and employ technological means to circumvent a technological measure, or to circumvent protection afforded by a technological measure, in order to enable the identification and analysis under paragraph (1), or for the purpose of enabling interoperability of an independently created computer program with other programs, if such means are necessary to achieve such interoperability, to the extent that doing so does not constitute infringement under this title.

(3)   The information acquired through the acts permitted under paragraph (1), and the means permitted under paragraph (2), may be made available to others if

the person referred to in paragraph (1) or (2), as the case may be, provides such information or means solely for the purpose of enabling interoperability of an independently created computer program with other programs, and to the extent that doing so does not constitute infringement under this title or violate applicable law other than this section.

(4) For purposes of this subsection, the term 'interoperability' means the ability of computer programs to exchange information, and of such programs mutually to use the information that has been exchanged.

What in the world did Congress have in mind when it drafted the above provisions on reverse engineering? Let us dig in and see. In brief, the provisions on reverse engineering permit a limited freedom to break someone's copy protection in order to reverse engineer portions of the copy protected program to achieve interoperability. However, Congress attached many strings. As we shall see, you can get yourself pretty tangled up if you find yourself relying on the reverse engineering provisions.

First, your *sole purpose* in reverse engineering must be identifying and analyzing those elements of the (copy protected) program that are necessary to achieve interoperability of an independently created computer program with other programs. What exactly does this mean? If I need to reverse engineer big company A's computer programs so that I can make a product that will interoperate with company B's programs, that is one thing. However, if I need to reverse engineer big company A's computer programs so that I can make a product that will interoperate with big company A's program, that may be something quite different. Consider this scenario.

You independently created a new video game that you developed on your Linux computer. Now you are trying to port your new game to the Xbox platform, but you can't get the Xbox to recognize your game. It turns out that Microsoft designed the Xbox operating system software so that only digitally signed code will run on it. Can you hack the security system in order to make your program interoperable with the Xbox? If you do, you certainly run the risk that Microsoft will come after you. You might argue that all you are doing is developing games that will help to make the Xbox platform more popular. Perhaps that is true and Microsoft will allow you to do so with their blessing. However, equally possible, Microsoft might view your efforts as falling outside their carefully orchestrated product roadmap. In which case, you might very well find yourself up to your neck in a very unpleasant legal quagmire. You see, it's really up to Microsoft. Some call this the "chilling effect" of the Digital Millennium Copyright Act. The act begins like a warm summer day, offering legitimate "reverse engineering" grounds for circumventing a protection measure, but it leaves many important questions unanswered. As a result, many conclude that the risk is too great. When you are hacking the software of a company that has more money than most

Third World countries, you just can't afford to gamble over what the words of this statute mean. Are you feeling the chilling effect?

Case in point. One MIT computer scientist by the name of Andrew Huang (also known by his friends on the Internet as "bunnie") authored a book entitled *Hacking the Xbox*. The book was to be a hands-on guide to programming Microsoft's Xbox computer system. Unfortunately for Huang, his publisher John Wiley & Sons (publishers of the popular "XXX for Dummies" series) dropped the title before publication, fearing Digital Millennium Copyright Act-related lawsuits. The chilling effect of the Digital Millennium Copyright Act stopped conservative Wiley in its tracks.

Second, you must be in possession of the copy protected program lawfully. If you buy the program, you are in lawful possession. But if you download it from the Internet without the copyright holder's permission, or if you borrow it from another, you are probably not in lawful possession and may not remove the copy protection to perform reverse engineering.

Here is a scenario that systems integrators and IT consultants may find familiar. You are an IT consultant for a number of large banks. These banks use a software program that they paid $300,000 to purchase and another $25,000 per year in maintenance fees. The software program is protected by copy protection, and it stores all data files in an encrypted form. The banks would like to migrate to a new software program, but they cannot make the transition overnight. Thus, they want to be able to run both the old and new systems in parallel for six months to one year. To maintain integrity of the banking data, it is necessary for the new systems to be able to read and write data in the encrypted form of the old program. You have been hired to make this happen. Can you hack the security of the old system in order to figure out how to make the two systems communicate? Oh, yes, there is one additional detail. To do this you will need to work with one of your customer's copies of the old software, and their license agreement specifically prohibits them from giving you access.

Third, you can't use the reverse engineering exception if the elements you are purportedly analyzing have already been made readily available to you. How "readily available" must something be? That is a good question. If a computer manufacturer makes its Software Development Kit (SDK) readily available to anyone who wishes to purchase it for the low, low price of $4999, are the software internals needed to make the manufacturer's software interoperate with your program readily available? Does it matter that you are only producing a $15 shareware MP3 volume control widget? Would the answer be different if you were producing a $20 million air traffic control system? What if you must also sign a license agreement stating that you will not develop a product that competes with the computer manufacturer's products? Unfortunately, the statute really doesn't answer these questions. Thus, the party who resorts to reverse engineering does so at his or her peril.

18.9   REMOVING COPYRIGHT MANAGEMENT INFORMATION—A DMCA VIOLATION OF THE SECOND KIND

If you have followed along so far you are to be congratulated. Rest assured, we are almost done. The remaining portion of the Digital Millennium Copyright Act deals with an aspect of copyright law that is a bit easier to understand.

When you signed your name at the top of your homework paper in grade school you were making a statement that this paper was *your* work. Every grade school child instinctively knows that if you erase Johnny's name from his paper and replace it with yours, you are cheating. The Digital Millennium Copyright Act simply gives Johnny a federal cause of action with which he can now sue you for removing his "copyright management information."

In fact, the Digital Millennium Copyright Act sets forth all manner of different violations, all of which amount basically to "cheating." The act provides:

(a) False copyright management information. No person shall knowingly and with the intent to induce, enable, facilitate, or conceal infringement—

   (1) provide copyright management information that is false, or

   (2) distribute or import for distribution copyright management information that is false.

(b) Removal or alteration of copyright management information. No person shall, without the authority of the copyright owner or the law—

   (1) intentionally remove or alter any copyright management information,

   (2) distribute or import for distribution copyright management information knowing that the copyright management information has been removed or altered without authority of the copyright owner or the law, or

   (3) distribute, import for distribution, or publicly perform works, copies of works, or phonorecords, knowing that copyright management information has been removed or altered without authority of the copyright owner or the law, knowing, or, with respect to civil remedies under section 1203 [of the copyright act] having reasonable grounds to know, that it will induce, enable, facilitate, or conceal an infringement of any right under this title.

In the context of a grade school homework paper, putting one's name on the paper is about as sophisticated as one needs to get. However, Congress needed to be a bit more all-inclusive in defining "copyright management information," lest someone might adopt a sophisticated way of cheating. Thus, Congress covered the waterfront:

(c) Definition. As used in this section, the term 'copyright management information' means any of the following information conveyed in connection with copies or phonorecords of a work or performances or displays of a work, including in digital form, except that such term does not include any personally identifying information about a user of a work or of a copy, phonorecord, performance, or display of a work:

(1) The title and other information identifying the work, including the information set forth on a notice of copyright.

(2) The name of, and other identifying information about, the author of a work.

(3) The name of, and other identifying information about, the copyright owner of the work, including the information set forth in a notice of copyright.

(4) With the exception of public performances of works by radio and television broadcast stations, the name of, and other identifying information about, a performer whose performance is fixed in a work other than an audiovisual work.

(5) With the exception of public performances of works by radio and television broadcast stations, in the case of an audiovisual work, the name of, and other identifying information about, a writer, performer, or director who is credited in the audiovisual work.

(6) Terms and conditions for use of the work.

(7) Identifying numbers or symbols referring to such information or links to such information.

(8) Such other information as the Register of Copyrights may prescribe by regulation, except that the Register of Copyrights may not require the provision of any information concerning the user of a copyrighted work.

18.10   MORE LOOPHOLES

The prohibitions against removing another's copyright management information would not be complete without a complementary set of loopholes. Here, Congress recognized that law enforcement should be allowed to remove someone's copyright management information if it is part of a lawful investigation of a computer crime.

(d) Law enforcement, intelligence, and other government activities. This section does not prohibit any lawfully authorized investigative, protective, information security, or intelligence activity of an officer, agent, or employee of the United States, a State, or a political subdivision of a State, or a person acting pursuant to a contract with the United States, a State, or a political subdivision of a State. For purposes of this subsection, the term 'information security' means activities carried out in order to identify and address the vulnerabilities of a government computer, computer system, or computer network.

The truth is, in the broadcast business, an author's copyright management information can be inadvertently omitted for a number of reasons. Because Congress had to keep the broadcast industry happy, it included the following sections describing under what circumstances a broadcaster will not be liable for violating the act. Congress created two different standards: one for analog transmissions and one for digital transmissions. Take note which set of provisions is more complicated:

(e) Limitations on liability.

  (1) Analog transmissions. In the case of an analog transmission, a person who is making transmissions in its capacity as a broadcast station, or as a cable system, or someone who provides programming to such station or system, shall not be liable for a violation of subsection (b) if—

   (A) avoiding the activity that constitutes such violation is not technically feasible or would create an undue financial hardship on such person; and

   (B) such person did not intend, by engaging in such activity, to induce, enable, facilitate, or conceal infringement of a right under this title.

  (2) Digital transmissions.

   (A) If a digital transmission standard for the placement of copyright management information for a category of works is set in a voluntary, consensus standard-setting process involving a representative cross-section of broadcast stations or cable systems and copyright owners of a category of works that are intended for public performance by such stations or systems, a person identified in paragraph (1) shall not be liable for a violation of subsection (b) with respect to the particular copyright management information addressed by such standard if—

    (i) the placement of such information by someone other than such person is not in accordance with such standard; and

    (ii) the activity that constitutes such violation is not intended to induce, enable, facilitate, or conceal infringement of a right under this title.

   (B) Until a digital transmission standard has been set pursuant to subparagraph (A) with respect to the placement of copyright management information for a category of works, a person identified in paragraph (1) shall not be liable for a violation of subsection (b) with respect to such copyright management information, if the activity that constitutes such violation is not intended to induce, enable, facilitate, or conceal infringement of a right under this title, and if—

   (i) the transmission of such information by such person would result in a perceptible visual or aural degradation of the digital signal; or

  (ii) the transmission of such information by such person would conflict with—

     (I) an applicable government regulation relating to transmission of information in a digital signal;

    (II) an applicable industry-wide standard relating to the transmission of information in a digital signal that was adopted by a voluntary consensus standards body prior to the effective date of this chapter; or

   (III) an applicable industry-wide standard relating to the transmission of information in a digital signal that was adopted in a voluntary, consensus standards-setting process open to participation by a representative cross-section of broadcast stations or cable systems and copyright owners of a category of works that are intended for public performance by such stations or systems.

  (3) Definitions. As used in this subsection—

    (A) the term 'broadcast station' has the meaning given that term in section 3 of the Communications Act of 1934 *(47 U.S.C. 153);* and

    (B) the term 'cable system' has the meaning given that term in section 602 of the Communications Act of 1934 *(47 U.S.C. 522).*

18.11   CONCLUSION—THE SIX-TOED CATS ARE PROBABLY WINNING

If you take away nothing else from this chapter, take away this. Digital Rights Management is a complex topic. Law is a complex topic. Do not, merely on the basis of what you have learned here, make any legal decision concerning what is or is not a violation of the Digital Millennium Copyright Act without consulting with a lawyer that you have retained to represent *your* interests. Copyright law, of which the Digital Millennium Copyright Act is a part, is an amalgamation of laws, exceptions, provisos, and loopholes that have been created over the years in response to pressures from numerous, diverse, special interest groups.

If anything can be said about the copyright law, it is this: the copyright law is filled with inconsistencies. If you ever feel dead certain that the copyright law *must* support what you are planning to do, chances are it does not. You have been warned.

Now on to a more important topic: the cats. We can close this chapter knowing that Hemingway's six-toed cats are being well cared for and will continue to propagate their feline legacy for generations to come. The Ernest Hemingway Home and Museum keeps these cats properly fed, and Nature, it seems, takes care of the rest. These cats lead a carefree life.

As for you and me, we are not as carefree as we once were. True, you can still record *Tarzan* to shift it to a more convenient time, as the Supreme Court said you could. But if the broadcast happens to be digital, and if that digital broadcast happens to contain a "protective measure" to prevent you from fast-forwarding through the commercials, then you had just better get used to it. You are not going to be able to lawfully remove those protective measures. Oh, and don't blame the manufacturer of your digital recorder for making the stupid thing work this way. They didn't have any choice either. Ah, how life has improved in the Digital Millennium.

INDEX